1994

Music AND *Society*

THE LATE
BAROQUE
ERA

Music and Society

THE LATE
BAROQUE
ERA

From the 1680s to 1740

EDITED BY GEORGE J. BUELOW

PRENTICE HALL
ENGLEWOOD CLIFFS, NEW JERSEY 07632

First North American edition published 1994 by Prentice Hall Inc.,
a division of Simon & Schuster, Englewood Cliffs, New Jersey 07632

First published in the United Kingdom 1993 by
The Macmillan Press Limited
Houndmills, Basingstoke, Hampshire RG21 2XS and London

Companies and representations throughout the world

ISBN 0-13-104340-4 (hardback)

ISBN 0-13-529983-7 (paperback)

Typeset by Florencetype Ltd, Kewstoke, Avon
Printed in Hong Kong

Contents

The Late Baroque Era

Illustration
Acknowledgments

The publisher would like to thank the following institutions and individuals who have kindly given permission for the use of illustrations appearing in this book:

Österreichische Nationalbibliothek, Vienna: 1, 49, 50, 53; Museo Civico d'Arte Antica, Turin: 2; Zentralbibliothek, Zurich: 3; Sotheby's, London: 4; Biblioteca Universitaria, Turin: 5; Civico Museo Bibliografico Musicale, Bologna: 6; Museo di Roma/photo Oscar Savio: 7; Biblioteca Apostolica Vaticana, Rome: 8, 17; Montreal Museum of Fine Arts (Adaline Van Horne Bequest)/photo Brian Merrett: 9; Biblioteca Museo Correr, Venice: 10, 11, 14; Galleria dell'Accademia, Venice/photo Alinari, Florence: 12; Istituto di Storia dell'Arte, Fondazione Giorgio Cini, Venice: 13; Staatliche Kunstsammlungen, Dresden: 15; Edizione Scientifiche Italiane: 16; Civico Museo d'Arte Antica, Milan/photo Saporetti: 18; Musée du Louvre, Paris/photo Réunion des Musées Nationaux: 19; National Gallery, London: 21; National Gallery of Scotland, Edinburgh: 22; Musée de Versailles/photo Réunion des Musées Nationaux: 23; Bibliothèque Nationale, Paris/photo Giraudon: 24; Archiv für Kunst und Geschichte, Berlin: 25; Staats- und Universitätsbibliothek, Hamburg/Freie und Hansestadt Hamburg: 26; Staatsarchiv, Hamburg: 28; Kupferstichkabinett, Dresden/photo Deutsche Fotothek, Sächsische Landesbibliothek: 29; 31–34 (Sax.Top.200); Schloss Fasanerie, Fulda/ Kurhessische Hausstiftung, Kronberg: 35; Staatliche Kunstbibliothek, Berlin: 36; Stadtgeschichtliches Museum/Rat der Stadt Leipzig: 37, 38, 39; Scheide Library, Princeton University: 41; Museum für Kunst und Gewerbe, Hamburg: 42; Stadtarchiv/Rat der Stadt Leipzig: 43; Deutsches Theatermuseum, Munich: 44, 45, 51; Residenz Museum, Munich/ photo Mansell Collection, London: 46; Universitätsbibliothek, Munich: 47; Kunstsammlungen Veste Coburg: 48; Národní Muzeum, Prague/photo Olga Hilmerová: 52; British Library, London: 54; Trustees of the British Museum (Department of Prints and Drawings), London: 55; National Portrait Gallery, London: 56, 57; Board of Trustees of the Victoria and Albert Museum, London: 58; Rijksmuseum, Amsterdam: 60; National Gallery of Victoria (Felton Bequest, 1940–50), Melbourne, Australia: 61; Polish Academy of Sciences: from J. Lileyko, *Zamek warszawski 1569–1763* (*The Warsaw Castle*) (Warsaw, 1984): 63; Gosudarstvennoe izdatelstvo literatury po stroitelstvu i arkhitekture: from *Russkaya arkhitektura pervoy polovini XVIII* (*Russian Architecture of the First Half of the 18th Century*), ed. I Grabar (Moscow, 1954): 64; Akademiia Nauk SSSR/Institut Istorii Iskustv Ministerstva Kultury SSSR: from *Russkoye iskusstvo pervoy chetverti XVIII veka* (*Russian Art from the First Quarter of the 18th Century*) (Moscow, 1974): 65

Abbreviations

AcM	*Acta musicologica*
AMw	*Archiv für Musikwissenschaft*
AnMc	*Analecta musicologica*
b	born
BJb	*Bach-Jahrbuch*
BurneyFI	C. Burney: *The Present State of Music in France and Italy* (London, 1771, 2/1773)
BurneyGN	C. Burney: *The Present State of Music in Germany, the Netherlands, and the United Provinces* (London, 1773, 2/1775)
BurneyH	C. Burney: *A General History of Music from the Earliest Ages to the Present* (London, 1776–89)
d	died
DTB	Denkmäler der Tonkunst in Bayern
DTÖ	Denkmäler der Tonkunst in Österreich
EDM	Das Erbe deutscher Musik
EM	*Early Music*
fl	*floruit*
Grove 6	*The New Grove Dictionary of Music and Musicians*
Grove O	*The New Grove Dictionary of Opera*
HawkinsH	J. Hawkins: *A General History of the Science and Practice of Music* (London, 1776)
HMT	*Handwörterbuch der musikalischen Terminologie*
JAMS	*Journal of the American Musicological Society*
JRMA	*Journal of the Royal Musical Association*
Mf	*Die Musikforschung*
MGG	*Die Musik in Geschichte und Gegenwart*
ML	*Music and Letters*
MQ	*The Musical Quarterly*
MT	*The Musical Times*
PRMA	*Proceedings of the Royal Musical Association*
RBM	*Revue belge de musicologie*
RdM	*Revue de musicologie*
RIM	*Rivista italiana di musicologia*

RMFC	*Recherches sur la musique française classique*
RMI	*Rivista musicale italiana*
RRMBE	Recent Researches in Music of the Baroque Era
SIMG	*Sammelbände der Internationalen Musik-Gesellschaft*
TVNM	*Tijdschrift van de Vereniging voor Nederlandse muziekgeschiedenis*
VMw	*Vierteljahrsschrift für Musikwissenschaft*
ZMw	*Zeitschrift für Musikwissenschaft*

Preface

The *Music and Society* series of books – eight in number, chronologically organized – were originally conceived in conjunction with a
series of television programmes of which the first was shown by
Granada Television International and Channel 4 in 1986. These
programmes were designed to examine the development of music in
particular places during particular periods in the history of Western
civilization.

The books have the same objective. Each is designed to cover a
segment of Western musical history; the breaks between them are
planned to correspond with significant historical junctures. Since
historical junctures, or indeed junctures in stylistic change, rarely
happen with the neat simultaneity that the historian's or the editor's
orderly mind might wish for, most volumes have 'ragged' ends and
beginnings: for example, the Renaissance volume terminates, in
Italy, in the 1570s and 80s, but contines well into the 17th century in
parts of northern Europe.

These books do not, however, make up a history of music in the
traditional sense. The reader will not find technical, stylistic discussion in them; anyone wanting to trace the detailed development of
the texture of the madrigal or the rise and fall of sonata form will
need to look elsewhere. Rather, it is the intention in these volumes to
show in what context, and as a result of what forces, social, cultural,
intellectual, the madrigal or sonata form came into being and took its
particular shape. The intention is to view musical history not as a
series of developments in some hermetic world of its own but rather
as a series of responses to social, economic and political circumstances and to religious and intellectual stimuli. We want to explain
not simply *what* happened, but *why* it happened, and why it happened when and where it did.

We have chosen to follow what might be called a geographical, or
perhaps a topographical, approach: to focus, in each chapter, on a
particular place and to examine its music in the light of its special
situation. Thus, in most of these volumes, the chapters – once past
the introductory one, contributed by the volume editor – are each

devoted to a city or a region. This system has inevitably needed some modification when dealing with the very early or very recent times, for reasons (opposite ones, of course) to do with communication and cultural spread.

These books do not attempt to treat musical history comprehensively. Their editors have chosen for discussion the musical centres that they see as the most significant and the most interesting: many lesser ones inevitably escape individual discussion, though the patterns of their musical life may be discernible by analogy with others or may be separately referred to in the opening, editorial chapter. We hope, however, that a new kind of picture of musical history may begin to emerge from these volumes, and that this picture may be more accessible to the general reader, responsive to music but untrained in its techniques, than others arising from more traditional approaches. In spite of the large number of lovers of music, musical histories have never enjoyed the appeal to a broad, intelligent general readership in the way that histories of art, architecture or literature have done: these books represent an attempt to reach such a readership and explain music in terms that may quicken their interest.

The television programmes and books were initially planned in close collaboration with Sir Denis Forman, then Chairman of Granada Television International. The treatment was worked out in more detail with several of the volume editors, among whom I am particularly grateful to Iain Fenlon for the time he has generously given to discussion of the problems raised by this approach to musical history, and also to Alexander Ringer and James McKinnon for their valuable advice and support. Discussion with Bamber Gascoigne and Tony Cash, in the course of the making of the initial television programmes, also proved of value. I am grateful to Celia Thomson for drafting the non-musical part of the chronologies that appear in each volume and to Julie Anne Sadie for the musical part in the Baroque volumes, and to Elisabeth Agate for her invaluable work as picture editor in bringing the volumes to visual life.

London, 1993   STANLEY SADIE

Chapter I

Music and Society in the Late Baroque Era

GEORGE J. BUELOW

Since the early nineteenth century, 'Baroque' has been used first in art criticism and later in musical historiography as a label defining the period in Western culture extending from approximately 1600 to around 1750. Significantly, its original application to music can be traced only to specific criticism of music written in France late in the period encompassed by this volume. It was in the 1730s that a few writers began to disparage the music of Jean-Philippe Rameau for being extravagant in style, bizarre, too dissonant and therefore in its original, pejorative context 'baroque'. The word itself originated with the Portuguese label *barroco*, for a misshapen pearl. Thus, for example, in 1739 Jean-Baptiste Rousseau declared in a letter that Rameau's opera *Dardanus* had inspired him to write a humorous ode containing the line 'distillers of baroque chords of which so many idiots are enamoured'.[1] In 1753 Jean-Jacques Rousseau accused the Italians of composing 'bizarre and baroque' music,[2] and in his *Dictionnaire de musique* (Paris, 1768) he formulated his well-known definition: '"baroque" music is that in which harmony is confused, charged with modulations and dissonances, in which the melody is harsh and little natural, intonation difficult and the movement constrained'.

In the early nineteenth century the distinguished Swiss art historian Jakob Burckhardt adopted the term to condemn art and especially architecture that he felt burst the bonds of Renaissance perfection of colour and design. More significant for the later widespread usage of 'baroque' with reference to style were the writings of Heinrich Wölfflin, whose book *Renaissance and Baroque* (1888) used the term, cleansed of its negative connotations, as a label for the period of art developing after the Renaissance. Musical historiography, at the beginning of the twentieth century still a young discipline, took the term and its general stylistic and conceptual implications as a means of defining the parameters of musical style found in post-Renaissance music and redundant before the so-called Classical period typified by the Viennese masters Haydn, Mozart and Beethoven. Once established, particularly in German scholarship, and perhaps most especially in the textbook by Manfred Bukofzer,[3] the term took on a life of its own which established the widespread belief that a Baroque period existed in music, originating at the turn of the seventeenth century and ending at the time of Johann Sebastian Bach's death in 1750. The time-span of some 150 years implied to Bukofzer and others that the period was divisible into distinct early, middle and late subperiods, and the 'late' Baroque came generally to encompass music composed between 1680 and 1740, or the period circumscribed generally by the essays in this book.

Such a simplistic concept of the Baroque in music history is fraught with problems, and periodization, especially of the Baroque, has received considerable criticism.[4] For the seventeenth century, a period of such musical inventiveness and orientation towards new musical styles, it is particularly misleading to imply by categories of early, middle and late that music developed organically from a simple to a complex style. The very notion of a single 'Baroque' style has no justification in the evidence. Indeed, one of the most obvious characteristics of music of the seventeenth century and of the early eighteenth is its extraordinary diversity: the invention of important new means of stylistic expression; the adaptation of old forms and styles that were welded to the new; the rise of nationalistic and individualistic compositional styles; and the frequent debates over which style should be considered the most successful. The prolixity of musical developments makes the concept of a single historical period for music problematical, and perhaps most challenging is any attempt to define a concluding borderline to these developments. Therefore, the label 'late Baroque' is a vague term without explicit meaning or time-frame. Nevertheless, it still serves as a convenient label for the abundance of musical creativity taking place during the last decades of the seventeenth century and the early decades of the eighteenth. To be more precise would be to misread that evidence; to abandon the concept and the evidence as it is found in the early eighteenth century would also lead to a gross misreading of what actually did occur in music and society in those decades.[5]

There was very little that was new in musical developments between the last decades of the seventeenth century and the early ones of the eighteenth. It is what happened to musical forms and styles in this period and how those changes are related to societal factors that concerns the essays in this volume. To enter the Baroque around 1670 or 1680 is in most instances to discover musical achievements already formed by the changes in music begun much earlier, going back at least to the beginning of the seventeenth century. In the sense creating a whole array of new styles and many new forms, most notably opera. This necessitated, at least in Italy and only for a while, the abandonment of polyphony, and led to a striking emphasis on melody and bass, made possible by the recent development of the thoroughbass as an essential aspect of all composition. In its goal of overt emotional expressiveness, and in reaching out to listeners with the tantalizing goal of involving them in the actual emotional participation, music began its irreversible evolution towards a primarily secular art that was eventually to erode and destroy the long-held stylistic distinctions between the sacred and the secular in musical expression.

For a while these innovative experiments remained isolated at prominent secular courts. The new type of solo song, monody, became the particular love of performers and audiences, and monodies were written by the hundreds in the early decades of the new century. It is not without importance to note that the composers were just as often amateurs, as well as professionals, and both groups consisted predominantly of singers. Many monody texts were love-poems, in which the conceits of expectation and disappointment of the lover and the frequent allusions to erotic experience were the pretext for unusually emotional outpourings of affective singing. The sudden popularity of this 'new music' – the title of Giulio Caccini's most famous collection of monodies, *Le nuove musiche* (Florence, 1602) – emphasizes just how radical the result of the experiments turned out to be, in a sense releasing the pent-up and largely frustrated Italian genius for impassioned solo song.

Of even greater significance, however, than the rediscovery of the power of song was the success of composers such as Cavalieri, Caccini and Peri in finding a musical style in which poetic texts could be sung in their entirety; thus they realized their dream of achieving the dramatic results that they thought the ancient Greeks had achieved. The *stile rappresentativo* or *stile recitativo* was the most significant breakthrough in finding a way to recite a text in tone. The earliest attempts, as in the *Euridice* operas by Peri and Caccini, already demonstrate the power of style in expressing intense emotions, such as those underlying the reporting of Eurydice's death in these operas. Claudio Monteverdi, in 1607, quickly developed the dramatic recitative to an art form of enormous subtlety and refinement in his opera for Mantua, *L'Orfeo*. This work, too, was meant for a sophisticated aristocratic audience, and in it Monteverdi introduced far more solo song to be contrasted with dramatically declaimed recitative. In the developing concept of opera that took place over the next few decades in the palaces of nobles, particularly in Rome, the relationship between dramatic reciting of texts and contrasting lyrical outbursts of songs of various kinds constantly changed. Indeed, the balance between the two was to remain in flux throughout opera history. It was, however, the very concept of joining these two newly invented styles into a play to be sung throughout that was to have enormous consequences for the future of Baroque music, as well as for the history of music in general.

In 1637 the first public opera house opened in Venice, and very soon Venice became the centre of opera development in the seventeenth century. The adaptation of the earliest forms of opera to suit the tastes of a ticket-buying audience, even if sophisticated and largely made up of Venetian aristocrats and foreign dignitaries, quickly forced the concept of opera into even more popular stylistic developments. During the first three quarters of the century, Venetian opera became the catalyst for the development of Baroque musical styles. While opera itself was transplanted only slowly beyond the Italian peninsula, by the end of the century it had become the most important and popular type of musical entertainment in the German courts, in the city of Hamburg, at the court of Louis XIV and, early in the eighteenth century, in London. Viewed from one perspective, the history of the late Baroque unfolds through the impact of operatic styles and forms on all music, sacred and secular.

MUSIC AND PATRONAGE

Throughout the final decades of the Baroque, Europe remained essentially as it had been, a society directed by court cultures. There were, of course, significant exceptions, such as the middle-class mercantile culture of such important German cities as Hamburg, Frankfurt and Leipzig, and the urban middle class of the Netherlands. At least north of the Alps and the Pyrenees, it was France and the court of Louis XIV that served as the supreme model with which all aristocratic life could be compared. By 1680 the Sun King, having crushed the hegemony of the Habsburgs, had effectively created the first superpower of modern Europe. He was acclaimed Louis le Grand by the Council of Paris, and, through a series of military victories achieved at great cost to French society, his political power was not only absolute but all-conquering. The artificial culture he created, which emanated from his sumptuous château of Versailles, was soon imitated elsewhere in Europe, both physically in the form of numerous pseudo-Versailles and intellectually in the adaptation of the French language, its literature, the arts and the social manners of French court life. Never before or since has a government so completely dominated the arts, and even more remarkably with the single-minded inspiration and direction coming from one man, the King of France.

The achievements in music were no less unprecedented than those in all the other areas of the arts. A predilection for dance and ballet had already been central to the musical life of Louis XIII's court, and his son was no less devoted to dance, both as a dancer himself and in his emphasis on dance and ballet at court. It was, however, during his reign that dance took on the formal and stylistic characteristics that came to be identified with French music in general and that infused almost all other forms of French musical developments, including opera. Fate played into the king's hands, by the appearance at his court of a young Italian musician, Jean-Baptiste Lully (Giovanni Battista Lulli, 1632–87), who quickly won the king's life-long approval as the composer to create the voice of French music. In 1653 Lully was named *compositeur de la musique instrumentale du roi*, in 1661 *surintendant de la musique et compositeur de la musique de la chambre* and in 1662 *maître de la musique de la famille royale*. The first part of his career Lully devoted largely to the composition of *ballets de cour*, but after 1672 he furthered the glory of French music by establishing in Paris the Académie Royale de la Musique, where he produced a new opera (*tragédie en musique*) almost each year. Lully became virtual dictator of music in France, and through various oppressive patents – licences issued by royal decree – he gained sole rights to the performance of all dramatic music throughout the nation. The effects of this unique control were twofold: (1) Lully's music became synonymous with French music, and the music of his ballets and operatic compositions achieved a stylistic unity that was new and opposed to the music of the Italians; (2) it froze music in France not only during Lully's lifetime but long after his death, as composers continued to imitate and emulate Lully's music as if it were the only music sanctioned by king and aristocratic audiences.[6] Lully's music became a cultural artefact, it represented Louis XIV's own *bon goût*, and it was one facet of the creation of a state culture meant to show the world French superiority over all other nations, most especially the Italian.

Italian music was not unknown at the French court, and during Louis' minority more than one Italian opera had been produced in Paris, notably through the efforts of Cardinal Mazarin. Its success was at best limited. Although a taste for Italian music, such as cantatas, probably existed among many French citizens, such an influence was almost totally expunged from the official court music composed by Lully. His music exudes classic restraint, with absolute faithfulness to the cadence and rhyme of the French text. Largely composed in recitative, there is nothing remotely suggestive of Italian aria style. The lyrical element in Lully's dramatic works tends to be brief and derived from the long tradition of the French *air de cour*, already established at the turn of the seventeenth century. Dramatic contrasts often come from a splendid employment of choruses and colourful originality in the use of the orchestra. Although Lully's *tragédies en musique* received performances at court, they were composed for the entertainment of Parisian society. The extraordinary success of Lully's commercial venture with opera confirms emphatically that court musical taste was also the accepted taste of the educated classes in Paris, as well as elsewhere in France and in other European centres where these works were performed.

The fact that several cultural and political centres in Italy had lavishly supported the arts since the Renaissance explains in part the enormous musical activity throughout Italy in the seventeenth and eighteenth centuries. In all cases, whether in Milan, Bologna, Venice, Rome, Naples or smaller cities, musicians depended on the munificence of the church and aristocratic Maecenas figures to support their creative careers. This must explain, in part at least, the singular musical vitality emanating from Italy and spreading out across Europe during the Baroque. No other Italian city equalled Rome in its ostentatious nurturing of the arts, including music. The pope and the Sacred College at the Vatican, more than 80 churches in the city, the various confraternities – societies of laymen – and the extraordinarily wealthy noble families (particularly the Ottoboni, Pamphili, Colonna and Ruspoli), as well as exiled royalty from other countries (such as Queen Christina of Sweden and Queen Maria Casimira of Poland), all contributed to Rome's dazzling musical culture, which was unrivalled throughout Europe.[7] Unlike the centrally controlled patronage of the French court, the variety and even competition among those promoting music as part of their cultural and political influence within the city gave Rome a superabundance of musical forms and styles. From the Vatican still emanated the demand that sacred music should be pure, dignified, 'ecclesiastical' and true to the sixteenth-century principles favoured in the works of Palestrina. The Sistine Chapel remained not just a holy sanctuary of the pope but also the sanctuary of the *prima prattica* and *a cappella* performing practices of vocal music. This preservation of a historically antiquated musical style through the authority of the Catholic church affected music not only in Rome but throughout the Catholic world as a style specifically identifiable with sacredness. The principles of sixteenth-century strict diatonic counterpoint were also to be adopted by Protestant composers seeking a style that evoked the same quality of the sacred and one that could be distinguished from the clearly secular origins of most Baroque music, as for example in Bach's use of the *prima prattica* in many of his vocal works, most especially in sections of the B minor Mass.

Sacred music was in particular supported and determined by several aristocratic families, for the heads of all three of the great families in this period – the Colonna, Pamphili and Ottoboni – were cardinals. It was, however, in their palaces that their impressive musical establishments provided extensive support to composers, singers and instrumentalists. Many of the most important names in Baroque music found employment there. Cardinal Pietro Ottoboni (1667–1740) lavishly financed musical events in his Cancelleria palace. He also contributed his own artistic ability as a poet by writing numerous librettos for operas and oratorios. Because of his many church duties, as curator of the Sistine Chapel and the Congregazione di S Cecilia (which was responsible for the music performed in the other Rome churches), he knew most of the musicians in the city. From 1690 to 1713 Corelli was employed as his orchestra director, and Alessandro Scarlatti also served in his employ. Every possible musical activity seems to have taken place at the palace, in his theatre and large halls, and in the gardens.[8] It was here that Corelli perfected his concept of the concerto grosso and performed for the first time many of the concertos later published as his op.6. Some idea of the extravagance of these occasions can be gained from a description of the performance of Alessandro Scarlatti's oratorio *Il regno di Maria Vergine assunta in cielo*, given in the courtyard of the palace on 23–4 August 1705:

> the orchestra, under the direction of Corelli, consisted of more than one hundred stringed instruments, plus trumpets and others, and the four best voices of the city sang the oratorio . . . For this important occasion a stage was erected on one side of the courtyard and was elaborately designed with balustrades, staircases, large twisted columns, and painted scenes representing the virtues; in the center, at an opening in the front balustrade, was a platform for singers. The audience was seated in open carriages that had previously been aligned so closely together that they touched one another. The most illustrious personages of Rome and environs attended the performances. Prior to the beginning of the oratorio on the first evening, a bell was rung, after which Pope Clement XI led the audience in devotions that included the *Ave Maria*, the *Gloria Patri*, and a prayer by the pontiff. At the end of the first part of the oratorio and throughout the second part, sumptuous refreshments were served.[9]

The tradition of oratorios performed in the prayer hall (the oratorio) of a Roman church had been established early in the seventeenth century. Three churches especially, S Girolamo della Carità, the Chiesa Nuova and the Crocifisso, supported and expanded this tradition into the eighteenth century. Performances increasingly took on the nature of entertainments, even though the custom of having a sermon between the two parts was largely retained. Given usually on Sundays and other feast days in the winter, oratorios grew in popularity as the works themselves increasingly took on more attributes of operas. Oratorios were also frequently presented in the palaces and in educational institutions. Their great popularity is especially emphasized by the long list of composers who contributed to this genre in Rome, including Alessandro Scarlatti, Stradella, Bernardo Pasquini, Caldara, Alessandro Melani, Ercole Bernabei, Foggia and numerous composers of lesser fame. Handel also contributed, writing *Il trionfo del Tempo e del Disinganno* to a text by Cardinal Pamphili and *La resurrezione* for a performance at the palace of the Marquis (later Prince) Ruspoli on 8 April 1708, for which an elaborate stage and scenery were specially constructed. The two performances on Easter Sunday and Monday employed an orchestra of some 45 instrumentalists conducted by Corelli.

It is impossible to estimate the numbers of musicians employed or the quantity of musical works created on demand by composers supported through the patronage of the churches and aristocratic families of Rome. In addition to all the sacred music commissioned for regular and special church services, to the major productions of operas and oratorios in the palaces of the wealthy, Cardinals Ottoboni and Pamphili and Prince Ruspoli all held weekly 'conversazioni' during the entire year, where friends, church dignitaries and the lords and ladies of patrician families, as well as diplomats, gathered informally for conversation, games and to hear newly composed music, usually chamber instrumental or vocal works such as cantatas and serenades. Alessandro Scarlatti, while in the service of both the Pamphili and Ottoboni families, wrote numerous cantatas. Antonio Caldara, who served Prince Ruspoli from July 1709 as *maestro di cappella*, wrote over a seven-year period some 150 solo cantatas and more than 50 chamber duets. The young Handel composed a large number of his Italian cantatas while living in the Ruspoli household, a musical experience that enabled him to absorb Italian musical style and practices to the degree that they became a basic concomitant of his own unique style.

No other city in Italy came close to Rome in its extensive support of music. Venice, however, was certainly second in providing an array of outlets for composers and performers in its churches, private palaces and opera theatres, and in its four *ospedali* (literally 'hospitals') – state-supported schools and homes for orphaned and unwanted girls. Each of them – the Ospedale della Pietà, the Ospedale degl'Incurabili, the Ospedale dei Mendicanti and the Ospedale dei Derelitti ai SS Giovanni e Paolo (the Ospedaletto) developed in the seventeenth century to include important and at times distinguished conservatories of music. From the eighteenth century these institutions provided one of the most important sources of income for many Venetian composers and instrumentalists. Some divided their employment between churches and the *ospedali*. For example, Giovanni Legrenzi was *maestro di coro* at the Mendicanti in 1683, but also vice-*maestro di cappella* at St Mark's from 1681, while being active as well as a composer of operas during the years 1681–4. The most famous of these four institutions was the Pietà, which by 1738 was reported to have 1000 girls enrolled. Antonio Vivaldi was employed intermittently as its *maestro di coro e violino*, 1704–38. Talented girls received a thorough musical education both as singers and instrumentalists from a small staff of instructors. They not only performed in the chapel, but often gave public concerts which became a notable attraction for both citizens and tourists. Some excelled as singers and instrumentalists, specializing in the harpsichord, violin, cello, viola d'amore, lute, theorbo or mandolin. Many continued to live at the Pietà in adulthood and became famous as soloists. It was for these performers that Vivaldi wrote most of his orchestral concertos, as well as most of his sacred vocal music.

Although Venice had no ruling aristocracy, it was home to numerous noble families, to this day still physically evident in their brilliantly conceived palaces lining the Grand Canal and other waterways of the city. Their support of the arts, including music, made Venice an exceptional cultural centre, matching its uniqueness as the island metropolis of the once great Venetian Republic. The first public operas, originating in 1637 and flourishing throughout the Baroque, could not have existed without aristocratic support. The many opera theatres functioning during the seventeenth and eighteenth centuries were all owned by the nobility, who either appointed a director to run them or leased them to an independent impresario or group of businessmen. As many as six different opera houses presented operas during Carnival and the autumn season, and opera was not only a focus of entertainment for aristocrats as well as wealthy merchants, foreign dignitaries and affluent tourists but was also a magnet attracting numerous northern composers and performing musicians to the city to experience first-hand the operatic vitality unequalled in any other Italian city. Venice was a meeting-ground for musicians and visiting dignitaries from all of Europe. Within private homes music was a focus of lavish entertainments, often held in honour of princes and rulers from other European states. For example, Johann David Heinichen (1683–1729) travelled to Venice from Leipzig in 1710 to learn first-hand about the Italian operatic style and to hear other forms of music by such major figures as Vivaldi, Gasparini, Pollarolo and Lotti. It was in the private home of a wealthy merchant, Bianchi, that he first met the visiting Prince-Elector of Saxony, who engaged him as a Kapellmeister to the court of his father at Dresden. Heinichen wrote numerous cantatas for the merchant's wife, Angioletta, a well-known singer, harpsichordist and patroness of the arts in Venice. She, in turn, arranged for Heinichen to compose a special cantata to honour the birthday of the Prince-Elector. In a report of that occasion we have a glimpse of the tradition of making music on the waters of the Grand Canal:

> [Heinichen's music] was performed from the water before the home (of the merchant), which stood . . . on the Grand Canal. Crowds of people gathered on the bridge and along the canal. As the first aria was sung, however, the clocks of the city began to strike, preventing the people from hearing. They began to indicate their vexation over this by stirring up such a loud noise that one could no longer hear the music. Madame Angioletta immediately asked them politely to be quiet to permit the music to continue. All became quiet again, though a repetition of the first aria was asked for, after which a tremendous cry of approval arose from the crowd; and the remainder of the serenade was received with no less approval.[10]

North of the Alps in Germany, musical patronage depended mainly on the absolute power attained by innumerable princes of large, small and even minuscule states. The rule of the German princes had been achieved after 1638, when the Holy Roman Empire for all practical purposes lost its former direct influence over the German states. By the end of the seventeenth century, Germany was divided and subdivided into geo-political regions in which a prince ruled over all aspects of life in his particular corner of Europe. The Catholic and Protestant churches, too, although allocated definitive regional powers as a result of the Thirty Years War, were largely subjugated to the will of the State. By the end of the century, apart from the Austrian territories controlled by Habsburgs, states such as Bavaria, Saxony and Brandenburg-Prussia clearly dominated the political landscape. A few smaller principalities, including Württemberg, Brunswick-Wolfenbüttel and Hanover, also played a smaller though significant role in supporting the growth of German culture. Whether in Vienna, Munich or Dresden, opera was the major court activity during the final decades of the seventeenth century and the early eighteenth. Enormous sums of money were lavished on producing Italian opera, which usually included employing Italian composers as well as the performing artists. Smaller courts such as those in Weissenfels, Ansbach, Bayreuth, Stuttgart and especially Brunswick-Wolfenbüttel also spent large sums on fairly regular performances of opera, and there were sporadic opera productions at even the smallest provincial courts. Not only opera but music of all kinds usually marked major state occasions, as each ruler in the German states, undoubtedly emulating the French court at Versailles, tried to outspend the others in dazzling his subjects and visiting dignitaries alike with a pomp and ceremony in which music played an essential role. Although a large part of the music heard at these grand festivities is lost, visual evidence survives in the sumptuous, copiously illustrated festival books that form a permanent record of these events.[11]

Sacred music, too, received considerable support because of the needs of the princely chapels. Court musicians not only took part in religious services but were frequently employed as teachers in associated schools, usually connected with the major churches. In Catholic regions such as Munich, the Jesuit college and church of St Michael, together with the related Seminarium Gregorianum, were particularly famous for training musicians. In other religious centres the Augustinians, Franciscans, Hieronymites and even the nunneries supported sacred music instruction and performances. While the predominant musical orientation in the southern Catholic courts of Germany was Italian, in the Protestant regions significant support both in secular and sacred music went largely to native composers and performers. A particularly well-documented example concerns the ruling house of Brunswick-Wolfenbüttel, where a tradition extending back into the Renaissance focussed on major musical activities. Already in the mid-seventeenth century, Duke Anton Ulrich established a court opera devoted primarily to Singspiel-like works sung in German. When a permanent opera theatre was built in 1690 in Brunswick, which was open to the public though supported by the court, a number of important German composers contributed to the repertory. These included Kusser, Erlebach, Schürmann, Keiser, Hasse and C. H. Graun. The court employment records indicate a large number of German singers and instrumentalists, but the ballet-masters and dancers generally came from France.

The cities of Protestant Germany, as well as smaller towns and princely courts gave extensive financial support to church musicians. This form of patronage was crucial to the north German development of a stylistically unique organ repertory. In Hamburg several generations of organists were pivotal in creating it, for example, Vincent Lübeck and Johann Adam Reincken. In Lüneburg, where J. S. Bach was a student, Georg Böhm was employed; in Lübeck, Buxtehude; and in Arnstadt and Mühlhausen Bach first found a job as organist. Bach's career is a particularly instructive example of eighteenth-century patronage in that he was supported by all its forms: as an organist in town churches; as a violinist, keyboard player, composer and Kapellmeister for the courts of Weimar and Cöthen; and as a composer of sacred music and Kantor in Leipzig, where he was also director of music for the city. Another important source of income for musicians in the cities was employment by the city government, both to perform at city functions, and also to be available for private entertainments, such as weddings.

Lastly, an important source of support in the larger cities came from the wealthy entrepreneurs who invested in musical performances. This is best exemplified by the establishment of the first public German opera house in Hamburg in 1678, as well as by the less successful one in Leipzig (1693–1720). The growth of public concerts is a notable development of the early eighteenth century, seen, for example, in the collegia musica founded in Hamburg, Leipzig and Frankfurt, and, as an outgrowth, in Telemann's famous Hamburg concerts that immeasurably enriched the musical life of that city. As the cities of Germany prospered in the new century, commercial public concert life was initiated or expanded in most places.

It was in London, however, that the entrepreneurial spirit thrived most successfully. The greater London area, by 1740, had a population of over 700 000 and was the largest city in the world. As is true of great cities in history and in the present, London contained all the strengths and weaknesses of a society overwhelmed by the poor and dominated by the wealthy. Unlike in other cities in states ruled by the aristocracy, English rulers, since the Restoration, no longer held absolute power, and actual support of music, while still a major feature of royal favour, was less significant than the freely developed organization of musical activities by individuals and groups of aristocrats and businessmen. The first half of the eighteenth century saw the establishment and growth of many musical institutions. Foremost among them, of course, was opera. Equally important, however, were the beginnings of a exceedingly rich and varied concert life that was to place London first among cities in this regard by 1800.[12] The public performance of music for profit transformed the culture of England in London as well as in the smaller cities. One reason for this was the rapid growth of amateur music-making within the families of the wealthy. As a status symbol, and also as a factor of family life, those in the upper levels of society pursued home music as an integral aspect of domesticity. This developing commitment to music beyond the confines of royal palaces affected all aspects of music as a business. Music publishing, directed to home consumption, grew significantly with the enormous variety of arrangements of instrumental and vocal music aimed at the amateur instrumentalist and singer. And London became the most attractive European city to foreign musicians, who flocked there seeking a share of the concert and operatic life.

Among those foreigners, it was, of course, Handel who most brilliantly illustrates how the social and cultural conditions in London affected a musician's career. Handel, though given some support throughout his working life by the royal household, was the first great composer to achieve substantial financial gains and also losses in the free marketplace of public music-making. Handel was a man of the world, cultivating political and social conditions to his advantage. When he settled permanently in London in 1712 it was for the purpose of supplying opera in the Italian style to the upper classes, and he succeeded brilliantly. When English society turned away from opera in Italian, Handel was soon forced to adapt to these changes in order to continue his career, and the result was the creation of the English oratorio. Among all the major composers of the late Baroque, only Handel freed himself from the age-old traditional patronage systems of court and church. As such, he was a model to be emulated as these patronage systems began to collapse amid the changing relationship of music to society.

STYLE AS A FOCUS OF CREATIVITY

The singularly rich and varied productivity of composers during the Baroque must be evaluated from various perspectives. This is necessitated in part by the unprecedented volume of music created during the period, but it is also the result of an avalanche of writings about music emanating from all of the European states. It is especially in the final decades of the Baroque that the intellectualizing of musical concepts stands out as a major achievement in the history of music. Seen from our perspective, it seems apparent that one of the most important developments of the seventeenth century which in a sense culminated at the turn of the eighteenth century was the achievement of myriad and often imprecise categories of musical styles. As has already been emphasized, the Baroque began with a decisive and intentional demand that composers find a new style of music to serve the meaning of words more faithfully. Monteverdi coined the phrase *seconda prattica* to dissociate his new music from that of earlier composers, and his new 'practice' was based essentially on a new and free employment of dissonances. By the end of the seventeenth century, styles of music as concept and in practice had burgeoned enormously. For example, in 1703 Sébastien de Brossard, the French composer, theorist and lexicographer, defined musical style in his *Dictionaire de musique* in the following way:

> Style is understood in music as the form and method that each person has especially for himself to compose, perform and to communicate. And all of these [forms and methods] are quite different, according to the measure of the genius of the composer, the country, and the people according to which the material, the place, the time, the subject, the expression etc. are rendered. Thus one says: the style of Carissimi, Lully, Lambert etc . . . The style of joyful and merry music is very different from that of the serious; the church style is very different from the theatrical or chamber styles;

the Italian style is sharp, colourful, expressive; the French in contrast, natural, flowing, tender. From these facts result various descriptive phrases in order to stress all of these different characteristics: the old and new style; the Italian, French, German styles; the Church, Opera, Chamber styles; the joyful, merry, colourful, sharp, moderate, expressive, tender, excited styles; the grand, sublime, galant styles; the normal, common, vulgar, fawning styles.

Johann Walther borrowed this definition for his *Musicalisches Lexicon* of 1732, the most important German music dictionary of the Baroque. He found, however, the list of styles incomplete and added further ones under the following rubrics: *Stilo choraico* (dance styles), *Stilo drammatico oder recitativo*, *Stilo ecclesiastico*, *Stilo fantastico* (instrumental improvisation), *Stilo hypochematico* (dance in the theatre), *Stilo madrigalesco* (word-related musical forms) and *Stilo sinfoniaco* (styles of music for various instruments). These and definitions found in other sources confirm two facts about music of the late Baroque: (1) writers on music did not have a simple definition of what constituted musical style; and (2) the diversity of styles lay at the heart of the concept of composing. By the beginning of the eighteenth century styles involved formal procedures, individual composers' methods, sociological factors – such as the place of performance – and, perhaps most crucially, national traits.

The impact of developments in Italian opera on music of the late Baroque, as well as on the later eighteenth century, was all-encompassing. Beginning with the establishment of the Italian forms of *opera seria* and *opera buffa* in the late seventeenth century and continuing with the reform of opera librettos by Metastasio, Italian opera became the most popular form of music for aristocrats and the middle class alike. The forms and styles of Italian opera infiltrated the music of all composers north of the Alps, even finally the French. Italian vocal and instrumental styles were equally appropriate to secular as well as to sacred music. Italian opera, as well as other Italian music using an operatic style such as the oratorio and cantata, was in the highest demand in every area of Europe and as far east as Russia. German composers who remained true to their own stylistic heritage based on contrapuntal vitality and characteristic melodic idioms either adapted in individual ways their musical language to the pervasive influence of Italian music, as did J.S. Bach, or, like Handel, went to Italy to learn first-hand about Italian musical styles and then fully committed their own musical developments to Italian concepts. This does not mean, of course, that the Italian ingredients of music forced a composer such as Handel to lose his identity and his unique musical style. But many composers of lesser genius than Handel in Germany certainly did not escape having their

2. Interior of the Teatro Regio, Turin, during a performance of Francesco Feo's opera 'Arsace': painting (1740) by Pietro Domenico Olivero

musical gifts absorbed by a generic Italian musical sound.

Even in France, where music had been frozen into stylistic formulae because of Lully's achievements and the king's desire to maintain a cultural distinction from the rest of the world, inroads of Italian style began to weaken the purity of the French style. This became true first in sacred music. Nevertheless, French musical style, epitomized in Lully's operas and François Couperin's harpsichord suites, did affect several generations of non-Italians, most especially German and English composers. This can be seen, for example, in the prominence of French overtures in their music and in their cultivation of the keyboard suite. Some foreigners came to Paris to study the music first-hand, especially the greatly admired and disciplined playing of the Paris orchestras. The French musical style, like the Italian, existed as an expressive means for composers to imitate.

By the end of the century, however, Paris began to resemble musically an island surrounded by the agitated waters of Italian music. The dyke had certainly been weakened with the death of Lully in 1687. His music was already seen by some critics as representative of the past, of the *anciens*, as opposed to the music of the *modernes*, composed by the Italians. It is at this time that a critical debate began that was to rage almost continuously for a century to decide whether French or Italian musical style was superior. One literary parody published in Paris in 1688 places Lully in the Underworld. Orpheus, however, has already learnt from an Italian musician of the problems with Lully and French music. He is told that Lully writes good symphonies and ballets and a few pleasant *airs* and dance-tunes with lively rhythms, but the operas are long and tedious, and Italians cannot understand why the French pay good money to hear the same thing 50 times over in one evening. The female singers are either inaudible or shrill, and the male singers cannot compare with Italian castratos. 'Few people leave the theatre after three hours attendance without a headache, and frequent yawning.'[13] It was, however, a short pamphlet by François Raguenet, a Rouen abbé, member of the Académie Française and a teacher at the Sorbonne – *Paralèle des italiens et des françois en ce qui regarde la musique et les opéra* (Paris, 1702) – that brought the argument into the open. He declared the superiority of Italian music – its boldness of melody, variety of affections and cleverness of stage design – and especially the greater intrinsic musicality of the Italian language. He preferred Italian methods of singing and acting and was especially excited by the remarkable voices and techniques of the Italian castratos. Raguenet's anti-French stance won the approval of Fontenelle, perhaps the most respected arbiter of taste in French society at that time. Of course, Raguenet was attacked almost immediately in French intellectual journals. But it was the appearance in 1704 of Jean Laurent Le Cerf de La Viéville's *Comparaison de la musique italienne et de la musique françoise* that became the definitive response and kept the critical battle raging for some time. Le Cerf was also from Rouen, and he had had a rigorous Jesuit education and was versed in ancient Greek and Latin literature. Dying at the age of 33, he had but a short career as a writer and poet. His response is composed as a set of dialogues in which he compared the arguments regarding French and Italian music to the older disagreements over the superiority of the ancients and the moderns.

The heart of Le Cerf's counter-attack concerns the continuing validity of French classical traditions, literary as well as musical, against the extravagance and poor taste of the Italians. For Le Cerf, French music's expressiveness appeals first to the intellect and then touches the emotions. This is in continuing agreement with many earlier theoretical pronouncements that music must give rise to affections in the listeners, affections that are in themselves intellectually rationalized concepts of emotions. In contrast, he criticized Italian music for its sensuousness, for appealing directly to the ear. French music is ruled by reason, it values moderation and simplicity. He made his most significant contribution, however, by adopting the French concept of good taste, *bon goût*, as an absolute standard of musical criticism, and for the first time equated the critical evaluation of music with its degree of beauty:

> I had often thought that, although we have in our language sufficient treatises on music, we have no treatise that enters into a discussion of the beauty of our music. There are only treatises concerned with mechanics and craftsmanship, if I may say so; treatises that teach the rules in a dry manner, and none of which teaches us how to feel the esteem we ought to have for compositions that follow these rules. Not one leads gentlemen to judge as a whole the worth of a symphony or an air.[14]

Le Cerf contended that one can judge the beautiful by developing a sense of good taste. For him, the composer who most fully achieved music with his concept of good taste – music that imitated the ancients' ideal of bringing together word and tone in a simple, affective manner – was Lully: 'If Lully had stayed in Italy and had only composed Italian music, he perhaps would not have brought it to the point of perfection to which he has led ours'.[15] Le Cerf was solidly French in his attitude that the intellect and not the emotions is the first aim of music, and that *bon goût* is the critical function of pure reason that can be applied systematically to music or to any of the other arts. Most significantly, good taste quickly becomes the key to criticism itself. Also important, Le Cerf advanced his definition of good taste to guide the amateur in gaining this critical acumen. He placed his trust in an educated public, the *honnêtes hommes*, to become *connoisseurs*, to be discerning critics free of slavishly following the rules of the craft, the science, which was characteristic of *sçavants*, who usually failed to understand the true worth of a musical composition.

Both Raguenet's and Le Cerf's essays were widely disseminated, and their influence can be seen in many aesthetic discussions emanating from Germany as well as England. In England, the critical opposition to Italian opera by some writers promoted a return to a former, English taste free of perceived excesses of a foreign style. John Dennis, in *Essay on the Opera's after the Italian Manner* (1706), feared the loss of British drama, one of the glories of England's past, to modern Italian opera, which he viewed as an absurd and pernicious invention. In Germany, however, the same debates over French and Italian musical styles were far less negative. Some writers suggested that perhaps the achievement of a true German style might be the result of combining the best aspects of both styles. As earlier with Le Cerf, German writers show a concern for their audiences and for the element of good taste as it affects both the quality of the music and the receptiveness of those who must be moved by it. Johann David Heinichen, a distinguished composer and writer on music, Kapellmeister at the Dresden court (1717–29), published an encyclopedic treatise on thoroughbass and the art of composition which reflects much of the current thought and practice of music in Germany of the early eighteenth century. In *Der General-Bass in der Composition* (1728) he formulated one of the clearest contemporary statements reflecting the influence of French thought and the central role that the concept of good taste now plays in the achievement of a successful musical style. To be a composer, after one has learnt the regular rules of theory and practice, Heinichen says one must seek appropriate experience:

> But what is it that one believes one must seek in the experience? I will give a single word defining the three basic *Requisita musices*, i.e., talent, knowledge and experience, as well as the true *fines musices* as the centre: this word is in four letters, *Goût*. Through diligence, talent and experience, a composer must achieve above all else an exquisite sense of good taste in music . . .
>
> The definition of *Goût, Gusto* or *guter Geschmack* is unnecessary for the experienced musician; and it is as difficult to describe in its essentials as is the true essence of the soul. One could say that good taste was in itself the soul of music, which so to speak it doubly enlivens and brings pleasure to the senses. The *Proprium 4ti modi* of a composer with good taste is contained solely in the skill with which he makes his music pleasing to and beloved by the general educated public . . . An exceptional sense of good taste is so to say the *Lapis philosophorum* and the principal key to musical mysteries through which human souls are unlocked and moved and by which the senses are won over.[16]

In his emphasis on the composer's responsibility to develop a style based on good taste, for the purpose of moving the souls of the general educated public, Heinichen echoed the opinions of French writers such as Le Cerf. It was Le Cerf who effectively opened the door to modern musical criticism both for the composer and for the listener, a criticism built on a foundation of distinguishing the positive and negative stylistic elements in French and Italian musical styles. Equally important, he raised the issue of the concept of the beautiful in music, which had previously had little or no actual identification as part of musical creativity. These issues of aesthetics and critical judgment, based on the growing debates about how music is discerned in styles, are undoubtedly among the most important new ideas to attract composers, theorists, critics, amateur musicians and knowledgeable listeners during the rest of the eighteenth century, and they were to remain particularly fertile as well for intellectual exploration in the nineteenth century.

INSTRUMENTAL MUSIC IN THE LATE BAROQUE

Music of the Baroque period was predominantly vocal in its forms and styles, and opera and operatic styles were primary factors in the origin and development of the largest amount of music written in the seventeenth century. Nevertheless, by the turn of the eighteenth century instrumental music had reached a level of sophisticated development that was to influence the future of music. From fairly elementary beginnings in the late Renaissance, a rich variety of instrumental forms and styles, keyboard music, chamber works and ultimately orchestral compositions were all in a sense poised for final Baroque stylistic developments in the crucial decades from the 1680s to the 1740s. Most of these instrumental works originated in Italy, where the composers were most often violinists. Inseparable from their frequent preoccupation with string music of increasing technical demands was the remarkable flourishing of string instrument building that began around 1680. The distinctive and ultimately classic concept of the modern violin was developed especially in Cremona by the Amati, but of course it was Stradivari who after 1690 created the ideal string instruments, with a beauty of tone and perfect form. The impetus behind this enhanced beauty and sensuousness of tone came from the human voice, which in operatic music had by this time completely captivated composers and audiences alike.

For much of the seventeenth century instrumental music was tied closely to vocal compositions – instrumental ritornellos in early operas and cantatas, orchestral introductions to operas labelled variously sinfonias or overtures, and other semi-dramatic vocal genres. Indeed, it was the highly disciplined orchestral playing in Lully's operas that gave the impetus for creating orchestras throughout much of Europe. The wish to emulate the glories of French operatic practice not only brought foreign musicians to Paris to experience and learn about Lully's orchestra but also influenced countless royal households to have their own orchestras. This not only led to a marked increase in the number of positions made available to instrumentalists, but sig-

3. Concert in the Shoemakers' Guild, Zürich: painting (mid-18th century) attributed to J. R. Dälliker

nificantly raised their technical and artistic standards. And the early orchestral repertory was preponderantly French, with overtures, suites of dances from ballets, and other incidental music from operas by Lully, Campra and Destouches. An orchestra, whether in the palace of a German principality or in the wealthy home of a noble Italian family in Rome or elsewhere in Italy, was as much a status symbol of power and wealth as a reflection of the most recent developments of musical taste. A large amount of instrumental music remained wedded to service functions, such as the organ in Protestant and Catholic ritual, the trio sonata as a substitute for sung portions of the liturgy, suites for social dancing or for background music at banquets, and town bands for civic celebrations. By the end of the seventeenth century, however, the upper levels of society profoundly influenced the expansion of music written for the non-functional purpose of simply listening or playing for individual and group pleasure. Most significantly, it was the greatly increased numbers of non-professional musicians, an amateur class, that created a largely new societal force affecting all aspects of music as an art and as a business.

Public concerts became a regular feature of musical life in the eighteenth century, although they originated in the previous century, first in England. There the new century witnessed the establishment of a number of concert enterprises in a variety of places such as dancing-schools and taverns. The latter were often hired by clubs for private music-making by the members or by concert promoters for concerts. Handel's oratorio *Esther* was given in 1732 in the Crown and Anchor Tavern in the Strand. It was there that in 1726 a group of aristocratic amateur musicians founded the Academy of Ancient Music, one of the first organizations with the purpose of restoring ancient sacred music. In 1678 an English music patron, amateur musician and charcoal-seller, Thomas Britton, established a series of Thursday night chamber music concerts in a room over his shop. The concerts were initially free and attracted a distinguished audience of both titled patrons and commoners. Other venues for concerts in London in the early part of the century included the Villiers Street Hall (Sir Richard Steele's Great Room), and rooms of dancing-schools such as Hickford's, Clarke's and Barker's. By the time Handel was giving public performances of oratorios, theatres with large auditoriums were needed to admit a sufficiently large audience to pay for the productions. The British love of attending concerts spread quickly beyond London to both large and small cities and towns. Another British innovation was the music given in the various pleasure gardens in London, as well as in other English cities; these evening concerts of vocal and instrumental music held from late spring to early autumn became one of the major institutions in eighteenth-century England supporting English composers and performers.

In France, the public concert outside of private royal and aristocratic gatherings developed more slowly. In 1725 Anne Danican Philidor established the Concert Spirituel; it was first active during Lent, but it later became one of the major concert institutions in Paris and remained so throughout the century. In Germany, public concert life in cities continued to depend in part on the tradition established in the previous century of the collegium musicum, which existed in Leipzig as well as in Hamburg and Frankfurt. As is well known, J. S. Bach took over the concerts of the Leipzig Collegium in 1729, which performed in a coffee-house. Telemann, who had first established the Leipzig Collegium, later created similar institutions in Frankfurt and Hamburg, and in Hamburg he became the manager of most of the popular public concerts; their success led to the building of that city's first public concert hall in 1761. In Italy notice has already been made of the vitality of concert life both in the palaces in Rome and in the conservatories in Venice. In Bologna, the Accademia Filarmonica, founded in the seventeenth century, was a catalyst for much of the concert life in a city of rich musical activities, including the sumptuous instrumental music created for use in the S Petronio basilica.

The interrelationships of society and its musical preferences, and the way in which these had an impact on composers, is clearly evident in the success of Arcangelo Corelli (1653–1713) and the spread of his music throughout Europe in the early eighteenth century. Corelli composed instrumental works only in the forms already standardized by the turn of the century – the violin solo sonata (with continuo), the church and chamber trio sonata and the string ensemble concerto. His published output was very small, consisting of only six collections of 12 pieces each. Corelli's initial fame was established in Rome, where he performed and conducted his and other composers' works in the palaces of Queen Christina of Sweden, the Pamphili and the Ottoboni. His pupils included some of the most important violinists and composers of the first half of the century, notably Castrucci, Gasparini, Geminiani, Somis and the Frenchman Anet. His two collections of church trio sonatas op.1 (1681) and op.3 (1689), and two sets of chamber trio sonatas op.2 (1685) and op.4 (1694) for continuo and two violins, became models of their kind – chamber music with moderate technical demands, exploiting the newly established balance between movements of vocal-like, bel canto melody and those of motivic contrapuntal textures enriched with numerous clashes of dissonances. The 12 solo violin sonatas of op.5 (1700) helped to establish the primacy of the solo sonata over the trio sonata. The popularity of both types of string music was in part the result of their appeal across the borders of national tastes, their collective style as a compendium of the state of violin artistry at the beginning of the eighteenth century. Their technical demands, though certainly not small, allowed skilled amateurs to experience the joys of violin ensemble and solo music in a purity and refinement that established a concept of style. It was to endure well into the century, especially in England, where Handel's instrumental concertos still reflected its influence.

Corelli's music was popular on a scale not known by previous composers of solo and ensemble string music, and the demand for it was quickly met by a rapidly expanding publishing industry in Italy, Paris, Amsterdam and London. Opp.1–5 appeared in numerous editions, as well as in a large variety of arrangements, selections and pastiches for various instruments and even for voice. Op.1 had 39 editions before the end of the century; op.2, 41; op.3, 37; op.4, 39; and op.5, 36; in addition, numerous manuscript copies are extant.[17] The growth of the market for music for the amateur as well as for the professional musician had grown impressively after 1700. Particularly popular, especially in England, were Corelli's 12 concerti grossi op.6 (1714), and these too not only received many new editions but also became the model for concertos by composers such as Geminiani, Gasparini, Venturini and Castrucci. Corelli's popularity in London is attested by the name of a music shop in the Strand, 'At the Sign of the Corelli's Head'.[18] According to Hutchings, 'over fifty music societies can be counted among subscribers to parts of concertos published in London between 1725 and 1750', not only in London, but also in Oxford, Norwich, York, Newcastle and even Aberdeen.[19] These parts were used by music societies and academies whose taste for Corelli seemed in its conservatism to lag behind the growing continental enthusiasm for the new form of the concerto that was coming especially from Venice.

Venice, however, was the place where the final Baroque development of the concerto took place. Corelli's concertos had simply placed the trio sonata as a solo (or *concertino*) group into the orchestral (*concerto grosso*) texture. There was no thematic contrast, and the only change of instrumental colour involved solo string sonority against doubled ensemble strings. These works retained the older, multi-movement forms of either contrasting fast and slow tempos or a suite of dances. The future of the concerto, however, lay in the singular changes in concept inaugurated in Venice by composers such as Albinoni, Alessandro and Benedetto Marcello and in particular Vivaldi. Each of these composers wrote operas, and their instrumental works are dependent on many aspects of instrumental practice and vocal style derived from Venetian opera. It was the phenomenal productivity and compositional brilliance of Antonio

149 365

4. Francesco Lorenzo Somis (cello) with his son Lorenzo (violin) and daughter Cristina (keyboard): drawing in black and white chalk on blue paper (1730s) by Lorenzo Somis (generations of the Somis family served at the Turin court)

Vivaldi (1678–1741) that was to make the solo orchestral concerto a definitive accomplishment of the late Baroque. Vivaldi composed around 500 concertos, mostly for performance by the girls and women of the Pietà. The 'red-haired priest' (*il prete rosso*), though handicapped from birth with an asthma-like condition, was not only an extraordinarily prolific composer but also a much-travelled virtuoso violinist and entrepreneur promoting the popularity of his own music, especially in Germany and Austria. The concerts at the Pietà, which he directed for long periods, were a magnetic attraction to Venetians as well as to the constant flow of foreign visitors to the city, including heads of state and influential diplomats and aristocrats. Pupils of Vivaldi, such as the distinguished German violinist at the Dresden court Johann Georg Pisendel, were also responsible for the popularity of Vivaldi's instrumental music outside Italy. Another indication of his contemporary fame is the large number of his scores that were published, approximately one fifth of the concertos, according to Talbot.[20] These called for a variety of solo instruments – one, two or four violins, some for two violins and cello, others for oboe or transverse flute. The earliest to be issued was the collection of 12 known as *L'estro armonico* (1711), published in Amsterdam by Roger, which had a remarkable success in Europe, influencing many composers. Not the least among them was J. S. Bach, who transcribed four of the concertos for harpsichord and two for organ; another organ concerto, BWV594, was transcribed from Vivaldi's op.7.

The success of Vivaldi's concertos across most of Europe, and the imitation of their formal and stylistic characteristics by other composers up to the mid-eighteenth century, was the result of Vivaldi's perception of what his audiences demanded of this new experience with concert music. The early eighteenth-century repertory had been anchored in vocal music and vocal styles – and, in Italy especially, in opera. Many writers of the period expressed uncertainty about or even opposition to purely instrumental music, for they thought it must be meaningless, affection-less, if words were absent. For them and for all those lovers of music who had been conditioned to find instrumental music as an accompaniment or support for the expression of a secular or sacred text, instrumental concertos must at first have proven a challenge to their comprehension and enjoyment. The concertos of Vivaldi and his contemporaries established the first large repertory of music for active listening and the pleasure derived from it, music that was not an accompaniment to operatic music or a background to another activity, social conversation, dancing or a sacred service. A variety of factors gave Vivaldi the opportunity to capitalize on a period in musical developments for which he was uniquely prepared. First, as is well known, he had a superbly trained orchestral ensemble at his disposal at the Pietà and an enthusiastic audience awaiting his newest works for that ensemble. Secondly, Vivaldi was without question one of the great violin virtuosos of the Baroque, and he had a complete command of the instrument, knowing how it could be used in the context of the string ensemble, and particularly how to dazzle his audiences in solo passages within a concerto. Lastly, and perhaps most importantly (though it is seldom stressed in the innumerable discussions of Vivaldi's instrumental works), he was a major opera composer; writing operas for Venice and other cities was the focus of the greatest part of his career. Vivaldi's instrumental concertos can be fully appreciated stylistically and in terms of their appeal to composers and audiences alike across Europe only in so far as they reflect an adaptation of Italian operatic style linked with the newest instrumental styles, notably virtuoso string playing. This is emphatically reflected in the more than 230 concertos that Vivaldi composed for the violin.

What did Vivaldi's audiences relish in these works? As far as one can generalize about this enormous number of compositions, they are structurally predictable. Most of them use a three-movement form that had already become familiar from the opera overture. Like these overtures, Vivaldi's concerto movements are usually organized in a pattern of I fast – II slow – III fast. The attentive listener could expect further guidance in the content of each movement: I ritornello form; II slow, often suggestive of the pathos of the serious affections found in opera arias; III a second ritornello or a dance-like movement. It was the brilliance of the concept of the ritornello, which Vivaldi developed from its use in operatic contexts, that gave 'meaning' to these concertos. In simplest terms, the opening orchestral ritornello presented all the relevant musical ideas, the invention of the movement. The solo instrument or instruments contributed new music that separated partial or complete returns of this familiar material and entertained through a more or less virtuoso style of the writing. The ritornellos provided constant plateaux of familiarity but also surprises, as the materials of the opening might come back incomplete, or in variations and with harmonic surprises. Yet listeners could never lose their way through the form. Within this easily perceived structure Vivaldi entertained with his inexhaustible variety of musical ideas: melodic motifs and phrases of symmetry and rhythmic vitality that are almost always memorable, that is, easily grasped and recognized in the course of the movement. The origins of these kinds of melodic material were certainly operatic, but Vivaldi's genius lay in his placing an indelible stamp of originality on them. The slow movements are most often long solos for violin, or another instrument such as oboe or flute, in which the composer placed in a non-verbal, instrumental context some of Italian opera's most expansive and beautiful bel canto arias, extended beyond the confines of length usually associated with an operatic context.

In the course of the rediscovery of his instrumental music in the twentieth century, Vivaldi has been criticized as a composer of little musical imagination who, Stravinsky supposedly once remarked, composed the same concerto over and over. This kind of criticism points up the problem of restoring any artwork out of its historical and social context. The sameness of form that many condemn in Vivaldi's works was a major factor in their viability as concert music in the eighteenth century. The perceived lack of thematic imagination or the sometimes disparaged simplicity of his themes was heard in Vivaldi's lifetime as a freshness and vitality emanating from the most recent operatic styles. Although his music quickly lost its popularity after his death, one cannot look at the closing phase of the Baroque without acknowledging the seminal influence of his music on the future. Vivaldi's concertos constituted the first substantial orchestral repertory for concert audiences, they established for more than a century the standard three-movement form of the concerto, and they popularized the appreciation of instrumental virtuosity as a vital part of concert music. In addition, Vivaldi's music had a direct effect on the first composers of the symphony, for example Giovanni Battista Sammartini. For northern composers such as Bach, the Vivaldian style became synonymous with Italian style. Bach's *Italian Concerto* BWV971, published for harpsichord by the composer in a collection also containing his *Overture in the French Style* BWV831, is a brilliant imitation of Vivaldi's concerto music. That a German composer of Bach's genius should wish to demonstrate his ability to write in the Italian style is only one more proof of the immense influence Vivaldi had on the music of his time. And that influence was the result of a composer responding to societal factors requiring him to create a repertory of instrumental music attuned to the popular taste of his audiences.

THE LEGACY OF THE BAROQUE IN MUSIC

Viewed from the wide perspective of the end of the twentieth century, musical developments in the seventeenth century and in the early decades of the eighteenth can be seen to have given birth to the modern world of music. The infinite variety of new music generated by the invention of opera and its related forms, and the increased importance and vitality of independent solo and ensemble forms, spawned a vast and constantly renewing repertory. But after more than a century of research and rediscovery, Baroque music is still hardly known in its broadest parameters, even by specialists. Thousands of opera scores, enormous amounts of vocal and instrumental chamber works, an inestimable quantity of sacred music – all remain unheard and largely unknown. The composers and works that have risen to the top of this immense corpus are often the superior artists and greatest works of their time, but they are nevertheless a meagre representation of the composers, singers, instrumentalists and dancers who gave European culture and society new dimensions of musical creativity. Yet the picture is clear enough. Almost every musical form and style that was to characterize the art music of the later eighteenth century and the nineteenth can trace its roots and often its substance to the Baroque. Certainly this is evident in the continuing relevance of opera to the present; the formulation and definition of the orchestra; the growth of chamber music, including the string quartet; the solo keyboard literature; and the concept of the symphony as it developed from the French overture and particularly the Italian opera overture. The achievement of the instrumental concerto is but one of the many new Baroque forms to enrich continuously the future of music.

Most of the theorists and most of the composers who communicated their ideas verbally maintained a single goal for music in this period: it must move the affections of the listener. This is not to say that music of earlier periods was without emotional substance, but in general that was secondary to technique and to structure. Clearly the sacred music of the great sixteenth-century masters, such as Lassus, often contains vivid emotional imagery, but the scale of emotional values was very limited both by the circumstance of purpose and the restrictions of musical style. Even the most dramatically expressive late Renaissance composers such as Gesualdo remained true to their heritage by using dissonance to underscore the meanings of individual words of great rhetorical power; they did not seek to move listeners through the total emotional impact of a text and its music. This approach changed in the new musical styles of subsequent centuries. Music became a language of identifiable emotions, and, from the beginnings of the Baroque, composers and writers on music reflected their commitment to this new goal by constantly discussing it. The resulting theories of musical expressivity established a basic criterion for music, affecting composers across the whole spectrum of European culture. The unanimity of viewpoint found among writers of the seventeenth and eighteenth centuries runs as a unifying thread through many treatises, prefaces to musical works, essays and other instructional documents. For example, Christopher Simpson (c1605–1669), an English composer, viol player and theorist, states:

> When you compose Musick to Words, your chief endeavour must be, that your Notes do aptly express the sense and humour of them. If they be grave and serious, let your Musick be such also: If Light, Pleasant, or Lively, your Musick likewise must be suitable to them. Any passion of Love, Sorrow, Anguish, and the like is aptly exprest by *Chromatick* Notes and Bindings. Anger, Courage, Revenge, etc. require a more strenuous and stirring movement.[21]

Heinichen worried as late as 1728 that composers were still poorly prepared to compose music of affective emphasis:

> What a bottomless ocean we still have before us merely in the expression of words and the affections. And how delighted is our ear, if we perceive in a well-written church composition or other music how a skilled composer has attempted here and there to move the emotions of an audience through his refined and text-related musical expression, and in this way successfully finds the true purpose of music.[22]

His contemporary and the outstanding German writer on music during the Baroque, Johann Mattheson (1681–1764), coined the term 'Klang-Rede' ('oration in sound') for all music, including instrumental works. And in the most succint aesthetic slogan of the time, he made clear the essential requirement of the affections to musical meaning: 'Alles was ohne löbliche Affecten geschiehet, heisst nichts, thut nichts, gilt nichts' ('Everything that occurs without laudable affections means nothing, does nothing, is worth nothing').[23]

In all the diversity that stands for Baroque music and its legacy to later musical developments, it is the factors of Italian culture, Italian music and Italian musicians that not only defined most of what was progressive about the historical period but also continued to dominate European musical culture until the end of the nineteenth century. Not only did Baroque music begin with the new expressive and formal concepts of Italian theorists and composers, but it was Italian music that almost totally conquered the European musical scene. Exactly why indigenous Italian musical expression, styles and forms did not become part of Italian high culture until the seventeenth century is a question that apparently remains unanswered. Although suggestions of Italian lyricism and expressiveness certainly colour earlier secular forms such as the frottola and madrigal, these forms and those of sacred music continued to be dominated by north European musical concepts, usually developed on Italian soil by foreigners from regions beyonds the Alps.

Fundamental to Italian musical sovereignty in the seventeenth and eighteenth centuries – in addition to the creation of new vocal forms and styles – was the related development of a new singing technique. Not only was it characterized by elaborately difficult vocal embellishments and passage-work, but it allowed singers to add new expressiveness to vocal music. Robert Donington gave an eloquent description of its effectiveness:

> The smooth, deep current of sound never falters, but its surface is a continual ripple of changing colours, modulations of volume, flexibility of tempo. The imagination is pure singer's imagination. And not only each note, but each word is made to live. The vowels are exploited for their varied colourings, the consonants for their variety of articulation and their full declamatory value. Caressed in this way fiercely and gently by turns, the words add another dimension to music.[24]

Although professional singers, both men and women, are known from the late Renaissance, especially at northern Italian courts, it was only after the establishment of new secular vocal forms that the profession expanded dramatically. Gifted women, whose careers as singers had always been severely restricted by the ban on their participation in sacred music, quickly found themselves in demand as professional opera stars. Their popularity both in Italy and across Europe was challenged only by the male castratos who were liberated by opera from their restricted service to the church; many of them became the most famous singers of the Baroque. The demand for Italian artists quickly resulted in the establishment of singing-teachers and conservatories of music, most notably in Naples. These had a unique effect on both the spreading influence of Italian singers and the training of many major Italian composers. For example, in the period between 1720 and 1750, composers trained in Neapolitan conservatories include Francesco Durante, Nicola Porpora, Francesco Feo, Nicola Logroscino, Leonardo Vinci, Leonardo Leo, Giovanni Battista Pergolesi and Niccolò Jommelli. The combination of a distinctly Italian concept of singing, a large number of com-posers gifted in exploiting it, and skilled singers trained to create it in the opera house and in the chambers of the wealthy, gave Italian music an international appeal that was equally appreciated abroad, in Munich and Dresden, St Petersburg, London and finally even Paris. In the long view, however, this Italian development was not only to influence singing technique and style into the twentieth cen-tury but also to lead to a domination of opera by Italian composers in the eighteenth and nineteenth centuries; though challenged by German and other composers, Italian composers still frequently dominate the major opera theatres to this day.

BACH AND HANDEL

An examination of the relationship between music of the Baroque and its future historical course cannot be concluded without reflect-ing briefly on the impact of Johann Sebastian Bach and George Frideric Handel on music history.[25] Of the two, Handel's place and importance in the subsequent history of music is less complex and easier to summarize. His posthumous fame as a composer was badly distorted. For the English, he became an icon of musical respectabi-lity and nationalism; for the Germans, he was wrongly cast in a companion role with Bach as one of the two greatest composers of German sacred music. His magnificent operas, largely composed for the London stage, were forgotten along with the eighteenth-century traditions of *opera seria*. Most curious and unfortunate, until the recent past, his international fame remained anchored on only one work, *Messiah*,[26] his most atypical oratorio. Despite these and other often incomplete or skewed viewpoints of what Handel achieved, he continued as a figure of considerable influence into the twentieth century. Indeed, outside the sacred music repertory, Handel 'is the only composer of the Baroque or earlier whose music has remained continuously before the public since his lifetime'.[27] In England Handel's reputation never faded away, although this reputation was based almost entirely on the creation and idealization of the English oratorio genre. After his death, on 14 April 1759, he was extolled repeatedly as a genius who had created the sublime in music, two catchwords that often defined achievement in English arts and letters in the mid-eighteenth century. For example, in the *Public Advertiser* (17 April 1759) the following acrostic appeared:

> **H**e's gone, the Soul of Harmony is fled!
> **A**nd warbling Angels hover round him dead.
> **N**ever, no, never since the Tide of Time,
> **D**id Music know a Genius so sublime!
> **E**ach mighty Harmonist that's gone before,
> **L**essen'd to Mites when we his Works explore.[28]

Handel's genius was compared with England's greatest literary figures, Dryden and Pope, and he was buried in Westminster Abbey, England's national shrine. His oratorios were transformed into national monuments when in 1784 a great commemorative festival was held in Westminster Abbey to celebrate the centenary of his birth (mistakenly thought to have been 1684). His music was subjected to a massive group of more than 500 performers. Commemorations such as this continued until 1791, when a total of 1068 musicians was involved. 'Handelomania' had become rooted in the English choral tradition. The Three Choirs Festival in England imitated these gigantic distortions of Handel's music, a performance style that can also be traced in the USA until the middle of the present century. To maintain Handel's music as a living tradition it was reworked in numerous adaptations. For a performance of *Messiah* in Berlin in 1786, Johann Adam Hiller reorchestrated and altered the score to produce, in his words, 'an entirely new score, as far as what Handel would himself have written at the present day'.[29] For performances in Vienna in the 1780s, Mozart also reorchestrated Handel's *Messiah*, as well as *Acis and Galatea*, the *St Cecilia Ode* and *Alexander's Feast*. Haydn's oratorio *The Creation* was strongly influenced by Handel, and Beethoven has been quoted as saying he believed Handel to be the greatest composer that ever lived.[30]

Between 1787 and 1797 Samuel Arnold published a collected edition of Handel's music, the first ever attempted for any composer. Although incomplete, it contained 19 of the oratorios and enabled numerous choral societies in England to perform Handel's music into the next century, when further English editions of this music appeared. Handel's music was, however, canonized in the 1850s when the German scholar Friedrich Chrysander began to produce his 100-volume edition of all Handel's works. Together with a similar project undertaken at the same time for the works of Bach, these two great musicological achievements inaugurated the modern age of musical scholarship and ensured that Handel and Bach would be the first composers to be placed in the pantheon of musical geniuses whose impact on subsequent developments in music is still difficult to estimate. In Handel's case, the influence came largely from his choral works: English composers of the nineteenth century seemed to be transfixed by their style and originality, and English choral music frequently imitated Handelian concepts until the mid-twentieth century. This influence also spread to composers of other nationalities.

With Bach, one confronts a great enigma in music history. In Friedrich Blume's memorable phrase, Bach's work 'ist genährt von der Vergangenheit und speist die Zukunft' ('was nourished by the past and feeds the future').[31] It is the fact of Bach's 'feeding' of the future of music that belongs among the most remarkable characteristics of any composer's impact on subsequent musical and general cultural history. The reception of Bach's music in subsequent centuries remains difficult to generalize about, and there is still no successful comprehensive overview of his impact on the nineteenth and twentieth centuries. The scope of the subject far exceeds any brief summary. It is not correct, however, to assume that Bach and his music were totally forgotten after his death in 1750. His second eldest son, Carl Philipp Emanuel, performed some of the sacred vocal music in Hamburg; the Bach tradition, especially for his keyboard music, was kept alive by former students; and numerous copies of the works circulated into the next century. In Vienna the musical circle organized by Gottfried van Swieten fostered performances of Baroque music, including Bach's. Both Mozart and Haydn knew some of his music, and Haydn owned a rare copy of the B minor Mass. Beethoven from his youth was well known for his performances from the *Well-Tempered Clavier*, and the influence of Bach's fugal style in his later compositions is incontestable.

The early nineteenth century saw a confluence of German developments placing upon Bach the mantle of the greatest native composer and the one who led the way for a German form of 'absolute' instrumental music. Johann Nicolaus Forkel, who published the first biography of Bach in 1802, gave a substantial impetus to making Bach a national hero. He spoke of his undertaking as contributing to 'the honor of the German name. The works which Johann Sebastian Bach has left us are an invaluable national patrimony, with which no other nation has anything to be compared'. Forkel considered Bach 'the first classic that ever was, or perhaps ever will be'. His purpose in writing the Bach biography had 'no other object whatever than to call the attention of the public to an undertaking the sole aim of which is to raise a worthy monument to German art, to furnish the true Artist with a gallery of the most instructive models, and to open to the friends of Music, an inexhaustible source of the most sublime enjoyment'.[32] In the early nineteenth century, E. T. A. Hoffmann, as well as Wackenroder and Tieck, raised aloft Bach's instrumental works as models of 'pure romantic essence'.[33] Bach's keyboard works and *The Art of Fugue* were seen as examples of the metaphysical achievement of textless music, music that could express 'inexpressible longing'. A model of German enthusiasm and pride in Bach's achievement appeared in the *Allegemeine musikalische Zeitung* in 1801, written by one Triest, a clergyman from Stettin:

> What joy for a patriotic resident of our Fatherland to know that the greatest, most profound harmonist of all previous time, who exceeded everything that Italy, France, England had done for pure music, who moved his musical world – which surely was accustomed to learned works – to amazement, and passed on to posterity still unequaled models, which would be considered like mysteries . . . that this man, I say, was a German! Proud and majestic shines the name of Johann Sebastian Bach before all German composers of the first half of the preceding century. He grasped with Newton's spirit everything that previously had been thought about and established as example, probed the depths so fully and successfully that he is considered to this day the rule-giver of authentic harmony.[34]

A growing interest in Bach's sacred vocal music also began at the turn of the nineteenth century, especially in Berlin. When Carl Friedrich Zelter assumed the direction of the Berlin Singakademie, he continued the practice already established by his predecessor of including Bach's works in the repertory. Two of his students, Felix Mendelssohn and the singer Eduard Devrient, caught up in Zelter's love for Bach, proposed to perform for the first time since its original performance the *St Matthew Passion*. This famous revival in 1829 of one of Bach's most imposing sacred works contributed to the growing movement in Germany that would view Bach as the great spokesman for German Protestantism and proclaimer of the Bible through music. He was to be called the 'fifth Evangelist', and a renewed interest in his cantatas and other sacred works such as the *B minor Mass* spread beyond Germany to other countries, including England and the United States.

Just as the growing interest in Handel's music had demanded an accurate and editorially competent publication of all his music, so too did the growing enthusiasm for performing Bach. In 1850, the centenary of his death, the Bach-Gesellschaft was founded with the support of the publisher Breitkopf & Härtel. A call for such an edition had been made as early as 1837 by Robert Schumann. Again revealing a particular interest in Bach's sacred works, the editors planned to publish as the first volume the *B minor Mass*. When they found that the primary manuscript source was unobtainable (being in the possession of the Swiss music dealer Hermann Nägeli, who refused access to it), they inaugurated the edition with a volume containing ten of the cantatas. The 46th and final volume was published in 1900. While the edition was often faulty in its scholarship and contained spurious works, it was largely free from editorial additions, included a critical commentary on sources, and established a general concept of the nature of the scholarly edition that was to influence numerous similar editions for other composers up to World War II. It also paved the way for a large number of practical performing editions of Bach's music, enabling the formation of numerous Bach festivals and the mounting of countless performances of his music.

A further landmark in the Bach revival was the achievement by Philipp Spitta of his epochal Bach biography, published between 1873 and 1880. This provided the first comprehensive examination not only of all Bach's music but also of the historical context in which he composed. Spitta gave for the first time a detailed picture of seventeenth-century German music as it laid the foundation for Bach's art, and he applied methods of musicological research (such as attempting to date compositions by dating the manuscript paper) that were to find their fullest development only in the next century. In his description and analysis of all Bach's music, the major emphasis for the first time in any Bach biography was on the sacred vocal music. Translated into English by Clara Bell and J. A. Fuller Maitland in 1883–5, Spitta's achievement remains monumental, despite certain factual inaccuracies uncovered by later research, and is still the single most comprehensive and influential source of information about Bach and his music.

Bach was deified in Hans von Bülow's famous slogan extolling the three B's, Bach, Beethoven and Brahms, the last two composers owing more than a little to Bach's patrimony. In our century, this German triumvirate has been a dominating force in the musical world. Bach scholarship has not only continued but expanded and achieved brilliant results: a revised chronology of the sacred works and a sophistication of research methods; new insights into Bach as man and into his music; new and often controversial theories regarding the performance of his music; and an expanded vision of the theoretical and aesthetic principles that influenced his work. In this century, the works of a number of composers, including Busoni, Bartók, Webern, Hindemith and Stravinsky, indicate that Bach's music continues 'to feed the future'. Bach has become part of popular culture (for example, the Swingle Singers) and has been satirized (Peter Schickele, as 'P.D.Q. Bach'). In the last analysis, however, the Bach enigma can best be seen in the astonishing popularity of his music with general audiences as well as with those specifically orientated to Baroque music. Music that is so uncompromising in technique, so complex in textures and melodic formulations, so wedded to intellectual premises of meaning, and so much the epitome of craft over easily assimilated expressive formulations would appear to be a music of little if any popular appeal. Yet as audience attendance at any major Bach concert will prove, quite the opposite is true. Despite the unlikely ability of audiences as a whole to decipher a great deal of the inner technical complexity of his music, Bach's perfection of design, his ethical spirit – his devotion to God – and certainly his supreme joy in his art and craft are clear to those who listen. It is perhaps as much the mystery of Bach's music as anything that attracts amateur and professional alike. It is in Bach's music that one sees, in the second half of the twentieth century, not only music formed by society, but society – or at least that part of society responding to music – formed and transformed by music.

NOTES

[1] *Correspondence de Jean Baptiste Rousseau et de Brosette*, ed. P. Bonnefon (Paris, 1911), ii, 280–81.

[2] 'Lettre sur la musique françoise', *Oeuvres complètes*, xiv (Paris, 1826), 22. See C. Palisca, 'Baroque', *HMT*, for further information regarding the French origins of the term.

[3] *Music in the Baroque Era* (New York, 1947).

[4] See, for example, C. Dahlhaus, 'Das 18. Jahrhundert als musikgeschichtliche Epoche', *Die Musik des 18. Jahrhunderts* (Laaber, 1985).

[5] Even Dahlhaus, ibid, who seeks to persuade that periodization is useless in musical historiography and who sets out to prove a unity of musical developments in the eighteenth century, finds it necessary to begin his eighteenth-century period in the 1720s!

[6] The ruthless suppression by Lully of talented composers that led to a certain sterility in French music during and after his lifetime is examined in Julie Anne Sadie's essay in this volume, 'Paris and Versailles'.

[7] See Chapter II, 'Rome: the Power of Patronage'.

[8] H. J. Marx, 'Die Musik am Hofe Pietro Kardinal Ottobonis unter Arcangelo Corelli', *AnMc*, no.5 (1968), 104–77.

[9] H. E. Smither, *A History of the Oratorio*, i (Chapel Hill, 1977), 276.

[10] J. A. Hiller, *Lebensbeschreibungen berühmter Musikgelehrten und Tonkünstler* (Leipzig, 1784), 137.

[11] For a particularly rich collection of this iconography see A. Bowles, *Musical Ensembles in Festival Books – 1500–1800: an Iconographic & Documentary Survey* (Ann Arbor, 1989).

[12] See W. Weber, 'London: a City of Unrivalled Riches', *Man and Music: the Classical Era* (London, 1989).

[13] F. de Callières, *Histoire poétique de la guerre nouvellement déclamée entre les anciens et les modernes* (Paris, 1688), as cited in G. Cowart, *The Origins of Modern Musical Criticism: French and Italian Music, 1600–1750* (Ann Arbor, 1981); my discussion is based on Cowart's excellent work.

[14] Cowart, *The Origins of Modern Musical Criticism*, 77.

[15] ibid 75.

[16] J. D. Heinichen, *Der General-Bass in der Composition* (Dresden, 1728), 20 (footnote i).

[17] H. J. Marx, *Arcangelo Corelli: die Überlieferung der Werke: Catalogue raisonné* (Cologne, 1980).

[18] A. Hutchings, *The Baroque Concerto* (New York, 1979), 256.

[19] ibid, 253 (footnote).

[20] M. Talbot, *Vivaldi* (London, 1978), 145.

[21] *A Compendium of Practical Musick* (London, 1667), 140.

[22] Heinichen, *Der General-Bass in der Composition*, 24.

[23] J. Mattheson, *Der vollkommene Capellmeister* (Hamburg, 1739), 146.

[24] *The Interpretation of Early Music* (London, 1963), 450–51.

[25] As late as 1931 the distinguished series *The Oxford History of Music* (2nd edn) continued to entitle the volume covering the eighteenth-century Baroque period 'The Age of Bach and Handel', the same title as used in the 1st edn (1901–5).

[26] Two major studies of Handel have helped significantly to clarify his historical significance and prodigious musical achievements: P. H. Lang, *George Frideric Handel* (New York, 1966); and C. Hogwood, *Handel* (London, 1985), especially 'Handel and Posterity', 232–76.

[27] W. Dean, 'Scholarship and the Handel Revival', *Handel Tercentenary Collection*, ed. S. Sadie and A. Hicks (London, 1987), 2.

[28] O. E. Deutsch, *Handel: a Documentary Biography* (New York, 1955), 818.

[29] Hogwood, *Handel*, 246.

[30] ibid, 248.

[31] *MGG*, i, 1017.

[32] *Über Johann Sebastian Bachs Leben, Kunst und Kunstwerke* (Leipzig, 1802); trans. in *The Bach Reader*, ed. H. T. David and A. Mendel (New York, 1945), 295–8.

[33] *Schriften zur Musik*, cited in C. Dahlhaus, 'Zur Entstehung der romantischen Bach-Deutung,' *BJb 1978*, 192.

[34] Triest, 'Bemerkungen über die Ausbildung der Tonkunst in Deutschland im achtzehnten Jahrhundert', *Allgemeine musikalische Zeitung*, iii (1800–01), 259; cited in Dahlhaus, *BJb*, 197–8.

Chapter II

Rome: the Power of Patronage

MALCOLM BOYD

Roma non ha tetto per accoglier la Musica, che ci vive mendica
(Alessandro Scarlatti, 1705)[1]

When Handel arrived in Rome at the beginning of 1707 he found a
musical culture whose artistic level surpassed that of all other
European capitals   (Hans Joachim Marx)[2]

The sharp contrast between these two views of musical life in Rome
during the early years of the eighteenth century cannot be accounted
for by any changes that took place there between May 1705 and the
early months of 1707, nor even by the way perceptions have altered
during the three centuries that separate the two writers. Professor
Marx goes on to speak of the oratorios, serenatas and secular cantatas that 'employed new effects to transport audiences to a hitherto
unknown state of sensual excitement . . . Listeners were enraptured
not only by the voices of the Papal singers, but also by the grand
sound of the large orchestras, the like of which had never been
heard'. Scarlatti, on the other hand, was writing as an opera composer at a time when papal authority had placed a ban on all
operatic performance, public or private, in Rome; the fact that circumstances had forced him to accept a subordinate post at the
basilica of S Maria Maggiore, as well as his failure to secure a
suitable position in Rome for his most gifted son, Domenico, also
helps to account for the disgruntled tone of his letter to Prince
Ferdinando. Taken together, therefore, the two quotations neatly
summarize the situation that faced the musician in Rome during
much of the period under discussion: difficulties as far as opera was
concerned, but plenty of opportunities elsewhere.

THE PAPACY AND CHURCH MUSIC

The influence and authority exerted by the popes in Rome during the
seventeenth and eighteenth centuries extended to virtually all aspects
of the city's cultural and spiritual life, far exceeding those of the doge

at Venice and the viceroy at Naples. This could hardly have been otherwise in a city which (according to the 1701 census) contained no fewer than 81 parish churches, as well as many more attached to religious brotherhoods, seminaries and private palaces, not to mention the numerous monasteries; in the same year the city's population of just over 140 000 included 63 bishops, 2824 priests, 1968 nuns, and 3811 monks and other 'religiosi'. As far as music was concerned, it was the Vatican that determined, by its example and when necessary by edict and censorship, what was played and sung in both the churches and the theatres, and even to some extent in the private palaces as well. The years 1670 and 1740 have been chosen as boundary dates for this chapter not merely because they serve as convenient 'round figures', but because they mark the beginning of one pontificate (Clement X) and the end of another (Clement XII). The papal succession during the whole of this period may be summarized thus:

1670–76:   Clement X (Emilio Altieri; *b* Rome, 1590)
1676–89:   Innocent XI (Benedetto Odescalchi; *b* Como, 1611)
1689–91:   Alexander VIII (Pietro Ottoboni; *b* Venice, 1610)
1691–1700: Innocent XII (Antonio Pignatelli; *b* near Naples, 1615)
1700–21:   Clement XI (Giovanni Francesco Albani; *b* Urbino, 1649)
1721–4:   Innocent XIII (Michelangelo dei Conti; *b* Rome, 1655)
1724–30:   Benedict XIII (Pietro Francesco Orsini; *b* Gravina, 1649)
1730–40:   Clement XII (Lorenzo Corsini; *b* Florence, 1652).

The advanced age reached by most popes at the time of their election should not be understood as indicating a high regard for long experience of the priesthood or a reverence for grey hairs; more often than not it reflected the political divisions attending the conclaves or else the personal ambitions of the cardinals. The election of an aged pope could be the means of shelving for a few years a difficult or impossible decision; besides, a reasonably frequent change of pontiff increased the chances of ecclesiastical preferment for all concerned. Five of the eight popes listed above were over 75 at the time of their election, and all but one were past what would now be regarded as retirement age. The exception is Clement XI, whose scholarly distinction and outstanding personal qualities made him an obvious choice to succeed Innocent XII in 1700; but his election, too, would certainly have been blocked by Austria's supporters if his sympathy for the French cause in the matter of the Spanish succession had been known at the time of the conclave. At 51 he was considered by many to be too young for the office. His pontificate was the longest during the period under consideration (the longest, in fact, since that of Alexander III, 1159–81), and in many other ways, too, it was the most important as far as music at Rome was concerned. Alessandro and Domenico Scarlatti, Corelli, Handel and Caldara were among the outstanding composers active in Rome during the first two decades of the eighteenth century, and the views and actions of Pope Clement XI directly affected much of the music they composed.

The popes and the Sacred College were very conscious of the responsibilities invested in them to preserve the ideal of a 'pure' church music, and this they attempted to do by both precept and example. The precept had in fact been formulated in the sixteenth century by the Council of Trent, which had outlawed the use of secular melodies and demanded a pious and uplifting style of musical setting which rendered the words at all times intelligible. (On other matters – including the use of instruments, which was of increasing concern to church authorities during the seventeenth and eighteenth centuries – the Council had been non-committal, or at best vague.) In the face of changing musical tastes, it was found necessary from time to time to reassert Tridentine principles, and even to go beyond them, notably in a bull of Alexander VII (1657), reaffirmed by the Holy Apostolic Visitation in 1665, by Innocent XI in 1678 and by Innocent XII in 1692. Church music was to be 'ecclesiastical, grave and devout'; it was to be sung by male voices only, out of sight of the congregation, and never by a solo voice (except possibly in short passages); while the organ was tolerated (except during Passiontide), the use of instruments associated with the theatre was frowned on.

It was perhaps only in the Vatican itself that these precepts were punctiliously observed. The papal singers, the Cappella Sistina, who sang the Mass and Office in the Sistine Chapel, were looked upon as guardians of the 'pure' tradition of Catholic church music. The prestige they had enjoyed in the sixteenth century declined somewhat during the seventeenth, but they continued to set themselves apart from other church musicians in Rome, maintaining their own standards, organization and discipline. Responsibility for the music performed in the other Roman churches rested with the Congregazione (later Accademia) di S Cecilia, founded in 1566 and still in existence today. From the Barnabite church of S Carlo ai Catinari, its headquarters from 1685, the Congregazione supervised the standards of the city's church music and controlled the activities of composers, organists, instrumentalists and singers.

Liturgical music in Rome, then, was on the whole conservative by the standards of other centres, such as Venice, but nevertheless extremely varied. The Cappella Sistina maintained a tradition of which the works of Palestrina were already recognized as the most perfect examples and exemplars. In the vast spaces of St Peter's the Cappella Giulia tempered sobriety with a more monumental approach, making use of organs and extending Palestrinian traditions in the direction of tonal harmony and polychoral effects. In the other churches and basilicas that maintained a *cappella* the character of the music depended largely on the tastes of the arch-priest and *maestro di cappella* concerned, and on their readiness to follow the Vatican lead. At patronal festivals, especially, the music might be on a quite lavish scale, with additional singers and instrumentalists hired for the occasion. The two extremes are represented in the Latin church music of two exact contemporaries who achieved their greatest fame as composers of secular music. On the one hand, the *a cappella* mass and motets that Domenico Scarlatti composed for the basilica of S Maria Maggiore and for St Peter's (where he was *maestro di cappella* from 1714 to 1719) exhibit a reverential, if not always technically orthodox, command of the *stile antico*, as the vocabulary of Renaissance polyphony came to be known. At the opposite extreme, the Vespers music composed by Handel for the Feast of Our Lady of Mount Carmel at the church of S Maria di Montesanto on 15–16 July 1707 exemplifies an uninhibitedly modern style. It includes parts for strings and oboes, but not for brass instruments, which were, however, occasionally used in Roman churches on festal occasions.

A feature of musical life at the Vatican peculiar to the period under discussion was the annual entertainment provided by the pope for the benefit of those cardinals who had attended Vespers on Christmas Eve and were remaining for the first Matins and Mass of Christmas Day. The entertainment took the form of a nativity cantata followed by a lavish supper in the Apostolic Palace. The earliest references to this practice date from 1676, when a 'dialogo', *Già molle di sudor al notte algente*, was performed. The composer is unknown, but all the pieces performed between 1679 and 1688 were the work of Giuseppe Pacieri, a *virtuoso* in the service of Cardinal Alderamo Cibo. Among the composers commissioned in subsequent years were Carlo Francesco Cesarini, Francesco Gasparini, and Alessandro and Domenico Scarlatti. These Christmas Eve celebrations continued each year until 1740, after which the new pope, Benedict XIV, was no longer prepared to meet the expense they entailed.

The music of only about half a dozen of these works has survived, but we know from librettos and contemporary accounts that there were usually five or six solo singers until 1705 and three or four after that date, together with instrumentalists (Antonio Bencini's score for 1730 included trumpets, horns, oboes, bassoon, strings and continuo) and sometimes a small chorus. The performers were chosen from the papal *cappella*, and they too were given supper after the performance, although separately from the cardinals and their guests. The works themselves are mostly called 'componimento' or 'cantata' in the librettos, but in length and structure they closely resembled an oratorio, especially those dating from after 1706, which were mostly divided into two parts like the normal oratorio of the period (see below).

MUSICAL PATRONAGE

It was by no means only in the domain of church music that the popes exercised their influence and authority; in fact, in secular music-making, and particularly opera, papal interference was perhaps even more keenly felt. The church's traditional (and to a large extent justified) mistrust of the theatre as a breeding-ground for moral turpitude and promiscuity continued to motivate papal attitudes. Against this must be set the fact that many cardinals, and even some popes, were themselves active in promoting plays and operas, and in some cases even in writing them. The result, during the years 1670–1740, was that periods of papal opposition to opera alternated with others when the genre was encouraged, or at least tolerated. The Barberini pope, Urban VIII (1568–1644), had actually been responsible for establishing opera at Rome, and Giulio Rospigliosi (1600–69), who wrote the librettos for most of Urban's productions, reigned as Pope Clement IX during the years (1667–9) immediately preceding the period under discussion. Among his successors it was the Clements who tended to be indulgent towards opera and the Innocents who were most often guilty of suppressing it. And what applies to opera applies also, in some measure at least, to other vocal genres in the vernacular – to the serenata, the cantata and even the oratorio.

Under the pope, and often in conflict with his rulings, an ecclesiastical and lay aristocracy wielded immense influence as patrons of music and the other arts in Rome. As munificent supporters of secular music in the early seventeenth century, the Barberini were succeeded above all by three cardinals (Colonna, Pamphili and Ottoboni), a marquis (Francesco Maria Ruspoli) and two exiled monarchs (Queen Christina of Sweden and Queen Maria Casimira of Poland). Friendly rivalry characterized much of their musical patronage, which encompassed all the current genres, both sacred and secular.

Cardinal Carlo Colonna was a member of an illustrious family which, since the late twelfth century, had included numerous cardinals, despite their frequent opposition to the Holy See. Carlo Colonna (1665–1739) was raised to the purple by Clement XI in 1706. In the pages of musical history he is remembered chiefly as patron of the annual feast of Our Lady of Mount Carmel, celebrated with considerable festivity and elaborate music at the Carmelite church of S Maria di Montesanto, one of the twin churches on the south side of the Piazza del Popolo. Alessandro Scarlatti and two of his sons (probably Domenico and Pietro) supplied music for this festival in 1703 and Handel in 1707. The celebrations of 1704 furnish an example of how papal authority could directly affect musical performance: on this occasion Pope Clement XI vetoed the erection of a gallery above the west door of the church because of the scandal caused the previous year when the congregation had turned its back on the high altar in order to listen to the music.

Benedetto Pamphili (1653–1730) was able to devote a considerable part of the fortune he inherited from his great-uncle, Pope Innocent X, to beautifying his palace on the Corso with paintings, furnishings and the sound of music. He sponsored operas and oratorios, and wrote texts for secular cantatas which were performed at his regular Sunday 'academies' or on other occasions. Corelli, Gasparini and two of the Bononcini brothers, Giovanni and Antonio Maria, were members of his household at one time or another, and among other composers who wrote works for him were Cesarini, Pasquini, Alessandro Scarlatti and Handel.

Handel's first oratorio, *Il trionfo del Tempo e del Disinganno* (1707), was composed to a libretto by Pamphili, but, as Winton Dean suggested in *The New Grove Dictionary of Music*, it may have been first performed at the Cancelleria, the grand palace of Cardinal Pietro Ottoboni (1667–1740) standing between what is now the Corso Vittorio Emanuele II and the Via del Pellegrino. During Ottoboni's occupation of the Cancelleria the palace housed a private theatre (rebuilt and extended by Filippo Juvarra in 1709), while in the Sala Riario and the Sala dei Cento Giorni of the *appartamento nobile* the cardinal received those guests who attended his regular 'academies' of vocal and instrumental music. Since the church of S Lorenzo in Damaso stood (and still stands) under the same roof, the Cancelleria might be said to represent a microcosm of the musical life of Rome, both sacred and secular. Like Pamphili, Ottoboni was a well-educated man of immense wealth and the grand-nephew of a pope – in Ottoboni's case Alexander VIII, who raised him to the purple in 1689. Again like Pamphili, he wrote oratorio librettos, and in fact opera librettos too, and employed the best composers of the day (though not in this case Handel) to set them to music. Ottoboni's *soirées musicales*, held at first on Mondays and later on Wednesdays, rivalled those of Pamphili, and from 1690 (when Pamphili left for Bologna, where he served as papal legate until 1693) they too were led by Corelli. Despite their shared interests and overlapping activities, the two cardinals were men of very different temperaments, as the Italian writer Roberto Pagano has trenchantly observed:

A mere comparison between the portraits of the two cardinals

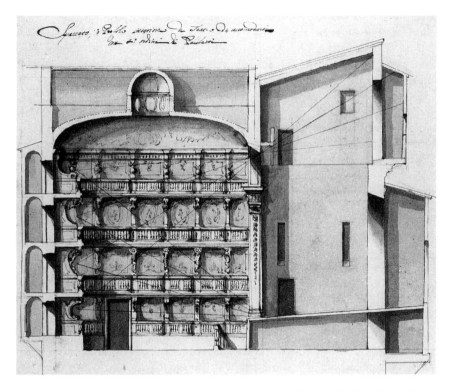

5. Design by Filippo Juvarra for the Teatro Ottoboni in the Palazzo della Cancelleria, Rome: longitudinal section showing the boxes of the auditorium (although Juvarra rebuilt and extended the theatre in 1709, it is not known to what extent this design was used in the final scheme)

reveals the greater success of the younger one as far as personal charm is concerned; but a thousand nuances tell us that, despite the delicacy of his features, Ottoboni lacked the fine discretion of Pamphili. The latter knew how to keep himself apart from all the complex political intrigues of the time, while Ottoboni was always on the lookout for personal advantage, for example in 1710, when he succeeded in having himself made cardinal protector of France while at the same time pretending not to be interested in the new, lucrative post.[3]

Closely associated with these two cardinals in the musical life of Rome, as well as in their membership of the Arcadian Academy (see below), was the marquis (from 1709, prince) Francesco Maria Ruspoli (1672–1731). Even wealthier than Pamphili and Ottoboni, Ruspoli shared with them the distinction of employing the best composers and musicians in Rome. During much of 1707–8 Handel lived as composer-in-residence at the Palazzo Bonelli, where he composed for Ruspoli the oratorio *La resurrezione* (1708) and many of his Italian cantatas, and from 1709 to 1716 Antonio Caldara served the prince as *maestro di cappella*.

Queen Christina of Sweden (1626–89), after her abdication and conversion to Roman Catholicism in 1654, lived the rest of her unorthodox life in Rome, where she quickly established herself in intellectual circles and gathered round her some of the leading writers, artists and musicians of her day. The *accademia* that she founded in 1656 survived her as the famous Arcadian Academy (see below). Christina was an enthusiastic supporter of opera, and the force of her personality, together with the high prestige she enjoyed as a convert from heresy, meant that she was one of the few people in a position to contest papal opposition to theatrical entertainments. Her support of Alessandro Scarlatti and other musicians in the controversy attending the early performances of his *Gli equivoci nel sembiante* (1679) did much to establish Scarlatti's reputation as an opera composer.[4] Other composers to benefit from Christina's patronage included Alessandro Melani, Pasquini and Corelli, who in 1681 dedicated his first published volume of sonatas to her.

Christina's long 'reign' in Rome, which ended with her death in 1689, was followed some ten years later by that of another queen, Maria Casimira (1641–1716), widow of King Jan III Sobieski of Poland. Undoubtedly aware of the role played by her illustrious predecessor, Maria Casimira set about rivalling the other maecenases with munificent patronage of the arts and a conspicuous 'presence' on the Roman stage. Queen Christina had made Alessandro Scarlatti her *maestro di cappella*; in 1711 Maria Casimira appointed Scarlatti's most gifted son, Domenico, to a similar position in her household. But comparisons between the two monarchs were made long before this. An oft-quoted pasquinade, which Francesco Valesio entered into his diary on 28 August 1700, gave voice to what many among the Roman intelligentsia must have been thinking:

> Nacqui da un gallo semplice gallina,
> vissi tra li pollastri e fui reggina,
> venni a Roma cristiana e non Cristina.

> A simple young hen, daughter of a Frenchman,
> she lived among the cockerels and was queen;
> she came to Rome a Christian and not a Christina.[5]

There is no doubt that Maria Casimira's reputation in modern times has suffered from a too ready acceptance of this contemporary judgment. As Valesio's diary as a whole makes clear, Maria Casimira enjoyed the esteem of the Roman aristocracy, the respect of the people and the ear of Pope Clement XI. Soon after her arrival in Rome she was admitted with particular ceremony into Queen

Christina's Arcadian Academy. Her household in the Piazza della Trinità de' Monti included singers and instrumentalists, and from 1708, when she had a small theatre installed in her palace, she employed some of the best Roman talents – including the stage designer Filippo Juvarra, the poet C. S. Capece and the composer Domenico Scarlatti – to put on opera performances which continued annually until 1714, when she left Rome to spend her last days in her native France.

THE ACADEMIES AND 'MUSICA DA CAMERA'

Cardinals, princes and exiled queens by no means exhausted the sources of musical patronage in Rome. Foreign ambassadors, notably those of Venice, Spain, Portugal, France and the Austrian Empire, were often zealous supporters of the arts, either for reasons of personal gratification or for propaganda purposes. The performance of a musical work, typically a serenata (see below), was an appropriate way of celebrating a political event or commemorating the birthday, betrothal, marriage etc. of a member of the ruling family. Musical patronage also went on in the *accademie*.

An *accademia* might be a more or less informal, ad hoc gathering at the invitation of a particular person (those of Cardinal Ottoboni, Cardinal Pamphili, Prince Ruspoli and Queen Christina have already been mentioned), or it might be a more formally organized society with a widely dispersed membership devoted to particular aims. As far as the latter type is concerned, there were in Rome a number of societies dedicated to promoting various artistic and scientific disciplines. The Accademia del Disegno di S Luca, founded in 1596, looked after the interests of painters, sculptors and architects. From 1702, at the instigation of Pope Clement XI, the academy organized an annual prizegiving ceremony at its headquarters next to the Palazzo del Campidoglio in which music, both instrumental and vocal, played a decorative role.[6] An orchestral sinfonia signalled the opening of the proceedings (Corelli supplied those for the years 1702–9, as well as supervising the music in general), and after the speeches and distribution of the prizes a cantata, composed specially for the occasion, was performed. Among the cantata composers are the names of Alessandro and Domenico Scarlatti, and it seems likely that Corelli himself wrote the cantata in 1702, although no vocal work by him is known to survive.

The Accademia di S Luca was not merely a cultural society handing out prestigious 'academy awards' each year. It had also a didactic role to play and, in addition, acted as a kind of trades union, making it difficult for non-members to find commissions in Rome. In a similar way the Congregazione di S Cecilia looked after the interests of church musicians (see above). Of the literary academies active during the period, the most important was the Accademia dell'Arcadia (Arcadian Academy), founded in 1690 but stemming from the private academy of Queen Christina of Sweden (see above). Practically every *littérateur* and person of quality in Rome was a member. They assumed the pose of nymphs and shepherds with legendary Greek or pseudo-Greek names, sometimes incorporating anagrams of their real names (Queen Maria Casimira, for example, became 'Amirisca'), and met at each other's 'huts' to discuss literary matters and exchange verses. Musicians were not usually accorded membership, and the admission of Corelli, Pasquini and Alessandro Scarlatti in 1706 seems to have been at the intervention of Cardinal Ottoboni ('Crateo' to the Arcadians), although Scarlatti, at least, was known as a poet as well; the composers Francesco Gasparini and Domenico Sarro and the singer Andrea Adami (a protégé of Ottoboni) were the only others admitted as musicians during the eighteenth century.[7] The part played by music at meetings of the Arcadians is not well documented. We know that operas composed for private theatres were sometimes repeated for the academy, and that music was included in the annual celebration of their protector, the infant Jesus; an oft-quoted account by the academy's first *custode* and chronicler, G. M. Crescimbeni, describes the impromptu setting by 'Terpandro' (Scarlatti) of verses by 'Tirsi' (the lawyer and poetaster G. B. F. Zappi).

Large-scale cantatas on the Nativity were performed in the Apostolic Palace on Christmas Eve, as mentioned above, but the musical genre *par excellence* of the academies, whether private or public, was the *cantata da camera* (chamber cantata). Its roots lay in the Florentine monody of the late sixteenth century, and the earliest volumes of cantatas were published in Venice; but throughout the seventeenth century, and well into the eighteenth, the cantata was associated particularly with Rome, where its combination of intellectual appeal and fine singing found a sympathetic audience. Its first outstanding and prolific masters were Luigi Rossi (*c*1597–1653) and Marco Marazzoli (*c*1605–1662), both in the service of the Barberini family in Rome, and Giacomo Carissimi (1605–74), whose cantatas are remarkable both for the variety of their subject matter and for their musical qualities and who was among the most prominent Roman composers of his generation. Alessandro Stradella (1644–82) was another leading composer of cantatas before he left Rome in 1677, but the most important heir to the tradition during the period under discussion was Alessandro Scarlatti (1660–1725), whose extant cantatas number over 700.

Classical myths and incidents from Roman history figure prominently in Scarlatti's early cantatas, as they had done in Stradella's, but by the end of the century cantata verse was firmly in the grip of Arcadian ideals and sentiments, and its subject matter was virtually restricted to situations of profane (and usually unhappy) love in a pastoral setting. But however repetitive the subject matter and however maudlin the sentiments of those articulating it, the verse itself was usually distinguished by some degree of verbal elegance and wit, and above all it lent itself to musical setting. Similarly, the music of the cantata, which in the mid-seventeenth century had responded to the text with a fluid sequence of recitative, aria and arioso, had by about 1700 crystallized into a succession of da capo arias (usually two or three) separated by recitative – a structure that imposed a stultifying predictability on the cantatas of the tyro and the ungifted, but challenged the best composers to exercise their imagination and invention in organizing the details of their cantatas. Little wonder that Scarlatti's were regarded, even during his lifetime, as material for the connoisseur. The only one to have achieved wide popularity in modern times is *O di Betlemme altera*, untypical (though by no means unique) in its use of string instruments and a sacred text (on the birth of Jesus); among the others are many fine works awaiting rediscovery by singers and publishers.

6. *Alessandro Scarlatti: portrait by an unknown artist, with music from his cantata 'Al fin m'ucciderete' (1705)*

To judge from the dated autographs and copies that have survived (which may not, however, be an entirely reliable indication), Scarlatti's second Roman period (1702–8) was a particularly prolific one for the composition of cantatas. Of special interest is a volume of 36, mostly autograph, in the University Library at Yale, which includes *Al fin m'ucciderete*, evidently a favourite among Scarlatti's contemporaries if the large number of eighteenth-century copies still extant is anything to go by; it appears also in an anonymous portrait of the composer now in the Civico Museo Bibliografico Musicale, Bologna (*see* fig. 6). Its text is no more remarkable than hundreds of others (the singer is tormented by jealous thoughts of the beautiful but scornful Clori), but close study of the Yale manuscript as a whole (including the several superscriptions that Scarlatti has placed on it) suggests that seemingly artificial and conventional cantata texts often reflected a particular event in the life of the composer or his patron.[8]

From this period date also most of the Italian cantatas of Handel. As a budding opera composer in Hamburg, Handel had, in the words of his biographer John Mainwaring, 'resolved to go to Italy on his own bottom, as soon as he could make a purse for that occasion'. He seems to have arrived in Florence in autum 1706, and he was almost certainly the 'sassone eccellente sonatore di cembalo e compositore di musica' whom the diarist Francesco Valesio reported as having astonished his hearers with his prowess on the organ of St John Lateran, Rome, on 14 January 1707. The archpriest of St John Lateran was at this time Cardinal Pamphili, and Pamphili may well have been the first of Rome's maecenases to enjoy the services of Handel as a composer; it was to Pamphili's words that Handel wrote his first oratorio, *Il trionfo del Tempo e del Disinganno*, in spring 1707. But Handel's most prominent Roman patron was undoubtedly Marquis Ruspoli, as a member of whose household he lived for much of 1707 and most of 1708. Ruspoli's household accounts have been carefully studied by Ursula Kirkendale, and they show that nearly 50 of Handel's Italian cantatas were composed, or at least copied, for performance at the *conversazioni* that Ruspoli held each Sunday at the Palazzo Bonelli in the Piazza de' Santi Apostoli.[9] Most of these would be performed by the famous soprano Margherita Durastanti, one of Ruspoli's musicians.

Handel undoubtedly knew and learnt from the cantatas of Alessandro Scarlatti and other composers at Rome, but his own cantatas are remarkable for their originality; indeed, they contain much that must have surprised and even puzzled his Italian colleagues. His way of often beginning the opening recitative of a cantata in the key of the first aria is a practice that Scarlatti had virtually abandoned by 1707 (none of the cantatas in the Yale volume mentioned above shows it). The effect is to tie the music too closely to a particular tonal centre, which Handel not infrequently avoids by ending the cantata in a different key from the one it started in – a practice almost unheard of among Italian composers. Scarlatti's chromaticisms might have prepared Ruspoli's *cognoscenti* for some of the harmonic audacities found in many of Handel's Italian cantatas, but the sheer dramatic intensity of works such as *O numi eterni* (on the Lucretia story), *Dietro l'orme fugaci* (Armida abandoned by Rinaldo) and *Dunque sarà pur vero* (Agrippina led to her death) is something rarely encountered in the Italian's vocal chamber music. Works such as these hold the clue, perhaps, to the reason why Handel's operas, rather than Scarlatti's, have been revived in modern times; they also help to show why Handel found it so convenient to draw upon his Italian cantatas for some of the music in his later operas and oratorios.

Instrumental chamber music also flourished in the academies. Writing about Ottoboni's *soirées* at the Cancelleria, Hans Joachim Marx tells us that 'quite often an *accademia* would begin with a trio sonata by Arcangelo Corelli. A small ensemble, consisting at the most of six violins and two violone or double basses, reinforced by a harpsichord, would perform these suite-like compositions'.[10] Marx is referring here to the trio sonata *da camera* (obviously with some doubling of the three parts), and Corelli's op.4, a set of 12 such works, was in fact published in 1694 with a title-page stating them to have been 'composte per l'Accademia dell'Em.^mo e Rev.^mo Sig.^r Cardinale Otthoboni'. Like the earlier op.2 set (1685), they consist mainly of dances (allemandes, correntes, sarabandes, gavottes and gigues), often preceded by a prelude in one or more movements.

Corelli was the most distinguished and the most revered among a large number of string players and composers of string music active in Rome by the end of the seventeenth century. Many of them were employed in one capacity or another at the church of S Luigi dei Francesi, which maintained a notable vocal and instrumental *cappella* under the direction of Alessandro Melani (1639–1703); Corelli himself played in it. Among earlier members of the *cappella* were Lelio Colista (1629–80), whose trio sonatas are widely regarded as being among the most important seventeenth-century examples of the genre; the violinist Carlo Caproli (c1620–92), whose music (which includes many chamber cantatas) has sometimes been confused with that of another violinist at S Luigi, Carlo Mannelli (1640–97); and the Milanese Carlo Ambrogio Lonati, who was in Rome between 1668 and 1677 and was for some years leader of Queen Christina's orchestra.

The trio sonata for two solo instruments and continuo, as cultivated by these and other musicians, was the most important genre of instrumental chamber music throughout most of the Baroque period. Alongside the chamber, or *da camera*, type mentioned above there was also the *da chiesa* sonata, intended originally for church performance (although in the eighteenth century these terms, insofar as they remained current, were increasingly associated with the music's structure and style rather than with its performance milieu). Corelli's op.1 (1681) and op.3 (1689) both contain 12 sonatas of the *da chiesa* type, each showing the same refined craftsmanship that characterizes all of his relatively small output.

The concerto as cultivated in Rome during this period was essentially the trio sonata 'writ large', making the most of the contrast to be obtained from a small group of soloists (the concertino) and a larger body of instruments (the ripieno or concerto grosso). As the title-page of Corelli's only published set of concertos (op.6) makes clear, these works could also be played as chamber music by simply omitting the ripieno parts, which rarely do more than double the solo lines in those passages where a bigger volume of sound is required. We are accustomed today to hearing the concertos of Corelli and other composers of the period played by small ensembles, such as the Academy of Ancient Music or the English Concert, which specialize in 'authentic' performances on period instruments with usually no more than two or three players to a part in the ripieno sections. But no less 'authentic' would be a performance of a Corelli concerto by an orchestra four or five times the size of these. We know, for example, that one of Corelli's concertos (not included in op.6) was performed as a sinfonia, or overture, to Lulier's oratorio *Santa Beatrice d'Este* when it was given in Rome in 1689; the orchestra on that occasion included 40 violins, 10 violas, 17 cellos and 7 double basses, as well as two trumpets and a trombone. The German composer and organist Georg Muffat, who visited Rome in the 1680s and heard concertos by Corelli performed there 'with the utmost accuracy by a great number of instrumental players', advocates using as many players as are available in the ripieno while always restricting the concertino to the three best string players, 'never assigning more to a part, unless in some unusually vast place where the players of the concerto grosso are exceptionally numerous, then assigning two at the most'.[11]

By 1714 the type of concerto represented by Corelli's op.6, which was published (posthumously) that year, was already being superseded in many of the main Italian and German musical centres. It survived in the conservative and largely amateur orchestral circles of England, and in the works of Corelli's pupils and others in contact with Rome. Among the most important of Corelli's pupils were Pietro Castrucci (1679–1752), one of several Roman musicians who followed Handel to London in the second decade of the eighteenth century; Giovanni Mossi (dates unknown), whose surviving works, like Corelli's, consist entirely of string sonatas and concertos; and Franscesco Geminiani (1687–1762), the most important composer of concerti grossi between Corelli and Handel, and another of those who emigrated to London (in 1714). Pietro Antonio Locatelli (1695–1764) may also have studied with Corelli. His later concertos are strongly influenced by the bravura style of the Venetians, but his op.1 (1721) seems to have been intended as a deliberate tribute to Corelli, consisting (like Corelli's op.6) of 12 concerti grossi, eight *da chiesa* and four *da camera*, with no.8 designed as a Christmas piece with optional pastorale movement. Corelli may not have been the only musician to be hailed as the 'Orpheus of his age', but few composers have so strongly and so widely influenced the music of their contemporaries and immediate successors.

THEATRES AND OPERA

As has already been mentioned, theatrical entertainments in Rome were very much subject to the whims and inclinations of the reigning pope. Sixtus V's edict of 1588 prohibiting women from appearing on stage in Rome might be circumvented in private theatres, but it inhibited actors and singers from visiting the city and discouraged the building and opening of public theatres; there were, in addition, long periods when any kind of theatrical performance was discouraged, if not absolutely prohibited.

The history of the famous Tordinona theatre illustrates the vicissitudes that attended any attempt to put on public opera in Rome between 1670 and 1740. It was, in fact, the first theatre in the city to open its doors to a paying public, and it would have done so during Carnival 1670 were it not for the death of Pope Clement IX, who had sanctioned its building, and the subsequent conclave to elect his successor. The opera-loving Queen Christina of Sweden and her major-domo, Count Giacomo d'Alibert, were the prime movers behind the Tordinona, and when it opened on 8 January 1671 it was to present an opera, *Scipione affricano*, which Francesco Cavalli had written for Venice seven years previously. Venetian operas, often (as in this case) including new music by Stradella, provided the main repertory for the theatre during its first four years. In 1675, a Holy Year, the theatre remained closed, and in fact it did not reopen for another 15 years. In 1676 Clement X was succeeded by Innocent XI, whose reputation for saying 'no' to any request earned him the nickname of 'Papa-Minga' ('minga' signifying the negative in Milanese dialect); it was not until the election of the Ottoboni pope, Alexander VIII, in 1689 that permission was granted for the Tordinona to resume operations.

7. Scene in the Piazza del Popolo at the opening of the carnival season: engraving (mid-18th century) by P. Sandley after D. Allon

On 5 January 1690 the theatre reopened with *La Statira* by Alessandro Scarlatti, to a libretto by Cardinal Ottoboni – an appropriate choice since the opera centres on the magnanimity of Alexander the Great in renouncing his empire because of his love for Statira, daughter of the Persian King Darius; two further Ottoboni operas were put on during the next season, but it was not long before revivals of recent, or fairly recent, Venetian operas began once more to dominate the repertory. The artistic climate was once again propitious for opera in Rome, and from 1692 a paying public could choose between mainly Venetian imports at the Tordinona and mainly new operas at the Capranica, formerly the private theatre of the Capranica family. This unusual situation was short-lived, however; after an expensive rebuilding of the Tordinona in 1695, making it one of the largest and best appointed theatres in Italy, ecclesiastical opposition hardened again, and in 1697 Pope Innocent XII ordered the complete demolition of the theatre. At the same time the Capranica, which had also been extensively refurbished in 1695 and had reopened with spectacular Venetian operas at increased prices, was forbidden to charge for admission, and it too was forced to close in 1698.

Political instability accompanying the War of the Spanish Succession, together with the suspension of Carnival during the years following the Roman earthquake of 1703, kept the public theatres closed even after Innocent XII had been succeeded by the more liberally inclined Clement XI. The Capranica did not reopen until 1711, after which its seasons included the premières of operas by Alessandro Scarlatti, Gasparini, Caldara, Giovanni Bononcini and Vivaldi. Some authorities mention a Roman première there in 1724 of Metastasio's first fully original opera libretto, *Didone abbandonata*, in a *rifacimento* of the setting by Domenico Sarro performed at Naples earlier in the year; from then until 1740 and beyond, composers associated with Naples, including Hasse, Porpora and Rinaldo di Capua, predominated at the Capranica. Meanwhile the Tordinona theatre remained in ruins until 1732, when its rebuilding was authorized by Pope Clement XII; after this date Neapolitan opera was in the ascendancy in that theatre as well.

Neapolitan composers provided the staple repertory for other public opera houses opened in Rome during the first half of the eighteenth century. The Teatro Alibert, opened in 1717 by Count d'Alibert's son Antonio and rechristened the Teatro delle Dame after its enlargement in 1726, was the scene of a fruitful collaboration between Metastasio and Leonardo Vinci which resulted in four operas for the 1728–9 and 1729–30 seasons; Neapolitan intermezzos became a speciality at the Teatro Valle in the 1730s; and the Teatro Argentina, inaugurated in 1732 with Sarro's *Berenice*, alternated

Neapolitan *opere serie* with spoken drama, intermezzos and other entertainments.

The opera repertory at Rome during the Baroque period has yet to receive complete scholarly documentation.[12] With the public theatres largely devoted to Venetian imports at the beginning of their history and to products of the Neapolitan school from about 1720, it might well be shown that the type of opera most truly representative of a Roman tradition was that cultivated in the private theatres of those patrons whose names have figured prominently in this chapter so far. A private theatre might be simply a room fitted out with a small stage and minimal scenery for a particular occasion; after the performance it would revert to its normal use. Alessandro Scarlatti's first opera (or, strictly speaking, the first of his to be staged), *Gli equivoci nel sembiante* (1679), was given in such an ad hoc theatre in the house of the architect Giambattista Contini in the Piazza Nicosia; it is a pastoral on an intimate scale, requiring only four singers, a small string band, no elaborate machinery and a single set. Many of the operas given in other private theatres, such as those of Colonna, Pamphili, Rospigliosi, Ruspoli, the various ambassadors and the religious colleges (the Collegio Clementino, the Seminario Romano and the Collegio Nazzareno), were on a similarly small scale.

Even when a patron could afford the luxury of a permanent, purpose-built theatre, such as those of Pamphili (in his palace on the Corso, 1684, designer Carlo Fontana), Ottoboni (in the Palazzo della Cancelleria, 1709, designer Filippo Juvarra) and Maria Casimira (in the Palazzo Zuccari, Piazza della Trinità de' Monti, c1708, designer unknown, perhaps Juvarra), they could not compete with the large public theatres in the possibilities they offered for operas on a heroic scale. Perhaps the most ambitious and elaborate of all the operas staged in these private Roman theatres was *Il Costantino pio*, C. F. Pollarolo's setting of a libretto by Cardinal Ottoboni, performed at the Cancelleria in 1710. The music has not survived, but the designs reproduced in the printed libretto give some idea of the work's unusual scale. Most other privately produced operas were on a more intimate level, and since the aristocratic patrons of opera in Rome were also members of the Arcadian Academy it is not surprising that pastoral comedies were popular in the private theatres, or that pastoral scenes should occur frequently in heroic operas as well.

Considering the difficulties attending opera production at Rome during the period under discussion, it is remarkable that the Roman theatres, both public and private, were served by some of the finest opera composers of the day. The papal ban on opera production during the period of Handel's residence in Rome (1707–9) robbed the Eternal City of its chance to sample the gifts of its most distinguished musical visitor as a composer for the lyric stage; Florence (with *Rodrigo*, 1707) and Venice (with *Agrippina*, 1709) were the beneficiaries. But Stradella, Alessandro and Domenico Scarlatti, Giovanni Bononcini and Gasparini – all of them among the leading Italian composers of opera – lived and worked for some years at least in Rome, establishing a distinctive, if short-lived operatic tradition there. It was, moreover, as Reinhard Strohm has observed, this Roman tradition that was to prove ultimately to be of the utmost importance to Handel as an operatic composer in London:

> By 1737–8 Handel must already have been well aware of the suc-
> cesses of the 'moderns'; not only had he already written for
> Carestini and Caffarelli, not only was Farinelli enjoying great
> acclaim in London in the works of Porpora and Hasse, but he
> himself had conducted, for example, Vinci's *Didone abbandonata* in
> 1737, in a version supplemented with much music composed by
> Hasse. In his own works, however, Handel takes another line. His
> models are Gasparini, Bononcini and Stradella (*Israel in Egypt*,
> 1738), and his *Concerti Grossi* op.6 were intended as a memorial to
> Corelli . . . Handel, at least in these years, shows himself attached
> to a musical tradition with a distinctively Roman basis.[13]

CONFRATERNITIES AND PALACES: ORATORIO AND SERENATA

Opera performances in Rome were concentrated into the period between Christmas and Lent and were specially popular during Carnival, which occupied the 11 days preceding Ash Wednesday; performances at other times of the year were infrequent. This did not mean, though, that the kind of music enjoyed in the theatre was denied the Romans for the rest of the year. At various times between Lent and Christmas, music of an operatic kind was available in the form of the oratorio (especially, but by no means exclusively, during Lent) and the serenata (especially out of doors during summer and autumn).

Rome had been the birthplace of oratorio. The Congregazione dell'Oratorio, a society of laymen founded in the spirit of the Counter-Reformation by Filippo Neri (1515–95), had received official recognition from Pope Gregory VIII in 1575; the society was widely referred to simply as the 'Filippini'. During the seventeenth century its meetings assumed the pattern of two sessions of prayers and singing separated by a sermon. The musical items gradually became longer and more important, taking the form of a semi-dramatic or contemplative enactment of an incident from the scriptures, presented in the vernacular without costume or gesture but with the biblical characters represented by different singers. As the form grew it began to fill the sessions both before and after the sermon, which accounts for the bipartite structure of most Italian oratorios in the late seventeenth and eighteenth centuries. The vernacular oratorios performed by the Filippini at their oratories (prayerhalls) adjoining the Chiesa Nuova and S Girolamo della Carità in Rome were joined before 1650 by Latin ones given during Lent by the more aristocratic Arciconfraternita del Santissimo Crocifisso at S Marcello. It may have been for this confraternity, or possibly for the German College where he was employed, that Carissimi wrote the first great masterpiece of the genre, *Jefte*. Latin oratorios continued annually at the Crocifisso until 1710 (and, exceptionally, in 1725, a Holy Year); the main composers during its later years were Stradella and Alessandro Scarlatti.

As with opera, public performances of oratorio by the confraternities were matched by private ones in the palaces of individual patrons – by and large the same patrons as supported the secular genre. Indeed, these privately sponsored oratorios were also in effect

8. Staged performance of G. B. Costanzi's 'oratorio' 'Componimento sacro' at the Palazzo della Cancelleria, Rome, in 1727, for the Accademia dell'Arcadia: engraving

secular occasions, the two parts of the work being separated not by spiritual refreshment in the form of a sermon, but by bodily replenishment in the form of food and drink, often both sumptuous and plentiful. Cardinals Pamphili and Ottoboni both wrote oratorio texts which were set by Pasquini, Scarlatti and others for performances at their respective palaces, and, as might be expected, Prince Ruspoli was an ardent patron of oratorio in such contexts. His *maestro di cappella*, Antonio Caldara (*c*1670–1736), composed at least nine oratorios for him between 1710 and 1715. A German traveller, J. F. A. von Uffenbach, described in his diary a performance of Caldara's oratorio *Abisai*, which he attended at Ruspoli's palace on 31 March 1715:

> In the evening the weekly concert at the palace of Prince Rospoli [*sic*] took place, which, because he spends so much on it each year, is the best here. Since he is pleased to see strangers and allows them to attend without introduction, we went along together and were led through many splendidly furnished rooms to an exceedingly grand and long gallery in which, as in the whole house, were incomparable paintings and silver artefacts. Everything was impressively lit, and on each side of the whole gallery chairs had been placed for the audience, with a raised area left free for the performers. On this were ranged a large number of players and seated in front of them three female singers together with a little castrato belonging to the [Imperial Habsburg] Ambassador, [Count Johann Wenzel] Gallas. They performed a magnificent concert, or so-called oratorio, which so enraptured me that I was convinced that I had never heard anything of the kind so perfectly done before in my life. Each time there is a completely new work composed and directed by the papal *maestro di cappella*, Caldara. Everyone listened so attentively to the excellent singers that not even a fly stirred except when a cardinal or a lady entered, whereupon everyone stood, but afterwards sat down again in their former places. I found also that none of the voices usually heard in the opera could equal these; the performance of a certain singer known as Mariotgi was particularly unusual and agreeable. The leading singer was the wife of Caldara; she was musically very able and could sing the most difficult things with great skill, but because she has a weak voice her singing did not please me as much as that of the other just mentioned. About halfway through the performance there was an interval during which large quantities of drinks, ices, cakes and coffee were brought in and offered to everyone. Then the second half of the work was given, so that altogether the performance lasted some four hours; but I would have been very pleased for it to have lasted 14 days, and left in pure amazement, never having experienced anything of the kind in my life before. The accompaniment included a violin which was uncommonly well played and many other instruments played to perfection. It was midnight when

we finished, but sleep did not prevent my listening to the very end with the greatest pleasure. There was a very large audience, which included many ladies and several cardinals, among them Cardinal Ottoboni, who never misses such things.[14]

An even more elaborate occasion had taken place at Ruspoli's palace seven years earlier, when Handel's oratorio *La resurrezione* was given on Easter Sunday 1708 as a sequel to Scarlatti's *Oratorio per la Passione* (words by Ottoboni), performed at the Palazzo della Cancelleria the previous Wednesday. Except in their actual quality, these works are typical of oratorio composition during the period. They consist of an instrumental sinfonia, or overture, followed by a succession of recitatives and ternary (da capo) arias, with the occasional duet or ensemble. The chorus, which Handel in England was to make an essential part of oratorio, was usually non-existent, though each of the work's two sections might end with a short *coro* in which all the solo singers joined.

The comparison between oratorio of this period and opera (which shared the same musical constituents of overture, recitative, aria and ensemble) has often been made; but it is the serenata rather than the opera that must be seen as the secular equivalent of the oratorio. Both genres are of approximately the same length (about half that of the average heroic opera); they are both normally divided into two parts (as distinct from opera's three or five acts), with refreshments served in the interval; they usually employ three to five singers (opera having more often eight to ten); and they were frequently supported by a very large orchestra (opera calling for a relatively small band). Moreover, as a social occasion the serenata was distinguished from the oratorio mainly by being performed out of doors during the summer months, rather than indoors during the rest of the year; but even this cannot always serve to distinguish one genre from another. The libretto might seem to be the determining factor, that of an oratorio being biblical, hagiographical or allegorical, that of a serenata celebratory and usually adulatory; but when (as often happens in a serenata) a patron is revered as though he were a saint and his supposed virtues are celebrated in allegorical terms, even this distinction falls away.

Accounts of serenata performances in Rome are numerous during the period under review. They were given mainly in the courtyards of palaces or in the squares and streets outside. The Piazza di Spagna was a favourite place, partly because of the several aristocratic houses there; it was especially popular from 1724, when the great stairway leading up to the Trinità de' Monti was built, providing an imposing 'stage' for such events. Before the 'Spanish Steps' were constructed Queen Maria Casimira often had serenatas performed from the bridge she had built in 1702 across the Strada Felice, leading from the Trinità de' Monti. During the seventeenth century the most spectacular serenatas were probably those put on by the Barberini family at their palace in the Via Quattro Fontane, and the splendour of these occasions was recalled on 24 August 1704, when the Prince of Palestrina, Urbano Barberini, had a serenata performed in the Piazza di Spagna for the wife of the Spanish ambassador. This is how Valesio described it:

> This morning wooden barriers were placed across the Piazza di Spagna from the palace of the Propaganda Fide to the doorway of the Spanish ambassador, with space left for people and carriages to pass in front of the houses opposite. In this space and in front of the palace doorway numerous open carriages were left without horses to reserve a place from where to hear the sumptuous serenata given this evening for the ambassador's wife, in celebration of the birth of the Duke of Brittany. The Prince of Palestrina Barberini, although loaded with debts, has borrowed a considerable sum of money which he has begun to spend on vanities such as this.
>
> Two hours after dusk there issued from the Barberini palace the magnificent procession of this serenata in the following manner. First, two men with torches preceded an open carriage drawn by six horses. The carriage itself was ornamented with gilt carvings, and its extremities, connected by further carvings and cupids, likewise gilded, were shaped like the poop and the prow of a ship. It carried various instrumentalists, nobly dressed with white plumes in their caps fastened with red and white tassels, of a kind normally worn in battle by the soldiers of the two crowns [the French and the Spanish]. Riding alongside this carriage was the Marquis Maculani dressed *alla disdossa* – that is, in a vest of rich brocade and with a white plume tied to his hat with a red and white clasp. Similarly dressed was Pompeo Capranica, who acted as coachman, but rode the horse on the left of the shaft instead of sitting on the coach-box as is customary, the horses themselves being adorned with numerous white and red ribbons. The second carriage was similarly filled with musicians dressed like those of the first; again in rich clothes, the Marquis [Ferdinando] Bongiovanni acted as coachman, while his son rode alongside. But the third coach was larger and more magnificent still, shaped like a boat with sails painted in gold chiaroscuro and other rigging, with at the rear a high poop ending in a bench on which were seated the three singers: the daughter of Laura who lives opposite the Chigi palace in the Corso, Cochina of the Monti household, and a girl, the daughter of a carpenter, who is in the service of the Princess of Palestrina. All three wore dresses of rich brocade in different colours given to them by the prince, but their heads were adorned in the same way with red and white ribbons. Also in the carriage were various cavaliers and gentlemen in fine coats. The prince himself served as coachman to this car-

riage, though he also rode on horseback; as well as a very fine outfit he wore in his hat a chain and clasp of rich jewels. Cavalier Aquilani rode alongside. The horses drawing this coach were adorned, even more than the others, with ribbons and other things, and the display ended with a noble carriage covered in dark blue velvet and drawn by two horses belonging to the said prince.

The three large coaches mentioned above were lit by 30 torches carried by as many footmen, dressed in the same livery as the prince provided at Naples when King Philip V of Spain went there. It consisted of close-fitting jackets of the finest cloth the colour of Isabella, with silver lace mixed with dark blue checks, a hat with a white plume and a white and red tassel, and red silk stockings. After leaving the Barberini palace in the Piazza del Duca, this magnificent cortège proceeded by way of the Strada della Madonna di Constantinopoli and the Dui Macelli (the entire route being thronged with people) to the Piazza di Spagna, already filled with carriages and people, some of them on platforms set up for hire. When the procession reached the place in the piazza which had been barricaded and kept empty (as explained above), it lined up beneath the balcony of the palace, where the ambassador and his wife, together with Cardinal [Forbin de] Janson and numerous ladies and cavaliers, were waiting. The torches were extinguished and wax candles lit, with crystal shades to protect them from the wind.

The orchestra and singers then began a serenata to words by the Abbé Bonaccorsi, in which Pallas and Juno complain of the judgment that Venus has won over them in the competition of the golden apple; but when Fame appears and tells them about the birth of the Duke of Brittany, the two goddesses decide to bestow on the infant all they had offered to Paris, Juno undertaking to create new worlds for the new hero. The serenata was received with universal satisfaction and cries of 'E viva!' The libretto had been printed, and in some copies wags had altered the words 'con licenza de' superiori' ['by permission of the authorities'] to 'con licenza de' creditori' ['by permission of the creditors'].[15]

As well as complimenting the wife of the Spanish ambassador and celebrating the birth of the Duke of Brittany, the Prince of Palestrina was obviously making a show of his support for Philip V's cause in the struggle for the Spanish succession. The performance was repeated the following evening in front of the palace of Cardinal Forbin de Janson in the Piazza Venezia.

It is, alas, only too typical of Valesio that he fails to mention the composer of this serenata, but it is unusual for him not to refer to the refreshments served to the audience, which on this occasion must surely have been (to use the diarist's favourite description) 'lautissimo'. Nor does his account contain precise reference to the number of musicians who took part, although they were clearly quite numerous. Observers frequently report as many as 100 or more instrumentalists, even for serenatas more modestly 'staged' than this one, although one suspects that such figures sometimes result from little more than guesswork. A serenata by Lulier, performed on 9 August 1694 at the palace of Cardinal Ottoboni (by whom Lulier was employed as composer and cellist), was described in one account as being accompanied 'with 100 string instruments', and in another 'with the accompaniment of 150 instruments'; the Ottoboni accounts show that 66 string players were paid for their services that evening.[16]

As far as the musical constituents of the serenata are concerned, there is little to distinguish the genre from opera and oratorio. An introduction, or sinfonia, was usually the only instrumental item, the rest of the work being composed mainly of recitative and da capo arias, with the occasional ensemble. A chorus, which today we would consider almost a *sine qua non* for a festive occasion with music, was only rarely used. Given the occasional nature of the serenata, it is not surprising that copies of the music have suffered even more than operas and oratorios from the ravages of time. But to compare contemporary descriptions of serenata performances, such as the one by Valesio quoted above, with the musical scores that have survived is to be reminded that the serenata was not, in fact, what we might think of today as a musical 'work', but rather an 'event' or 'spectacle' in which music played a part (and perhaps not, to most of those present, the most important part).

*

It is in fulfilment of a similarly decorative role that music as a whole is to be understood in Rome during the years 1670–1740. Just as the statues, fountains and colonnades of Bernini adorned the city's public squares, so the music of Corelli, the Scarlattis, Caldara, Gasparini, Handel and a host of lesser men adorned its churches, palaces, theatres and oratories. For much of this music-making Rome had been dependent on the support of a relatively small number of musical patrons, and when the last and perhaps the most important of these, Cardinal Pietro Ottoboni, died on 28 February 1740 an important chapter in Rome's musical history was brought to a close.

NOTES

[1] 'Rome has no roof to shelter Music, which lives here like a beggar'; letter to Prince Ferdinando de' Medici, dated 30 May 1705, quoted in M. Fabbri, *Alessandro Scarlatti e il Principe Ferdinando de' Medici* (Florence, 1961), 58.

[2] H. J. Marx, 'The Instrumentation of Handel's Early Italian Works', *EM*, xvi (1988), 496.

[3] *Scarlatti, Alessandro e Domenico: due vite in una* (Milan, 1985), 77.

[4] The account of these performances in F. A. D'Accone, *The History of a Baroque Opera: Alessandro Scarlatti's 'Gli equivoci nel sembiante'* (New York, 1985) contains much valuable information on the production of opera in Rome at this time.

[5] The play on words here is not only between 'Christian' and 'Christina', but also on the double meanings of *gallo* ('cock' or 'Frenchman') and *pollastri* ('cockerels' or 'Poles').

[6] The ceremonies are fully documented in F. Piperno, 'Anfione in Campidoglio', *Nuovissimi studi corelliani: Fusignano 1980*, 151–209.

[7] See F. della Seta, 'La musica in Arcadia al tempo di Corelli', ibid, 123–50.

[8] MS Osb.2, compiled between October 1704 and September 1705, has been aptly described by Reinhard Strohm as a 'cantata diary'; see his interesting description of the MS in 'Scarlattiana at Yale', *Händel e gli Scarlatti a Roma: Rome 1985*, 113–52.

[9] U. Kirkendale, 'The Ruspoli Documents on Handel', *JAMS*, xx (1967), 222–74.

[10] 'Die Musik am Hofe Pietro Kardinal Ottobonis unter Arcangelo Corelli', *AnMc*, no.5 (1968), 113.

[11] G. Muffat, Preface to *Ausserlesene Instrumental-Music* (Passau, 1701); trans. in O. Strunk, *Source Readings in Music History* (New York, 1950; 1981, in 5 vols.), iii, 89–92.

[12] A chronological history of operas produced in Rome during the seventeenth century is being prepared by Lorenzo Bianconi, Lowell Lindgren, Margaret Murata and Thomas Walker. Meanwhile some useful documentation is available in L. Lindgren, 'Il dramma musicale a Roma durante la carriera di Alessandro Scarlatti (1660–1725)', *Le muse galanti: la musica a Roma nel settecento*, ed. B. Cagli (Rome, 1985), 35–57.

[13] *Essays on Handel and Italian Opera* (Cambridge, 1985), 92.

[14] Diary of J. F. A. von Uffenbach (University Library, Göttingen), quoted in U. Kirkendale, *Antonio Caldara: sein Leben und seine venezianisch-römischen Oratorien* (Graz, 1966), 74. Uffenbach was incorrect in stating that Caldara was *maestro di cappella* to the pope.

[15] *Diario di Roma*, ed. G. Scano and G. Graglia (Milan, 1978), iii, 150–54.

[16] L. Lindgren, 'Il dramma musicale a Roma', 56.

BIBLIOGRAPHICAL NOTE

M. Andrieux's *Daily Life in Papal Rome in the Eighteenth Century* (London, 1968; originally in French as *La vie quotidienne dans la Rome pontificale*, Paris, 1962) lacks scholarly documentation, but it provides a lively picture of Roman society during the period and contains a useful bibliography. Andrieux's account may be supplemented, by readers of Italian, by the fascinating *Diario di Roma* of Francesco Valesio, ed. G. Scano and G. Graglia (Milan, 1977–8); this covers the period 1700–42, except for a gap from 11 March 1711 to 23 December 1724 and smaller lacunae elsewhere.

Biographies of Queen Christina of Sweden are numerous, though many of them mix fact with fiction; among the more readable and reliable of recent books on her is G. Masson, *Queen Christina* (London, 1968). Cardinal Benedetto Pamphili has been the subject of a detailed biography by L. Montalto, *Un mecenate in Roma barocca* (Florence, 1955), which draws extensively on the Doria-Pamphili archive in Rome but which must be read with caution as far as the information on music is concerned; H. J. Marx's 'Die *Giustificazioni della Casa Pamphilj* als musikgeschichtliche Quelle', *Studi musicali*, xii (1983), 121–87, covering the years 1677–1709, forms an important appendage to Montalto's book. *Marysieńka* by K. Waliszewski (Paris, 1896; Eng. trans. Lady Mary Loyd, London, 1898) remains essential reading on Queen Maria Casimira of Poland, but it devotes little space to her years in Rome and none at all to her musical patronage. For Rome's other two important patrons of music, Cardinal Ottoboni and Prince Ruspoli, one must rely on articles in periodicals, notably, for the former, H. J. Marx, 'Die Musik am Hofe Pietro Kardinal Ottobonis unter Arcangelo Corelli', *AnMc*, no.5 (1968), 104–77, and, for the latter, U. Kirkendale, 'The Ruspoli Documents on Handel', *JAMS*, xx (1967), 222–74.

For information on the church's prescriptions for sacred music, see R. F.

Hayburn, *Papal Legislation on Sacred Music, 95AD to 1977AD* (Collegeville, MN, 1979). For a survey of the music itself, G. Stefani's *Musica e religione nell'Italia barocca* (Palermo, 1975) may be recommended. The articles on Rome in the *Enciclopedia dello spettacolo* and *Grove 0* contain much valuable information on Roman theatres and their repertories, and A. Cametti's *Il teatro di Tordinona poi di Apollo* (Tivoli, 1938) is of fundamental importance. Roman opera of the period is not usually given much attention in general histories, but some idea of the operatic situation is conveyed in books on specific composers (e.g. Handel and the two Scarlattis); see also the literature mentioned in notes 4, 12 and 13 above. Information on the *cantata da camera* in Rome is similarly diffuse; a useful starting-point is provided by the article 'Cantata' in *Grove 6* and its accompanying bibliography. Much information about the nativity cantatas performed annually at the Vatican is contained in C. Gianturco's '"Cantate spirituali e morali", with a Description of the Papal Sacred Cantata Tradition for Christmas', *ML*, lxxiii (1992), 1–33, and H. J. Marx's 'Römische Weihnachtsoratorien aus der ersten Hälfte des 18. Jahrhunderts', *AMw*, xlix (1992), 163–99. For oratorio the standard text is now H. E. Smither, *A History of the Oratorio*; the period under discussion is covered in chapters 5 and 6 of volume i (Chapel Hill, 1977). The serenata during the greater part of the period is expertly dealt with in T. E. Griffin's doctoral dissertation, *The Late Baroque Serenata in Rome and Naples* (University of California, Los Angeles, 1983). A more recent volume touching on various aspects of music at Rome during the late seventeenth and early eighteenth centuries is *Händel e gli Scarlatti a Roma*, ed. N. Pirrotta and A. Ziino, containing papers read at an international conference in Rome in June 1985.

Chapter III

Venice in an Era of Political Decline

ELEANOR SELFRIDGE-FIELD

The Venetian Republic had enjoyed a century of undisputed power and a millennium of growth as the seventeenth century neared its end. Its endurance and stability greatly recommended its enlightened form of government – a doge elected by his fellow executives, a legislative assembly consisting of all male nobles above the age of 21, and a judiciary subdivided into an intricate network of small chambers to oversee domestic, territorial and foreign affairs. Venice commanded holdings reaching from the edges of the Piedmont and the southern slopes of the Alps, across the plains north of the Adriatic and down the eastern Adriatic coast into the Peloponnese. The arc formed by the modern-day cities of Bergamo, Brescia, Verona, Vicenza, Padua, Treviso, Belluno, Udine, Trieste, Split and Dubrovnik fell within the bounds of the Most Serene Republic in 1680. Corfu and the smaller islands of the Ionian Sea also lay within its maritime provinces. 'The Hinge of Europe', as William McNeill termed Venice in his history of the Republic,[1] was uniquely situated to bear witness to cultural diversity. Muslim and Christian, Protestant and Catholic, Pontine and Levantine Jew encountered one another in the lagoon city. Diversity was tolerated and oddity was prized. Camels and elephants captured in distant battles were put on display in the piazzetta near the Doge's Palace. At Carnival in 1687 the appearance of African pygmies caused a sensation on the piazza.[2] Turkish coffee was introduced to Europeans by the Venetians at about the same time: like the camels and elephants, it was one of the spoils of the war with the Ottoman Empire.

While retaining all these holdings during the last two decades of the seventeenth century and the first two of the eighteenth, Venice began to feel the undertow of a shifting tide in the balance of power, as the Austrian Empire claimed much of the future Yugoslavia and Hungary from the Ottomans. The alliance of the Venetians with the Austrians seemed to work more to the benefit of the latter than of the former. Symbolically, no land was more sacred to the Venetians than the Peloponnese, known to them as the Morean peninsula. Won in the hard-fought battle of Lepanto in 1574, the Morea was lost in 1688, regained in 1699 and lost for good in the Peace of Passarowitz in 1718. What was lost in time was ennobled in memory to a degree that was to have profound implications for the arts.

SACRED MUSIC IN THE MOST SERENE REPUBLIC

In a world of large monarchies and small principalities, the integrated structure of Venetian society was unique. While Venice was not a democracy in the modern sense, power was vested in society as a corporate entity rather than in any single individual or small group of individuals. Although it was a tiered society, the elite stratum was relatively large. In the city of Venice itself, where the population was around 100 000, there were approximately 3000 male nobles by the early eighteenth century.

The ducal basilica – St Mark's

As a conspicuously corporate entity without an absolute ruler, Venice thrived on institutional diversity. Reflecting this diversity, music assumed many roles and satisfied many needs. The basilica of St Mark's, adjacent to the Doge's Palace, with its five Byzantine domes and its gold mosaic interior, was centrally important, since it was there that the doge worshipped on special occasions. Other dignitaries accompanied him on the more significant feasts.

The function of music at St Mark's was ultimately to represent with proper decorum the best interests of the doge and the Republic. It needed to express (1) the ceremonial importance of the office of the doge; (2) the stability of the Republic; (3) the perpetual (so the Venetians believed) dominion of the Republic over the Adriatic Sea; (4) the dignity of the Venetian government; and (5) the strength of the Venetian nobility. At the same time it needed to satisfy the needs of the church for orthodoxy, liturgical suitability and conformity with papal directives. The practical limits of space and budget also required accommodation. Aesthetic considerations had to operate within the confines imposed by all these factors. While it is easy to read these prescriptions as a formula for a draining conformity to detail, it is remarkable to behold the array of novelties to which they gave rise. Each requirement was satisfied in a different way, with the result that services of great variety were the norm.

A ceremonial sense was conveyed by the care with which personal attire and the decor of the sanctuary were regulated. The positions of the most important members of society could be read from the colour of their robes and the decorations they wore. The liturgical importance of the occasion could be calculated from the numbers and lengths of candles burning within the basilica. The use of instruments of different kinds and in different configurations reinforced the messages conveyed in visible ways. The numbers of *piffari*, who played herald trumpets and trombones to mark the doge's arrival at the basilica in the sixteenth century, slowly increased as they assumed other functions and other roles. String players were present by 1600, and such wind instruments as cornetts and bassoons were used throughout the seventeenth century. The rapid evolution of instrument technology around 1700 caused ripples only slowly in Venice's paramount church. The indoor use of brass consorts declined as woodwind instruments such as the oboe came into use. A pair of natural trumpets may have been used for the performance of a *Te Deum*, which was often performed to mark a naval victory, although no surviving music with obbligato trumpet parts can be associated with St Mark's. Recorders, despite their occasional appearance in Venetian painting, were probably never used inside the basilica because, through their classical association with lasciviousness, they violated papal dictate. The bassoon, however, remained a special favourite of the Venetians.

The large complement of string players who formed the basic orchestra at St Mark's were for the most part Venetians. Many of the brass players, singers and organists were also from Venetian families that had produced generations of musicians. The arrival of woodwind instruments brought cultural diversity to the *cappella*, for many of the oboe *virtuosi* active in Italy were German. Thus the oboe brought with it new perspectives on musical style and performance; its unfamiliar sound undoubtedly stimulated the curiosity of listeners, while its difficulties with intonation limited the harmonic variety of pieces in which it was to be used. In this last respect, the oboe had a pronounced influence on musical style.

The strength, endurance and dignity of the Venetian government were expressed more subtly in the regularity with which the musical calendar was maintained. Feasts were divided into five general classes of liturgical importance. The performing resources included a choir, an orchestra, four organists, small groups of *piffari*, and, as the eighteenth century dawned, itinerant *virtuosi* such as the Florentine violinist Francesco Maria Veracini (1690–1768), who appeared on especially important occasions. Performance space was not limited (as many history books and disc notes mistakenly suggest) to the two fairly large lofts that straddle the altar: the smaller boxes underneath and somewhat forward of these lofts, special stalls erected for particular occasions, and the lectern from which the Epistle was read (known locally as the *bigonzo*) are all known to have been used for small groups on particular occasions.[3]

The main groups were frequently used in divisions, so that one half of the orchestra might play on one feast of a particular class and the other half on the next feast of the same kind. The organists alternated at a single instrument to provide music for lesser feasts but provided music in combination for the greater feasts. It is im-

9. *The interior of St Mark's: painting (c1755) by Antonio Canaletto; the two 'bigonzi' (tubs) can just be seen either side of the iconostasis (screen)*

portant to appreciate the possibilities that these rotational schemes allowed. The apparent reduction in orchestral staff from 34 in 1685 to 23 in 1708 may actually have meant a dissolution of the platoon system and a stabilization of the group at 23 (as opposed to 17). The inevitable result of this large number of options was that scarcely any two feasts were ever treated in exactly the same way.

Composers providing music for St Mark's thus had great latitude in the performing resources on which they could draw. The spiritual thrust of the music was increasingly entrusted to the trio medium in both vocal and instrumental music. In the trio, the two upper parts could converse, contest and concur with grief-filled dissonances and consoling resolutions. The medium was well suited to the piety of countless motet texts of the time. Almost none of these works is in the modern repertory, and a very large percentage of all that were composed does not survive.[4]

One can acquire some notion of their musical style from the large number of trio sonatas that do survive, especially from the period between 1690 and 1710. The early publications of Antonio Caldara, Giorgio Gentili, Tomaso Albinoni and Antonio Vivaldi all explored the trio medium. On solemn occasions there was a turning-away from the grandiose and the imposing, even at St Mark's. Vivaldi's father was one member of a trio engaged in 1689 to provide special music at the basilica. The addition of a string trio to the other groups available built on a foundation of 50 years' or more duration that required a violin solo at the Elevation of the Host at Christmas, Easter and other high feasts. These routines were well known to Antonio Caldara (c1670–1736), who served as an alto and a cellist at the basilica in the 1690s.

It was for lesser feasts not attended by the doge that a mere handful of singers would have sung without accompaniment from a choirbook by the lectern, as shown in Canaletto's late drawing (1766) of the interior of St Mark's, and in fig.9; from this position they could be better heard by the ordinary worshippers in the nave.

Monasteries, convents, ospedali

Conspicuous as it was to the foreign visitor and central as it was to the impression of greatness that the Republic sought to project, the basilica was not a church of much personal consequence to the vast majority of Venetians. There were many dozens of monastic and parochial churches, all with organs, many with choirs and a few with instrumental ensembles. Monks and nuns played musical instruments, as can best be determined from surviving accounts, with interest, vigour and imagination. Plucked string instruments, especially the theorbo, seem to have been favoured at the church of S Maria Gloriosa de' Frari, the site of a Franciscan monastery in which Claudio Monteverdi (1567–1643) had spent his last years. Brass instruments were equally popular, it seems, among nuns and priests. Organs, both portable and non-portable, were more or less ubiquitous. The English visitor Thomas Coryat had counted '143 paire of organs' in Venice in 1611.[5] Even small convents seem to have had at least two permanent organs, and organ lofts were apparently convenient nooks for surreptitious drinking and clandestine rendezvous, to judge from the frequency with which organists (and sometimes their charges) were disciplined for misbehaviour of one kind or another.[6]

The most striking institutions that supported music in the early eighteenth century were the four *ospedali*. These were charitable institutions whose general function was to provide shelter and education for several thousand female orphans. Increasingly, from the end of the sixteenth century, they had taken on the function of providing exquisitely lovely and exceptionally moving sacred music for their benefactors. In the pages of *Pallade veneta*, a Venetian journal initiated in 1687, we read of princes enraptured by the playing of lutes and theorbos, of ordinary listeners clustered on balconies and at windows to overhear concerts for which the seating was vastly inadequate, of religious conversions affected by moving motets, and of mourners 'with hearts of ice turned to cascades of water' by the delicacy and sentiment with which music tailored to the occasion was sung and played.[7] So highly regarded was this music that by 1700 noblemen were seeking places for their musically talented daughters among the selective ranks of these groups of able indigents.[8]

Quite in contrast to St Mark's, where convention was the rule, the *ospedali* were committed to personal expression. Formality was superseded by conviction. Since the avowed social purpose of the *ospedali* was to instruct, the music they most promoted was the one genre that was essentially didactic – the oratorio. In Catholic Italy oratorios of the earlier Baroque period had been religiously solid but musically ponderous: they sometimes ran to several hours, were tediously verbose and often lacked melodic interest or definable musical structures. This was acceptable to audiences of cardinals in Rome but it ill suited the needs of the young charges of the Venetian *ospedali*. Since oratorios were not staged, they could not appeal, as Venetian opera so commonly did, to the sense of vision; they could appeal only to the ear.

What sets and costumes were to the Venetian theatres, musical instruments seem to have become to the Venetian *ospedali*. This cannot be deduced from surviving works, since few of the hundreds of oratorios composed for these institutions between 1680 and 1750 are known from anything other than their printed librettos. It can be deduced, however, from such information as inventories of instru-

10. Organ loft of one of the Venetian ospedali: watercolour from 'Gli abiti de Veneziani ... dipinti nel secolo XVIII' of G. Grevenbroch

ments held by the *ospedali*, documentary accounts of performances, and the large number of instrumental works, especially introductory sinfonias and complementary concertos, that seem to be the residue of these lost vocal compositions.

The account books of the four *ospedali*, which devoted themselves entirely to the care of female charges, included payments not only for the violins, violas, cellos and harpsichords used in the opera houses but also, in the later seventeenth century, for viols, double basses and organs. In the early eighteenth century such esoteric bowed instruments as the double-strung viola d'amore were acquired by the Ospedale della Pietà, and by the 1720s instruction on the oboe and transverse flute were regularly provided.

The aim of oratorio was not simply to inform but to stir the emotions and to evoke a spiritual response. To this end, the matter of performing technique received concentrated attention in the four *ospedali*. Singers were trained to develop a number of special ornaments that used the throat and tongue in different ways to create special effects appropriate to particular texts, or, as usually happened, to illustrate particular metaphors. Many metaphors were drawn from the natural world of streams, birdcalls and tempests. Human emotions were likened in oratorio and motet texts to running brooks, pining doves and raging storms. Sacred and secular were not compartmentalized in Venice; they were studiously entwined.

Instrumental obbligatos in Venetian oratorios were used to suggest natural or spiritual states. While violins could be either bright or melancholy, other instruments were often typecast. The running quavers of plucked instruments could represent the relentless passage of time or the approach of danger. Transverse flutes playing limping dotted-note rhythms were favoured imitators of birdcalls. Oboes and more obscure kinds of woodwind, such as the single-reed chalumeau,[9] were serious, sometimes even tragic in import; they could be harbingers of death, but their particular function was often to suggest spiritual triumph in the face of earthly tragedy (as for instance in recounting the lives of saints and martyrs). Instruments thus became emblematic and reinforced the didactic purpose of the text.

The most cherished repertory from early eighteenth-century Venice is probably the large corpus of concertos composed by Antonio Vivaldi (1678–1741) for the Pietà. The fact that mechanical advances made some of the wind instruments, such as the oboe and eventually the clarinet, moderately playable was undoubtedly essential to the development of this repertory, but its principal motivation may have come from the oratorio. It was customary to introduce the longer vocal works with instrumental pieces such as sinfonias. Oratorios were composed in two halves, with concertos and solo improvisations filling some of the intermissions.

The roster of solo instruments for which Vivaldi composed concertos – flutes, oboes, bassoons and lutes, as well as violins and cellos – closely matched the emblematic emphases of oratorios. The elaborate ornaments cultivated among vocalists to enable listeners to respond emotionally to texts drew greater attention to instrumentalists who mimicked their techniques. The natural imagery towards which vocal texts were so inclined thrived in the concerto literature too: the 'Four Seasons', the 'Bullfinch' and the 'Tempest' (among the most familiar concerto subtitles), when considered as suggestive approaches to musical expression, all had countless grounds for invention within the vocal literature.

Musicians and patrons as members of society
Census reports in Venice rigidly distinguished between artisan, citizen and nobleman. Although most musicians came from the artisan

73

class, some came from the citizen class, and in the eighteenth century some, such as Alessandro Marcello (1669–1750) and his brother Benedetto (1686–1739), came from the nobility. Among artisans music was viewed as a heritable occupation: fathers not only coached their children; they bequeathed their musical posts to them. An entrenched guild system, reinforced by inherited rights of survivorship, made it all but impossible for those destined for another trade to enter the formal ranks of civic musicians.

Young foreign musicians came to Venice in considerable numbers, especially in the second decade of the eighteenth century. The examples of the visiting Saxons Johann David Heinichen (1683–1729) and Johann Georg Pisendel (1687–1755) suggest the lasting effect that such visits had: Heinichen is still remembered for his figured bass tutors of 1711 and 1728, and the violinist Pisendel is remembered for his 25-year tenure, from 1730 until his death, as director of the court orchestra in Dresden. Conversely, Venetians were often invited by the dignitaries who visited Venice to make music abroad; these comings and goings were arranged in many instances by diplomatic personnel. The performances most crucial to a performer's chance to gain wider renown may have been the myriad private ones that were given during dinners and parties in the family and ambassadorial palaces that lined the Grand Canal. Antonio Lotti (c1667–1740), the most highly regarded opera composer of the time and a longtime organist and *maestro di cappella* at St Mark's, won a long-term invitation from the Electoral Prince of Saxony, Friedrich August, who was honoured by a series of special entertainments during a 17-month stay in Venice (1716–17). Lotti and his wife, the opera singer Santa Stella, returned from three triumphal years in Dresden (1717–20) with horses and carriages that, while being of little value in the lagoon city, facilitated their use of a country villa and brought them other privileges that lesser mortals could only dream of.

Native patronage of music was diffuse within Venetian society. Noblemen who aspired to high office usually found it advantageous to be conspicuous patrons of the arts, but the reasons for this are convoluted and may not necessarily tell us much about what was valued or why. The governors of each of the *ospedali* and the 12 procurators of the basilica had positions of particular political prestige and musical influence: they could determine the overall scope of the musical establishment, but they seem rarely to have interfered in the conduct of musical affairs. Vivaldi had a slowly deteriorating relationship with the administrators of the Pietà which may have been prompted by his many absences in connection with opera productions elsewhere.[10]

ACCOMMODATIONS TO POLITICAL DECLINE

Centuries of conquest had engendered an elaborate network of contacts between Venice and the rest of the world. From the time of the Crusades the Venetians had been conscious of the existence of the Levant and from the time of Marco Polo's travels they had been chroniclers of the exotic. In the eighteenth century their diplomatic missions stretched from London to Damascus, and part of many young noblemen's education was to serve in junior posts in scattered locations outside the Veneto. The nobility of the eighteenth century were highly aware of life and customs abroad.

Because Venice had been an extremely important centre of publishing in the sixteenth and seventeenth centuries, it was a magnet to aspiring authors and readers. Religion and natural history were the most heavily represented fields in book-lists of the time. The strength of the publishing industry had made Venice an obvious target of the Inquisition. Subtle relationships between diplomacy, propaganda and censorship were of very great importance as the Republic started, ever so slightly, to loosen its grip as a political force. Since literacy was largely limited to clerics and nobles, many authors were either priests or members of the government. Relatively few books were condemned, but every piece of writing sent to press was reviewed by not one but a total of six bodies before publication could proceed.[11]

Music had been published in Venice since early in the sixteenth century. The texts of musical works were included in the body of writing that was regularly submitted to censors. It is, in fact, because of these restrictions that texts were printed in tiny books (*libretti*), where they were divorced from the musical score, and it is a tribute to the diligence of Venetian record-keeping that so many of these books survive when the music does not.

This uncoupling of text from music had broader implications. Because authors knew that texts would be read by several juries of influential people, there was a strong incentive to produce writings that would flatter the values that these juries sat to protect. Subject matter, especially for major works between 1680 and 1720, came to be allied with the interests of the State through parallels drawn from history and legend. Heroes, whether taken from the histories of the ancient Near East, Greece or Rome, from medieval chivalry or even from Teutonic mythology, were always depicted in positions of power with which Venetians and their allies could identify. The defeat of heathens in any time or place was seen to promote the interest of the Holy League in repulsing the advance of the Ottomans. The fall of Teutons recapitulated the glory of early Venice in defeating the Huns. Military triumphs, such as those of Alexander the Great, were likened to Venetian naval triumphs. The frailties of kings and the cunning intrigues of empresses were associated, in the Venetian mind, with the frailties and intrigues of rulers they too had known. To this extent opera was a form of propaganda, since its overriding purpose seems to have been to promote through an orthodox view of history a uniformity of commitment to meeting present-day challenges.

While oratorios were ostensibly sacred in import, it is remarkable to see the degree to which biblical heroes and early church martyrs were subjected to political delineation in oratorio texts. G. D. Partenio's *Tomaso Moro*, given at the Mendicanti in January 1688, was a gloss, by way of sixteenth-century English history, on the pregnancy of Mary of Modena, the wife of James II; it celebrated the triumph of Catholicism (somewhat prematurely, with regard to the English throne). Among works for which the music survives, Vivaldi's oratorio *Juditha triumphans* is also illustrative: while the story is taken from the Apocrypha, it is clear in the retelling of 1716 that Judith represented the Venetians and her drunken adversary, Holofernes, the Turks as they were seen not in biblical times but in the early eighteenth century. Indeed, the story of Judith's triumph over Holofernes was a favourite subject of Venetian painters, such as Piazzetta, in the first half of the eighteenth century.

The double meaning of texts was perhaps most delightful to Venetians in the serenata literature, but it is largely indecipherable in our time. Serenatas were usually written for a single performance on an occasion made special by the fortunes of royalty or nobility; they could celebrate births, marriages, name-days, treaties, arrivals and departures. They involved fewer characters than operas and were less elaborately staged, since they were usually given not in theatres but in gardens and ballrooms; the characters were often generic ones, such as Muses or Virtues, while in the pastoral serenata they were pining shepherds and fickle shepherdesses. There is a growing suspicion, however, that, in the guise of such innocent tales, comments on the acts and attitudes of men of power were perceptible to a knowing audience while remaining imperceptible to bodies of censors.[12]

Sadly, the triumphs sought by the Venetians in endless wars and distant battles had so drained the Republic's treasury by 1690 that increased revenues were sought in every sphere of commercial activity. This had unfortunate consequences for Venetian music printing, since new levies were imposed at a time when new techniques of production were being developed in northern Europe. Northern publishers had easy access to a growing bourgeois market. The distinguished Venetian families in whose hands music printing had been carried on since the first decade of the sixteenth century

11. *The dramatic cantata (or serenata) 'Il ritratto della Gloria donato all'Eternità' by Domenico Freschi, performed in the hall of the Villa Contarini, Piazzola sul Brento, on 7 August 1685 (the instrumentalists were girls from the conservatory established by Marco Contarini in Piazzola): engraving from 'L'orologia del piacere' (1685) by the librettist Francesco Maria Piccioli*

were dying out in the last years of the seventeenth. Venetian composers from Marc'Antonio Cavazzoni, Claudio Merulo, Gioseffo Zarlino and Andrea and Giovanni Gabrieli to Monteverdi, Francesco Cavalli, Giovanni Legrenzi and the young Caldara had benefited from good access to music printing of the highest quality.

This advantage was lost to Albinoni, Vivaldi, Lotti and the

Marcellos, who saw only their early works published in Venice. Such composers became increasingly dependent on presses in France, the Netherlands and eventually England.[13] Recent studies have cast considerable doubt on the reliability of attributions to Venetians and other Italians from the presses of Estienne Roger, Michel-Charles Le Cène and François Boivin, many of whose prints were further reprocessed by English presses such as that of John Walsh. The implication is that the 'late' works by figures such as Vivaldi and perhaps Benedetto Marcello may not have been by them at all. Some works feigned legitimacy by paying thematic homage to such figures;[14] others were offered under respected names merely to create a market. It is clear from either case that Venetian composers were suffering enormous losses of prestige and custom with the decline of Venice as a world power.

Life at home was not without opportunities for compensation. The phenomenon of Venice, with or without a bright political future, was a great lure to tourists, and several kinds of visitor regularly arrived there. Representatives of foreign governments frequently came to inform, to be informed and to negotiate. Italian noblemen and their families, in common with diplomats from abroad, often maintained residences so that they could partake of the Republic's entertainments and stay current with political developments. By the second quarter of the century the grand tour, in which young men from wealthy families abroad, especially England, were shown the main sights of Continental culture, had become an institution; it rapidly attracted the scions of prosperous merchants of the Netherlands and the northern German provinces.

The grand tour engendered an enormous market for souvenirs, which could take the form of view paintings (a need to which Canaletto and Guardi responded generously), books of arias or manuscripts of single musical works. Aria books contained the most versatile or celebrated numbers from the repertory of one theatre or one season; except for the continuo, instrumental parts were usually eliminated to facilitate amateur performance. Single musical works such as cantatas and concertos may also have found a market among tourists. Vivaldi boasted in 1733 that he had discontinued the practice of sending to press 12 works as a set; it was of more financial benefit to sell single works in manuscript.[15]

Venetians responded to the creeping commercialization of their culture in predictable ways. They retreated to their drawing-rooms, to their villas on the River Brenta and to their private lives. To a remarkable degree for a culture so accustomed to visual splendour, Venetians indulged themselves anew in the life of the mind. This they did in their almost ubiquitous academies. These were not institutions of formal education but assemblies of the nobility that met on a weekly basis to converse and debate. Academies were hospitable to the arts: many regularly presented cantatas and other music to complement readings of poetry and drama. From the 1680s there were academies at which unusual musical instruments were introduced: over the course of a lifetime Alessandro Marcello amassed a collection of instruments that ranged from sixteenth-century crumhorns to such experimental instruments as a vertical harpsichord of recent manufacture and a novelty whose promise was not at first recognized, a fortepiano.[16]

It was in the academies where the breadth of learning of the Venetian nobility could most clearly be seen. In the 1690s, 1700s and 1710s the academies were havens of inventiveness. Geography, world exploration, astronomy, natural science and mechanical invention were among the most commonly and lavishly pursued subjects. The publications of these groups, which appeared irregularly,[17] contain an amazing wealth of descriptions and speculative illustrations that anticipate the accomplishments of later ages (near-equivalents to typewriters, cars and punch-cards are described). The strength of Venetian interest in engineering is evident in such paintings as Canaletto's view of the water entrance of the Arsenal: the masts of moored ships, the regulation of the suspension bridge, the idiosyncrasies of the Venetian 24-hour clock (the day began at sundown, which was represented in the 3.30 position of the modern clock), even the carefully calculated asymmetry of the gondola were all part of this legacy of mechanical innovation. The difference between the attitude of Venetian academics and that of later inventors was that the Venetians were by and large content with speculation. They had no interest in development or production; they were not entrepreneurs. Nothing sealed the fate of the Republic so securely as its satisfaction with inventive ideas to the exclusion of their actualization. In the end, Venice was colonized by improvements on its own inventions, a turn of events aptly represented by the fortepiano, which became a practical and popular instrument in the hands of German and Austrian makers a half-century after its invention in Padua.

THE GREAT DEBATE

While there was a general course to events, it was the cross-current of conflicting values within this flow that had the greatest consequences for music. The great dialogue within Venice in the first half of the eighteenth century – the widespread but ardently contested dialogue between the ancients and the moderns – was one that was not in most respects particular to Venice.

The 'beloved past', to use Peter Gay's apt term,[18] was championed by antiquarians almost to the point of deification. The ancient past, especially of Greece, the Holy Land and Rome, was venerated as an age in which culture had attained perfection. To replicate that perfection was merely a matter of reinstituting the same techniques and values. In the same spirit in which operas and oratorios promoted the cause of the Republic by analogy, antiquarianism promoted it by inference. The Venetians imagined themselves to have a special relationship with the Holy Land because of their hospitality to centuries of crusaders. However tenuous their hold on the Morea had become, they saw themselves as the liberators of the Greeks from the Turks and of Christians from heathens. Alone among Italian cities of prominence, they had no history extending back to Roman occupation, so they had no adversarial relationship with Roman history. The ancient past was a convenient substitute for Venetian prehistory.

Modernism, on the other hand, was rooted in social change. The same mercantile class who made tours to Venice and took away its view paintings, its lace, its glass and its concertos had less patience with the acquisition of skills that required decades to cultivate: the rigours of ancient languages and the tediousness of historical chronicles were not for them, and neither were counterpoint or *solfegge*. This audience wanted easily mastered skills and easily understood works of art.

These two perspectives necessarily engendered very different responses. Antiquarianism prompted not so much the preservation of the status quo as a conscious search for the past and the espousal of values that had been traditionally maintained by the musical establishment. This meant the continued study of counterpoint and support for conservative viewpoints on other aspects of composition and performance. Modernism was more selfconscious, more orientated towards exhibitionism, and in consequence more allied with performance than with composition. Benedetto Marcello was the preeminent antiquarian, Vivaldi the pre-eminent modernist.

Antiquarianism in music and drama

While antiquarianism may seem limited as a source of intellectual stimulation, it was not so in Venice. There were six points of reference in antiquarianism that influenced Venetian music: (1) the idyll of rural innocence; (2) emphasis on mythology; (3) sympathy towards drama; (4) the scope allowed for satire; (5) respect for rhetoric; and (6) enthusiasm for the restoration of cultural artefacts.

Pastoral simplicity (1) ran somewhat counter to the grain of the Baroque age. Elaboration and ornamentation were supported in Venetian opera until, in the second decade of the eighteenth century, the poet and dramatist Apostolo Zeno (1668–1750), a native son, began to call for a new order of things in which self-important display would be discarded.[19] The image of the lovelorn shepherd was extraordinarily pervasive in secular vocal music because it supported by suggestion the Arcadian culture that academicians were attempting to revive. The Arcadia of mythology was the Morean peninsula of Venetian conquest.

The musical emphasis in works that derived their texts from Arcadian legend was on simplicity. When shepherdesses sang cantatas and serenatas for private audiences the performances were innocent of the guttural gymnastics that filled Venetian theatres. In the absence of such superficial devices composers were under pressure to

12. *The Concert: painting (1741) by Pietro Longhi (1702–85)*

create well-formed melodies that transparently encased texts. There was a new interest in singing styles and vocal control. Not surprisingly, the Venetian who composed the largest number of secular cantatas, Benedetto Marcello, was also the one who most concerned himself in the early eighteenth century with the reform of singing.[20] The arias of some of his cantatas from the second decade of the century are so highly lyrical that they may be said to illustrate the slightly later style known as 'Neapolitan bel canto'.

Innocence and simplicity as found in Virgilian eclogues hardly represented the whole thrust of the classical revival. Athenian tragedy and heroic mythology (2) were rejuvenated, especially in Venetian opera of the 1720s and 30s. The subject matter was more easily adapted than the musical style. Operas began to be differentiated according to whether they were dramas, pastorals or 'actions'. But not all dramas (3) were operas. In his long dramatic cantatas, Marcello emphasized long, declamatory recitatives in which emotional expression sometimes took on the guise of frenzy or madness. Extreme emotional turbulence could be expressed by harmonic digressions to keys that were otherwise avoided because of lingering tuning problems – D♭ major and F♯ major, for example. The same subject matter, when set by modernists, continued to concentrate on the elaboration of particular words. Emotional agitation was expressed in both camps by enormous vocal leaps.

In familiarizing themselves with the literature of antiquity, much of it only then being made available in vernacular translation for the first time, the Venetians did not fail to note with interest the satires (4) of Horace and Lucretius. In his depictions of the lives of his fellow Venetians, the painter Pietro Longhi called attention to a thousand small eccentricities and evidences of artificiality (fig.12). In music, it was Marcello who most extended himself in imitation of such models. His comic madrigals debating the musical virtues versus the moral vices of the castratos who took female roles in opera, his cantata cast in the form of a letter to the singer Vittoria Tesi in which the ornamentation styles of other opera singers are mimicked, and in particular his celebrated mock treatise *Il teatro alla moda*, in which he outlined (with tongue in cheek) the ingredients required for a successful opera – all these works thinly disguised the contempt in which he held such practices. In *Il teatro alla moda* the anonymous author offered 'useful and necessary advice to poets, composers, musicians of one and another kinds, impresarios, instrumentalists, stage engineers and painters, comedians, costume designers, prompters, copyists, protectors and mothers of *virtuose*'. All three works were created around 1720. At roughly the same time Anton Maria Zanetti, a nobleman and a historian of Venetian art, created dozens of caricatures of Venetian musicians: self-centred prima don-

13. The singer Vittoria Tesi: caricature by Anton Maria Zanetti (1680–1757)

nas, portly organists and dozing choirmasters all fell prey to his pen.

Rhetoric (5) was a more serious matter and one about which, in the Venetian context, we know rather little. The existence of rhetorical devices and their musical equivalents – a topic to which considerable attention was paid in German writings of the time – can be inferred only from actual musical practices. The aim of evoking a personal response to music, as expressed in documents of the time, can be said to have been a rhetorical intention. One response of Venetian antiquarians was to couple particular texts with certain interval sequences; a modernist response was to elaborate important words with extreme ornamentation. Interrogative pronouns, in the former case, were often set to an ascending 4th, which produced an emphatic effect; words representing elements of nature and passions were frequently set, in the latter case, with a great many notes to the main syllable. The word 'cara' was more frequently prefaced with a grace-note appoggiatura than any other word.

When it came to literal imitations of the art of antiquity, the boldest stroke of the classical revival in Venetian music was Marcello's effort to base some of his settings of the first 50 psalms of David (1724–6) on chants of the diverse Hebrew sects resident in Venice. To honour the practices of antiquity (6), these were treated with appropriate modesty: some settings were not harmonized, and male voices were favoured throughout. Obbligatos for cello or for two violas suggested the austere shading that Marcello thought appropriate to music he believed had ancient origins.[21] Although they are little known today, Marcello's psalms were profoundly influential not only in Venice but throughout Europe, and not only in his own time but throughout the eighteenth and nineteenth centuries. The prefaces that appeared in the eight volumes in which they were published constituted a manifesto for the classical revival itself. 'Nobility' and 'simplicity' were praised, and testimonials in support of Marcello's views and his new style of composition were offered by a host of poets and composers, including his teacher Francesco Gasparini and his German contemporaries Johann Mattheson and Georg Philipp Telemann. The fact that Marcello was a nobleman may have attracted more attention in some quarters than his music, but since there were also Austrian and German rulers of the time who distinguished themselves as composers, this should not have seemed so unusual then as it does today.

There was no real consensus on the merits of Marcello's music. German writers extolled its melody, English writers its harmony; the Italians and French looked to it for models of contrapuntal practice. Publishers of sheet music loved it a little too well: they stripped out lyrics, transposed, rearranged and retexted the result, producing short pieces that enjoyed a big market because of their practicality but bore little relation to the original material.

Through the sustained popularity of psalms quoting musical material from what was taken for antiquity, searches for exotic music of all kinds began in the later nineteenth century. In a curious if convoluted sense, the twentieth-century study of 'ancient and oriental' music, and its elaboration into the field of ethnomusicology, owe some debt to the Venetian conception of musical classicism.

Modernism

Marcello's relationship to antiquarianism was diametrically opposed by Vivaldi's relationship to modernism. The son of a barber who also played the violin at St Mark's and, for a time, in the Ospedale dei Mendicanti, Vivaldi had a practical ability in playing the violin which was evidently superior. His formal education came through his training as a priest. He was especially responsive to the shifting tides that were reshaping European society, although he probably had no conscious perception of these changes, and it must be said that he was highly individual in his accommodation of the values promoted by the enlightened world beyond Venice and beyond classicism. Four primary emphases filtered through to Vivaldi from this broader sphere: (1) invention; (2) classification; (3) self-reference; and (4) simplification.

Invention for its own sake was a motto of the early eighteenth century. It meant not simply the design of mechanical devices but also the creative use of materials. For Bach, keyboard works with mutually imitative parts were inventions. In Italy, unaccompanied works, such as those for violin by the Trentine composer Francesco Antonio Bonporti (1672–1749), were occasionally called inventions. Vivaldi did not use the title 'invention', but he promoted the concept of inventiveness in his endlessly creative scoring combinations. A player of the violin (and probably also the viola) in an environment brimming with string players, he nonetheless chose to accommodate oboists, flautists and many other wind instrumentalists. He stretched the capabilities of commonly used instruments such as the violin to their limits and explored the usefulness of both obsolescent and nascent instruments such as the chalumeau, clarinet and viola d'amore.

Vivaldi and Albinoni (1671–1751) both responded to a growing sense of natural order in the universe by observing fundamental distinctions of genre (2). The sonata, the sinfonia and the concerto were differentiated at the start of the eighteenth century. The ensemble sonata was played with one instrument to a part. The trio sonata, scored for two melody instruments (usually violins) and, in the Venetian literature, a cello as well as a keyboard continuo, was the dominant sub-species between 1690 and 1710. The solo sonata flourished in the next decade, as did works ambiguously scored for string bass (*violone*) or keyboard continuo. Accompaniment on a plucked instrument such as the lute or archlute enjoyed a brief vogue over the same years. Around 1700 the sinfonia might closely resemble a sonata on the page, but many instruments played to one part. Sinfonias often served to introduce extended vocal works, and many were based on schemes of rhythmic definition and contrast borrowed from the French *ouverture*.

The earliest concertos from Venice, which were by Albinoni and were published in 1700, were based not on the alternation of solo and tutti passages but on the elaboration of the first violin part of a sinfonia by the addition of a *violino de concerto* – a clear predecessor of the *violino principale* of the concerto. Only 11 years later Vivaldi's earliest set of concertos, op.3, involved the use of one, two or three instruments (drawn from the familiar combination of two violins and cello) to develop episodic material in alternation with a tutti ritornello. From there Vivaldi went on to create a large repertory of works in which one or two violins (or, more rarely, a cello or bassoon) assumed progressively more daring solo passages.

This selfconsciousness of the individual instrumentalist (3) developed in parallel with an interest elsewhere in portraiture and the biographical novel. In fact, the concept of self-awareness was one that was considered to have been ushered in by the rise of a middle class. The prospering individual was less interested in likenesses of figures from history and mythology than in confirmation of his own existence and individuality. The new creed held that glory and greatness could be found in the lives of the humble. Through musical virtuosity and the employment of appropriate playing techniques, the role of soloist in the concerto could be likened to the role of a self-made individual in society.

The concept of simplification practised by the modernists (4) was not the same one cherished by the classicists. The modernists kept the elaboration of concepts simple, while the classicists concentrated on keeping performance simple. For Vivaldi, this meant a turning-away from the complexities of counterpoint towards the delineation of individual parts by the simpler and more audible means of timbre. It meant the use of melodic sequences, which were slightly varied repetitions, in preference to spinning out long lines from short motifs. It meant harmonic regularity. At times, it meant the composition of music by formula. The codification of the tonal system, urged on by such diverse phenomena as the limited range of the natural trumpet and the need of continuo players to find appropriate harmonies quickly, represented a somewhat formulaic approach to music. In specific cases material as simple as the descending scale provided a skeleton both for single movements within works and even for the series of tonalities on which successive movements of long vocal works were based.[22]

The general tenor of the debate between classicists and modernists can be seen from the long succession of short quips in Marcello's *Il teatro alla moda* (1720). Vivaldi and some of his associates in theatrical affairs were satirized on its front page, and it is generally assumed that much of the musical invective within was intended to relate to his practices.

*

There were some common threads running through both fabrics. An absorption in proportional relations likened Vivaldi's concertos and Canaletto's heavily dramatized paintings of Venetian buildings. Canaletto was often careful to frame his subjects with generous borders of less compelling material. Shadows give a sense of depth, staircases of height, and balconies of length in the architectural portrayal of what would otherwise be dull, flat space. In much the same way the orchestra frames the concerto soloists, who provide surface details in successive musical episodes.

Naturalism was also pervasive throughout the repertory. Certain elements of the classicists' Arcadia, which concentrated on rural innocence, were different only by way of emphasis in the modernists' more comprehensive view of the physical world. In the text associated with Vivaldi's 'Four Seasons' concertos from op.8 (1725), the effects of weather on temperament were stressed. In Marcello's oratorio entitled *Il pianto e il riso delle quattro stagioni* ('The Sorrows and Joys of the Four Seasons') the emphasis was devotional: the aim was not to delight and inform but to instruct and inspire. The specific images suggested were different, but the intended effect of immersion in empirical reality was common to these and many other efforts of the same kind.

OPERA AND SOCIETY

There were several levels of reality associated with the Venetian theatre. Life as depicted on the stage strived for verisimilitude to a degree that makes it seem, to twentieth-century tastes, ludicrously

14. *Interior of an unknown Venetian theatre, showing 'incognito' boxes and members of the audience wearing masks: engraving from Zaccaria Seriman's satire 'I viaggi d'Enrico Wanton . . .' (1749)*

artificial. Misnomers, anachronisms and blatant machinations were commonly employed. The world of visual illusion that was created on the stage was so opulent that modern means of stage production seem almost pedestrian by comparison.

On the other hand, Venetian theatres were small. They seated only a few hundred people who were predominantly in boxes that were leased perennially by the same families. Those who sat in the parterre saw the stage poorly, since the orchestra was not in a pit; they also suffered occasional indignities, such as having the residue of meals consumed by box-holders discarded on to their heads. Apart from numerous choruses and groups of dances, casts were small and orchestras were of chamber dimensions.

The theatres served a multitude of social purposes. One was to provide a meeting-place for rendezvous that might have been illicit under any other circumstances. Operas were given only during Carnival, which was not exclusively the pre-Lenten season but referred to any time during which masks were permitted. To some approximation, masks were permitted when the Great Council was in recess. Only when masks were worn were Venetian nobles allowed to hold discourse with foreigners (whose identities were ostensibly concealed not only physically but also by the adoption of pseudonyms). Venetian opera was in a sense allied not with the interests of the Republic *per se* but with the interests of some of its most powerful nobles.

The complex calendar of openings maintained by Venice's main theatres was almost as ritualized as the liturgy at St Mark's. The splendid Teatro di S Giovanni Grisostomo, run by the august Grimani family, usually had a première on the feast of St Stephen (26 December). Other major theatres – S Salvatore, S Angelo and S Cassiano – usually had premières on ensuing evenings. A second round of openings began in the middle of the winter carnival and lasted until the start of Lent, when the public theatres were closed.

In the late seventeenth century the first operas of Carnival were often dedicated to Roman nobles and almost equally often treated episodes from Roman history or mythology. Between 1700 and 1725 operas given at this time were usually composed by seasoned Venetian composers such as Gasparini (1661–1727) and Carlo Francesco Pollarolo (*c*1653–1723). Between 1725 and 1740 Neapolitan composers such as Leonardo Leo (1694–1744), Leonardo Vinci (*c*1690–1730) and Nicola Porpora (1686–1768) held sway. The second operas of Carnival were often dedicated to foreign (especially German and English) patrons. The Germans seem to have liked stories derived from Gothic history and legend, while the English were drawn to more exotic subjects – from Persia, Ethiopia and even China. Many of the composers most favoured during this season

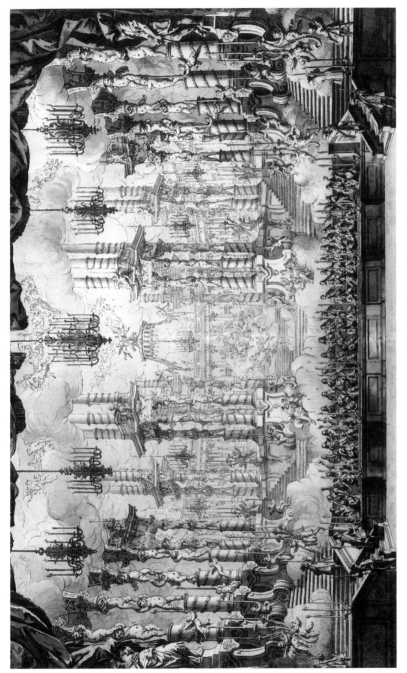

15. *Design by Antonio Jolli for the backdrop (representing 'La reggia della Dea Flora', with musicians seated in front) for the ball in honour of the visit of Frederick Christian, Crown Prince of Saxony and Poland, at the Teatro S Giovanni Grisostomo on 1 March 1740 after the final opera performance (G. A. Giai's 'Adriano in Siria') of the carnival season*

were German (Heinichen, Hasse) or had strong German ties (Lotti, Vivaldi).

The autumn opera season, which gained a following in the first years of the eighteenth century, seems to have catered for Italian, predominantly nearby patrons who were not celebrities. In fact, the lower tiers of the nobility, those of insufficient means to have villas to which to retreat in autumn, seem to have provided much of the patronage. This was the season for which many Venetian composers, including Caldara, Albinoni and Giovanni Maria Ruggieri (*fl c*1690–1720) wrote their first operas. Satirical works and other low-budget productions were a special predilection. The spring season, which coincided with the Ascension Fair, was initiated in the 1720s. By this time the winter carnival season had lost ground, and an increasing number of operas lacked designated patrons. Spring became a season for pastorales, and one in which foreign composers, such as Gluck, increasingly took an interest.

Venetian opera became what all of Venetian culture was destined to be in the modern world – part of a service economy. With increasing regularity it imported composers and performers. The styles of music and manners of performance witnessed in Venice became less and less Venetian. The image of an international emporium that had been promoted for generations to attract Carnival visitors now became a year-round reality. Philosophical predispositions became immaterial to the long-term progress of music, for an interest in meeting ever-changing requirements for fashionability, as defined by strangers, had taken charge.

Venetian composers looked elsewhere for patronage. Many church musicians and violinists emigrated only as far as Padua, where Giuseppe Tartini formed his 'school' of violin playing, the Scuola delle Nazioni. Others were attracted especially to London, Vienna, Dresden and St Petersburg in the 1730s, 40s and 50s. Venetian singers and instrumentalists took jobs in smaller cities like Lyons and Brussels as readily as in larger ones like Berlin and Paris. Remnants of Venetian musical tradition were cast like bread on the waters of European culture, and the music that was heard in Venice in the later eighteenth century was progressively less memorable – and less Venetian.

NOTES

[1] W. H. McNeill, *Venice: the Hinge of Europe* (Chicago, 1974).

[2] Exotic details of Venetian life such as these are given in the very numerous weekly news sheets and monthly journals that flourished between 1680 and 1720; for further information on this kind of material, see E. Selfridge-Field, *Pallade veneta: Writings on Music in Venetian Society, 1650–1750* (Venice, 1985).

[3] This thesis is put forward for the first half of the seventeenth century by the late J. H. Moore, *Vespers at St. Mark's: Music of Alessandro Grandi, Giovanni Rovetta, and Francesco Cavalli* (Ann Arbor, 1981); it is likely that it pertained to a diminishing extent as time passed.

[4] Very little sacred music from Venice was printed after 1690. Letters and other accounts indicate that many motets were written for the major churches and *ospedali*, but new liturgical works, especially masses and Vesper psalms for the churches, were rare; stocks amassed over preceding decades were evidently adequate for most needs.

[5] T. Coryat, *Coryat's Crudities* (London, 1611), 289.

[6] Disciplinary actions in the major churches, where all the musicians were male, are rarely noted. Male teachers and music directors in the convents and *ospedali*, where all the residents were female, were reprimanded for quite trivial offences. Numerous dismissals for reasons of behaviour are recounted in G. Ellero, J. Scarpa and M. C. Paolucci, eds., *Arte e musica all'Ospedaletto: schede d'archivio sull'attività musicale degli ospedali dei Derelitti e dei Mendicanti di Venezia* (Venice, 1978).

[7] See, for example, the accounts of funerals in E. Selfridge-Field, *Pallade veneta*.

[8] D. Arnold, 'Orphans and Ladies: the Venetian Conservatoires', *PRMA*, lxxxix (1962–3), 35.

[9] The chalumeau was in use in only a few places in the middle decades of the eighteenth century; a useful study is C. Lawson, *The Chalumeau in Eighteenth-Century Music* (Ann Arbor, 1981).

[10] Vivaldi claimed to have composed almost 100 operas; music for some 20 and librettos for another 30 or so survive.

[11] On the workings of the Venetian press, see E. Selfridge-Field, *Pallade veneta*, chap. 2.

[12] On the allegorical interpretation of some of Vivaldi's serenatas, see M. Talbot, 'Vivaldi's Serenatas: Long Cantatas or Short Operas?', *Antonio Vivaldi: teatro musicale, cultura e società: Venice 1981*, 88ff.

[13] In fact, after almost two centuries of relying almost entirely on printed music for all musical performances except opera, the Venetians had to revert to the use of manuscripts for most sacred, secular and instrumental performances. Operas and oratorios, because of their length and ephemeral nature, were never committed to print, but audiences were always provided with printed librettos containing the text.

[14] E.g. Vivaldi's op.13, a collection of six sonatas for flute or other melody instrument. Philippe Lescat has recently shown that these works, which include quotations from Vivaldi's earlier music, were composed by Nicolas Chédeville.

[15] Reported in the correspondence of Edward Holdsworth and cited in M. Talbot, 'Charles Jennens and Antonio Vivaldi', *Vivaldi veneziano europeo: Venice 1978*, 71.

[16] The core of this collection is now housed in the Museo Nazionale di Strumenti Musicali in Rome; it remains uncatalogued. Alessandro Marcello's fortepiano is one of three surviving specimens by the instrument's inventor, Bartolomeo Cristofori; built in 1724, it is the least decorative but the best preserved. Cristofori lived in the marshes near Padua, where the Marcellos had a summer villa.

[17] The most comprehensive of the academic publications was the *Galleria di Minerva*, which appeared in six very large volumes, 1696–1717; new publications were the main focus of the *Giornale de' letterati d'Italia*, initiated by Zeno in 1710 and published regularly for 30 years.

[18] P. Gay, *The Enlightenment: an Interpretation*, i: *The Rise of Modern Paganism* (New York, 1966), 30ff.

[19] The standard work on this subject is R. Freeman's *Opera without Drama: Currents of Change in Italian Opera 1675–1725* (Ann Arbor, 1981). Zeno's role in the reform of opera and what that reform meant are subjects re-evaluated in a series of articles by R. Strohm in *Informazioni e studi vivaldiani*, ix–xii (1988–91).

[20] What Marcello valued most highly was 'taste', somewhat in contrast to the vocal gymnastics that had become *de rigueur* for aspiring singers; he was the teacher of one of Venice's most noted prima donnas, Faustina Bordoni (1700–81), and of several less well known *virtuose*.

[21] The foundation of Marcello's perceptions of what ancient music sounded like seems to have rested with living traditions in the Venice of his day (Venice had three distinct Jewish traditions in its ghetto, which was near Marcello's home). He retrieved two Greek hymns from writings of the ancients and was an avid reader of French and Italian translations of the writings of antiquity.

[22] See Vivaldi's oratorio *Juditha triumphans*, in which eight movements representing the dramatic core of the work begin on successive tonalities of the descending B♭ major scale.

The Late Baroque Era

BIBLIOGRAPHICAL NOTE

There is no general history of Venetian music, nor is there any up-to-date social history of Venice in which the role of music is clearly delineated. P. Molmenti's eight-volume *Venice: its Individual Growth from the Earliest Beginnings to the Fall of the Republic*, trans. H. F. Brown (London, 1906–8), gives a good sense of the scale of things. In matters of detail and interpretation it is superseded by myriad subsequent studies in such journals as the *Archivio veneto* and in diverse monographs. A rich source of information on musical events is the contemporary periodical *Pallade veneta*, musical extracts of which are reproduced and annotated in E. Selfridge-Field, *Pallade veneta: Writings on Music in Venetian Society, 1650–1750* (Venice, 1985), which contains an introductory commentary and a calendar of documents in English.

Genre studies of sacred music are greatly indebted to F. Caffi's *Storia della musica sacra nella già cappella ducale di San Marco in Venezia dal 1318 al 1797* (Venice, 1845–55), which has recently been reissued in facsimile but has never been translated. Increasingly, however, the information that Caffi provided is being refined by sophisticated archival research. The documentary history of Venetian sacred music over four centuries (1400–1800) has been profoundly augmented by the research of Gastone Vio, whose findings, which relate mainly to the lives of individuals and institutions, are reported in a host of Italian scholarly journals, such as the *Bollettino dell'Istituto italiano Antonio Vivaldi*, in the proceedings of conferences held at the Fondazione Giorgio Cini in Venice and in monographs on Venetian churches. *Women Musicians of Venice: Musical Foundations, 1525–1855*, by J. L. Baldauf-Berdes (Oxford, 1993), is a richly documented history of music in the *ospedali*.

Stylistic histories containing chapters on specific genres of Venetian music include several studies of the 1960s and 70s, such as W. S. Newman's *The Sonata in the Baroque Era* (Chapel Hill, 1959, rev. 2/1966), A. Hutchings's *The Baroque Concerto* (New York and London, 1961, rev. 3/1973) and H. Smither's *The Oratorio in the Baroque Era* (Chapel Hill, 1977). D. and E. Arnold's *The Oratorio in Venice* (London, 1986) contains a chapter on the period from 1700 to 1740 and a listing of 573 works performed in the *ospedali* up to 1770.

Studies that trace the progress of one kind of music over several generations include E. Selfridge-Field's *Venetian Instrumental Music from Gabrieli to Vivaldi* (Oxford, 1975) and E. Rosand's *Opera in Seventeenth-Century Venice: the Creation of a Genre* (Berkeley, 1991). A total of approximately one dozen facsimiles of operas from the period 1680 to 1740 are scheduled to appear in the series Drammaturgia Musicale Veneta published by Ricordi (Milan, 1983–); many volumes are prefaced by book-length introductory essays that collectively constitute an important source for the study of the history of Venetian opera. Although the bibliography of Venetian opera up to 1680 is voluminous, little of a comprehensive nature has been written on its subsequent history except in specialized studies and a few dissertations. Short articles, supported by numerous illustrations of costumes and stage design, appear in M. Collins and E. Kirk, eds., *Opera and Vivaldi* (Austin, 1984).

As for individual composers, Vivaldi is the best served. The first volume of Marc Pincherle's path-breaking two-volume study *Antonio Vivaldi et la musique instrumentale* (Paris, 1948) is available in C. Hatch's translation as *Vivaldi: Genius of the Baroque* (New York, 1957). M. Talbot's *Vivaldi* (London, 1978) is a short, up-to-date account which includes biographical material, while his *Vivaldi* (London, 1979), a BBC Music Guide, concentrates on particular aspects of the repertory. A. Kendall's *Vivaldi* (London, 1978) emphasizes biography and draws heavily on letters and contemporary accounts of Venetian life. The definitive catalogue of Vivaldi's works is P. Ryom's *Répertoire des oeuvres d'Antonio Vivaldi* (Copenhagen, 1986–); volume i, covering the instrumental works, appeared in 1986; volume ii is forthcoming.

Current research is reported in *Informazioni e studi vivaldiani*, the annual bulletin of the Istituto Italiano Antonio Vivaldi.

Among other composers, Albinoni is served by M. Talbot's *Tomaso Albinoni: the Venetian Composer and his World* (Oxford, 1990). The reach of Venetian music into the Habsburg domain is well covered in B. W. Pritchard, ed., *Antonio Caldara: Essays on his Life and Time* (Aldershot, 1987). The music of Benedetto and Alessandro Marcello is catalogued and discussed in E. Selfridge-Field's *The Music of Benedetto and Alessandro Marcello: a Thematic Catalogue with Commentary on the Composers, Repertory, and Sources* (Oxford, 1990).

Chapter IV

Naples: a City of Entertainment

CAROLYN GIANTURCO

It has been said that through the centuries the Neapolitans' 'two refuges from suffering were music and religion',[1] and it could be added that even religion often expressed itself in music. Certainly the people had much cause for suffering, which emanated from both political events and natural disasters. Moreover, the frequency of such circumstances invalidates the statement that the years under discussion here 'are perhaps the dullest in Italian history',[2] at least when applied specifically to Naples; on the contrary, the history of Naples in the years 1680–1740 is a lively one, and one that may be documented through its music – composed to celebrate or to alleviate, depending on one's point of view, the consequences that politics and nature imposed on the people. The string of rulers governing Naples understood the power of entertainment to pacify their subjects; they also found such secular and religious occasions attractive themselves. Local nobility emulated them in both attitudes; and the lower classes were grateful for whatever came their way of a pleasant nature. Of all the adornments of baroque Naples, it might be said that music was the richest and was indulged in the most frequently.

HISTORICAL AND POLITICAL BACKGROUND

One of Europe's capitals, Naples was praised by John Evelyn as having 'certainly one of the richest Landskips in the World';[3] at the time of Milton it was already being said that 'There Spring is everlasting; a piece of the sky fallen to the earth; blessed Campania, the most beautiful shore not only of Italy but of all the globe of earth'.[4] In 1503 Naples came under King Ferdinand II ('the Catholic') of Aragon, and every few years until 1707 a new viceroy arrived from Spain to govern the city; when he left he was sure to be laden with Neapolitan treasures – paintings, sculpture, furniture. This was obviously much to the people's displeasure, as they made clear in their attempted revolt of 1647. The year 1656 was specially disastrous, as a plague in Naples reduced the inhabitants from 360 000 to approximately 160 000. (Only slowly did the city recuperate, the population numbering 185 000 in 1688 and 300 000 in 1742.) In 1659 they were hit again, this time by one of the relatively frequent and terrible earthquakes that shook the terrain. In 1665 Philip IV of Spain died, and his sceptre passed to Charles II, the last of the Habsburgs to rule Spain. In the 1670s, while there was tremendous famine, the French attacked. It is no wonder, then, that the Neapolitan people refused to raise the 300 000 ducats that Charles expected in 1675 as a wedding present.

The 1680s brought still another viceroy, Gaspar de Haro, who tried his best to wipe out the bandits for which Naples was infamous as well as to curtail its rampant illegal feudalism. Before the decade was over another earthquake shook the city, and Francisco de Bonavide replaced De Haro. In the 1690s there was another plague, another earthquake, Mount Vesuvius erupted, and the French attempted further attacks. Under the viceroy Luigi Francisco de la Cerda bandits thrived and the government was dishonest; whether through stupidity or connivance, the viceroy even let some Genoese merchants export grain, at a time when famine was starving the Neapolitan people.

When Charles II died in 1700, leaving the Spanish throne to the Bourbon King Philip V (grandson of Louis XIV of France), the Neapolitans – made desperate by two centuries of suffering and continual robbing by the Spanish nobility with Madrid's consent and despondent after the latest eruption of Vesuvius and their consequential plight – looked to the Bourbons' enemy, the Habsburg Emperor Charles VI, as their saviour. Unfortunately, their efforts to effect a change failed, and in 1702 another new Spanish viceroy arrived in Naples.

Juan Emanuel Fernandez Pacheco was a benevolent and cultured man, but he could do little to assuage the ravages of the earthquakes that hit the city in March and again in April. Philip V's visit (16 April–2 June) brought some relief: he reduced the tax on grain and flour and cancelled the university's overdue taxes, which amounted to about two and a half million ducats. Nevertheless, demonstrations in Naples were openly pro-Austrian, and when the Austrian army arrived in Livorno the viceroy knew he could not depend on his subjects' loyalty as the enemy continued south. As it turned out, the Austrians, in the name of Charles VI, entered Naples on 7 July 1707 without bloodshed. They had already been welcomed at Aversa by Francesco Mancini (1672–1737) and other court musicians; to celebrate their victory Mancini had composed and performed a *Te Deum* for the occasion (as a reward he was appointed court music director).

The Neapolitans' first joys quickly turned to bitter disappointment, however, as they realized that their new king did not plan to give them independence. The new viceroy, Georg Adam von

Martinitz, revealed that the only appreciable difference the people would find was that instead of being under Spanish rule they were now under Austrian. Libraries were soon sacked and volumes sent to Austria; and the university was abandoned for some time. For the next 27 years the only consolation was that several viceroys were Italian. The riots that broke out in 1723 were, in such conditions, to be expected.

After the death of Maria Luisa of Savoy, Philip V of Spain married the ambitious Isabella (Elisabeth) Farnese in 1714. Their son Charles (Don Carlos) crossed the Pyrenees at the age of 15, arriving with an English-Spanish-Tuscan navy in Livorno in 1732. He carried on to Florence, where Grand Duke Gian Gastone greeted him as his successor (thereby infuriating the Austrians). Charles left there on 24 February 1734; when he arrived at Maddaloni on 9 April he received homage from 18 Neapolitans, who gave him the keys to their city. At Aversa, Francesco Mancini once again had court musicians welcome the new ruler, and thus secured his position of music director. After only five days' battle, the fortress of Sant'Elmo fell, and others quickly followed. By 10 May the capital was ready to receive Charles Bourbon. The people were happy – as they had been at the arrival of many previous rulers – forgetting all past suffering and hoping for a better future.

On 15 May 1734 news arrived that Philip V renounced all his rights to Naples in favour of his son. The young Charles travelled all over his new kingdom, and on 3 July he was officially crowned King of the Two Sicilies. Naples finally became autonomous, albeit attached to Spain. Even though the new king at first preferred hunting, fishing and the arts to governing, his ministers managed to set various reforms in motion, notably regarding finance, which had been left in a disastrous state by the Austrians. In 1738 Charles married Princess Maria Amalia of Saxony and in 1740 a daughter was born to them. The same year Emperor Charles VI of Austria died, and the War of Austrian Succession broke out. Although Naples tried to stay neutral, it was forced to send troops to help Spain, Charles proving himself a courageous leader at the Battle of Velletri. In the meantime another terrible earthquake shook Naples. In 1746 Philip V died, Isabella was set aside and Ferdinand VI succeeded to the Spanish throne. After 25 years of ruling Naples, however, Charles was called to succeed Ferdinand VI as King Charles III of Spain, and so left his southern kingdom in 1759.

In the complex game of European struggle for power, Naples clearly played a major role. To the locals it was, instead, simply a game of survival. The hardships caused by famine, poverty, drought, earthquakes and volcanic eruptions were sufficient to make their lives miserable. To these sufferings were added the misfortune and humiliation of living under foreign rulers – the Spanish, the Austrians, and again the Spanish. However, some aspects of life in Naples remained constant – one of them was the music. Moreover, music was often produced as a direct response to political or natural events. Some of these musical occasions were intended only for the nobility; at others the nobility and lower classes could have attended together; still other musical occasions were principally for the populace. To look in turn at these three categories of music-making in Naples will allow us to appreciate the kinds of music that were being written and performed in the years 1680–1740; at the same time we will better understand the Neapolitans (and their foreign 'guests'), for whom the music was created.

OPERA FOR THE NOBILITY

Contemporary accounts of Naples frequently refer to opera. It was clearly a preferred entertainment of the viceroy, as well as the one he offered to his important visitors. For example, in summer 1718 an opera was given in the royal palace for Admiral Byng, captaining an English ship on its way to Sicily. The prestige of the guests is affirmed by the gifts offered to the admiral's son and cousin: silver glove-cases, swords of gold and walking-sticks decorated one with diamonds and the other with gold. When the admiral returned the following July, he and the viceroy heard another opera, Sarro's *Alessandro Severo*, in the Teatro S Bartolomeo.[5] Opera was also performed to welcome the arrival of a new viceroy, perhaps at the Teatro dei Fiorentini, where Wolfgang-Annibale von Schrattenbach was taken in 1719 to hear G. P. di Domenico's *Lisa Pontegliosa*. It was also the means of celebrating an event in the life of a ruler (even in his or her absence) – a birthday, name-day or wedding-day: in 1680 *Elice* and *Arsinda d'Egitto* were given in the palace for the birthdays of Marie Louise and Charles II of Spain respectively: *I rivali generosi* was heard in 1700 for the birthday of Emperor Joseph I of Austria; and *Porpora's Faramondo* was given on 19 November 1719 (the feast of Elizabeth) in honour of the Austrian Empress Elizabeth.

Festive days were spread throughout the year, and visitors might arrive in any season; so the court could hear opera at almost any time. In 1722, for example, the viceroy heard operas at Carnival (Vinci's *Lí zite 'ngalera* at the Teatro dei Fiorentini), in April (*La noce di Veneviento* at the same theatre, as entertainment for the princes of Bavaria), in August (*Leo's Bajazete imperador de' Turchi* at the royal palace, to celebrate the birthday of Empress Elizabeth; and Vinci's *La festa di Bacco* at the Fiorentini), in September (at the Teatro S Bartolomeo), in October (at the Fiorentini) and in November (Vinci's *Pubblio Cornelio Scipione* at S Bartolomeo, to celebrate

The Late Baroque Era

Charles's name-day, and again in that theatre on the Empress Elizabeth's name-day). He began 1723 by attending two operas in January (Mancini's *Trajano* at S Bartolomeo and, considering this 'good but tedious, being long and tragic', he asked for Sarro's *Partenope* to be put on again, which it was, with new arias and delightful intermezzos)[6] and others in February (Porpora's *Amare per regnare* at S Bartolomeo and Leo's *La mpeca scoperta* at the Fiorentini); Lent interrupted his routine, but in April he was back at the opera (*Le pazzie d'amore* by Falco at the Fiorentini); in this pleasant way his year's diet of opera made a full round.

The theatres

The beginnings of this most popular form of musical entertainment in Naples makes for an interesting tale.[7] It was in 1618 that a group of actors headed by the Ferrarese Pier Maria Cecchini inaugurated a theatre for spoken plays, the Teatro della Commedia Nuova dei Fiorentini, with *Il pastor fido* and *La Idropica*. The theatre had 34 boxes and 310 seats in the orchestra; later on it often hosted companies of Spanish actors and, in fact, throughout the seventeenth century was referred to as the 'Commedia Spagnola'. The Teatro S Bartolomeo, built in 1621 by the governors of the Santa Casa degli Incurabili (who had the *jus repraesentandi* for every sort of spectacle in the city), offered Neapolitan plays by Neapolitan authors; it was rectangular in shape, with two rows of boxes along its side and a third level of simple seats (the *loggione*). Only in 1644 is there any notice of opera proper in Naples, when 'the very beautiful opera *Galatea*' by the Roman composer Loreto Vittori was given in the palace of the Prince of Cariati, probably by a company from Rome; this private performance was judged 'marvellous, beautiful, with lovely scenes' and was attended by 'almost all the nobility of ladies and cavaliers'.[8]

While other operas may have been given as entertainment for the nobility and their guests, nothing is known of them. In 1650, however, the royal palace, which had also presented plays in one of its great salons which had been adapted for the purpose, began to mount operas on a regular and different basis. In that year the viceroy, Count d'Oñate, invited a travelling company, the Febiarmonici, to perform,[9] mainly as a way of affirming the government's authority after subduing the 'Masaniello' revolution of 1647. The operas were given in a pavilion called 'del Pallonetto' (from its use for the game of pelota); but since it was transformed into a 'sumptuous theatre with boxes' by the company, and since they also paid for the 'variety of costumes of the personages, as well as for the well ordered scenery with many views of several kinds', he allowed them to charge an entrance fee of 'five carlini a head at the door . . . 2 other carlini for the seat, and 4 ducats for every box, one of which was occupied by Signor Viceroy who also paid'.[10] For these reasons it may be considered the first opera theatre in Naples open to a paying public (although the 'public' would have been an exclusively aristocratic one).

After some alterations by Giovan Battista Balbi to accommodate the needs of the new genre, the Teatro S Bartolomeo also began to offer opera from 1654. On 6 February 1681 the bitter cold encouraged patrons to light fires in their boxes (although this was forbidden); one fire was not properly extinguished and razed the theatre to the ground. It was to be restructured in 1682 and again in 1696, when the viceroy ordered that it be made 'larger and more magnificent, in conformity with other theatres in other cities' and the rows of boxes be increased from two to five. In 1699 Ferdinando Galli-Bibiena supervised additional changes, intended to permit the use of large stage machines. However, certain limitations inherent in the theatre's structure brought about its demolition in 1737. For several years it had been Naples's largest theatre and, despite complaints about its inadequacies for opera, it played an important role in the history of opera there.

Offering its stage to opera only in 1681, the Teatro dei Fiorentini, by contrast, was the home of comic opera. Originally intended as a small prose theatre for the nobility, it too was adapted to accommodate opera, intended there mainly for the middle and lower classes. It had 22 boxes, each furnished with four straw chairs without backs, and six more boxes called 'corridors'; in the orchestra there were 16 rows of seats, with 16 seats per row. It could seat a total of 256; and it was illuminated with two torches called 'splendours'.

Inaugurated in 1724, the Teatro della Pace (also known as the Teatro del Vico della Lava) was said to be quite small with only three rows of boxes. Its fare of comic opera (performed by 'singers of mediocre ability', or so it was complained) was also frequented mainly by the lower classes. Since the rooms above and below the theatre were said to be used for immoral activities, performances stopped in 1749. On quite another level was the Teatro Nuovo, also opened in 1724, built by Giacinto de Laurentiis and Angelo Carasale to a design by Domenico Antonio Vaccaro. It is considered the first opera theatre – certainly in Naples but perhaps also in general – built according to modern, functional criteria; although the basic area was small (80 square 'palms'), it had 140 seats in the orchestra and five rows of 13 boxes each, seating a total of 1000 people. The architecture, acoustics and lighting caused one commentator to remark that 'from the impossible was born the possible' and others to maintain that it need not envy the well-established Teatro S Bartolomeo, except in size. The Teatro Nuovo alternated comic operas with prose comedies in Italian and Neapolitan dialect.

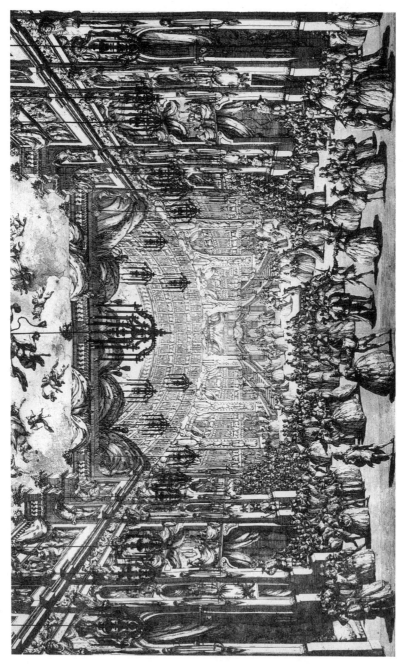

16. Auditorium of the Teatro S Carlo, Naples, built in 1737 to the designs of D. G. Metrano, viewed from the stage: engraving by Luigi de Lorrain after Vincenzo Re, showing the theatre adapted for a festival ball

In 1736 Charles decided that Naples needed a new theatre for serious opera on a par with other European theatres. The project was assigned to Giovanni Antonio Medrano, brigadier of the royal troops. Perhaps because of his inexperience he was given as aide Angelo Carasale, the able and proven builder of the Teatro Nuovo. The new theatre, called Teatro S Carlo in honour of the Bourbon king, was completed in the record time of eight months and 20 days and offered 14 boxes and 213 seats more than the S Bartolomeo. The writer Francesco Milizia criticized opera theatres saying that in general they were shameful and deserving of change, both inside and out; he described 18 theatres which he claimed were the only acceptable ones in all Europe and which included the Teatro S Carlo, about which he had to say the following:

> The royal theatre of Naples, constructed in 1737 according to the plan of engineer and brigadier D. Gio. Metrano, is also a horseshoe; that is to say, it is a semicircle, of which the extremities are elongated in almost parallel lines, which come closer together as they approach the scene [stage]. The largest diameter of the orchestra is about 73 Parisian feet, and the smallest is 67, and there are six rows of boxes, with a superb royal box in the middle of the second row [Charles Burney, the English music historian, reported that it occupied the space of four regular boxes]. The construction is all in stone, the staircases are magnificent, entrances, cloak-rooms, corridors are spacious; the entrance is divided into three sections; it has some decoration which could be more majestic and more significant.[11]

Burney described the lighting:

> In the front of each box there is a mirrour, three or four feet long, by two or three wide, before which are two large wax tapers; these, by reflection, being multiplied, and added to the lights of the stage and to those within the boxes, make the splendour too much for the aching sight.[12]

Librettos

Most of the serious operas presented in Naples were Venetian in origin.[13] It was not that the Neapolitans were disinterested in writing for the theatre, or that they failed to understand what was required. Proof of the contrary is to be found in the several literary academies that the city boasted, and in authors such as Andrea Perrucci, whose treatise on drama reveals him as an astute scholar of the theatre. In the first place, Perrucci was practical, as the following passage about plays reveals: 'About the length of a Work, choose one neither so short that it leaves one unsatisfied, nor so long that it causes boredom, agreeing with those who said that it should last not more than four and not less than three hours'.[14] Perrucci abhorred ridiculous and 'unnatural' situations, such as when a stage set forced a woman dressed grandly to enter with her back to the audience.[15] Instead, he believed that in order to achieve the true objective of performance, that is 'to move the affections to love, to anger, compassion, justice, praise, or intense dislike',[16] the actor had to 'transform himself into that personage which he represented, as though he had been transformed into him, forgetting his own real state so that the more he expresses himself naturally, the more he will achieve the desired results, and receive applause'.[17] These were typical attitudes of the period, but Perrucci and others were nevertheless generally called on simply to add prologues, intermezzos and the occasional aria to a Venetian libretto, or perhaps a comic scene, which pleased Neapolitan audiences more than Venetians as time went on.

From the 1640s onwards Italian opera plots were normally based on an episode from classical history. The intention, however, was not documentary but narrative – a lively, passion-filled, heroic tale, often relying on mistaken identity and disguise. The ending was always happy, no matter how difficult to bring about nor how absurd the contriving. Comic scenes between lower-class characters – servants or soldiers – served to relieve the seriousness of scenes for the noble characters. There might also be scenes for allegorical figures, gods and goddesses, or magicians.

By the end of the seventeenth century plots were generally less complicated and had fewer characters (reduced from 10–20 to 6–10). Invented characters were introduced only rarely and the number of comic scenes reduced (except in Naples, where they were much appreciated). Librettists were influenced at this period both by the classical tragedies of Corneille and Racine and by Italian Renaissance pastoral literature, which greatly interested them.

A typical sort of plot for the beginning of the eighteenth century – one that was heard in Venice, Naples and London – is *Gl'amanti generosi*. The text, by Giovanni Pietro Candi, was first set to music by Benedetto Vinaccesi for the Teatro S Angelo, Venice, in 1703; it was revised for presentation at the Teatro S Bartolomeo in Naples in 1705, with music by the Neapolitan composer Francesco Mancini. During the course of the opera[18] there is a fight between the protagonist, Idaspe, and a lion; one wonders how it was feigned (it is only one of several moments when someone's life is in danger). Disguise also figures largely: Idaspe and his uncle Dario are dressed as moors – among the most common of exotic disguises – a dramatic device that doubtless reflects the Turkish threat that loomed over Europe for so long. After much confusion, events are resolved: the tyrant unexpectedly becomes a benevolent ruler, and the two couples who have been struggling throughout the opera are joyfully united in matrimony. An important aspect of the libretto is its comedy. Six of the characters are 'serious', while two – a soldier and a maidservant – are comic. These last have an extended scene in each act in which their light, amusing banter centres on his love for her and her coy behaviour (Act 1, in fact, ends with their scene, affording it a prime position).

The Neapolitans' particular delight in such comic scenes is also revealed in operas such as *Il trionfo di Camilla, regina de' Volsci*, Silvio Stampiglia's first opera libretto, written in 1696 in Naples and set to music by his main collaborator Giovanni Bononcini. The libretto admits Virgil's *Aeneid* as a source, stating that 'the rest is invented'. Much of the 'invention' is comedy: one scene in Act 1 (scene xii), three in Act 2 (scenes vii, xvi and xviii, during which there is also a dance) and two scenes in Act 3 (scenes iii and x). Six scenes are thus allotted to a nurse and a servant – two characters extraneous to the principal plot and much lower in station than the other six – indicating that while the opera was indeed 'serious' in its main intent, comedy offered a goodly balance.

The comic intermezzo

Towards the end of the seventeenth century there was a tendency to eliminate comedy from the typical serious opera libretto and instead to insert comic scenes between the acts. Throughout the seventeenth century intermezzos had often included dance and allowed for scenic transformations; they could be either humorous or serious. Now that comedy had been removed from the main opera, the comic type of intermezzo prevailed. Its foolish characters did not disturb the main libretto and were often unconnected with it; the intermezzo could then travel independently from theatre to theatre and from opera to opera. This general trend emanated from Venice. When serious operas were presented in Naples, however, comedy continued to be added until about 1720; moreover, comic intermezzos were inserted as scenes within an opera itself, as with Tomaso Albinoni's inter-mezzo *Pimpinone*, given as an integral part of *Engelberta* (music by Antonio Orefice, *fl* 1708–34, and Mancini) in Naples in 1709.[19] The final elimination of comedy from serious opera in Naples was eventu-ally accomplished through the contact that Neapolitan composers enjoyed with other operatic centres.

Neapolitan composers such as Leonardo Vinci (*c*1690–1730), Nicola Porpora (1686–1768) and Leonardo Leo (1694–1744) became leading figures in Venice and the Veneto, and some spent long periods there. They were made to cultivate the comic intermezzo and acquired a liking for it. In the three intermezzos performed with a serious opera (two between Acts 1 and 2, one as the penultimate

17. Leonardo Vinci: caricature by the Roman artist Pier-Leone Ghezzi (1674–1755)

scene of Act 3), the two characters – stock *commedia dell'arte* types – often included a humble but cunning servant-girl, shepherdess or widow who manages to ensnare her partner and get him to marry her. Supernatural aspects might also be present, as well as one or more mute characters. As Michael Talbot points out: 'Much of the humour derives from the well-worn antitheses: youth versus age; male versus female; wealth versus impecuniosity; gullibility versus guile'.[20] Musically, comic intermezzos consisted of three short parts, each containing one or two arias and a concluding duet. The aria texts were usually longer than in serious opera because of the music's syllabic, rapid, declamatory style which, to achieve a substantial length in the set pieces, necessitated more words than a florid vocal style.

The eventual popularity of comic intermezzos in Naples may be seen in the steady stream that Johann Adolf Hasse (1699–1783) was asked to compose for insertion between the acts of serious operas at the Teatro S Bartolomeo on his arrival in the city:[21] *Miride e Damari* (with *Il Sesostrate*), May 1726; *Larinda e Vanesio* (with *Astarto*), December 1726; a revision of his Venetian intermezzo *Grilletta e Porsugnacco* (with Albinoni's *L'incostanza schernita*), November 1727; *Carlotta e Pantaleone* (with *Attalo, re di Bitinia*), May 1728; *Scintilla e Don Tabarano* (with Pietro Scarlatti's *Il Clitarco*), autumn 1728; *Merlina e Galoppo* (with *L'Ulderica*), January 1729; *Dorilla e Balanzone* (with *Tigrane*), November 1729; *Lucilla e Pandolfo* (with *Ezio*), autumn 1730; and *Arrighetta e Cespuglio* of about the same time. The genre achieved international fame when G. A. Federico's *La serva padrona* in the delightful setting by Giovanni Battista Pergolesi (1710–36) (first heard in Naples in 1733 with the composer's serious opera *Il prigioniero superbo*) was performed with enormous success in Paris in 1752; it was taken up as an example of 'natural' and pleasing Italian music to pit against the stylized French *tragédie lyrique*. As a result of the ensuing controversy, the so-called Querelle des Bouffons, more Neapolitan comic intermezzos by Pergolesi, Gaetano Latilla (1711–88), Leo, Niccolò Jommelli (1714–74) and others were presented in Paris.

Metastasio

Together with the elimination of comic characters from eighteenth-century serious opera and the insertion of comic intermezzos between its acts came a standardization of the type of plot and of the formal structure of serious opera. It was due in great part to Apostolo Zeno (1668–1750) and to Pietro Metastasio (1698–1782), a Roman lawyer who went to Naples as a young man in 1719, began to write poetry for music, and then went on to Rome, Venice and finally Vienna as court poet, achieving enormous success as a librettist. Comparing Zeno and Metastasio, Burney wrote:

> If the musical dramas of Apostolo Zeno are compared with those of his predecessors and contemporaries, they will be found infinitely superior to them in conduct, regularity, character, sentiment, and force. But Metastasio's refined sentiments, selection of words, and varied and mellifluous measures, soon obscured the theatric glory of Zeno.[22]

Metastasio wrote 27 three-act *opera seria* librettos, which were set by many different composers, totalling over a thousand settings. The frequency with which his librettos were presented to the Neapolitans is a testimony of their favourable appreciation of his work. Between 1723 and 1773, 25 of them were given a total of 60 different 'runs' in Naples, constituting an extraordinary diet of one man's realization of the eighteenth-century concept of opera. In the 1780s Stefano Arteaga's history of opera in Italy dedicated several pages to

Metastasio; Arteaga defined the particular qualities that made the poet's texts so apt for music:

> No-one better than he has known how to bend the Italian language to the nature of music, now making the sentences of recitative vibrate; now leaving aside those words which because they are too long, or have an awkward and sustained sound, are not suitable for song; now often using shortened words and those forms which end in an accented vowel, such as *ardì, piegò, farà*, which greatly help to smooth out the diction; now artificially mixing seven-syllable lines with those of 11 syllables to give the sentence variety which suits the harmonic interval and the pace of whoever has to sing it; now cutting the verses in half in order to shorten the sentences and render the pauses more sweet; now using rhymes discreetly but not in a fixed way, according to the pleasure of the ear and to avoid excessive monotony; now finally with singular ability suiting the diversity of the metres to the various passions, making use of short lines for the affections which express listlessness so that the soul, so to speak, does not have the force to finish the sentiment . . . No-one better than he has understood the needs of opera in accommodating the lyrical style to drama in such manner that neither the embellishments of the one ruin the [theatrical] illusion of the other, nor the naturalness of the latter thwart the ability to describe of the former.[23]

Metastasio's consummate skill in writing beautiful lyrical Italian served to enhance the historical plots he favoured, in which characters are meant to be noble and heroic in the face of moral or physical danger. He believed in the happy ending as being the natural consequence of right and reason's triumph over adversity. Of course, the singer-actors also had to be taken into account, and the number of arias assigned to each was determined by the importance of each role; in addition, after an aria, the singer was permitted to leave the stage. Theatrical conventions such as these naturally conditioned the structure, and the drama, of Metastasio's librettos.

But this was obviously just what the period, and certainly Naples, wanted, as is clear from Burney's account of the reception given to Metastasio's dramatic cantata *Gli orti esperidi*, set to music by Porpora for the birthday of the Empress Elizabeth in 1721:

> Indeed, the tradition says, that this drama [which Burney called *The Gardens of the Hesperides*] had an effect upon the audience in general, which Naples had never before experienced. The recitative was hardly begun, when the spectators formed a more curious spectacle than the actors themselves: so great was the change in their behaviour and mode of listening that was instantly produced. Violent noise and unbridled clamour, used to reign in every part of

that theatre, and could never be subdued but with great difficulty, even when some capital singer had a favourite air to perform; and it was no sooner over, than the din was renewed with such vehemence, that even the orchestra could not be heard. But now, every one delighted by the new and decorous arrangement of the scenes, original beauty and sweetness of the verse, the force of the sentiments, the texture of the parts, and all the wonders of Metastasio's dramatic poetry, was forced, almost insensibly, into profound silence and attention. The companions of Dido while Eneas was relating the tragical events which happened at the siege of Troy, could not have listened with more eagerness than the Neapolitan audience did at this representation. Universal curiosity was excited, and enquiries made, after the author.[24]

Besides offering an insight into the typical behaviour of a Neapolitan audience, Burney's account points out how unusual and wonderful Metastasio's texts seemed at the time. Moreover, Metastasio was given the blessing of other men of letters; and since he himself was a musician, composers and singers felt that they too had an ally in him. He had conquered all factions, and he managed to dominate them for a century.

Staging – the visual element

Another aspect of *opera seria* closely related to the libretto is the visual one. In Stampiglia's *Il trionfo di Camilla, regina de' Volsci* of 1696, for example, 14 *mutazioni* (set-changes) were executed: Act 1 required four – involving both interiors and exteriors – and Acts 2 and 3 five each. The visual marvels of the sets and of changing them enraptured theatre-goers, and had critics and painters (the 'inventors of the scenes') continually discussing what they should be and how they should be achieved. Arteaga described the great strides made in this area:

The art of making very small places seem spacious and grand, the ease and rapidity of quickly changing a scene, the manner of artificially varying the strength of the lights, and above all the invention of the incidental points, or rather, the manner of viewing the scene at an angle, brought the science of illusion to its summit. The great secret of the arts is the presenting of objects in such a manner that fantasy does not stop where the senses stop, but that there always remains something for the spectator to imagine which the eye does not see and the ear does not hear. Thus, to break away sometimes from perspectives that reach a central point and which are, so to speak, the end of visual and imaginative capability, was like opening an immense career for the industrious and restless imagination of those who, from a distance, look on the scenes.[25]

Arteaga acknowledged that the Galli-Bibiena brothers from Bologna, Ferdinando and Francesco, played decisive roles in bringing about such changes in the theatre; they both worked in Naples at the turn of the eighteenth century.

Sets and the machinery to change them or to manufacture a visual effect were constructed not just for the main opera but also for any prologue to the drama. Such a section might serve as something new added to an opera that had been first presented elsewhere, or might pay homage to the chief guest in the audience, or might simply prepare the audience for the story.[26] *La schiava di sua moglie*, heard in Naples in 1672 with music by Francesco Provenzale (*c*1626–1704), had both an Anteprologue and a Prologue; they required special equipment, which was designed by Gennaro delle Chiavi, named specifically in the libretto. A contemporary account of what occurred in the prologue to *Artaserse*, given at the Teatro S Carlo in 1738 with music by Leonardo Vinci, gives some insight into the delights one could witness at the opera theatre. After remarking on the richness of the dress of all the nobility and court, the chronicler went on to relate that at the beginning of the drama there was

> a very beautiful Prologue for five characters, figuring Notte [Night], Venere [Venus], Amore, Partenope and Sebeto. There appeared meanwhile a wood, with countryside, and hills, and to the right was shown Partenope dressed in a royal manner, upon a golden seat at the top of a staircase, sleeping, and about her various nymphs also sleeping upon various rocks. To the left one observed Serbeto who was still sleeping, leaning against his urn, from which clear and limpid waters ran, and about him in a circle various shepherds also sleeping. In the air to the left one saw Notte in a four-wheeled chariot drawn by two black horses, dressed in blue sprinkled with golden stars, crowned with poppy flowers; to the right one discerned another chariot drawn by two doves, in the centre of which was located Venere crowned with roses and myrtle, and on whose head resplended a very shining star. Amongst all however one admired [most] the chariot of Amore, drawn by four white horses in which was Amore with white wings, arrows and bow, and with a heraldic emblem burning in his hand, and at the same time one discerned peeping through on the Horizon the shining Moon, and at the end of the Prologue, during the chorus's [cries of] Long Life, and a resounding firing of rifles and cannons, a great number of Sonnets were dispersed throughout the audience by flying cupids.[27]

In the eighteenth century, because of Charles's specific preference, operas had dance scenes between the acts instead of comic intermezzos. For *L'Andromaca* in 1742, the 'engineer, and painter of the scenes and inventor of the machines', Vincenzo Re, had to provide all that was needed: in addition to the seven indoor and outdoor scenes for the opera proper, he created the following two for the respective entr'actes:

> The Shore of the Sea, and in its midst the Residence of Neptune formed by many rocks and seashells, on which several sea Nymphs are seated, and the four principal rivers, and at the top Neptune with Tetide, who will be pulled to the shore by seahorses; [and a] Shepherd's Hut.

Musical style

It was, of course, the music that brought to life the plays with their wonderful scenery – recitatives alternating with arias accompanied either by a simple continuo bass or by the orchestra. In the seventeenth century many arias were accompanied by continuo alone, as in the earliest operas by Alessandro Scarlatti (1660–1725), and they would usually have been preceded or followed by a few bars of orchestral ritornello; in an accompanied aria, the orchestra (initially strings and continuo) might have played only between the vocal phrases. Later, orchestral participation became more continuous, and in the eighteenth century arias were normally accompanied throughout by the orchestra. In Naples this development was paralleled by a particular interest in achieving variety of instrumental accompaniment throughout an opera. Mancini's *Gl'amanti generosi* of 1705 is scored for two violins, viola, trumpet and continuo. The trumpet plays not only in the opening sinfonia but also in the aria 'Empia stella, nemica e rubella' (Act 2 scene xiii), where its traditional association with battle serves to highlight the singer's accusation that the stars are warring against him, notably in long, brilliant *fioriture* for voice and trumpet. In scene xvii of the same act the soprano aria 'Torna la speme in sen' is accompanied by two harpsichords. While it was normal at this period to have two harpsichords in an opera orchestra as continuo instruments (perhaps one accompanying recitatives and the other the set pieces), Mancini conceived the role of these harpsichords, with their fully written-out parts, as melodic, rhythmic and timbral accompaniment in the full sense of the word.

As far as the continuo was concerned, Porpora's *Flavio Anicio Olibrio* of 1711, for example, specifies a lute, archlute, violone (viola da gamba), cellos and double bass as continuo instruments (presumably with a harpsichord). They do not seem to have played together all the time, but were grouped differently from aria to aria. Moreover, the violins are sometimes divided, sometimes in unison, and occasionally there is a 'violino solo'. So, even though the orchestra comprised only strings and continuo, it did not always play as a set unit but offered a variety of accompaniment during the opera, which added greatly to the interest. This continual change of instrumentation is a typical feature of Neapolitan opera and is found throughout the eighteenth century.

The variety increased, of course, whenever there were more instruments, such as two trumpets, two oboes and two horns in addition to strings and continuo, which became the standard ensemble: one sees it, for example, in the opera *L'Olimpiade*, which Pergolesi wrote in Naples but which was performed in Rome in 1736. An additional surprise is to be found there in the aria 'Torbido in volto' (Act 3 scene iv), where two orchestras are called for: in the *prima orchestra* there are parts for two violins, viola, cello and continuo; and in the *seconda orchestra*, two violins, viola, horns and continuo. The two groups alternate in a manner reminiscent of double choirs or of a concerto grosso; the singer may be accompanied by one orchestra or the other, and the orchestras even alternate in the middle of a vocal phrase.

Variety of musical style is also a hallmark of Neapolitan *opera seria*. Although it is often said that late Baroque music is based on the insistent repetition of small motifs to such an extent that the rhythm has been called 'motoric', that is anything but true for Naples. A single motif is never repeated over and over again; rather, different motifs combine to make up a musical phrase, just as in prose as opposed to poetry. Neapolitan composers also had a penchant for dotted rhythms: they filled their vocal and instrumental parts with patterns of alternating long and short notes, producing a characteristic effect peculiar to their music. Rests frequently punctuate phrases, as though to suggest conversation among the vocal and instrumental forces. Because downbeats are not stressed, the result is of lightness and movement, but not 'the smooth and linear style of Venetian composers'.[28] The instrumental bass lines tend to be active, often motivic, polarizing with the voice rather than merely supporting it. Vocal parts are virtuoso, with bar upon bar of *fioriture*. The vocal line is often angular, filled with leaps that serve to surprise and delight. Correct declamation of the text, initially crucial to opera composers, is often sacrificed in favour of an interesting musical idea.

The Neapolitan composer's contrapuntal skills are not tested in his operas. Only one part at a time has relevant motivic material (except where two parts imitate one another), the others serving simply to fill out the texture, unlike, for example, the Roman operatic style, better known for 'the complexity of its orchestral parts . . . and contrapuntal floridity'.[29] This is especially true of the strings, which often accompany the voice with series of repeated notes and thus create a dramatic environment but no new musical material. The general practice of having all parts phrase and pause together, as in the later eighteenth century, was not yet current; what one sees in Naples at this time is simply a tendency towards that style.

While all the music heard in opera theatres in Naples, both instrumental and vocal, was designed for competent professionals, the most striking was conceived for singers. As everywhere in Italy, the castrato reigned supreme, and Naples boasted the presence of some of the most famous: Giovanni Francesco Grossi, known as 'Siface' from his stupendous performance in 1671 of a role of that name in Cavalli's opera *Scipione affricano*; Matteo Sassano, known fondly as 'Matteuccio'; Nicolò Grimaldi, called simply 'Nicolini'; Carlo Broschi, known as 'Farinelli'; Domenico Cecchi, known as 'Il Cortona'; and Gaetano Majorano, called 'Caffarelli'. Among the women who sang similar roles were the famous Maria Anna Bulgarelli-Benti, called 'La Romanina' (it was she who finally convinced Metastasio to turn from law to librettos); Lucia Nannini, called 'La Polacchina'; Maria Maddalena Musi, known as 'La Mignatti'; and Faustina Bordoni (the future wife of Johann Adolf Hasse).

It comes as no surprise that, with singers of this calibre, Neapolitan serious opera was filled with difficult passages of splendour and sheer virtuosity. Throughout Italy, first-rate sopranos and contraltos, both male and female, were always given such music, and bass singers (actually rather bass-baritone in range) were also allotted important roles and were expected to be agile. Exceptional in Naples – and noteworthy for the history of singing – is the role of the operatic tenor. Elsewhere in Italy the tenor was given comic or unsympathetic roles, often those of old men and women, but in Naples the tenor was more on a par with the castrato. Porpora's *Flavio Anicio Olibrio* of 1711 and *Amare per regnare* of 1723, for example, both have florid tenor parts. Such regard for the tenor voice was normal in France, where the castrato was abhorred as unnatural, but Naples too played a part in properly evaluating this voice.

OTHER ARISTOCRATIC ENTERTAINMENTS

For nearly 20 years, from 1684 to 1702, Alessandro Scarlatti dominated the musical scene in Naples as court *maestro di cappella*. His operas were for the palace theatre or for the Teatro S Bartolomeo, which was supported by the court. In addition, during his lifetime he wrote more than 600 smaller-scale vocal works for the Italian nobility. Several years spent in Rome at an early age no doubt encouraged his development as an excellent composer in the chamber style. In fact, some felt that Scarlatti's style, competent and full of wonderful subtleties, was better suited to an intimate gathering in the viceroy's palace than to a theatre, where the audience, according to the impresario F. M. Zambeccari, could not appreciate his skill and

18. A Musical Gathering: painting (c1725) by an artist of the Neapolitan School (? Giovanni Amalfi)

wanted something not thoughtful but 'happy and bouncy'.[30] Whether this evaluation of Neapolitan audiences was true, the nobility, especially the court, clearly had much use for music at their private entertainments.

From contemporary accounts, it is clear that these parties were intended to impress the guests, and the first way was through the food. In April 1722, for example, the viceroy, Marcantonio Borghese, arranged a meal for the Bavarian princes which had 60 courses;[31] and at a gathering offered by the viceroy Wolfgang-Annibale von Schrattenbach to some military and nobility in July 1720, the guests – seated on a large gondola – were served

> refreshment in great abundance, and without a shadow of economizing one saw coffee, and tea of rare quality, beer, and liquors of perfect making, cold fruit of many kinds, perfect hot chocolate, and cold, sweets, jams, fruits in syrup, & other similar things made by excellent caterers.[32]

At a *festa* even the music seems not to have taken precedence over the food. Everything was on the level of extravagant 'pleasure'. The music might have been for a ball, such as that given by Prince Caracciolo in February 1734 at which the viceroy and his wife were present, where 'there was a generous distribution of all sorts of exquisite refreshments, and sweets';[33] or an *accademia*, an evening of music like the 'sumptuous' one offered by Prince Ardore to some German nobility in May 1723 at which the best *virtuosi* performed and a 'very great quantity of selected refreshments of various sorts' was served.[34]

On Sunday 1 September 1720, another magnificent evening was organized, which again included music. The contemporary chronicler deserves quoting in full in order for us to savour the richness of the private occasions at which music was offered. This party was arranged by Schrattenbach in the great hall of the royal palace, and included a

> serenata in praise of the Most August Ruler intitled *Scherno festivo tra le ninfe di Partenope*, performed in a beautiful theatre, which figured a delicious wood with a view in the distance of the sea. [It was] sung by first-rate male and first-rate female virtuosos with 140 instruments. That whole great hall appeared to be a clear day because of the reflection of great lights, which shone off the great number of mirrors, and because of the diversity of the noble crystal chandeliers. The nobility spent the evening enjoying that noble entertainment, & enjoying themselves in the games in the said hall, and in the other apartments furnished with several tables; and here His Eminence, not neglecting to practise his usual grandness, time and again made them enjoy with diversity of refreshment and sweets the acts of [his] generosity.[35]

From a historical point of view, a most notable party was given on the following Wednesday, 4 September 1720, when Metastasio's first important poem for music was heard. It had been set by Porpora, and one of his young students, the castrato Farinelli, made his début in it. The entertainment was offered by Prince Caracciolo after the viceroy's celebrations the same day for the empress's birthday. A contemporary account shows that the music was only one of the many *divertimenti* provided by the thoughtful host.

> In his lodge he had a delicious garden made, in the midst of which, in a beautiful theatre, he had performed by six voices a serenata intitled *Angelica e Medoro*, dedicated to Prince Zinzendorff. That ended, all the ladies and cavaliers entered the apartment of the said prince, where one saw [it] all well adorned with costly furniture, and splendour of lights; & there one passed the time at the gaming-tables, & meanwhile to all was given every sort of refreshment, sweets and chilled fruits, which one saw in diverse forms, also *al naturale*. From there one went on to the ballroom; after 9 o'clock Italian time [around 3 or 4 a.m.] 40 of the cavaliers and ladies had a noble supper, which ended at daybreak.[36]

The chronicler continued to say that the serenata was performed again the following Saturday, with the same setting, for all the royal ministers and tribunal lawyers. Metastasio's *Angelica* is a short, light pastoral play. The plot is from Ariosto, but the poet dressed it in elegant language, structured it for musical setting and divided it into two parts, adding a concluding *licenza* in praise of Elizabeth. There are six characters – nymphs and shepherds – scored by Porpora as three sopranos, two contraltos and a bass; the orchestra consists of two sections of violins and one of violas, two trumpets, two oboes, bassoon and continuo (including cello and double bass). As with opera, recitative alternates with da capo aria, the instrumentation is varied and the style of the vocal writing is similarly demanding.

In addition to such spectacular music, simpler works were given at aristocratic gatherings. Secular cantatas – small dramatic scenes, again in recitative and aria form, for one or more voices – were the usual fare. Single arias, duets and trios were also performed as chamber music, as well as madrigals, such as Scarlatti's *Cor mio, deh non languire*, for four sopranos and one contralto, intended to be performed round a table. Sacred cantatas too were given during Lent or Advent and for other religious feasts; those by Francesco Feo (1691–1761), bearing such titles as *La morte del giusto e del peccatore*, are typical examples. Like their secular counterparts, sacred cantatas were scored for one or more voices and continuo, with or without other instruments, and usually followed the standard pattern of alternating recitative and da capo aria.

There was also a repertory of instrumental music to delight the nobility. The lute, guitar and harp had always been favoured for indoor diversion in Naples; drums and wind instruments were played out of doors, as at the funeral of the head of the Theatine Fathers in April 1720.[37] The skill of local instrumentalists is attested to by Burney's account of Corelli's visit to Naples in 1702,[38] when 'the Neapolitan band executed his concertos almost as accurately at sight, as his own band [in Rome] after repeated rehearsals, when they had almost got them by heart'. Corelli was also 'astonished beyond measure to hear Petrillo, the Neapolitan leader, and the other violins, perform that which had baffled his skill' when rendering a piece by Scarlatti. Some composers specialized in instrumental music: Nicola Fiorenza (*d* 1764) left 15 concertos for various combinations of instruments (which could also have been given in church, where Burney said concertos were performed in 1770), as well as nine symphonies; and Gaetano Greco (*c*1657–*c*1728) was particularly noted for his keyboard works. But most composers wrote both vocal and instrumental music.

Yet another type of musical entertainment enjoyed by the nobility – a most intriguing one, since no trace of the genre remains – consists of comedies with music, which were improvised in the Neapolitan *palazzi*. A reference of January 1723 mentions them as part of the festivities held at the royal palace for Carnival;[39] since the performers are called *virtuosi*, the loss of any musical documentation is all the more disappointing. That comedies would have been improvised is no surprise in a country where the *commedia dell'arte* prevailed; and these plays certainly had songs interspersed. The reference, however, is not to rough actor-singers, travelling from one public square to another, but – through the term 'virtuoso' – to performers who were musically trained and excellent singers, perhaps attached to a court, theatre or chapel.

SACRED MUSIC

By the end of the seventeenth century there were more than 500 churches in Naples, testament to the important role of religion in Neapolitan life.[40] Belief and devotion aside, the church was another means by which the nobility could manifest its importance and through which the poor could hope for some alleviation of its misery. 23 religious institutions had a permanent group of musicians (a *cappella musicale*), or at least an important organist (who would have directed a choir); among the leading institutions were the royal chapel, the cathedral, the Oratory (home of the 'Filippini'), the Annunziata and the four conservatories. The women's convents, too, had regular directors of music. It is easy to deduce from these statistics, as well as from contemporary accounts and manuscript sources, that much of the music heard in Naples was sacred; and its quality and importance were often on a par with opera.

The court had its own chapel, where sacred music was enjoyed only by the aristocracy. The viceroy and his entourage assisted regularly at services in the royal chapel to celebrate a ruler's birthday or name-day, or the birth or wedding of a member of the royal family; on such occasions the *Te Deum*, a hymn of praise and thanksgiving, was always sung by the musicians in his employ. When music was performed in public churches, however, the aristocracy was either absent or was joined by other classes; here, too, a *Te Deum* might have been heard, as on the occasion in October 1723 when one was sung continually in all the Neapolitan churches to celebrate the empress's pregnancy,[41] or in the Augustinian church of S Maria della Verità in December 1720, when the pope recovered from a sickness,[42] or at the church of the Carmine in May of the same year for an armistice.[43]

Public religious services in general required music, and there would have been even more of it during the special seasons of Christmas, Lent and Easter. Some would have been instrumental –

trio sonatas and concertos – performed at moments when an audible pronouncement of the liturgy was not required; most of it, however, was vocal, and quite varied in genre and style. It is surprising to find that, so many years after his death, many masses were still being written 'alla Palestrina' – *a cappella* works for soprano, alto, tenor and bass using continuous imitation. There were also masses with wind and string accompaniment; some bore the title *Gloria*, indicating that only the Kyrie and Gloria were set (including the opening text of the Gloria traditionally intoned by the celebrant). One such work by Feo, scored for four voices, two oboes, two violins, flute and continuo, is sectional, with voices and instruments used in varying combinations throughout.

The many extant *Te Deum* settings are also varied. Because of the joyful nature of their occasions they are always splendid; one by Francesco Fago (1677–1745) for five soloists and chorus with two trumpets, two oboes, violins and continuo abounds in vocal *fioriture* and brilliant passages for an excellent trumpeter. Two other texts that received considerable attention were Psalm 1, *Miserere mei Deus*, and the *Stabat mater*. Among the extant settings of the former is one by Leonardo Leo for two four-part choirs and continuo which offers traditional polyphony resounding from two groups of voices, and one by David Perez (1711–78) for four soloists, chorus and continuo where, throughout its 20 sections, the verses alternate between plainchant and polyphony. The beautiful and extremely moving scene of Mary at the crucifixion of her dying son depicted in the *Stabat mater* received still more inspired settings, such as Pergolesi's, which Dent praised for its 'grace and charm'.[44] The musical gamut in motets is a large one, running from *a cappella* Palestrina-style works to simple pieces for a single voice and continuo or elaborate compositions for voice and large instrumental ensemble, either of which might favour only arias or might prefer a more dramatic presentation through the use of both recitative and aria.

An extremely popular service in Naples was the Forty Hours Devotion: the Host would be exposed and venerated, and at the end there would be a Benediction. A detailed description of one held in January 1736 at the church of S Diego reveals the architectural and theatrical aspects of the event, as well as the religious one. This particular occasion in fact boasted the three elements usually encountered in important Neapolitan sacred feasts: an 'apparatus', a structure similar to a theatrical set built for a specific place and occasion and intended to fit over an already existing indoor or outdoor structure; music; and a procession. At S Diego all admired

> the magnificent sacred pomp of the great machine, apparatus and
> illumination situated on the main altar, formed like an ample niche,

which frontispiece was decorated with cloths of silk, and in its midst rose up a tall pyramid, decorated with various works, and genial invention, at whose sides one saw statues of angels, who supported lighted candles, and at the top there was a multitude [of them] climbing up two spacious staircases. The columns of the church [were] adorned with cloths of silk, on each pedestal and capital one admired horns of plenty, well ordered and full of candles. The altar [was] abundant with much silver. And both morning and evening one heard select voices directed by the *maestro di cappella* Nicolò [Francesco] Fago, as well as three moving sermons of erudite Fathers of the said convent. On the last evening then [there was] a solemn procession with the accompaniment of 80 cavaliers, among which D. Pompeo Piccolomini of Aragon carried the standard; they were followed by a multitude of religious of the mentioned place, all with lighted torches, and after these the religious dressed respectfully in copes and surplices, with the assistants to the Father Guardian, who carried the Monstrance, going about the large square, and then gave Benediction.[45]

For the feast of Corpus Domini in June 1720, the engineer Filippo Marinelli designed an apparatus for the cathedral, where the miraculous blood of S Gennaro, patron saint of Naples, was kept and seen to liquefy once a year (another occasion on which music was heard). The apparatus consisted of a catafalque with a beautiful, silver-covered altar; above it was a painting of S Gennaro, who held the two phials with his blood from which great light shone. There was also a very lovely fountain representing Mount Parnassus with the muses on it; water was said to flow playfully from it, and it emitted the song of several birds, the combined result being 'a harmonious concert'.[46]

Though not part of the liturgy, the oratorio was another genre of sacred music cultivated in Naples. Oratorios were sometimes performed in private palaces, as was the *Oratorio per la festività del glorioso S Nicola vescovo di Mira* by Michele Falco (?1668–after 1732), given at the home of Domenico Celentano in 1709; but usually they were composed for the various lay confraternities, as was the *Oratorio per la festività di S Gaetano* by Domenico Sarro (1679–1744), composed for the Congregazione degli Orefici (the jeweller's guild) and heard at the church of S Paolo in 1712, or for religious orders (such as Leo's *Oratorio per la Ss Vergine del rosario*, heard at the cloisters of S Caterina a Formiello in 1730. At this period the oratorio was a two-part play based on an episode from the Old or New Testament, from the life of a saint or from church history. There were usually four to six characters, one of whom may have assumed the function of narrator, although this role was not always included. The setting was structured as recitative and aria, perhaps with some choral ensembles, with accompaniment either for continuo alone or with other instruments added to it; the musical style was similar to that of contemporary opera, but there was no stage action.

Stage action was, however, a feature of the three-act sacred music dramas favoured by, among others, the Oratorians (a religious order founded in Rome in the late sixteenth century by Filippo Neri) for their didactic value. Some of these sacred operas made use of Neapolitan dialect (see below), often for the simpler characters, such as fishermen and shepherds; there are humorous scenes, in which these characters are confused when talking to someone representing Christian authority – a saint or an angel – and need to have doctrine and morality carefully explained to them. The most famous example is Andrea Perrucci's *Il vero lume tra le ombre, overo La spelonca arricchita per la nascita del Verbo Umanato* of 1698, which was given in Naples year after year. During Lent or in the summer sacred operas were performed in convents, palaces and city squares. From 1656 conservatories, whose students were always connected with performances of church music, had had their better students compose sacred operas as 'end of course' compositions. Such was *Li prodigi della Divina Misericordia verso li devoti del glorioso Sant'Antonio da Padova* by Francesco Durante (1684–1755), which was performed in a public square in 1705, Leo's *Santa Chiara o L'infedeltà abbattuta*, presented first at the Conservatorio della Pietà dei Turchini in 1713 and then repeated in the square of the viceroy's palace, and Feo's *Il martirio di Santa Caterina*, given in the same conservatory the following year. One of the last examples, and one of the very few with surviving music, dates from 1731 – Pergolesi's *Li prodigi della Divina Grazia nella conversione e morte di San Guglielmo duca d'Aquitania*, composed at the end of his training at the Conservatorio dei Poveri di Gesù Cristo.[47] The plot calls for almost everyone to be in disguise, and for the scene to change continually as an Angel and the Devil each try to win over the soul of Guglielmo; it is his servant Cuòseno's conversion that is the source of humour, as he impudently and foolishly argues in dialect with the other-world characters. Accompanied and *secco* recitative, as well as 'serious' da capo arias, are mixed with lighter, comic music.

POPULAR ENTERTAINMENTS

The rise of comic opera

Comic opera was first encouraged by aristocrats (probably to rival the court's patronage of *opera seria*). Like sacred music drama, it made much use of Neapolitan dialect,[48] which since the fifteenth century had been widely used in serious literature, as well as in government documents that predated the introduction of Spanish rule in 1503. Some literary classics had even been translated from Italian and Latin into the Neapolitan language (Tasso's *La Gerusalemme liberata*, Virgil's *Aeneid*). Prose comedies had long been improvised in dialect by *commedia dell'arte* companies, and some plays were actually written down in the language (e.g. the anonymous *Mezzotte*, 1701; Nicola Maresca's *La Deana o Lo Lavenaro*, 1706). Another genre that used it was the cantata, an aristocratic entertainment; the few examples in Neapolitan would probably have been written for the local nobility rather than for those few foreigners who understood the language. A delightful example is Scarlatti's *Ammore, brutto figlio de pottana*, where Cicco complains of his resistant love Zeza in colourful, amusingly vulgar language. The setting is for tenor (a natural voice, not that of a castrato) and continuo.[49]

The several strands of comedy in music (comic scenes and comic intermezzos) and in dialect (sacred operas and cantatas) intertwined and, together with an explicit opposition on the part of intellectuals to the existing literature, resulted in the first comic opera in Neapolitan dialect[50] – *Cilla*, with text by Francesco Antonio Tullio and music by Michelangelo Faggioli (1666–1733), presented more than once at the palace of the Prince of Chiusiano from 26 December 1707 into January 1708.

Just before this, in 1706, the impresario Serino, released by the Teatro S Bartolomeo, tried unsuccessfully to win that public over to the Teatro dei Fiorentini by presenting serious operas with comic intermezzos. Nicola Pagano (Alessandro Scarlatti's brother-in-law) and two lawyers, Boraggine and De Rano, then attempted to attract another sort of public, the non-aristocratic classes, with suitable entertainment. The memory of an unpleasant episode of 1696 would have still been fresh in the mind: on that occasion, to celebrate the queen's name-day, the viceroy Luigi de la Cerda had had a serenata performed with 150 instruments and five singers in the square in front of the royal palace for all the people to enjoy; but it was a failure, and, much to the viceroy's consternation (as it had been expensive to produce), the public was abusive.[51] The enterprising lawyers also realized that any entertainment would have to be offered at reasonable prices. In the wake of private performances of Neapolitan comedy in music, Boraggine and De Rano became convinced of the viability of that genre as a new economic venture and rented the Teatro dei Fiorentini for the purpose. During the opening season at the Fiorentini in 1709, the works presented were *Lollo pisciaportelle*, with text by Nicola Orilia and music by Michele Falco, *Patrò Calienno de la Costa*, with text perhaps by Nicolò Corvo and music by Antonio Orefice, and *Lo spellechia finto razullo*, with text by Carlo de Petris and music by Tommaso de Mauro (*fl* 1701–9).

Although the first comic opera librettists were mainly lawyers, they were serious writers, sincerely critical of the fantastic and complicated world of serious opera and in favour of simple, clear and 'natural' theatre with contemporary relevance. Comic librettos, in fact, portrayed aspects of life in the little streets and gathering-places of the colourful lower classes of Naples – their habits, their ways of expressing themselves, their psychology. They also made fun of *opera seria*, perhaps as a necessary affirmation of identity by a cultured and proud community under humiliating foreign domination. The plays expressed the writers' 'freedom', however, mainly in their choice of language, Neapolitan dialect; the plots took their point of departure from the Latin comedy popular in the sixteenth century and – in spite of the usual depiction of contemporary classes – soon became rigid in their situations, characters, affections and intrigues (the state censors would also have kept a librettist's 'freedom' in check).

Li zite 'ngalera by Bernardo Saddumene, set to music by Leonardo Vinci in 1722, is a good example of the three-act genre;[52] this 'commeddeja' was presented in the 'Triato de li Shiorentine' (the Teatro dei Fiorentini, as stated on the libretto, which is written entirely in dialect, including the frontispiece, dedication, list of characters etc.). Comic opera quickly became so popular that the two new theatres that opened in 1724, the Teatro della Pace and the Teatro Nuovo, both presented it. Until about 1720–30 impresarios were concerned more with the quality of the librettos than with the music. The earliest comic opera composers were anonymous, or of second rank; sometimes the work was a collaboration by various composers, and 'popular' songs were often inserted as arias. The performers were actors rather than singers, or singers not good enough to find work elsewhere; but their voices were the right ones for their roles, not of the wrong sex or 'unnatural', as in serious opera.

From the second decade of the eighteenth century, however, composers of quality began to use their talents in the service of these comedies. Some used the structures and styles of *opera seria* – *secco* and accompanied recitative, and da capo arias; certainly these known procedures could be used with effect when a libretto had aristocratic or serious roles. At the same time, a new sort of libretto required a new style of music, the adoption of such comic techniques as already existed in intermezzos, cantatas and sacred opera.

One such technique was that of exaggerating the mannerisms of serious opera: a *fioritura* might be put on an unimportant word where its stress was ridiculous; awkwardly large leaps might be given to a *buffo* bass, rendering the character unstable and excited; extremely rapid speech in music, speech continually broken up with pauses, staccato stuttering and the imitation of animal noises might all be used as comic effects. In general, the florid style of serious opera played little part; instead, arias were syllabic settings of simple lines and were at first quite short. Unusual or irregular rhythms, suggesting fun or silliness, came to typify comic operas such as *Ciommetella correvata* (text by Pietro Trinchera, music by Nicola Logroscino, 1698–1765/7) of 1744. An unorthodox change from a major tonality in an opening phrase to a minor one afterwards was used to depict a sad thought coming into a character's mind – an exaggeration of the earlier 'pathetic' style and a mannerism accomplished with great effect by Pergolesi in Bastiano's aria 'Con queste paroline' from *Il Flaminio* of 1735.

Ensembles were more frequent in comic operas. A delight in single voices on the part of both audiences and singers had made serious opera a series of solo pieces; but in comedy the emphasis was more on the story, and when necessary (or simply interesting, amusing or convenient to a plot) characters joined together for duets, trios and so forth. Normally an act would end with an ensemble. These early finales were quite short (simple binary or ternary structures), but later, notably in the 1750s and 60s, through the influence of the Venetian librettist Carlo Goldoni, finales began to involve more characters and more events leading up to the end of the act; composers accordingly wrote continuous pieces, incorporating several structures, resulting in a succession of musical sections, uninterrupted by recitative. The finale was the the most important structural invention of comic opera, a testimony to the freedom from restrictive theory that was enjoyed by its writers and composers.

The first Neapolitan comic operas were entirely in dialect. Then, during the 1718–19 season, the impresario at the Fiorentini offered three comedies in 'Tuscan' (i.e. Italian): *Il gemino amore* (music by Orefice), *Il trionfo dell'onore* (music by Scarlatti) and *La forza della virtù* (music by Feo). Although the experiment was not repeated, Italian was thereafter mixed with dialect in comic librettos, and was used either for a serious role or as a means of ridiculing a character. In his libretto for *La noce de Veneviento* of 1722, Saddumene explained that he was obliged to have some characters speak a more civilized ('tuscanized') Neapolitan, 'in order not to make our language too difficult for certain foreigners in the cast'. Therefore, for realism's sake, and because of a theatre's desire to employ non-Neapolitan singers, comic operas began to encompass various social and educational levels of Neapolitan dialect, as well as Italian.

Comic opera was expressly aimed at a lower-class audience, and was successful in capturing it. At the same time it appealed to some of the nobility, who attended with great delight, and even to some of the viceroys. Writing in 1724, a chronicler makes quite clear the wide range of classes present when he says that 'the new opera in the Neapolitan language that began Saturday evening of last week [at the Fiorentini] was done to the greatest satisfaction not only of the nobility but to every level of person'.[53] There were, however, other aristocrats and members of the court who were suspicious of the use of dialect and local flavour and were critical of the libertine behaviour of the actor-singers. King Charles, for example, never attended any of the comic opera theatres; and the only comic opera performed at the theatre he had built, the Teatro S Carlo (*La locandiera*, text by G. A. Federico, music by Pietro Auletta), in 1738, was given in order that his newly arrived queen could see a uniquely Neapolitan entertainment. Comic opera was tolerated by members of the court, but it took more than half a century for them to be won over to it.

Other popular entertainments

Another category of 'non-aristocratic' music, popular song, was heard on the streets and in the squares. There had always been a large repertory of songs in the Neapolitan dialect – colourful, staccato, full of soft and double-stopped consonants – and there remained so in the period under discussion. Many have not survived their oral transmission, but some were written down: one famous example is *So' le sorbe e le nespole amare*, which Leonardo Vinci put into his comic opera *Lo cecato fauzo* (1719). Like most popular songs, it is syllabic and strophic and talks of love; it mentions fruits which are bitter when unripe but which, if one has patience, will mature and can be eaten; and the concluding moral is that love goes the same way for one who knows how to wait. Many songs make reference to *gelosie* (the window-shutters so necessary in the hot climate), which are usually seen as hiding a beloved, as in *La nova gelosia*. The beautiful sea bordering on Naples is often mentioned, as is water in general, a precious and scarce commodity, as for example in *Fenesta vascia*, in which a scorned young man threatens to go away and sell water, though his pitcher will be full of tears.

It was probably this sort of music – gems of simple (though not naive) wisdom – which was heard during the public entertainments offered by the government to the people. On several occasions each year there would be a series of floats representing the various categories of worker, such as butchers and farmers. They would parade down the Strada di Toledo to the square in front of the royal palace (now the Piazza del Plebiscito), where at a signal the people would be allowed to raid a *cuccagna*, a type of maypole (normally greased), from the top of which food was hung. Carnival was a period when this would happen week after week, as well as on special occasions for the government. On 4 November 1720, the Feast of St Charles (the name-day of the Emperor Charles VI of Austria), the following *festa* was described:

In the midst [of the square] one saw a great, well-designed *cuccagna* representing the triumph of Bacchus for the fertile production of wine this year, following above a float drawn by two tigers, holding a cup in one hand, and in the other a stick decorated with bunches of grapes, & next to him a huge bottle [*fiasco*] full of delicate liquor which Mother Earth produced for the refreshment of her followers, inviting each one to satisfy himself in order to sing happily of her glories; around the float on the parts sticking out of the pedestal were seated many priests of Bacchus, some playing, some drinking, & others singing to their god. The support of the pedestal, as well as that of the outer walls, were all covered with chickens, bread, veal, cows, sheep, *casci* [a type of cheese], lard, hams, *provature* and *casciacavalli* [other types of cheeses], decorated with festoons of flowers, and on the sides of the said support there were two great pyramids used by the priests decorated with every sort of food, with four cattle pretending to support them. At about 10 p.m., since a very ornate [structure covered with] rich material was erected on the principal balcony of the royal palace for all that flowering nobility, His Eminence [Viceroy Schrattenbach] ordered the sacking, and with special jubilation and common satisfaction it followed without disturbance, all exclaiming the generosity and grand spirit of His Eminence, who in such calamitous times tried to keep his beloved people happy.[54]

That a ruler would want to keep his subjects happy and quiet was only to be expected. That it was done traditionally in such an attractive, ornate and theatrically splendid manner was not solely the foreigners' doing: they may have paid for the festivities, but it was the Neapolitans who created and built the various structures necessary to their success. Moreover, music always played some role in people's private and public entertainments.

THE NEAPOLITAN SCHOOLS

More than a century ago Francesco Florimo wrote a history of the 'Neapolitan school of music';[55] a student and later teacher, librarian and archivist at the conservatory of music in Naples, he dedicated himself to furthering an appreciation of Neapolitan music. Because of his writings, and because of the lack of detailed knowledge of music elsewhere in Italy and abroad, the term 'Neapolitan school' has been adopted and perpetuated to refer to a particular style of eighteenth-century music: it was said to originate in Naples and then to spread elsewhere, and was seen as the basis for the Classical style. In an age when music and musicians travelled all over Europe, however, a single source for a new style is highly unlikely.[56]

The Neapolitans certainly participated greatly in the fermentation and experimentation of new musical ideas, and in their transmission. Neapolitan composers, instrumentalists and singers were requested to manifest their skills in all the major and minor centres for music-making. That they were extremely well trained was due to the four schools of music that operated in Naples: the S Maria di Loreto, the S Onofrio a Capuana, the Pietà dei Turchini, and the Poveri di Gesù Cristo. They had opened in the sixteenth century as institutions for orphans and foundlings; the first three were under the jurisdiction of the viceroy, and the last under the archbishop. The young boys supplemented the income of these institutions by participating in the music-making of the various palaces and churches, so that music education began to assume a position of importance; it was a fine education, and included singing, counterpoint and instrumental tuition.

By the eighteenth century the conservatories enjoyed a reputation of respect and attracted students from all over Italy. Even an established family of musicians such as the Puccini of Lucca sent their offspring Domenico (grandfather of Giacomo) to Naples; and, of course, Pergolesi went to Naples to study (from Iesi), as did Fago (from Taranto in Apuglia), Vinci (from Strongoli in Calabria), Farinelli (from Andria in Apuglia), Caffarelli and Logroscino (from Bitonto in Apuglia), Sarro (from Trani in Apuglia) and so on. It was the fact that Naples had as many as four good music schools capable of training highly professional musicians, that the schools were able to recruit their students from all over Italy, and that these students then passed their training and standards of musicianship on to others elsewhere that made the situation in Naples unique. The most famous contemporary institution for music education outside Naples was probably the Pio Ospedale della Pietà in Venice, where Francesco Gasparini and Antonio Vivaldi taught; but their students were, with rare exceptions, confined to making music at the *ospedale*; neither as performers nor as composers did the girls have the potential to exert the influence that was available to the young men in Naples.

One should perhaps acknowledge the impressive results and germinating effects of the professional Neapolitan schools of music, rather than attempt to assign to them, and to all musicians in Naples, the reponsibility for a style that within in a few years was to be found throughout Europe; the conservatories certainly deserve credit for turning Naples into one of Europe's paramount centres for music.

NOTES

[1] 'Naples', *Encyclopedia Britannica* (London, 15/1984).
[2] H. Hearder and D. P. Waley, *A Short History of Italy* (Cambridge, 1967), 98.

[3] J. Bowle, ed., *The Diary of John Evelyn* (Oxford, 1983), 88.

[4] J. Arthos, *Milton and the Italian Cities* (London, 1968), 106, n.1.

[5] The principal sources for notices of Neapolitan opera performances are the librettos, as well as the contemporary MS and printed accounts listed in the Bibliographical Note. The notices on Admiral Byng appear in the *Diario ordinario*, nn.181, 319 (2 Aug 1718, 18 July 1719).

[6] *Diario ordinario*, n.857 (26 Jan 1723).

[7] The history of the Neapolitan theatres that follows is based largely on V. Gleijeses, *La storia di Napoli* (Naples, 1987), and U. Prota-Giurleo, *Breve storia del teatro di corte e della musica a Napoli nei secoli XVII–XVIII*, i (Naples, 1952).

[8] *I-MOs: Avvisi e notizie dall'estero*, busta 35, 1644; cited by D. A. d'Alessandro, 'La musica a Napoli nel secolo XVII attraverso gli *avvisi* e giornali', *Musica e cultura a Napoli dal XV al XIX secolo: Naples 1982*, 162.

[9] The history of this company is traced in L. Bianconi and T. Walker, 'Dalla *Finta pazza* alla *Veremonda*: storie di Febiarmonici', *RIM*, x (1975), 379–454. I am grateful to Lorenzo Bianconi for having read a first draft of this chapter.

[10] Quoted from an *avviso* in *I-MOs*; cited in Bianconi and Walker, 'Dalla *Finta pazza*', 379.

[11] *Trattato completo, formale e materiale del teatro* (Rome, 1771, 2/1794), 82.

[12] *BurneyFI*, 336.

[13] L. Bianconi, 'Funktionen des Operntheaters in Neapel bis 1700 und die Rolle Alessandro Scarlattis', *Colloquium Alessandro Scarlatti: Würzburg 1975*, 13–111.

[14] *Dell'arte rappresentativa, premeditata, ed all' improvviso* (Naples, 1699), 80.

[15] ibid, 124.

[16] ibid, 9–10.

[17] ibid, 106.

[18] A plot summary is published with the facsimile of Mancini's score in H. M. Brown, ed., *Italian Opera 1640–1770*, xviii (New York, 1978).

[19] The preface to Michael Talbot's edition of Albinoni's *Pimpinone*, RRMBE, xliii (1983), contains a clear introduction to the genre of the comic intermezzo; it also acknowledges a debt to the excellent work of Charles E. Troy, *The Comic Intermezzo: a Study in the History of Eighteenth-Century Italian Opera* (Ann Arbor, 1979).

[20] ibid, p.xi; the statement is valid for other works as well as *Pimpinone*.

[21] For a list of Hasse's dramatic works, see the article on him by Sven Hansell in *Grove O*.

[22] C. Burney, *Memoirs of the Life and Writings of the Abate Metastasio* (London, 1796), i, 57.

[23] *Le rivoluzioni del teatro musicale italiano dalla sua origine fino al presente* (Bologna, 1782, rev. 2/1785), ii, 83–4, 89. An interesting evaluation of Metastasio is in J. Brown, *Letters upon the Poetry and Music of the Italian Opera* (Edinburgh, 1789); more recent studies include E. Surian, 'Metastasio, i nuovi cantanti, il nuovo stile: verso il classicismo: osservazioni sull *Artaserse* (Venezia 1730) di Hasse', *Venezia e il melodramma nel settecento: Venice 1973–5*, i, 341–62; and D. Heartz, 'Metastasio, "maestro dei maestri di cappella drammatici"', *Metastasio e il mondo musicale: Venice 1985*, 315–38.

[24] Burney, *Memoirs of . . . Metastasio*, 28–9.

[25] Arteaga, *Le rivoluzioni*, ii, 76–7; his ideas here are based on F. Algarotti, 'Saggio sopra l'opera in Musica' [1755], *Opere del Conte Algarotti* (Livorno, 2/1764), ii, 303.

[26] Unless stated otherwise, the following information on scenery is taken from the relevant librettos.

[27] *Diario ordinario*, n.3196 (21 Jan 1738).

[28] L. Bianconi and T. Walker, 'Production, Consumption and Political Function of Seventeenth-Century Italian Opera', *EMH*, iv (1984), 247.

[29] idem.

[30] Letter by Zambeccari (16 April 1709), quoted by R. Strohm, 'Alessandro Scarlatti und das Settecento', *Colloquium Alessandro Scarlatti: Würzburg 1975*, 166.

[31] *Diario ordinario*, n.747 (21 April 1722).

[32] ibid, n.477 (30 July 1720).

[33] ibid, n.2585 (16 Feb 1734).

[34] ibid, n.902 (11 May 1723).

[35] ibid, n.492 (3 Sept 1720).

[36] ibid, n.495 (10 Sept 1720).

[37] ibid, n.433 (16 April 1720).

[38] *BurneyH*, ii, 439–40.

[39] *Diario ordinario*, n.857 (26 Jan 1723).

[40] For a discussion of this role, see R. De Maio, *Società e vita religiosi a Napoli nell'età moderna* (Naples, 1971); on the establishments offering sacred music, see D. Fabris, 'Generi e fonti della musica sacra a Napoli nel seicento', *La musica a Napoli durante il seicento: Naples 1985*, 415–54.

[41] *Diario ordinario*, n.966 (5 Oct 1723).

[42] ibid, n.539 (17 Dec 1720).

[43] ibid, n.444 (14 May 1720).

[44] E. J. Dent, *Alessandro Scarlatti: his Life and Works* (London, 1905, 2/1960 with addns by F. Walker), 187–90.

[45] *Diario ordinario*, n.2887 (24 Jan 1736).

[46] *Diario ordinario*, n.453 (5 June 1720).

[47] For a discussion of this work, see G. Salvetti, 'Musica religiosa e conservatorii napoletani: a proposito del *San Guglielmo d'Aquitania* di Pergolesi', *Musica e cultura a Napoli dal XV al XIX secolo: Naples 1982*, 207–15.

[48] Helpful for an understanding of the use of dialect in general is P. Martorana, *Notizie biografiche e bibliografiche degli scrittori del dialetto napolitano* (Naples, 1874); its connection with comic opera is seen best in E. Battisti, 'Per una indagine sociologica sui librettisti napoletani buffi del settecento', *Lettura*, viii (1960), 114–64.

[49] A facsimile edition, as well as a transcription of the text in poetic layout, appears in M. Boyd, *Cantatas by Alessandro Scarlatti (1660–1725)*, The Italian Cantata in the Seventeenth Century, ed. C. Gianturco, xiii (New York, 1986), no.24.

[50] Battisti, 'Per una indagine . . . librettisti napoletani', offers a clear presentation of the early history of Neapolitan comic opera and is the basis for much of what appears here.

[51] *I-Ta* Lettere ministri, Due Sicilie, *mazzo* 6: *avviso* (31 July 1696); cited by T. Griffin, 'Alessandro Scarlatti e la serenata a Roma e a Napoli', *La musica a Napoli durante il seicento: Naples 1985*, 358.

[52] The score is in H. M. Brown, *Italian Opera 1640–1770*, xxv (New York, 1979), the libretto ibid, lx (New York, 1979).

[53] *Diario ordinario*, n.1107 (29 Aug 1724); the opera was *Lo pazzo apposta*.

[54] *Diario ordinario*, n.519 (5 Nov 1720).

[55] F. Florimo, *La scuola musicale di Napoli e i suoi conservatori, con uno sguardo sulla storia della musica in Italia* (Naples, 1880–83).

[56] For an understanding of some of the changes made to Neapolitan comic opera when it was exported, and for a discussion of comic opera in Rome and Tuscany, see P. Weiss, 'La diffusione del repertorio operistico nell'Italia del settecento: il caso dell'opera buffa', *Civiltà teatrale e settecento emiliano*, ed. S. Davoli (Bologna, 1986), 241–56.

BIBLIOGRAPHICAL NOTE

Historical background

In addition to the article 'Naples' in the *Encyclopedia Britannica* (15/1984) and H. Hearder and D. P. Waley's *A Short History of Italy* (Cambridge, 1967), a general history of Naples is to be found in the *Enciclopedia italiana di scienza, lettere ed arti*, known commonly as the *Treccani* (Rome, 1951), which offers a brief overview. V. Gleijeses' *La storia di Napoli* (Naples, 1987) is in one volume but is clear and complete, touching on all aspects of Neapolitan history and culture. For these same reasons (and because each chapter is written by an expert), see also *Storia di Napoli*, vols.vi–viii (Naples, 1970), for the period in question.

Theatre music

The first study devoted to Neapolitan theatres was B. Croce's *I teatri di Napoli (secolo XV–XVII)* (Naples, 1891; repr. 1968). Continuing Croce's work and adding more detail on music theatres and on other music in Naples, the fruit of excellent archival work as well as of an awareness of music sources, is U. Prota-Giurleo's 'Breve storia del teatro di corte e della musica a Napoli nei secoli XVII–XVIII', *Il teatro di corte del palazzo reale di Napoli* (Naples, 1952), 19–146. M. F. Robinson's *Naples and Neapolitan Opera* (Oxford, 1972) is the only monograph on the subject: it is both an excellent summary of earlier research and a clear presentation of a more detailed study of the texts and music of serious (which he calls 'heroic') and comic opera in Naples; it also offers a comprehensive bibliography of the subject up to 1968. F. Degrada's 'L'opera napoletana', *Storia dell'opera*, ed. G. Barblan and A. Basso, i/1 (Turin, 1977), 237–332, is a good survey of Neapolitan opera in the seventeenth and eighteenth centuries and takes account of research published after Robinson's monograph. Two studies by Lorenzo Bianconi and Thomas Walker, while not devoted exclusively to Naples, shed new light on the beginnings of opera there and on the connections between Neapolitan and Venetian opera: respectively, 'Dalla *Finta pazza* alla *Veremonda*: storie di Febiarmonici', *RIM*, x (1975), 379–454; and 'Production, Consumption and Political Function of Seventeenth-Century Italian Opera', *EMH*, iv (1984), 209–96. While these articles deal mainly with serious opera, Graham Hardie has documented 'Comic Operas performed in Naples, 1707–1750', *Miscellanea musicologica: Adelaide Studies in Musicology*, viii (1975), 56–81, and 'Neapolitan Comic Opera, 1707–1750: some Addenda and Corrigenda for *The New Grove*', *JAMS*, xxxvi (1983), 124–7. The fundamental study on the comic intermezzo is C. E. Troy, *The Comic Intermezzo: a Study in the History of Eighteenth-Century Italian Opera* (Ann Arbor, 1979).

Education

Francesco Florimo presented original archival research on the history of the Neapolitan conservatories in *La scuoia musicale di Napoli e i suoi conservatori, con uno sguardo sulla storia della musica in Italia* (Naples, 1880–83), which includes valuable accounts of teaching staff and students in each period; he also offers further information on opera and sheds light on the sacred music performed in Naples. For the conservatories, one must also see S. Di Giacomo, *I quattro antichi conservatorii musicali di Napoli*, i (Milan and Naples, 1924), and H. Hucke, 'Verfassung und Entwicklung der alten Neapolitanischen Konservatorien', *Festschrift Helmuth Osthoff zum 65. Geburtstag* (Tutzing, 1961), 139–54.

Other music

Much information may be gleaned from contemporary accounts of happenings in Naples. Some of these so-called *avvisi* – reports from diplomats sent regularly to their courts – are in manuscript, others were printed. While the former may be found only in state archives throughout Europe, for the latter see D. Confuorto, *Giornali di Napoli dal mdclxxix al mdcic* (Naples, 1930), i–ii; *La gazzetta di Napoli* (for the relevant years); and *Diario ordinario d'Ungheria* (from October 1718 *Diario ordinario*) (Vienna and Rome, for the relevant years). Most contemporary accounts presented here are from this last source, and this is the first time that they have been cited.

Despite the above bibliography, much research still needs to be done on music in Naples, as regards both the documentation and the music, which is still largely unstudied, apart from opera. An enormous impetus in this direction has been achieved with the publication of proceedings from two conferences held in recent years in Naples: *Musica e cultura a Napoli dal XV al XIX secolo: Naples 1982* and *La musica a Napoli durante il seicento: Naples 1985*. New research into sacred, secular, vocal and instrumental music is published in these reports for the first time, together with bibliographical information as to research (published and ongoing) relevant to individual topics; these important volumes also indicate where future research might fruitfully be pursued.

The Late Baroque Era

Although single articles have been devoted to individual aspects of a composer's production, none of those who worked in Naples has had a monograph, catalogue or whole conference devoted to him, apart from Alessandro Scarlatti and Pergolesi. For Scarlatti, see, among others: E. J. Dent, *Alessandro Scarlatti: his Life and Works* (London, 1905, 2/1960 with addns by F. Walker); G. Rostirolla, 'Catalogo generale delle opere di Alessandro Scarlatti', *Alessandro Scarlatti*, ed. R. Pagano and L. Bianchi (Turin, 1972), 319–595; *Colloquium Alessandro Scarlatti: Würzburg 1975*; and the edition of his operas initiated by D. J. Grout (Cambridge, MA, 1974–). For Pergolesi, see M. E. Paymer, *Giovanni Battista Pergolesi 1710–1736: Thematic Catalogue of the Opera Omnia, with an Appendix listing Omitted Compositions* (New York, 1977); F. Caffarelli's edition of the music is not acceptable. For biographical information and for a discussion of a composers' works, see the relevant entries in *Grove 6*, which is also useful for its historical explanations of genres. To these may be added: T. M. Gialdroni's 'Le cantate profane da camera di Domenico Sarro: primi accertamenti', *Musicisti nati in Puglia ed emigrazione musicale tra seicento e settecento: Lecce 1985*, 153–211 (which includes a thematic catalogue of Sarro's secular cantatas), and 'Le cantate celebrative a Napoli dal 1737 al 1798', *IMSCR, xv Madrid 1992* (in preparation); and S. M. Shearon's *Latin Sacred Music and Nicola Fago: the Career and Sources of an Early Eighteenth-Century Neapolitan Maestro di Cappella* (diss., U. of North Carolina, 1992), and 'Nicola Fago and the Neapolitan Musical Environment of the Early Settecento', *IMSCR, xv Madrid 1992* (in preparation). For information on theatre music (librettists, composers, genres, performers, theatres, architects, set designers), see the relevant entries in *Grove O* and in *Enciclopedia dello spettacolo*.

Most Neapolitan music is in manuscript, the largest single collections being in the libraries of the Conservatorio Statale di Musica 'S Pietro a Majella' and the Oratorio dei Filippini, Naples; the first is especially rich in operas and librettos, the second in sacred music (however, they have both been closed for several years). The next best collection of Neapolitan music is in the British Library, London. Some Neapolitan opera scores are published in facsimile in the series *Italian Opera 1640–1770*, ed. H. M. Brown (New York, 1977–84); the relevant librettos appear in facsimile in the companion series *Italian Opera Librettos*.

Chapter V

Paris and Versailles

JULIE ANNE SADIE

PROLOGUE: THE DEATH OF LULLY

Few can have grieved over the early demise of Jean-Baptiste Lully in March 1687; some may be forgiven for thinking it his just reward. For 30 years he had shaped musical taste at the courts of the Regent Anne of Austria and, from 1660, Louis XIV. He used his unprecedented influence with the king for personal gain, creating musical theatre that was the envy of every court in Europe, ruthlessly suppressing talented younger contemporaries and amassing a fortune exceeded by musicians only in modern times. To judge by the reception of *Armide* in 1686, Lully was at the very height of his powers just as the tide was turning for Louis XIV. His operas were being performed not only in Paris and at Versailles, but also at the courts of the Low Countries, Germany and Italy.

Lully had trained a small circle of composers to administer the performances of his works at the Académie Royale de Musique – his eldest son Louis (1664–1734), Pascal Collasse (1649–1709), Jean François Lallouette (1651–1728), Henry Desmarets (1661–1741) and Marin Marais (1656–1728). On his horrible death – the result of inadvertently wounding his foot three months earlier while beating time in a performance of his *Te Deum*, ironically in celebration of the king's heroic recovery from illness – it fell to them, *faute de mieux*, to supply the Académie, primarily with revivals of Lully's works, while gradually and with limited success introducing their own Lullian tributes and those of their contemporaries.[1]

During Lully's lifetime, writers such as Racine, Boileau-Despréaux, La Fontaine, La Bruyère and Saint-Evremond (who wrote in exile from London and published in Paris in 1684) challenged the Lullian myth in poetry and prose. Few entrepreneurs and musicians had dared – much less were allowed – to present serious alternatives to his *spectacles*. Those that did – Molière (1622–73), Pierre Perrin (*c*1620–1675) and Robert Cambert (*c*1627–1677), Jean Granouillet de La Sablières (1627–*c*1700), Henry Guichard (*fl* 1670-early 18th century) and Lallouette – suffered injustice and even exile.

The Late Baroque Era

When in 1679, for example, Lallouette challenged Lully's exclusive *privilège* by presenting an opera of his own in Paris, it was quickly suppressed by order of the king. The mixture of fear and admiration that Lully engendered in life is evident in the surviving satirical accounts of his probable reception on Mount Parnassus.

The most uncompromising account was published within a year of Lully's death by François de Callières, in his *Histoire poétique de la guerre nouvellement déclamée entre les anciens et les modernes* (1688). In a vain effort to deprive Lully of *entrée* to Parnassus, an Italian musician informs Orpheus of Lully's practice of producing only one new work annually – an intolerable state of affairs (by comparison with Venice, for example), compounded by his refusal to present other composers' operas. The French public is reprimanded for colluding in the name of fashion, and likewise Lully, for his rushed and shoddy productions. Lully dismisses the charges as inconsequential prattle and invites Orpheus to join him in creating 'an opera that will be worth money to us', a loathsome proposal Orpheus heartily rejects.

In *Le triomphe de Lulli aux Champs Elysées* (1687), Lully survives a trial, defended by the muse Polyhymnia against musical and moral charges brought against him by a group of French musicians, and is honoured by Apollo and the heroes of his operas.[2] In yet another version by Antoine Bauderon de Sénecé (formerly a valet of the queen's chamber), Lully presents himself to the gods, who require him to conduct a performance of his music before a distinguished audience, during which he assaults one of the violinists for ornamenting his part.[3] Afterwards he is made to give an account of his life, interrupted by damaging testimony from his former rivals and colleagues, before being exonerated and declared worthy of a monument.

One and maybe two musical scenarios exist, both dating from 1725, though that by François Couperin (1668–1733) may have been composed as much as a dozen years earlier (after the death of Arcangelo Corelli in 1713). Couperin would have been familiar with the literary models, for there are many correspondences in his programmatic *Concert instrumental sous le titre d'Apothéose composé à la mémoire immortelle de l'incomparable Monsieur de Lulli*, which followed by a year the publication of his rather more *galant Apothéose de Corelli* (1724). In a second, anonymous work entitled *Mélophilètes, idylle en musique*,[4] the *ombres* of both Lully and Corelli take part, as in Couperin's allegorical apotheosis. In 1708 Evrard Titon du Tillet commissioned a two-metre high bronze sculpture of Mount Parnassus with statuettes of Lully and distinguished departed French writers, in an attempt to generate interest in erecting a much larger version at Etoile (where the Arc de Triomphe now stands).[5]

Public criticism of Lully and his music came from his former colleagues in the theatre, in particular the members of the Ancien Théâtre Italien, or Comédie Italienne, at the Hôtel de Bourgogne (in the rue Mauconseil) and those of the Comédie Française at the Théâtre Guénégaud in the Palais-Royal. Parodies of Lully's music and Jean-Baptiste Quinault's texts – especially *Roland* and *Armide* – were the staple of the comedians both during and after Lully's death. The monotony of Lullian opera, the unpredictability of the machinery and its perceived unsuitability as entertainment for virtuous women proved particularly fertile themes. But if Lully's competence as a composer was often debated, his successors fared even worse: in Barante's *La Fontaine de sapience* (1694), one of the characters claims to have composed an opera in spite of knowing nothing of music. Overriding the criticism was the myth, abetted by such hagiographers as Charles Perrault (whose eulogy appeared in 1696), Grimarest (the Lullist author of the *Traité du recitatif* which appeared in 1707), Le Cerf de La Viéville and Titon du Tillet, who honoured Lully above all French musicians in his biographical lexicon (written to publicize the sculpture) *Le Parnasse François*, which first appeared in 1727.

THE SPECTRE OF ITALIAN MUSIC

In the year of Lully's death, Charles Perrault read his famous panegyric poem 'Le siècle de Louis le Grand' at a meeting of the Académie Française, formally elevating Louis XIV and Lully to the status of Ancients: the king was compared to Augustus and Lully proclaimed 'l'Orphée du nouvel âge'. Because not all Perrault's colleagues were in accord, a celebrated literary quarrel erupted over whether the modern French surpassed the Ancient Greeks. Wishing to join the fray, writers on music, notably François Raguenet and Le Cerf de La Viéville, took their cue from Perrault's *Parallèle des Anciens et des Modernes* of 1692 and substituted French music, typified by Lully, for the writings of Ancients; their dispute lay in whether the Italians or the post-Lullians (many of whom were greatly influenced by Italian music) were to assume the mantle of the Moderns.

Although Raguenet entitled his 1702 comparison of the two musics *Paralèle des italiens et des français*, it has little in common with Perrault's seminal *Parallèle*: after a show of objectivity, it radically and unambiguously asserts the superiority of Italian music, with particular reference to opera. Le Cerf, Lully's self-appointed apologist, employed the dialogue format of Perrault's *Parallèle* in his three-volume *Comparaison de la musique italienne et de la musique française* (1704–6). The *Comparaison* was intended as much more than merely a reply to Raguenet's provocative tract; it is, in fact, an extended

19. Louis XIV: portrait (1694) by Hyacinthe Rigaud

(some would say rambling and haphazard) investigation into the aesthetics of French and Italian music of the day.

Le Cerf traded on the impression of chimeric power conferred by the anomaly of Lully's Italian origins and French achievements. While this had often been viewed as a liability, the duality of his patrimony and his uniquely popular French image nevertheless conferred a kind of universality on his music, difficult for either side to deny. Perrault wrote of Lully's music in *Les hommes illustres* that 'Nothing is comparable to the beauty of the operas he composed. Since in these works he united the genius of his nation with the refinement and ornaments of ours, there is almost nothing that the Italians can do to supersede them'.

Responding in his emotional *Défense du Parallèle* (1705), Raguenet concurred, while roundly condemning the post-Lullians, declaring that if parity between Italian and French styles was to be achieved, a French-born composer would have to repeat Lully's feat by conquering Italian taste. Le Cerf deftly dismissed this suggestion, observing that 'Italy's unhappiness was that she had lost Lully and we had gained him'. The debate was fanned, one imagines, in a plethora of ephemeral communications, and by Nicolas de Boisregard Andry, a friend and medical colleague of Raguenet, who published reviews in the influential *Journal des sçavans*, until the untimely death of the 33-year-old Le Cerf in 1707.[6]

The dispute continued without Le Cerf and Raguenet: in November 1713 the *Mercure galant* published a 'Dissertation sur la musique italienne et française par M. de L. T.', which summarized the views of Raguenet and Le Cerf and proposed to unite 'the wise and ingenious taste of the Italians' with 'the natural and simple taste of the French', a compromise already being promoted by French composers of sonatas and cantatas and one very like 'les goûts-réünis' of Couperin. Jacques Bonnet, a parliamentary treasurer, included the *Mercure* essay in the first volume of the *Histoire de la musique et de ses effets depuis son origine jusqu'à présent* (a collaborative effort with other members of the Bonnet-Bourdelot family), which appeared with exquisite timing in 1715, the year in which the dedicatee and great patron of Italian music, the Duke of Orléans, became Regent of France; subsequent editions during the 1720s incorporated the whole of Le Cerf's *Comparaison* as volumes ii–iv, without acknowledging Le Cerf by name.

Raguenet, who, it is whispered, took his own life in 1722, had the satisfaction of witnessing the assimilation of Italian genres and performing practices into French music. But he would also have been aware of the extent to which French composers retained their essential orientation, never fully acquiescing to Italian models. As Noël-Antoine Pluche later remarked in *Le spectacle de la Nature* (1732): 'We [the French] no longer admire our music by exclusion, a pettiness which would dishonour us, thereby impoverishing us'.

MUSICAL PEREGRINATIONS TO PARIS

No aspiring French composer at the turn of the century could fail to have been touched by Lully, if not by his domination while he lived, then by the artistic crisis initiated by his departure which was to continue in different guises well into the reign of Louis XV. As early as June 1683 the *Mercure* had demurred about the long-term effects of Lully's absolutism and the damaging effect of suppressing new and innovative musical theatre. But as the writer in the *Mercure* well knew, Paris audiences made do with a diet, laced with nostalgia, of Lully and his satirists, while members of the royal family circle were commissioning private performances of newly composed music. The dauphin and his wife presided over performances at the royal *châteaux* of dramatic works by the precocious young Elisabeth-Claude Jacquet (1666/7–1729), Desmarets, Michel-Richard de Lalande (1657–1726), Claude Jean-Baptiste Boesset (1665–1736) and Marais, whose *Idylle dramatique* of 1685 was praised in the *Mercure galant*. Among these only Marais ever answered directly to Lully, and it was to be expected that he would dedicate his first book of *pièces de violes* to his mentor in 1686 and later collaborate with Louis Lully – at best a mediocre composer – on *Alcide* (1693).

The new generation of French composers did not hesitate to look to the Italians for inspiration. It is more difficult to know how influential were the italianate qualities of the music of Marc-Antoine Charpentier (1643–1704) – much of it composed for the italophile cousin of the king, the Duchess of Guise, who died in 1686, with its deeply expressive harmonies and imaginative orchestration; it may have fired fresh expectations in these younger composers and performers, hungry for new and stimulating influences. It would seem, however, that Charpentier's proximity to Lully worked against him. The Académie audiences, accustomed to the classic simplicity of Lully's style, fought shy when in 1693 a gifted contemporary such as Charpentier (aged *c*50) presented his *Médée*, with modernisms of harmony, counterpoint and foreign-sounding accompaniments.

The Italians themselves had never actually been out of favour with Louis XIV. Guided by Cardinal Mazarin in his youth, the king had always taken a keen interest in Italian music. As far back as 1645 Mazarin had imported Italian singers, Atto Melani (1626–1714) preeminent among them, to sing in performances of Francesco Sacrati's Venetian opera *La finta pazza* (1641) and then in Francesco Cavalli's *L'Egisto, re di Cipro* (1643), and in the première of Luigi Rossi's *Orfeo* (1647), supervised by the composer himself. Lully himself must have owed something of his initial success at court to being Italian and, as a consequence, was never able entirely to exclude his fellow countrymen from Paris and the royal *châteaux*: Chantilly, Fontainebleau, Meudon, Marly, Saint-Germain and Versailles.

On the contrary, the king continued his policy (instigated by Mazarin) of granting preferment and naturalization to Italian musicians to the end of his reign: since 1659 he had maintained a *cabinet italien*, led by the tenor Giovanni Francesco Tagliavacca, which included women and castratos; his Grande Bande employed Italian instrumentalists; individual players, such as the violinist Pietro Alberti (*fl* 1697–1706) in 1697, are known to have played for his private music; and, throughout his reign, the records of the Menus Plaisirs list castratos among his Chapelle singers.[7] Couperin composed some of his 1704 *versets* for the Chapelle castratos Hiacinte Mazza (*fl* 1694–1729) and Antonio Paccini (*d* 1745), who was the subject of a drawing by Antoine Watteau. The French public retained an uneasiness about the castratos: the chevalier of Le Cerf's dialogues, for example, commented that after a few arias their voices became irritating. Nevertheless, Lully used the Swiss 'dessus italien' (the French term for a castrato) Antonio Bagniera (1638–1740) in the 1677 production of *Alceste*. Among the the Bourbon family members, the king's brother and nephew (the dukes of Orléans) as well as his own children – the Princess of Conti and the dauphin in particular – all patronized Italian musicians.

Philippe II de Bourbon (Duke of Chartres until 1701, then Duke of Orléans and finally Regent of France from 1715 until his death in 1723) was unique among the Bourbons: a composer as well as a patron of music, and a versatile linguist. He played the flute, viol and harpsichord and was taught first by the theorist Etienne Loulié (*c*1655–*c*1707), then by Charpentier, both of whom were associated until 1686 with the cultured and devout Duchess of Guise, the italophile cousin of the king. With Charpentier the duke collaborated on an opera, *Philomèle*, performed at the Palais-Royal in 1694 (the year after *Médée*). Later, in 1705, with the assistance of his *maître de musique* Charles-Hubert Gervais (1671–1744), he produced *Penthée*: they collaborated again in 1712 and 1716. From the 1690s he played the discerning patron of André Campra (1660–1744) and later of the young François Colin de Blamont (1690–1760); he was probably influential in Charpentier's 1698 appointment as *maître de musique* at the Sainte-Chapelle and that of Nicolas Bernier (1665–1734) in 1705. Marais, the king's faithful servant, dedicated his second book of *pièces de viole* (1701) to the duke.

Philippe had not always been warmly received at court, in part because of his own behaviour, in part because of that of his parents, Monsieur and Madame (the Princess Palatine). His father, the younger brother of the king, was bisexual (preferring on the whole men to women), to the consternation of Louis XIV, whose negative views on homosexuality were well known, while the duke's mother – in love with the king and at the same time ambitious for her son – was hopelessly at odds with the king's secret wife, Madame de Maintenon.[8]

In particular, Philippe rankled the fastidious king with his dissipation and debauchery. His wife, Françoise-Marie of Bourbon (the illegitimate daughter of Louis XIV, whom Philippe had been forced to marry in 1691), finally sought refuge at Versailles and Saint-Cloud rather than continue to endure the humiliation of living at the Palais-Royal with her husband's mistresses and the persistent rumours about the exact nature of the close relationship he maintained with their eldest daughter, the Duchess of Berry (whose husband was heir to the throne from 1712 until his death in 1714). Philippe's espousal of Jansenism (which served precariously to counterbalance the power of the Jesuits), his possible role in the alleged Spanish *coup d'état* of 1709 and his often tactless extravagance gave the king cause for further disquiet. However, in the event, Philippe took his duties as

The Late Baroque Era

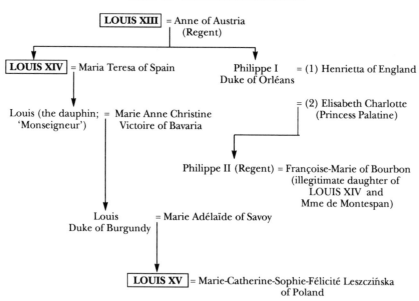

Table V.1 THE BOURBON SUCCESSION

Regent to heart and faithfully served the interest of the young Louis XV.

The duke's love of contemporary Italian music was reinforced by his experiences during the Italian military campaign, which in 1706 took him to Turin and Venice. In addition to Gervais, his musical household included a mixture of Italian musicians and French neophytes – Giovanni Antonio Guido (*d* after 1728), Michele Mascitti (1663/4–1760), François Duval (1672/3–1728), Jean-Baptiste Stuck (1680–1755), Antoine Forqueray (1671/2–1745), Bernier and Jean-Baptiste Morin (1677–1754); Morin's revolutionary collections of sonatas and cantatas (settings of the duke's literary protégés J.-B. Rousseau, La Motte and Fontenelle) were subsidized by the duke in the first years of the eighteenth century. Like other members of the nobility, Philippe had his daughters tutored in singing and on the harpsichord.

Most of the Italians who settled in France came not to conquer but to please, consciously adapting their compositional styles to suit prevailing French tastes. Theobaldo di Gatti (*c*1650–1727), like Lully a Florentine, followed him to Paris and in 1677 joined the Académie orchestra as a bass violinist. Because of this connection, he was among the first after Lully's death to be allowed to present a *tragédie en musique*, *Coronis* (1691), at the Palais-Royal theatre and certainly the first post-Lullian Italian composer to do so. However, his inclusion of a long *air* with an Italian text in his successful 1701 *tragédie en musique, Scylla*, was hardly innovative: Lully did it in the *Ballet de la raillerie* (1659) and in *Psyché* (1678), while among the dramatic works of the 1690s Charpentier's *Médée* and Campra's *L'Europe galante* contain Italian-style *airs*.

In 1678 the Roman composer Paolo Lorenzani arrived, in good time to witness the premières of Lully's finest *tragédies en musique*. He stayed for 16 years, enjoying the patronage of the queen (until her death in 1683), the royal mistress Madame de Montespan, the Prince of Condé and Cardinal Mazarin's nephew. At the height of his favour, Lorenzani was despatched to Italy by the king to recruit five castrato singers for the Chapelle. His music – including a *pastorale, Nicandro e Fileno* (1681), a *sérénade en forme d'opéra* (1682) on which he collaborated with Lalande and, eventually, a full-length opera, *Orontée* (1688) – were performed at the *châteaux* of Fontainebleau and Chantilly. Then in 1693 an invitation to take up the post of *maestro di cappella* at the Vatican was proffered, providing the right opportunity to return to Rome. Lorenzani accepted it, but not before presenting Louis XIV with a specially printed collection of 25 *motets*, perhaps in the hope of prolonging his stay by acquiring the *sous-maître* post vacated by Nicolas Coupillet (before 1650–after 1713) which went instead to Lalande.

In the following decade the Venetian composer Antonia Bembo (*c*1640–*c*1715) waited (apparently in vain) upon the king's ear with vocal chamber music, including psalm settings, two *Te Deum* and an opera dedicated to him. As the patron of Elisabeth-Claude Jacquet – who later married the organist Marin de La Guerre (*d* 1704) – Louis XIV should in principle have been disposed towards another gifted woman composer, but as Italians gained appointments only as singers in the Chapelle or performed in theatrical productions, and women gained formal court posts only towards the end of the Regency, her opportunities would have been limited. Until mention of her in contemporary memoirs or an account of a performance of her opera *L'Ercole amante* (1707) comes to light, she will remain an enigma.

It is tempting to speculate that, had Bembo lowered her sights and sought the patronage of the Paris-based aristocracy, her music might have been performed and printed, instead of languishing in the Bibliothèque Nationale for over 200 years. The patronage of the Duke of Orléans enabled the newly arrived violin virtuoso Michele Mascitti to issue his first collection of sonatas from Henry Foucault's Paris shop in 1704; that of the wealthy financier Antoine Crozat supported his later collections. Stuck, a cellist of Italian and German descent known as 'Batistin', settled in Paris in 1705 (though he is known to have composed an opera, *Il Cid*, for the 1715 Livorno

Carnival) and published four books of cantatas (which interestingly mix French and Italian styles) with the support of the Princess of Conti and the Duke of Orléans. To judge from contemporary memoirs, the dukes and duchesses of Burgundy and Berry as well as the visiting Prince of Monaco and Elector of Bavaria must also be counted among the important music patrons of the day.

At much the same time there arrived another Italian violinist, Giovanni Antonio Piani (*b* 1678; known in Paris as Jean-Antoine Des Planes) and the outstanding cellist of his day, Angelo Maria Fiorè (*c*1660–1723). With the patronage of the Count of Toulouse, who enabled him to publish an innovative collection of violin sonatas, Piani stayed until 1721, when he took up a post at the Vienna court. By contrast, Fiorè – a member of the entourage of the visiting Savoy ambassador – remained only a few months. There were other foreign musicians attached to diplomatic missions in Paris, including the violinist Luigi Madonis (*c*1690–*c*1770), who performed at the Concert Spirituel in 1729 and published a set of sonatas in 1731 while in the service of the Venetian ambassador. The circumstances that prompted the Venetian double bass player Giuseppe Fedeli, also called Joseph Saggione (*fl* 1680–1733), to settle in Paris around 1700 remain a matter for speculation, though it would seem that he was recruited (perhaps by Michel Pignolet de Montéclair) for the orchestra of the Académie Royale de Musique. In 1715 he published a collection of violin sonatas and in 1728 three *recueils d'airs français dans le goût italien*.

Meanwhile, the keyboard player Joseph-Nicolas-Pancrace Royer (*c*1705–1755) and the violinist Giovanni Pietro Ghignone (1702–74), both Savoyards, arrived in Paris about 1725. Royer sought naturalization immediately, while Ghignone (better known as Jean-Pierre Guignon) waited until 1741, when Louis XV appointed him *roy et maître de ménestriers*. Royer composed for the fair theatres before taking up a post as *maître de musique* at the Opéra; his appointment was marked by performances of *Pyrrhus*, his *tragédie en musique*. His *ballet-héroïque Zaïde, reine de Grenade* (1739) remained in the repertory for more than 30 years. Royer's acceptance into the French musical establishment was sealed by a court appointment in 1734 – the first of several, culminating in that of *maître de musique de la chambre du roi* in 1753; he proved a vital and inspiring director of the Concert Spirituel from 1748 until his death in 1755.

Guignon, a pupil of Somis, appeared on the same programmes as the French violinist Jean-Baptiste ('Jacques') Anet (1676–1755), a pupil of Corelli, during the 1725 showcase season of the Concert Spirituel (which had been inaugurated with Corelli's 'Christmas Concerto') and on his own, playing sonatas and concertos, over the next quarter of a century. Hubert Le Blanc claimed, in his *Défense de la basse de viole* (1740) that Guignon had 'the most beautiful bow-stroke in Europe':

> A single down-bow lasts so long that the memory of it makes one breathless to think of it, and it seemed like a stretched silken cord which (in order not to be boring with the bareness of a single sound) is surrounded with flowers, with silver festoons, with gold filigrees mixed with diamonds, rubies, garnets and above all with pearls. One saw them spill out from his fingertips.[9]

Such hyperbole could not, however, excuse his contentious and sometimes violent behaviour towards his French colleagues Anet, Jean-Marie Leclair *l'aîné* (1697–1764), Jean-Joseph Cassanéa de Mondonville (1711–72) – with whom he became involved in a legal dispute – and other musicians.

In the seventeenth century many Germans and Austrians – Johann Fischer (1646–1716/17), Johann Sigismund Kusser (1660–1727), perhaps Johann Philipp Förtsch (1652–1732), certainly Johann Caspar Ferdinand Fischer (*c*1670–1746), Rupert Ignaz Mayr (1646–1712) and the Alsatian-born Georg Muffat (1653–1704) – went to Paris specifically to work with Lully. In the decade after Lully's death, the legacy of those associations bore fruit in the form of collections, published abroad, of orchestral overtures and suites in his (the accepted French) style. After studies with Lully, Muffat eventually took up a post at the Salzburg court in 1678; at the beginning of the 1680s the archbishop granted him leave to go to Rome to continue his studies with Corelli. On his return to Salzburg in 1682, Muffat arranged for the printing of his *Armonico tributo*, the supreme seventeenth-century Germanic example of what Couperin later called 'les goûts-réünis', combining Corellian concerto features with Lullian articulation and dances. To the *Florilegium primum* (1695) he appended his autobiography, providing important information about Lully and his practices. To the *Florilegium secundum* (1698) he added a multilingual preface in which he described how to perform 'ballets à la françoise'.

German visitors to the French capital seeking to acquire a familiarity with the French style included the Darmstadt court viol player Ernst Christian Hesse (1676–1762), in Paris from 1698 until 1701, who (according to the eighteenth-century lexicographer Gerber) succeeded in studying simultaneously with the two most distinguished exponents of French viol playing, Marais and Forqueray, and Pantaleon Hebenstreit (1667–1750), who in 1705 created a sensation with his cumbersome dulcimer, which Louis XIV eponymously dubbed 'the Pantaleon'. Hebenstreit and his instrument became the impetus for Abbé de Châteauneuf's *Dialogue sur la musique des anciens à Monsieur de **** (1725), which was supposed to have taken place in

1705 at the fashionable salon of Ninon de L'Enclos, a great friend of Madame de Maintenon. Her own position, on the side of French music, would seem to be confirmed by her presidency over concerts of lute and harpsichord music. Johann Friedrich Armand von Uffenbach (1687–1769), in Paris in 1715 and 1716 to study the lute with the elderly Gallot 'le jeune' (*d* 1716), may also have frequented her salon.[10]

In 1714 the distinguished Dresden court organist Christian Pezold (1677–1733) and violinist Johann Georg Pisendel (1687–1755) accompanied the Prince-Elector of Saxony to Paris. Another Dresden musician, Johann Joachim Quantz (1697–1773), visited Paris for eight months from August 1726. He may have been encouraged to come by his flute teacher, the Provençal Pierre-Gabriel Buffardin (*c*1690–1768), who had performed at the Concert Spirituel earlier that year while on leave from Dresden. Quantz had his flute modernized by the addition of a second key, attended concerts – later writing with particular pleasure of the performance by Guignon, Forqueray and the flautist Michel Blavet (1700–68; Blavet, unlike Quantz, was later to decline a post at the court of Frederick the Great) – and arranged for the publication by François Boivin of a collection of *Sonates italiennes* (1729). Quantz's exposure to French music served as the basis for the far-reaching, if retrospective, assessment of the French style in his *Anweisung die Flöte traversiere zu spielen* (1752). The enterprising Georg Philipp Telemann (1681–1767) travelled to Paris in 1737 to supervise the printing of two editions.

One of the most devotedly francophile Germans was the viol-playing music patron Maximilian II Emanuel, Elector of Bavaria, who was governor of the Spanish Netherlands from 1691. On his frequent visits to Paris he obtained librettos and scores, and made the necessary arrangements to mount Lully operas in Brussels[11] with the combined forces of his German-Italian Kapelle and the French musicians and dancers lent to him in 1694 by Louis XIV, who was eager to secure his support in the War of the Spanish Succession. The elector was the younger brother of the dauphine, Marie Anne Christine Victoire, Princess of Bavaria (*d* 1690), and was at one time considered as a possible husband for one of the daughters of Monsieur. Equally a lover of chamber music and women, the elector patronized a number of prominent French musicians – among them the *outré* singer said to have been his mistress, Mademoiselle Maupin (1670–1707), the viol players Hilaire Verloge (known as 'Alarius', *c*1684–1734), Marais and Forqueray, the violinist Anet, the harpsichordists Louis-Nicolas Clérambault (1676–1749), Jeanne Dandrieu (1695–*c*1760), Elisabeth-Claude Jacquet de La Guerre, Louis Marchand (1669–1732) and the Flemish oboist Jacques Loeillet (1685–1748) – as the dedications of their sonatas and cantatas attest.

Later, in 1703, Maximilian II Emanuel joined Louis XIV in a coalition against the Habsburg emperor, only to find himself forced to seek exile in the South Netherlands in 1704, following the defeat of his army by the English. Louis XIV honoured his debt by providing Maximilian with a further place of temporary exile in 1709 at Compiègne and a Parisian *pied-à-terre* at Saint-Cloud (near his controversial friend and fellow italophile the Duke of Orléans), from where Maximilian continued to visit the city and nearby *châteaux* before returning to Munich in 1715.

The Stuart kings of England were francophiles. Charles I married Henrietta Maria of France. During the Commonwealth era Charles II lived in exile in France, where he acquired a taste for Lully's music and the trappings of Louis XIV's *musiques de cour*; when he returned to England he took French musicians with him, whom he chose openly to favour over his English ones. His band, modelled on Lully's Vingt-quatre Violons, was further subdivided into two groups of 12 for chamber music. John Banister (*c*1624–1679), its leader from 1662 until 1666, and Pelham Humfrey (1647–74) were sent to Paris (1660–62) to acquire mastery of Lully's style and method of training his musicians; according to Samuel Pepys, Humfrey returned home 'an absolute Monsieur'.

At the turn of the century two English visitors partook of the musical life of Paris and on returning home wrote at length of their experiences. Dr Martin Lister, who accompanied the Earl of Portland on a diplomatic mission to France, spent six months in Paris, observing and recording in *A Journey to Paris in the Year 1698* (London, 1698) how the citizens diverted themselves:

> I did not see many opera's not being so good a Frenchman, as to understand them when sung. The opera, called *l'Europe Gallante*, I was at several times, and it is look'd upon, as one of the very best. It is extremely fine, and the musick and singing admirable: the stage large and magnificent, and well filled with actors: the scenes well suited to the thing, and as quick in the removal of them as can be thought: the dancing exquisite, as being performed by the best masters of that profession in town: the cloathing rich, proper and with great variety.

In Campra's *L'Europe galante* (1697) Lister would very probably have heard the supreme Lully interpreter Marie Le Rochois (*c*1658–1728), who was also appearing in the production by the Académie Royale de Musique of André Cardinal Destouches' *Issé*, which had opened on 17 December 1697.

Lister also attended performances of Molière plays at the Comédie

20. Harem of Sultan Zuliman in Campra's opéra-ballet 'L'Europe galante' (1697): engraving from the libretto, 'Recueil général des opéra', vi (1703). The sultan is seen here with his two rival sultanas, Zaïde and Roxane.

Française and enjoyed the low life frequenting the Lenten fair in the *quartier* of St Germain, where the Italian comedians performed plays with music by some of the best French composers:

> The place where it is kept, well bespeaks its antiquity; for it is a very pit or hole, in the middle of the *fauxbourg*, and belongs to the Great Abbey of that name. You descend into it on all sides and in some places above 12 steps; so that the city is raised above it six or eight foot.
>
> The building is a very barn, or frame of wood, tiled over; consisting of many long allies, crossing one another, the floor of the allies

unpaved, and of earth, and as uneven as may be: which makes it very uneasie to walk in, were it not the vast croud of people which keep you up.

The great Rendezvous is at night, after the play and opera are done; and raffling for all things vendible is the great Diversion.

Joseph Addison (1672–1719) arrived in France in September 1699, on the first leg of a trip that took him to Venice, Florence, Vienna and Hamburg before he returned to London in February 1704. In Paris he attended performances of the Académie, where he must have heard Lully's *Thésée* (with Mlle Desmatins taking the role of Medea and Mlle Maupin that of Minerva) and probably a revival of Lully's *Atys*, which began its run on New Year's Eve 1699. Inspired by all he had heard, Addison sought to foster a uniquely English style of opera by writing an opera libretto, *Rosamond*, which was set by Thomas Clayton (1673–1725) in 1707 and later, with more success, by Thomas Arne (1710–78). His views on Lully and on French opera are recorded in the *Spectator* (1711–12).

The younger Henry Eccles (1675/85–1735/45), a violinist, joined the household of the French ambassador in London, the Duke d'Aumont, and in December 1713 accompanied the duke and his wife Madame de Villequier back to Paris. In 1720 he published there a collection of sonatas, incorporating movements by Giuseppe Valentini (1681–1753) and F. A. Bonporti (1672–1749). Eccles's second collection appeared in Paris three years later.

French provincial musicians flocked to Paris and Versailles, no less attracted to Paris by the glamour of Lully's operas – which were performed, with permission, in Marseilles, Toulon, Avignon, Arles, Montpellier, Grenoble, Chalon and Aix-en-Provence[12] – and the favourable opportunities the capital and court offered. Many of them even gained a certain pre-eminence over their Paris-born colleagues for their fresh perspectives: the influential *organiste du roi* from 1678, Nicolas-Antoine Lebègue (*c*1631–1702), came from Laon; one of his pupils, François Dagincour (1684–1758; also an *organiste du roi*, from 1714 to 1730), came from Rouen. The Lyons-born Jesuit Claude-François Ménestrier travelled extensively throughout Europe and to England before settling in Paris, where in 1681 he published *Des représentations en musique anciennes et modernes*. Yet another organist, the gifted and flamboyant Louis Marchand, and the exquisite leading soprano actress of the Académie, Marie Antier (1687–1747), were also from Lyons, where music-making and a flourishing publishing trade were second only to those in Paris. The avid collector of contemporary music and author of the *Dictionnaire de musique* (1703), Sébastien de Brossard (1655–1730), was Norman;[13] the doughty defenders of Italian and French musical aesthetics, Raguenet and Le

Cerf, were both from Rouen; the resourceful Jean-Baptiste Matho
(*c*1660–1746) was Breton; Jean-Baptiste Moreau (1656–1733),
Racine's sometime collaborator, and Jean-Philippe Rameau (1683–
1764), who visited Paris from 1706 to 1709 before settling there at the
end of the Regency (in 1722), were Burgundians; and, besides
Campra, Jean François Salomon (1649–1732), the composer of the
popular jingoistic Académie opera *Médée et Jason* (1713), and the
aristocracy's 'musicien des grâces' Jean-Joseph Mouret (1682–1738),
were Provençals.

MUSICAL PEREGRINATIONS FROM PARIS

Study abroad had been strongly discouraged for Paris-based musicians during the Lullian era. Charpentier's career was almost certainly compromised, though his music incalculably enhanced, by his
sojourn in Rome, probably under Giacomo Carissimi, in the 1660s.
Médée, his superbly crafted essay in post-Lullian *tragédie en musique*,
suffered from prejudice: in spite of the title role being taken by Le
Rochois and the enthusiastic patronage of Monsieur and the dauphin, only ten performances were given during the 1693–4 Carnival
season. It was never revived, which was usually an indication of
failure; but the *Mercure galant* of December 1693 had praised it highly
(the librettist Thomas Corneille often wrote for the journal), reporting that the king had accepted Charpentier's dedication and describ-
ing the composer laconically as 'an able man' who had included in
the opera 'very fine things'. The royal printer Christophe Ballard,
who published the full score in 1694, also published parodies of two
airs from *Médée* in collections of *parodies bachiques*, which appeared in
1695 and were reprinted in 1696 and 1702.

   Médée remained a *cause célèbre* for Lullists, provoking comment not
only a decade later, when Le Cerf chided Charpentier (who was
literally on his deathbed) for his 'wretched opera', 'harsh, dry and
stiff in the extreme'. Even a decade after his death, Jean de Serré de
Rieux wrote in *Les dons des enfants de Latone* (1714) of Charpentier's
misuse of 'haute science' to overwhelm his listeners and, as late as
the 1740s, Claude Parfaict dismissed the opera with faint praise in
his *Histoire de l'Académie Royale de Musique* as a work that only foreigners would regard as a masterpiece. Brossard provides the contemporary voice of reason in the annotated catalogue of his music
collection which he prepared for presentation to the king's library in
1724:

> It is unquestionably the most expert and exquisite of all [the oper-
> as] that have been published, at least since the death of Mr de
> Lully; and although thanks to cabals of the envious and ignorant it

was not received by the public as well as it deserved or even as well as many others, it is this one, more than any other opera without exception, from which may be learned the essentials of good composition.[14]

In vain, the Lullian protégé Henry Desmarets had petitioned his master to be allowed to study in Italy, only to be fobbed off with the vague excuse that his command of 'the French style' might in some way be irrevocably damaged. This attitude was quickly abandoned once Lully was gone, enabling French musicians to travel to Italy specifically to hear the latest music and absorb its style. Among the first were the versatile singer and viol player Michel Pignolet de Montéclair (1667–1737) and the gifted young violinist Jacques Anet.

Montéclair's command of contemporary vocal and chamber music idioms was manifested as early as 1695 when his 'Adieu de Tircis à Climène' appeared in Ballard's *Recueil d'airs sérieux et à boire*. From his first book of cantatas (1709) onwards he mingled French and Italian styles, yet went on to publish in 1736 his *Principes de musique*, the definitive treatise on early eighteenth-century French vocal practices. Anet is said to have studied for at least three years in Rome with Corelli, who in turn was so moved by his playing that he gave Anet his bow. Anet returned to Paris about 1700 via Germany and Poland, where he played for August II ('the Strong').[15] Abbé Pluche (*Le spectacle de la nature*, 1732) later succinctly described Anet's laissez-faire approach to contemporary music:

> He wasn't interested in the origin of a piece. German, Italian, English music, to him it was the same. If he found it noble or gracious, he played it and surrendered himself as appropriate for the sake of accuracy of intonation and the singular energy of his gestures.

Nor were Montéclair and Anet exceptional: innumerable links were forged with foreign cities and courts from the turn of the century onwards. Lallouette composed a concerto grosso and had it performed while visiting Rome in 1689; the illustrious bassoonist of the Grande Hautbois, Jacques-Martin Hotteterre (1674–1763), probably acquired his sobriquet 'le Romain' as a result of studies in Rome.

Just after the turn of the century, Jean-Philippe Rameau briefly visited Milan, even before his first trip to Paris. Turin was the destination of Jean-Marie Leclair *l'aîné* in 1726 and Louis-Gabriel Guillemain (1705–70), who went to study with the highly regarded violinist Giovanni Battista Somis (1686–1763) some time before 1729. Leclair's newly acquired *italienismes* proved a treat for the audiences of the Concert Spirituel in 1728, and Somis himself performed there in 1733. One of Somis's pupils, perhaps the frenchified

Guignon, may have organized the Paris publication of his op.4 sonatas in 1726, and even his opp.7 and 8 sonatas, which appeared in 1740.

French musicians were never particularly sought after in Italy, though their expertise must have been required to mount performances of Lully's operas in 1687 at Modena (where a niece of Mazarin was duchess) and in 1696 in Mantua. However, at the Savoy court in Turin the longstanding tradition of patronage for French music and musicians continued throughout this era.[16] Lallouette served the duchess regent in 1678, following his banishment from Paris for having boasted of composing some of Lully's *Isis*. François Couperin's cousin Marc-Roger (or Marco Roggero) Normand (1663–1734) emigrated there in 1688, serving the Prince of Carignano (hereafter 'Carignan') until his appointment in 1699 as court organist.

Many German courts employed French dancing-masters. From 1666 until 1705 the Celle court maintained a French orchestra of 16 players under Philipp La Vigne (*d* 1706). The violinist Jean-Baptiste Farinel (1655–1726), who was born in Grenoble and had worked at the Savoy court, held *Konzertmeister* appointments at Hanover and Osnabrück during the 1680s and 90s. French music and manners were highly valued at the Dresden court, where in 1715 Buffardin took up his post, remaining there until 1750, when he returned finally to Paris. Louis Marchand, having earlier resigned his post as *organiste du roi* at Versailles to tour abroad, turned tail in Dresden when in 1717 he contrived to avoid taking part in a competition with Johann Sebastian Bach (1685–1750); that same year the violinist Jean-Baptiste Senaillé (*c*1688–1730) began a two-year stay at the Dresden court. At Kassel, Leclair and Pietro Locatelli (1695–1764) performed together in 1728.

In England there were many who did not approve of Charles II's 'French music', among them Sir Bernard Gascoigne, who in 1664 urged the Secretary of State to advise the king to rid himself of 'those Frenchmen that are not worth a fiddlestick'. Nevertheless, in 1666 the Frenchman Louis Grabus (*fl* 1665–94) rose to the highest echelons of English court music when he became Master of the King's Musick and leader of both French-inspired string bands, the 24 Violins and the 12 Violins, posts he retained until 1674. He was joined in London that year by Lully's exiled rival, Robert Cambert (*c*1627–1677), who briefly presided over a Royal Academy of Musick (which employed the 24 Violins) at the Theatre Royal in Bridges Street, Covent Garden, and by the violinist Michel Farinel (*b* 1649), who married Cambert's daughter.

Also in 1674, a number of French wind players were recruited for performances at Whitehall of the masque *Calisto* by Nicholas

Staggins (*d* 1700) and John Crowne (*c*1640–1712). Among them was James Paisible (*d* 1721), who stayed on in the employ of another of Cardinal Mazarin's nieces and later became a member of the King's Musick. Hortensia Mancini's house in Paradise Row, Chelsea, was the scene of a daily academy, frequented by the expatriate opera critic Charles Marguetel de Saint-Denis, Seigneur de Saint-Evremond, among others. French music was much in vogue in London when, in 1676, Louis XIV sent a troupe of three male French singers, who relied on two resident French flautists (possibly Paisible and François Le Riche, who had recently obtained a court post) and Cambert as harpsichordist to play for Charles II; the music they performed included excerpts from Lully's *Cadmus et Hermione, Alceste, Thésée* and *Atys* (among which the 'Sommeil' proved very popular). During James II's short reign French musicians continued to take part in court music, and many would have been repatriated when the king accepted Louis XIV's offer of asylum in 1689.

During the 1690s more French names appear in the register of Chapel Royal musicians. Charles (François?) Dieupart (?after 1667–*c*1740) provided instrumental music for the London stage during the first decade of the eighteenth century. In 1706 Giuseppe Fedeli arrived in London with French dancers, who performed in his opera *The Temple of Love* at the Haymarket Theatre. In 1707 the son of the influential French viola da gamba pedagogue Monsieur de Sainte-Colombe (*d* before 1701) visited Edinburgh, leaving behind an important manuscript collection of his father's music; in London in May 1713 he gave a benefit concert at Hickford's Room.

But ultimately it was Italian musicians, not the French, who gained a lasting foothold in the London theatre – in no small part because the operas they brought with them were composed for smaller commercial theatres such as those of Venice and Naples and were better suited to the London theatres than were the ostentatious, heavily subsidized French *tragédies en musique*. A sympathetic reception would have thus greeted the annotated English translation of Raguenet's *Parallèle* (*A Comparison between the French and Italian Musick and Opera's*), published anonymously in London in 1709. The only significant French performer to appear in London during the early part of the century was the dancer Marie Sallé (1707–56), the great rival of La Camargo (1710–70); John Rich, the proprietor of the Lincoln's Inn Fields Theatre, engaged Sallé along with four other French dancers for the 1725 season, which included performances of Jean-Féry Rebel's *divertissement* of 1715 *Les caractères de la danse*. She returned to London several times to perform at the Drury Lane Theatre and in Handel productions at Covent Garden, before her retirement in 1740.

The Spanish court was less welcoming to French musicians, in spite of a continuing Bourbon presence there in Marie-Louise d'Orléans (Charles II's consort) and, from 1701, Philip V. Henri Guichard, an *intendant* in the service of Louis XIV's uncle, Gaston d'Orléans, accompanied his employer's daughter Marie-Louise to Madrid in 1679; he brought along a contingent of French musicians, among them the peripatetic violinist Michel Farinel, with whom he intended to found an academy for the performance of French opera.

According to the December 1700 issue of the *Mercure galant*, Jean-Féry Rebel (1666–1747) and Michel de La Barre (*c*1675–1743/4) headed another group of French musicians who travelled to Madrid with Louis XIV's grandson, the Duke of Anjou, for his coronation as Philip V, King of Spain. They were joined there in 1701 by Lully's one-time protégé Henry Desmarets, who remained in royal service until 1707. Any vogue for French music at the Spanish court was short-lived, and while Philip V's consort, Marie-Louise of Savoy (sister of the Duchess of Burgundy), retained in Pierre Rameau (*fl* early eighteenth century) a French dancing-master, both she and her husband preferred to patronize Italian musicians, actors and artists. In command of the French troops deployed in Spain in 1707, the Duke of Orléans – who cherished a slender claim to the Spanish throne (which, to his uncle's despair, nearly led to his being charged with treason in France) – would much have enjoyed the music at the court.

PRINTED MUSIC AND ARTISTIC PRESTIGE

Lully would not have been unaware during the last years of his life of the dramatic influx in Paris of manuscripts and editions, particularly of sacred Italian music. However, he could hardly have foreseen the flowering of *recueils d'airs italiens* published by Ballard, among them one devoted to the music of Lorenzani (1695) and another to that of Gatti (1696). Of the Lorenzani *airs*, Ballard revealed in the preface that he had initially to be persuaded by friends that there was a sufficient number of people devoted to the Italian language and music to warrant their issue. Gatti wrote in the bilingual preface to his collection (dedicated to the Princess of Conti) that one must be prepared to consult a practitioner of the Italian style because it had proved impossible to notate all the ornaments appropriate to the music. Italianate chamber music for violins and continuo written in the early 1690s by French composers – who included Brossard, Rebel and the keyboard players Clérambault (still in his teens), Couperin and La Guerre – circulated in manuscript, while solo suites for the lute, harpsichord and viol were usually privately engraved and distributed by the sheet (*en blanc*), often by the composer himself.

21. *Michel de La Barre and other musicians (thought to be the viol player Marin Marais and the wind players Louis and Nicolas Hotteterre): painting (c1710) attributed to Robert de La Tournières [Levrac]. The music is copied from La Barre's 'Troisième livre de trios, pour les violons, flûtes et hautbois' (1707)*

The opening of two music shops – in 1692 Foucault's 'à la règle d'or', where Marais' newly engraved trio suites were available in partbooks, and five years later that of the Amsterdam printer Etienne Roger, who specialized in French and Italian editions – gave further encouragement to informal societies of musicians and music lovers who gathered in private homes to hear and perform their latest acquisitions. Possession of a copy of the 1689 Roman edition of Corelli's op.3 trio sonatas, for example, would have been certain to cause a *coup d'éclat*. Marais' trios were followed in 1694 by La Barre's collection of trio suites and in 1697 by those of Montéclair, which took the form of an orchestrated *Sérénade* for three contrasting trios of flutes with bass viol, oboes with bassoon and violins with cello. La Barre's second set appeared in 1700, and the *haute-contre* Thomas-Louis Bourgeois (1676–c1750) had a further set printed in 1701 (though no copy seems to have survived). The first French composer to publish trio sonatas was Jean-François Dandrieu (c1682–1738), in 1705.

The salons of respected musicians such as Marie-Françoise Certain (d 1711), La Guerre, Marais, Couperin and Clérambault provided a forum for students and colleagues to air their latest works before having them engraved. Titon du Tillet (*Le Parnasse François*, 1732) remarked of La Certain that 'as she gave extremely fine concerts in her home [near the Palais-Royal], the very best composers brought along their music, which was always performed with considerable success', and Le Blanc (1740) portrayed her as an important arbiter of French and Italian taste. An accomplished harpsichordist, Certain had at one time been a mistress and muse of Lully and, along the way, acquired six manuscript volumes of his ballets and five of his operas, as well as dozens of printed editions, including the *grands motets*.[17]

But as a collector of Lulliana Certain was not alone: Loulié amassed a great number of manuscripts while in the service of the Duchess of Guise and then made them available to be copied and sold by Foucault, who from about 1694 advertised Lully's music in manuscript and authorized printed copies from Ballard. The opera scores went on being printed well into the 1720s, in line with the revivals, not only in Paris but in the provinces and abroad. Among the antiquarian 'curieux' who scooped them up, Brossard admitted willingness to pay relatively large sums for manuscripts of the original Lully ballets, which were never printed.

In 1726 Couperin reminisced in the preface to *Les nations* about the tentative début of his own early ensemble *sonades* in the 1690s: impassioned by his love for the works of Corelli and Lully, he had felt compelled to compose a trio sonata, which he then had played by musicians whom he had earlier heard perform Corelli's music so well. In order to ensure that his own work might appeal to the audience, he pretended it had been composed by an Italian from the Turin court whose name he gave as an anagram of his own. Only when '*la sonade* was devoured with alacrity' did Couperin lay claim to its authorship; even then, however, he was not ready to commit this music to print.

The arrival in Paris of copies of Corelli's op.5 violin sonatas, published in Rome in 1700, undoubtedly encouraged the production of engraved editions of French music, which document – insofar as publication dates reveal anything about the probable dates of composition – the critical transition from the French suite to an italianate French sonata. Already in 1701 Louis Heudelinne (*fl* 1700–10), a shadowy figure, published the first collection of French suites for a single treble viol which, in accordance with performing traditions, were intended to be accompanied by a bass viol. There followed in 1702 La Barre's suites for transverse flute, again accompanied by a courtly bass viol as well as a theorbo.

Then, in 1703, Bernier took out a *privilège* to publish cantatas, though Morin appears to have been the first actually to issue a collection of cantatas (the feebleness of which Pierre-Louis d'Aquin de Château-Lyon later noted, in his *Siècle littéraire de Louis XV* of 1753, 'les a fait oublier'). In that same year Brossard provided definitions of 'sonata' and 'cantata' in his *Dictionnaire de musique*, along with a *Traité de la manière de bien prononcer les mots italiens*, observing that never had there been more taste and passion for Italian music than now existed in France. In the very next year, in fact, Duval, who had been much praised for his performances of Corelli, became the first Frenchman to publish violin sonatas, which he dedicated to his employer, the Duke of Orléans.

The desire to produce acceptably modern music, while somehow acknowledging French traditions, moved Rebel (newly appointed in 1705 as leader of the king's Vingt-quatre Violons) to issue his first printed *oeuvre*, a collection of violin suites, with *recitante* parts for the bass viol; even in 1707, when La Guerre became the first French woman composer to publish sonatas for violin (just as with *Céphale et Procris* in 1694 she had been the first woman to compose a *tragédie en musique*), she too seemed to feel obliged to frenchify them by incorporating short *récits* for bass viol. Meanwhile, Charlotte Massard de La Tour prepared a Paris edition of Corelli's op.5 which appeared in 1708 (Foucault delayed his until 1719), and manuscript transcriptions of the sonatas became the rage; those for the bass viol were conceived for and performed by the italophile player Antoine Forqueray and his admirers who, ironically, cared more for novelty than tradition.

The first Paris collection of overtly italianate violin sonatas was eventually published in 1710 by a pupil of Piani, Jean-Baptiste Senaillé, though Ancelet, writing retrospectively in his *Observations sur la musique, les musiciens, et les instrumens* (Amsterdam, 1757), assumed that Senaillé had deliberately contrived complicated bass lines to appease the virtuoso bass viol players who might have been expected to accompany. The convention of retaining a bass viol in French-style chamber music ensembles was observed by the promising young violin virtuoso Leclair in his op.2 trio (1728) and by Telemann in the two sets of 'Paris Quartets' from the 1730s, culminated in Rameau's *Pièces de clavecin en concerts* (1741) and finally was marginalized in the quartet sonatas of Jean-Baptiste Quentin *le jeune* and Louis-Gabriel Guillemain later in the 1740s.[18]

Throughout this period, but particularly in the first decades of the new century, Parisian engravers and printers found it fiendishly difficult to keep up with their burgeoning order-books. Remarks contained in the prefaces to the *pièces* of Couperin and Marais reveal that they, and others of their perfectionist ilk, preferred to wait upon the mastercraftsmen and -women, among them Baussen, Hüe, Du Plessy and Roussel. The *Mercure de France* of November 1713 reported that

> cantatas and sonatas spring up under our very feet, a musician no longer arrives without a sonata or cantata in his pocket, and there are none who do not wish to write a work and have it engraved and beat the Italians at their own game: poets can scarcely keep pace with them, and indeed there are even some texts that have suffered more than once the torture of italianate music, so that here we are suffocated by cantatas.[19]

By contrast, the Italian cantatas of such composers as Alessandro Scarlatti (1660–1725) and Giovanni Bononcini were known to Parisian italophiles from manuscript copies; Bononcini's *Meslanges de musique latine, françoise et italienne* was not published in Paris until 1725.

Although copies of all French editions of vocal and instrumental music were deposited in the king's library (now part of the Bibliothèque Nationale) and others were presented to patrons, colleagues and students, most were sold to aristocratic and bourgeois pupils in Paris and the provinces. To facilitate the playing of this music, an easier repertory, such as *petits airs*, *brunetes* and menuets, as well as practical treatises, increasingly became available (the last had been anticipated by the *traités de viole* of Danoville and Jean Rousseau in 1687, followed by those for other instruments of Saint-Lambert in 1702, Hotteterre 'le Romain' in 1707, Montéclair in 1709 and 1711–12 and Couperin in 1717). From 1694 onwards amateur pupils, more often than not young women,[20] published their *airs* in Ballard's serial collections, alongside those of the most distinguished musicians of the era.

Musicians such as Marais, Lalande, Marchand, Montéclair and

Couperin were much in demand as teachers, and accordingly the status of musicians in general rose: their portraits were painted and engravings after them circulated; the most eminent were elevated to the minor aristocracy.[21] Though musicians, like writers and artists, were usually invited by a duke or duchess merely to provide entertainment at private gatherings, they were also deemed desirable company in their own right: during the 1690s, for example, Couperin and the fabulist La Fontaine frequented the salon of the Duke d'Aumont. They would, however, have expected to perform at some point in the evening: D'Aquin de Château-Lyon (son of the organist Louis-Claude Daquin) recorded an occasion 'chez Madame la Duchesse de B' at which the invited guest was Marchand; when asked to play, he refused at first and then played with bad grace, prompting the duchess to dismiss him with 'Taisez-vous, Marchand . . . vous nous enuiez'. Nevertheless, the inclusion of dozens of musicians in Titon du Tillet's exclusive parnassic society, and – as in the cases of Lully, Lalande, Marais, La Guerre, Campra and Destouches – their commemoration on bronze medallions, reflects their higher profile in French cultural life.

The gestures of respect accorded Le Rochois on her death at the age of about 70, on 9 October 1728, by her colleagues and fans were indicative of the great affection she had inspired throughout her long career. Her funeral and interment at St Eustache were attended by musicians of the Académie Royale de Musique and other distinguished persons, and were followed one month later by a memorial service at Notre Dame des Victoires. However, according to Titon du Tillet, the second occasion was marred by a *coup d'authorité*: those in charge of arranging the memorial service had neglected to secure permission from the Archbishop of Paris to use musical instruments in the church and were made to regret it. With Campra and members of the Académie ready to perform, and the church filled with invited guests, an emissary from Cardinal Noailles adjourned the service to the chapel (in which Lully was, in fact, interred), where the musicians were forced to perform the *De profundis* in *faux bourdon*.

SEARCHING FOR CYTHERA

Turn-of-the-century Paris, wearied by the terminal effects of absolutism described in Abbé Fénélon's book *Télémaque* (1698), was alive to change. Parisians turned their backs on the stiffness of court etiquette in favour of a more gracious – though just as self-conscious – way of life. In the theatre, gods and historical heroes were replaced by earthy *commedia dell'arte* characters, mythical and medieval settings gave way either to modern domestic ones or to exotic worlds where the strictures of French court life had no relevance and great human

22. *Fête vénitienne: painting by Jean-Antoine Watteau (1684–1721); the dancers are accompanied by a musette*

issues were held at bay. Such scenarios were promoted by Antoine Houdar de La Motte, Jean-Baptiste Rousseau, and other opera and cantata librettists who favoured the more trivial preoccupations idealized in Campra's *L'Europe galante* (1697) and *Les festes vénitiennes* (1710). The literary portraiture of Jean de La Bruyère's *Les caractères, ou Les moeurs de ce siècle* (1699) was echoed in the many musical portraits found in the published instrumental chamber music of such composers as Marais, Couperin and Rameau (though the last admitted in the preface to *Les pièces de clavecin en concerts* of 1741 that the titles of some of his pieces were suggested by friends after they had been composed).[22]

The paintings of music-making by Antoine Watteau, who arrived in Paris only in 1702, capture the escapism and search for the exotic of those early years of the century: musicians playing flutes, theorbos, guitars and viols – often garbed in whimsical costumes and positioned in relaxed outdoor settings – are glimpsed in pursuit of pleasure, contributing to a *fête galante* among friends rather than rendering a service to their social betters. Flutes, hurdy-gurdies (*vielles*) and bagpipes (*musettes*), as well as keyboard instruments and the feminine *pardessus de viole*, became the familiar provenance of amateurs, who played music for its own sake.

Watteau was discovered by Pierre Crozat (officially *trésorier des Etats de Languedoc* and, at court, paymaster of the order of Saint-Esprit), at whose frequent concerts in his Paris home in the rue de Richelieu Watteau would have met and heard perform musicians including Couperin, whose 'La Raphaéle' (Ordre viii) may refer to a painting in the Crozat collection (Joseph-Antoine Crozat was a passionate art collector).[23] Watteau may also have frequented the concerts held in the 'sallon de Mr Bertin', which featured 'un fort joli cabinet d'orgues', where on at least one occasion a cantata by André Cardinal Destouches (1672–1749) was performed; Destouches described the performance, declaring that 18 performers had made as much noise as 50, in a letter to the Prince of Monaco (23 December 1709).

Raguenet wrote that not only the cantatas but entire operas by Bononcini were known to a growing circle of italophiles; the minimal production requirements of most Italian operas suited private performances quite nicely. The Marquis de Dangeau's diary contains references to the dauphin's presence on such occasions. Librettos and scores of the latest operas were offered for sale so that scenes and music from dramas could be privately performed at the *hôtels* of the aristocracy as well as in the more modest salons of the performers themselves. Dangeau in fact put on performances of an Italian opera, *Viva il amico del re*, in June 1704.

THE PATH OF SACRED MUSIC

Lorenzani's earlier success had proved that italophilia was not confined to secular music. Le Cerf remarked on the excellent performances given by French singers, whom he felt pronounced Latin well in motets but Italian very badly in Italian arias. Churches provided venues for concerts of Italian sacred music, while clerics such as Nicolas Mathieu (following the example of his elder colleagues René Ouvrard and Claude-François Ménestrier) arranged more intimate gatherings *chez lui*, in the *quartier* of St-André-des-Arts. On such occasions Italian music, by Francesco Cavalli (1602–76), Carissimi, Legrenzi, Melani and Alessandro Stradella (1644–82), was performed.[24]

Italian sacred music was also performed at Versailles: in 1688, for example, the royal music librarian André Danican Philidor (c1647–

1730) copied a book of 'petits motets et elevations' for the Chapelle, which included 32 works by Carissimi and seven by Antonio Foggia (*c*1650–1707). In December 1701 Dangeau remarked that, in the company of Madame de Maintenon, Monseigneur and the Princess of Conti, the king heard a Lalande motet performed 'à la manière italienne', which he claimed to be 'fort à la mode'.

The *louisquatorzien motet*, politicized, though not significantly shaped, by Lully as the sacred counterpart to his allegorical operas, was brought to a new and sublime level of perfection by Lalande and his protégés, prominent among them Campra, Destouches, Bernier, Jean-François de La Porte and Blamont. Blamont called Lalande 'the Latin Lully' in his prefatory note in the lavish posthumous edition (1729) of Lalande's motets. Lalande had lived to see his music, and the *grand motet* in particular, rise to new prominence at the Concert Spirituel, the public concert series in Paris which was held at the Tuileries palace from 1725. Blamont attributed the popularity of Lalande's motets to the composer's ability to be 'profound and learned on the one hand, simple and natural on the other' and on his ability 'to touch the soul by richness of expression and vivid pictorialism'. D'Aquin praised him unreservedly: '*Lalande* transports you to Heaven, he inspires the respect and love of the Divinity'.

Of all those who at one time had been barred from advancement by Lully, Lalande took greatest advantage of the vacuum created by his death to make his way to the upper echelons of the music establishment at court, which since 1683 had been officially in residence at Versailles. Whether by providence or clever design, Lalande gradually gained exclusive control over the Chapelle, a position he achieved by 1714 and one that afforded him a remarkable degree of intimacy with the king, surpassed only by that once enjoyed by Lully. The price for this privilege was, apparently, a degree of artistic freedom; according to Lalande's first biographer, Tannevot, at a certain point the king came to regard Lalande's motets, like Lully's operas, as icons of his regime and thus not susceptible of improvement even by the composer himself – a view apparently not shared by Lalande, who returned again and again to his manuscripts, refining and modernizing his music to suit new occasions. The chapel as a focal point for the court and, more particularly, the rituals of worship gradually replaced the more frivolous *divertissements* of the earlier part of the reign.

There were, of course, bastions of traditional French sacred music in Paris – Notre Dame, St Germain-l'Auxerrois, the convents of the Feuillants and the Théatins, but especially the Sainte Chapelle, on the Ile-de-la-Cité next to the Parlement, where Gregorian chant and *faux bourdon* were sung. Nevertheless, the prestige of the *maître de musique* (charged with directing the services, instructing the choristers and composing) was second only to that of the *sous-maîtres* of the Chapelle Royale, which helps to explain why Charpentier should have been appointed to that post in 1698. His tenure there coincided exactly with that of the organist Marin de la Guerre. Charpentier was succeeded by Nicolas Bernier, Marais' son-in-law and one of the Duke of Orléans' circle.

Charpentier himself was under no illusions about the twists and turns of his career: his own ghost in the cantata *Epitaphium Carpentarij* wryly remarks that 'I was a musician, thought to be among the good ones by the good and among the ignorant ones by the ignorant'.[25] The fact is that the best composers of the day did provide works, particularly *Te Deum* settings to celebrate births, the good health of the monarch and military victories, that were performed more often than not in the presence of a royal patron. Louis XIV made a rare visit to Paris in 1706 to attend the inauguration of St Louis-des-Invalides, at which a *Te Deum* by Lalande was performed by the *musiques de cour*.

The Collège Louis-le-Grand, a Jesuit boys' school in the rue St Jacques, had for many years catered to a faithful following of royal and ecclesiastical connoisseurs by commissioning progressive works such as Charpentier's *tragédies en musique Celse Martyr* (1687) and *David et Jonathas* (1688), the acts of which served as *intermèdes* to Latin plays; the *Mercure galant* of March 1688 did not hesitate to call *David et Jonathas* an opera. The performances, given by the pupils, took place in one of three venues, according to the season: there were courtyard theatres for the summer and Carnival productions, and a 'salle des actions' for winter productions and rehearsals. A decade later the Collège presented music by the versatile André Campra, *maître de musique* at Notre Dame, whose *opéra-ballet L'Europe galante* (1697) had recently taken Paris audiences by storm.

THE LURE OF THE EXOTIC

Supported by the powerful patronage of the dukes of Orléans and Sully and the Duchess of La Ferté, Campra presented *L'Europe galante* for the first time on 24 October 1697 at the Palais-Royal – though at first anonymously, being eager not to incur the wrath and censure of his ecclesiastical superior, the Archbishop of Paris. But the experimental *opéra-ballet*, with its macaronic text (in French, Spanish, Italian and pseudo-Turkish) by La Motte, proved such a phenomenal success that Campra followed it two years later with *Le carnaval de Venise*, incorporating a miniature, five-scene Italian opera, *Orfeo nell' inferi*. A popular chanson of 1697:

> Quand notre Archevesque scaura
> L'Auteur du nouvel Opéra,
> De sa Cathédrale Campra
> Décampera.[26]

made nonsense of his subsequent attempt to credit his younger brother with the composition of the second work and a number of *airs*, so it is hardly suprising that he resigned his post at Notre Dame in 1700 (never having taken orders), though many people, Le Cerf among them, were disappointed that Campra had abandoned sacred music for the theatre. Voltaire expressed that sentiment in his *Epître à Madame de Fontaine-Martel*:

> Au Curé préférent *Campra*
> Vous avez Loge à l'opéra
> Au lieu d'un Banc dans la Paroisse.

Ballet de cour, refashioned as *opéra-ballet*, was back in vogue.

By seizing on the Venetian carnival theme Campra had tapped the French public's peculiar delight in escapism – indulging in masquerade and imaginary travel to exotic places – an astute hunch that Campra again pursued in 1702 by contributing a *Sérénade vénitienne* (text by Antoine Danchet) to a *divertissement comique* of previously unpublished 'fragments de Lully'. It was called *Cariselli*, after the fifth *entrée*, which was composed of da capo arias with Italian texts. Taking his cue from Campra, Destouches used the Venetian carnival theme a year later in his *comédie-ballet Le Carnaval et la Folie*.

When in 1710 Campra composed the *opéra-ballet Les festes vénitiennes*, the little six-scene opera contained within it was in French, not Italian, which was surely symptomatic of a symbolic coming of age among post-Lullian composers. Two years earlier, in 1708, Campra had written in the preface to his first book of cantatas that he had tried to mix in his music the vivacity of Italian music with the gentleness of the French. In *Les festes vénitiennes* he may have felt that the conventions were sufficiently established to make it no longer necessary to rely on the Italian language to convey a sense of style already implicit in the music.

Lully would not have foreseen the impact of the patronage of Philippe de Bourbon (who was only 13 at Lully's death). Writing in retrospect, Hubert Le Blanc, a *sécretaire d'état de la guerre* during the Regency, credited the duke with having 'honoured the combats of French and Italian harmony with his presence'.[27] As a member of the bourgeois professional class, Le Blanc would inevitably have been excluded from such an exclusive aristocratic forum and might have resented the fact, as he presented it, that the duke 'held the door himself, allowing only distinguished lovers of the arts or the elite among performers to enter'. Whether or not this was so, numerous instrumental and vocal works of Philippe's musicians from the first decade of the eighteenth century bear testimony to his delight in celebrating the different qualities embodied in the two styles, as for example in Stuck's otherwise unremarkable opera *Méleagre* (1709), which begins with a debate between the two musics.

THE COURT OF LOUIS XIV

At Versailles and at the other royal *châteaux* there was a clear social division between *musique de cour* and *musique privée* and, accordingly, between those who were required to attend the former and those privileged to be present at the latter. Music composed and directed by Lalande as *surintendant de la musique de la chambre* is said to have accompanied every ceremonial event of the king's day, from dawn to dusk. Resident courtiers were required to attend daily Mass, at which the musicians of the Chapelle would usually perform one *grand motet* and two *petits motets* by Lalande (though not in the existing chapel at Versailles, which was under construction for 20 years before its completion in 1710).

Music for dancing also had to be prepared for the regular evening *appartements* on Wednesdays, Thursdays and Sundays and for the Saturday-night balls. For general entertainment spoken plays, regularly employing a handful of musicians and dancers, were performed as early as 1685 in the Salle de Comédie. To celebrate military victories and royal births, marriages and recoveries from illness and to mark deaths, Lalande could draw on the combined forces of the *musiques de cour* (Chapelle, Chambre and Ecurie) to perform a *Te Deum, De profundis* or *Dies irae*.

Between 1684 and 1701 Louis XIV had an inner apartment constructed at Versailles, comprising the Cabinet des Chiens, the Salon du Petit Escalier, the Cabinet des Coquilles, the Cabinet aux Tableaux and the Petite Galerie, where only members of his family and a few distinguished guests attended him. When not presiding over regular and lengthy meetings with his ministers, Louis XIV took keen pleasure in the private concerts organized by Madame de Maintenon and Clérambault for the king's most intimate circle. The extent to which members of that circle actually took part in these entertainments is illustrated by an entry from 15 April 1700 in Dangeau's diary, recording the performance in Madame de Maintenon's rooms at Meudon of a motet by the Count of Ayen, in which the Duke of Burgundy, Monsieur de Chartres, the Count of Toulouse, the Princess of Conti and Madame de Villequier took part.

As late as 1714 chamber music was performed by the finest court musicians – Couperin, Anet, the flautist René Descoteaux (*d c*1699),

Table V.2 THE DESCENDANTS OF LOUIS XIV

```
La ──────────▶ Marie Anne de Bourbon          ┌─▶ Louis, Duke of
Vallière                 =                     │   Burgundy
                   Prince of Conti             │      = ──────▶ ┌─────────┐
                                               │   Marie Adélaïde │ LOUIS  │
                                               │   of Savoy       │   XV   │
                                               │                  └─────────┘
┌─────────┐                                    ├── Philippe, Duke of
│ LOUIS   │ = (1)Maria ──────▶ Louis 'Monseigneur'   Anjou,
│  XIV    │      Teresa              =               King of Spain
└─────────┘              Marie Anne Christine Victoire    =
                         (sister of Maximilian II    Marie Louise
                         Emanuel, Elector of Bavaria)   of Savoy (sister
                                                        of the Duchess
                                                        of Burgundy)

                                               └── Charles, Duke
           = (2)Mme de                             of Berry
                 Maintenon                            =
                                                   Marie-Louise-
                                                   Elisabeth
                                                   (daughter of
                                                   Philippe II, Duke
                                                   of Orléans)

                              ┌── Louis-Auguste
                              │   Duke of Maine
                              │        =
                              │   Anne-Louise-Bénédicte of
                              │   Bourbon Condé

                              ├── Louise-Françoise,
                              │   Mlle de Nantes,
                              │   'La Duchesse'
              Mme de          │        =
              Montespan ──────┤   Duke of Bourbon-Condé

                              ├── Françoise-Marie
                              │        =                   Louis I
                              │   Philippe II, Duke of Orléans  Duke of Orléans
                              │   (Regent)

                              └── Louis-Alexandre
                                  Count of Toulouse
                                       =
                                  Marie-Sophie-Victoire
                                  de Noailles
```

the viol players Marais and Forqueray and the theorbo player Robert de Visée (c1660–c1732), to name but a few – almost daily in Madame de Maintenon's rooms: *grande musique* on Wednesdays, Fridays and Sundays, and *petite musique* on Tuesdays and Thursdays. The Princess of Conti – described by Dr Lister as 'without dispute one of the most graceful and handsomest women in France' – was also known to have presided over 'une très belle musique', again performed by the best musicians of the *musiques de cour* twice a week (usually on days when there was no music *chez* Madame de

Maintenon). These were not, of course, the only private concerts given and attended by the aristocracy while in attendance at court.

After fulfilling her duties to the king, Madame de Maintenon devoted her remaining energy to the founding (1686) and administration of the Maison Royale de St Cyr (where in fact she retired in 1715 to live her last four years).[28] It was a school for some 250 daughters of indigent military officers, very near Versailles, where Clérambault could conveniently serve as organist. She attended performances, often in the company of the king, prepared by the boarders, and prevailed on the eminent French dramatist Racine to collaborate with Jean-Baptiste Moreau on two dramatic works, *Esther* (1689) and *Athalie* (1691), for them to perform. Moreau and Lalande also produced a setting of Racine's *Cantiques spirituelles*, suitable for the young ladies, which was published in 1695. Perhaps flushed with success, Moreau, ever the ambitious provincial, soon overstepped Madame de Maintenon's finely developed sense of propriety with what she at least considered to be a lascivious *divertissement* – *Zaïre* (c1694), the offending text of which, by Alexandre Lainez, resulted in Moreau's virtual exile to Languedoc as *surintendant de musique*.

But for all the novelty of the occasional *concert exquis d'airs italiens*, Lully's operas never lost their lustre in the eyes and ears of Louis XIV. A propos this is Le Cerf's anecdote about Anet, who, having played an Italian work, was commanded to play an *air* from *Cadmus et Hermione*, after which the king made his famous pronouncement: 'Voilà mon goût à moi, voilà mon goût'. Privately, the king continued to enjoy unpublicized performances of single acts of operas and ballet *entrées* and was regularly joined on these occasions by a small group of intimates at the Grand Trianon, until the autumn of 1697, when he ordered the ten-year-old theatre to be dismantled.

The more musical of the courtiers often took part in these entertainments: in 1700, for example, the Duke of Maine (once a pupil of Couperin) took a role in a performance of *Alceste* organized by the Princess of Conti. In more private moments, the king himself could be overheard whistling or singing Lully's tunes, which seem to have provided a useful diversion on the many sad occasions, such as the death of his brother (from a stroke) in 1701, when – according to the memoirs of the captious Duke of Saint-Simon – the king was observed taking undue pleasure in excerpts from Lully's panegyric prologues with his granddaughter-in-law, the Duchess of Burgundy.

On visits to the nearby home at Meudon of the dauphin and his unofficial second wife, Mademoiselle de Choin, and that of the exiled English Catholic monarch James II, affectionately known as 'Roi Jâques', and his queen, Maria of Modena, at Saint-Germain-en-Laye, Louis XIV had ample opportunity to attend performances of other operatic and, in particular, Italian fare. On a visit to Fontainebleau in 1703, the widowed Queen Maria was entertained during the *soupers* with concerts of Italian music, replacing the usual Lalande *symphonies*; according to the November *Mercure galant*, they were performed by two Romans, the Pasqualinis, who were accompanied by musicians of the Duke of Orléans and the *musiques de cour*.

During the court's annual sojourn in late summer and autumn at Fontainebleau, untried *pastorales*, ballets and operatic works by composers such as Lalande[29] who were not associated with the Académie were performed, along with excerpts from the new Académie operas in rehearsal for the next Carnival season. As the services of Académie musicians, dancers and the French and Italian comedians were required, the Paris theatres were forced to close, a situation that proved to be a financial hardship to the companies and a deprivation to those seeking entertainment in Paris. Still other performances organized by the courtiers themselves took place in the relaxed atmosphere at Fontainebleau.

Throughout the rest of the year, a dozen short trips to Marly were undertaken by between 50 and 60 invited members of the court. It was traditional, for example, to interrupt the Carnival festivities at Versailles with journeys to Marly for the privileged few who were invited by the king. Marly was a small country house, designated the Pavillon du Roi, to which were added (before 1686) 12 further Pavillons des Seigneurs and six amphitheatres for performances of drama and opera and evenings of *masquerade*. Certainly, at the end of the reign, musical entertainment could not be taken for granted, nor could one expect to hear the latest music: it was at Marly that Louis XIV finally heard the popular tempest scene from Marais' *Alcyone* (1706) – five years after its première in Paris. Indeed, one could not be certain that there would be any music at all, according to Dangeau (whose diary ends about this time), and so it was both ironic and inevitable that many of the courtiers dreaded having to attend the king there. Of course, all of this – the migrations and the entertainments – ceased on Louis XIV's death, including the *voyages* to Fontainebleau, which were resumed only in 1724. Not until the era of Marie Antoinette did music again function so vitally in the rituals of court life.

THE END OF A REIGN

Because of France's role in the War of the League of Augsburg (1688–98), Louis XIV seems to have felt less inclined throughout the 1690s and, indeed, to the end of his reign, to authorize court performances of new *tragédies en musique* at Versailles. He replaced them with less costly masquerades, in which courtiers were expected to join the professional singers, actors and dancers. He personally involved himself in the strategies of the war and wanted to be seen by his people to be trimming the excesses of court life as the disastrous economic effects of the prolonged series of territorial wars, and the famine of 1694, began to be felt.

The strain did occasionally show: in 1694 the usually indomitable king was forced to spend a week in bed. Still, far more terrible was the suffering wrought by the War of the Spanish Succession (1702–13) – especially the crushing defeat at the Battle of Blenheim in August 1704 – and, for the Bourbon dynasty in particular, the smallpox epidemic of 1711–12, which claimed the lives of three dauphins, among them Louis XIV's son Louis, to whom he had delegated much of the responsibility for the court's artistic activities during this period.

Louis de France (1661–1711), known at court as 'Monseigneur', was considered by the Parisians the most popular member of the royal family. The Marquis de Sourches (who was married to Lully's granddaughter) and the Marquis de Dangeau record many occasions on which he attended performances by the Académie and presided over a lively circle of the intelligentsia who patronized, among other things, Italian music and musicians. He served with distinction in the army and shared his father's love of hunting, art collecting, *spectacle*, *musique de chambre* and *haute cuisine*.

In January 1688 Dangeau reported that, with the king looking on, the dauphin directed rehearsals of a ballet at Marly, which was performed on a double bill with a comedy and repeated at Versailles the following month. Widowed in 1690 with three sons (the dukes of Burgundy, Anjou and Berry), he maintained a degree of autonomy from his father by living at Meudon and convening his own circle of advisers; in 1699 he commissioned a *comédie en prose* from F. C. Dancourt with music by Lalande, which the king never saw. At Marly, Meudon and Fontainebleau he hosted *appartements* and balls; during one on 18 March 1700, Sourches reports, two singers dressed as parrots were accompanied by a theorbo player dressed as a tiger.

The dauphin also authorized private entertainments for his friends. Following a day of hunting on a bright July day in 1702 in the Forest of Sena, the Monseigneur dined with his half-sister, the Princess of Conti, at Villeneuve St Georges. Music was performed by the Académie singers Jacques Cochereau (c1680–1734), Gabriel-Vincent Thévenard (1669–1741), Mademoiselle Maupin and Marguerite-Louise Couperin (c1676/9–1728), along with court instrumentalists – Descoteaux, Philibert (fl 1667–1717), Visée and Forqueray; during the interval, the courtiers played Lansquenet (a popular Parisian game of chance). Later that year he had Matho's *Coronis* (destined never to be mounted in Paris) privately performed at Fontainebleau. Had he lived to succeed his father, court music might well have regained the vigour and vision of the Lullian years, which his own broad musical and theatrical tastes would have imbued with cosmopolitanism.

Exceptions to the official policy of visible austerity maintained at Versailles were inevitably made. In 1697 the signing of the Treaty of Ryswick and the wedding of the Duke of Burgundy (the son of Monseigneur and the second of the ill-fated dauphins) to Marie Adélaïde of Savoy prompted the performance of Destouches' *pastorale héroïque*, *Issé*, at the Grand Trianon. For the wedding in 1698 of the king's niece Elisabeth-Charlotte of Orléans to Léopold, Duke of Lorraine, a new production of Molière's *Mirtil et Mélicerte* (1666) was mounted, with music by Lalande, followed a month later by a lavish revival of *Le bourgeois gentilhome* with Lully's original music.

The proclamation of the Duke of Anjou as King of Spain, following the death of Charles II in November 1700, occasioned the performance of *Danaé*, an opera specially written for the occasion by the court musician Anne Danican Philidor (1681–1728). Of the Carnival celebrations that followed, the Duke of Saint-Simon wrote that he for one 'never saw the light of day in the last three weeks before Lent'.[30] But above all, Lully's music remained throughout a useful, potent symbol of the Sun King's reign, and his most popular operas – *Alceste*, *Atys* and *Roland* – were specially staged for state visits, such as that of the Spanish ambassador in December 1701, when it was important to maintain an outward appearance of splendour.

CRISES OF OPERATIC PROPORTIONS

Because of the king's near-pathological reluctance to spend time in Paris after 1672, two of Lully's operas, *Phaëton* (1683) and *Roland* (1685), had their premières at Versailles and five others – *Thésée* (1675), *Atys* (1676), *Isis* (1677), *Proserpine* (1680) and *Le triomphe de l'Amour* (1681) – took place at Saint-Germain-en-Laye. Other members of his family regularly attended the performances at the Palais-Royal and represented him on opening nights. Had war and famine not intervened one might have expected the operas and ballets of Pascal Collasse, Lully's most trusted protégé, to have secured the same privilege, especially given his impressive portfolio of court appointments: from 1683 he was one of the four *sous-maîtres* of the Chapelle and, from 1686, both *compositeur de la musique de la chapelle* and *compositeur de la musique de la chambre*.

But, as the *Mercure historique et politique* pointed out after the première in November 1687 of Collasse's faithful completion of Lully's *Achille et Polixène* (only the overture and first act existed), imitation of the master did not necessarily ensure success. The Italian comedians were less circumspect: in their parody, *La plainte de Priam*, Lully's ghost confronts Collasse and the librettist, Jean Galbert de Campistron, with the failure; they in turn blame ambivalence and a decline in taste on the part of opera audiences. In spite of the mixed reception given to *Achille*, Collasse was deeply gratified by the response to *Thétis et Pélée* in 1689. With ballet *entrées*, fresh-sounding recitatives, clear departures from Lullian form (such as the interruption by the chorus of warriors of the prologue's 'Air de la Nuit'), colourful orchestration and a revolutionary second-act tempest, it seemed to launch post-Lullian tragedy in new directions. When, within a month of its première, a performance in the Salle de Comédie at the Grand Trianon was arranged, Collasse must have imagined his future was secure. That it was a remarkable work is reflected in a letter (mentioned above) written 20 years later, in 1709, by Destouches to the Prince of Monaco, in which he referred to the revival he had just attended and the work's undiminished power to dazzle audiences.

Assured of a pension of 100 pistolets and the gift of a house from Lully's will, Collasse presumed, one supposes rightly, that the public would appreciate hearing more unknown 'airs de violon' by the departed Lully, and so included some he apparently salvaged (after Lully had rejected them) in *Les saisons* (1695) – but for the absence of 'modern' characters, the first real *opéra-ballet*. However, its success ignited the jealousy of the Lully family, who successfully instituted a lawsuit to disinherit him. Obviously under pressure, Collasse drew a clear distinction between his music and that of Lully in the preface to the 1696 edition of the ballet:

> The author of the music of this ballet has not judged it appropriate to mix the music of the late Monsieur de Lully with his own . . . He realized that such a *mélange* would distress the family of Monsieur de Lully, to whom he has taken great pains to express (on all occasions that have presented themselves) *marques d'estime* and the respect he has for the memory of this incomparable man.

Unappeased, the Lullys exacted further retribution: a disclaimer inserted in some of the copies of Collasse's ballet *La naissance de Vénus* (1696) informed purchasers that in fact 'almost all the instrumental and some vocal pieces are by Lully'. Collasse's reputation was fatally compromised, and his operas were hissed by their audiences and became juicy carrion for the comedians. Self-evidently more than merely an exponent of the Lullian style, Collasse had inherited a poisoned chalice. Dismissed by his former colleagues as half mad, he turned in desperation to alchemy and ended his life in 1709.

The career of Henry Desmarets provides another cautionary tale. In spite of his propitious connection with Lully and promising talent (an opera and a motet by him had already been performed at Versailles as early as 1682), he never developed into a first-rate composer. When he failed in 1683 to win one of the *sous-maître* posts in the royal chapel, his relative youth was blamed. Without patronage Desmarets was reduced to ghosting motets for the *sous-maître*, Nicolas Coupillet, who forfeited his coveted post when in 1692 he was exposed, after failing to keep up payments to Desmarets. The post might then justifiably have gone to Desmarets had Lalande – no doubt eager to limit the damage caused by the scandal – not blocked it. Desmarets turned to opera, but, despite the warm reception accorded to *Didon* in 1693, his next five operas (perhaps too hastily conceived) proved outright failures.

Seeking solace in love, Desmarets eloped with a young woman to Brussels, an act for which he was condemned to death *in absentia* by a Paris court. Fortunately, a recommendation from a friend, Matho (*maître de chapelle* to the Duke of Burgundy), enabled him to find work at the Spanish court as *surintendant de la musique* to Philip V. In Paris, Matho and one of the Philidors took steps to keep his musical reputation alive. Ballard agreed to print Desmarets' *airs* in his *recueils*, and Campra was secured to complete Desmarets' score of *Iphigénie en Tauride*, which was performed by the Académie in 1704; Philidor printed and distributed his *grand motet Cum invocarem* in 1714. Meanwhile, Desmarets had returned to France in 1707, taking up a post with the Duke of Lorraine. In 1722 he requested and received a royal pardon from the regent, but by then it was too late to rekindle the approbation of the Paris opera public. His application for a post at Versailles, following the death of Lalande in 1726, also came to nothing, and he reluctantly retired to Lorraine.

The only post-Lullian to gain the distinction of having his operas premièred at court belonged to the minor aristocracy, the dashing erstwhile musketeer André Cardinal Destouches, who was destined for many marks of royal favour. Although the protégé of Campra, Destouches was at first, by virtue of his breeding, considered only a talented amateur, but in many ways he became Lully's successor at the Académie and at court. His correspondence reveals a man of uncommon warmth who, despite his success, retained modest expectations for his music.[31]

Thanks to his friendship with Antoine de Grimaldi, Prince of Monaco from 1701, Destouches' *Issé* graced the 1697 royal wedding of the Duke of Burgundy. Beginning in that year, he was accorded the privilege of rehearsing and performing his new operas at the royal *châteaux*; excerpts were given at evening *appartements*. As with Lully, the king made suggestions and, in the case of *Issé*, declared that no music since that of Lully had given him so much pleasure. The result was a temporary turning-point for the waning fortunes of *tragédie en musique*. Both *Amadis de Grèce* (1699), with its chorus of animated statues in the prologue and the *sommeil* that opens Act 1, and his Rococo masterpiece *Omphale* (1701)[32] were also warmly received.

Destouches no doubt savoured the pleasure Louis XIV took in the Carnival performance of *Omphale* at Marly in 1702, but was naturally disappointed the following year when the king failed to attend the performance of *Le Carnaval et la Folie*. Factors other than disaffection contrived to keep the king from this and other performances, including those of Lully's *Atys* and the Duke of Orléans' *Penthée* – namely the death of James II and his own faltering health, which had been exacerbated by the pressures of matters of state. Destouches continued annually to present his new works at Fontainebleau, even though none was ever as successful as the early ones. Even his ultimately highly acclaimed collaboration with Lalande on *Les élémens* (1721–5) was not initially admired and required several revisions.

In a departure from his usual policy of excluding members of the aristocracy from positions of power, the king appointed Destouches to the prestigious post of *inspecteur général* of the Académie Royale de Musique in 1713, a post he was to hold, along with the directorship (only from 1728) until 1730. Court appointments came later: he acquired the post of *surintendant de la musique de la chambre* in 1718 and, after Lalande's death, that of *maître de musique de la chambre* as well. Destouches' appointment to the newly created post of *inspecteur général* was part of the king's larger scheme to revitalize the Académie, which was suffering from low morale and spiralling debt.

The construction of an auxiliary building in the rue St Nicaise known as the 'Magasin' began in 1712, and during the next two years new regulations governing the administration of the Opéra were put into force. The effect was to restore Lullian order: each season was to begin with a new tragedy, followed by revivals, and in the summer another new tragedy, followed by a ballet; unsuccessful works were to be replaced without ado by stock revivals of Lully operas.[33] As in Lullian times, each new work panegyrized the king's pursuit of peace. They included Destouches' *Callirrhoé* (1712), Campra's *Télèphe* (1713), Destouches' *Télémaque* (1714) and Bourgeois' novel *ballet lyrique*, *Le divertissement du roi* (1714).

The king's intervention, so near the end of his life, is evidence of both his enduring vision of the Académie and the frailty of absolutism: his lack of attention to opera in the years after his move to Versailles had led to a decline in standards of performance and decorum. As early as 1694 the *Mercure galant* made public the deploring behaviour of the *siffleurs* who drowned out unpopular opera singers, and in 1698 Dr Lister marvelled why anyone even attended the Opéra:

> There are great numbers of the Nobility that come daily to them,
> and some that can sing them all. And it was one thing, that was
> troublesome to us Strangers, to disturb the Box by these voluntary
> Songs of some parts of the Opera or other. That the Spectators may
> be said to be here as much Actors, as those employed upon the very
> Stage.

Later, in 1732, Voltaire was to observe wryly in a letter to his friend
Pierre Robert le Cornier de Cideville that 'the opera is a public
meeting place where people assemble themselves on certain days,
without knowing why'.

The accepted absence of the king from court *spectacles* (even those
mounted by the dauphin at Fontainebleau), observed by Dangeau as
early as October 1703, also led to a similar decline in attention to
etiquette, according to the Duke of Saint-Simon. Yet, to his dying
day, Louis XIV observed strict routines few others could match.
According to the *Mercure galant*, a week before his death on 1
September 1715, he celebrated his saint's day by listening to the
trumpet and drum fanfare beneath his balcony, the Vingt-quatre
Violons during his *souper* and finally a concert of chamber music
before retiring.

The king was a firm believer in fresh air and exercise. He bravely
endured the clysters, leeches and purges his physicians regularly
visited upon him (Dangeau and Sourches graphically recount their
effects). Though he enjoyed remarkably good health, with age came
infirmities: after the 1686 fistula operation, which occasioned the
thanksgiving celebrations of 1687 so fatal to Lully, Louis XIV found
it difficult to sit very long or walk any distance. By 1688, the attacks
of gout he had been suffering since about 1681 had became quite
intense, confining him to an astonishing variety of wheelchairs, *bar-
ouches* and carriages designed to suit every occasion; and by 1701
(aged 62) he had lost all of his teeth. His stoicism was admirable. He
appeared on the battle front as late as 1693 and was rumoured by the
Duke of Saint-Simon to have fathered children as late as 1705. But
certainly the picture of Louis XIV at Versailles was very different –
and altogether more human – than the glorious image portrayed by
the painter Hyacinthe Rigaud in 1694 (see fig.19 above).

Many factors besides the health of the septuagenarian monarch
contributed to the increasing sobriety at court: the limitations of one
man's rule over half a century, the privations caused by the prolonged war over the Spanish Succession, unseasonable weather, and
contagious diseases (in particular measles and smallpox), which
wiped out two (almost three) generations of legitimate heirs to the
French throne. All plans for expanding the facilities at Versailles,
with the exception of the chapel, were held in abeyance. The lowest

point came in 1709. A terrible frost caused famine and, ultimately, bread riots in Paris. Concern over the growing national debt forced the consignment of royal silver to the Mint. Even the Académie revivals of Lully's *Roland* and *Atys* failed. Then, the French army suffered a terrible defeat at Malplaquet, causing the Princess Palatine ('Madame') to remark that 'Versailles was full of bandages and crutches'. The miseries of war continued for two more years, until the death of Emperor Joseph I in 1711, which paved the way for the historic treaties of Utrecht (1713–15) and peace in Europe.

ESCAPE FROM VERSAILLES

Life at Versailles at the end of the reign bored many of the younger courtiers, and even members of the king's immediate family grew restive. Gradually they spent less and less time there, retreating instead to Paris or their nearby country houses, where they set up their own musical establishments and entertained when and as they wished. At their town houses in Paris, they mixed with society and partook of a wider variety of theatrical and musical fare. Prominent among this set were the dauphin (until his death in 1711), his half-sisters Madame la Duchesse and the Princess of Conti, the Duchess of La Ferté, the Prince of Condé (also known as 'Monsieur le Prince') and, of course, the Duke of Orléans, who from 1692 had made the Palais-Royal his official residence. By 1706 the Duke of Burgundy had stopped attending concerts in accordance with his religious beliefs (he had also sold the jewels he had inherited from his mother and distributed the money among the poor). By contrast, lesser nobles, having contributed much of their wealth to the war efforts, were forced by necessity to marry the daughters of the rich bourgeoisie, which inevitably bound them more closely to Paris. By the autumn of 1714, the *Mercure galant* noted that members of the court living in Paris travelled to Fontainebleau only when the prospect of outdoor *spectacles*, such as those honouring the visiting Elector of Bavaria and Elector of Saxony, justified the trip.

Few hesitated over an invitation to Sceaux, the country residence of the Duke and Duchess of Maine since around the turn of the century. The duke was Madame de Maintenon's favourite among the king's illegitimate children, though his eccentric and headstrong duchess was much frowned upon. Exiled by choice from Versailles, the vivacious and insomniac Duchess of Maine successfully occupied herself by devising exceedingly popular impromptu all-night entertainments in which music figured prominently. At first Matho composed much of the music: in 1706 his *comédie-ballet La Tarentole* was performed before a distinguished audience, which included the dauphin and the dukes of Orléans, Burgundy and Berry. There were many, not least the Duke of Saint-Simon, who strongly disapproved of the extravagance of her parties, which culminated in a series of 16 *spectacles* between 31 July 1714 and 15 May the following year; these came to be known as the 'Grandes Nuits de Sceaux' (chronicled by Abbé Genest in *Les divertissements de Sceaux*, 1725).

About 1708 Jean-Joseph Mouret, newly arrived from Avignon, ambitious, and already as much courted for his charm as for his ability, joined the Maines' service, composing and superintending the performances of ballets, operatic works and cantatas in which he was associated with Marchand, Bernier, Bourgeois and Blamont, who were also nominally in the duchess's employ. Mouret's most important composition for Sceaux was his innovative lyric comedy *Le mariage de Ragonde et de Colin*, performed there in December 1714. By that time Mouret had already begun turning his energies towards Paris, where he was forging links with the Académie. In August the Académie gave the première of *Les festes ou Le triomphe de Thalie*, which Mouret was obliged to dedicate to the Duchess of Maine.[34]

Les festes de Thalie, as the ballet became known, portrayed with verve and charm contemporary French women in a prologue and series of three *entrées* ('La fille', 'La veuve' – later 'La veuve coquette' – and 'La femme'), to which a fourth, 'La Provençale', was later added. Initially it caused a scandal, which was deftly countered in October with the addition of 'un nouvel acte' entitled 'La critique des Festes de Thalie', but it quickly gained the affection of a public weary of tragedy. In this work Mouret took the spirit of Campra's innovations one step further and, with his subsequent appointment by the regent in 1717 as the composer-director of the Nouveau Théâtre Italien, effectively superseded Campra as the establishment's most popular composer of theatre music.[35]

But even Mouret could not effect a renaissance for the *tragédie en musique*, which now suffered virtual eclipse, weakened by poor librettos, cliché music and gestures of desperation; this was exemplified by Louis de Lacoste's *Philomèle* (1705), which depicted taboo themes of incest, infanticide and mass suicide so realistically that members of the first-night audience were said to have panicked.[36] The opera-going public sought refuge in topical comedy and ballet genres, such as Rebel's *Les caractères de la danse* (1715), Montéclair's *opéra-ballet Les festes de l'été* (1716) and Blamont's fashionable (through more conservative) *ballet héroïque* requiring elaborate stage machinery, *Les festes grecques et romaines* (1723).

If the *cabale* liked a first performance, places for subsequent performances were immediately booked. If they smelt a whiff of conservatism, the run could be doomed, as was *Les élémens* in 1721. According to Destouches, it was considered by the public to be too long, too serious (each of the four *entrées* forming a separate *tragédie en musique*) and danced by only 'petits seigneurs'; but, as was often the case when a work failed at the Palais-Royal, the elite Tuileries audience adored Destouches and Lalande's *opéra-ballet*. When Mouret's operas succeeded, as *Pirithoüs* did in 1723, it was in spite of the libretto and because of the lighter elements, such as the *divertissements*, which swayed opinion.

Destouches soldiered on as *inspecteur général*, at first in tandem with a series of *directeurs* and then on his own, until 1730, when he was succeeded by Campra. To raise money, masked balls at the Opéra were inaugurated in 1716 on Mondays, Wednesdays and Saturdays during Carnival, while the *comédiens italiens* (the Nouveau Théâtre Italien), welcomed back to Paris by the regent that year, were allowed to perform there on evenings when there was no opera. In a desperate attempt to enliven the operas themselves, Destouches eventually resorted to interleaving Italian intermezzos ('frenchified' with dances by Mascitti) between the acts and, in 1729, authorized performances of two Italian comedies at the Opéra, which were not very well received.

Although the regent had his own box at the Opéra, which in any event was adjacent to the Palais-Royal, his more enthusiastic patronage of the Opéra-Comique, the Nouvelle Comédie Italienne and the Nouveau Théâtre Italien seriously undermined the stature of the Académie Royale de Musique. When he died, at the end of 1723, his Italian comedians were automatically subsumed as *ordinaires du roi*, and plans to refurbish the Salle de la Comédie at Fontainebleau were set in motion. But while he took many French sopranos as mistresses, he apparently did not otherwise presume to further their careers.

Only months before his death, the regent authorized the issue of passports for Giovanni Bononcini (said to have been offered a post with the regent's last official mistress, Marie Thérèse, Duchess of Falari) and the great Italian singers Francesca Cuzzoni (*c*1698–1770), Margherita Durastanti (*fl* 1700–34), Senesino (*d* 1759), Gaetano Berenstadt (*fl* 1708–34) and G. M. Boschi (1698–1744) to travel from London. Attempts by the regent (and later the Prince of Carignan) to mount genuine Italian opera, as in London, would have undoubtedly failed, since it remained the preserve of connoisseurs.[37]

PARIS DURING THE REGENCY

When in 1715 Philippe, Duke of Orléans, became regent, he moved the court to Paris, installing little Louis XV in the Tuileries palace with an appropriate entourage and himself at the Palais-Royal. The court returned to Versailles only in 1722, when Louis XV came of age. During the Regency, even the annual trips to Fontainebleau were suspended. For the musicians the return to Paris provided a

23. The Regent Philippe of Orléans with the young Louis XV: portrait, French School, early 18th century

welcome respite from travelling to and fro, often spending long periods away from their families. Those who now held posts in both royal *musiques* had hardly more than to cross the rue Saint-Honoré between the Tuileries palace and the Palais-Royal. In addition to the daily regime of chapel and chamber music and evening entertainment, there were official functions, such as the visit in March 1721 of the Turkish ambassador which occasioned a performance of Lully's *Thésée*. For others, there was the Académie, also close at hand, so that most musicians (as the addresses on the title-pages of their music and tutors reveal) lived in the neighbouring *quartiers*.

At first the amusements deemed appropriate for the young Louis XV included exhibitions by fire-eaters, acrobats and *dresseurs d'animaux* – accompanied by violins, to be sure – as well as comedies (which usually employed at least four musicians). In 1718 *ballet de cour* was revived at the Tuileries, enabling the king to learn to dance in the company of his courtiers to music specially composed by Lalande, Destouches and Rebel. Early in 1720 the regent joined his nephew in performing Lalande's *entrées* for Corneille's *L'inconnu* and then, at the end of the year, in Lalande's *Les folies de Cardenio*, which inaugurated the newly renovated Salles des Machines.

Seemingly oblivious to the terrible economic vicissitudes occasioned by the collapse in 1720 of both the banking system devised by the regent's Scottish gambling companion John Law and the 'South Sea Bubble', the court indulged in the annual Carnival pleasures which the diarist Edmond-Jean-François Barbier described on 18 January 1721 as 'magnifique et bien rempli'. The stunning performances that year by the Académie's *première actrice* Marie Antier, particularly in *opéra-ballets* in which the king danced, such as *Les élémens*, won her an appointment as a *musicienne de la chambre du roi*. Johann Christoph Nemeitz, a German visiting Paris at much this time, commented in his memoir *Séjour de Paris* (Leiden, 1727) on the number of excellent concerts that one could attend, especially if one could sing or play. Among those to which he gained entry were series hosted by the Duke d'Aumont, Clérambault, Abbé Grave, Mademoiselle de Maes and the Mesdemoiselles Ecuiers.

The king's recovery from a possibly dangerous illness in the summer of 1721 had occasioned great celebrations, including performances of a *Te Deum* by the musicians of the Sainte-Chapelle and Notre Dame, illuminations after dark and a street concert presented by the Opéra, and an all-comers ball, given by the Comédie Italienne. Afterwards Barbier noted that 'never had health been celebrated to this degree nor so lavishly'. The next important occasion requiring extraordinary musical forces was Louis XV's saint day (since the reign of Louis XIII, 25 August had been traditionally celebrated as the 'fête du roi'), for which this year a Mass by Dornel, specially commissioned by the Académie Française, was performed, followed by a concert, given by the forces of the Académie Royale de Musique, and fireworks. Though he had weathered his ordeal, the king's health, and more important the fate of the throne, now preoccupied those loyal to Louis XIV.

The hastily contrived engagement of the boy king to the five-year-old Princess of Asturia was abandoned in 1722, but not before she had been brought to Paris and made to endure grown-up celebrations in their honour, including a visit – the first for each of them – to the Opéra to see a special performance of Lully's *Phaëton* and attend a ball, at which, according to Barbier, two orchestras of 150 players, set up at opposite ends of the room, performed in alternation, except when the king danced.

Louis XV was crowned at Reims on 25 October 1722, several months in advance of his legal majority. Though few present were probably the wiser, an incident over the music for the service threatened to mar the occasion: the musicians of the *musiques de cour* had

24. *The coronation of Louis XV at Reims Cathedral, 25 October 1722 (musicians from both the Grande Écurie and Musiques de Cour took part in the ceremony): engraving from Antoine Danchet, 'Le sacre de Louis XV, roy de France et de Navarre dans l'église de Reims, le dimanche xxv octobre MDCCXXII' (Paris, 1732)*

prepared Lalande's latest version of his 1684 *Te Deum*, which *surinten-dant* Blamont was to conduct, but a Gregorian plainsong version was substituted at the last moment.[38] The regent had been among those who honoured the king with celebrations in the weeks beforehand, treating him to a 'foire idéale' at Villers-Cotterets (north-east of Paris), where there was a fine Renaissance *château* with gardens by Le Nôtre and a royal hunting-ground. According to the November *Mercure*, singers, dancers and *symphonistes* (including trumpet marine players and 40 *cors de chasse*!) from the Opéra, together with the best Italian comedians, were engaged for the event; Mouret composed the music and Louis-Guillaume Pécourt (?1651–1729) was the choreographer.

Earlier that year, Jean-Philippe Rameau had arrived in Paris, determined to oversee the printing of his 450-page *Traité de l'harmonie*, which was respectfully reviewed in the October-November issue of the *Journal de Trévoux*. Though on his earlier visit (1706–9) he had held organ posts at the Collège Louis-le-Grand and with the Mercedarians and had won a further post as organist at Ste Madeleine-en-la-Cité (a post he was forced to forfeit when he refused to give up the others), he seems not to have sought posts either in Paris churches or at court. It was not an unpropitious moment to seek royal employment, since Lalande was just preparing to shed most of his court responsibilities in favour of a pension and a knighthood. Instead, Rameau chose to collaborate with his fellow *dijonnais* the poet Alexis Piron on music for the fair theatres. It was probably through Piron that he made important friendships with the librettist Louis Fuzelier and the tax farmer and music patron Alexandre-Jean-Joseph Le Riche de la Pouplinière, whose musical establishment he eventually joined.[39]

Couperin had nearly all of his known music printed during the last 20 years of his life (1713–33), including four books of *pièces de clavecin* (1713, 1716–17, 1722, 1730), his treatise *L'art de toucher le clavecin* (1717), his three *Leçon de Ténèbres* (1713–14), and the evocatively titled collections of duo and trio chamber music. These comprised the *Concerts royaux*, which had been performed in the concerts of 'petite musique' during the last months of Louis XIV's life but published only in 1722; a second collection of *concerts* entitled *Les goûts-réünis* (1724); the two substantial apotheosis works honouring Corelli (1724) and Lully (1725); and two publications which may be considered supreme examples of their genres – *Les nations* (1726), comprising sonata-suites (whose gestation spanned more than 30 years) honouring in turn the French, Spanish, Austrians and Italians, and the two sublimely refined suites for bass viol, whose publication in 1728 coincided, perhaps not insignificantly, with the death of Marais. In the preface to *Les goûts-réünis*, Couperin admitted that 'I always admire works of merit, without taking exception to authors or nations'. Writing about music-making in Couperin's era in his *Observations sur la musique, les musiciens, et les instrumens* (1757), Ancelet despaired of 'the endless and exhausting disputes between different partisans of French and Italian Music', asserting that both have their respective merits and that 'one must judge the taste of a musician by the choice of music he performs'.

These attitudes were in concord, broadly, with those of the regent. He preferred private concerts – indeed almost anything private – and in the summer months arranged intimate gatherings of a dozen friends (never including his wife) at Saint-Cloud, where they dined grandly and enjoyed music and fireworks over the Seine. He was likewise entertained: in August 1721, the Marshal d'Estrées gave a dinner party for the regent and his current mistress, Madame d'Averne, at Bagatelle on the edge of the Bois de Boulogne, where they were treated to 'fêtes de musique'. But these events did not go unnoticed by ordinary citizens, who professed to be greatly shocked by what Barbier described as 'the triumph of adultery and vice in public', and the regent's already colourful reputation suffered. The Duke of Saint-Simon, his stalwart friend, understood him better than most:

> Never was there a man born with so many gifts, such facility and eagerness to use them, never one whose private life was so idle, so much given up to dullness and boredom . . . Finally the low and knavish company which he kept, and from among whom he chose those boon companions, whom he openly referred to as his *roués*, drove better men from his side.[40]

On 2 December 1723 the regent died, not wholly unexpectedly, of apoplexy – not in his beloved Paris but at Versailles, where lately he had been compelled to attend the court. During his stewardship he had fought to loosen the bureaucracy of absolutism, attempted to invest his fellow noblemen with power (though they proved themselves no longer fit after generations of idleness), and sought to reform taxation and to institute a banking system. It all came to naught. He compounded these failures by his own sorry legacy, leaving France after eight years of regency morally and spiritually impoverished to an extent not achieved by the wars, famine and epidemics of the previous reign. His finest hours as a patron of music had predated the Regency, during the decades around the turn of the century when he was in his prime and not yet burdened with the conundrums of state, though as caretaker of the throne he did succeed in institutionalizing Italian music and theatre.

The 13-year-old king was taken in tow by the Duke of Bourbon until 1726, when Cardinal Fleury became his first minister. Although Louis XV was quite unformed in his musical preferences (a state of affairs that sadly persisted), a token semblance of tradition, clearly weakened by the tone of the Regency, was maintained at Versailles. Lalande was succeeded in 1723 by *sous-maîtres* Campra, Bernier and Gervais – all of whom owed much to the departed Duke of Orléans – and the ambitious *surintendant* Blamont, variously the protégé of the Duke of Orléans, the Duchess of Maine and Lalande himself. Blamont considered himself Lalande's rightful heir, emboldened by the success in Paris of *Les festes grecques et romaines*, on which he had collaborated with Fuzelier earlier that year. The competitive spirit between members of this quartet, both artistic and administrative, for control of the increasingly infrequent ceremonial occasions must have been predictable from the moment of their appointment.

PUBLIC CONCERTS AND THE DECLINE OF VERSAILLES

Although the court had settled again at Versailles, it was still to Paris that one went to hear new music: *plus ça change*. In addition to Crozat's own private concert series (initiated at the beginning of the Regency), he joined forces with the Marchioness of Prie (the Duke of Bourbon's mistress), together with her circle of friends, who included the Countess d'Evreux, the Marchioness de Castellane and Madame de La Mésangère, to sponsor a subscription concert series at the Tuileries palace. From 1724 the series, in which only professional musicians performed, was known as the Concert Italien. Cuzzoni's appearance in one of the summer concerts that year must have been a *coup*.[41] Encouraged by the popularity of these concerts, Anne Danican Philidor, the son of the royal music librarian André Danican Philidor *l'aîné*, conceived a much grander scheme to create a concert series open to the public during Lent and at other times in the church calendar when opera was not performed. Through his connections (Philidor had served in all branches of the *musiques de cour* and had directed concerts for the Duchess of Maine and Prince of Conti), he secured the use of the Salle des Suisses in the Tuileries palace and the services of the musicians of the Académie and *musiques de cour*.

From its beginning, the Concert Spirituel, as it became known, was well attended, charging an admission of four *livres* per person. Large-scale choral works, especially *grands motets*, were performed along with virtuoso solo and orchestral music. Performers from abroad were attracted and introduced new genres (especially instrumental ones) to Paris audiences. The inaugural concert on 18 March 1725 (Passion Sunday), lasting two hours, included on the programme both French and Italian music: the violinists Guignon and

Anet appeared as soloists, alternating with *grands motets* and instrumental music by Lalande – which became the staple of the series until 1770 – and Corelli's 'Christmas Concerto'. Altogether the performance required 60 musicians. The *Mercure de France*, which reported on each concert, remarked of this historic occasion that 'it would be very difficult to find anywhere else a more perfect combination of singers and players'.

The centrepiece of Le Blanc's *Défense de la basse de viole* (1740) is a dramatization of the struggle for supremacy between traditional French and progressive Italian music at the newly created Concert Spirituel. He employed a heady mixture of mythological and literary allusions as scenery, and musical instruments as characters: Lady Viola da Gamba is made to defend herself against the ambitious Sultan Violin and his upstart minion, the Violoncello. At issue is not so much their relative powers to delight the sensibilities or move the spirit as whose tone carried best in a public concert hall: 'The Lords and Ladies who had come to the concert, enjoying the quarrel, gave ear to it as willingly as they would have to the music'. When, after initial representations, the ladies appeared to be siding with the viol, the violin took the offensive. But even while the final judgment, diplomatically praising the viol as a chamber instrument and deeming the violin better suited to concert halls, was being delivered, the ladies were stifling their boredom caused by the repetitious ornamentation of Somis and Geminiani, only to be revived by the suitably elegant and cosmopolitan flute playing of Blavet. The viol, armed with dances and *pièces de caractère*, apparently retained its place at court until the middle of the century, thanks first to the patronage of the regent and then of the king, both of whom, Le Blanc assures us, possessed first-hand knowledge of the instrument.

After the *débacle* of the first royal engagement, the Duke of Bourbon (abetted by the Marchioness of Prie) chose pragmatically on behalf of the king, seeking not to disturb the delicately poised relationships between the Princes of the Blood nor to introduce any substantial foreign influence, with the ultimate intention of securing the succession by means of an heir at the earliest possible date. The new queen, Marie-Catherine-Sophie-Félicité Leszczińska, was seven years Louis' senior and, as the daughter of the exiled Polish King Stanislaus, brought neither wealth nor power to the marriage. The wedding took place on 4 September 1725 at Fontainebleau in the Chapelle de la Trinité, not without incident. The royal congregation had assembled and the *sous-maître* Bernier was in his place, preparing to conduct his scheduled *Te Deum*, when *surintendant* Blamont, flaunting decency and decorum, challenged him for the baton. Eventually the diplomatic remonstrations of the Duke of Mortemart and the Bishop of Rennes persuaded Bernier to step down, but in the rush belatedly to begin the service Blamont was forced to conduct Bernier's music, no doubt to his discomfiture and the amusement of the musicians.[42] Afterwards, the royal couple were entertained by *musique en canal* as they strolled in the gardens, an indoor concert and two Molière plays. The celebrations, spanning the entire *voyage* of 1725, also included performances of a *divertissement* by Blamont, *Le retour des dieux sur la terre*, and a new *opéra-ballet* by Destouches, *Les stratagèmes de l'Amour*.

Despite Le Blanc's assertions to the contrary, Louis XV's ambivalence towards music seems clear enough. Though his parents, the Duke and Duchess of Burgundy, had been ardent patrons of music, they died before imparting any influence to him. According to Barbier, the regent tried repeatedly to interest him in opera, but Louis XV was by all accounts a shy and indecisive monarch who daily sought refuge from his people and difficult matters of state by hunting in the relative solitude of his royal preserves. On the rare occasion when he did show interest, it was after a day's hunting and not without some form of protest; during the five-hour performance of Campra's *Tancrède* on 30 March 1729 he had 300 soldiers stand guard. He had little in common with his wife, who was an ardent music lover and a harpsichordist. To her distress, the king maintained a succession of official mistresses, pre-eminent among them Madame de Pompadour, herself a talented actress with musical pretensions, and he kept a private brothel at the nearby Parc aux Cerfs.

The queen lived quietly and dutifully bore him 11 children (seven survived), in whom she took pleasure in instilling something of her passion for music. Soon after settling at Versailles, she requested there be 'concerts chez la reine'. Destouches and Blamont took on this task and organized frequent concerts of a distinctly conservative vein; the memoirs of the Duke of Luynes, who was a close confident of the queen, chronicle concert performances of extracts from operas and Concert Spirituel programmes. Because of the minimal demands made by the king on the *musiques de cour*, there was no need to set up a separate musical household. Although her *accouchements* sometimes delayed her departure on the annual *voyage* to Fontainebleau, it was not until the beginning of October 1728 that she made her first visit to Paris, where, according to Barbier, 'she viewed with astonishment the crowds of people'.

LES GOÛTS-RÉUNIS

In 1726, the year in which the style-conscious Quantz was drawn to Paris, the 'reforms' propounded for so long in chamber music by Couperin manifested themselves in the theatres. Quantz arrived in

August, the month in which the Italian comedians Dominique, Romagnesi and Riccoboni *le fils*, collaborating with Mouret, gave the première of *Les comédiens esclaves* at the Nouveau Théâtre Italien. In this, their own version of 'les goûts-réünis', dances and other music were interleaved between the three acts, each cast in a differently mixed genre, the first in a *goût pastoral*, the second a *tragédie burlesque* and the third emulating *opéra comique*. Such was its popularity that it became part of the company's permanent repertory. The revival in 1726 of Rebel's *Les caractères de la danse* – choreographed 'symphonies' originally composed in 1715 for the acclaimed Académie dancer Madame Françoise Prévost (1680–1741) and popularized by her graceful pupil Marie Sallé (at the Foire St Laurent in 1718, in London in 1725, and at the Opéra in 1729, when she and her partner abandoned their masks) – inaugurated a new era of solo dancing which immediately made a cult figure of the débutante Marie-Anne Cupis de Camargo, also a pupil of Prévost.

The first evidence of what was to become a highly successful collaboration between the violinists François Rebel (1701–75), son of Jean-Féry Rebel, and François Francoeur *le cadet* (1698–1787) was presented at the Opéra in 1726: *Pyrame et Thisbé* was a reform *tragédie en musique*, which, apart from the recitatives and the chorus that opens the prologue, made few concessions to Lullian traditions. The textures are italianate, with elaborate vocal lines, instrumental obbligatos and lively running and arpeggiated basses. Quantz must surely have attended the performances, which began on 15 October, and have enjoyed the prominence Rebel and Francoeur accorded to the flutes.[43]

At the Concert Spirituel Quantz would have heard Blavet perform flute concertos and Marie Antier, Claude-Louis-Dominique de Chassé de Chinais (1699–1786), Marie Pélissier (1707–49) and perhaps even Catherine-Nicole Le Maure (1704–86) – who made her début there in March 1727, the month Quantz departed – sing in motets by Lalande, who had died just before Quantz arrived. Whether he met Crozat or the Prince of Carignan and attended glittering concerts in their homes or, for that matter, any of the amateur concerts of the society of Mélophilètes (patronized by the Prince of Conti, who died a few months later), is less certain; he may well have paid calls on Marais, Couperin, Destouches, Mouret, Montéclair or Rameau. He did hear and later praise the playing of professional musicians such as the flautist Jacques-Christophe Naudot (*c*1690–1762), the viol players Forqueray and Roland Marais (*b* 1680) and the violinists Anet and Guignon.

Philidor's last brainchild, the Concert Français,[44] was probably conceived after Quantz's return to Dresden. It provided a venue for the performance of concertos, solo motets, cantatas and *cantatilles*, sung by some of the best Académie singers, notably Antier and Le Maure. The repertory was predominantly French, though not exclusively so, and competed with the more parochial Concert Italien for its audiences. Like its rival, the Concert Français took place twice a week at the Tuileries palace. For a time the concerts went well, owing to astute programming (the repertory was steeped in familiar favourites such as Clérambault's *Orphée*), but the final concert, on 2 November 1733, closed ceremoniously with Lalande's *De profundis*. As with the failure of the aristocratic Titon du Tillet to garner support for his retrospective literary and musical Parnassus through the publication in 1727 of his preliminary *Description du Parnasse François*, the predictable charms of the Concert Français gradually bored a public which was growing steadily more outward-looking. The Concert Spirituel succeeded because it featured the best of the Académie singers and promoted new and often foreign virtuoso instrumentalists, who performed their latest concertos, setting them against familiar grandiose French choral repertory which provided continuity and effectively framed the concerts.

In attendance at these and other concerts was the young La Pouplinière,[45] who had retired at the age of 28 from the Mousquetaires to take up the lucrative appointment of a *fermier général*. During the 1720s he became an intimate of the Crozat family, near whom he lived and through whom he developed a passionate love of the arts. His progress as a patron was spurred on by his rivalry with another tax farmer, the powerful Prince of Carignan, Victor-Amédée-Joseph of Savoy, who during the 1730s served as the *inspecteur de l'Opéra* and whose nearby home at the Hôtel de Soissons during those years was the scene of countless celebrated concerts, many of them dress rehearsals for imporant new Académie productions. Writing to the Prince of Monaco on 6 June 1730, Destouches described a concert of the latest Italian music *chez* Carignan, performed by six Italian and four French musicians, who, to the general amazement of all, surpassed the Italians. He attributed their success to the fact that, whereas anyone could play Italian music, it required taste and experience to perform in the French style: 'un capucin est plus aisé à peindre qu'une jolie femme'.[46]

Rameau seems to have enjoyed some sort of special status in the prince's establishment in the months immediately following the triumph of *Hippolyte et Aricie* in 1733, before taking up a more permanent appointment in 1736 with La Pouplinière.[47] Carignan numbered among his personal musicians such luminaries as Blavet, Anet, Guignon and Antier, whom the prince claimed as his mistress. It was over the affections of Antier that the two *mélomanes* crossed swords in 1727: La Pouplinière, discovered with her by Carignan *in flagrante delicto*, gracefully retired – not without some kudos – first to Provence and then to eastern France and the Low Countries, occupying himself with compiling a *Journal du voyage de Hollande*. On his return to Paris in 1730, La Pouplinière began attracting intermingling circles of writers, philosophers, actors, painters and musicians to his home in the rue Neuve des Petits-Champs. His mistress from about 1734, Thérèse Boutinon Deshayes (who later became his wife), studied the harpsichord with Rameau and would have encouraged Rameau's appointment, though La Pouplinière would, in any event, have gained great satisfaction from having lured Rameau away from Carignan.

Rameau must have aspired to be an opera composer after visiting Paris in 1706–7. He undoubtedly attended performances of Marais' *Alcyone* and would have been greatly influenced by its pervasive chamber-music style, its rustic effects and the extraordinary drama of the storm. Certainly, Rameau considered his cantatas from the 1720s and his contributions to the *foire* productions as his apprenticeship, and by 1727 had begun searching for a suitable literary collaborator. He immediately encountered reluctance, in part because of his growing reputation as a theorist: in 1726 he had published his seminal *Nouveau système de musique théorique*, which temporarily overshadowed his accomplishments as a composer. Among those who declined to work with him was Destouches' cousin La Motte, to whom Rameau afterwards wrote in 1727, imploring him to make enquiries about the reception of his cantatas and incidental music for the Théâtre Italien:

> You will then see that I am not a novice in the art and that it is not obvious that I make a great display of learning in my compositions, where I seek to hide art by very art; for I consider only people of taste and not at all the learned, since there are many of the former and hardly any of the latter.[48]

Fortunately, the discerning Simon-Joseph Pellegrin agreed to collaborate with Rameau, who approached him after hearing *Jephté* (1732), on which Pellegrin had collaborated with Montéclair. Rameau had doubtless known Montéclair for many years, and in 1729 and 1730 they had been involved in a lively exchange in the *Mercure* regarding Rameau's theory of the *basse fondamentale*. Rameau must have taken a keen interest in the music of *Jephté*, whose revolutionary scoring – particularly the imaginative deployment of instruments and choirs on and off stage – demonstrably influenced *Hippolyte et Aricie*. *Jephté*, like Charpentier's privately performed sacred opera *David et Jonathas* of more than 40 years earlier, was based on a biblical text. Montéclair and Pellegrin's foray into public 'sacred opera', and even the ill-fated *Samson*[49] of Rameau and Voltaire, closely parallel the critical juncture in Handel's career, at exactly the same date, when he began turning from Italian opera to English oratorio.

Jephté was rapturously hailed at its first performance on 28 February 1732, in which Antier (whose career had suffered little from the distractions of her affairs with tax farmers), Le Maure and La Camargo all took part. The unsuccessful intervention of the Archbishop of Paris only served to fuel its already well deserved popularity. Voltaire was among those who had reservations: writing to Cideville on 8 March 1732, a week after the première, he expressed anger that sacred subjects did not enjoy the same success at the Opéra that profane subjects did at the Comédie, while admitting that he preferred the depraved morals of the public to their scruples: 'I very humbly beg the pardon of the *Old Testament* if it bored me at the Opéra'.[50] The following spring, the Concert Spirituel paid Montéclair a rare compliment by including in the programme for 2 April a *Pange lingua* set to the music of 'Nous vivons dans l'innocence' from Act 4 of *Jepthé*. Montéclair's opera was revived in Paris seven times in ten years and performed four times at Versailles.

Voltaire, best known to us by his monumental *Siècle de Louis XIV* (which he began assembling in 1733), had contemplated writing an opera libretto as early as 1723. The wake of controversy following the première of *Hippolyte et Aricie* on 1 October 1733 stirred his enthusiasm and his disdain – for Voltaire was an exceedingly complex, not to say vain, character. He wrote to Cideville: 'The music is by someone called Rameau, who has the misfortune to know more about music than Lully. He's a pedant in music: he's meticulous and tiresome'.[51] Nevertheless, while Rameau was still associated with the powerful Prince of Carignan, Voltaire agreed to collaborate on *Samson*. However, his correspondence reveals him to be not remotely conciliatory enough to accommodate Rameau's views on the relative importance of music and text. While Acts 3 and 5 were rehearsed in 1734, any plans to mount the work at the Opéra were abandoned.

Fortunately, Rameau's collaboration with Pellegrin in 1733 had a quite different outcome. D'Aquin, for whom Rameau was 'l'Orphée de nos jours', admired Montéclair's *Jephté*, which he felt could not have been performed in Lully's time. He observed, however, that *Hippolyte et Aricie* was even more challenging and that 'day by day we make new progress'. For many, *Hippolyte et Aricie* became the most important French opera of the eighteenth century, not least for its beauty and craftsmanship.

EPILOGUE

The death of Couperin *le Grand* in 1733, the year of *Hippolyte et Aricie*, like that of Lully, serves as a convenient marker within the larger period of French history known as the Ancien Régime. As with 1687, or any other date, the death of one man could not stem the tide of old practices and irrelevancies, enabling a pristine new era to be ushered in. Indeed, the mixtures of old and new, foreign and indigenous, are what enrich this particular period of music history and thus should be neither suppressed nor regularized. Such writers as Le Cerf, Titon du Tillet, Voltaire and D'Aquin, like musicians such as Charpentier, Couperin, Destouches, Montéclair and Rameau, were deeply aware that the years expressed in musical historiography as the Lullian and Rococo eras were unprecedented, perhaps never to be equalled, in the life of French culture.

NOTES

[1] See A. Ducrot, 'Les représentations de l'Académie royale de musique à Paris au temps de Louis XIV (1671–1715)', *RMFC*, x (1970), 19–55; H. Lagrave, *Le théâtre et le public à Paris de 1715 à 1750* (Paris, 1972); L. E. Brown, *The tragédie lyrique of André Campra and his Contemporaries* (diss., U. of North Carolina, 1978); C. Wood, *Jean-Baptiste Lully and his Successors: Music and Drama in the tragédie en musique 1673–1715* (diss., U. of Hull, 1981); J. de La Gorce, 'L'Opéra et son public au temps de Louis XIV', *Bulletin de la Société de l'histoire de Paris et de l'Isle-de-France*, cviii (1981), 27–46; repr. in *The Garland Library of the History of Western Music*, xi (New York, 1986); R. Fajon, *L'opéra à Paris du Roi Soleil à Louis le Bien-Aimé* (Geneva, 1984); S. Pitou, *The Paris Opéra: an Encyclopedia of Operas, Ballets, Composers and Performers* (Westport, CT, 1983–5); J. de La Gorce, *L'Opéra à Paris au temps de Louis XIV: histoire d'un théâtre* (Paris, 1992); see also *Grove 0*. See also S. Milliot and J. de La Gorce, *Marin Marais* (Paris, 1991), 154–262: Marais' *Alcyone* (1706) was among the most successful post-Lullian operas, in part because of the tempest scene (making effective use of the extremes of range provided by double basses and violins), which was incorporated into a 1707 revival of Lully's *Alceste* and quoted by Campra in *Les festes vénitiennes* (1710).

[2] *F-Pn* MS 6542, no.173, f.260, attributed to Nodot; H. Prunières, 'Le triomphe de Lully aux Champs-Elysées', *ReM*, vi/3 (1925), 92–105.

[3] An echo of this is to be found in J. L. Le Cerf de La Viéville, *Comparaison de la musique italienne et de la musique françoise* (Brussels, 1704–6), ii, 128, writing about Lully's rehearsal method: 'It is true that more than once in his life he broke a violin on the back of him who failed to followed his lead. The rehearsal finished, Lully called him, paid him thrice over for his violin and took him to dinner'.

[4] M. Brenet, *Les concerts en France sous l'ancien régime* (Paris, 1900), 165.

[5] E. Titon du Tillet: *Le Parnasse François* (Paris, 1732). See also J. Colton, *The Parnasse François: Titon du Tillet and the Origins of the Monument to Genius* (New Haven and London, 1979); J. A. Sadie, 'Parnassus Revisited: the Musical Vantage Point of Titon du Tillet', *Jean-Baptiste Lully and the Music of the French Baroque: Essays in Honor of James R. Anthony* (Cambridge, 1989), 131–57; Titon du Tillet's main biographical entries on musicians have been extracted and published separately by M. F. Quignard in *Evrard Titon du Tillet: vies des musiciens et autres joueurs d'instruments du règne de Louis le grand* (Paris, 1991).

[6] A. Cohen and J. A. Sadie, 'Le Cerf de La Viéville, Jean Laurent'; 'Raguenet, François', *Grove 0*.

[7] L. Sawkins, 'For and Against the Order of Nature', *EM*, xv (1987), 315–24. Several other court castratos sang at the Concert Spirituel, including Francisco Antonio ['Francisque'] La Fornara (*d* 1781) in 1727, and later Antonio Albanese (1729–1800), whose 42 performances (1753–64) included the Paris première of Pergolesi's *Stabat mater*.

[8] E. Forster, *A Woman's Life in the Court of the Sun King: Letters of Leselotte von der Pfalz, 1652–1722* [Elisabeth Charlotte, Duchess of Orléans] (Baltimore and London, 1984).

[9] H. Le Blanc, *Défense de la basse de viole contre les entreprises du violon et les prétentions du violoncelle* (Amsterdam, 1740), 96; trans. B. Garvey Jackson, *Journal of the Viola da Gamba Society of America*, xi (1974), 31. See also L. de La Laurencie, 'Un musicien piémontais en France au XVIIIe

siècle: Jean-Pierre Guignon, dernier "Roy des violons"', *RMI*, xviii (1911), 711; M. Pincherle, 'Jean-Pierre Guignon et la morale', *Monde musicale* (1926); repr. in *Feuillets d'histoire du violon* (Paris, 1927), 40.

[10] J.-B. de La Borde, *Essai sur la musique ancienne et moderne* (Paris, 1780), iii; 129; E. Preussner, *Die musikalischen Reisen des Herrn von Uffenbach: aus einem Reisetagebuch des Johann Friedrich A. von Uffenbach aus Frankfurt a. M. 1712–1716* (Kassel and Basle, 1949); W. Braun, 'Lully und die französische Musik im Spiegel der Reisenbeschreibungen', *Jean-Baptiste Lully: Saint-Germain-en-Laye and Heidelberg 1987*, 271–85.

[11] These were not the first performances in the Low Countries: Lully's operas had already been given in Brussels and Antwerp as early as 1682 and in Amsterdam in 1687. See C. B. Schmidt, 'The Geographical Spread of Lully's Operas during the Late Seventeenth and Early Eighteenth Centuries: New Evidence from the Livrets', *Jean-Baptiste Lully and the Music of the French Baroque*, 183–211; F. Noske, 'L'influence de Lully en Hollande (1670–1700)', *Jean-Baptiste Lully: Saint-Germain-en-Laye and Heidelberg 1987*, 591–8.

[12] H. Schneider, *Der Rezeption der Opern Lullys im Frankreich des Ancien Régime* (Tutzing, 1982).

[13] Y. de Brossard, *Sébastien de Brossard: théoricien et compositeur: encyclopédiste et maître de chapelle 1655–1730* (Paris, 1987).

[14] Trans. H. W. Hitchcock. See also H. W. Hitchcock, *Marc-Antoine Charpentier: catalogue raisonné* (Paris, 1982), 360–62; H. W. Hitchcock, 'Marc-Antoine Charpentier', *The New Grove French Baroque Masters* (London, 1986), 79–81; C. Cessac, *Marc-Antoine Charpentier* (Paris, 1988), 379–404; H. W. Hitchcock, *Marc-Antoine Charpentier* (Oxford, 1990), 4.

[15] While in Poland Anet very probably met the future king, Stanislaus Leszcziński, whose daughter Marie became the consort of Louis XV; later, in 1737, Anet took up the post of first violinist at his exiled court in Lunéville. See Antoine, 'Note sur les violinistes Anet', *RMFC*, ii (1961–2), 81–93.

[16] M.-T. Bouquet, 'Quelques relations musicales franco-piémontaises au XVIIe et au XVIIIe siècles', *RMFC*, x (1970), 5–18.

[17] M. Le Moël, 'Chez l'illustre Certain', *RMFC*, ii (1961–2), 71–9; P. Ranum, 'Mr de Lully en trio: Etienne Loulié, the Foucaults and the Transcription of the Works of Jean-Baptiste Lully (1673–1702)', *Jean-Baptiste Lully: Saint-Germain-en-Laye and Heidelberg 1987*, 309–30. In 1702 Ballard's edition of *Les Fragments de Monsieur de Lully* (a ballet completed by Campra) includes a report on the 'Etat des opéras en musique par Monsieur de Lully', dividing them into three categories: those that had never been issued, those out of print and those that could still be purchased unbound; it goes on to state that, other than the 'Fragments', none of Lully's 23 ballets had ever been printed, nor his 'Elévations'. See also J. R. Anthony, 'Towards a Principal Source for Lully's Court Ballets: Foucault vs Philidor', *RMFC*, xxv (1987), 77–104.

[18] J. A. Sadie, *The Bass Viol in French Baroque Chamber Music* (Ann Arbor, 1980).

[19] Trans. from D. Tunley, *The Eighteenth-Century French Cantata* (London, 1974), 15.

[20] J. A. Sadie, '*Musiciennes* of the Ancien Régime', *Women Making Music*, ed. J. Bowers and J. Tick (Urbana and Chicago, 1986), 191–223.

[21] After Lully, the first French musicians to be painted include Marais, André Danican Philidor (*c*1647–1730), Rebel, Marchand, Louis and Nicolas Hotteterre, La Barre, Couperin, Lalande, Campra and, later, Rameau and Jean-Baptiste-Antoine Forqueray (1699–1782). See J. Huskinson, 'Les ordinaires de la Musique du roi, Michel de La Barre, Marin Marais et les Hotteterre d'après un tableau du XVIIe siècle', *RMFC*, xvii (1977), 15–28. Couperin was admitted to the order of Latran, Campra became a Chevalier de Saint-Lazare, and, beginning with Lalande in 1722, musicians (including Blamont and Rameau) were admitted to the exclusive order of the Chevaliers de Saint-Michel; Rameau was granted letters of nobility in 1764.

[22] Milliot and La Gorce, *Marin Marais*, 130–32, 136–9; J. Clark, 'Les Folies Françoises', *EM*, viii (1980), 163–9; W. Mellers, *François Couperin and the French Classical Tradition* (London, 1950; rev. 1987), 380–467; J. R. Stevens, 'The Meanings and Uses of *Caractère* in Eighteenth-Century France', *French Musical Thought, 1600–1800* (Ann Arbor, 1989), 23–52. See also C. Girdlestone, *Jean Philippe Rameau: his Life and Work* (New York, 1957; rev., enlarged 1969), appx B, 569–603.

[23] R. McQuaide, *The Crozat Concerts 1720–1727: a Study of Concert Life in Paris* (diss., New York U., 1978). See also Brenet, *Les concerts en France*, 160–63.

[24] M. Le Moël, 'Un foyer d'italianisme à la fin du XVIIe siècle: Nicolas Mathieu, curé de Saint-André-des-Arts', *RMFC*, iii (1963), 43–8; A. Cohen, 'The Ouvrard-Nicaise Correspondence (1663–93)', *ML*, lvi (1975), 356–63; W. Witzenmann, 'Sébastien de Brossard als Carissimi-Sammler', *Mf*, xxxv (1982), 255–62.

[25] Trans. from Hitchcock, *Charpentier* (1990), 5. See also M. Brenet, *Les musiciens de la Sainte-Chapelle du Palais* (Paris, 1921), and Cessac, *Charpentier*, 405–18.

[26] *F-Pn* Chansonnier Maurepas, 9 (1697), f.269.

[27] *Défense*. Le Blanc (also an *abbé*, Doctor of Law and amateur viol player) was forced to retire temporarily to Flanders in 1723, when he might have had time to write his discursive *Défense* before being rehabilitated in 1726; his sojourn there might explain why the *Défense* was subsequently published, albeit posthumously (Le Blanc died in 1728), in Brussels.

[28] T. Lavallée, *Madame de Maintenon et la maison royale de St-Cyr (1686–1793)* (Paris, 1862); M. Bert, 'La musique à la maison royale de Saint-Louis de Saint-Cyr', *RMFC*, iii (1963), 55–71; iv (1964), 127–31; v (1965), 91–125.

[29] B. Coeyman, *The Stage Works of Michel-Richard Delalande in the Musical-Cultural Context of the French Court, 1680–1726* (diss., City U., New York, 1987); P. F. Rice, *The Performing Arts at Fontainebleau from Louis XIV to Louis XVI* (Ann Arbor, 1989).

[30] *Historical Memoirs of the Duc de Saint-Simon*, ed. and trans. L. Norton (London, 1967), i, 160.

[31] Raguenet (1705, p.127) and Le Cerf (i, p.136) crossed swords over the latter's uncompromising assessment of Destouches as a musically illiterate enthusiast: 'M. des Touches est saisi de la fureur de faire des Opéra; il produit des Simphonies qu'il ne sauroit même noter. C'est un homme qui ne sait ni lire ni écrire, & qui fait un Livre admirable'.

[32] *Omphale* later became the subject of the 'Querelle des Bouffons', which was preceded by F. W. von Grimm's *Lettre sur Omphale* (Paris, 1752); see P.-M. Masson, 'La "Lettre sur *Omphale*" (1752)', *RdM*, xxvii (1945), 1–19.

[33] L. Rosow, 'From Destouches to Bertin: Editorial Responsibility at the Paris Opera', *JAMS*, xl (1987), 285–309.

[34] R. Viollier, *Jean-Joseph Mouret: le musicien des grâces 1682–1730* (Paris, 1950), 45–59; see also F. Moreau, 'Une oeuvre oubliée: l'Impromptu de Villers-Cotterêts', *Jean Joseph Mouret et le théâtre de son temps* (Aix-en-Provence, 1982), 39–58.

[35] From 1717 there was no love lost between the Duchess of Maine and the Duke of Orléans – not merely because she lost Mouret's services to the regent's comedians but, even more important, because of his role in depriving her husband of a place in the order of succession to the throne.

[36] T. Raimond, *Lettre critique sur Philomèle, tragédie* (Paris, 1705); C. Masson, 'Journal du Marquis de Dangeau, 1684–1720', *RMFC*, ii (1961–2), entry for 19 Nov 1705; Fajon, *L'Opéra à Paris*, 192–4.

[37] M. Barthélemy, 'L'Académie Royale de Musique et l'opéra italien de Londres en 1723', *RBM*, x (1956), 161–2; L. Lindgren, 'Parisian Patronage of Performers from the Royal Academy of Musick (1719–1728)', *ML*, lviii (1977), 4–28; K. Vlaardingerbroek, 'Faustina Bordoni applauds Jan Alensoon: a Dutch Music-lover in Italy and France in 1723–4', *ML*, lxxii (1991), 538–9.

[38] J. E. Morby, 'The Great Chapel-Chamber Controversy', *MQ*, lviii (1972), 386.

[39] G. Sadler, 'Rameau, Piron and the Paris Fair Theatres', *Soundings*, iv (1974), 13–29.

[40] *Historical Memoirs*, ii, 426–38.

[41] A reference to Cuzzoni's performance of a psalm setting by Bononcini at Fontainebleau on 8 Sept 1724 appears in *Journal et mémoires de Mathieu Marais . . . sur la Régence et le règne de Louis XV (1715–1737)*, ed. Lescure (Paris, 1863), iii, 91–2.

[42] Morby, 'The Great Chapel-Chamber Controversy', 387–8; Rice, *The Performing Arts at Fontainebleau*, 135–6.

[43] Rebel and Francoeur (both in their early twenties) accompanied General Bonneval to Prague for the coronation of Charles VI in 1723, when they would have attended the performance of Fux's *Costanza e Fortezza* and possibly made the acquaintance of Quantz, C. H. Graun (1703/4–1759), Antonio Caldara (*c*1670–1736) and J. D. Zelenka (1679–1745).

[44] D. Tunley, 'Philidor's "Concerts français"', *ML*, xlvii (1966), 130–34; Tunley, *The Eighteenth-Century French Cantata*, appx B.

[45] G. Cucuel, *La Pouplinière et la musique de chambre au XVIIIe siècle* (Paris, 1913).

[46] Quoted from A. Tessier, 'Correspondence d'André Cardinale des Touches et du Prince Antoine Ier de Monaco', *ReM*, viii/2 (1926), 97–114; viii/4 (1927), 107–17, 209–24.

[47] G. Sadler, 'Patrons and Pasquinades: Rameau in the 1730s', *JRMA*, cxiii (1988), 314–34.

[48] Trans. from Girdlestone, *Jean-Philippe Rameau*, 10.

[49] C. Girdlestone, 'Voltaire, Rameau et Samson', *RMFC*, vi (1966), 133–43; C. Kintzler, 'Rameau et Voltaire: les enjeux théoriques d'une collaboration orageuse', *RdM*, lxvii (1981), 139–68.

[50] *Oeuvres complètes de Voltaire*, xxiii: *Correspondence*, i (Paris, 1880), 248.
[51] Trans. from Sadler, 'Patrons and Pasquinades', 316.

BIBLIOGRAPHICAL NOTE

General

To approach the music of the era 1687–1733 it is necessary first of all to master the life and times of Louis XIV, who reigned from 1660 until his death in 1715, as well as that of his *maître de musique extraordinaire* Jean-Baptiste Lully, whose death in 1687 marks the starting-point of this essay. In F. Bluche's *Louis XIV* (trans. M. Greengrass, Oxford, 1990) we have an important and eminently human biography of the king; in P. Burke's *The Fabrication of Louis XIV* (New Haven and London, 1992) we learn how his public image was crafted; but a balanced, in-depth study of Lully has yet to appear. For two decades our view of this era has been emphatically influenced by the historian R. Isherwood's brilliantly conceived *Music in the Service of the King: France in the Seventeenth Century* (Ithaca, 1973), which effectively bridges the chasm between monarch and first musician; the chapter on 'The End of the Reign' is particularly apposite here. The court diaries of the Marquis de Dangeau (*Journal de la cour de Louis XIV*) and Marquis de Sourches (*Mémoires sur la règne de Louis XIV*) and reports in the *Mercure* all greatly add to our knowledge of music-making in Paris and at the court at Versailles.

Important perspectives on the interregnum between Louis XIV and Louis XV, a historical period too often glossed over, may be acquired from J. H. Shennan's monograph *Philippe, Duke of Orléans: Regent of France 1715–1723* (London, 1979), J. C. Petitfils's *Le Régent* (Paris, 1986) and L. Norton, ed. and trans., *Historical Memoirs of the Duke of Saint-Simon* (London, 1967; in three vols., covering the period 1691 to 1723). A. Tessier's edition of the correspondence between Destouches and the Prince of Monaco (1709–31; *ReM*, viii, 1926–7) addresses musical matters almost exclusively, while the more general memoirs of Mathieu Marais (ed. M. de Lescure, 1863), covering 1715 to 1737, and Edmond-Jean-François Barbier (pubd 1866), which take up where Saint-Simon's leave off, are also well worth consulting. The unprecedented biographical detail and rich anecdotage contained in E. Titon du Tillet's *Le Parnasse François* (Paris, 1732) and L. D'Aquin de Château-Lyon's *Siècle littéraire de Louis XV, ou Lettres sur les hommes célèbres* (Amsterdam, 1753) underscore the soaring status of musicians during the era. A historical overview may usefully be gleaned from A. Cobban's *A History of Modern France*, i: *1715–1799* (Harmondsworth, 3/1984), while *A New History of French Literature*, ed. D. Hollier (Cambridge, MA, and London, 1989) provides valuable, up-to-date summaries of the literary issues and documents that often affected composers and inspired parallels in the musical literature.

No musically minded student of the post-Lullian era will want to be without J. R. Anthony's pioneering survey *French Baroque Music from Beaujoyeulx to Rameau* (London, 1974, 2/1978; enlarged Fr. trans., 1981), nor indeed the trusty *New Grove French Baroque Masters* (London, 1986), to which Professor Anthony generously contributed. The work of an older generation of French scholars – Brenet (Marie Bobiller), Borrel, Cucuel, Ecorcheville, Lajarte, La Laurencie, Masson, Pincherle, Prunières, Quittard, Tessier and, more recently, Barthélemy, Dufourcq, Launay, Lesure and Viollier – continue to reward study. Details of the lives of the musicians, their librettists and patrons are to be found in the long-awaited *Dictionnaire de la musique en France aux xviie et xviiie siècles* (Paris, 1992), edited by Marcelle Benoit, in *Grove 6* and in J. A. Sadie's more concise, gazetteer-style *Companion to Baroque Music* (London, 1990). A. P. de Mirimonde's *L'iconographie musicale sous les rois Bourbons* (2 vols., Paris,

1975–7) elegantly dresses their profiles, and to his commentary may be added the broader views of A. Blunt's *Art and Architecture in France* (Harmondsworth, 1953) and M. Levey's *Rococo to Revolution: Major Trends in Eighteenth-Century Painting* (London, 1966). The continuing, luxuriant flowering of recordings by period specialists has greatly increased our familiarity with their music.

Source material

We are remarkably, even unprecedentedly, well endowed with source materials for what is often called the French Classical era, thanks in no small part to the efforts of François Lesure, who facilitated the publication by Minkoff and others (notably Slatkine and Pendragon) of superbly produced facsimile editions of manuscript and engraved musical scores, contemporary treatises and commentary – precious among them F. Raguenet's *Paralèle des italiens et des français en ce qui regarde la musique et les opéra* (Paris, 1732).

The painstaking archival work inspired by Norbert Dufourcq has yielded a rich harvest of extracts from royal and municipal records, journals and memoirs, many of which were published by the Parisian firm of A. & J. Picard, separately and between the covers of the now sadly discontinued *Recherches sur la musique française classique* (*RMFC*). Pre-eminent today among the legion of archivists is Marcelle Benoit, whose monumental companion volumes *Musiques de cour: chapelle, chambre, écurie: recueil de documents 1661–1733* and *Versailles et les musiciens du roi: étude institutionnelle et sociale 1661–1733* (Paris, 1971) serve as inexhaustible resources about the employment of musicians at court. C. Pierre's *Histoire du Concert Spirituel 1725–1790*, published by the Société Française de Musicologie (Paris, 1975), with an index of concert programmes prepared by A. Bloch-Michel, is similarly invaluable to any investigation of this era. A. Devriès's work on eighteenth-century French publishers documents the proliferation of French music.

Composers and music

The *catalogue raisonné* of the music of Marc-Antoine Charpentier, meticulously prepared by H. Wiley Hitchcock, has stimulated great interest which, with the recent commencement of the issue of Charpentier's complete works in facsimile, should ensure his rightful place alongside Lully. But while Catherine Cessac has provided a substantial monograph on Charpentier (Paris, 1988) and Sylvette Milliot and La Gorce one on Marin Marais (Paris, 1991), we lack similar up-to-date assessments of Lully and Rameau. The 1983 Rameau and 1987 Lully tercentenaries stimulated important new research – much of which has already found its way into conference reports, *Festschriften* and journals – and prompted exhibitions and festivals which have greatly popularized these composers and their times. Yet their music and that of their contemporaries, such as Michel-Richard de Lalande, to name the most important, still lacks critical collected editions and remains largely the preserve of research libraries, most notably the Bibliothèque Nationale in Paris. J. R. Mongrédien's *Catalogue thématique des sources du grand motet français (1663–1792)* (Paris, 1984) is an important landmark in the revival of the noble genre of sacred music in which Lalande excelled. The German scholar Herbert Schneider has produced an excellent catalogue of the works of Lully, and catalogues for Lalande and Rameau are promised by Lionel Sawkins and Sylvie Bouissou. The unprecedented success of the French film *Tous les matins du monde* (1991), loosely based on the life and music of Marin Marais, serves to confirm the current widespread interest in French music and manners of this era.

Young American, Antipodean and English scholars continue to turn out pertinent dissertations under the supervision of French specialists such as Albert Cohen,

David Fuller, Graham Sadler, David Tunley and Neal Zaslaw. L. Rosow's *Lully's 'Armide' at the Paris Opéra: a Performance History, 1686–1766* (diss., Brandeis U., 1981) and P. R. Rice's *The Performing Arts at Fontainebleau from Louis XIV to Louis XVI* (Ann Arbor, 1989) interpret, expand and greatly enhance our knowledge of the sources. The doctoral research of David Fuller and Bruce Gustafson are usefully joined to form the basis of *A Catalogue of French Harpischord Music 1699–1780* (Oxford, 1990). Oxford University Press's quarterly journal *Early Music* has devoted whole issues to Lully and Rameau and has been a frequent outlet for a new research in English on French Baroque performing practice.

Increasingly, young French scholars – inspired by the examples of Catherine Massip (François Lesure's successor at the Bibliothèque Nationale), Jérôme de La Gorce (Centre Nationale des Recherches Scientifiques) and Jean R. Mongrédien (Professor at the Sorbonne's Centre d'Etudes de la Musique Française aux XVIIIe et XIXe Siècles) – are producing substantial biographies (a realm hitherto occupied by writers in English such as Edith Borroff, Cuthbert Girdlestone and Wilfrid Mellers) and surveys, notable among them R. Fajon's *L'Opéra à Paris de Roi Soleil à Louis le Bien-Aimé* (Geneva, 1984), C. Kintzler's *Poétique de l'opéra français de Corneille à Rousseau* (Paris, 1991) and J. de La Gorce's *L'Opéra à Paris au temps de Louis XIV: histoire d'un théâtre* (Paris, 1992). As to the future, the Centre de Musique Baroque de Versailles, founded in 1987, must be seen as a powerful potential benefactor, through its lavish festivals at Versailles – reminiscent of the *spectacles* of Louis XIV's day – and the intoxicating prospect of the production of databases on a scale unimaginable to an individual scholar.

25. *Distant view of Hamburg: engraving (c1750) by J. G. Ringlin after Friedrich Bernhard Werner*

Chapter VI

Hamburg and Lübeck

GEORGE J. BUELOW

At the turn of the eighteenth century, Hamburg, with a population of some 75 000, was, after Vienna, the second largest city in the empire. Originally one of a number of towns loosely interconnected commercially by the Hanseatic League, Hamburg had in the seventeenth century outgrown in size and economic development the other league members.[1] In the eighteenth century the free, imperial city-state of Hamburg became one of the most important commercial and cultural centres in northern Europe. With its magnificent geographical position on the Elbe river, only 60 miles from the North Sea, and connected by a system of rivers and canals to central and eastern Europe, Hamburg and its harbour thrived on shipping and trade. While much of central and northern Europe had been laid waste by the Thirty Years War and other terrible conflicts in the seventeenth century, Hamburg, through the foresight of its government, remained neutral, aided notably by the superiority of its fortifications. Europe was entangled in almost continuous conflicts throughout the seventeenth century, but Hamburg dealt with most of the warring factions to its advantage both economically and politically. Even when Denmark and Sweden frequently threatened its peace and freedom and eventually surrounded it with their armies, Hamburg managed to find the means to extricate itself from impending foreign domination.

As a free, imperial city-state, Hamburg had only a loose political connection with the German Reich and its emperor. It was free of domination by any aristocratic forces that ruled most of the other cities and towns on the continent as well as in England. Hamburg's government consisted of a Senat (city council) formed from the most important patrician families who were elected for life and who elected their successors. A citizen's assembly (Bürgerliche Kollegien) had representatives elected from each of Hamburg's five parishes, although the franchise was limited to only a few of the richest landowners of the parishes. Therefore, the assembly grew less and less representative of the ever-growing merchant class of the city. This led to frequent and serious disagreements between the city and the merchants. The assembly's powers were limited to giving consent to any legislation passed by the Senat before it could become effective, and also to control over the city treasury. Members of the Senat could not hold titles of nobility, although through their wealth and their membership of Hamburg's upper class the city government was in effect elitist. The clashes between the ruling body and disenfranchised burghers led to bitter internal political strife at the end of the seventeenth century that culminated in a revolutionary uprising in 1698. This forced the emperor to appoint an imperial commission to restore law and order. For several years Hamburg experienced political anarchy until a new constitution was formed in 1709. This brought the Senat and the assembly into a more democratic balance. However, voting privileges continued to be restricted to the wealthiest merchants, and the democratic process remained in the hands of fewer than about 10% of the city's population.

It was, however, commerce that drove the mechanism of life in Hamburg, and the benefits that accrued to its citizens were visible on both the social and cultural levels. The atmosphere of freedom that permeated the city was apparent to visitors. Charles Burney, for example, found 'the streets . . . crowded with people who seem occupied with their own concerns; and there is an air of chearfulness, industry, plenty, and liberty, in the inhabitants of this place, seldom to be seen in other parts of Germany'.[2] The social responsibility of its citizens was frequently praised. Already in the sixteenth century Hamburg had built a *Seefahrerarmnenhaus* for unemployed seamen, as well as rent-free housing for widows and others who were destitute. An orphanage existed from the seventeenth century. Hamburg also led the way in establishing charitable hospitals. Of course, such examples of social conscientiousness depended on the great wealth of so many of the Hamburg burghers.

The city flourished not only because of its citizens' financial prowess, but also because it attracted wealth from various foreign enterprises. Hamburg was known to be one of the most cosmopolitan cities in Europe. Refugees from other parts of the continent, for example the Dutch provinces, had flooded it during the seventeenth century, and foreign immigrants continued to seek out its political protection into the next century. Because of its commercial and political dealings with many foreign governments, Hamburg attracted consular and ambassadorial enclaves and numerous diplomats. Especially significant in this regard was the long-established relationship with England that had granted the Hanseatic city special protective trade treaties. After the Elector of Hanover ascended the British throne as George I, this relationship was further strengthened. And although Hamburg did not have a native nobility, it became the temporary home for many nobles who often had to abandon their lands in the face of conflict. Others made it a practice to settle in the city for the winter season in order to take part in its cultural and social life. This large influx of foreigners greatly affected the cultural make-up of Hamburg. The combination of diplomats, nobility, and wealthy patrician and merchant families created an ideal population for developing the arts in the eighteenth century; these groups had the money and the leisure time to enjoy the dramatic and musical arts, and they collected the visual arts for their numerous elegant homes both within the city and outside the walls, where they built summer gardens and villas. Gardens became a prominent feature of the landscape, some modest, others elaborate and modelled after French classical designs. Many travellers to Hamburg in the eighteenth century observed the unusual beauty of the garden areas on its periphery.

Although Hamburg did not have a university until the nineteenth century, its intellectual community was particularly large in both the sciences and the humanities. This was partly the result of the strong support for intellectual education emanating from the Latin school, the Johanneum, founded in 1529, and also from the Akademische Gymnasium, opened in 1613. The latter, while not granting degrees, was meant to train the best Hamburg students for a university education, and its curriculum was in a practical sense equal to the first levels of a university education. Both institutions could boast specially renowned faculties.

Several societies of scholars contributed to the richness of intellectual life, for example the Teutsch-übende Gesellschaft, which published a journal devoted to the German language and its literary usage. English influences quickly brought to Hamburg the most recent developments in British philosophy and literature. The first German weekly was published in Hamburg in 1713 by Johann Mattheson, *Die Vernünfftler*, a translation and imitation of the popular *Tatler* and *Spectator*. Another publication, *Der Patriot*, modelled on the *Spectator*, was a highly successful journal of the Patriotische Gesellschaft, whose membership included many of the outstanding literary figures in the city; published between 1724 and 1726, it was designed to improve the tastes and morals in Hamburg as well as elsewhere, and it was a significant voice in the rapidly growing influence of English Enlightenment philosophy.

As these examples of Hamburg's political and social make-up suggest, the city had become by the turn of the eighteenth century an ideal political and socio-economic society for the cultivation of the arts. The wealth of its institutions, the coming and goings of many aristocrats and their entourages, the large foreign population, the preservation of its physical well-being, all made Hamburg particularly well suited to the establishment of the first public opera house outside Venice. Another aspect of Hamburg's distinctive culture was the strong literary traditions that had developed in the seventeenth century. The opera that opened on the Gänsemarkt in 1678[3] was from the beginning strongly supported by the city's leading writers and poets who provided librettos. These included: Christian Heinrich Postel (1658–1705), Christian Friedrich Hunold (1681–1721), Friedrich Christian Feustking (1678–1739), Johann Ulrich von König (1688–1744), Lucas von Bostel (1649–1716), Joachim Beccau (1690–1755) and Barthold Feind (1678–1721).

OPERA IN HAMBURG, 1678–1738

The impact of opera touched many aspects of the city's life and culture. The success of this new theatrical-musical art form during the first decades of the eighteenth century affected most of the institutions of music and perhaps even strengthened the city's economy by attracting the wealthy from other parts of north Germany. Johann Mattheson (1681–1764), Hamburg's distinguished native composer, critic, music journalist and lexicographer, made the following illuminating point as to why opera was valuable to a republic like Hamburg:

> Through celebrated performances [in the opera house] great princes and lords are often persuaded to stay and to bring their households to stay in a city, procuring for them frequent supplies of food-stuffs. Scholars, artists, artisans come along too, and the city takes on the kind of eminence with a good opera as it has with good banks. For the latter are for service, the former give pleasure; the latter serve to give security, the former [serve] to instruct. It is almost always true that where the best banks are found so too are found the best opera houses.[4]

Many among Hamburg's outspoken intellectuals agreed with Mattheson that pleasure was not the only goal of opera, but that it must also serve a moral-didactic purpose. And Mattheson insisted that opera brought together all the artistic disciplines, as well as philosophy:

> a good opera theatre is nothing less than an advanced school of many of the fine arts, including together and simultaneously architecture, scenography, painting, mechanics, dancing, acting, moral philosophy, poetry and most especially music, united most pleasantly and always giving new demonstrations for the edification and pleasure of distinguished and sensible spectators.[5]

The early and virulent attacks upon opera by Pietist ministers had largely been muted in the 1690s, as the Lutheran orthodoxy, the faculties of theology and jurisprudence at the universities of Wittenberg and Rostock and the city council all vigorously disagreed with the Pietists' views that opera was immoral and the work of the Devil. Even the philosopher Gottfried Wilhelm Leibniz (1646–1716) published his view that opera was a new form of entertainment developed out of Christian church music, and in itself contained nothing either good or evil.[6] Johann Wolfgang Franck[7] and Johann Philipp Förtsch dominated the repertory in the first years. A change came about in 1691 when Johann Georg Conradi (*d* 1699) was engaged and for three years composed a series of works for each season, including *Die schöne und getreue Ariadne* (1691); this is the earliest extant complete score for an opera written specifically for Hamburg.[8] Conradi's music mixes Venetian, German and – significantly – French styles, an innovation enriching the Hamburg operatic repertory. The opera opens with a typical French (i.e. Lullian) overture, ceremonious in its slower tempo and dotted rhythms and followed by a faster, somewhat imitative section. Several solos are written for chaconne basses, and the opera ends with an extensive *Passacaille* for solo and chorus, and probably dancers, representative of the tradition established by Lully. The vocal style, with largely simple melodic lines and a notably mellifluous flow in several duets, has a French character. While the score seldom gives specific indications for instruments, it contains significant evidence of the growing importance of the orchestra in opera at Hamburg: about half the 38 arias in the three acts have orchestral accompaniment, and there is considerable orchestral support in solo ensembles and in a number of accompanied recitatives and ariosos.

A continuing interest in French music is seen in a performance in 1692 of *Achille et Polixène*, left incomplete by Lully at his death and completed by Collasse. Lully's German student Johann Sigismund Kusser held the post of opera director briefly, and between 1693 and 1695 composed several operas for Hamburg which were also indebted to French music for various aspects of their style. However, a notable event took place in 1694 – a performance of Reinhard Keiser's *Basilius*. Keiser, more than any other, was the composer who gave Hamburg its illustrious reputation for having one of the great opera houses in Europe.

The Age of Keiser

Reinhard Keiser (1674–1739) was born near Weissenfels and as a boy received his education at the Leipzig Thomasschule. He seems to have been largely self-taught in music. From 1692 to 1695 he lived in Brunswick, where he wrote several operas for the important commercial opera house opened there in 1691 with the enthusiasm and financial support of the ruling house of Brunswick-Wolfenbüttel. Around 1697 Keiser went to Hamburg, where, with several interruptions, he remained for the rest of his career as a composer and, for a period, as director of the opera. One can speak of an 'age of Keiser' in Hamburg, for each year between 1696 and 1717, except for the year 1708, he contributed at least one and sometimes several operas to the repertory. During this period few other composers gained entry to the Gänsemarkt theatre, important exceptions being Johann Mattheson, Christoph Graupner and the young George Frideric Handel. Handel had come to the city from his native Halle at the age of 19 in 1704 to play the violin and harpsichord in the opera orchestra. Undoubtedly he was attracted to the city because of its famous opera, and it was here that he first learnt many of the important aspects of writing and producing operas that would be a central focus of his career in Italy and in London. Between 1718 and 1738, except for Telemann and Handel, Keiser remained the most popular box-office attraction for the Hamburg opera public.

His contemporaries recognized Keiser as the embodiment of the German musician. One critic commented that he was 'perhaps the greatest original genius in music that had ever appeared in Germany'.[9] Mattheson called Keiser the 'premier homme du monde'[10] and 'the greatest opera composer of the world.[11] His enormous output of between 60 and 65 complete, three-act operas was almost entirely written for Hamburg; of these only 17 survive.

Keiser's operatic style cannot be characterized in a few words. Even the 17 extant scores remain to be studied in detail and in themselves do not fully establish the gradual changes in musical direction that the composer took over his long career. What, then, can be said to explain the success of Keiser? First, he was immensely gifted with a fecundity of melodic invention, and to this must be added his understanding of the human voice and how best to display its virtues. Not only did he write countless melodies of memorable beauty (which so impressed Handel that he re-used or adapted many of them in his own works), but he also created virtuoso and somewhat italianate show-pieces that gave performers a highly prized opportunity for vocal pyrotechnics and the audience the pleasure of experiencing the seemingly impossible in singing. Keiser also entertained by his splendid use of the orchestra. The colourful and expressive treatment of solo instruments, often in subtle and affective concerted passages interacting with the voice, as well as extensive programmatic passages that colourfully paint scenes and emotions, all made Keiser the first German composer to employ the orchestra in opera with originality and new dramatic effects.

Keiser was an eighteenth-century, typically eclectic composer, who combined in his operas numerous styles identifiable as being

26. Title-page of the libretto of Keiser's opera 'Die entdeckte Verstellung oder Die geheime Liebe der Diana' (1712; revised 1724)

influenced by French, Italian and German music. In the last category are passages that use various 'popular' tunes of the time in north Germany, secular and sacred *lieder*, street cries and folksongs, as well as various dances. Many of Hamburg's important literary figures, particularly Christian Heinrich Postel, wrote his librettos, which were often adaptations or translations of librettos used by Italian composers. Their subjects ranged widely over almost every type of opera plot popular in the late seventeenth and early eighteenth centuries: Greek mythology, Roman legend, biblical stories, historical plots from Italian, French, Spanish and German sources, and some based on topical or local events. While most of the operas are serious in tone, they almost always contain secondary comic characters, a *sine qua non* for the Hamburg audience. Mattheson, perhaps, says it best when summing up Keiser's achievements: 'in the period in which he flourished, there was no other composer, especially in tender vocal pieces, who composed [music] so rich, so natural, so flowing, so attractive, and for the most part, so clearly, intelligently and rhetorically'.[12]

The Hamburg opera season was long, normally lasting from the beginning of the year through to December, closing for Lent and other religious observances. Documents recording attendance figures and ticket receipts are rare, although Mattheson gives important data of this kind for the decade between 1695 and 1705, the period of Keiser's initial success. Table VI.1, drawn with some modifications from Mattheson's account,[13] indicates a considerable fluctuation in audience attendance for the different years.

Table VI.1 REPERTORY AND FINANCIAL DATA FOR THE HAMBURG OPERA, 1695–1705

Director	Year	Opening/Closing	No. of Performances	New Operas	Receipts (marks)
Kremberg	1695	7 Jan–5 Dec	108	6	19 697
Schott	1696	2 Jan–30 Dec	112	4	17 895
Guest perf. Kiel	1696		13		3 854
	1697	27 Jan–2 Dec	103	3	16 155
Guest perf. Kiel	1697		14		3 665
	1698	3 Jan–2 Dec	117	4	21 694
Bronner-Kordes	1699	4 Jan–19 Dec	113	7	22 838
Schott	1700	2 Jan–22 Dec	112	2	15 560
	1701	3 Jan–19 Dec	65	4	11 381
	1702	16 Jan–8 Dec	117	10	18 438
Schott's widow	1703	2 Jan–7 Dec	72	3	13 138
Keiser-Drüsicke	1704	2 Jan–5 Dec	94	3	13 863
	1705	7 Jan–23 Dec	23	1	6 158

Between 1700 and 1717 performances for the year consisted on average of four to six operas, of which three to four were new to the audiences. In contrast, between 1718 and 1738, of the 246 operas performed, 71 were new to the repertory, about double the number of different works performed each year.[14] Up to 1717 Keiser composed some 45 operas for Hamburg. Operas written by other composers to Italian texts were invariably presented in German translation, like Handel's *Rinaldo* in 1715 and his *Amadigi di Gaula* in 1717. Of particular significance regarding the encroachment of Italian influences into the Hamburg opera was the insertion into Keiser's opera *Claudius* (1703) of 11 arias in Italian, distributed evenly among the principal characters. Subsequently, almost every opera produced at the Gänsemarkt theatre included Italian-language texts, which appeared also in German translation in the librettos sold to the audiences. The reasons for this corruption of the purity of the German libretto with Italian aria texts are not clear: it would seem that both composers and singers (most of whom were German) preferred the sound and singability of the Italian language.

The last two decades of repertory opera in Hamburg were dominated by Georg Philipp Telemann (1681–1767). He came to the city in 1721, and his comic opera, *Der geduldige Socrates*, had a highly successful première in January. He received dual appointments as Kantor of the Johanneum, with the responsibility to supply music to the five city churches, and also as music director of the opera. Before the opera went bankrupt in 1738, Telemann gave audiences another dozen or more major works, comic as well as serious. He was also a participating composer in various pasticcios, particularly popular in this period, as well as being responsible for adapting and arranging operas by other composers, including Handel.

Telemann's gifts make him a major figure in opera history. He had already refined those gifts in Leipzig, where in 1701 he was made director of the opera and where, he recounted in his autobiography, he wrote some 20 stage works.[15] He composed in a mixture of styles reflecting the changing musical trends of the early eighteenth century. Of his many operas only a handful remain, and among those, in addition to *Socrates*, is *Pimpinone* (1728), an intermezzo inserted between the acts of Handel's *Tamerlano*. *Pimpinone* is a highly accomplished *opera buffa*, written several years before the now more famous Italian exemplar *La serva padrona* by Pergolesi. Humour, comical and satirical, are particular strengths of Telemann's light and *galant* works, although he also wrote in the *opera-seria* style that reflected the traditions of Hamburg opera so successfully maintained by Keiser. When the opera house closed its doors in 1738, Telemann had devoted 17 years to its musical success. He was, however, to remain a major catalyst in the musical, educational and cultural life of the city for another 29 years.

HAMBURG'S CHURCHES

The pre-eminent place that Hamburg had held earlier in the seventeenth century on account of the richness and variety of the organ music heard in its churches depended on the master organists and composers who lived there. As has been described elsewhere,[16] the rich tradition of organ music in Hamburg originated in part from students of the Dutch master Sweelinck, including Jacob Praetorius and Heinrich Scheidemann. One of the reasons organists continued to be attracted to Hamburg was the excellence of the instruments in the city churches. The Jakobikirche, Johanniskirche and Nicolaikirche all possessed superb organs by the famous north German builder Arp Schnitger (1648–1719); the last instrument, with its four manuals and 60 speaking stops, has been judged his greatest achievement.

It was probably the unique qualities of the Nicolaikirche instrument that attracted Vincent Lübeck (1654–1740) to that church in

1702, a position he held until his death. Though he was praised by his contemporaries for his virtuosity and sought out as a teacher, his compositional gifts are hard to judge today: only nine organ works by him survive, seven preludes and fugues related in form and style to similar works by Buxtehude, a chorale fantasy on *Ich ruf zu dir Herr Jesu Christ* and an incomplete partita of six variations on *Nun lasst uns Gott dem Herren*.

Most influential and famous among the organists in Hamburg was Johann Adam Reincken (1623–1722), who had studied with Scheidemann at the Catharinenkirche and later became his assistant and, in 1663, his successor. He remained a renowned virtuoso organist and teacher for 57 years until he died, just short of reaching 100. Many came to hear him perform or to study with him on the Catharinenkirche organ, including Georg Böhm – later organist at Lüneburg, some 30 miles to the south of Hamburg, where Johann Sebastian Bach was a student at the Michaelisschule between 1700 and 1702. During this period Bach himself came more than once to Hamburg to hear the great Reincken perform and, perhaps, also to experience opera for the first time at the Gänsemarkt theatre. In 1720 he returned to Hamburg from Cöthen, performed on several Hamburg organs, including the one at the Catharinenkirche, where before a distinguished audience that included the 97-year-old Reincken, he played for two hours, with a half-hour improvisation on the chorale *An Wasserflüssen Babylon*. Reincken, according to Bach's son C. P. E. Bach, is credited with saying after that performance: 'I thought this art was dead, but I see it still lives in you'. Bach had come to Hamburg, apparently, as one of eight candidates for the position of organist at the Jakobikirche. Even though he did not participate in the actual performance competition on 28 November, he was approached by the church committee to fill the position. Bach turned them down. Somewhat later, Johann Mattheson, in one of his many observations about musical life in Hamburg, suggested that the reason was Bach's refusal to pay simony of 4000 marks into the church coffers, which the successful candidate, Johann Joachim Heitmann, did contribute after his election. Mattheson's words of scorn offer a glimpse into this form of ecclesiastical graft:

> I remember, as will still a large number of parishioners, that some
> years ago a certain great virtuoso [Bach], whose merits have since
> earned him an important cantorate [at Leipzig], presented himself
> as an organist in a town of no small size [Hamburg], performed on
> many of the finest organs, and aroused the admiration of everyone
> for his mastery. But there also appeared among other incompetent
> journeymen, the son of a wealthy artisan [Heitmann], who could
> execute preludes better with thalers than with his fingers. It was he
> (as might easily be guessed), who gained the post, although almost

everyone was angered by it. It was just at Christmastime, and the eloquent chief preacher, who had not willingly participated in this simony, took as his text the Gospel story of the angel's music at the birth of Christ . . . closed his sermon with the remarkable pronouncement that went something like: He was certain that if one of the angels of Bethlehem had come down from Heaven, played divinely, and wished to become organist at St J[akob], but had no money, he could only fly away again.[17]

Very few organ works by Reincken survive and they give but a glimpse into this composer's virtuosity and achievements. The lengthy chorale variations on *Was kann uns kommen an für Not* and *An Wasserflüssen Babylon* are outstanding examples of north German keyboard technique. The latter work, especially, presents almost an encyclopedia of variation procedures built up from a chorale melody and illustrates aspects of Reincken's keyboard artistry for which he was famous. These are models of chorale variation that Bach himself was to emulate, even if with his own unique craftsmanship. But most of Bach's technical devices are already found in Reincken's work: elaborate passages of runs and broken-chord figurations requiring exemplary finger technique, motet-like passages of contrasting textures, various forms of imitations of the chorale melody and its constituent motifs, double pedals, echo effects and dazzling passages of hand-crossings. *An Wasserflüssen Babylon* is one of the most typical and powerful examples of organ music that would frequently have been heard in Hamburg's churches.

The final decades of the seventeenth century witnessed a steady decline in the quality and diversity of vocal music in the city's five main churches. The outstanding organization of church music that had been developed under the Kantors Erasmus Sartorius, Thomas Selle and Christoph Bernhard[18] began to disintegrate after Bernhard's death and the appointment of his successor, Joachim Gerstenbüttel (c1650–1721). His tenure, which continued until his death, endured a multiplicity of problems: a government faced with political strife and financial crises; the reduction of the number of singers employed in the city's Kantorei; the decline in the number and ability of the city musicians (*Ratsmusikanten*) to six aging and often incompetent players; and the growing competition with the opera (after 1678) to attract soloists. More than anything it was the increasing popularity of opera in the city that diminished the role of church music in Hamburg's culture. It was also during this period, as has been noted, that several orthodox ministers attacked the forms of sacred music, especially the cantata, as typifying the inroads made by operatic music into the church, an influence they blasted as unchristian and the work of the Devil. Gerstenbüttel was unequal to the many challenges facing his cantorate, and after 46 years he died

27. Georg Philipp Telemann: portrait engraved by G. Lichtensteger

an embittered man, who had failed to bring the changes into church music that were required to satisfy public taste for a music more attuned to secular forms and style, especially as found in opera.

These conditions, however, changed dramatically with the fortunate and wise election by the city council of Georg Philipp Telemann to succeed Gerstenbüttel. Between 1721 and Telemann's death in 1767 music in the churches, as well as at the opera and in public concerts, became exceptional and vital aspects of Hamburg's musical image. As Kantor of the Johanneum, Telemann was the director of music for all five of the main city churches, as well as civic music director for music performed at various city ceremonies and celebrations. In addition to acting as director of the opera, he took upon himself the establishment of numerous public concerts. Indeed, Telemann's extraordinary energies expended in composing, directing and publishing his own music – largely engraved by himself – makes him one of the most productive composers in history.

Under Telemann's leadership, music in the churches took a leap forward in quality and modernity of style. It is, however, impossible to tell how adequate many of his performances were, and undoubtedly they fluctuated in competence during his 46-year tenure. Telemann was expected to compose two new cantatas for each Sunday in the church year, one to be performed before the sermon and one after. He published several complete cycles of cantatas, including the well-known *Harmonischer Gottes-Dienst*. Among the remaining more than 1000 sacred cantatas, the majority of which are lost, the greatest number were performed in Hamburg. These cantatas are modern in the sense that they use the Neumeister reformed cantata texts, with free sacred poetry laid out in alternating recitatives, arias and choruses and composed in contemporary operatic style. Many are for a solo voice, one instrument and continuo. However, seen in their totality, the majority of the surviving cantatas are scored for four or more voices, and over half have accompaniments for strings and wind instruments, sometimes brass also, in various combinations. The style of Telemann's sacred vocal music was heavily indebted to his creative activity as an opera composer, but during his long career this style developed significantly from a late Baroque concept to a mid-eighteenth-century style often described as *Galant*. In his music written after 1730 there is a decided turn towards simplicity and symmetrical thematic constructions, and an elimination of the unifying device of expressing only a single affection in each piece. Textures become generally uncomplicated, and the continuo line is frequently eliminated – all attributes suggesting Telemann's importance as a composer who is astride the significant musical changes occurring between the Baroque and the Classical styles.

Performing forces in the churches varied considerably. In the Petrikirche Telemann directed seven singers, male and female,[19] 17 instrumentalists, three trumpeters and a timpanist. In the Nicolaikirche there were seven singers, 16 instrumentalists, three trumpeters and a timpanist. The Catharinenkirche musicians comprised two singers and seven instrumentalists, the Jakobikirche six singers, 17 instrumentalists, three trumpeters and a timpanist, and the Michaeliskirche only one singer, nine instrumentalists, one trumpeter and a timpanist. However, vocal and instrumental forces were augmented, at times by adding amateurs from the community. For example, the celebrations in 1730 for the 200th anniversary of the Augsburg Confession included more than 100 performers heard in all five churches on the same day.[20]

In addition to Telemann's remarkable production of cantatas, he wrote a new Passion for every year during Lent, a tradition that had already been established in the preceding century. These 46 works were composed to the Gospels in four-year rotation. Each work was performed in all the important churches, beginning on the third Sunday in Lent (Oculi) at the Petrikirche, on the fourth Sunday (Laetare) at the Nicolaikirche, on the fifth Sunday (Judica) at the Catharinenkirche, on the Friday before Palm Sunday at the Jakobikirche, on the Monday after Palm Sunday at St Maria

Magdalena and on the Tuesday at St Gertrud. Telemann also wrote much sacred music for various other reasons. He wrote the installation music for some 40 pastors and deacons, each including two cantatas as well as other incidental compositions. The burial services for distinguished citizens, such as the Bürgermeister, required some 11 funeral cantatas. In addition to the music he composed for the 200th anniversary of the Augsburg Confession (25–6 July 1730), he composed cantatas for the 100th anniversary of the Westphalian Peace (30 October 1748) and for the celebration of 200 years of religious peace (5 October 1755). The consecration of new churches or new altars also required him to compose music for the ceremonies: in this category fell one of Telemann's last official responsibilities, for the dedicatory ceremonies on 19 October 1762 of the reconstructed Michaeliskirche, which 11 years earlier had been destroyed by fire. It was here, on 25 August 1764, that Telemann conducted the burial-service music composed by Mattheson for his own interment, when Telemann's friend and Hamburg's great music critic and music theorist was buried in the crypt of the church to which he had donated 44 000 marks for the installation of a new great organ.

PUBLIC CONCERTS IN HAMBURG

Musical life in Hamburg in the eighteenth century grew immeasurably richer with the institution of frequent public concerts. As early as 1660 Matthias Weckmann had instituted a Collegium Musicum in the city, which performed on Thursdays in the refectory of the cathedral. Although successful in presenting music by many of the best composers of the period and in attracting singers and instrumentalists, both professional and amateur, the concerts did not continue after Weckmann's death in 1674. In the early eighteenth century there were public concerts for a ticket-purchasing audience, although they were sporadic at best. For example, in October 1708 John Abell, a well-known English countertenor, gave a recital in the Drillhaus, the exercise-hall built for the city militia and a favourite place for musical events. In March 1716 a concert with choruses and instruments was given at the Niederbaumhaus, the first half devoted to Keiser's music, the second to Mattheson's. Christoph Wideburg, an opera Kapellmeister, performed his new oratorio, *Die vernügte Sehnsucht der liebenden Sulamith* in the Drillhaus in December 1718.[21] Many more performances probably took place, but at this time concerts were not always reported in Hamburg's newspapers. Clearly, however, the vitality of concert life changed once Telemann became involved.

Immediately on taking up his duties as Kantor, Telemann re-established the Collegium Musicum, which he directed at first in a room in his home and later (on Mondays and Thursdays) in the Drillhaus. Telemann's enthusiasm for and expertise with this kind of public concert had begun in his student days at Leipzig University; here he had founded a Collegium with fellow students which quickly became a focus of musical life in Leipzig. Also, during his years in the employ of the city of Frankfurt, he had directed the Collegium of one of the city's private clubs, the Frauenstein. In Hamburg his Collegium became the means to entice audiences into numerous public concerts, and notices in the newspapers reveal an extraordinary activity on Telemann's part in presenting concerts almost continuously until shortly before his death.[22] Even though other composers and performers also appeared frequently before paying audiences in Hamburg, Telemann took the role of virtual concert manager for the city.

The music Telemann presented varied widely and included repetitions of cantatas and Passions first performed in the churches, as well as music written for various private celebrations. Much of the music, of course, was written specifically for public concerts, including some of his oratorios. Telemann's decision to repeat performances of cantatas and other sacred works in public locations made a breakthrough that overturned an ancient tradition forbidding the Kantor to perform sacred music outside the church. Indeed, Telemann's first public appearance in the summer of 1722 brought forth protests from a group within the city council:

> Because the current Kantor Telemann has thought to perform for money his music in a public inn where all manner of disorder is possible; and moreover makes free to perform operas, comedies, and similar entertainments likely to arouse bawdiness, even outside the ordained market days, and all without the consent of this most excellent Council and Citizenry; so the *Oberalten* of the Council seek a decree that for such music the Kantor shall be most earnestly disciplined and forbidden further such doings.[23]

The council, however, took no action and Telemann was free to bridge the age-old gap between sacred music as ritual and sacred music as entertainment. This incident may have caused him to have second thoughts about his position in Hamburg, or perhaps other factors influenced him in September to petition the council to release him from his contract, so that he could accept the offer to become the new Kantor in Leipzig. However, the Hamburg officials bargained with him, and he decided to stay, making way, after some further deliberations, for Leipzig to choose Johann Sebastian Bach for that position.

A year later Telemann seems to have found the cultural atmosphere of Hamburg all that he had hoped for, and he wrote to a friend

The Late Baroque Era

– Johann Friedrich von Uffenbach – contrasting the state of music in Frankfurt, his former employer, with that in Hamburg:

> While music meanwhile goes downhill there, here it is climbing up; and I do not believe that there is anywhere such a place as Hamburg where the spirit of one working in this science can be more encouraged. A great advantage is added to this by the fact that, besides the presence of many persons of rank here, also the most prominent men of the city – including the entire city council – do not absent themselves from public concerts. Likewise the reasoned judgment of so many connoisseurs and intelligent people give opportunity for concerts. Not less important is the opera which now is at its greatest flowering, and finally the *nervus rerum gerendarum* [the nerve of all things, i.e. money], which does not adhere too strongly to music lovers.[24]

Telemann's concerts frequently included music composed for various private performances, especially those for annual celebrations held by civic and military groups. The city council gathered for an elaborate 'Petri- und Matthäimahl' every 21 February for the councillors, repeated on 24 February for distinguished ambassadors, church dignitaries and other prominent citizens. The officers of Hamburg's militia gave an annual banquet towards the end of August. These occasions and others required from Telemann, as well as from other composers, a large repertory of music, including choral and orches-

28. (a) Celebration banquet of the citizen-captains in the Drillhaus, Hamburg: engraving (1719) by Christian Fritzsch

28. (b) detail showing the musicians' balcony

tral compositions. Telemann composed 40 so-called *Kapitänsmusiken* between 1722 and 1763, each consisting of a large-scale oratorio and a serenade; each received a public performance shortly following the private occasion for which it was commissioned.[25]

One of Telemann's most popular works, repeated frequently over the years at public concerts, was the music he wrote for the centennial celebration of the Hamburg Admiralty on 6 April 1723; the text was by Michael Richey, professor of Greek at the Gymnasium. A serenade with voices was introduced by an orchestral overture with dances, bearing the following descriptive titles for the movements: (1) Overture – the Stillness, Undulations, Unrest of the Sea; (2) Sarabande – the Sleeping Thetis; (3) Bourrée – the Awakening Thetis; (4) Loure – the Amorous Neptune; (5) Gavotte – the Playful Naiades; (6) Harlequinade – the Merry Tritons; (7) Tempest – the Stormy Aeolus; (8) Antique Minuet – the Pleasant Zephyr; (9) Gigue – the Ebb and Flow of the Tides; and (10) Canaris – the Merry Sailors.[26]

Also frequently programmed by Telemann for his public concerts were Passion-Oratorios and oratorios based on other biblical subjects, most of which were first presented privately. They include his setting of Brockes's *Der für die Sünden der Welt gemarterte und sterbende Jesus*, which was also composed by Keiser, Mattheson and Handel; Ramler's *Der Tod Jesu*, later to be made famous in C. H. Graun's setting; an oratorio based on Klopstock's *Der Messias*; and his most popular oratorio, *Seliges Erwägen des Leidens und Sterbens Jesu Christi* (1728). The last was performed almost yearly in churches, as well as in concert. All this concert activity apparently finally convinced the city of the need for a hall built exclusively for concerts: in 1761 a 'new concert hall on the Kampe, in the midst of newly built houses' opened, the earliest structure built specifically for this purpose in

Germany, and in subsequent years Telemann frequently presented programmes there.

Although Telemann certainly dominated concert life for four decades, the city also enjoyed many concerts by various virtuoso performers. In August 1722 the harpsichordist Conrad Friedrich Hurlebusch gave concerts in the Hof von Holland. Margaretha Susanna Kayser, one of the opera's most distinguished singers, gave a concert in February 1724. A concert at the Drillhaus in 1727 featured four Waldhorn players, one of whom played two instruments simultaneously! In May 1730 Dominichina Pollone, also from the opera, performed a serenade by the organist at the Petri- and Johanniskirche, Herrn Hencken, who played on a 'Klockenspiei'; a lutenist also performed on the same programme. In 1734 two unidentified flautists appeared in the Kaiserhof, presenting a concerto by Vivaldi and music from a Hasse opera. In 1736 three child prodigies, the Kröner sisters, gave several concerts in the Drillhaus to the amazement of audiences. In 1738 Leopold Chevalier performed on the flute 'extraordinary new Italian compositions'. In 1740 Mingotti's touring opera company came to the city and, in addition to staging operatic works, his vocal celebrities gave concerts; they included Francesca Cuzzoni, Marianne Pircker, the castrato Giacomo Zaghini and the baritone Giovanni Antonio Cesari. In 1749 'a famous harpist will be in the city with a David's harp'. In the Kaiserhof in May 1753 an audience heard 'one of the best virtuosos' on the oboe and transverse flute; and in July of the same year two performers from the Netherlands exhibited their skills on the cello and bassoon. In February 1755 Giovanni Battista Locatelli presented nine singers in a selection of arias, and an orchestra played 'many new symphonies'.[27] Since documentation of concert life in Hamburg is very incomplete, it is possible to surmise an even richer musical culture. Telemann's achievements were critical to the entirely changed circumstances of musical life in Hamburg. His determination to be free to give concerts under his own supervision and for his own profit made Hamburg one of the first cities in Germany not only to eliminate the barriers between sacred and secular music but also to make the composer a free agent without restrictions imposed by either church or state. Like Handel in London, Telemann became the earliest representative of the musician-entrepreneur, but unlike Handel, he managed to achieve this freedom while remaining employed by the city-state of Hamburg.

LÜBECK

Lübeck, once one of the most powerful and strategic cities in the Hanseatic League, did not continue to prosper during the seventeenth century. Earlier, its geographical location on a fine harbour opening into the Baltic Sea had been advantageous, because commerce in the Middle Ages and the Renaissance had been strongly centred on this part of the world. After 1600, however, it was Hamburg that flourished by maintaining and expanding its commercial enterprises through shipping with western countries, especially with merchants from England and the Netherlands.

By the end of the seventeenth century Lübeck's population had grown only to about 27 000, only a third of Hamburg's at approximately the same time. Musical life up to the middle of the eighteenth century changed only slightly from what had earlier been established.[28] The five main churches of the city – the Jakobikirche, Petrikirche, Aegidienkirche, Catharinenkirche and Marienkirche – continued to support music in their services. The Marienkirche, in particular, the official church of the city council, still placed great emphasis on music. Indeed, it was the appointment of Dieterich Buxtehude (c1637–1707) in 1668 as organist and 'Werkmeister' (secretary, treasurer and business manager) at the Marienkirche that assured the spread of Lübeck's musical fame far beyond the city's walls.

Buxtehude succeeded Franz Tunder to one of the most prestigious organist's posts in northern Europe. Of Danish origin, Buxtehude was the most important composer of German organ music before Johann Sebastian Bach. He was equally significant in the development of the German sacred cantata and the German oratorio.[29] The established service at the Marienkirche required him to play at the main Sunday morning service and at the afternoon service on Sundays and feast days, as well as in the afternoon before Vespers. The congregational hymns were preceded by organ preludes, although usually the organist did not accompany the hymn-singing. Buxtehude was also expected to supply music, instrumental as well as vocal, for Communion. The choir, of course, was not his responsibility, but rather the Kantor's, who trained the boy's chorus at the Catharinenkirche; it was this choir that participated in the services at the Marienkirche, especially on the most important feast days.

Specific details of the major ecclesiastical and musical events at the Marienkirche were seldom recorded in the kind of detail one would wish to have today, although fortunately there is a record of the musical part of the services relating to the Christmas season 1682–3, for the first and second days of Christmas, New Year's Day and Epiphany.[30] In the morning service for each the Kyrie and Gloria were performed in Latin by vocal and instrumental forces, including vocal soloists and the choir (*capella*). On Christmas Day the same forces, ten instrumentalists, eight vocal soloists and eight choral voices, also performed the Credo and Sanctus. The afternoon services also included concerted vocal and instrumental works before and after the sermon, two before and two after. On each of the four feast days the first work was a motet for eight voices without instruments, with a Latin text on two of the days and German on the other two. The second work was often in several movements with various scorings, but omitting the choir. For example, on Christmas Day, the work appears to have been a concerto-aria cantata for two sopranos, alto, tenor, bass and 12 instruments (two violins, two violas, two clarinos, two cornettos, three trombones and a dulcian). The Latin *Magnificat* usually came after the sermon, composed in modern concerted style with solo and choral voices, and instruments. On New Year's Day the *Te Deum* replaced the *Magnificat* and in 1683 the score included five vocal soloists, five in the choir and ten instrumentalists. The final musical composition in the afternoon was usually a large concerted German motet. The instrumentalists who participated in these elaborate services were paid by the church, although seven of them belonged to the municipal musicians (*Ratsmusikanten*) and also received a salary from the city.

No surviving documentation names the composers whose music so enriched the services at the Marienkirche during occasions such as those described here. Most of the musical treasures of the Lübeck churches are lost, although one considerable body of music is extant in Vienna.[31] That reveals something at least of the extensive library of music that could be drawn upon for performances. The majority of titles are settings of the Mass Ordinary in Latin; some are *Missa brevis* settings (short masses, setting only the Kyrie and Gloria), but most are compositions of the entire Ordinary by Italians and Catholic composers of northern Europe. Among the collections of sacred works are two of the most popular anthologies by Germans, the *Florilegium portense* (1618–21) by Erhard Bodenschaft and the *Promptuarium musicum* (1611–13) by Abraham Schadaeus. Other German composers whose music was at one time in the repertory of the Marienkirche include Samuel Capricornus, Andreas Hammerschmidt, Hieronymus Praetorius, Johann Staden, Johann Schein, and Heinrich Schütz, represented by one work, the *Symphoniarum sacrarum*, part iii. Well-known Italians whose compositions are listed in the inventory are Maurizio Cazzati, Domenico Freschi, Alessandro Grandi, Paolo Quagliati and Giovanni Rovetta. The collection is clearly incomplete, however, containing no music printed after 1674 nor what would have been an extensive number of manuscripts. Noticeably, no works of Buxtehude are found there. While Buxtehude's position did not require an involvement with the performance of vocal music, it seems likely that he did frequently direct concerted vocal music at the Marienkirche. His own sacred vocal works – various concerto-aria cantatas – suggest they were written for both Communion services and as music to precede the sermon. The tradition established earlier in the seventeenth century in which the organist joined with two *Ratsmusikanten*, a violinist and sometimes a lutenist, to play music during the distribution of Communion undoubtedly continued. It was probably for this purpose that Buxtehude's trio sonatas were intended. He also composed occasional vocal music – arias with various instrumental ensembles – which were performed outside the church, at weddings and probably also for funeral services.

Abendmusiken concerts

Buxtehude's predecessor, Franz Tunder (1614–67), had established the practice of giving *Abendspiele*, weekly organ recitals, on Thursday at the Marienkirche. These so pleased the wealthy townspeople that Tunder was encouraged to expand the programmes to include instrumentalists and singers. Buxtehude developed this tradition and placed even greater significance on the concerts by moving them to the last two Sundays in Trinity and the second, third and fourth Sundays in Advent, from 4 p.m. to 5 p.m. Some of his programmes consisted of choral and solo vocal works, but he also composed several large oratorios for orchestra, chorus and soloists. The greater number of performers necessitated the addition of four new balconies to the walls of the church. These *Abendmusiken* – public concerts, free of charge to the public – became famous throughout Europe. A guidebook for Lübeck from 1697, in its description of the Marienkirche, gives expression to the pride the city felt in this early example of public concerts:

> On the west side, between the two pillars under the towers, one can see the large and magnificent organ, which, like the small organ, is now presided over by the world-famous organist and composer Dietrich Buxtehude. Of particular note is the great Abend-Music, consisting of pleasant vocal and instrumental music, presented yearly on five Sundays between St Martin's and Christmas, following the Sunday vesper sermon, from 4 to 5 o'clock, by the aforementioned organist as director, in an artistic and praiseworthy manner. This happens nowhere else.[32]

Unfortunately, none of Buxtehude's compositions for the *Abendmusiken* survives, and only a few of the librettos remain to give any idea of the scope of the music. A libretto of 1678 for a two-part oratorio, *Die Hochzeit des Lamms*, indicates a scoring for six soloists, a heavenly choir, 11 violins, three violas, three violas da gamba, two trumpets and trombones. In 1684 spring catalogues for the Frankfurt and Leipzig book fairs announced the imminent publication of two dramatic works in five parts by Buxtehude: *Himmlische Seelenlust auf*

The Late Baroque Era

Erde and *Das allerschrecklichste und allerfreulichste*. No evidence has been found that these works were published, but the five-part form suggests the usual eighteenth-century practice of extending a single work over the five Sundays of an *Abendmusiken* season. In 1705 Buxtehude gave two special concerts on 2 and 3 December: the first presented an oratorio, *Castrum doloris*, commemorating the death of the Emperor Leopold I; the second, *Templum honoris*, celebrated the accession of Joseph I as Holy Roman Emperor. The young Johann Sebastian Bach had arrived in Lübeck that autumn, after a lengthy trip of some 280 miles from Arnstadt, and he probably heard these especially brilliant performances of two Buxtehude oratorios. Bach had come to the city to hear Buxtehude play, and the experience was apparently so rewarding in so many ways that he stayed for almost three months. Buxtehude's music and his command of the organ were lasting influences on Bach's own unique achievements as a performer on and a composer for the instrument.

The Lübeck *Abendmusiken* remained a vital musical tradition throughout the eighteenth century, although none of Buxtehude's successors brought to these concerts works of the distinction that he had achieved; they were Johann Christian Schieferdecker (1679–1732), Johann Paul Kunzen (1696–1757), his son Adolf Carl Kunzen (1720–81) and Johann Wilhelm Cornelius von Königslow (1745–1833). The practice begun by Buxtehude of composing an oratorio in five parts to be performed over all five Sundays was usually maintained. Only two oratorios have survived World War II – Adolf Kunzen's *Moses in seinem Eifer gegen die Abgötterey in den Wüsten* and *Absalon*. A third, anonymous work, *Wacht! Euch zum Streit*, has been variously ascribed to and denied the authorship of Buxtehude. Most recently, Kerala Snyder has concluded that it is the work that Buxtehude composed for the *Abendmusiken* of 1682.[33]

Public concerts and opera in Lübeck

Most of the music heard outside the churches continued to be performed in homes or at private events of various kinds. Weddings and other social gatherings remained significant opportunities for the town musicians to earn money. The earliest records of public concerts begin only in 1733, when Johann Paul Kunzen, the second organist to succeed Buxtehude at the Marienkirche, established a subscription concert series, presented in rooms of his quarters at the Marienkirche until 1734, when they were given in a theatre. Since Kunzen had lived in Hamburg for ten years from 1723, his motivation for originating concerts for a ticket-buying public was probably inspired by Telemann's successes. From 1752 he also sold tickets to those who wished to attend the final rehearsal of the *Abendmusiken*, which often included fine soloists brought from Hamburg.

The first public performance of an opera in Lübeck occurred in June 1746, when the famous touring Mingotti opera company presented an opera entitled *Ipermestra* and an intermezzo, *Grullo e Moschetta* (composers unknown). The same company returned again in 1752 to stage six operas and intermezzos; one of the works was entitled *Artaxerxe* and was perhaps by the Dresden court composer Johann Adolf Hasse. Performances took place in a theatre on the Beckergrube which was completely renovated in 1753; it consisted of 120 seats, 200 places for standing, a box for town officials in the parquet and 11 boxes with 80 seats in the balcony. This was the opera house that was to remain in use until 1905.[34]

NOTES

[1] Concerning Hamburg and the Hanseatic League see G. J. Buelow, 'Music in the Hanseatic Cities in the Seventeenth Century', *The Early Baroque Era*, ed. C. Price, *Man and Music*, iii (London, 1993).

[2] *BurneyGN*, ii, 236.

[3] Concerning the opening of the opera house on the Gänsemarkt in 1678 and its early repertory see Buelow, 'Music in the Hanseatic Cities'.

[4] J. Mattheson, *Der musicalische Patriot* (Hamburg, 1728), 176.

[5] J. Mattheson, *Die neueste Untersuchung der Singspiele* (Hamburg, 1744), 84.

[6] G. W. Leibniz, *Sämtliche Schriften und Briefe*, iii, no.444, p.513, as cited in G. Flaherty, *Opera in the Development of German Critical Thought* (Princeton, 1978), 22–3.

[7] Regarding Franck's importance to Hamburg opera and its repertory see G. J. Buelow, 'Hamburg Opera during Buxtehude's Lifetime: the Works of Johann Wolfgang Franck', *Church, Stage, Studio: Music and its Contexts in 17th Century Germany*, ed. P. Walker (Ann Arbor, 1989), 127–41.

[8] It is described in G. J. Buelow, 'Die schöne und getreue Ariadne (Hamburg, 1691): a Lost Opera by J.G. Conradi Rediscovered', *AcM*, xliv (1972), 108–21.

[9] J. A. Scheibe, *Über die musikalische Composition* (Leipzig, 1773), p.liii.

[10] J. Mattheson, *Das neu-eröffnete Orchestre* (Hamburg, 1713), 217.

[11] J. Mattheson, *Grundlage einer Ehren-Pforte* (Hamburg, 1740), 133.

[12] ibid, 129.

[13] Mattheson, *Der musicalische Patriot*, 197–9.

[14] Data from R. D. Lynch, *Opera in Hamburg, 1718–1738: a Study of the Libretto and Musical Style* (diss., New York U., 1979); Lynch has extrapolated this information from P. A. Merbach, 'Das Repertoire der Hamburger Oper von 1718 bis 1750', *AMw*, vi (1924), 354–72.

[15] Mattheson, *Grundlage einer Ehren-Pforte*, 359.

[16] Buelow, 'Music in the Hanseatic Cities'.

[17] Mattheson, *Der musicalische Patriot*, 316.

[18] See Buelow, 'Music in the Hanseatic Cities'.

[19] Women in church choirs had been strictly banned for centuries; it was Mattheson who took credit for first introducing professional female singers into a performance of an oratorio in Hamburg Cathedral (17 Sept 1716) and then again in later performances (see his comment in *Grundlage einer Ehren-Pforte*, 203).

[20] J. Sittard, *Geschichte des Musik- und Concertwesens in Hamburg vom 14. Jahrhundert bis auf die Gegenwart* (Altona and Leipzig, 1890), 40.

[21] H. Becker, 'Die frühe Hamburgische Tagespresse als Musikgeschichtliche Quelle', *Beiträge zur Hamburgischen Musik-Geschichte*, ed. H. Husmann (Hamburg, 1956), 24–5.

[22] A summary of Telemann's public performances, by year, is in E. Klessmann, *Georg Philipp Telemann in Hamburg, 1721–1767* (Hamburg, 1980), 181–233.

[23] Sittard, *Geschichte des Musik- und Concertwesens in Hamburg*, 61.

[24] *Georg Philipp Telemann Briefwechsel*, ed. H. Grosse and H. R. Jung (Leipzig, 1972), 213.

[25] Only nine of the oratorios and one serenade are extant. Further regarding this important form of concert music, see W. Maertens, 'Georg Philipp Telemanns Hamburger "Kapitäns-musiken"', *Festschrift Walter Wiora* (Kassel, 1967), 335–41.

[26] W. Menke, *Das Vokalwerk Georg Philipp Telemanns* (Kassel, 1942), Anhang 4.

[27] Data from Becker, 'Die frühe Hamburgische Tagespresse', 26–8, and Sittard, *Geschichte des Musik- und Concertwesens in Hamburg*, 68–81.

[28] See Buelow, 'Music in the Hanseatic Cities'.

[29] Buxtehude's career and music are fully discussed in K. J. Snyder, *Dieterich Buxtehude, Organist in Lübeck* (New York, 1987).

[30] *Natalitia Sacra, Oder Verzeichnüss aller Texte, Welche in bevorstehenden Heiligen Feste, als Weinachten, Neuen Jahr und Heil. drey Könige allhie zu St. Marien sowohl Vor- als Nachmittag, theils vor und nach den Predigten, theils auch unter der Communion mit genugsamer Vocal-Hülffe sollen musiciret werden* (Lübeck, 1682), as given in Snyder, *Buxtehude*, 483–4.

[31] This large collection of music was transferred to Vienna from Lübeck in 1814; it is described by C. Stiehl, *Katalog der Musik-Sammlung auf der Stadtbibliothek zu Lübeck*, Anhang I: 'Musik-Sammlung der St. Marienkirche zu Lübeck, seit 1814 der Gesellschaft der Musikfreunde in Wien angehorend', *Program des Katharineums zu Lübeck* (Lübeck, 1893).

[32] *Die Beglückte und Geschmückte Stadt Lübeck: was ist Kurtze Beschreibung der Stadt Lübeck So wol Vom Anfang und Fortgang Derselben In ihrem Bau, Herrschafften und Einwohnern* (Lübeck, 1697); Eng. trans. in Snyder, *Buxtehude*, 57.

[33] Snyder, *Buxtehude*, 211.

[34] W. Pfannkuch, 'Vom Musiktheater in der Beckergrube bis zur Franzosenzeit', *800 Jahre Musik in Lübeck*, ii: *Dokumentation zum Lübecker Musikfest 1982* (Lübeck, 1983), 83–9.

BIBLIOGRAPHICAL NOTE

Most of the literature on Hamburg's political and cultural history is in German. A major work is E. Klessmann's *Geschichte der Stadt Hamburg* (Hamburg, 1981). Two important articles dealing with the political, cultural and economic conditions in Hamburg during the first half of the eighteenth century are H. W. Eckardt, 'Hamburg zur Zeit Johann Matthesons: Politik, Wirtschaft und Kultur', and J. Rathje, 'Zur hamburgischen Gelehrtenrepublik im Zeitalter Matthesons', both in *New Mattheson Studies*, ed. G. J. Buelow and H. J. Marx (Cambridge, 1983). A useful summary of Hamburg's history in the eighteenth century appears in B. D. Stewart, *Georg Philipp Telemann in Hamburg: Social and Cultural Background and its Musical Expression* (diss., Stanford U., 1985). Some of the most important primary sources for a variety of information on Hamburg and its cultural as well as musical milieu are found in the works of the great Hamburg composer, theorist and journalist Johann Mattheson, including: *Der musicalische Patriot* (Hamburg, 1728), *Grundlage einer Ehren-Pforte* (Hamburg, 1740) and *Die neueste Untersuchung der Singspiele* (Hamburg, 1744).

The literary foundations of Hamburg's opera are made clear in G. Flaherty, *Opera in the Development of German Critical Thought* (Princeton, 1978). The classic study of Hamburg's Baroque opera remains H. C. Wolff's *Die Barockoper in Hamburg (1678–1738)* (Wolfenbüttel, 1957). A comprehensive study of the Hamburg opera in its final two decades, based on an examination of all the librettos, is by R. D. Lynch, *Opera in Hamburg, 1718–1738: a Study of the Libretto and Musical Style* (diss., New York U., 1979). Further studies about specific aspects of opera in Hamburg include G. J. Buelow, 'Hamburg Opera during Buxtehude's Lifetime: the Works of Johann Wolfgang Franck', *Church, Stage, Studio: Music and its Contexts in 17th Century Germany*, ed. P. Walker (Ann Arbor, 1989), 127–41, and 'Die schöne und getreue Ariadne (Hamburg, 1691): a Lost Opera by J.G. Conradi Rediscovered', *AcM*, xliv (1972), 108–21; H. J. Marx, 'Geschichte der Hamburger Barockoper: ein Forschungsbericht', and K. Zelm, 'Die Sänger der Hamburger Gänsemarkt-Oper', both in *Hamburger Jb für Musikwissenschaft*, iii: *Studien zur Barockoper*, ed. C. Floros, H. J. Marx and P. Petersen (Hamburg, 1978); H. J. Marx, 'Politische und wirtschaftliche Voraussetzungen der

Hamburger Oper', and K. Zelm, 'Zur Verarbeitung italienischer Stoffe auf der Hamburger Gänsemarkt-Oper', both in *Hamburger Jb für Musikwissenschaft*, v: *Die frühdeutsche Oper und ihre Beziehungen zur Italien, England und Frankreich*, ed. C. Floros, H. J. Marx and P. Petersen (Laaber, 1981); and W. Braun, *Vom Remter zum Gänsemarkt: aus der Frühgeschichte der alten Hamburger Oper (1677–1697)* (Saarbrücken, 1987).

The standard work for the history of public concerts in Hamburg remains the venerable study by J. Sittard, *Geschichte der Musik und Concertwesens in Hamburg vom 14. Jahrhundert bis auf die Gegenwart* (Altona and Leipzig, 1890). For Telemann's career in Hamburg, see E. Klessmann, *Georg Philipp Telemann in Hamburg: 1721–1767* (Hamburg, 1980); W. Menke, *Das Vokalwerk Georg Philipp Telemanns* (Kassel, 1942); and the valuable collection of letters, *Georg Philipp Telemann Briefwechsel*, ed. H. Grosse and H. R. Jung (Leipzig, 1972).

The most important work concerning Buxtehude's life and career, as well as a rich account of Lübeck's historical and cultural background, is found in K. J. Snyder's *Dieterich Buxtehude, Organist in Lübeck* (New York, 1987).

Chapter VII

Dresden in the Age of Absolutism

GEORGE J. BUELOW

Of all the cities in central Germany during the late Baroque era to symbolize the Age of Absolutism, Dresden was the foremost example of cultural achievements attained in the cause of political ambition. Before its destruction in World War II, Dresden was often called the Florence on the Elbe and presented a cityscape of magnificent buildings – the electoral palace, the Zwinger, the court churches and opera house – that recalled a period in the history of Saxony unequalled before or after in the splendour of its physical beauty. With the break-up of the empire at the end of the Thirty Years War (1648), the Saxon princes began a determined development to place themselves at the centre of German political influence, an influence that could be challenged at that time only by Bavaria. When Friedrich August I ('August the Strong') succeeded to the electoral throne in 1694 Dresden had already become a cultural centre of elaborate, court-directed festivities. Three years later he was elected King of Poland, and the Saxon-Polish alliance seemed to achieve the goals envisaged by earlier rulers, Johann Georg II (1656–80), Johann Georg III (1680–91) and Johann Georg IV (1691–4). It was, however, a fragile union, threatened first by the bellicose Swedes and later by the rapid rise to power of Brandenburg-Prussia, which in the mid-1750s under the guidance of Frederick the Great destroyed Saxony's short-lived centrality in German power politics.

Dresden had already achieved musical significance earlier in the seventeenth century, even before the appointment of Heinrich Schütz as director of the court Kapelle. Trained in Italy by Giovanni Gabrieli and intensely interested in Italian musical developments throughout his career, Schütz became a major catalyst in bringing the German polyphonic style into a union with the new seventeenth-century Italian concertato and operatic styles. Italian musicians were already a prominent influence in court musical organizations in the mid-seventeenth century. Schütz shared the position of Kapell-meister with Giovanni Andrea Bontempi and Vincenzo Albrici and had as his vice-Kapellmeister Marco Gioseppe Peranda; solo singers, too, were largely imported from south of the Alps. The first Italian opera performed in Dresden was *Il Paride* by Bontempi, a multi-talented castrato and composer; it was given as part of the festivities celebrating the marriage of the elector's daughter in 1662. Bontempi's *Dafne*, composed in 1671 with Peranda, remains the first fully extant opera in German (the score for Schütz's *Dafne*, composed to a German translation of Rinuccini's libretto and already heard by the court at Torgau in 1627, is lost). The first important German opera house was completed during the reign of Johann Georg II. A theatre and opera house of impressive grandeur; with a capacity of 2000, it was inaugurated in 1667 with *Teseo*, composed by either Bontempi or Giovanni Andrea Moniglia, author of the libretto. The new theatre was incorporated into the yearly displays of elaborate festivities, notably for the carnival season, but also as part of celebrations for royal baptisms, weddings and visiting nobility and for other occasions. At great expense these celebrations brought together all manner of entertainment – sports, plays both serious and comic, hunting, banquets, fireworks, ballets and, frequently, Italian opera.

One of Johann Georg III's first responsibilities upon becoming ruling prince in 1680 was to reduce the expenses of the court Kapelle. He dismissed all the Italian musicians and made Christoph Bernhard (1628–92), Schütz's former pupil, director of a German Kapelle. Sacred music at court remained, however, strong in numbers of performers. As well as an unspecified number of chapel boys, the first chorus included (in addition to Bernhard) a vice-Kapellmeister and organist, one alto, tenor and bass, three violins, a bassoon and three trumpets. The second chorus consisted of the court Kantor, an organist, one alto, two tenors, one bass, two cornetts, three trombones and two kalkants (organ-bellows operators). Also available to the Kapelle were 14 court trumpeters and a timpanist, as well as six French violinists.[1] The new elector, like his father before him, had spent considerable time in Venice, where he had learnt to favour Italian music above all other, and especially Italian opera. This led in 1685 to his establishing a permanent Italian opera company and re-engaging the popular Venetian opera composer Carlo Pallavicino, who had earlier served his father as Kapellmeister. At the same time, Margherita Salicola, whom the elector had heard in Venice, was brought as prima donna to Dresden from Mantua, where she had been the favourite of Duke Carlo IV. Since she came secretly from Mantua, without the duke's permission, a diplomatic crisis of some consequence arose between Mantua and Dresden. She sang for the first time at the Dresden opera during the carnival season of February 1686 in *Alarico*; further triumphs at Dresden included her Armida in Pallavicino's *La Gierusalemme liberata* in 1687 and in 1689 her appearance in his *Antiope*. The latter work was left unfinished on the composer's death and was completed by Nicolaus

Adam Strungk (1640–1700), who became the new court Kapellmeister.

Johann Georg IV inherited his family's great love for music and theatre and, having lived for a time in Venice, maintained the Dresden court's cultivation of Italian music. In his short reign – two and a half years – he continued the artistic traditions laid down by his father. For his marriage to the Margravine of Brandenburg-Ansbach at Torgau in April 1692 the Dresden Kapelle was engaged for a ballet, *Le feste di Cupido*, in which men and women of the court participated; the Prince of Brandenburg brought 'Italian music' to the celebrations. Carnival season at Dresden the next year included performances of two operas, *Camillo generoso* and *L'Arsinoe*. With the permission and support of the new elector, Strungk went to Leipzig, where he had an opera house constructed and established a new Italian opera company to perform during the three annual fairs.

29. (a) *Banquet celebrating the 49th birthday of Friedrich August I (August the Strong) on 12 May 1718: drawing by Johann Friedrich Wentzel*

29. (b) detail showing the musicians' gallery

Strungk proposed to the elector that the Leipzig opera might serve as a training-school for musicians who could subsequently be employed by the Dresden court.

Friedrich August I (1694–1733), known as 'August the Strong', brother of Johann Georg IV, gained the Saxon throne in April 1694 and was responsible for creating the most brilliant and extravagant period in the cultural history of Dresden. His musical training came from Christoph Bernhard. He travelled extensively throughout Europe, including Spain and Portugal, and in Paris acquired a life-long devotion to French poetry and theatre. But like his grandfather, father and older brother, experiences in Venice impressed on him the significance of Italian composers and performers, and of Italian opera. He was a hedonist who reportedly had 354 natural children and who saw in cultural exhibitionism substantial political values, as had the French king, Louis XIV. The city gained its famous Baroque façade with the employment of the architect Matthäus Daniel Pöppelmann (1662–1736), who built the Zwinger palace as the dramatic, theatrical centre of the court, with its intricate combination of arches, columns and balconies (see fig.30). Other building projects (completed in 1719 for the wedding festivities of the crown prince and Maria Josepha, daughter of the emperor) included the enlargement of the adjacent palace, the decoration of the Taschenberg palace for the crown prince, the fitting out of the Turkish palace in the upper garden and new furnishings for the Dutch (later Japanese) palace, as well as numerous newly laid-out gardens, fountains, an outdoor theatre, triumphal arches and much more. The Italian Baroque was also represented by Gaetano Chiaveri's Hofkirche. A companion architectural jewel to the Zwinger palace was the new opera house 'am Zwinger', which the elector ordered to be constructed in just one year for the festivities of 1719 (see fig.32 below).

The achievement of Pöppelmann and Alessandro Mauro, it was the largest in Germany at the time and representative of the elaborately decorated late Baroque style.[2] It remained a centre for opera in Germany until it was destroyed by fire in the May revolution of 1849.

Music continued to be only one of the arts helping to define the elector's intention to project the image of Dresden and Saxony as a model of absolute political influence. Considerable court expenditure was required to sustain his love of the French theatre. Between 1700 and 1705 a French theatrical troupe including dancers and musicians resided at court; most of their performances, however, were given at the Warsaw court. In 1708 a new French group of actors, dancers and musicians was engaged for the Dresden court that was directed by the famous French dancer Louis de Poitier.[3] As early as 1695, for the carnival season, August planned the main parade as a magnificent procession of pagan gods and goddesses, consisting of 11 groups, each deity or two preceding a festival wagon. Musicians, directed by the Kapellmeister Strungk, were integrated into each segment of the procession, with their costumes and instruments determined by the context or character of each troupe. The first group was devoted to Jupiter and Juno with 32 musicians in Harlequin and Pulcinella costumes. August dressed as the god Mercury followed on horseback. Another pageant wagon presented the Seven Deadly Sins, with an accompaniment of six bagpipers. Mars and Bellona were assisted by shawms, trumpets, timpani and long-drums. For Neptune's wagon with sirens, nymphs and wind gods, there were eight oboists, and two bassoonists dressed as satyrs. The eighth group, led by Apollo in his sun-chariot, was followed by 12 musicians playing oboes, bagpipes, guitars and fiddles. The goddess Aurora, impersonated by Countess Aurora von Königsmark, one of the elector's mistresses, had an ensemble of eight musicians – two singing from an open music manuscript, while others played oboes and violins in pairs, a harp and a lute. Perhaps the most elaborate of the wagons represented Mount Parnassus with the Nine Muses, who were represented by women playing the lute, violin, cello, harp, trumpet, cornett, guitar and psaltery. It was reported that this procession was the most elaborate and impressive event ever staged in Dresden.[4]

In 1697 August converted to Catholicism in order to solidify his and his heirs' claims to the Polish throne and thereby raise Dresden to the first rank of princely courts in Europe. His action was not without serious religious consequences in the court itself and in the principality. Much of the nobility, including the Electress Christiane Eberhardine of Brandenburg-Bayreuth, refused to embrace the Catholic religion. On being elected King of Poland, August converted the Dresden opera theatre into the court Catholic church, and the court Kapelle was required to take on the double function of

30. Inner court of the Zwinger Palace, Dresden (1709–28; designed by Matthäus Daniel Pöppelmann): engraving (1758) after Bernardo Bellotto (self-styled 'Canaletto' after his better-known uncle, Antonio)

serving both Protestant and Catholic worship. By 1708 the king was seeking Catholic boys for his Kapelle and, helped by the efforts of the Jesuits, boys were enlisted from neighbouring Bohemia. Court documents of 1710–15 indicate that the Catholic chapel consisted of two or three boy sopranos, one or two altos, one or two tenors, two or three violins, a double bass and an organist. A rich repertory of sacred music, largely unknown today, was created for this court chapel, notably by the Kapellmeister (from 1721) Johann David Heinichen (1683–1729) and his assistant (from 1729 Kapellmeister) Jan Dismas Zelenka (1679–1745).[5] In addition, court musical activities were greatly expanded with the dual responsibilities for court functions in both Dresden and Warsaw. Between 1709 and 1719 the court orchestra became famous throughout Europe. Among its many distinguished members were J. B. Volumier (c1670–1728), its leader, succeeded by J. G. Pisendel (1687–1755); F. M. Veracini, a court composer and violinist; Christian Pezold (1677–1733), a court composer and organist; S. L. Weiss (1686–1750), a theorbo player; J. D. Zelenka, a double bass player; P. G. Buffardin (c1690–1768), a flautist; and Johann Christoph Richter (1700–85), an oboist.

The zenith of cultural display, as well as the climax of the Dresden court's reputation for spending vast sums of money on enormously elaborate festivities, was reached in 1719. The occasion was the

221

31. *Te Deum in the Catholic court chapel, Dresden, following the marriage in Vienna of Prince Friedrich August of Saxony and Archduchess Maria Josepha of Austria, 3 September 1719: drawing by Carl Heinrich Fehling*

marriage of Crown Prince Friedrich August to Maria Josepha, daughter of the Emperor Joseph I, which was the culmination of the efforts of the Saxon elector and King of Poland to command European political power; for through this marriage he not only retained influence in Polish lands but could now envisage Saxon politics joined by heredity to those of the empire. Court preparations for the wedding festivities began apace. As early as 1716 the crown prince, while spending a year in Venice, engaged Heinichen as one of the court Kapellmeisters. In addition, he was commissioned to engage an Italian opera troupe led by the composer Antonio Lotti and his wife the soprano Santa Stella, which among others would also include the soprano Margherita Durastanti, the contralto Vittoria Tesi, the castrato Senesino, the tenor Francesco Guicciardi and the bass Giuseppe Maria Boschi.

The wedding took place on 20 August in Vienna. In the theatre of the Favorita palace a festive performance of the opera *Sirita* by Antonio Caldara was performed, as well as the cantata *L'Istro* by Francesco Conti. The bridal party arrived on 2 September at Pirna, just south of Dresden on the Elbe, where the the princess boarded the Buccentauro, a replica of the Venetian state gondola. Travelling by water and accompanied by a fleet of other ships and gondolas, she was met by the king at Dresden and proceeded into the city in a magnificent parade of the military corps, nobles and city officials, in more than 100 decorated coaches. From the triumphal arches and church towers musicians performed, and trumpeters and timpanists welcomed the procession at the palace. Beginning the next day, and almost continuously until 30 September, musical, theatrical, sports and other kinds of elaborate entertainment were held. The central theme of all the events was that of the gods of the seven planets and their effect on mankind and especially on royalty. On 3 September the royal highnesses and the court attended a *Te Deum* in the electoral Catholic chapel (fig.31). That evening the new opera house was dedicated with a performance of Lotti's *Giove in Argo*. On the evening of 5 September, French, and on 6 September, Italian, plays were given. Another opera by Lotti, *Ascanio, ovvero Gli odi delusi dal sangue*, was performed on 7 September. On 10 September the celebrations were dedicated to the sun god, Apollo, and in the afternoon a performance of Heinichen's serenade *La gara degli dei* was sung by performers representing Mercury, Apollo, Diana, Mars, Venus, Jupiter and Saturn. In the evening a serenade by 64 trumpets and eight timpani introduced a fireworks display. A high point of the musical events was the production of Lotti's new opera, *Teofane*, given in the new opera house on 13 September (fig.32).

All the arts and sciences seem to have united in this [creative]

32. Interior of the Dresden court theatre (designed by Pöppelmann, with interior decoration by Alessandro Mauro) with the performance of Lotti's opera 'Teofane', 13 September 1719, that formed part of the marriage celebrations (note the ostentatious royal box at the back of the theatre): drawing by C. H. Fehling

33. Festival of Diana on the River Elbe, 18 September 1719, with Kapellmeister J. D. Heinichen directing his 'Serenata fatta sulla Elba': drawing by C. H. Fehling

breath of air. The extraordinary payments which the king grants the players have attracted the best and most excellent masters of this art to Dresden from Italy, the great school of music. When Senesino and Berselli sing, to Lotti's directions, however, one hears everything that [such] beautiful and tender music has to offer. The whole orchestra is manned by the best instrumentalists. The stage is actually smaller than the one in Vienna, but its complement [of performers] is incomparable.[6]

Five days later a festival in honour of Diana, goddess of the moon and hunting, reached its climax in a performance of Heinichen's *Serenata fatta sulla Elba*, an elaborate serenade performed on the Elbe on a superbly decorated ship in the form of a gigantic seashell (fig. 33):

After the court was seated on the right-bank of the Elbe, there appeared the gilt- and silvered ship, constructed like Diana's chariot and drawn by four seahorses down river. There, on board was the goddess herself with her nymphs, such as Climene, Daphne, Niese and Alcippa, next to the royal musical ensemble, who were all clad in green taffeta, and who, as they approached the royal hunting tent [on shore] sang an Italian cantata with all sorts of instruments, entitled *Diana upon the Elbe*. When this was over, Diana and her nymphs, as well as the entire musical ensemble, debarked, where they watched the hunt.[7]

Among the numerous other court activities during these remarkable days of celebration was the performance on 23 September of a French *divertissement*, *Les quatre saisons*, with text by the French actor Jean Poisson and music by the second Kapellmeister Johann Christoph Schmidt (fig.34). The stage was constructed in the open air in the middle of the great palace gardens. There were interpolated ballets danced by members of the court, and the singers and members of the orchestra numbered more than 100, all in the service of the elector. The widely touted brilliance of these events during a month-long celebration attracted large numbers of tourists and artists to Dresden. Among those who came to experience music, especially opera, was Georg Philipp Telemann (1681–1767), who undoubtedly had contacts with many of the court musicians; later he was to dedicate a violin concerto to the Dresden Konzertmeister J. G. Pisendel. Handel lived in Dresden for several months, played for the court, and renewed his acquaintance with Lotti; he also had contacts with the illustrious singers, several of whom (including Berselli, Senesino, Durastanti and Boschi) he was later to engage for performances of his operas in London.

34. Performance of J. C. Schmidt's divertissement 'Les quatre saisons' in the gardens of the Zwinger Palace, 23 September 1719

Nothing approaching the quality and quantity of cultural display was ever again to be achieved in Dresden. In 1720 the entire Italian opera ensemble was summarily dismissed by the elector when he learnt that Berselli and Senesino had created an embarrassing scene during the rehearsal of Heinichen's opera *Flavio Crispo*; Senesino had accused the composer of not knowing how to set the Italian text, tore up the music and threw it at his feet. This incident may have presented the elector with an unanticipated excuse to eliminate the burdensome costs of the Italians, who had never enjoyed his personal admiration. Indeed, after the departure of the Italian opera company, August re-established to some prominence French actors and musicians, who dominated court entertainments both in Dresden and in Warsaw as well as in several country palaces such as Moritzburg and Pillnitz. Court festivals continued both for the yearly carnival celebrations and for other court ceremonies, such as the marriage in 1725 of one of August's natural daughters. The crown prince and princess, however, rather quickly began to restore the Italian wing of court musicians, at first primarily for service in church and chamber music. In September 1726 the crown princess ordered the performance of a comic Italian opera, *Calandro*, by the court composer Giovanni Alberto Ristori (1692–1753), to celebrate the return of her husband from Warsaw. The following year Ristori's comic work *Un pazzo ne fà cento, ovvero Don Chisciotte*, based on Cervantes, was the musical centrepiece to the carnival celebrations. By 1730 the strength in Italian singers and musicians had reached numbers even greater than in 1719.

It was in 1731 that the German composer Johann Adolf Hasse (1699–1783), trained largely in Italy, and his wife, the famous prima donna Faustina Bordoni Hasse (1700–81), first came to Dresden. Hasse had been in Italy since 1722, studying with Nicola Porpora and Alessandro Scarlatti; for seven years he was court composer at Naples, and his achievement in mastering the form and style of Neapolitan opera led to further successes in Venice. In 1730 the Saxon ambassador to Venice invited Hasse and his wife to come to Dresden in 1731, although already by 1730 Hasse had begun to use the title *maestro di cappella* of the Dresden court. He and his wife arrived in Dresden in the summer of 1731, and on 13 September his opera *Cleofide* was heard in the Dresden opera house, where over the next 32 years he was to perform 34 of his operas. The cast was outstanding, and included Faustina Bordoni. Johann Sebastian Bach, who travelled from neighbouring Leipzig to Dresden on several occasions, was in the city and gave an organ recital. It is most likely that he heard a performance of the opera, since according to Forkel, his first biographer, Bach knew the Hasses, who 'had come often to Leipzig and admired his great talents'. Forkel continues:

The Late Baroque Era

'[Bach] was therefore always received in an exceedingly honorable manner at Dresden, and often went thither to hear the opera. He generally took his eldest son with him. He used to say in joke some days before his departure: "Friedemann shan't we go again to hear the lovely Dresden ditties?"'[8]

The Hasses left Dresden again, performing operas around Italy in cities such as Turin, Rome, Venice and Bologna. When August died in 1733 and his son Friedrich August II gained the throne, Hasse was recalled to Dresden, where he arrived early in 1734. His appointment as Kapellmeister began on Good Friday with his oratorio *Il cantico de' tre fanciulli* in the Catholic court church. From that year until 1763 Hasse and his wife spent long periods in Dresden, but they were also frequently in Italy, often lived in Vienna and much later retired to Venice. Hasse's operas to librettos by Metastasio became models of eighteenth-century *opera seria* and made Dresden court opera internationally famous. In addition, Hasse contributed a major body of sacred music for the court Kapelle. His music, with its roots deep in the early eighteenth-century Classical tendencies of Neapolitan opera, had already in its formal and expressive character left behind any concept of the Baroque as a style. Only in the elaborateness of the staging, the magnificence of the costumes and the spectacular vocal gifts of the mainly Italian singers did Hasse's operas reflect the continuing tradition of cultural display developed by the Saxon electors over some six decades. When August II died in 1763, his son Friedrich Christian came to power; he discontinued all elaborate court extravagance, and discontinued Hasse's services. For Dresden, the great Baroque Age of Absolutism had ended.

NOTES

[1] See M. Fürstenau, *Zur Geschichte der Musik und des Theaters am Hofe zu Dresden*, i (Dresden, 1861), 262–3; further factual data for this article has been drawn from this classic study of music and theatre at the Dresden court.

[2] Further description and pictures of the opera house are in H. Schnoor, *Dresden: vierhundert Jahre deutsche Musikkultur* (Dresden, 1948), 67–73.

[3] Valuable information regarding the musical organizations at the court of August the Strong is found in I. Becker-Glauch, *Die Bedeutung der Musik für die Dresdener Hoffeste* (Kassel, 1951), 20–29.

[4] Information from E. A. Bowles, *Musical Ensembles in Festival Books, 1500–1800* (Ann Arbor, 1989), 387–404, which also includes several delightful reproductions of scenes from the procession.

[5] A major study of the music for the Catholic court chapel in this period is by W. Horn, *Die Dresdner Hofkirchenmusik 1720–1745* (Kassel, 1987).

[6] Quoted from Bowles, *Musical Ensembles in Festival Books*, 438, who takes the passage from G. Pietzsch, *Sachsen als Musikland* (Dresden, 1938), 52.

[7] Ibid; in addition, a set of engravings, all scenes related to the wedding festivities, is given on pp.440–47.

[8] *The Bach Reader*, ed. H. T. David and A. Mendel (New York, 1945), 335; (rev. 2/1966).

BIBLIOGRAPHICAL NOTE

Although the development of music in Dresden, especially at the Saxon court during the Baroque, was particularly important, the literature is quite limited. For the period circumscribed by this essay, only a few studies, largely in German, stand out as major sources of information. Despite its origins in the mid-nineteenth century, the fundamental work remains that of Moritz Fürstenau (1824–89), a flautist in the Dresden royal Kapelle and librarian of the private royal music collection. His comprehensive (for its time) history of music and theatre at the Dresden court appeared in two volumes: *Zur Geschichte der Musik und des Theaters am Hofe der Kurfürsten von Sachsen, Johann Georg II, Johann Georg III, und Johann Georg IV* and *Zur Geschichte der Musik und des Theaters am Hofe der Kurfürsten von Sachsen und Könige von Polen, Friedrich August I (August II) und Friedrich August II (August III)* (Dresden, 1861–2, facs., 1971). Almost nothing of significance followed Fürstenau's work until the publication of I. Becker-Glauch's *Die Bedeutung der Musik für die Dresdener Hoffeste bis in die Zeit Augusts des Starken* (Kassel, 1951). With her extensive research in the available archives in Dresden (many of them still difficult to find, or lost in the aftermath of World War II), Becker-Glauch greatly expanded upon Fürstenau's account of the elaborate court festivals that established Dresden's fame as an outstanding cultural centre.

A good overview of music in Dresden during the Baroque is contained in H. Schnoor's *Dresden: vierhundert Jahre deutsche Musikkultur* (Dresden, 1948). For a fine study of sacred music at the Dresden court during the late Baroque, see W. Horn, *Die Dresdner Hofkirchenmusik 1720–1745* (Kassel, 1987). A number of vivid iconographical representations of Dresden court festivals appear in E. A. Bowles, *Musical Ensembles in Festival Books, 1500–1800: an Iconographical & Documentary Survey* (Ann Arbor, 1989). *Oper in Dresden: Festschrift zur Wiedereröffnung der Semperoper*, ed. M. Rank and H. Seeger (Berlin, 1985), includes among the essays three of significance to the late Baroque: M. Rank and H. Seeger, '"Was Dafne gibt, das bleibt!": der Kontinuitätsgedanke in der Dresdner Operngeschichte'; J. L. Sponsel, 'Das Festjahr 1719'; and O. Landmann, 'Die Dresdner "Ära Hasse" (1733–1763)'. The only major study of Hasse's operas is F. L. Millner's *The Operas of Johann Adolf Hasse* (Ann Arbor, 1979). Early in this century a important study of Hasse's sacred music also included a useful thematic catalogue: W. Müller, *Johann Adolf Hasse als Kirchenkomponist* (Leipzig, 1911). The oratorios are examined in M. Koch, *Die Oratorien Johann Adolf Hasses: Überlieferung und Struktur* (Pfaffenweiler, 1989). A number of specialized studies concerning various aspects of Hasse's operas and sacred music appear in *Colloquium Johann Adolf Hasse und die Musik seiner Zeit: Siena 1983*, published in *AnMc*, no.25 (1987).

Chapter VIII

Brandenburg-Prussia and the Central German Courts

BERND BASELT

Only consider the great vogue music enjoys everywhere! Soon there will be not even a little village, especially in Thuringia, where both vocal and instrumental music do not thrive and flourish wonderfully and exquisitely everywhere. If there is no organ, then vocal music is, at the least, accompanied and embellished by one, five or six fiddles, something that could hardly have been found even in towns in the old days.

Such were the terms in which Michael Altenburg of Erfurt (1584–1640), a pastor and composer, described the flourishing musical culture of central Germany before the devastation of the Thirty Years War (1618–48).[1] Even later, however, when the country had recovered from the damage inflicted by the war, the population of central Germany found an intrinsic part of their intellectual identity in music, so that Wolfgang Carl Briegel (1626–1712), court Kapellmeister of Gotha, thought it proper to state proudly:

The noble land of Saxony is to be praised above others, more particularly because the Divine Service in public worship is conducted there with both choral and figural singing[2] in so fine and sprightly a manner. Leaving aside the excellent music now found in the famous cities of Saxony, it is well known that there are few villages in that noble land that do not have a little organ in their church, as well as other musical instruments, with which they praise God most diligently. Young people there are very well versed in music: on Sundays and feast days music is made not only *choraliter* but also *figuraliter*, and very often in tiny villages, so that it is a joy and a wonder to hear it.[3]

The historical development of German music in the age of absolutism and the Enlightenment took place, for the most part, in the areas mentioned in the two quotations above. The eastern part of the former German Empire – especially Brandenburg, Saxony and

Thuringia – was a special reservoir of brilliant musical talent which had produced the three great 'S' composers of the seventeenth century – Heinrich Schütz (1585–1672), Johann Hermann Schein (1586–1630) and Samuel Scheidt (1587–1654). They were followed in the eighteenth century by three no less important representatives of central German music – Georg Philipp Telemann (1681–1767), George Frideric Handel (1685–1759) and Johann Sebastian Bach (1685–1750). These names, of course, are only *primi inter pares*; but their birthplaces, and some of the places where they lived and worked, lie within the geographical area whose politics and economics were principally controlled by the major central German states of Prussia (Brandenburg) and Saxony.

The political situation typical of Germany in the seventeenth century, and to some extent in the eighteenth too, was based on particularism. The sweeping changes in power politics and the social transformations that took place in Europe during the eighteenth century were slow to obtain a foothold in the many small states and independent cities of central Germany. It was a gradual process, for these only nominally independent political entities were always passive, never actively participating in developments affecting Europe as a whole and always dependent on the great powers that beset them; splintered as they were by particularism, they had hardly any political say in the period following the Thirty Years War. But their almost chaotic multiplicity of forms, related to individual, regionally determined development, brought considerable momentum into artistic and intellectual affairs. That is particularly evident in the field of music.

Many of the most famous seventeenth- and eighteenth-century masters of German music were born in Saxony and Thuringia. Indeed, until the middle of the nineteenth century, central Germany could probably boast the largest number of notable musicians in all the German-speaking lands: Schumann and Wagner came from the area, while Liszt was court Kapellmeister of Weimar, in the heart of Thuringia, for almost two and a half decades. This may be put down to the wealth of musical centres, both large and small, the courts that had orchestras, and the cities that had ensembles of church and town musicians, as well as to the obvious musical talent of Saxons and Thuringians.

The principal musical centres of central Germany extend from the east of Brandenburg-Prussia (with its capital, Berlin), through the Anhalt principalities of Cöthen (now Köthen), Bernburg, Dessau and Zerbst, the great trade centres of Magdeburg, Halle and Leipzig, and the electorate of Saxony with the world-famous court Kapelle of Dresden, to the western and southern parts of Thuringia. The Saxon principalities of Weissenfels, Merseburg and Zeitz – principalities of secundogeniture, as they are technically described – organized their court music on the Dresden model. They were imitated and complemented by the neighbouring cities and residencies of Thuringia, which included the old university centres of Erfurt and Jena, the courts of Weimar and Gotha, the Schwarzburg courts of Rudolstadt and Sondershausen, and the courts of Altenburg, Meiningen and Eisenach. It was here that typically German, and specifically Protestant central German, musical genres arose and developed, like the motet, the *geistliches Konzert* and the cantata. There were also secular genres, such as German-language opera (alongside the famous Italian opera at the Dresden court), and French instrumental chamber music (keyboard and orchestral suites) and its Italian counterpart (solo and trio sonatas, solo concertos and concerti grossi), as well as German song both sacred and secular (Lutheran hymn and *Gesellschaftslied*).

BRANDENBURG-PRUSSIA

When economic and cultural life in central Germany slowly stabilized again after the devastation and destruction of the Thirty Years War, the centrally administered forms of state that were introduced, headed by rulers regarded as absolute monarchs, brought a new intellectual attitude known as the Enlightenment. In many respects, the Enlightenment influenced the whole of society, although religious fears, dogmas and prejudices could still exert surreptitious influence on the foundations of new thinking and new intellectual endeavours. One of the first German states where the new ideas took hold was Brandenburg, under the 'Great Elector', Friedrich Wilhelm (1620–88, elector from 1640), and his son Friedrich III (1657–1713; Friedrich I, King of Prussia, from 1701). Friedrich's second wife Sophie Charlotte (*d* 1705), daughter of Elector Ernst August of Hanover, was particularly well educated and artistically inclined, and was the first to help the new Prussian court achieve some musical importance.[4]

Berlin

Under the Great Elector, the Berlin court Kapelle became a modern string ensemble, while church music, which had suffered as a result of quarrels between Lutherans and Calvinists, was reorganized and talented musicians were encouraged. Specially prominent among them was the Kantor of the Nikolaikirche, Johannes Crüger (1598–1662), who composed motets and hymns (to texts by Paul Gerhardt, Johann Heermann and Johann Franck). Under the next elector, Friedrich III, later Friedrich I, King of Prussia (who like his grandson Friedrich II, known as Frederick the Great, was particularly

35. Johann Joachim Quantz, a member of the Dresden court Kapelle from 1727 until 1741, when he moved to Berlin to enter the service of Frederick the Great: portrait by an unknown artist

fond of the flute), and his wife Sophie Charlotte, the transformation of the Kapelle into what was for its time a modern orchestra was complete.[5] Italian virtuosos were attracted to the court, including Attilio Ariosti (in Berlin, 1697–1703), Francesco Antonio Pistocchi (1696–7) and Giovanni Bononcini (1702–4), and orchestral and chamber music and opera were encouraged.

Under the special patronage of Sophie Charlotte, a fervent admirer of the Italian composer Agostino Steffani, with whom she corresponded (he was Kapellmeister to her father in Hanover), the residence at Lietzenburg (later Charlottenburg castle) became a centre for chamber music and opera. Outstanding musicians, both German and foreign, played in the court orchestra: prominent among its German members were Johann Georg Linike (*c*1680–after 1737, later leader of the orchestras in Weissenfels and Hamburg) and Gottfried Pepusch,[6] while for the names of the French and Italians we may turn to Telemann's account of his impressions of Berlin in his autobiography of 1739:[7]

The Late Baroque Era

36. *The Berlin Royal Opera House (1741–3; designed by Georg Wenzeslaus von Knobelsdorff),
with St Hedwig's Cathedral behind: engraving*

> Travelling from Leipzig, I twice visited Berlin; I heard Giov.
> Bononcini's opera *Polyphemo*,[8] and another work (but concealed by
> my friends, since admission was allowed only to a few people) in
> which most of the parts were sung by persons of high rank, includ-
> ing a margravine who later married and went to Kassel,[9] while
> Queen Sophia Charlotte herself accompanied on the keyboard, and
> the orchestra for the most part consisted of Kapellmeisters and
> orchestra leaders, as for instance: Padre Attilio Ariosti; the brothers
> Antonio and Giovanni Bononcini; principal Kapellmeister Rieck;
> Ruggiero Fedeli; Volumier [*par corruption* Woulmyer]; Conti; La
> Riche; Forstmeier, etc.

The death of Queen Sophie Charlotte (5 February 1705) meant
the end of Italian opera at the Prussian court for the time being.
Thereafter, Singspiels and sung ballets were performed, but only at
major court festivities. When Friedrich Wilhelm I, the 'Soldier
King', succeeded his father in 1713, one of his first economy
measures was to disband the court orchestra and dismiss all the
musicians, so that he could invest funds in armaments. Not until the
mid-eighteenth century, after the Seven Years War (1756–63), was
music at the Prussian court reorganized, under the famous flautist
king Friedrich II (Frederick the Great), in a quite different form and
on a new basis. Musicians recruited at the time included Carl
Heinrich Graun (*c*1703–1759) as Kapellmeister, his brother Johann
Gottlieb (*c*1702–1771) as leader of the orchestra, C. P. E. Bach
(1714–88) as harpsichordist, and Johann Joachim Quantz (1697–
1773) as chamber musician and court composer. Together with the
Benda brothers – Franz (1709–86), Johann (1713–52), Georg (1722–

95) and Joseph (1724–1804) – they had already served in the Rheinsberg Kapelle maintained by Friedrich while he was still crown prince.

Zerbst

Among the Prussian-owned residencies of Anhalt-Bernburg, Anhalt-Cöthen, Anhalt-Dessau and Anhalt-Zerbst, only Cöthen (under J. S. Bach, 1717–23) and Zerbst (under J. F. Fasch, 1722–58) were of musical significance. Zerbst, an independent principality from 1603 until 1793, owed its musical fame to Johann Friedrich Fasch (1688–1758)[10] in particular. His many tasks as the moving spirit of court music at Zerbst included the provision of church music; he wrote at least ten cycles of church cantatas, 35 masses for Zerbst and Dresden, several Passions, settings of Latin psalms for the Catholic court chapel in Dresden, and many birthday cantatas and serenades for members of the Zerbst princely house. Besides, he provided instrumental music for courtly display and entertainment, including overtures, concertos, sinfonias and chamber music for a variety of ensembles,[11] and had been involved with opera at Bayreuth and Naumburg before his Zerbst appointment;[12] his opera *Berenice* (a revision of *Lucius Verus*, Naumburg, 1711) was given in Zerbst in 1739. Fasch kept in close contact with his contemporaries: Christoph Graupner in Darmstadt, Gottfried Heinrich Stölzel in Gotha and Bach in Leipzig, as well as Johann David Heinichen, Johann Georg Pisendel and Jan Dismas Zelenka in Dresden, and he wrote vocal and instrumental compositions for them. Other musicians who worked at Zerbst were the violinist and horn player Carl Höckh (1707–72) and the organist Johann Georg Röllig (1710–90), who was later Kapellmeister; for two years Röllig taught the harpsichord to Princess Sophie Auguste Friderike of Zerbst, who later became Empress Catherine the Great of Russia.

Halle

Of the two major Prussian cities of Magdeburg and Halle, famous as the birthplaces of Telemann and Handel, Magdeburg was severely damaged in the Thirty Years War and was slow to recover from its destruction. After its annexation by Prussia it became chiefly a garrison town and a fortress and did not regain cultural influence until the late eighteenth century. Halle, on the other hand, had attained a musical importance of its own in the seventeenth century (despite its proximity to Leipzig), chiefly through the presence there of Samuel Scheidt. The music theorist, historian and composer Wolfgang Caspar Printz, writing in 1690, named Scheidt as one of the three great 'S' composers: together with Schütz and Schein, he salvaged and maintained the high reputation of German Protestant church music after the devastation of the Thirty Years War. The son of a prosperous citizen of Halle, Scheidt studied in Amsterdam with the great Dutch organist and composer Jan Pieterszoon Sweelinck and returned to Halle as court organist (from 1609), court Kapellmeister (1620–25 and again from 1638) and city music director (from 1620). He composed chiefly sacred choral music and works for organ, and greatly influenced the development of German organ music in the later seventeenth century and the early eighteenth.

By the time of Scheidt's death (1654), after the end of the Thirty Years War and the Peace of Westphalia (1648), Halle was only a nominal possession of the Saxon court. The archdiocese of Magdeburg, to which Halle belonged at the time, was granted to the electorate of Brandenburg as part of the peace treaty. After the death of Duke August of Saxony in 1680, Halle became the possession of Brandenburg-Prussia, and the court of his successor, Duke Johann Adolf I of Saxony (ruled 1680–97), moved to Weissenfels, 30 km from Halle, taking its musicians with it.

These years were not happy for Halle. As a result of the great plague epidemics of 1681 and 1683, when 6000 people (almost 60% of the city's inhabitants) fell victim to the disease, the population had fallen to only about 5000 by 1684. The next two decades, however, saw a significant change for the better: the new Brandenburg government turned its attention to increasing the population, and Halle became a refuge for hundreds of Huguenots, driven from France after the revocation of the Edict of Nantes in 1685. The French colony was organized as early as September 1686: the cathedral became its church (Handel was later appointed organist there). After 1692 Jewish merchants and businessmen exiled from the archdiocese since the fifteenth century returned to the city, along with a large number of members of the German Reformed Church from the Palatinate, who had emigrated to Berlin. Halle's population structure was completely reorganized with the integration of these new citizens, as were its economy and its cultural and intellectual structures. The Francke Foundations were set up in 1692 and soon became a centre of Pietism. On the basis of its scholarly reputation, the university, officially inaugurated on 1 July 1694, made Halle a focal point of intellectual development in Germany.

During the second half of the seventeenth century and the beginning of the eighteenth most Halle musicians were of only local importance, except for David Pohle, Christian Ritter and Friedrich Wilhelm Zachow (see below). Ritter (*b* c1645) served as chamber organist and was regarded as a gifted composer in his day. He later lived in Hamburg and died there some time after 1720. During the 1660s, when David Pohle (1624–95) became Kapellmeister to the administrator, Duke August of Saxony, music in Halle reached a relatively high standard. In 1677 the court Kapelle comprised 18 musicians and could call on choirboys and the town choir, besides five civic musicians and three violinists who could be brought in to supplement the orchestra. Pohle was thus able to direct a musical ensemble of some size in the performance of secular and sacred works in the polychoral concerto style, even when large forces were required; and during his time in Halle early forms of Singspiel were given at the Comödienhaus. When Johann Philipp Krieger (1649–1725) joined the Kapelle as a chamber musician and chamber organist on 12 November 1677 (probably replacing Christian Ritter, who had left for Dresden), Pohle's responsibilities were considerably reduced; soon afterwards Krieger was appointed deputy Kapellmeister and then Kapellmeister. Pohle went to the ducal courts of Zeitz and Merseburg as Kapellmeister (both, like Weissenfels, Saxon courts of secundogeniture).

After the court's move from Halle to Weissenfels (see below) in 1680, Krieger spent four decades successfully developing a rich musical life there. Brought up in Nuremberg with his younger brother Johann (1651–1735), Krieger was a highly skilled composer and harpsichordist who had travelled throughout Europe, studying with Kaspar Förster the younger in Denmark and then in Italy, notably with Cavalli and Legrenzi in Venice and with Carissimi in Rome. During his tenure the musical life of Halle and Weissenfels acquired an international character, which is reflected in Krieger's inventory of the sacred music he performed in Weissenfels between 1684 and his death in 1725. Besides numerous Italian composers such as Maurizio Cazzati, Legrenzi, Ziani, Carissimi, Carlo Grossi, Pollarolo, Ruggiero Fedeli, Palestrina and others, the best-known composers of northern, southern and central Germany are well represented. Krieger himself also features there, with 2150 of his own works, ranging from older genres such as the *geistliches Konzert* for a variety of forces, small or large, to modern cantatas with 'reformed' texts (recitative-da capo arias) by the theologian and poet Erdmann Neumeister. His secular works comprise two collections of trio sonatas for violin, viola da gamba and continuo (1688 and 1693), overtures for wind ensemble (1704), and harpsichord and organ works, as well as many dramatic compositions, ten of which are known from printed librettos. In these music dramas Krieger skilfully combined the Italian aria form with the German song style, in a personal musical language, tinged with emotion, that still sounds fresh and original today.

University life in Halle offered great intellectual stimulation. Remarkably progressive trends in the philosophical sciences as taught in the university, represented first by Christian Thomasius and after 1706 by Christian Wolff, made Halle one of the centres of the German Enlightenment, and this attracted many progressively minded students. Handel matriculated on 10 February 1702 at Halle University, at a time when particularly fruitful academic discussions were taking place. Among other disputes, there was a controversy about the use of music in church which complicated matters, although it barely affected the actual performance of music by organists and Kantors in the churches. Disputes about sacred music smouldered for some time at Halle and certainly contributed to the arguments in favour of discarding Latin texts for sacred music performed in Halle churches after 1699–1700.

Around the end of the seventeenth century and the beginning of the eighteenth, the most important musical figure in Halle was certainly Friedrich Wilhelm Zachow (1663–1712), Handel's first and only music teacher. Appointed organist of the Marienkirche in 1684, Zachow belongs to that generation of composers whose personalities left a deep mark on the musical history of central Germany in the three decades between the death of Schütz in 1672 and the first creative achievements of Bach and Handel. Zachow's surviving works give evidence of a characteristic, personal style of great individuality, notable for its wealth of stylistic ideas in a period of transition between needing to satisfy the requirements of the aristocracy or the guilds and developing a more accessible, popular tradition of music that suited the early Enlightenment and the evolution of its thinking. The Enlightenment brought a new spirit into music: Handel may be regarded as its most significant and its greatest representative.

While Zachow as an organist could continue in the best traditions of Halle as established by Scheidt, as a composer of cantatas he depended greatly on the Leipzig influences of his early youth, which account for the dramatic style of many of his cantatas. He may have received practical tuition in the operatic style through links with the Weissenfels court, where Krieger's development of a new phase of early German opera provided a good example. Or he may have had instruction through personal contact with Schütz's pupil Johann Theile (1646–1724), who had earned a great reputation as a Kapellmeister and opera composer in Gottorf, Hamburg and Wolfenbüttel, and in 1686 was appointed Kapellmeister to the court of Merseburg, whence he made frequent visits to Halle.

Zachow's connections with Theile are confirmed by official documents from the Halle law courts. In 1690 Theile fought a duel with a student at Halle University, in the latter's room; the student was quite badly injured, and Theile himself received a dagger wound. The participants' seconds, who witnessed the fight, were Johann Christian Grosse and Zachow, described in the records when the matter came to court as 'the two organists concerned in these incidents'. Luckily, both Theile and Zachow emerged comparatively lightly from the case. Zachow was also among the church musicians of Halle reproved in a resolution of 22 August 1695 for their preference for a dramatic style of cantata: 'That in their churches the many and long performances of non-devotional and inaudible figural music, in which none but the Kantors and organists take pleasure, be moderated, and pious songs of penance and thanks in which the *sanctus coetus* may join be sung instead'. Such hostility to artistic and dramatic styles greatly affected the musical life of Halle in the eighteenth century, and it is often regarded as one of the reasons why the young Handel left his native city so early.

THE SAXON PRINCIPALITIES

On the death of Elector Johann Georg I of Saxony in 1656, the division of his inheritance led to the founding of the Albertine collateral lines and three independent principalities: Saxe-Merseburg (which existed until 1738), Saxe-Weissenfels (until 1746) and Saxe-Zeitz (until 1718). These courts maintained proficient musical ensembles of their own, and for a short period music flourished in their residencies, exerting considerable influence in central Germany.

Merseburg

The thousand-year-old city of Merseburg an der Saale, originally founded as a fortress on the eastern frontier of the Holy Roman Empire and in its feudal heyday a famous seat of German kings and a site of imperial diets and large trade fairs, developed a very active musical life, in both city and court, in the second half of the seventeenth century and the first half of the eighteenth.[13] As in many other central German cities, the guild of the *Stadtpfeifer* (civic musicians, literally 'town pipers') was the basis of musical life in Merseburg and had great influence on it. In 1653, shortly after the end of the Thirty Years War, during which Merseburg suffered damage on numerous occasions, a 'companie' of four *Stadtpfeifer* was set up; together with over 100 civic musicians from 40 places they formed the 'Collegium of Instrumental Music of Upper and Lower Saxony'. This guild drew up statutes for itself,[14] with 25 articles ruling on the allocation of commissions in the face of competition, examinations to become a journeyman and a master, and matters concerning status and employment. Besides their general duties to provide music for such social occasions as weddings, christenings, funerals and the 'convivial gatherings' of town guilds, the civic musicians of Merseburg had to undertake to join in the performance of sacred music under the direction of the Kantor in Merseburg Cathedral and in the city church on Sundays and feast days. Quantz's biography[15] relates that in 1707, after his father's death, Quantz went to Merseburg as a ten-year-old boy to be apprenticed as a civic musician to his uncle, Justus Quantz (or Quantus), who had acquired citizenship of Merseburg in 1690 and was to hold the post of director of civic music until his death in 1708. He was succeeded by his son-in-law Johann Adolf Fleischhack, with whom the young Quantz completed his apprenticeship, becoming a journeyman before he left Merseburg in 1716. After various travels he settled in Dresden.

There were court musicians at Merseburg as early as 1656, when Duke Christian, administrator of the Merseburg foundation since 1650 and still 'Inspector' of the Dresden court Kapelle in Schütz's time, set up a court music ensemble on the Dresden model in his residency at Merseburg castle. The court Kapellmeisters were among the most famous and productive of central German musicians. David Pohle was Kapellmeister at all three Saxon courts of secundogeniture after 1660. Replaced by J. P. Krieger as director of the court music at Halle (see above) and Weissenfels, Pohle went next to the court of Saxe-Zeitz; when the Kapelle there was disbanded in 1682 he moved to Saxe-Merseburg and remained there until his death in 1695.

Pohle was among the most outstanding pupils of Schütz. His extensive output as a composer[16] ranges over almost all the musical genres of the time; as well as sonatas and orchestral suites, written as *Tafelmusik* and for court entertainment, he composed a great deal of sacred music, ranging from the *geistliches Konzert* for a considerable number of performers to the concerto-aria cantata for solo voice. He also made valuable contributions to secular vocal music: in Halle, along with Philipp Stolle (1614–75), Pohle had been one of the principal exponents of early German opera; and his 12 lovesongs (to texts by Paul Flemming, 1650) for two voices with instruments were valuable additions to the body of the German *Gesellschaftslied*.

On a par with Pohle was Johann Theile, born in the nearby cathedral city of Naumburg, who was in charge of the Merseburg orchestra as court Kapellmeister after 1690, having given up the post of Kapellmeister in Wolfenbüttel in order to spend the evening of his life nearer his birthplace. Theile's activities at the court probably came to an end with the death of Duke Christian in 1694, but he left the city of Merseburg a fine memorial by publishing in 1708 a catalogue of all his sacred works (23 masses, eight *Magnificat* settings and 12 psalms). He was described by his contemporaries as 'the famous Kapellmeister of Merseburg' and 'the father of contrapuntists'.

In the early eighteenth century the court Kapelle of Merseburg was directed by among others, Jakob Christian Hertel (*fl c*1667–

*c*1726), father of the famous violinist Johann Christian Hertel (1699–1754), Johann Gottlieb Graun (1703–71), Christian Heinrich Aschenbrenner (1654–1732) and Christoph Förster (1693–1745). When the last Duke of Merseburg, Moritz Wilhelm, died childless in 1738, the principality of Saxe-Merseburg reverted to the electorate of Saxony and ceased to exist as an independent state. Its court Kapelle came to a sudden end too, at almost the same time as those of the neighbouring courts of Weissenfels and Zeitz; the orchestra was disbanded, and the musicians had to earn their bread elsewhere.

Weissenfels

Nearby Weissenfels, a residency from 1680 under dukes Johann Adolf I (ruled 1680–97), Johann Georg (1697–1712), Christian (1712–36) and Johann Adolf II (1736–46), was in its musical prime under the court Kapellmeister J. P. Krieger, who directed the ducal Kapelle from 1680 until his death in 1725. The first big musical occasion to take place at the Weissenfels court under Krieger was the consecration of the castle church on 1 November 1682, when there was a performance of his fine polychoral setting of Psalm cl for 66 voices; musicians from neighbouring courts (Merseburg, Zeitz, Eisenberg and Gotha) were enlisted to swell the ranks of the performers. The court then held a series of six special services to celebrate the completion of the castle complex of Neu-Augustusburg, built between 1663 and 1682 on the Klemmberg ('white cliff') above the city. This Baroque residency was named after Duke August, its builder, who was Duke of Saxe-Weissenfels but ruled as administrator in Halle until his death in 1680.

As early as 1673, nine years before the consecration of the castle church, an organ was built there by Christian Förner (inventor of the hydraulic wind-pressure gauge[17]) and there was 'a newly furnished theatre in the new Augustusburg' (mentioned in several printed librettos) in the castle's south wing. After November 1685 German operas by Krieger, Telemann, Keiser (*Almira*, 30 July 1704) and Johann August Kobelius were performed there, and visiting opera companies from Leipzig and Hamburg gave performances. Another musician of high standing who served in the Weissenfels court Kapelle was Johann Beer (1655–1700), a native of Upper Austria, who was a 'musician and alto singer' there from 1676 and was appointed leader of the orchestra in 1685. He composed vocal and instrumental music, but is best known as the author of satirical novels and polemical pamphlets (*Jan Rebhu*, *Musicalische Discurse*, 1690). Other orchestral leaders at Weissenfels included Pantaleon Hebenstreit (served 1698–1707), who won considerable fame with the dulcimer-like instrument (the 'pantaleon') that he invented around 1690, while the piano was still in its infancy. Johann Georg

Linike (1711–21) came to Weissenfels from the court Kapelle of Brandenburg-Prussia and later became leader of the orchestra of the Hamburg opera.

In 1725 Johann Philipp Krieger was succeeded as court Kapellmeister at Weissenfels by his son Johann Gotthilf Krieger. J. S. Bach's relationship with the Weissenfels court was extensive. In 1713, while in Weimar, he had already dedicated the secular cantata *Was mir behagt, ist nur die muntre Jagd* BWV208a to Duke Christian on his birthday; Bach's second wife, Anna Magdalena Wilcke, came from Weissenfels, where her father Johann Caspar Wilcke was court trumpeter; and Bach himself served as an honorary court Kapellmeister from 1723 until the Kapelle was disbanded in 1736.

Zeitz

The third Saxon principality of secundogeniture, Zeitz, is closely connected historically with the bishopric of Naumburg.[18] Its first duke was Moritz, the youngest son of the Elector Johann Georg I of Saxony, who had his first residency in Naumburg as administrator of the bishopric but moved to Zeitz in 1663. At the same time a court Kapelle was built up for him by Schütz, who in old age often came to Zeitz from his home in Weissenfels and was appointed honorary court Kapellmeister. He found musicians for the Kapelle, trained several choirboys himself and provided the court with his own compositions. The first full court Kapellmeister, Johann Jakob Löwe von Eisenach (1629–1703), was appointed in 1663, on Schütz's recommendation, from Wolfenbüttel, where he had been court Kapellmeister since 1655, but he left Zeitz for Lüneburg after only two years. His fine suites and sonatas for instrumental ensemble and his secular songs were of considerable importance to seventeenth-century German music; his two-part *Sonaten* were written in Zeitz and printed in nearby Jena in 1664. Löwe von Eisenach's successors were the orchestral leaders Clemens Thieme (until 1668) and Heinrich Gottfried Kühnel, who, together with David Pohle, directed the music at the Zeitz court until 1681. After the death of Duke Moritz in that year the court Kapelle was disbanded; no more musicians were appointed at Zeitz for ten years. Under Duke Moritz Wilhelm, the first new Kapellmeister was the singer Johann Franciscus Beyer. He was succeeded in 1698 by the violinist Christian Heinrich Aschenbrenner (fresh from his post at Merseburg), who held the post until the Kapelle was again disbanded, after the death of the last duke in 1718.

Opera in Zeitz and nearby Naumburg was at its peak between 1705 and 1716. A magnificent opera house was built in Naumburg but was destroyed in a great fire in the city in 1716. German operas were performed there at the instigation of the Duke of Saxe-Zeitz, composed by, among others, Heinichen,[19] J. F. Fasch and G. H. Stölzel (later Kapellmeister of the Gotha court).

One of the principal figures in the musical life of Zeitz was Johann Polykarp Büchner, formerly a bass singer at the Weissenfels court, who went to the Michaeliskirche in Zeitz as Kantor after the Weissenfels court Kapelle was disbanded in 1736. Johann Ludwig Krebs (1713–80), probably the best known of Bach's pupils, was organist at the castle in Zeitz from 1744 until 1756 and then at the Altenburg court until his death. Georg Christian Schemelli (*c*1680–1762), known for his widely used book of hymns, *Musicalisches Gesang-Buch* (1736), worked for some 30 years in the city. The hymn-book contains the following note in its foreword: 'The melodies to be found in this song-book are in part quite newly composed by his honour Herr Johann Sebastian Bach, Kapellmeister to the electoral court of Saxony and *director chori musici* in Leipzig, and in part have been improved by him in the thorough bass'.

THURINGIA

The Thuringian duchies of Weimar, Jena, Gotha and Eisenach derived their existence from the partition of the possessions of the Ernestine line of Saxony in the sixteenth century. The Weimar, Eisenach and Coburg lines came into existence in 1572. In 1603 Weimar was divided into the duchies of Weimar and Altenburg, and in 1640 the duchy of Weimar was further divided into Eisenach, Gotha and Weimar. Finally, Weimar was divided yet again into three duchies in 1662 and 1672, and the lines of Jena (which survived until 1690), Eisenach (until 1741) and Weimar emerged, while Gotha produced seven new ruling houses in the period from 1680.

Weimar

Under Duke Wilhelm IV of Saxe-Weimar (1598–1662), known for his 'singular and inborn pleasure in music',[20] Weimar acquired its first efficient court Kapelle, which had to satisfy the duke's taste for Italian concertos and sonatas as well as for German music drama. Once again, Schütz kept an eye on the Weimar Kapelle from his home in Dresden in 1647–8, and in 1652 he was still advising its director, Drese, on the strength, composition, range of instruments and repertory of a good court orchestra. Adam Drese (*c*1620–1701), court Kapellmeister from 1652 to 1662, had studied in Warsaw with Marco Scacchi and in Italy, possibly with Johann Rosenmüller in Venice, and had been a court musician at Weimar since at least 1645. The Weimar court poet, Georg Neumark, worked closely with him. The Kapelle reached its prime in 1658, when there were 18 musicians, eight trumpeters and drummers, and the civic musicians, who joined the court music in 1623.

After Duke Wilhelm's death in 1662, almost two decades passed before Weimar can be said to have had any real court music again. In 1683 the duchy came to a curious arrangement whereby there were several simultaneously reigning dukes, the older dukes heading the government, while their younger relatives acted as co-regents. This, and their religious differences, led to many disputes between them, as we know from the biography of Bach and other sources. Duke Wilhelm Ernst ruled from 1683 to 1728, with two co-regents – his younger brother Johann Ernst III and (from 1707 to 1728) his nephew Ernst August, who ruled alone from 1728 to 1748. Ernst August became an adherent of the Pietist movement within central German Protestantism after studying in Halle, where he had come into contact with August Hermann Francke; his uncle, on the other hand, favoured orthodox Lutheranism (the differences between them were not outwardly settled until after a mediatory congress in 1723, but even then complete agreement was not achieved[21]). Under these rulers Weimar became a little centre of Thuringian musical culture.[22] Music at the court reached its peak at the turn of the century; around 1700 the Kapelle under Johann Samuel Drese (court Kapellmeister from 1683 to 1716) and his deputies Johann August Kühnel (served 1688–95) and Georg Christoph Strattner (served 1695–1704) consisted of 13 instrumentalists and nine singers, male and female.

In 1703 Bach spent several months as a lackey and violinist in the private orchestra of Johann Ernst III before going to Arnstadt as an organist. One of the sons of Johann Ernst III's second marriage, Prince Johann Ernst of Weimar (1696–1715), composed music: in 1718 Telemann published six violin concertos that the prince had written during a nine-month course of lessons in composition from Johann Gottfried Walther, who was town organist in Weimar from 1707 and a court musician, 1721–8. Other members of the Drese family also held the post of Kapellmeister: in addition to Adam and Johann Samuel, the latter's son Johann Wilhelm, who had already served in the Weimar Kapelle as a copyist, musician and deputy Kapellmeister, was Kapellmeister from 1717. It is well known that he was preferred over Bach, who had been appointed organist (1708) and was thus personally involved in the quarrels at court. Bach's duties included playing the organ, leading the orchestra (from 1718) and writing instrumental music (which included his famous keyboard arrangements of concertos by Italian masters, such as the nine from Vivaldi's opp.3, 4, 7 and 8,[23] and church cantatas. Bach also taught the sons of Johann Ernst III[24], and he often played in the private orchestra of the co-regent, Ernst August.

Bach's annoyance at being passed over in favour of Johann Wilhelm Drese in 1717 for the post of court Kapellmeister is said to have led to his famous confrontation with Wilhelm Ernst. The appointment of Drese had been preceded by an offer made by the court to Telemann, but he had turned it down. Thereupon the post of Kapellmeister was given to the less accomplished Johann Wilhelm Drese, whose study tour in Italy in 1702 had been financed by Wilhelm Ernst. Disappointed in being passed over, Bach gave notice. He had already established contacts with the Anhalt court in Cöthen through the agency of Ernst August, who was married to Princess Eleonore Wilhelmine, sister of Prince Leopold of Anhalt-Cöthen. Wilhelm Ernst, however, refused to let Bach go, and even imprisoned him for some months before he was allowed to leave Weimar. After Ernst August became sole ruler in 1728, the court Kapelle was much reduced, and it was not enlarged again until much later: music played a negligible part at the court between 1728 and 1740.

Erfurt

The city of Erfurt, with a strong musical tradition dating back to the Middle Ages and the Reformation, when it was maintained by its many monasteries and religious foundations, owes its cultural significance not least to the college founded there to promote learning; its university status was confirmed in 1392. Erfurt University is thus one of the oldest of German educational institutions. Martin Luther studied there from 1501 to 1505 and received his musical training there. Once again it was the civic musicians, along with the city's *chorus musicus* and the instrumental musicians of the Gymnasium, who were most active and influential in civic musical life. As with so many Thuringian cities, members of the extensive Bach family lived in Erfurt and did much for its musical culture. Johann Bach (1604–73) lived and worked in Erfurt after 1634; he married Hedwig Lämmerhirt as his second wife, his nephew Johann Ambrosius Bach (1645–95) married Hedwig's younger stepsister Maria Elisabeth, and their marriage produced the most famous of all the Bachs, Johann Sebastian. The posts of town musicians were firmly in the hands of members of the Bach family. As well as Johann Bach, who was also organist at the Predigerkirche from 1638, his brother Heinrich (1615–92, later organist in Arnstadt) and his three sons Johann Christian (1640–82), Johann Aegidius (1645–1716) and Johann Nicolaus (1653–82) were all *Stadtpfeifer* in Erfurt, where several held in succession the post of director of the town music. Johann Sebastian Bach's father Johann Ambrosius was also a violinist in the Erfurt town ensemble from 1667 to 1671, when Duke Johann Georg I of Eisenach appointed him musician at his court.

As important in the musical history of Erfurt as its town musicians, however, were its organists. Johann Bach was succeeded by two outstanding organists and composers of organ music – Johann Effler (later court organist in Weimar) and from 1678 to 1690 Johann Pachelbel (1653–1706), whose first published organ work, the *Musicalischen Sterbens-Gedancken* (four variations on chorale tunes relating to death), appeared in Erfurt in 1683 under the influence of the plague epidemic that raged there in 1682–3; Pachelbel's young wife was among its victims. Pachelbel left Erfurt in 1690 for Stuttgart but subsequently returned to Thuringia, serving as city organist in Gotha from 1690 to 1695. While in Erfurt he trained a number of gifted pupils, including Johann Sebastian Bach's eldest brother, Johann Christoph (1671–1721), Andreas Nicolaus Vetter (1666–1710, court organist at Rudolstadt from 1691) and Johann Heinrich Buttstett (1666–1727). The style of imitative part-writing in Pachelbel's chorale-inspired works, both instrumental and vocal, greatly influenced composers before and including Bach – a fruitful contribution made by Erfurt to the musical culture of central Germany.

Buttstett is known for his literary dispute with Mattheson over solmization and the traditional teaching of sacred music in his treatise *Ut, mi, sol, re, fa, la, tota musica et harmonia aeterna, oder Neueröffnetes, altes wahres, einziges und ewiges Fundamentum musices* (Erfurt, 1716–17). He held the post of organist at the Predigerkirche in Erfurt from 1691 to 1727 and, besides organ music, composed a series of cantatas and masses, printed in Erfurt in 1720 as his op.1. His most prominent pupil was Johann Gottfried Walther, born in Erfurt in 1684. Erfurt also fostered the talents of music theorists such as Johann Philipp Eisel (*Musicus autodidactus, oder Der sich selbst informierende Musicus*, Erfurt, 1738) and in particular Jakob Adlung (1699–1762), Buttstett's successor as organist of the Predigerkirche and from 1741 a teacher at the grammar school; Adlung's treatises *Musica mechanica organoedi* (1726) and *Anleitung zu der musikalischen Gelahrtheit* (1758, with a foreword by the Eisenach organist Johann Ernst Bach) were quoted frequently and in much detail. Johann Christian Kittel (1732–1809), a famous pupil of Johann Sebastian Bach, was born and brought up in Erfurt and was an organist there from 1756 until his death.

Gotha

Musical life in Gotha received a major stimulus from the *Gothaer Schulmethodus* (1642), a manual for schoolteachers, and from the *Cantionale sacrum* (Gotha, 1646–8), a collection of three-part sacred songs for use by school choirs written by composers of the mid-century, some with Gotha connections. Music at the Gotha courts, however, began in 1646 with the consecration of the castle church on the Friedenstein, the court residence.[25] Duke Ernst I (1601–75), nicknamed 'the Pious', had moved his court to Gotha in 1641 and he founded a court Kapelle there about 1650. Its outstanding figure was Wolfgang Carl Briegel (1626–1712), who became Kapellmeister in 1664; he later moved to Darmstadt. He was succeeded in 1670 by Georg Ludwig Agricola and then by the Altenburg court musicians Wolfgang Michael Mylius (from 1676), a former pupil of Christoph Bernhard in Dresden) and Christian Friedrich Witt (Kapellmeister, 1713–16). Under Gottfried Heinrich Stölzel (Kapellmeister from 1719) the court music was reorganized and enlarged; Stölzel's creative versatility – his work comprised operas, instrumental music and an extensive body of church music[26] – temporarily made Gotha a centre of Thuringian musical life. Even so notable a musician as Telemann was associated with it for a short period (1708–12).

Eisenach

The duchy of Saxe-Eisenach, ruled from 1672 to 1741 by the four dukes Johann Georg I (ruled 1672–86), Johann Georg II (1686–98), Johann Wilhelm (resident in Jena from 1690) and Wilhelm Heinrich (1729–41), was an independent residency. Since Wilhelm Heinrich left no heirs, it reverted on his death to Weimar. The musical life of Eisenach[27] can be divided into three periods on the basis of its resident musicians, its repertory and its documented performances. From 1672 until about 1700 music at court evolved gradually and was systematically organized, though without a real court Kapelle. Under the gifted but unstable Daniel Eberlin (1647–1715), who was appointed Kapellmeister at Eisenach three times in succession, church music was regularized and court and civic musical life were integrated. The last attained considerable importance chiefly through the activities of several members of the Bach family.

Johann Ambrosius Bach was employed from 1671 until his death in 1695 as a town and court musician in Eisenach; his son Johann Sebastian was born there, close to the Wartburg, on 21 March 1685. Johann Christoph Bach (1642–1703), who came from Arnstadt, was town organist from 1665; his motets and cantatas[28] show that he was probably the best composer of the family before Johann Sebastian. His successor as organist at the Georgenkirche was Johann Bernhard Bach (1676–1749), son of Johann Aegidius Bach, director of the town music in Erfurt; he joined Duke Johann Wilhelm's Kapelle in 1703 as a harpsichordist and wrote chorale preludes and orchestral suites, some of which Johann Sebastian copied in his own hand. Johann Bernhard Bach's son Johann Ernst (1722–77) studied law in Leipzig and then succeeded him as town organist; he practised as a lawyer in Eisenach and was also an industrious musician and composer.

During the second, and the most important, period at Eisenach, 1700–30, the court Kapelle was reorganized (1708) and chamber music, now in the hands of Pantaleon Hebenstreit, was raised to a very high standard. Telemann came from Sorau in 1708, together with other well-qualified musicians, to join the Eisenach Kapelle, and after Hebenstreit's departure he acted as court Kapellmeister until 1712. In 1717 the court again succeeded in engaging him as unofficial Kapellmeister; Telemann showed gratitude to Eisenach all his life and wrote serenades, concertos and sacred music for the city.

The third and final period of court music at Eisenach, 1730–41, saw Johann Adam Birckenstock (1687–1733) as director of music and leader of the orchestra. He was succeeded as Kapellmeister by Johann Melchior Molter (1695–1765) and as leader of the orchestra by Johann Christian Hertel (1699–1754). Hertel's son Johann Wilhelm (1727–89) later became leader of the orchestra and court Kapellmeister in Mecklenburg-Strelitz. The well-known lutenist Ernst Gottlieb Baron (1696–1760) went to Eisenach from Gotha and worked there between 1732 and 1737. The court Kapelle was disbanded after the death of the last duke, Wilhelm Heinrich, in 1741; thereafter, music in Eisenach was dependent on the city.

Rudolstadt

The state of Schwarzburg-Rudolstadt, though small, is of considerable significance for the musical history of central Germany because of the musicians who worked there.[29] The house of Schwarzburg had ruled the city and administrative region of Rudolstadt since the mid-sixteenth century. After the Peace of Westphalia in 1648, which brought the sufferings of the Thirty Years War to an end, the independent county of Rudolstadt gained greater political and cultural importance under Count Albert Anthon (ruled 1662–1710), who was granted the hereditary title of prince by the Emperor Joseph I in 1710. Influenced by his long-term mentor, later his chancellor, Ahasverus Fritsch (1629–1701), Albert Anthon was widely educated, interested in the arts and popular among his subjects, and carried a high reputation. A special interest in music developed at Rudolstadt under his rule, and court music was properly organized for the first time.

At Albert Anthon's wedding in 1665, and in the two following years, a series of six dramatic performances with musical interludes took place at the Heidecksburg in Rudolstadt; these events are known in literary history as the Rudolstadt Festivals. Music played a quite important part in them. The count commissioned works from various musicians – including Johann Samuel Drese, Kapellmeister at Weimar – integrated the town choir with the court music and organized sacred music in the castle chapel over several decades. Finally, he engaged the gifted Georg Bleyer as deputy Kapellmeister (served until 1677), sent him to be trained at the court's expense in

Italy and France, and built up the basis of what was to become a well-stocked music library; its contents are known from two extensive catalogues. Bleyer was a musician of real significance: the orchestral pieces in his *Lust-Music* (Leipzig, 1670–71) and *Zodiacus musicus* (Amsterdam, 1688) show an early French influence, and he was also outstanding as a composer of sacred music.

Under the influence of the two countesses, Aemilie Juliane and Ludaemilie Elisabeth, and the chancellor Fritsch, a strongly pro-Pietist trend in intellectual life developed at Rudolstadt. It was publicly expressed in the Geistliche Fruchtbringende Jesusgesellschaft, founded by Fritsch in 1676 with the encouragement of the Pietist theologian Philipp Jakob Spener. Albert Anthon's son Ludwig Friedrich (1667–1718), the first to bear the title of prince, further increased the number of court officials, and under the Princes Friedrich Anthon (1697–1744) and Johann Friedrich (1721–67) music at court saw another period of considerable growth, as Rudolstadt moved towards its nineteenth-century role as an important centre of culture in northern Thuringia.

The first significant court Kapellmeister at Rudolstadt was Philipp Heinrich Erlebach (1657–1714), who may be numbered among the most important and gifted composers of German Protestant church music in the period directly before Bach and Telemann.[30] As court Kapellmeister from 1681 until his death, he also made a great contribution to secular music. Among his works were operas and serenades, orchestral suites 'after the French style and manner' (1693), trio sonatas in the Italian manner (1694), sonatas and *Tafelmusik*. His sacred vocal works include cantatas (some with texts by Erdmann Neumeister), masses and works in the oratorio style (*Historia nativitatis, Historia Passionis, Historia Resurrectionis, Actus Pentecostalis*). Under him and his successor, the court Kapelle grew to over 25 members; the list of its instruments mentions an organ, three harpsichords, two spinets, a clavichord, two theorbos, a harp, four tenor violas da gamba, two smaller violas da gamba, a violone, seven violins, six viols and a whole range of wind instruments.

Dramatic works performed at Rudolstadt in this period range from the customary serenatas, ballets and pastorals to full-length operas. Two three-act operas by Erlebach – *Die Plejades, oder Das Siebengestirne* (1693) and *Die siegende Unschuld* (1702) – were composed during his time as Rudolstadt. Their librettos and surviving arias indicate that by about 1690 German music drama had developed some degree of independence from the standard Italian recitative and da capo aria form and from the French (specifically Lullian) style of instrumental writing, as well as from the earlier German preference for strophic songs with continuo and orchestral ritornello, and was approaching a certain identity of its own, with some formal consolidation.

The Late Baroque Era

Erlebach's successors at Rudolstadt included the well-known violinist Johann Graf (1680–1745), whose violin sonatas (opp.1–3, 1718, 1723, 1737), with their virtuoso double-stopping technique, are akin to the early German violin music of such composers as J. J. Walther and Biber and suggest Corelli as a formal model. Graf was also outstanding as a composer of cantatas and operas. After his death Christoph Förster succeeded him as court Kapellmeister. Förster, a Thuringian, had been leader of the court orchestra in Merseburg (where he was taught by Heinichen) and had visited Prague in 1723 for the famous coronation festivities of the Emperor Charles VI, an occasion at which many celebrated musicians gathered. Since the 1740s Förster had maintained artistic contacts with the Schwarzburg courts of Sondershausen (where sacred vocal works by him still survive) and Rudolstadt. Initially appointed deputy Kapellmeister, he was promoted full Kapellmeister at Rudolstadt in 1745 but died only a few weeks later. He won lasting fame in central Germany with his orchestral suites and sinfonias, his violin sonatas with harpsichord obbligato (adventurous for their time) and his church cantatas, but few of his works survive.

With the deaths of Graf and Förster in 1745 the Rudolstadt court lost two leading musicians in rapid succession. After an interim period of two years, during which Graf's eldest son Christian Ernst directed the Kapelle, a suitable successor was eventually found in 1747 in Georg Gebel the younger (1709–55); initially appointed leader of the orchestra, he became Kapellmeister in 1750 and raised the standard of court music to its former high level. A prolific composer, he wrote at least 12 operas, over 100 instrumental works (sinfonias, concertos and chamber music) and several hundred sacred works for the Rudolstadt court; over 200 of his church cantatas, two Passion oratorios and a Christmas oratorio survive.

*

Among the great host of central German composers of the first half of the eighteenth century, the most famous representatives today are Bach and Telemann, but in their own time and place others were of equal standing. The prominent position of central German musical culture in the seventeenth and eighteenth centuries, with its great wealth of works in all genres, shows that a survey based on only a selection of those works that are now recognized as masterpieces must inevitably be superficial. A lack of sources compels the exclusion of a great number of works by musicians who were much admired in their own day. Music in central Germany developed qualitatively – even in the smallest of residencies, cities and towns – and consistently, in a manner rarely seen in any other time or place.

Brandenburg-Prussia and the Central German Courts

The feudalism of princely absolutism in central Germany, with its intellectual background and social motivating force in the shape of the Enlightenment, provided exemplary conditions for the development of art and culture in general and of music in particular.

NOTES

[1] Foreword to *Erster Theil neuer lieblicher und zierlicher Intraden mit 6 Stimmen* (Erfurt, 1620).

[2] 'Choral' implies unaccompanied vocal music (e.g. motets, chorales); 'figural' implies larger-scale vocal music, usually in cycles, performed with instrumental accompaniment (e.g. *Geistliche Konzerte*, cantatas, masses etc., for soloists, chorus and orchestra).

[3] Foreword to *Evangelisches Hosianna* (Frankfurt, 1677).

[4] C. Sachs, *Musik und Oper am kurbrandenburgischen Hof* (Berlin, 1910).

[5] In 1712 the Berlin court Kapelle had more than six first violins, five second violins, two violas, five cellos, four oboes and four bassoons, as well as a 12-man band of trumpeters and drummers; see Sachs, *Musik und Oper*, 67.

[6] Not Johann Christoph Pepusch (1667–1752), who received a thorough musical education in his native city of Berlin before going to the Netherlands in 1698 and England in 1700; he was not a member of the Berlin court Kapelle.

[7] The 1739 autobiography was published by J. Mattheson in *Grundlage einer Ehren-Pforte* (Hamburg, 1740); ed. M. Schneider (Berlin, 1910), 359.

[8] Bononcini's *Polifemo* (libretto by Attilio Ariosti), given its première in 1702 in Lietzenburg castle, is the only surviving Berlin opera of this period; ed. G. Kärnbach (Berlin, 1938).

[9] Luise Dorothea Sophie, who married the hereditary Prince Friedrich of Hessen-Kassel.

[10] For the extensive literature on Fasch, see *Johann Friedrich Fasch (1688–1758): Zerbst 1983* [=*Studien zur Aufführungspraxis und Interpretation von Instrumental Musik des 18. Jahrhunderts*, xxiv (1984)]; see also R. Pfeiffer, *Die Überlieferung der Werke von Johann Friedrich Fasch auf dem Gebiet der DDR* (diss., U. of Halle, 1986). An autobiography by Fasch was printed by F. W. Marpurg, *Historisch-kritische Beyträge zur Aufnahme der Musik*, iii (Berlin, 1757), 124ff, repr. in *Studien zur Aufführungspraxis und Interpretation von Instrumental Musik des 18. Jahrhunderts*, xv (1981).

[11] Most of Fasch's instrumental works are in *D-Dlb*.

[12] R. Brockpähler, *Handbuch zur Geschichte der Barockoper in Deutschland* (Emsdetten, 1964), 259, 288–9.

[13] R. Langer, 'Merseburg', *Bedeutende Musiktraditionen der Bezirke Halle und Magdeburg*, ed. Verband der Komponisten und Musikwissenschaftler der DDR, Bezirksverband Halle/Magdeburg, i (Halle, 1981), 33ff.

[14] 'Kaiserliche Confirmation der Artickel dess Instrumental-Musicalischen Collegii in dem Ober- und Nieder-Sächsischen Creiss, und anderer interessierter Oerter: 1653'; see R. Wustmann, 'Sächsische Musikantenartikel (1653)', *Neues Archiv für Sächsische Geschichte und Altertumskunde*, xxix (Dresden, 1908), nos.1 and 2, pp.104–17.

[15] 'Herrn J. J. Quantzens Lebenslauf, von ihm selbst entworfen', in F. W. Marpurg, *Historisch-kritische Beyträge zur Aufnahme der Musik*, i (Berlin, 1755), 197ff.

[16] See G. Gille, *Der Schützschüler David Pohle (1624–1695): seine Bedeutung für die deutsche Musikgeschichte des 17. Jahrhunderts* (diss., Martin Luther U., Halle, 1974).

[17] See J. C. Trost (the younger), *Ausführliche Beschreibung des Neuen Orgelwercks auf der Augustus-Burg zu Weissenfels* (Nuremberg, 1677).

[18] A. Werner, *Städtische und fürstliche Musikpflege in Zeitz* (Bückeburg, 1922).

[19] The only surviving stage work from Naumburg is Heinichen's *Paris und Helene* (1710), which had its première in Leipzig in 1709; the score was in the library of the Berliner Singakademie (in *D-B*) before World War II and is thought to have perished.

[20] A. Aber, *Die Pflege der Musik unter den Wettinern und wettinischen Ernestinern: von den Anfängen bis zur Auflösung der Weimarer Hofkapelle 1662* (Bückeburg, 1921), 144.

251

The Late Baroque Era

[21] See G. Mentz, *Weimarische Staats- und Regentengeschichte vom Westfälischen Frieden bis zum Regierungsantritt Carl Augusts* (Jena, 1936).

[22] W. Lidke, *Das Musikleben in Weimar von 1683 bis 1735*, Schriften zur Stadtgeschichte und Heimatkunde, no.3 (Weimar, 1954).

[23] BWV593, 594 and 596 for organ, BWV 972, 973, 975, 976, 978 and 980 for harpsichord; see K. Heller, *Antonio Vivaldi* (Leipzig, 1991), 319ff.

[24] As well as the arrangements of Vivaldi that he made in Weimar (see n.23), Bach transcribed several of Prince Johann Ernst's concertos for keyboard instruments (BWV592 and 595 for organ, 982, 984 and 987 for harpsichord).

[25] M. Schneider, 'Die Einweihung der Schlosskirche auf dem Friedenstein zu Gotha im Jahre 1646', *SIMG*, vii (1905–6), 308ff; A. Fett, *Musikgeschichte der Stadt Gotha: von den Anfängen bis zum Tode Gottfried Heinrich Stölzels (1749)* (diss., U. of Freiburg, 1952).

[26] F. Hennenberg, *Das Kantatenschaffen Gottfried Heinrich Stölzels* (Leipzig, 1976).

[27] C. Oefner, *Das Musikleben in Eisenach 1650–1750* (diss., Martin Luther U., Halle, 1975).

[28] Ed. M. Schneider, *Altbachisches Archiv*, EDM, 1st ser., i, ii (Leipzig, 1935).

[29] On the musical history of Rudolstadt see P. Gülke, *Musik und Musiker in Rudolstadt* (Rudolstadt, 1963) [special edn in the series Rudolstädter Heimathefte].

[30] B. Baselt, *Der Rudolstädter Hofkapellmeister Philipp Heinrich Erlebach (1654–1714): Beiträge zur mitteldeutschen Musikgeschichte des ausgehenden 17. Jahrhunderts* (diss., Martin Luther U., Halle, 1963).

BIBLIOGRAPHICAL NOTE

Literature

Books on the development of musical culture in central Germany are listed in R. Brockpähler's excellent *Handbuch zur Geschichte der Barockoper in Deutschland* (Emsdetten, 1964); this also lists about 50 cities and royal seats in which early German operas were performed and gives a short history of the development of musical culture, with a catalogue of operas. A standard work of a similar nature for sacred music is F. Blume's *Geschichte der evangelischen Kirchenmusik* (Kassel, 1965), with its numerous musical examples, facsimiles and lavish illustrations. E. W. Böhme's *Die frühdeutschen Oper in Thüringen* (Stadtroda, 1931) is an important study of opera sources.

The studies of individual cities, royal seats and composers mentioned in the above notes contain detailed information on regional musical history. In particular, C. Sachs's *Musik und Oper am kurbrandenburgischen Hof* (Berlin, 1910), on Prussian musical culture, and A. Werner's *Städtische und fürstliche Musikpflege in Weissenfels* (Leipzig, 1911) and his *Städtische und fürstliche Musikpflege in Zeitz* (Bückeburg and Leipzig, 1922), on musical life in Saxony and Thuringia, are important, as are a number of dissertations submitted at Halle University on Pohle, Fasch, Erlebach and the musical culture of Gotha, Eisenach, Weimar and Rudolstadt. On musical life in Halle, W. Serauky's monumental monograph *Musikgeschichte der Stadt Halle* (5 vols., Halle and Berlin, 1935–43) is distinguished from smaller, local studies by its encyclopedic nature. The extensive literature up to 1945 on the history of music in central Germany is listed in R. Schaal's *Das Schrifttum zur musikalischen Lokalgeschichteforschung* (Kassel, 1947). For more recent literature, and for information on individual musicians and cities in central Germany the entries in *MGG*, *Grove 6* and *Grove O* provide useful starting-points.

Sources

Much of the music of this period remains in manuscript in Germany, in the major regional and university libraries and local archives. The standard collected editions *Denkmäler deutscher Tonkunst* (DDT) and *Das Erbe deutscher Musik* (EDM) include a large number of vocal and instrumental works by composers from central Germany, but these represent only a fraction of the surviving music from the region.

Chapter IX

Leipzig: a Cosmopolitan Trade Centre

GEORGE B. STAUFFER

Without question, our picture of music-making in Leipzig during the second half of the Baroque period is dominated by the figure of Johann Sebastian Bach. The portrait commonly painted by Bach scholars, however, is not entirely flattering: Bach's heated disputes with the town council, his frequent and prolonged trips to Berlin and Dresden and his attempt to find employment elsewhere are raised as signs of Leipzig's provincialism. Leipzig is often presented as the religiously conservative town that failed to provide Bach with an adequate outlet for his talent, much in the fashion of Salzburg with Mozart. While that picture furthers the nineteenth-century notion of Bach as a misunderstood artist, it does grave injustice to Leipzig. For by the time Bach arrived in 1723 Leipzig stood as an attractive, vital metropolis, a town that indeed made demands on its musicians but also offered them unusual financial security, greatly varied opportunities for composition, and admiring, knowledgeable auditors. Leipzig fostered such important figures as Johann Friedrich Fasch, Christoph Graupner, Melchior Hoffmann, Johann Georg Pisendel, Johann Adolph Scheibe, Nicolaus Adam Strungk and Georg Philipp Telemann. Moreover, it placed its illustrious Thomaskantors – Johann Kuhnau, Johann Schelle and Bach – before an international forum.

Like Hamburg and Frankfurt, Leipzig was a trade city. Although it fell under the jurisdiction of the Elector of Saxony in Dresden, its affairs were governed by the town council, an elected body of powerful, prosperous citizens. The council, as opposed to a monarch, duke or bishop, ruled on all aspects of daily life, from the design of buildings and parks to the sequence of church services and the festivities accompanying trade fairs. Since the elector received tax monies on merchandise sold at the fairs, it was in his interest to maintain close ties with Leipzig and to promote its economic well-being through patronage and licence. But it was the council that shaped Leipzig's cultural development. In retrospect, we can see that

the seeds for the town's great nineteenth-century musical achievements – the Gewandhaus concerts, the opera and the musical criticism of Schumann (whose *Neue Zeitschrift für Musik* was originally
called *Neue Leipziger Zeitschrift für Musik*) – were planted during the
second half of the Baroque era by the plutocratic hand of the council.

For Leipzig, the period around 1680–1740 was one of unprecedented growth and prosperity. Like most other German cities,
Leipzig suffered deep devastation in the seventeenth century during
the Thirty Years War (1618–48). The town was besieged five times
and occupied by Swedish troops, and during the course of the struggle its population dropped from approximately 17 500 to 14 000.
With its strong commercial foundation, however, Leipzig was able to
recover rather quickly. Still, progress was interrupted by local strife
and devastating epidemics. The last great plague occurred in 1680,
when the town's population, now almost 20 000, was reduced by
more than 3000 deaths in the short period between August and
December. Of 757 houses in the inner city, 150 stood empty.

From this low point Leipzig staged a remarkable comeback. Both
economically and culturally, it flourished without a crippling disrup-
tion until 1756, when the Seven Years War with its ten million taler
retribution payment to Prussia placed the town on a downward
course – a slide that was not to be reversed until the nineteenth
century. In 1753 the population reached its highest point in the
eighteenth century, 32 384. For Leipzig, then, the second half of the
Baroque period was a bright era. In the secular sphere the annual
fairs established it as one of Germany's foremost cosmopolitan
centres, and the income generated from trade and industry enabled
private citizens to refashion the town architecturally. In the sacred
sphere, the Thomasschule with its outstanding Rektors and Kantors
made Leipzig the Lutheran capital of central Germany.

ECONOMY

Leipzig, from its earliest days to the present, has been a crossroads
city, connecting east with west, north with south. Located just above
the confluence of the Pleisse, the Parthe and the Weisse Elster rivers,
it has thrived on commerce stemming from its position on vital trade
routes. Recently discovered artefacts suggest that a settlement
existed at the present site of Leipzig as early as 700. By the eleventh
century the settlement had developed into a fortified city, formally
called 'Urbs Libzi'. In 1170 'Urbs Libzi' was granted municipal
status.

Leipzig's transformation from a moderately active Saxon city to a
teeming commercial town took place during the Renaissance. The
discovery between 1470 and 1520 of silver deposits in nearby

Freiberg, and then of valuable ores in Schneeberg, Annaberg and Marienberg, brought industry from the field (fur trading) into the shop (fine-metal working). Leipzig entrepreneurs quickly capitalized on the changing economy, exploiting the foreign markets made available by the annual fairs. The Fugger family of Augsburg and others invested heavily in Leipzig ventures. At the same time the Emperor Maximilian I granted royal trade privileges, steering commerce to Leipzig while restricting business in competing cities. By the second half of the sixteenth century Leipzig rivalled Frankfurt and Hamburg as a mercantile centre. Led by its council of independent businessmen, Leipzig displayed the first noble signs of material success: a large group of stately buildings constructed or refashioned in the High Renaissance style, structures such as the Rathaus (Town Hall) and the Waage (Weighing House), both of 1556–8.

After 1680 Leipzig merchants turned to manufacturing in the manner of France and the Netherlands, and profits burgeoned. The Leipzig work-force benefited greatly from two waves of skilled immigrants: French Huguenots, who fled the revoked Edict of Nantes in 1685, and Salzburg Protestants, expelled from Austria in 1732. The growing membership in the town guilds gave strength to the *Kleinbürger*, while the selective membership of the town council assured that the interests of the *Grossbürger* would be carefully protected. By 1747 local industry counted 19 factories, 2000 artisans and 10 550 working men (between the ages of 14 and 60). The further extension of trade routes – west to the Atlantic, east to Moscow, south to Italy and north to the North Sea – increased the quality and sophistication of available goods and made Leipzig ever more international.

THE FAIRS AND THE BOOK TRADE

Certainly it was the *Messe*, or trade fair, that gave Baroque Leipzig its international stamp. There were three fairs annually: the New Year's Fair (*Neujahrs-Messe*), which began on 1 January; the Easter Fair (*Oster-Messe*), which began on Jubilate Sunday (the third Sunday after Easter), normally in April or May; and the St Michael's Fair (*Michaelis-Messe*), which began around St Michael's Day, 29 September. The 1497 edict of Maximilian I had stipulated that each fair should run for one week and that the town's church bells were to ring for a quarter of an hour to announce the start. During the sixteenth century the fairs became such a commercial success that they were gradually lengthened. In the week before the opening (*Handelswoche* or *Böttcherwoche* – 'Commerce Week' or 'Cooper's Week'), foreign retailers were allowed to set up and clean their stalls and begin selling wares three or four days in advance of the official start. In the week after the fair (*Zahlwoche* – 'Accounting Week'), merchants who obtained proper permission were allowed to continue to sell goods while taxes were being assessed. By the mid-seventeenth century the average Leipzig fair lasted about three weeks.

The Easter and St Michael's fairs can be traced back as far as the twelfth century, when they were mentioned in contemporary documents. The New Year's Fair was added in 1458, by decree of the Elector Friedrich III. The position of the Leipzig fairs was greatly enhanced by Maximilian I, who, in return for an excise tax, confirmed the city's right to hold three fairs annually and forbade neighbouring towns such as Magdeburg, Meissen and Naumburg to start new fairs. In 1507 Maximilian went further, granting Leipzig exclusive fair rights for a radius of 15 *Meilen*, approximately 70 miles. Merchants entering the prescribed area during fair-times could not circumvent Leipzig but instead had to go through it and display their goods for sale for a period of three days before they were permitted to move on. Such regulations were strictly enforced. In 1518, for instance, the Fuggers were fined heavily for taking a detour around Leipzig. By dint of monopoly, the Leipzig fairs (called *Märkte*, or 'markets', until the term *Messe* came into vogue in the second half of the seventeenth century) flourished. As German culture and economy turned increasingly to the East, Leipzig's rank as a trade city rose. By 1700 Leipzig eclipsed Frankfurt and stood as Germany's principal *Messestadt*.

Goods were sold from booths erected in the streets, in the open market place in front of the town hall (see fig.37), in the arcades (*Gewölben*) of the ground floors of buildings and in special commercial structures bearing names such as *Pelzhaus* ('Furriers' Hall') or *Gewandhaus* ('Clothiers' Hall'). It was one of these commercial structures, the New Gewandhaus, erected in 1781, that also served as recital hall for the ensemble that evolved into the Gewandhaus orchestra of today. By the late seventeenth century the demand for display space in the inner city was so great that private houses were built in a way that maximized the amount of first-floor area that could be used as commercial arcades. The fairs were thus a critical factor in Leipzig's distinctive Baroque architectural style (see below).

Many of the goods sold at the fairs were produced locally: gold and silver work, velvet and silk cloth, linen and other textiles, oil cloth, silk stockings, paper, shoes, wigs and, increasingly, books. Equally attractive, however, were imported items, from France, the Netherlands, England, Bohemia, Poland, Lithuania, Russia, Austria and Italy. Then, too, there were products from other German towns – Hamburg, Lübeck, Cologne, Frankfurt, Nuremberg and elsewhere. During the fairs tradesmen were granted special protection, and

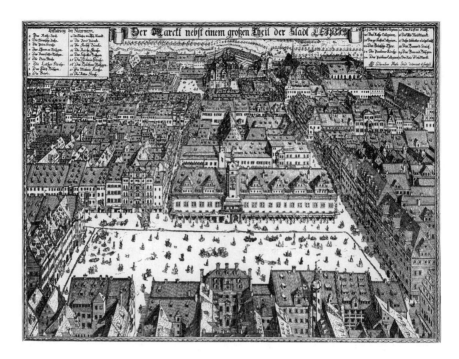

37. View of the Leipzig Markt, or market place, dominated by the Renaissance town hall (centre, with commercial arcades and tower), with Baroque mansions, including that of Dietrich Apel (the tallest building, to the right of the town hall), where the Saxon elector stayed during his visits: engraving (1712) Johann Georg Schreiber

guards were increased at the borders and town gates. If a merchant's papers were in order, and if he paid the proper excise tax, he gained the right to sell whatever he wished, without local intervention. When several vendors sold shrunken Turks' heads at the Easter Fair in 1684, it created a public scandal; but the vendors were not incarcerated, nor were their wares seized.

The availability of shrunken heads reflects the exoticism of the Leipzig fairs. Visitors could savour a cup of imported Turkish coffee or purchase an ivory crucifix from Florence, a wool sweater from England or even tobacco from America. They could also expect to encounter street musicians, jugglers, tightrope walkers, fire-eaters, giants and midgets, snake charmers and a great menagerie of animals – elephants, apes, tropical birds etc. Such attractions drew curiosity-seekers in great numbers and made the fairs truly colourful events. While fully exploiting the economic potential of the fairs, the town council also exercised a strong hand in keeping order: an ordinance of 1581 stipulated in unambiguous terms that itinerant performers had to leave Leipzig once the fairs were over.

Visitors came not only to watch street performers but to observe each other as well. With the ready availability of local and imported fabrics, a strong system of factory labour and a large furriers' guild, Leipzig became a fashion centre during the Baroque era. The chic apparel that was sold and worn in the town, especially during fair-times, led to the epithet 'Klein-Paris'. Sperontes's famous song collection *Singende Muse an der Pleisse*, published in four volumes between 1736 and 1745, features a frontispiece showing fashionably attired couples in Leipzig, drinking coffee, listening to music, and observing other well-dressed pairs promenading along the edge of the Pleisse River, in front of the Klein-Bosischer Garten (see fig.38). Sold during the fairs (the first part was released at the St Michael's Fair, 1736), the *Singende Muse* volumes contained pleasant, uncomplicated, strophic songs – perfect, *galant* leisure-hour entertainment for a middle-class audience.

Sperontes's collection was but one of many music publications produced in Leipzig and sold at the fairs. Leipzig offered the raw

38. *Divertissement along the River Pleisse, just outside the Ranstätt Gate, overlooking the Promenade and Klein-Bosischer Garten (the Thomaskirche is seen in the view of Leipzig in the background): engraving by C. F. Boetius from Sperontes, 'Singende Muse an der Pleisse' (Leipzig, 1736)*

materials needed by printers: metal for type and engraving-plates; imported (from other parts of Germany as well as from other countries) ink and paper for printed pages; and leather for bindings. Equally important, the fairs offered publishers the opportunity to display and sell their books directly to an international market, thus reducing the need for a network of foreign agents. The fairs brought the readers to the publishers, as it were. Many publishers settled in Leipzig; others came only during fair-time, from Augsburg, Frankfurt, Nuremberg and other printing centres. The visiting printers normally rented space in booths or set up temporary quarters in local print shops.

The strongest competitor in the book trade was Frankfurt, whose business surpassed that of Leipzig in the sixteenth century. During the seventeenth century, however, Leipzig steadily gained ground. By the last quarter of the seventeenth century the great industry of Leipzig's printers, combined with heavy tariffs imposed on foreign books sold in Frankfurt, enabled Leipzig to take the top position. Leipzig's printers included such important figures as Friedrich Lanckisch (1618–67), editor and publisher of the famous Biblical Concordance;[1] Johann Heinrich Zedler (1706–51), editor of the ambitious, 64-volume *Universal-Lexikon*;[2] and Bernhard Christoph Breitkopf (1695–1777), whose friendship with Johann Christoph Gottsched, professor of poetry and philosophy at the university in Leipzig, led to many notable literary projects (Breitkopf printed cantata texts and title-pages for Bach, but no music; it was his son Johann Gottlob Immanuel Breitkopf, 1719–94, who later built the firm into one of the most important music-printing houses in Europe). But of equal importance for Leipzig's musicians was a host of lesser printers – Johann Bauer, Johann Köhler, Christoph Ernst Sicul, Johann Adolph Boetius, Johann Gottfried Krügner, Johann Christian Langenheim, Immanuel Tietz and others – who stood ready to publish cantata texts and small collections of keyboard or ensemble music.

Leipzig borrowed from Frankfurt the idea of printed catalogues listing the volumes available at approaching fairs. Frankfurt's first catalogue, published by the Augsburg book dealer Georg Willer, appeared in 1564. Leipzig followed suit in 1594, with a catalogue printed locally by Henning Gross; Gross's firm continued to publish Leipzig book catalogues until 1759. Within each catalogue books were listed by topics, commonly in the order theology, law, medicine, philosophy, history, geography, poetry, music and foreign-language volumes ('Peregrini Idiomatis').

The book market enabled Leipzig's composers to see and buy the very latest music publications. During fair-times Bach could have purchased such trend-setting German collections as Vincent

Lübeck's *Clavier Übung* (Hamburg, 1728), a volume of keyboard dance suites; Johann Joachim Quantz's *Sei sonate a flauto traversiere solo* (Dresden, 1734), six *galant* sonatas for flute and harpsichord; or Johann Mattheson's *Die wol-klingende Finger-Sprache* (Hamburg, 1735-7), a collection of 12 keyboard fugues. All of these would have been of great interest to Bach, since he was working on similar projects (the six partitas, the flute sonatas and the *Art of Fugue*) at approximately the same time each publication appeared. In the realm of theory, Bach could have bought almost any of Mattheson's 22 publications, which treated in exhaustive detail French, Italian and German music practices and, in a number of cases, even discussed Bach's own compositional style. Johann Heinrich Buttstett's *Ut, mi, sol, re, fa, la, tota musica* (Erfurt, 1716), which defended past procedures, and Barthold Heinrich Brockes's *Harmonische Himmels-Lust* (Hamburg, 1744), a translation of James Thomson's enlightened poem *The Seasons* (which later served as the model for Gottfried van Swieten's text for Haydn's oratorio), were also available. Bach did not have to leave town to keep abreast of musical tastes; the fairs kept him *au courant*.

In addition, the fairs gave Leipzig's composers an incentive to print their own works. Even though the practice of distributing music in handwritten copies was very widespread in Germany during the Baroque period, composers nevertheless attempted to disseminate selected works to a broader audience through printed editions. Two methods of printing were commonly used. The first was typesetting, which resembled book printing in the sense that the music was set with small, movable pieces, each of which included a note-head, stem, flag (or flags), and a segment of staff lines. The second was engraving, which reproduced the image of a handwritten manuscript via copper plates. From an aesthetic standpoint engraving produced more pleasing results; but copper plates were expensive and could be used for limited runs only, of no more than a few hundred copies. Movable type was more durable and could be used for larger runs. In general, movable type was employed for ensemble music, engraving for keyboard works. Both types of printing were available in Leipzig at one time or another during the Baroque period. By 1700 or so, however, engraving emerged as the prevalent method. Of the Leipzig printers, Bauer and Köhler set music in movable type. Tietz, Boetius, Krügner and others practised music engraving.

Johann Christoph Pezel (1639–94), Leipzig *Stadtpfeifer* (town piper) from 1670 to 1681, turned to local printers to publish a number of important collections of ensemble music; they were dedicated to the town council or influential merchants and placed on sale at the fairs. All of Kuhnau's keyboard collections were engraved by Leipzig publishers and sold at the fairs; the famous 'Biblical Sonatas'

(*Musicalische Vorstellung einiger biblischer Historien*), engraved by Tietz in 1700, remained available even after the composer's death in 1722. The *Vier und zwantzig neue quatricinia* by the *Stadtpfeifer* Gottfried Reiche (1667–1734) were printed by Köhler in 1696 and sold at the Easter Fair the same year. Reiche was a highly esteemed trumpet player first for Kuhnau (1706–22) and then for Bach (1723–34).

Bach, too, earmarked his editions for fair sale. The six partitas of the first part of the *Clavierübung*, for instance, were printed by Krügner. The second and third partitas were advertised in the *Leipziger Post-Zeitungen* on 19 September 1727, in time for sale at the St Michael's Fair on 5 October. The advertisement added that the series would continue at each coming fair – an ambitious schedule to which Bach was unable to keep. The third *Clavierübung* volume (the so-called German Organ Mass), engraved in part by Krügner, was prepared for the Easter Fair of 1739 but did not appear until the following autumn, at the St Michael's Fair. For the *Musical Offering* Bach used two printers: Johann Georg Schübler, in Zella, for the engraved music plates; and Breitkopf for the printed title-page and dedicatory foreword. A payment slip from Breitkopf reveals that Bach ordered 200 copies of the title-page, a figure that probably represents the average run for most of Bach's publications. The second part of the *Clavierübung*, consisting of the Italian Concerto and the French Overture, was engraved by Johann Weigel of Nuremberg. During fair-times, however, Weigel set up shop in Leipzig, in the merchant Peter Hohmann's house in Peterstrasse; it was there that the volume was available for purchase during the St Michael's Fair of 1735. Thus Bach did not have to venture to Nuremberg when he wished to use Weigel, who was more experienced at music engraving than Leipzig printers and consequently produced more handsome results.

It is quite possible, too, that Bach fashioned the contents and titles of his collections to suit the tastes of fair visitors. The first *Clavierübung* volume contains French-style dance music; its title – which translates as 'Keyboard Practice, consisting in Preludes, Allemandes, Courantes, Sarabandes, Gigues, Minuets, and other Galanteries, Composed for Music Lovers, to Refresh Their Spirits' – makes a special point of the collection's *galant* side. The second volume shows a similarly cosmopolitan bent: 'Keyboard Practice consisting in a Concerto after the Italian Taste and an Overture after the French Manner . . . Composed for Music Lovers, to Refresh Their Spirits'. Such music would have appealed to the international sentiments of buyers at the fair.

ARCHITECTURE AND LANDSCAPED GARDENS

The extraordinary success of local industry and foreign commerce in Leipzig produced a class of wealthy, culturally ambitious business-men. Johann Heinrich Wolff (1690–1759), a merchant who traded on an international scale, was typical. The Address Book of 1742 (*Die jetzt florirende Kauffmannschafft in Leipzig*) describes him as dealing in great varieties of Italian silk, Dutch threads, English and Turkish yarns, and gold and silver wares – all of which were obtained directly from foreign traders. From his shop located on the street level of the town hall, Wolff also sold learned publications, including Zedler's *Universal-Lexikon*, to an impressive list of subscribers. When he married Susanna Regina Hempel on 5 February 1728, he commissioned Bach to write music for the ceremony: the cantata *Vergnügte Pleissenstadt* BWV216 was the proffered composition.

The ability to ascend quickly through the ranks is illustrated by Peter Hohmann (1663–1732). Born into a poor family in Cönnern, Hohmann moved to Leipzig at the age of 23 and took a job as a clerk in the shop of David Fleischer and Augustin Kober. When Kober died in 1693, Hohmann became half-owner of the shop. Seven years later he became sole owner, when Fleischer stepped aside. Through shrewd monetary transactions, and by efficiently providing supplies for wars on the Rhine and in Spain, Italy and Hungary, Hohmann soon amassed a fortune. In 1715 he joined the town council, and in 1717 he was ennobled by Charles VI and given the title 'Hohmann Edler von Hohenthal'. In 1723 he passed on his business to his sons Peter and Christian Gottlieb, and to his brother-in-law, the wealthy banker Michael Koch. At the time of his death in 1732 Hohmann owned a dozen country houses and three large, specially built mansions in town: one on the market place, one in the Katharinenstrasse and one in the Peterstrasse (it was in the Peterstrasse dwelling that Bach's second *Clavierübung* volume was sold during fair-time). Hohmann's remarkable rise demonstrated what an industrious person could accomplish in Leipzig – a lesson that surely was not lost on the town's Kantors. While the Thomaskantor had little chance to be ennobled, he did have the right to send his sons to the university, which was an important step up the social ladder. And Bach even speculated directly in business ventures: at the time of his death he owned a share in an ore mine at Klein Vogtsberg.

Working through the town council, Hohmann and other affluent businessmen strongly influenced Leipzig's architectural styles. The council monitored the building of both private and public structures, scrutinizing plans and granting licences for construction. Not surprisingly, the members of the council preferred pragmatism to pretence. Existing buildings were often remodelled and extended upwards – sometimes to a height of five storeys – rather than razed. Over-large rooms were avoided, as were space-squandering exterior double stairways. Architectural flourishes were restricted primarily to decorative façades. Most important, however, in both private and public buildings, was the concern for commercial space: the street level was commonly devoted to *Gewölben* – vaulted chambers that could be used for shops and storage.

The Börse am Naschmarkt ('Business Exchange on the Confectionery Market Place') symbolized the new architectural era. Located behind the town hall, it was built between 1678 and 1687 at the request of the Merchants' Corporation to the town council. It was the first large, public Baroque structure in Leipzig and displayed the type of practical eclecticism that was to become standard. The building, two and a half storeys high and strongly rectangular in shape, included ostentatious touches, such as an elegant, free-standing double stairway in front, leading to the upper floor, and large, noble statues of Apollo, Mercury, Venus and Athene on the corners of the flat, balustraded roof. For Leipzig, the four gods held special allegorical significance and often appeared in local verse (as in the text of Bach's cantata *Erwählte Pleissenstadt* BWV216a, which features a dialogue between Apollo and Mercury). Apollo was associated both with moral good and with the higher developments of civilization, such as law, philosophy and the arts; Mercury was the Roman god of traders and merchants; Venus was the Roman goddess of vegetation and later identified with Aphrodite, but she was also the bringer of good fortune; and Athene was the guardian goddess of Athens, a free city viewed by Leipzig citizens as the historical counterpart of their own town.

At the time of construction, the free-standing stairway was criticized by several members of the town council, who pointed out that although it was visually pleasing its steps 'would not be comfortable to climb in rain, snow or ice, especially by the many elderly citizens who invariably visit the Exchange during the St Michael's and Easter fairs'.[3] While the steps were retained in the Exchange, they were not included in later buildings. The strongly symmetrical structural elements of the Exchange reflected Italian influence. By contrast, the building's façade, decorated with sculpted garlands placed on the vertical pilasters and horizontal cornices surrounding the windows, reflected the Dutch tradition. The street floor was given over to vaulted rooms that were rented out to shopkeepers; the upper space was devoted to business.

The Exchange marked the beginning of a building spree that was to continue unabated until the outbreak of the Seven Years War in 1756. Moreover, in a number of critical ways, it established the pattern for structures that followed: first, architectural elements were borrowed from existing schools but combined in original ways; second, there was a strong concern for pragmatism; and third, there was the firm, omnipresent hand of the town council. The council soon proceeded to appoint a series of master builders, who in the short span of approximately 75 years reshaped almost one third of the inner city. The first builder hired after the completion of the Exchange was Johann Gregor Fuchs (1650–1715), whom the council lured from Dresden, overruling the objection of the Leipzig builders' guild. In Dresden Fuchs appears to have worked with the court architect Matthäus Daniel Pöppelmann (1662–1736), builder of the famous Zwinger complex. In Leipzig Fuchs was named *Ratsmauermeister* – the council's master mason.

Fuchs's first Leipzig project was perhaps his most important: the large mansion built between 1701 and 1704 for burgomaster Conrad Romanus. The house was a true town palace, constructed on a site at the corner of the Katharinenstrasse and Brühl that earlier had accommodated three plots. The house had two outer façades, each lined with three and a half storeys of majestic windows grouped into symmetrical units. At the centre of each façade stood an elaborate doorway, framed by weighty pilasters and topped by an impressive gable. The gable, in turn, was echoed on each side of the roof by smaller gables, and the roof was crowned with a mighty belvedere, which commanded a grand view of the town. The two façades were joined at the corner by a two-storey bay window, a carry-over from the Renaissance. Rich decorative work strengthened the overall impression. As with the Exchange, the ground floor of the Romanushaus, as it came to be called, was devoted to sales and storage areas. But the most critical part of the plan was the inclusion of an open central courtyard, connected by direct passage-ways to both Katharinenstrasse and Brühl. The central court provided even more commercial space, since it could be lined on all sides with small shops and booths.

In constructing the Romanushaus, Fuchs borrowed ideas from town palaces in Vienna and Prague. Nevertheless, he was able to create a new, forceful concept of the merchant mansion. His last work, a large house overlooking the market place (Markt 11; later called Äckerleins Hof), built for Peter Hohmann, shows the vertical extension of the Romanus style. Situated on a narrow plot running from the Markt through to the Klostergasse, the house rose imposingly to a height of four and a half storeys. The market façade contained four horizontal rows of seven windows each. These rows were divided vertically into three groups by pilasters. Both pilasters and cornices were decorated with hanging garlands. The central door was flanked on each side by three columns, which in turn were crowned by large statues. Directly above the door stood the head of

265

Mercury. The lively, richly ornamented façade was topped by a finely divided mansard roof, whose gabled windows and cupolas were arranged in such a way that they mirrored the symmetries of the lower façade. And as in the Romanushaus, Fuchs once again included an open central courtyard in his design.

The overall impression created by the Hohmann house is one of noble purpose: strong vertical elements are balanced by the play of surface embellishment. But nothing seems wasteful or too extravagant. The tall, symmetrically divided façade and the central courtyard were retained as ideals by the master builders who followed Fuchs: Christian Döring (1677–1750), Georg Werner (1682–1758) and Friedrich Seltendorff (d 1778). Their designs maximized both residential and commercial space in the very narrow plots that commonly existed in the inner city. Koch's house (Markt 3/Reichsstrasse 15), a mansion built by Werner between 1735 and 1739, shows the extent to which these principles could be carried. The building was constructed on a very narrow site stretching from the market place to the Reichsstrasse. To utilize the space fully Werner fashioned not one but two central courts, connected by corridors to the two streets. Today, this type of building is sometimes termed a *Durchgangshof* – a large edifice with central courtyard and passage-way. The *Durchgangshof* is perhaps the most distinctive symbol of Leipzig's Baroque architectural style.[4]

With the encouragement and imprimatur of the town council, the master builders transformed Leipzig from a Renaissance city to a Baroque showplace. Major projects included the construction of large private mansions on the Katharinenstrasse, Peterstrasse and market place, the rebuilding of the Peterstor (Peter's Gate) in 1722–3 and the expansion of the Thomasschule in 1731–2. Of the private mansions, the most famous was the large house built by Fuchs in 1706–7 for the merchant Dietrich Apel. Located catercorner to the town hall on the market place (see fig.37 above), Apel's house, as it was called at the time, rose majestically to a height of four and a half storeys. The electors Friedrich August I and II stayed there on their visits to Leipzig, and from its windows they listened to student serenades conducted by Kuhnau and Bach. The Peterstor was designed by Pöppelmann, whose plans were personally approved by Friedrich August I; it was executed in the progressive French Regency style, much in vogue in Dresden, with the result that it exhibited far less surface decoration than Fuchs's buildings. The Thomasschule, rebuilt by Werner, showed the usual upward extension (from three storeys to four and a half, in this case) of the Leipzig Baroque period. But it also displayed a simplification of surface decoration, pointing to a more 'natural' architectural style (see fig. 39b). This progressive tendency, looking towards the approaching

(a)

(b)

39. The Thomasschule: (a) in 1723 (left, with the Thomaskirche, centre), before the 1732 rebuilding by Georg Werner; (b) engraving by Johann Gottfried Krügner

rationalism of the Enlightenment, also appeared in the mansion Werner built soon afterwards for Breitkopf.

The churches, too, profited from the building craze. The Barfüsserkirche and Petrikirche were renovated, the façade of the Paulinerkirche was rebuilt in the Baroque style and the Johanniskirche was equipped with a Baroque tower designed by Werner. But it was the merchant homes that attracted the greatest attention. They were greatly admired, and engravings of them were widely circulated. *Die Civil-Baukunst*, written by Nicholaus Goldmann, edited and enlarged by Leonhard Christoph Sturm and financed by the merchant Georg Bose (who owned Goldmann's manuscript),[5] systematically analysed the Leipzig techniques; it quickly became the standard text on civic architecture.

Equally impressive were the promenades and gardens that sprang up around Leipzig, just outside the city walls. On the west side of the town a long, public promenade lined with linden trees was established for the diversion of citizens and visitors (see fig.38 above). On large plots wealthy merchants built expansive gardens, with geometrical arrangements of trees and shrubs. The flat, moist terrain was ideal for plants and fountains alike. Often, the gardens also included a villa (*Lustschloss*) or coffee-house (*Caffeeschrank*). As with town mansions, so with landscaped gardens: the merchants were guided by both aesthetic and pragmatic concerns, and consequently fountains and flowers were combined with fruit-bearing trees. The most famous gardens during the Baroque period were the Gross-Bosischer Garten, owned by Caspar Bose (*d* 1700) and located just outside the city wall at the south-east corner of the town; the Klein-Bosischer Garten, owned by Bose's brother Georg (*d* 1700) and located along the Pleisse on the west side of the town; and Apel's garden, built for Dietrich Apel and also along the Pleisse on the west side of the town, opposite the Thomaskirche.

The Bose gardens were designed by Leonhard Christoph Sturm (1669–1719), editor of *Die Civil-Baukunst*, who was called to Leipzig by the Bose brothers in 1690. Sturm visited the Netherlands in 1697 and Paris in 1699, and the trips greatly affected his Leipzig work. Indeed, documents from the time describe his gardens as being in the 'französisch-holländisches Geschmack'. The layout of the Gross-Bosischer Garten, recorded in a contemporary engraving, reveals clearly the happy balance between extravagance and practicality. The engraving shows a villa of modest size, framed by ornate, French-style flower-beds and standing before a semicircular orangery, which rests in a lowered amphitheatre. The amphitheatre arrangement served to shield sensitive flowers and citrus trees from the wind. Within the amphitheatre are a decorative fountain, two more French flower-beds, and a number of Dutch-style flower-beds, with plants arranged in neat, radiating rows. Outside the amphitheatre stretch rectangular beds of food plants and groves of fruit trees. To the left, well out of sight of the villa, stand long work-sheds, in which crops could be dried and stored.

The promenades and gardens symbolized Leipzig's transformation from a walled to an open city, from a Medieval-Renaissance to a Baroque town. The new and renovated buildings, together with the walks and gardens, were sources of great pride and optimism. They demonstrated what free citizens could accomplish through their own endeavours. A song from Sperontes's *Singende Muse* collection captured the spirit well:

Das angenehme Pleiss-Athen	The pleasant Athens-on-the-Pleisse
Behält den Ruhm vor allen,	Holds glory for all,
Auch allen zu gefallen:	And for all, pleasure:
Denn es ist Wunderschön.	For it is exceedingly beautiful.
An tausend andern Orten	At a thousand other places
Trifft man von jeden Sorten	One encounters all sorts of diversion,
Gewiss wohl kein Vergnügen an,	But certainly none
Das mehr ergötzen kan,	That can amuse more,
Als hier bey unsren Linden	Than here under our lindens
Daraus die Anmuth selber sprisst,	From which charm herself springs,
Im Überfluss zu finden,	Is found in abundance,
Und stets beysammen ist.	And is constantly present.
Geht in und um und vor die Stadt,	Go in and around and before the city,
Und zeigt der Neu-Begierde	And observe the new longing
Was hier und dort vor Zierde	For embellishment that here and there
Die Gegend in sich hat!	The region possesses!
Geht und bemerckt aufs beste	Go and note in the best possible way
Die prächtigsten Palläste,	The magnificent palaces,
Und was Verordnung, Kunst und Fleiss	And what order, skill and industry
Wohl zu ersinnen weiss;	Can indeed conceive;
Das wird den Ausschlag geben:	This will decide the issue:
Weil alles, alles ungemein,	Since all find all quaint,
Hier muss ein englisch Leben!	Here it must be an angelic life!
Hier muss ein Eden seyn![6]	Here it must be an Eden!

By 1750 Leipzig was a city of the future. The contrast with its old commercial rival, Frankfurt, could not have been greater. While Leipzig stood transformed, Frankfurt retained its medieval and Renaissance appearance, a fact that impressed the young Goethe, who visited Leipzig in 1765 to study law. In a letter to his sister written in December of that year, he too, like Sperontes, praised Leipzig as an earthly paradise:

The gardens are as magnificent as anything I have ever seen in my life. I will try to send you a view of the entrance to Apel's Garden, which is regal. The first time I saw it, I believed I was entering the Elysian fields.[7]

And later, in his autobiography *Dichtung und Wahrheit* (1811–33), he recalled:

To the observer, Leipzig does not bring to mind an ancient age. Rather, this monument announces a more recent era, one of great industry, affluence and abundance. To my mind, the unbelievably splendid buildings, which turn their faces to two streets and which encircle enclosed courts with sky-high walls, contain an entire bourgeois world. They are great citadels – indeed, cities within the city.[8]

This was the town in which the Thomaskantors Schelle, Kuhnau and Bach worked.

CHURCH LIFE AND SACRED MUSIC-MAKING

Saxony stood at the very centre of the German Reformation, geographically and politically. It was the home and battleground of Martin Luther (1483–1546), a Saxon born in Eisleben. Luther's famous dispute with Johann Eck took place in Leipzig. When Luther was declared a fugitive in 1521 after the Diet of Worms, he was granted refuge in the Wartburg Castle by the Saxon Elector Friedrich III ('Frederick the Wise'; 1463–1525); and at the height of the conflict with Rome, Luther was given strong support by Friedrich's successor, Johann Friedrich I (1503–54), who became an ardent Lutheran and led the conversion of Saxony. On Whitsunday 1539, when Luther returned to Leipzig to preach in the Thomaskirche, he was greeted as a conquering hero. Over the course of the next 150 years Saxony became one of Europe's strongest bastions of Lutheranism.

From a practical standpoint, Luther's call for individual responsibility and freedom from papal control appealed to both Saxon nobles and peasants, who equally deplored the drainage of local funds to Rome. Merchants and businessmen found Luther's doctrine of personal freedom exhilarating, and they were quick to perceive the financial advantages of confiscating church property. Indeed, in Leipzig, the town council's prestige and power were greatly enhanced by Reformation policies. The properties of the Augustinian Thomaskirche, the Franciscan Barfüsserkirche and the Dominican Paulinerkirche were seized and transferred from Roman to council jurisdiction. The cloister of the Barfüsserkirche and the monastic properties of the Thomaskirche were sold in 1543; the cloister of the Paulinerkirche was given to the university the following year.

During the first half of the eighteenth century Leipzig's position as a Lutheran stronghold gained new significance. In 1697 the shadow of Catholic domination spread over Saxony when Elector Friedrich August I ('August the Strong'; 1670–1733) converted to Catholicism in order to become ruler of Poland (as August II). At first Saxony was little threatened by the conversion: the Peace of Westphalia (1648) protected the rights of both Lutherans and Catholics – of the Corpus Evangelicorum and the Corpus Catholicorum. But pressure from Rome and restiveness in Poland soon forced August to affirm his Catholic faith in more than a token way: in 1708 he ordered the court opera house in Dresden to be rebuilt and dedicated as a Catholic chapel (the Hofkirche im Theater), and in 1717 he agreed to spend no more than three months of each year in Saxony.[9]

The Lutheran-Catholic conflict became specially acute within the royal family, for August's wife, Christiane Eberhardine of Brandenburg-Bayreuth, remained Protestant and insisted also that her children be raised as Protestant. Against her wishes the crown prince, the future Friedrich August II, was taken off to Bologna, where he was confirmed in the Catholic faith in 1712. August I, fearing unrest in Saxony, kept news of the conversion a secret until 1717. In the meantime Christiane Eberhardine moved to Torgau, then to Pretzsch on the Elbe. When she died in Pretzsch on 5 September 1727 she was hailed as a Protestant martyr, and Leipzig, which had never wavered in its Protestantism, was chosen as an appropriate site for a large commemoration service. The service was held with great solemnity in the Paulinerkirche on 17 October. Gottsched composed a funeral ode, which was set to music by Bach (the cantata *Lass, Fürstin, lass noch einen Strahl* BWV 198). The event, described in unusual detail in contemporary publications, affirmed Leipzig's position as Saxony's Lutheran centre.

The preceding 30 years had witnessed a sharp intensification of Lutheran worship in Leipzig. In 1694 the town council voted for new midweek Communion services in the two principal churches, the Nikolaikirche and the Thomaskirche. Still, so great was the attendance at Sunday services there that the council soon authorized the renovation of two dilapidated Catholic churches – the Barfüsserkirche and the Petrikirche – for Lutheran use. The Barfüsserkirche was reopened, as the Neue Kirche, in 1699; the Petrikirche was dedicated in 1712. Moreover, the Paulinerkirche, used previously only for academic events, was also rebuilt and opened for public worship in 1710. By the second decade of the eighteenth century Leipzig was, as an oft-quoted church ordinance of 1710 put it, a 'Kirchen-Staat' – a city of churches.[10] The pervasive influence of the

The Late Baroque Era

Lutheran church in Leipzig life can be measured from the frontispiece of Sperontes's *Singende Muse* (fig.38 above): although the couples in the portrait are engaged in secular diversions, the Thomaskirche stands prominently in the background – a stark symbol of Leipzig's orthodox Lutheran tradition – and the woman in the foreground listening to music wears a crucifix.

The music in Leipzig's principal churches was placed under the supervision of a single director, the Thomaskantor. The Thomaskantor post existed at least as early as 1435, when it was occupied by Johannes Steffani from Orba. When the monasteries were disbanded in 1543, the Thomasschule, a city choir- and grammar-school, was formed on the grounds of the Thomaskirche. The Thomaskantor became a member of the school's teaching staff, answerable to the town council and third in command behind the Rektor and the Superintendant. The Thomaskantor was required to provide music for services in the Thomaskirche and Nikolaikirche, to direct the musical studies of the Thomasschule students (who ranged in age from 12 to 23), and to teach certain academic subjects at the school, chiefly Latin and the catechism. This last requirement became a point of contention for a number of Thomaskantors, including Bach. In the seventeenth century, possibly during the tenure of Sebastian Knüpfer (Kantor from 1657 to 1676), the Thomaskantor's title was extended to *director musices Lipsiensis* ('director of city music in Leipzig'). This confirmed that the Thomaskantor was by that time also responsible for providing civic music at public events, at the command of the town council. Finally, when new public worship services were initiated in the Neue Kirche and Petrikirche, the Thomaskantor was placed in charge of the music there, too. In the Paulinerkirche, the Thomaskantor's responsibilities extended only to special university occasions.

To provide music in the churches, the Thomaskantor had at his disposal a group of singers and instrumentalists of greatly differing abilities. The singers were drawn from a pool of 50 to 60 Thomasschule students, who by Kuhnau's time were divided into four choirs of 12 to 16 singers, depending on talent. The best singers participated in the first and second choirs, which performed concerted polyphonic music (that is, cantatas and similar pieces with instrumental accompaniment) in the Nikolaikirche and the Thomaskirche.[11] The third choir performed polyphonic music, such as motets, at the Neue Kirche, and the fourth choir, composed of the most modestly talented boys, sang unison chorales at the Petrikirche. The first choir was conducted by the Thomaskantor; the others were conducted by prefects – older pupils appointed as conductors.

For instrumentalists, the Thomaskantor could rely on a core of eight professional players: four *Stadtpfeifer* (town pipers), three

Kunstgeiger (skilled fiddlers) and one apprentice fiddler. Despite their titles, the *Stadtpfeifer* and *Kunstgeiger* commonly played a wide range of instruments. At times the positions were occupied by extremely competent players, such as the senior pipers Johann Pezel and Gottfried Reiche, who have already been mentioned with regard to music publishing. Pezel was a highly skilled string and brass player; Reiche was one of the most outstanding trumpeters in central Germany – a fact that was not lost on Bach, whose Leipzig trumpet parts were extremely taxing.[12] But not all the players were so gifted, and since the appointments were normally for life, many *Stadtpfeifer*, and *Kunstgeiger* remained in their posts long after they had passed their prime. In a memorandum to the town council, Bach was rather pointed about the limitations of the pipers and fiddlers:

> Modesty forbids me to speak at all truthfully of their qualities and musical knowledge. But one must remember that they are partly *emeriti* and partly not at all in such *exercitio* as they should be.[13]

The small orchestra of approximately 18 to 20 players (the figure given by Bach) was rounded out by students drawn from the Thomasschule and the university.

By far the most demanding task the Thomaskantor faced was the ongoing provision of service music for Sundays and high feasts. The first choir performed in alternate weeks at the Nikolaikirche and Thomaskirche. At these churches the main Sunday service, Hauptgottesdienst, started at 7 a.m. and lasted three to four hours. In addition to bolstering congregational hymn-singing at Hauptgottesdienst, the first choir was expected to perform a motet at the beginning of the service, a cantata after the Gospel and a second concerted piece (either the second half of the cantata or another musical work altogether) during Communion. The motet was normally a Latin-texted, Renaissance *a cappella* work, often drawn from a printed collection such as Erhard Bodenschatz's *Florilegium portense* (1618–21). The cantata was more important, musically and theologically, since its German text was normally based on the Epistle or Gospel reading of the day or on a hymn sung by the congregation. The cantata served as an important supplement to the liturgy: placed just after the Gospel, it prepared the way for the heart of the service – the Creed, the sermon and the Eucharist. The cantata was a substantial piece, commonly 20 to 30 minutes in length, and the Thomaskantor was expected to provide new works from his own pen.

It was Johann Schelle (1648–1701) who introduced the German 'liturgical cantata' into the Leipzig service. Assuming the Thomaskantor post in 1677, he taught Latin and the catechism at the Thomasschule, directed the music at the Thomaskirche and

Nikolaikirche and, after 1679, supervised the music for academic events at the Paulinerkirche as well. At first Schelle's substitution of German-texted pieces of his own composition for the Latin works of Italian origin that had traditionally followed the Gospel met with opposition. Most other large cities had long before moved away from using only Latin-texted works in the Lutheran service. In Dresden, for instance, where Schelle studied, Schütz had composed concerted works with German texts for the royal chapel at least as early as the 1620s. Nevertheless, Leipzig, with its conservative tradition, was loath to make the change. The controversy came to a head when the burgomaster Christian Lorenz von Adlershelm instructed Schelle to restore the Latin settings during the Christmas season of 1683. Schelle took the matter before the town council and won his appeal.

Schelle's cantatas based on scripture readings represent the most important part of his output. In collaboration with the pastor Johann Benedict Carpsow he also introduced the chorale cantata, a work based on a hymn whose melody was sung by the congregation and whose text formed the subject of the day's sermon. Even through Bach's tenure, many parts of the Leipzig Hauptgottesdienst remained in Latin, in the spirit of Luther's eclectic Reformation service: the Collect, Response and Preface, and at times the Kyrie, Gloria and Credo as well. Thus to members of the congregation not conversant with Latin, the German cantata, based on scripture or hymn, became a central part of the service – so much so that printed copies of the cantata text were made available. A 1715 account specifically praised the practice:

> It has been the custom for some time for the esteemed Kantor to have the texts of the music printed beforehand, under the title *Kirchen-Music*, so that the music, especially on high festivals, may be heard with greater devotion and that everyone can follow along.[14]

A number of the printed librettos have survived; they normally appear in the form of a small booklet, containing the texts to a half-dozen or so works.

Schelle performed his duties well, achieving fame as a teacher and composer. Among his students were Reinhard Keiser (1673–1739), the famous Hamburg opera composer, and Christoph Graupner, Kapellmeister in Darmstadt. Although Schelle was described in Walther's *Musicalisches Lexicon* of 1732 as having composed 'viele Music-Stücke und Jahrgänge', few of his compositions are extant today. The 'Jahrgänge', or yearly cycles, would have been groups of 60 or so sacred cantatas, one for each Sunday and high feast day of the year. To judge from the surviving compositions, Schelle's cantatas commonly consisted of an orchestral sinfonia and opening chorus

40. Title-page of J. G. Walther's 'Musicalisches Lexicon' (Leipzig, 1732)

40. Title-page of J. G. Walther's 'Musicalisches Lexicon' (Leipzig, 1732)

followed by sections for chorus, soloists or instruments. Some of the settings, presumably written for special feast days or perhaps for services during fair-times, appear to have been quite elaborate. In *Lobe den Herrn*, a scripture cantata, Schelle called for 26 parts, divided into three instrumental groups and a chorus of 'concertino' (solo) and 'cappella' (tutti) forces. Despite these notable achievements, when Schelle died in 1701 the Leipzig church music programme was in a state of decline and ready for rebuilding.

The rebuilding was undertaken by Schelle's capable colleague

Johann Kuhnau (1660–1722). Appointed organist at the Thomas-kirche in 1684, Kuhnau came to the Thomaskantor post with impressive credentials. By 1701 he had published four collections of keyboard music, as well as a satirical novel on contemporary music practices, *Der musicalische Quack-Salber* (Dresden, 1700). Just as important to the town council was the fact that Kuhnau was university-trained. He received a law degree in Leipzig in 1688, and his dissertation, a learned Latin tome on the laws of church music, was published the same year. By 1700 he had developed a flourishing law practice. Indeed, he had represented Nicolaus Adam Strungk in the opening of the new opera house in 1693 – an action that was not without later irony, as we shall see. Kuhnau also studied maths, Greek and Hebrew. Walther praised him in the *Musicalisches Lexicon* as one gifted 'in Theologia, in Jure, in Oratoria, in Poesi, in Algebra & Mathesi, in linguis exoticis, und in Re Musica'. Obviously, Kuhnau was well suited for the academic instruction required at the Thomasschule.

During Kuhnau's tenure the duties of the Thomaskantor grew to include the supervision of music for the newly opened Petrikirche and Neue Kirche and for the new services at the Thomaskirche and Nikolaikirche. The Thomaskantor was also expected to direct personally the music at large funeral services and, as in the past, to provide pieces for civic events (such as visitations of the Saxon elector) that fell under the jurisdiction of the town council. For church cantatas Kuhnau relied mostly on his own compositions, written in the manner of Schelle. They commonly began with an instrumental sinfonia, followed by an opening chorus (except in solo cantatas), recitatives and arias. For special celebrations, such as the 300th anniversary of the university in 1709 or the 200th anniversary of the Reformation in 1717, Kuhnau wrote a number of large, brilliant pieces, sometimes calling for as many as three choirs of voices.

Despite Kuhnau's impressive production of cantatas and occasional works, his term as Thomaskantor was not without strife. First, he was frequently ill, so much so that as early as 1703 the town council asked Telemann to stand ready to assume the Kantor position, should Kuhnau expire.[15] Second, the burgomaster Romanus granted Telemann the privilege of writing music for the Thomaskirche – a clear infringement of the Thomaskantor's prerogatives; and the privilege was continued for Melchior Hoffmann after Telemann's departure. Finally, Kuhnau experienced difficulty maintaining his performing forces, in part because the quality of voices in the Thomasschule declined as academic standards rose and in part because the university students were enticed away by secular pursuits – the opera and the collegia musica. In a memorandum of 1709 to the town council Kuhnau complained:

The greatest problem with this music [the church music for Sunday morning] is caused by the opera and the music-making in the Neue Kirche. For as soon as most of the students . . . have been trained at the expense of the Kantor's hard work and given enough proficiency to be useful, they immediately long to join the company of the opera singers, therefore doing nothing helpful, and they seek their dismissal before it is due, often with immodesty and defiance . . . This was recently the case with our best bass, Herr Petzold, who was given permission to sing in the opera, or the talented descantist, Herr Pechuel, whom the most honorable council did not prevent from spending time in Weissenfels and also from singing in the opera in Naumburg . . . and naturally where opera is allowed [in Leipzig], it is also great fun to frequent public coffee houses . . . and to spend evenings on the streets, or in some other way make music with lively company.[16]

Kuhnau's complaint about the Neue Kirche reflected the fact that the Neue Kirche organist traditionally directed a collegium musicum, a student ensemble that performed *galant* secular music in gardens and coffee-houses. Kuhnau died in 1722 without resolving these conflicts. His successor was to deal with them in a most direct way.

Bach was elected Thomaskantor on 22 April 1723 – but only after the town council had been unable to obtain Telemann or Graupner. From the council's viewpoint, Telemann and Graupner were better choices: both were well known locally, having made music in Leipzig at an earlier time; both had studied law at the university, making them specially qualified for the academic teaching required at the Thomasschule; and both had extensive experience composing church music – by 1723 each had written at least five yearly cycles of cantatas. Bach's output of church works was far more modest – a single incomplete cycle – and his academic credentials (three years of choir school in Lüneburg) far less impressive.

Nevertheless, in his first years as Thomaskantor and *director musices Lipsiensis* Bach approached his responsibilities with great industry. Beginning on the first Sunday after Trinity (30 May) 1723, he proceeded to compile in short order five yearly cantata cycles, each containing approximately 60 works. In the first cycle, assembled in 1723–4, he drew heavily on his incomplete series of 25 or so cantatas from the Weimar years, filling in the gaps with new pieces. There can be no doubt that Bach's expectations were great. Although there is no unifying concept in the first cycle, the works are remarkably expansive in scale and richly inventive. Many of the concluding chorales, for instance, include obbligato instrumental interludes – a feature absent in most later cantatas. For the second cycle, assembled in 1724–5, Bach adopted a more encompassing artistic plan.

41. Johann Sebastian Bach: replica (1748) by Elias Gottlieb Haussmann of his 1746 portrait showing the composer holding a copy of his six-part canon BWV1076

Starting with the first Sunday after Trinity (11 June) 1724, he composed a series of chorale cantatas, each based on the text and melody of the 'sermon hymn' (the hymn sung by the congregation immediately after the sermon) of the Sunday or feast day in question. It is possible that Bach, like Schelle, collaborated with the minister, who would have used the same hymns as the basis for weekly sermons. The chorale cantatas are among Bach's most refined and accessible vocal works – so much so that Philipp Spitta, the great nineteenth-century Bach biographer, mistakenly viewed them as the culminating creation of the composer's later years.

For reasons that are not entirely clear, Bach required more time to assemble his third yearly cycle. It stretched over the period 1725–7 and contains a good number of works for solo voice instead of chorus, a fact that suggests growing difficulties with performing forces. The fourth cycle appears to have been assembled during the years 1728–9 to texts by Picander (the *nom de plume* of Christian Friedrich Henrici), one of Bach's favourite local poets. While the librettos of the fourth cycle are known through Picander's published works, only nine of Bach's settings have survived. The fifth cantata cycle has thus far defied reconstruction, since most of the cantatas in it have been lost.

During his first seven years in Leipzig Bach also wrote a number of brilliant sacred works for special occasions: the *St John* and *St Matthew* Passions for Good Friday services (continuing the Passion tradition started by Kuhnau in 1721), the *Magnificat* (in its E♭ form) and the Sanctus in D major (third movement of bwv232) for Christmas Day services, and a series of large motets for funerals. For both cantatas and special works Bach had to supervise the copying of parts, a task usually carried out by Thomasschule students. He also had to coach many of the instrumentalists and train the vocalists through daily singing lessons. Finally, he had to direct the performance in the Thomaskirche or Nikolaikirche. To these duties were added Latin instruction (for which Bach paid an assistant), the production of music for civic events and the fulfilment of outside commissions.

There can be no doubt that unusual care was expended on sacred music during fair-times. Merchants were forbidden to sell on Sundays, which meant that church services and church music were the chief form of social activity that day. In an appeal for better performance forces, Kuhnau had pointed out to the town council that it was specially necessary to produce good music on 'feast days and during the fairs, since visitors and distinguished gentlemen would certainly want to hear something fine in the principal churches'[17] – that is, in the Thomaskirche and the Nikolaikirche. Certainly it is not by chance that Bach created a number of his most ambitious and festive pieces for Sundays that occurred during fair-times, works such as the cantatas *Singet dem Herrn ein neues Lied!* bwv190 and *Sie werden aus Saba alle kommen* bwv65 (both of which would have fallen during the New Year's Fair, 1724) and *Herr Christ, der einige Gottessohn* bwv96 (which would have been performed during the St Michael's Fair, 1724).

Around 1729 Bach's extraordinary production of church works suddenly came to a halt. Only 13 new cantatas can be assigned to the period after 1729 – an average of less than one per year – and most were written to fill gaps in the existing yearly cycles. Moreover, the large works that were assembled after 1730, the *St Mark Passion* (1731), the *Christmas Oratorio* (1734–5) and the *Mass in B minor* (1748–9), rely heavily on parody technique, that is, on the rearrangement of previously existing material. Why Bach turned his back on sacred music around 1729 has been the subject of much recent debate.[18] Certainly he suffered through annoying squabbles with the town council over the fees and prerogatives of the Thomaskantor. These arguments began as early as 1723, when Bach requested the right to supervise the music in the Paulinerkirche not only for university ceremonies but also for the new Sunday services. Kuhnau had received payment for conducting the new services, but after his death the council had assigned them to the organist of the Nikolaikirche.

When the council refused to change this arrangement, Bach appealed to the Saxon elector, but to no avail.

Then, too, there was Bach's pointed complaint, issued in the famous 'Short but Most Necessary Draft for a Well-Appointed Church Music' of August 1730, about the quality of the vocalists and instrumentalists available to him. Bach claimed that boys with no musical talent whatsoever were being accepted into the Thomasschule, and he reproached the council for undermining his instrumental ensemble by withdrawing the stipendia for student players that had been available in the days of Schelle and Kuhnau. Bach noted with envy the orchestra in Dresden, in which the musicians, paid by the elector, were 'relieved of all concern for their living, free from chagrin, and obliged each to master but a single instrument'.[19] As with Kuhnau's memoranda, Bach's 'Draft' appears to have gone unanswered.

Certainly these factors contributed to Bach's diminishing interest in liturgical music. But it is just as likely that he simply began to look for other compositional challenges, once he had written a large body of cantatas that could be re-used year after year. In March 1729 Georg Balthasar Schott, organist of the Neue Kirche and director of the collegium musicum founded by Telemann, left Leipzig to become Kantor in Gotha. According to a longstanding tradition, the directorship of the 'Telemann' Collegium should have fallen to the next organist of the Neue Kirche; but by April 1729 Bach had assumed the directorship himself, thus shifting the weight of his responsibilities from the Kantor side of his job to the *director musices Lipsiensis* side. Thinking, perhaps, of the Dresden orchestra, Bach may have preferred to work with an instrumental ensemble of university students rather than with a vocal chorus of boys from the Thomasschule.

In any case, in the 1730s Bach focussed the bulk of his energies on the production of secular music for the collegium. In the 1740s he turned more and more to private projects, such as the publication of his keyboard music and the assembling of manuscript collections like *Das wohltemperirte Clavier*, book 2, and the great 18 chorales BWV 651–8. Bach never returned to church music with the concentrated vigour of the years 1723–9, and when the town council convened in 1750 to choose his successor, the burgomaster Stieglitz declared that the Thomasschule needed 'a Kantor, not a Kapellmeister'.[20] The council found such a person in Gottlob Harrer, whom they had auditioned the year before. But in a sense, they misunderstood the progressive direction in which music in Leipzig was heading.

CIVIC LIFE AND SECULAR MUSIC-MAKING

If sacred music blossomed in Leipzig between 1680 and 1740, secular music certainly did as well. It is quite understandable that Leipzig's businessmen and university faculty would desire musical diversion, and that cosmopolitan visitors to the fairs would seek similar entertainment. As civic life prospered, so did secular music-making. By 1700 those in search of music outside the church could visit the opera, listen to a collegium musicum performance at a coffee-house or wine garden, observe ceremonial music presented on a grand scale for public events, or even attend dancing-classes.[21]

The most visible symbol of growing interest in secular music was the public opera house erected in 1693. Built by Nicolaus Adam Strungk (1640–1700), court Kapellmeister in Dresden, the house was a bold financial venture, since it was not supported by a court. Strungk was granted a ten-year licence by the Elector Johann Georg III, who believed the undertaking would enrich the arts in Leipzig and provide a training-ground for Dresden musicians too. Certainly the idea of a Leipzig opera company did not spring out of the blue. Earlier in the seventeenth century a series of student productions was well received; later, Johann Velten (*d* 1692) and his troupe of performers presented plays with great success. Both the student productions and the plays took place during fair-times. Velten's death in 1692 may have spurred Strungk to fill in the gap with opera. Strungk acquired a plot on the Brühl, just inside the city wall at the northeast corner of the town, and commissioned the Italian architect Girolamo Sartorio to construct a building of modest size but stately appearance. Sartorio, builder of opera houses in Hanover, Amsterdam, Hamburg and other cities, was assisted with the interior by Tarquinio Bernardelli.

Although Leipzig was late getting into the opera business (the public opera in Hamburg had started in 1678), conditions were highly favourable for success. From the start, opera in Leipzig was linked with the annual fairs. According to the terms of his licence, Strungk was required to present 15 performances during each fair, a figure that does not seem unreasonable in light of the fact that by the end of the seventeenth century the fairs normally extended over a three-week period. Strungk obviously hoped to capitalize on the combined patronage of wealthy citizens, university students and fair visitors. The house was inaugurated on 8 May 1693, during the Easter Fair, with a performance of Strungk's *Alceste*. Paul Thymich, an instructor at the Thomasschule, fashioned a German libretto from Aurelio Aureli's well-known Italian text. Thymich's wife Anna Catharina performed the role of Alcestis.

Local composers, local performers and German – or mostly

German – texts were to become mainstays of the Leipzig opera. Strungk wrote at least eight works for Leipzig. Telemann claimed to have written more than 20, supplying pieces even after he moved from the town. In addition to Strungk and Telemann, Christian Ludwig Boxberg, Gottfried Grünewald, Johann David Heinichen, Melchior Hoffmann and Johann Gottfried Vogler composed prolifically for the Leipzig stage. All of them studied at one point or another at the Thomasschule or at the university. The Leipzig operas commonly concerned classical themes: Strungk's *Nero* (1693) or *Agrippina* (1699), Telemann's *Jupiter und Semele* (1716) or *Die Satyren in Arcadien* (1719), or Heinichen's *Hercules* (given in 1714), for instance. But comic subjects were well received, too: Grünewald's *Der ungetreue Schäffer Cardillo* (1703) or Heinichen's *Der angenehme Betrug oder Der Karneval in Venedig* (given in 1709), for example. Like opera elsewhere, Leipzig productions often dwelt on the spectacular. Strungk's *Phocas* (1696) called for a burning tower, a wild bear and a storm.

For its singers the Leipzig opera relied principally on students for the male roles and on wives and daughters for the female roles. Grünewald, Telemann, Graupner, Fasch, Heinichen and many others took time from their academic studies to sing in the opera. In addition to Thymich's wife Anna Catharina, Strungk's daughters Philippine, Magdalena Anna and Elisabeth Catharina are known to have participated in Leipzig opera performances. This reliance on local talent contrasted with practices at wealthy courts such as Dresden and Hanover, where Italian singers, including castratos, formed the centrepieces of the vocal ensemble. In Leipzig the instrumentalists, too, were drawn chiefly from the student ranks – the *Stadtpfeifer* and *Kunstgeiger* do not seem to have assisted. After Strungk's death in 1700 the directorship of the opera was assumed by Telemann, who ran the operation with great vitality between 1702 and 1704. He was extremely successful in attracting student singers and players to the opera, an achievement that was bitterly resented, as we have seen, by Kuhnau, whose forces were proportionately depleted. When Telemann left Leipzig in 1704, the opera was run mainly by Hoffmann, who served as principal director until his death in 1715.

Unfortunately, very little music from the Leipzig opera has survived. The repertory can be reconstructed in part from extant librettos, which reveal a strong resistance to the Italian-texted arias that flourished in Dresden, Berlin and other opera centres supported by royal patronage. In Leipzig, German prevailed, undoubtedly because of the bourgeois nature of the audience. Until 1709 or so, arias in languages other than German were used only for special effects, as dialect songs in *Singspiel*-like works. After that time, Italian-texted arias appeared together with German-texted pieces, but the latter continued to predominate.[22] Elsewhere, Italian took over.

The Leipzig librettos were normally derived from the standard Italian texts of Aureli, Giulio Cesare Corradi, Nicolò Minato and others. The German versions show a marked tendency toward informality. In many instances *opera seria* gods were transformed into highly personalized figures, speaking to the audience of everyday situations in everyday language. In the text of *Aeneas*, presented at the Easter Fair in 1710, for instance, we find Aeneas, the hero of antiquity, dispensing practical advice on amorous courtship:

Ein Kleiner Streit	A little dispute
In Liebessachen	In affairs of love
Dient offtermahls an Zunders statt	Quite often serves instead to kindle
Und kann die Flamme stärker machen.	And can make the flame stronger.
Wenn zwei verliebte Hertzen	When two hearts in love
Stets lachen, spielen, schertzen,	Constantly laugh, play and jest,
So kriegen sie bey guter Zeit	They become, in time,
Einander satt.[23]	Tired of one another.

This is quite like the platitudinous tone of many of Bach's cantata texts, such as the bass aria of *Christ unser Herr zum Jordan kam* BWV7, first performed on St John's Day 1724:

Merkt und Hört, ihr Menschenkinder,	Children of mankind, note and listen
Was Gott selbst die Taufe heisst.	To what God himself said about Baptism.
Es muss zwar hier Wasser sein,	This must, indeed, be water
Doch schlecht Wasser nicht allein.	But not wretched water alone.
Gottes Wort und Gottes Geist	For God's word and spirit
Tauft und reiniget die Sünder.[24]	Baptizes and purifies sinners.

In the opera, it is Homer's *Aeneid* that is made more accessible; in the cantata, it is the first stanza of Luther's hymn *Christ unser Herr zum Jordan kam*.

After Hoffmann's tenure the Leipzig opera declined. Hoffmann and his predecessors, Strungk and Telemann, had been able to use student players and singers, which undoubtedly helped to keep expenses low. After 1715 the opera lacked a charismatic leader, one who could supply new compositions and motivate local musicians to perform them. Debts accumulated, and by 1720 operations at the Leipzig opera ceased. Sartorio's opera house fell into a state of disrepair, and in 1729 it was torn down.

After that time opera was provided now and then during the fairs by itinerant Italian troupes, which performed on temporary stages set up outdoors in front of the Peterstor or indoors in the Reit-Haus (Riding-House). The most famous visitors were the Mingotti brothers, Angelo and Pietro, whose virtuoso ensembles sometimes included castratos. Of a 1744 Easter Fair performance of the opera *Adelaide, Königin aus Italien* and the intermezzo *Amor fa l'uomo cieco*, the Leipzig resident Johann Salomon Riemer reported:

> Pietro Mingotti was here with two castratos as well as many other virtuosos, among whom were two women soloists, Rosa Costa and Ms Stella, who were incomparable to hear, and who received the most gracious applause because of their singing.[25]

In 1746 the Mingotti troupe again visited during the Easter Fair. On 3 May, according to Riemer, it presented *Argenide* 'in the presence of the elector', with 'ballets by the Italian Dance Master Porzi'. On 6 and 9 May the fare was *Semiramis*, again with the elector attending. The troupe's stay concluded two days later with *La finta schiava*, featuring Turkish dress and Turkish dances. Although such performances won wide acclaim, a permanent opera company was not re-established in Leipzig until the construction of the Schauspielhaus in 1766.

Secular music was provided on several other fronts by professional and amateur musicians. The four *Stadtpfeifer* and four *Kunstgeiger* hired by the town council were required to play ensemble music daily from the tower of the town hall (*Turmmusik*, or 'tower music') and to be available to perform at weddings, feasts and other special occasions, in addition to their weekly church duties. So great were the day-to-day demands on the professional players that when Johann Caspar Gleditsch was elevated from *Kunstgeiger* to *Stadtpfeifer* in 1719 his new contract stipulated that he could not spend a night away without written permission from the council. It is also worth noting that the instruments used by the pipers and fiddlers for civic events were owned by the council and housed in the town hall, not in the Thomaskirche.

For tower music, the *Stadtpfeifer* and *Kunstgeiger* undoubtedly used pieces for wind ensemble, a combination whose sound would best carry over the expansive open space of the market place. Pezel's widely disseminated *Hora decima musicorum Lipsiensium* (1670), written for five-part cornett and trombone ensemble and dedicated to the town council, and Reiche's equally well-known *Vier und zwantzig neue Quatricinia* (1696), written for four-part cornett and trombone ensemble, are fine examples of Leipzig tower music. Chorales, too, seem to have been favourite fare. A 1747 inventory of music stored in the town hall includes the now-lost item 'five chorale books and 122 wind pieces . . . which the late *Stadtpfeifer* Gottfried Reiche himself composed, little by little'.[26] Since Schelle, Kuhnau and Bach did not leave behind any works of this nature, it seems safe to assume that the tower repertory was the bailiwick of the *Stadtpfeifer* rather than of the Kantor.

However, it was the duty of the Thomaskantor, as general music director of Leipzig, to supply compositions for public events. This consisted of writing occasional works for the town council, the Thomasschule or the university. In addition, the Thomaskantor was often asked by nobles and wealthy citizens to compose music for weddings, birthdays, house consecrations and similar celebrations. This resulted in a substantial body of secular music, which was often recycled into the sacred repertory via parody technique (Bach's *Christmas Oratorio*, for instance, was derived from the reworking of a series of secular cantatas). The income from secular composition was considerable, and it represented a critical supplement to the Thomaskantor's annual salary.

By far the most important vehicle for secular music-making was the collegium musicum, a gathering of amateur student players, who normally performed under the direction of a professional leader. During the seventeenth century a number of collegium groups emerged from time to time in Leipzig: a 'Collegium Gellianum' is mentioned in 1641; Pezel formed a highly successful collegium in 1672; and Kuhnau started an ensemble of 'Studiosi' in 1688. These seem to have been groups of modest size and ambition, consisting, perhaps, of 15 or 20 players meeting to read through secular chamber music. Kuhnau stated, tongue-in-cheek, perhaps, that the practice had redeeming social value:

> The musicians in cities commonly hold a collegium musicum every week or two. That is indeed a laudable undertaking, in part because it provides them with the opportunity to refine further their excellent art, and in part, too, because they learn from the pleasing harmonies how to speak together concordantly, even though these same people mostly disagree with one another at other times.[27]

In the seventeenth century the collegium musicum played a relatively small role in Leipzig's musical activities. Its importance increased when Telemann formed a new group in 1702. Telemann's entrepreneurial talents were as great as his musical gifts, and under his guidance the collegium became a much more formal organization. The ensemble convened on a weekly basis, and the quality of its concerts improved markedly. According to Telemann's own account, his group grew to 40 players and performed regularly not just for townspeople and fair visitors but for the elector and other nobles as well. Telemann succeeded in giving the collegium a high degree of stability by linking its directorship with the post of organist at the Neue Kirche, a position he won in 1704 with the promise that he would bring his band of student players with him. This, together with the opera, drained Kuhnau's resources for Hauptgottesdienst at the Thomaskirche and the Nikolaikirche and set up a rivalry between the Thomaskantor and the Neue Kirche organist that remained bitter during Kuhnau's lifetime.

After Telemann's departure his collegium continued to be run by the Neue Kirche organist: first by Hoffmann (1705–15), then by Vogler (1715–19) and then by Schott (1719–29). Bach's decision to step in as Schott's replacement in 1729 and run the 'Telemann' collegium himself thus represented an important break in the sequence. In 1736 Bach appears to have relinquished the collegium directorship, at which point it reverted once again to the Neue Kirche organist, Carl Gotthelf Gerlach, who headed the group until at least 1747, apparently with Bach's intermittent participation. Running simultaneously with the 'Telemann' collegium for many years was a second student group, directed from 1723 to 1756 by Johann Gottlieb Görner (1697–1778), organist first of the Paulinerkirche, then of the Nikolaikirche and finally of the Thomaskirche. That Leipzig could support two groups – and eventually three – during the first half of the eighteenth century mirrors the growing enthusiasm for secular ensemble music.

Contemporary publications periodically announced the collegium meetings. These announcements reveal that each collegium usually met once a week, outdoors in summer and indoors in winter. The sessions were open to 'Cavaliers und Dames', and they were normally free. In some instances, however, text sheets were printed, for which there may have been a charge. For 'special concerts', such as the 1743 session in which a visiting bass singer, one 'Mr Fisher', performed, the audience was assessed a nominal fee. During the fairs the activities of the collegia were stepped up in order to supply more music for the out-of-town visitors. Bach and Görner seem to have been on good terms, for the schedules of their groups were coordinated quite carefully. A 1736 account reports that Görner's collegium normally convened each Thursday evening from 8 o'clock to 10 o'clock in the Schellhafer hall, and Bach's collegium each Friday evening during the same hours in Zimmermann's coffee-house. At fair-time, however, both groups met twice per week: Görner's on Monday and Thursday evenings, and Bach's on Tuesday and Friday evenings. In this way, collegium entertainment was provided on four out of five weekdays.

Zimmermann's coffee-house, the site of Bach's collegium meetings, was located at Katharinenstrasse 14, a four-and-a-half-storey Baroque building constructed by Döring around 1715. The coffee-house consisted of two adjoining rooms of modest size: one was approximately 8 x 10 metres, the other approximately 5.5 x 10 metres. In summer the collegium moved outside, to Zimmermann's coffee-garden 'vor dem Grimmischen Thore'. In these intimate settings, Bach presented a great variety of secular compositions: cantatas, concertos, instrumental suites, chamber pieces and solo harpsichord works. Of the collegium cantatas, the so-called 'Coffee Cantata', *Schweigt stille, plaudert nicht* BWV211, is perhaps the best known. Its humorous text, written by Picander, tells of an irascible father and his recalcitrant daughter who refuses to give up coffee. Like the Baroque architecture of Leipzig, the work subtly combined beauty with practical concerns: while musically entertaining, the cantata also served as a type of singing advertisement for Zimmermann's establishment.

For concertos, Bach capitalized on his own gifts as a keyboard player, as well as on the talents of his sons and students, writing (or arranging, from pre-existing works) a series of ambitious, innovatory pieces featuring the harpsichord. The repertory includes eight works for one harpsichord BWV1052–9, three works for two harpsichords BWV1060–62, two works for three harpsichords BWV1063–4 and finally the Concerto in A minor for four harpsichords BWV1065, a *pièce de résistance* arranged from Vivaldi's Concerto in B minor for four violins. In the single concertos Bach undoubtedly played the demanding solo part himself. In the multiple concertos he most probably played the first harpsichord part – by far the most difficult technically – and delegated the remaining, less demanding parts to his sons and students.

A good number of the instrumental suites and other chamber pieces such as the three viola da gamba sonatas BWV1027–9 and the B minor Flute Sonata BWV1030 appear to date from the 1730s and 40s and also seem to have been intended for collegium performances. The B minor Flute Sonata may have been written for one of the documented Leipzig visits of the famed Dresden flautist Pierre Buffardin. Of the works for harpsichord alone, it is likely that the second volume of *Das wohltemperirte Clavier*, compiled between 1738 and 1742, stems from collegium sessions. Unlike the first volume, which survives in a book-like, reference format, the second volume is written on fold-out sheets – the most practical layout for public performance, since it greatly reduces page-turns; in addition, the second volume shows an unusually high number of lighter, dance-derived pieces, suggesting that Bach wished to exploit composition styles that would have appealed to an audience of bourgeois 'Cavaliers und Dames'.

Another traditional function of the collegium was the performance of music paying homage to the Saxon elector. Works were written for the elector's name-day and birthday, for the anniversary of his election or coronation and for his visits to Leipzig. They were often

42. An outdoor collegium musicum performance, by torchlight, during an 'illumination' in nearby Jena: from the 'Jenaer Stammbuch', c1740

presented alfresco on the market place, in conjunction with general celebrations. At times they were played at night, by torchlight, as part of town 'illuminations' (see fig.42). During his visits to Leipzig the elector normally resided at Apel's Baroque mansion, located on the market place, next to the town hall. In these instances, 'homage music' was presented in front of Apel's house, so that the elector could formally receive it.

17 homage works can be documented for Bach. One of the most ambitious pieces is the cantata *Preise dein Glücke, gesegnetes Sachsen* BWV215, written for trumpets and drums, flutes, oboes, strings and two four-part choruses. Bach later re-used the festive music of the opening chorus, 'Preise dein Glücke', for the Osanna of the *Mass in B minor*. The cantata was performed in the presence of Friedrich August II during his visit to Leipzig on 5 October 1734. The town celebrated with an illumination of unusual size and splendour, which was described in detail by Riemer:

On the 5th [of October], the Coronation Day of His Royal Majesty was celebrated in the greatest gala style . . . At seven in the evening a cannon was fired as a signal, and then the whole town was illuminated. The Rathaus tower and the balcony were very splendidly decked out with many variegated lamps; the towers of St Thomas' and St Nicholas' were beautifully and properly illuminated from the balcony to the belfries, and this could be seen for some miles out into the country . . .

And the illumination lasted until twelve o'clock. Many people came in from the country to see it, and at seven o'clock in the morning one could still see some lamps burning. About nine o'clock in the evening the students here presented the Majesty and his family with a most submissive evening serenade [Cantata no.215] with trumpets and drums, which the Hon. Capellmeister, Johann Sebastian Bach, Cantor at St Thomas', had composed. For this, six hundred students carried wax tapers, and four Counts acted as marshalls in presenting the music. The procession made its way up to the King's residence [Apel's house] . . . When the text was presented, the four Counts were permitted to kiss the Royal hands, and afterwards his Royal Majesty together with his Royal Consort and the Royal Princes did not leave the windows until the music was over, and listened most graciously, and liked it well.[28]

For large homage pieces with trumpets Bach supplemented his student ensemble with the *Stadtpfeifer*. In the case of Cantata no.215 this had an unexpectedly unhappy outcome: the trumpeter Gottfried Reiche, overcome by smoke and the unusual demands of Bach's score, suffered a stroke on arriving home after the performance and died the next morning.

Viewed as a whole, Bach's collegium music shows progressive tendencies. The harpsichord concertos are unusually accessible and outgoing, and many pieces in the second *Das wohltemperirte Clavier* volume are strikingly 'modern'. But the vocal works, especially, contain passages that lean towards the *galant*. Many pieces, including Cantata no.215, carry the label 'dramma per musica' and feature dialogues among allegorical figures. In many ways such cantatas resemble concert operas, and there can be little doubt that they fulfilled an opera-like role, especially after 1720, when the public opera house closed. Two cantatas from the Bach circle, nos.203 and 209, even have Italian texts, bringing them into line with the operas and intermezzos performed by the Mingotti brothers.

The progressive features of Bach's secular compositions were not lost on contemporary observers. In 1729 Martin Fuhrmann, a fair-visitor from Berlin, reported:

When I was at the Easter Fair in Leipzig recently . . . I had the good fortune to hear the world-famous Mr Bach. I thought the

Italian Frescobaldi had polished off the art of keyboard playing all by himself, and Carissimi was a most valued and cherished organist. But if one were to put the two Italians with their art on one side of the scales and the German Bach on the other, the latter would far outweigh them . . .[29]

And in defending Bach against the criticisms of Johann Adolph Scheibe in 1738, Christoph Lorenz Mizler pointed out:

Anyone who heard the music that was performed by the students at the Easter Fair in Leipzig last year, in the Most High Presence of his Royal Majesty in Poland, which was composed by

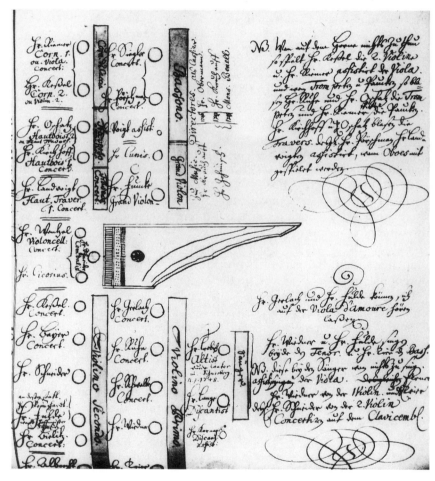

43. *The layout and personnel of the 'Gross Konzertgesellschaft', 1746–8; this group, the third collegium in Leipzig, represents the beginning of the Gewandhaus tradition (that of a large-scale, publicly funded orchestra): drawing from the chronicle of Johann Salomon Riemer, 1748*

Capellmeister Bach, must admit that it was written entirely in accordance with the latest taste, and was approved by everyone. So well does the Capellmeister know how to suit himself to his listeners.[30]

The public's appetite for this type of music kept increasing. By 1747 the number of collegia meeting regularly had grown to three: Gerlach's group, Görner's group and a new ensemble 'under the direction of the merchants and other people'. The new ensemble proved to be the most important. It quickly attracted the best players, including Gerlach, and soon developed into the 'Gross Konzertgesellschaft' ('Grand Concert Society'), whose exact membership and disposition for the years 1746–8 was recorded in a contemporary sketch by Riemer (see fig.43). The society represented the first formal move towards a town orchestra, a publicly funded ensemble performing in a concert hall with a regular subscription series. This was the beginning of Leipzig's great nineteenth-century Gewandhaus tradition, for which the secular music-making of the late Baroque era clearly paved the way.

NOTES

[1] *Concordantiae Bibliorum germanico-hebraico-graecae* (Leipzig, 1669).

[2] *Grosses vollständiges Universal-Lexikon aller Wissenschaften und Kunst* (Leipzig, 1732–54).

[3] W. Hentschel, 'Die Alte Börse in Leipzig und ihr Architekt', *Abhandlungen der Sächsischen Akademie der Wissenschaften zu Leipzig: philologisch-historische Klasse*, lvii/4 (1964), 14.

[4] Of the four buildings discussed, the Exchange and the Romanushaus remain standing today; Hohmann's house and Koch's house were destroyed in World War II.

[5] *Nicolai Goldmanns vollständige Anweisung zu der Civilbaukunst* (Leipzig, 1696); the volume served as the foundation for a number of later publications on civic architecture edited or written by Sturm.

[6] Sperontes (Johann Sigismund Scholze), *Singende Muse an der Pleisse* (Leipzig, 1736; repr. Leipzig, 1964), 53–4.

[7] Letter of 12 Dec 1765 to Cornelie Goethe; quoted from *Goethe-Briefe*, ed. P. Stein (Berlin, 1902–5), i, 29.

[8] *Dichtung und Wahrheit*, pt i, bk 6; quoted from *Goethes Sämtliche Werke*, xxxii, xxxvii (Stuttgart and Berlin, n.d.).

[9] Indeed, when August I died in 1733 his body was buried in Kraków, and only his heart was returned to Dresden, in a silver capsule.

[10] The significance of the title of the 1710 ordinance (*Leipziger Kirchen-Staat – das ist, deutlicher Unterricht vom Gottesdienst in Leipzig*) was first pointed out by A. Schering, *Musikgeschichte Leipzigs*, ii: *Von 1650 bis 1723* (Leipzig, 1926), 6. It is true that a small Catholic chapel was established in Leipzig, in the Pleissenburg, for use by the French and Italian community and by the elector on his visits. Nevertheless, the unassailably Lutheran character of Leipzig's churches stood in direct contrast with the religious dichotomy in Dresden, where the Frauenkirche (1726–36), designed by the German architect Georg Bähr as an affirmation of the Lutheran faith, was soon matched by an equally impressive monument to the Catholic faith, the Hofkirche (1739–55), designed by the Roman architect Gaetano Chiaveri.

[11] One must keep in mind that during the Baroque period boys generally reached puberty at a later age than they do today: it was not at all unusual for a boy to retain a high voice until his 16th or 17th year; thus Kantors had a more extended period in which to train boy sopranos and altos to sing difficult part-music.

[12] So taxing, in fact, that they contributed to Reiche's demise; see the discussion of cantata BWV215 below.

[13] *Bach-Dokumente*, ed. W. Neumann and H.-J. Schulze (Leipzig and Kassel, 1963–79), i, no.22; trans. derived from H. T. David and A. Mendel, eds., *The Bach Reader* (New York, rev. 2/1966), 121.

[14] C. E. Sicul, *Neo annalium Lipsiensium Continuatio II: oder des mit 1715ten Jahre Neuangegangenen Leipziger Jahrbuchs Dritte Probe* (Leipzig, 1717), 570.

[15] The council acted with similar tactlessness towards Bach, auditioning Gottlob Harrer for the Thomaskantor position in June 1749, over a year before Bach died.

[16] Quoted from the full memorandum of 17 March 1709, which is reprinted in *St. Thomas zu Leipzig: Schule und Chor*, ed. B. Knick (Wiesbaden, 1963), 124–6.

[17] Schering, *Musikgeschichte Leipzigs*, ii, 18.

[18] It was only in the 1950s, with the more accurate dating of Bach's vocal works through modern source-critical methods, that the remarkable concentration of cantata writing during the period 1723–9 was discerned.

[19] The entire draft is given in *Bach-Dokumente*, i, no.22, and, in Eng. trans., in David and Mendel, eds., *The Bach Reader*, 120–24.

[20] *Bach-Dokumente*, ii, no.614.

[21] The Leipzig address books of the time list several resident French dancing-masters; in addition, a number of dance manuals were printed in Leipzig and sold at the fairs, including Samuel Rudolph Behr's *L'art de bien danser, oder Die Kunst wohl zu Tanzen* (Leipzig, 1713) and Gottfried Taubert's impressive 1176–page tome *Rechtschaffener Tantzmeister, oder Gründliche Erklärung der Frantzösischen Tantz-Kunst* (Leipzig, 1717).

[22] While the use of macaronic texts strikes modern sensibilities as odd, it was quite common in German and English opera in the eighteenth century.

[23] Quoted from Schering, *Musikgeschichte Leipzigs*, ii, 465.

[24] W. Neumann, ed., *Sämtliche von Johann Sebastian Bach vertonte Texte* (Leipzig, 1974), 163.

[25] Quoted from F. Reuter, 'Die Entwicklung der Leipziger, insbesondere italienischen Oper bis zum siebenjährigen Kriege', *ZMw*, v (1922–3), 7.

[26] G. Wustmann, *Aus Leipzigs Vergangenheit* (Leipzig, 1885), i, 320.

[27] *Der musicalische Quack-Salber* (Dresden, 1700), chap. 1.

[28] G. Wustmann, *Quellen zur Geschichte Leipzigs* (Leipzig, 1889), i, 259; trans. adapted from David and Mendel, eds., *The Bach Reader*, 432–3.

[29] *Bach-Dokumente*, ii, no.268; trans. from David and Mendel, eds., *The Bach Reader*, 441.

[30] ibid, ii, no.436; trans. from David and Mendel, eds., *The Bach Reader*, 249.

BIBLIOGRAPHICAL NOTE

The literature on Leipzig presents a number of problems. First, the reader must be conversant with German, since most accounts are in that language. Secondly, political events – the rise of the Nazi Party in 1933, the Communist takeover in 1945 and the Cold War – have produced a long period in which objective, international scholarship has not been possible in Saxony. For reliable information one must commonly turn to pre-World War II studies, even though such material is obviously in need of updating. And thirdly, Leipzig itself has changed radically in the last 50 years in terms of its appearance. Many Baroque buildings were destroyed in the war (or razed soon afterwards for Socialist projects) and replaced with structures of a distinctly utilitarian stamp. As a result, Leipzig has been less attractive to art historians than it once was. It is hoped that the recent political changes in eastern Europe will produce a more favourable climate for scholarship.

General

Of recent volumes, H. Füssler's *Leipzig* (Leipzig, 1966) is the best general survey. W. Volk's *Leipzig* (from the Historische Strassen und Plätze Heute series; Berlin, 2/1979) is strong on architectural history and contains an extensive bibliography.

Leipzig: a Cosmopolitan Trade Centre

R. A. Gräbe's *Leipzig: ein Bildwerk zum 800jährigen Stadtjubiläum* (Augsburg, 1965) is essentially a picture-album with a short but reliable introductory text. The 'Leipzig' entries by P. Young in *Grove 6* and by R. Eller, G. Hempel and P. Rubhardt in *MGG* summarize the chief historical developments with regard to music. The ambitious three-volume bibliography compiled by H. Heilemann, *Bibliographie zur Geschichte der Stadt Leipzig* (Weimar, 1971–7), is, alas, heavily weighted toward Socialist concerns.

Of pre-World War II material, L. Woerl's *Illustrierter Führer durch Leipzig und Umgebung* (Leipzig, 1914) is a wonderfully detailed guidebook; it is specially helpful to the modern visitor in search of historical Leipzig, since it presents descriptions and locations of sights now greatly altered, renamed or gone altogether. G. Wustmann's publications *Aus Leipzigs Vergangenheit* (Leipzig, 1885–1909), *Leipzig durch drei Jahrhunderte: ein Atlas zur Geschichte des Leipziger Stadtbildes* (Leipzig, 1891) and *Geschichte der Stadt Leipzig: Bilder und Studien* (Leipzig, 1905) contain charming but nevertheless carefully researched essays on specialized topics (such as the search for Bach's bones in the nineteenth century); they are seminal reading for anyone interested in Baroque Leipzig. Wustmann's *Quellen zur Geschichte Leipzigs* (Leipzig, 1889–95) reproduces documents from the time, including the important chronicle kept by the Leipzig citizen Johann Salomon Riemer from 1714 to 1771.

Social, political and economic history

Fine discussions of the social and political climate of eighteenth-century Germany can be found in W. H. Bruford's classic *Germany in the Eighteenth Century: the Social Background of the Literary Revival* (Cambridge, 1935) and in G. Parry's 'Enlightened Government and its Critics in Eighteenth-Century Germany', *Historical Journal*, vi (1963), 178–92. On Leipzig in particular, the standard economic history remains E. Kroker's *Handelsgeschichte der Stadt Leipzig: die Entwicklung des Leipziger Handels und der Leipziger Messen* (Leipzig, 1925), which also contains detailed sketches of the town's most important businessmen. L. Finscher's 'Central and Northern Germany at the Time of Johann Sebastian Bach: Political and Social Conditions', *Johann Sebastian Bach: Life, Times, Influence*, ed. B. Schwendowius and W. Dömling (Eng. trans., Kassel, 1977), 9–22, compares Leipzig politics with those in Berlin and Dresden. Leipzig's literary figures are described in G. Witkowski's *Geschichte des literarischen Lebens in Leipzig* (Leipzig and Berlin, 1909). Detailed population figures are given in W. Volk's *Leipzig* (mentioned above) and by Pevsner (see below).

The fairs and the book trade

For the fairs, too, E. Kroker's *Handelsgeschichte der Stadt Leipzig* (see above) is the most important source of information. P. Voss's *The Growth of the Leipzig Fair* (Leipzig, 1933) is one of the few accounts in English. H. Kirsch's *Die Leipziger Messe* (Leipzig, 1957) is Marxist-orientated, as is *800 Jahre Leipziger Messe* (Leipzig, 1965).

The fair catalogues are reproduced in *Codex nundinarius Germaniae literatae* (Halle, 1850–77). The music collections advertised in the catalogues are discussed and listed in A. Göhler, 'Die Messkatalog im Dienste der musikalischen Geschichtsforschung', *SIMG*, iii (1901–2), 294–376, and *Verzeichnis der in den Frankfurter und Leipziger Messkatalog der Jahre 1564–1759 angezeigten Musikalien* (Leipzig, 1902). K. J. Snyder's *Dieterich Buxtehude: Organist in Lübeck* (New York, 1987), 307–11, gives an admirably clear summary of late seventeenth- and early eighteenth-century music-printing practices. J. H. Zedler and his *Universal-Lexicon* are discussed in G. Quedenbaum, *Der Verleger und Buchhandler Johann Heinrich Zedler, 1706–1751* (Hildesheim and New York, 1977). H. von Hase's 'Breitkopfsche Textdrucke zu Leipziger Musikaufführungen zu Bachs Zeit', *BJb*, x (1913), 69–127, discusses the texts Bernhard Christoph Breitkopf printed for Bach, Gerlach and others, whereas R. Elvers, ed., *Breitkopf und*

The Late Baroque Era

Härtel: 1719–1968: ein historischer Überblick zum Jubiläum (Wiesbaden, 1968) concentrates on the later development of Leipzig's most famous music-publishing house.

Architecture and landscaped gardens

The central study of Leipzig architecture is N. Pevsner's *Leipziger Barock: die Baukunst der Barockzeit in Leipzig* (Dresden, 1928), which includes floor plans and photographs of a number of Baroque buildings that fell victim to World War II. H. Füssler, ed., *Leipziger Bautradition* (Leipzig, 1955) contains fine essays on Leipzig's various building periods, including H. Bethe's excellent 'Leipzigs Barockbauten' (pp.125–50), which draws heavily on Pevsner but corrects various points. W. Volk's *Leipzig* (see above), also based on Pevsner, presents a clear summary of Leipzig's architectural styles. H. Füssler and H. Wichmann's *Das alte Rathaus zu Leipzig* (Berlin, 1958) gives a wonderfully thorough description of the genesis of the town hall, with 119 photographs of every nook and cranny. N. Powell's *From Baroque to Rococo: an Introduction to Austrian and German Architecture from 1580 to 1790* (London, 1959) is good on general trends but unfortunately says little about civic building.

The definitive study of landscaped gardens in Saxony is still H. Koch's *Sächsische Gartenkunst* (Berlin, 1910); chapter 4 (pp.37–183) treats Baroque gardens in great detail, including the most important sites in Dresden and Leipzig.

Music and musicians

A. Schering's *Musikgeschichte Leipzigs, ii: Von 1650 bis 1723* (Leipzig, 1926) and *Muskigeschichte Leipzigs, iii: Das Zeitalter Johann Sebastian Bachs und Johann Adam Hillers* (Leipzig, 1941) remain the best general studies of music-making in Leipzig during the second half of the Baroque period, covering sacred and secular practices. On many points they are greatly in need of revision, however.

On sacred music-making, A. Schering's *Johann Sebastian Bachs Leipziger Kirchenmusik* (Leipzig, 1936) sets the standard, though it, too, requires revision in the light of recent findings. The interplay of music and liturgy is discussed in G. Stiller's *Johann Sebastian Bach und das Leipziger gottesdienstliche Leben seiner Zeit* (Berlin and Kassel, 1970), reissued in translation as *Johann Sebastian Bach and Liturgical Life in Leipzig* (St Louis, 1984). W. Horn's *Die Dresdner Hofkirchenmusik 1720–1745* (Kassel, 1987) contains a detailed description (pp.13–31) of the political intrigue surrounding the 'Dresden situation' and its effect on Lutheran practices in Saxony. B. Knick, ed., *St. Thomas zu Leipzig, Schule und Chor* (Wiesbaden, 1963) tells the story of the Thomaskirche and Thomasschule through pictures and selected documents. F. Ostarhild's *St. Nikolai zu Leipzig* (Leipzig, 1964) gives a comparable account for the Nikolaikirche.

On secular music-making, G. F. Schmidt's 'Die älteste deutsche Oper in Leipzig am Ende des 17. und Anfang des 18. Jahrhunderts', *Festschrift zum 50. Geburtstag Adolf Sandberger* (Munich, 1918), 209–57, surveys the Leipzig opera from 1693 to 1720 and presents an annotated list of the surviving textbooks. F. Reuter's 'Die Entwicklung der Leipziger, insbesondere italienischen Oper bis zum siebenjährigen Kriege', *ZMw*, v (1922–3), 1–16, focusses on the visiting Italian troupes that performed after 1722. E. Preussner's *Die bürgerliche Musikkultur* (Kassel, 2/1950) presents a fine general survey of music in middle-class German culture, while A. Schering's 'Die Leipziger Ratsmusik von 1650–1775', *AMw*, iii (1921), 17–53, examines the music provided for the Leipzig town council. The most important account of the 'Telemann' collegium musicum under Bach's direction is W. Neumann's 'Das Bachische Collegium Musicum', *BJb*, xlvi (1960), 5–27, which sets forth many new documents and corrects Schering in many regards. Unfortunately, an up-to-date, full-length study of Leipzig collegium practices has yet to be written. Two stimulating discussions of Bach's involvement with secular music-making in the 1730s and 1740s are R. L. Marshall's 'Bach the Progressive: Observations on his Later Works', *MQ*, lxii (1976), 313–57 (repr. in R. L. Marshall, *The Music of Johann Sebastian Bach*, New York, 1989, pp.23–58), and C. Wolff, 'Bach's Leipzig Chamber Music', *EM*, xiii (1985), 165–75.

Helpful summaries of the lives and works of Schelle, Kuhnau, Bach, Pezel, Reiche and other Leipzig musicians can be found in *Grove 6* and *MGG*. Kuhnau's *Der musicalische Quack-Salber* has been reissued in modern reprint (Berlin, 1900) and still makes for lively reading. The *Grove 6* 'Bach' entry has been reprinted as an independent paperback volume, *The New Grove Bach Family*, by C. Wolff and others (London, 1983); it includes a succinct survey of Bach's life and achievements, as well as a complete work-list and bibliography.

As might be expected, the literature on Bach is quite extensive. C. Wolff's *Bach Bibliographie* (Kassel, 1985) presents 413 pages of items, and that does not include the deluge of material from 1985, the Bach tercentennial year. In terms of biography, P. Spitta's *Johann Sebastian Bach* (Leipzig, 1873–80; Eng. trans., 1884–99), though greatly outdated in many ways and incorrect on matters of chronology, nevertheless remains a monumental achievement. Its broad description of the music culture of central Germany in Bach's time is specially admirable. M. Boyd's *Bach* (London, 1983) is a useful summary and incorporates the findings of recent research. The seventeenth- and eighteenth-century documents pertaining to Bach's life are presented in their entirety, in the original languages, in the *Bach-Dokumente*, ed. W. Neumann and H.-J. Schulze (Leipzig and Kassel, 1963–79). *The Bach Reader*, ed. H. T. David and A. Mendel (New York, rev. 2/1966), presents a fascinating selection of the more important documents, in English translation. Finally, *Johann Sebastian Bach: Life, Time, Influence*, ed. B. Schwendowius and W. Dömling (Eng. trans., Kassel, 1977), contains highly readable essays on Bach and on the art, music and politics of his time.

Chapter X

Courts and Monasteries in Bavaria

ROBERT MÜNSTER

Present-day Bavaria, comprising Old Bavaria (Upper Bavaria, Lower Bavaria and the Upper Palatinate), Franconia and Swabia, acquired its present unity and form only at the beginning of the nineteenth century. In considering the late Baroque period, therefore, a number of factors in the political and cultural history of the area recommend a survey of its musical history under several separate headings.

OLD BAVARIA

The Munich court before 1679

Under Dukes Albrecht V (ruled 1550–79) and Wilhelm V (1579–97), who were lovers of the arts, Munich had been one of the most important musical centres of Europe. Roland de Lassus, highly esteemed by his patrons in the ruling house of Wittelsbach, built up an ambitious international repertory at the court, a considerable part of which survives (now in the Bavarian State Library). Honoured by both the German Emperor and the King of France, Lassus ranked among the great geniuses of musical history for the universality and richness of his creative work: he brought the Renaissance vocal style to a peak of perfection. After his death in 1594, economic measures meant severe cutbacks in the musical life of the court. Wilhelm's son Maximilian I (1597–1651), who became the first Elector of Bavaria in 1623, was a serious-minded ruler and inclined to remain aloof; he concentrated more on the welfare of the state than on cultivating the arts. Bavaria was a stronghold of exclusive Roman Catholicism. In line with the Catholic revival that Maximilian encouraged, at court sacred music took precedence over secular. Lassus's successors, Johannes de Fossa from the Netherlands and Lassus's own two sons, continued his tradition on a more modest scale. But around 1620 Rudolph de Lassus and Georg Victorinus introduced to Munich the

44. *Auditorium of the opera house in the Salvatorplatz, Munich (completed in 1654), commissioned by Ferdinand Maria from Domenico Mauro and Francesco Santurini: engraving by Michael Wening after Domenico Mauro (note the central elector's box, added in 1685)*

new basso continuo style, which had originated in Italy. In 1635 an Italian, Giovanni Giacomo Porro, from Rome, was appointed Kapellmeister (his wealth of vocal compositions, which have not survived, were probably destroyed in the Residenz fire of 1674), and thereafter Italian musicians played a leading part at the Munich court, continuing to do so until the end of the eighteenth century.

During the Thirty Years War (1618–48) Bavaria was one of the German states worst affected by privations and pestilence. The Swedish invasions of 1632 and 1634 in particular brought severe suffering. Entire villages were laid waste, and the population was drastically reduced: in 1620 Munich had 22 000 inhabitants; in 1650 they numbered only 17 000. Understandably, these troubled times put an end to almost all continuous development in musical life. Not until 1648, with the Peace of Westphalia, could a systematic new start be considered. In his old age Elector Maximilian I prepared for the introduction to Munich of musical drama, but the first independent opera house of any size in Germany, the Salvatortheater (fig. 44), though commissioned by Maximilian, was not opened until 1654, three years after his death.

The Late Baroque Era

The early history of opera in Munich began in 1653 on the occasion of the wedding of Elector Maximilian's successor Ferdinand Maria (1654–79), with the performance of the dramatic cantata *L'arpa festante* by the court chaplain, poet and composer Giovanni Battista Maccioni (*d c*1678). The extremely gifted Electress Henriette Adelaide of Savoy now took a lead in court life: she was responsible for the appointment of Italian poets, artists and musicians, and her personal co-operation helped promote concerts, music drama and ballet. A notable appointment, unique at this period, was that of a German, Johann Kaspar Kerll (1627–93), to the post of Hofkapellmeister in Munich in 1656. Kerll had, however, studied in Italy with, among others, Carissimi, and he brought Baroque opera in Munich to its prime. At least ten of his dramatic works were magnificently staged between 1657 and 1672 (they are now all lost). Apart from his organ works and sacred music, his only surviving work is a Jesuit drama composed for performance in Vienna. The range of Kerll's sacred music extends from the traditional Palestrinian style to modern concertante works. His masses (1689) and his *Cantiones sacrae* (1669) are among the most important contributions made by south German composers to the sacred music of the Baroque period.

Under Kerll the number of court musicians at Munich was increased by almost a third, 15 more being added to the original 14 singers, 17 instrumentalists and three organists. In 1673 the temperamental Kapellmeister left for Vienna after altercations with some of the Italian court musicians, but in 1684 he was back in Munich, to spend his last years. His successor as Kapellmeister from 1674 was Ercole Bernabei (1622–87), previously *maestro di cappella* of the Cappella Giulia in the Vatican. Bernabei's strength was his mastery of the *stile antico* employed by Palestrina's followers, but he also composed madrigals and some solo secular cantatas.[1]

In 1670 a treaty of alliance with France, aided by the electress, brought closer links between Bavaria and France in the last few years of Ferdinand Maria's reign. This reorientation had an effect on music too: the Lullian style was introduced to Munich by the composer Melchior d'Ardespin (*c*1643–1717), who became music teacher to Ferdinand Maria's son and heir Maximilian Emanuel.

The Munich court up to the 1750s

On his father's death Elector Maximilian II Emanuel (1679–1726), then aged 18, assumed rule in Bavaria. Max Emanuel was bold and ambitious, but he also had an outstanding feeling for art and a musical talent above the average. Pageantry, hunting, dancing and other diversions were part of the way of life at court, and they had musical accompaniment whenever possible.

As a consequence of the defence treaty concluded between Bavaria and Austria in 1683, Max Emanuel's Bavarian army took part in the Turkish war, contributing substantially to the defeat of the Turks at Vienna the same year. In 1685 Max Emanuel married the emperor's daughter Maria Antonia, thus giving his heirs a claim to the Spanish inheritance. He achieved the height of his fame as the 'Bavarian Hercules' by his bold capture of Belgrade in 1688, an event celebrated in music even outside Bavaria, with such works as the recently rediscovered opera *La costanza gelosa negl'amori di Cefalo e Procri* by Carlo Francesco Pollarolo, performed in Verona in 1688.[2] These campaigns meant severe economy measures at the Munich court: in 1689 musical expenditure was reduced by a seventh. In the same year Max Emanuel concluded a treaty of alliance with France, and in 1692 the King of Spain made him Governor of the Spanish Netherlands. The elector and his court now led a life of luxury in Brussels, and most of his court musicians moved from Munich with him. The incumbent Kapellmeister, Giuseppe Antonio Bernabei (?1649–1732), a son of Ercole, remained in Munich with some musicians, to provide music for the Divine Service at the court, but the organist Pietro Torri (*c*1650–1737), by now the most outstanding musical figure in Max Emanuel's entourage, accompanied the elector to Brussels with a select company of singers and instrumentalists. Torri, from Peschiera on Lake Garda, had previously been employed at the court of the Margrave of Bayreuth; in Brussels he rose to the position of court Kapellmeister and was responsible for church music and oratorios. At the opera, directed in Brussels by Pierre Antonio Fiocco (*c*1650–1714), a native of the city, the works staged were mainly by Lully: some 20 singers (male and female), about 50 choristers and up to 20 instrumentalists were employed. These performances, together with the great court festivals, swallowed up large sums. The financial situation of some of the musicians, however, bore no relation to the general expense: the list of payments for the year 1701 shows that the larger part of salaries due for the preceding few years had never been paid.

Max Emanuel's court in Brussels conformed to the French style. In music, as in other matters, it was the brilliant court of Louis XIV that the elector sought to emulate; there is no record at this period or later of musical connections with the composers of the imperial court in Vienna. Music was a part of Max Emanuel's daily life. From 1670 onwards he heard music every evening and often took part himself, playing the viola da gamba. In 1681 he appointed the brilliant Italian composer Agostino Steffani (1654–1728) director of his chamber music. Steffani, and later Torri, wrote for him many Italian chamber cantatas and duets, which are among the best of the period. There was always great demand for music to be performed in small gatherings, with one or two solo instruments (violin, viola da gamba, recorder or flute, oboe) and continuo.

Max Emanuel suffered a severe personal loss in 1699 with the death of his son Joseph Ferdinand, who was not yet seven years old and had been named by King Charles II of Spain as his sole heir. The Bavarian dream of the Spanish inheritance was over. In 1701 Max Emanuel returned to Munich. The elector now stood between France and the emperor in their struggle for the Spanish inheritance. In 1701 a rift opened up between Bavaria and the Austrian imperial house, not least because of the elector's patronage of a French theatrical company; a theatre had been built for it in the Residenz. In 1702, to ensure his hold on the Netherlands at least, Max Emanuel made a treaty of alliance with France. That, however, meant war with Austria, a war in which Max Emanuel was initially successful, having the advantage of surprise. But in August 1704 Bavaria lost the Battle of Blenheim against the Austrians and their English allies, and Max Emanuel was forced into exile. Once again, he turned to Brussels. Some of his own musicians followed him again, among them the recently engaged Italian cellist Evaristo Felice dall'Abaco (1675–1742), but most stayed in Munich, where they had to live in poverty-stricken circumstances during the Austrian occupation. Those who could enter the service of other patrons did so, but most had no alternative but to exist in wretched conditions, barely able to subsist on occasional donations or charitable aid from such sources as the Jesuits.

Even now, however, Max Emanuel was unwilling to deprive himself of music. In exile, he extended his circle of musicians by appointing Netherlanders and French musicians to new posts, and he kept in close touch with his brother Joseph Clemens, Elector of Cologne, who was also in exile and spent some time in Lille. Neither brother was willing to do without opera, although the meagre funds provided by the King of France would often not even cover the hire of horses for musicians' inevitable journeys. But even in this situation attempts were made to emulate as far as possible the court in Paris: of an opera by Pietro Torri, commissioned by and performed for Joseph Clemens in 1713, the elector wrote: 'tout le monde est satisfait de mon opéra . . . il surpasse celui de Paris!'.[3]

Several of Torri's major operas from this period of exile survive. His sacred oratorios in Italian and French, performed in place of operas during Lent, were rediscovered only a few years ago, and they too are important.[4] In the tradition of Lully, they show Torri as a significant pre-Handelian oratorio composer. Their subjects were generally Old Testament figures (*Abelle, Giacobbe, Elia, Gionata, Abramo*) or saints (*Santo Genesio, Santo Vinceslao, Santo Landelino*). The phrase 'Oratorio teatrale' in some of their titles indicates stage performance (such works were also later staged in Munich: according to the account of a court lady, Torri's *Abelle* was performed 'like an opera' when it was revived at the Salvatortheater in 1734). Orchestral accompaniment was mainly strings and continuo; *Giacobbe*, written during the court's exile, also calls for two flutes, two oboes, three trumpets, three *corni di caccia* and two violas da gamba, one of which was played by Max Emanuel himself, as the original score shows. Music was the breath of life to him, particularly in his time of greatest need.

When Max Emanuel returned to Munich after the peace of 1715, he immediately reorganized and extended his Hofmusik, despite a huge burden of debt. Several musicians from France and the Netherlands had accompanied him back from exile, among them the wind player and composer Jacques Loeillet (1685–1748), who remained in the service of the Munich court until 1732, at a high salary. G. A. Bernabei was still court Kapellmeister, responsible for sacred music, but Torri, whose title was *Hofkapelldirektor*, had the more influential position: he was in charge of opera, and also, in collaboration with Dall'Abaco, of Max Emanuel's chamber music.

Until the elector died in 1726, musical life at the Munich court flourished more than ever. Opera in particular earned for the court, in its first and last decades in Munich, a reputation as one of the most brilliant musical centres of Europe. The operas of Ercole Bernabei, like those of his predecessor Kerll, are lost. The Kapellmeister G. A. Bernabei was mainly concerned with sacred music; his few surviving stage works are notable for their noble, cantabile melodic lines, and his beautiful wedding serenata *Venere pronuba* of 1688 is set throughout for double ensemble. Like several other dramatic serenades that were staged not in the theatre but in a hall of the Munich Residenz, this work – like Kerll's earlier *Antiopa giustificata* (1662) – must have been performed on two stages set up opposite each other. The most important dramatic composer of Max Emanuel's court was the highly cultured Agostino Steffani, one of the leading composers of the late Baroque period, who first arrived at the Munich court as a boy of 13. Of his five operas for Munich, the last, *Niobe, regina di Tebe*, is the most important; it was produced four times at Carnival 1688, with great success. Act 1 includes a brilliantly conceived aria for King Amfione, with four solo violas da gamba playing concealed on stage, in which the king seeks release in music from the cares of his royal office. Torri included this scene unaltered, no doubt at the elector's request, in his cantata *La reggia dell'armonia* of 1714: at the end of 'his period of exile, during which he had suffered heavily, Max Emanuel must have seen himself reflected in this scene, which shows how music at court, apart from its function

45. *Design by Domenico and Gasparo Mauro for the moonlit garden scene in Steffani's opera 'Servio Tullio', performed in celebration of the marriage of Elector Maximilian II Emanuel to Maria Antonia, Archduchess of Austria, in 1686*

of absolutist display, could also serve the expression of personal emotion.

Steffani went to the court of Hanover as Hofkapellmeister in 1688, but between 1696 and 1701 he was frequently with Max Emanuel in Brussels as a Hanoverian envoy. The early works of Torri, the most productive of the elector's opera composers, were much indebted to Steffani. With Venetian operatic style as a starting-point, Torri took Lully's French operas as a model while he was in Brussels, and finally, after his return to Munich, took up the older, Neapolitan style. His *Andromaca* of 1717 still mainly reflects a French model, but with *La Merope* of 1719 he firmly established an italianate style, retaining, however, the characteristically French use of the chorus. Some 35 of Torri's operas, dramatic serenades and cantatas survive.

Max Emanuel always played a part in the preparations for court opera performances: he had a hand in the casting, and almost certainly in the choice and form of the libretto. In the early years he hardly ever missed rehearsals; after 1715 he left the task of attending them to his son Carl Albrecht. A large-scale opera had an average of five rehearsals, the last a dress rehearsal; the first rehearsals were held in a hall in the Residenz (a practice still common in 1780–81, when Mozart's *Idomeneo* was in production in Munich). Special occasions called for additional expense: G. A. Bernabei's festival opera *Il segreto d'Amore*, with a ballet by Melchior d'Ardespin, performed in 1690 for the visit of the Emperor Leopold I, called for no fewer than 15 rehearsals. Each opera was usually given five or six actual performances, normally beginning at five in the afternoon and lasting for five or six hours, including intervals. Smaller-scale operas might be produced in smaller halls or, in the summer, in the castles of Dachau and Nymphenburg or outside in the castle grounds.

The librettos of these operas, almost always in Italian, were printed, some also in German translation; for example, an edition of 1200 copies of Bernabei's *L'Eraclio* was printed in 1690. German opera took a subordinate role: apart from *Lisimen und Calisto* by the court musician Veit Weinberger (1681) and G. A. Bernabei's dramatic cantata *Der Jahrmarkt* (or *La Fiera*, 1691), we know from printed librettos of only three others performed between 1694 and 1701, during the Austrian occupation and Max Emanuel's absence in the Netherlands. Like the incomplete and anonymous *Leoldo und Elona* (1694), the only surviving one, they must have been parodies of contemporary Italian operas and seem to have been performed not in the court theatre but possibly in the great chamber of the Munich town hall.

The elector was extremely interested in Italian singers, the best of whom were much esteemed in their day. Virtuoso performers like the alto castrato Antonio Maria Bernacchi, whom Handel later regarded highly, and the celebrated soprano castrato Filippo Ballatri were members of his Hofmusik at certain times. Ballatri's annual salary of 3500 gulden was higher than that of any other musician or singer throughout the whole of the eighteenth century, some ten times more than the usual amount paid. These singers, much admired and in great demand, were sometimes given permission to make long tours, thus spreading abroad the fame of the Munich Hofmusik. Among female singers, the famous Faustina Bordoni performed in Munich in 1722–3. There were fewer German than Italian solo singers; some of the most gifted, like the bass Philipp Jakob Seerieder and the Munich soprano Rosina Schwarzmann, were sent to Italy for training; Schwarzmann became well known, appearing at the Teatro S Giovanni Grisostomo in Venice several times between 1730 and 1738. A number of instrumental players were also given a chance to study in Italy or in Paris.

Around 1680 Max Emanuel's Hofmusik consisted of 30 court musicians (assistant Kapellmeisters, organists, singers) and 12 instrumentalists. In addition, there were 17 trumpeters, who did not actually belong to the Hofmusik but were brought in when needed. These figures do not include all the performers: young musicians often played for some time without remuneration until a position became vacant. With the increasing importance of instrumental music and the development of the orchestra, particularly for use in opera, the Hofmusik had by 1688 expanded to 17 instrumentalists, 31 court musicians and 15 trumpeters. The string section in particular was further extended.

Despite this increase in personnel, the number of court musicians was often not enough for large-scale operas, tournaments or balls. The ranks were swelled on such occasions by city and parish musicians. The Munich city musicians' guild was founded in 1650 'to extirpate and eradicate all disreputable boastful folk, and such vagrant and noxious fellows', that is, to ensure that the city had a properly organized musical life. The guild's task was to provide for the musical requirements of church festivals, weddings and dances. Its members' occasional duties at court brought a welcome addition to their meagre income, but only a few succeeded in getting regular court employment.

Besides court balls, Carnival entertainments requiring extra musicians included what were known as the Shrovetide Races. These revelries were held, at considerable expense, in the Turnierhaus. In 1721 the great Carnival procession through the city which preceded them had no fewer than 40 separate sections, representing hunters, farmers, all kinds of professions and callings, characters from Italian comedy, fools, children etc. Each section had its own music, illustrating its particular character. The instruments played were *corni da caccia*, violins, string basses, hurdy-gurdies, lutes, guitars, harps, trombones, tambourines, castanets, triangles and children's instruments, in all kinds of different combinations. The music (which survives in a version for keyboard) provides intriguing glimpses of a world of popular music-making that is otherwise lost through lack of original sources.[5]

Court musicians' contribution to sacred music made up a considerable part of their duties. Max Emanuel attended Mass daily. Large-scale performances of musical settings of the Mass took place only on feast days and holidays, but during the church year a smaller body of musicians performed plenty of works which were sung frequently but are now mostly lost. Like dramatic music, sacred music was composed almost exclusively by musicians from the court itself, notably Kerll and Ercole and G. A. Bernabei (the last was also a priest). Some of G. A. Bernabei's works were still being sung at court well into the nineteenth century, notably during Lent. As well as the traditional polyphonic *stile antico*, some pieces, for instance by Torri, used soloists, chorus and instruments in a concertante style, while others, though to a lesser extent, called only for solo voices.

Many vocal works in the more traditional style, such as the six masses that G. A. Bernabei composed on the occasion of Max Emanuel's return from exile in 1715, were still sung from choirbooks, as they had been in Lassus's time. That tradition was to continue at the Frauenkirche (later the cathedral) until the nineteenth century. Franz Xaver Murschhauser (1663–1738), an organist and leading composer of organ music who had been a pupil of Kerll, was choirmaster there from 1691 until his death. High Masses with trumpets and drums were performed at court on special feast days. Bernabei wrote 14, and Torri also provided masses for church festivals, both in Brussels and in Munich, some requiring four trumpets and drums. These works were given in addition to the sacred oratorios that were performed during Lent, usually in the court chapel.

The most important composer of instrumental music at court was Dall'Abaco, who was in Bavarian service from 1704 to 1742. His sonatas and concertos have been claimed as 'perhaps the purest manifestation of the majestic type of Italian chamber music at its full maturity'.[6] During the years of exile, when he dedicated his 12 *concerti da chiesa* to the elector, he was much influenced by French music, particularly the suite. Although his output was not extensive in comparison with those of his Italian contemporaries such as Albinoni, it has a marked character of its own. The *Concerti a più istrumenti* op.5 (*c*1719) includes an early cello concerto. Dall'Abaco not only played in court concerts for Max Emanuel and his son Carl Albrecht but also organized 'academies' in his own house which may be seen as the precursors of private concerts given in Munich in the later eighteenth century.

Albinoni was highly regarded in Munich: he dedicated his *Concerti a cinque* op.9 to Max Emanuel in 1722 and in the same year took part in the first performance of his opera *I veri amici*, which was written for Munich. The elector, as a passionate music lover, accepted a number of dedications from other contemporary composers. These helped a composer's reputation and usually brought a welcome financial reward. Besides Bavarian composers such as Georg Christoph Leuttner (1644–1703), Johann Christoph Pez (1664–1716) and Rupert Ignaz Mayr (1646–1712), Steffani and the French composer Louis-Nicolas Clérambault dedicated works to him; Max Emanuel had heard and admired Clérambault's cantatas of 1710 in Paris. Michele Mascitti, a pupil of Corelli, issued his sonatas for violin op.4 (Paris, 1711) with a dedication to the elector.

After the death of Max Emanuel in 1726 his son Carl Albrecht succeeded him and ruled until 1745. His reign saw the beginning of the artistically productive rococo period in Bavaria, internationally famous through painting, sculpture and architecture. Carl Albrecht's first aim was to reduce the enormous burden of debt left by his father of 26.8 million gulden, and the Hofmusik was initially cut back. An order even went out that the ends of candles used in the theatre and by musicians were to be retrieved for re-use. However, after about four years the elector abandoned his policy of economy. Music drama continued as before; indeed, casting and production were more expensive and more lavish than ever. Opera composers in electoral service included Torri (until his death in 1737) and the Italians Giovanni Battista Ferrandini (*c*1710–1791), Bernardo Aliprandi (*c*1710–*c*1792), Francesco Peli and Giovanni Porta (?*c*1690–1755), who joined the court in 1737. None was outstandingly brilliant, but they were mostly able musicians. Bernabei and Dall'Abaco remained responsible for sacred and instrumental music.

Carl Albrecht's chief interest lay in opera. He had first appeared on stage at the age of 18, dancing in an opera by Torri, and now he acted as a kind of director at rehearsals. Almost all the operas performed were commissioned by him from musicians in his service; a notable exception, however, was *Alessandro nell'Indie*, given in 1735, composed by Leonardo Vinci, an exponent of the Neapolitan school who had died in 1730. Only one German, the chamber composer Joseph Anton Camerloher, seems to have been commissioned: his *La clemenza di Tito*, however, planned for performance in 1742, could not be staged for political reasons until 1747 after the deaths of its composer and of the elector – when it was given for the wedding of Carl Albrecht's successor Maximilian III Joseph.

The year 1740 ushered in troubled times: the Habsburg emperor, Charles VI, had died without male heirs, and Bavaria claimed the succession: the result was the War of the Austrian Succession. A few days after Elector Carl Albrecht was crowned Emperor Charles VII of Germany in Frankfurt on 12 February 1742, Austrian hussars occupied Munich. Once again the country was plunged into privation and horror. By the time the emperor was able to return to Munich, on 23 October 1744, he was mortally ill; he died in 1745, leaving an onerous legacy to his 18-year-old son Maximilian III Joseph. The young elector was obliged to give up his hereditary Austrian lands. During his reign he devoted his efforts to improving the economy, developing cultural and scientific pursuits and steering clear of warlike confrontations. He was fond of music, played the viola da gamba extremely well and composed sacred music and concertos. But the former high artistic level of music at court, which had declined sharply after the death of Max Emanuel for lack of new creative talents among both composers and performers, could not now be recovered. This must have been partly the influence of the elector himself, a fervent supporter of the kind of stereotyped Neapolitan virtuoso opera promoted by his court Kapellmeister

46. Maximilian III Joseph playing the viol, with two of his sisters: portrait (1758) by Johann Nikolaus de Grooth

Andrea Bernasconi, at Munich from 1755. In 1777 the elector had no position vacant for Mozart; he thought Mozart's music too new and unusual. Although no authoritative assessment of music at the court of Maximilian III Joseph can be made, it is clear that eighteenth-century changes in style received little stimulus from Munich.

The smaller courts

The smaller courts of Bavaria, musically less important than Munich, took the great courts of the time as their models and tried to emulate them within their limited capacities. Giovanni Battista Mocchi, a pupil of Carissimi, was the leading personality at Neuburg, the capital of the small principality of the Junge Pfalz ('Young Palatinate'). In 1685 the Hofmusik of this court consisted of the Kapellmeister, six or seven singers and nine or ten instrumentalists. German opera enjoyed a short season of popularity here in

1678–9, under Mocchi and his successor Johann Paul Agricola (*c*1638–1697). After 1685, when the court had moved to Düsseldorf and then to Heidelberg, the Hofkapelle visited Neuburg only occasionally, for family festivals; it was disbanded in 1742, when the Pfalz-Neuburg line died out and Neuburg merged with the Palatinate. Musical activity in the Upper Palatinate was restricted to the town of Amberg and various monasteries; otherwise the region is notable only as the birthplace of a number of fine musicians, including Christoph Willibald Gluck, who was born in Erasbach, near Neumarkt, in 1714.

The Prince-Bishops of Freising, Eichstätt and Passau maintained strong musical establishments. As well as serving as bishops, these prelates were also the temporal rulers of their provinces and, unlike rulers at the Munich court, they generally appointed German musicians to leading positions. The court music of Freising had a good reputation, largely due to the presence there of Kapellmeisters such as Rupert Ignaz Mayr, one of the leading south German composers of Baroque music of the period, and Placidus von Camerloher (1718–82), whose music foreshadowed the pre-Classical style. Camerloher accompanied the bishop to Bonn, Düsseldorf and Paris, and between 1744 and 1763 he was director of chamber music in Liège. The main emphasis at Freising was on sacred and instrumental music, notably symphonies for chamber orchestra, but didactic music drama was performed as well. This genre was also well represented at Eichstätt, together with sacred music. The court Kapellmeisters there were, successively, Johann Caspar Prentz, Anton Deichel (*c*1662–1712) and Joseph Meck (1690–1758).[7] The musicians at court in 1745 comprised four singers, five violins, a cello, a double bass, two oboes, an organist, five trumpeters and a drummer. Here, and in general at other small courts, the musicians were primarily employed in some other capacity – as valets, chamberlains or court officials – and had to provide musical services in addition. As a rule they could play more than one instrument, so that a variety of combinations of instruments was possible.

In Passau, which had always been in close cultural contact with Vienna because of its position on the Danube and its longstanding historical links with the city, outstanding exponents of Baroque instrumental music were at work: from 1690 to 1742 music at court was directed successively by Georg Muffat (1653–1704) and Benedict Anton Aufschnaiter (1665–1742). In their own compositions they adopted an independent attitude towards the French suite and the Italian concerto grosso. While Muffat was considered one of the best south German organ composers of the time, Aufschnaiter also left a considerable legacy of good sacred music. Passau Cathedral, like the cathedral churches of Freising and Eichstätt, was an important centre of sacred music, as can be seen from the wealth of musical material it once possessed, most of it now surviving only as documentary records in inventories. The breadth of the repertory was remarkable, and it included a great deal of instrumental music.

Musical activity at the courts of these ecclesiastical rulers differed from that at secular courts because of the special emphasis placed on sacred music, but there was a place for secular celebrations too. As well as solemn masses with drums and trumpets, the courts wanted concerts, *Tafelmusik* at mealtimes and music drama. However, there is no record of operatic performances here until the second half of the eighteenth century.

Musical life outside the courts

Together with the religious enthusiasm of the Baroque period, which found eloquent expression in Bavaria in the building of many churches and monasteries, a great age of theology began in the mid-seventeenth century. Its achievements lay principally in the realms of moral theology and canon law. The Jesuits too were active in promoting and establishing the Catholic reform movement, particularly through educational work in their religious foundations in Munich and elsewhere; pupils from a wide social background received from the Jesuits a thorough grounding in music, as well as in other subjects. The most gifted were recruited as schoolboys to be singers and instrumentalists in the performance of sacred music in the annual Latin school plays and so-called Lenten meditations. Jesuit music drama, performed to celebrate various festivals of the church year or the end of the school year, provided a model for other orders to emulate, in particular the Benedictines and Augustinians. In its early form it was also a major influence on opera. The grandly conceived 'sacred comedy' *Philothea*, by the Jesuit Johann Paullinus, is regarded as the first German oratorio. With an instrumental accompaniment of strings, trombones and organ, it was performed several times in Munich and elsewhere and appeared in print in 1669; it made a great impression on the Elector Ferdinand Maria and the rest of the audience, many of whom are said to have had tears in their eyes. Lenten meditations were performed on Sundays in Lent each year as a series of three, four or five sacred dramas with incidental music, like cantatas; they might be described as dramatically staged sermons for Lent. Most of their music is lost, but a three-part collection made by the Jesuit Franz Lang, *Theatrum affectuum humanorum* (1717), provides the texts and music of 67 such works performed in Munich; the composers, including G. A. Bernabei, were all from Bavaria.[8]

Monasteries throughout the area, particularly in Old Bavaria and Swabia, were also important as centres of musical life. In the area that is now modern Bavaria there were 80 houses belonging to the

Benedictines and Augustinians alone before the closure of the monasteries in 1803. Liturgical music was not confined to plainchant. Leading sixteenth-century musicians such as Senfl and Lassus had sent sacred works to the abbeys; and at the beginning of the seventeenth century instrumental music also made its way into the liturgy. During the seventeenth century monastic composers appeared increasingly, composing chiefly for their own monasteries but also publishing their works. Among the Benedictines, for instance, Sebastian Erthel of the monastery at Weihenstephan published music from 1611 to 1617, Rufinus Sigel of Seeon published sacred concertos in 1630, and Valentin Molitor of Kempten published works from 1668 to 1692. Developments in typography during the seventeenth century afforded good opportunities for the distribution of their music. Munich, Ingolstadt and Kempten, Passau and Innsbruck, were all major centres of printing until Augsburg took the lead in the early eighteenth century. The Protestant publisher Johann Jakob Lotter (*c*1683–1738), examples of whose publications can still be found throughout Europe, admitted that the music he published by Marianus Königsperger (1708–69), a monk at the Benedictine abbey of Prüfening, had laid the foundations of his fortune. Masses, litanies, Vespers and smaller sacred works, as well as instrumental and organ music, appeared in great quantities, and were also an important part of the church music repertory outside the monasteries. German sacred solo songs with continuo, such as the Bogenberg pilgrim songs by the Benedictine monk Balthasar Regler of Oberaltaich (1679) or the Marian song collections (1710–30) of Gotthard Wagner of Tegernsee, another Benedictine, are among the most valuable contributions that monastic composers made to the genre.

More numerous than printed works were the many manuscript works that were in circulation; these are now largely lost. Printed music was expensive, and represented only a small part of a wealth of musical material that still cannot properly be surveyed. As well as sacred music, chamber music was performed in the monasteries, and there was *Tafelmusik* at mealtimes when guests visited, at New Year and Shrovetide and on other occasions. The performers were mostly members of the monastic orders: in many religious houses a good singing voice or the ability to play at least one instrument was a condition of admission. Where the resident talent was inadequate, musicians were recruited from the country round about or from among the monks' pupils. On great festival days the elector himself frequently offered the services of court musicians. Monasteries did not merely provide an essential service in training the choirboys necessary for church services; the musical instruction that was offered in the monastery schools, their own abundant repertory of sacred music and their performances of music drama gave large sections of the rural population their only chance of hearing any kind of art music.

Italian models determined the style of the music. The influences of Munich, Salzburg and – in the Upper Palatinate – Bohemia are clearly discernible in the different repertories. On the other hand, there were remarkably few points of contact with significant musical institutions in Austria. In the musical activities of the monasteries, as well as in their repertories, there is clear evidence of their proximity to local forms of folk music. The Cistercian composer Remigius Falb of Fürstenfeld, for example, wrote in the foreword to his *Pastorellae symphoniae* op.2 of 1755 that he wished to unite the 'church' style with the 'country' style. Sacred instrumental music and church sonatas show an attempt to write in a way that was not too elaborately artistic and admitted popular elements, as for instance in the small concertos contained in the masses (1743; fig.47) of the Cistercian Alberich Hirschberger of Raitenhaslach. Songs in German played a significant part in the Mass, and some appeared in print. 'Pastorals' – pastoral songs with instrumental accompaniment sung in church at Christmas, usually before the sermon – were popular with congregations; some familiar Christmas carols derive from them.[9] Some of the powerful and direct Baroque sermons of the time have literary merit; their most famous exponent was Abraham a Santa Clara, who sometimes preached in Bavaria.

An important source for popular songs of the time is the manuscript collection *Rhitmorum varietas* (1646) made by the Benedictine monk Johannes Werlin of Seeon, comprising some 3000 songs from printed and manuscript sources, many of which are now lost.[10] The ways in which ordinary town and country people made music in the Baroque period can generally be gleaned only from their reflection in art music or from pictorial sources. In the first half of the eighteenth century the foundations had already been laid for the many German dances or *Ländler* that became popular in such numbers at a later period. The chief musical instruments of the countryside, particularly used to accompany dancing, were the bagpipes, shawm, pipe, dulcimer and hurdy-gurdy.

The many instrument makers active at this period include organ builders such as the Freundt family of Passau and the Egedacher family of Straubing, as well as Johann Fux in Donauwörth and Kaspar Kurz in Ingolstadt. An extremely well restored organ built by Fux in 1736 survives in the famous Cistercian monastery church at Fürstenfeld. Besides organ builders, other notable instrument makers were working at this time, particularly in southern Bavaria. Matthias Klotz (1653–1743) of Mittenwald started the famous Mittenwald violin-making tradition around 1700 in his native moun-

47. Title-page of the collection of masses and other works, 'Philomena Cisterciensis' (Burghausen: Luzenberger, 1743), by Alberich Hirschberger, with a view of the monastery of Raitenhaslach where he worked

tain village; members of the Walch family devoted themselves to making woodwind instruments in Berchtesgaden from around 1650 for over 200 years; and Jakob Hochbrucker is said to have invented the first single-action pedal harp in Donauwörth in about 1720. Some of the instruments they made are now valuable museum exhibits.

FRANCONIA

The courts

Unlike Old Bavaria, Franconia and Swabia were split into many small territories before the collapse of the Old Empire, around 1790, which was brought about as a result of the French Revolution. Numerous principalities, counties and other demesnes enjoyed the exercise of sovereign rights. Franconia contained the ecclesiastical principalities of Bamberg, Würzburg and Eichstätt (the last is now part of Upper Bavaria; see above), the margravates of Ansbach and Bayreuth, 11 other independent counties, four bishoprics, and the Protestant free imperial cities of Nuremberg, Rothenburg, Windsheim, Schweinfurt and Weissenburg. In Swabia (see below) the number of small sovereign states, both ecclesiastical and secular, was even greater.

The secular courts of Ansbach and Bayreuth were outstanding as musical centres. Both these margravates were ruled by members of the house of Hohenzollern, and they thus had strong musical links with north Germany. Johann Wolfgang Franck (1644–?c1710) was Kapellmeister at Ansbach from 1672 to 1678, when he had to flee following a murder committed out of jealousy. For a short time his successor was the unstable Johann Sigismund Kusser (1660–1727), a friend of Lully. Both were important figures in the history of early German opera, which, together with Lully's operas, flourished at Ansbach under the Margrave Johann Friedrich. Franck's opera *Die drei Töchter Cecrops* (1679) is among the earliest extant operas in German. The introduction of violin playing 'à la française' under Margrave Johann Friedrich (*d* 1686) shows the margrave's interest in French musical culture; in 1698–9, however, Giuseppe Torelli (1658–1709), the Italian master of the concerto grosso and violin concerto, was employed as *maestro di concerto* at the Ansbach court. His pupil Johann Georg Pisendel (1687–1755), a former Ansbach choirboy, became one of the leading musicians and composers of the Dresden Hofkapelle. Several more operas were produced under the direction of Francesco Antonio Pistocchi (1659–1726), appointed Kapellmeister in 1696, but in 1703 the number of court musicians was severely reduced. For over half a century there were no more notable musical developments in Ansbach.

Early German opera made an appearance in Bayreuth in 1662, in the time of Margrave Christian Ernst, with *Sophie*, an anonymous Singspiel. Regular performances of operatic works, however, most of them in German, did not begin until 1699. The repertory shows clear parallels with that of the Hamburg Gänsemarkt theatre, a major operatic centre of the time, and with that of the duchy of Saxe-Weissenfels. Around 1715, under Margrave Wilhelm, up to six operas a year were performed at Bayreuth, and members of the court participated actively. There were productions of both Italian and German works by such composers as Antonio Lotti, Stefano Benedetto Pallavicino, Gottfried Heinrich Stölzel and Telemann.

The period between 1735 and 1758 was a high point in the musical history of Bayreuth. The power behind it was the clever and gifted Margravine Wilhelmine, sister of King Frederick the Great of Prussia. As Margrave Friedrich's wife, she used her influence to encourage enlightened absolutism. She was responsible in Bayreuth for fine rococo architectural creations such as the Neue Schloss and the Eremitage, and for some imaginative landscaped gardens. Music and drama flourished under her influence. Important composers such as the Graun brothers, Johann Gottlieb and Carl Heinrich, Franz Benda and Johann Joachim Quantz visited the court, and the margravine herself was a composer of some ability. Italian opera was popular, and so was French ballet. 1748 saw the opening of the magnificent opera house built by Joseph Saint-Pierre and Carlo and Giuseppe Galli-Bibiena, which still stands today. Other productions were staged in castles and in open-air theatres. The court Kapellmeister was Johann Pfeiffer (1697–1761) of Nuremberg, the singers were Italian and the instrumentalists German. Among them were musicians distinguished in their own right, such as the lutenist Adam Falckenhagen (1697–1761) and the three Kleinknecht brothers – Johann Wolfgang (1715–86), Jakob Friedrich (1722–94) and Johann Stephan (1731–91) – all of whom were also composers. The period of Bayreuth's musical glory ended with the margravine's death in 1758.

The musical establishment at the court of the Prince-Bishop of Würzburg, documented as early as 1600, developed fully between 1720 and 1746 under the rule of Johann Philipp Franz von Schönborn and his brother and successor Friedrich Carl von Schönborn. The Schönborns were responsible for encouraging much creativity in art and architecture; the 'goût Schönborn' was spoken of with admiration in German princely courts of the time. Balthasar Neumann, one of the leading architects of the period, was commissioned by the Schönborns to design and build many churches and castles in Franconia. His masterpiece was the Residenz at Würzburg, with its fine frescoes by Giovanni Battista Tiepolo. The Franconian-German baroque style of the Schönborn period achieved a happy synthesis of lordly generosity and popular piety, in which music too had its place. Leading court composers included, besides German musicians, the two Italians Fortunato Chelleri (c1686–1757) and Giovanni Benedetto Platti (c1700–1763); the former is of interest for his oratorios, cantatas and church music, the latter for his instrumental works, which point the way to the pre-Classical style. There were particularly strong musical links with Rome, Venice and Vienna. Details of the musical repertory of Würzburg do not survive, but some idea of its abundance can be gauged from Count Rudolf Franz Erwein von Schönborn's collection of music in Wiesentheid castle which covers the period 1685–1735. Rudolf Franz Erwein was another brother of the two Prince-Bishops of Würzburg. He acquired most of his collection of music, which survives almost intact and comprises some 150 printed and 500 manuscript works by about 200 composers, in the course of his extensive travels. The count bought the most up-to-date musical works in France, Italy and Vienna; the names in his collection range from Corelli to Johann Adolf Hasse (called Sassone, 'the Saxon'), who was very popular in Italy. Since he was an enthusiastic cellist, cello music is particularly well represented in the count's collection.[11]

The court of the princes of Löwenstein-Wertheim-Rosenberg in the years leading up to 1750 exemplifies the kind of musical activity to be found at the courts of the smaller Franconian principalities on the Main. Details of the music that was performed there are lost, but other documents show that the court had links with musical activities in Würzburg, Mainz, Mannheim and Kassel, as well as with Franconian monasteries on the Main, such as Neustadt, Amorbach and Triefenstein. Further afield, there were contacts with Dresden, Prague, Vienna, Paris, Venice and Naples.[12] Clearly, even rulers of the smaller states were anxious to keep up with the musical world at large.

Another Catholic prince-bishopric in the area was Bamberg, where the post of Hofkapellmeister dates back to the sixteenth century. From about 1640 to 1667 Georg Mengel held the position, but it subsequently fell vacant. Mengel and the well-known court organist and composer Georg Arnold (1621–76) wrote in a characteristically early Baroque style; among their works are polychoral and concertato masses, as well as small-scale motets.[13] As the Prince-Bishops Lothar Franz and Friedrich Carl von Schönborn each held two princely sees from 1693 to 1746 and spent most of their time in Mainz or Würzburg, the main emphasis at Bamberg was on church music. The court oboist and violinist Johann Jakob Schnell (1687–1754), the leading German exponent of the musical Baroque style in Franconia at the time of the Schönborns, lived in Bamberg from at least 1714 until his death; most of his works were chamber music, and he was also active as a music publisher.

Nuremberg: a free imperial city

In the Protestant imperial cities organized musical life was slow to redevelop after the Thirty Years War. *Stadtpfeifer* and other professional civic musicians, institutionalized during the sixteenth century, played for the festivals of the trade guilds, for private parties and dances and in church. In the country, village schoolmasters usually provided sacred music in the Catholic churches. Where funds allowed, printed sheet music was bought, some of it from south German publishers, but much music circulated only in manuscript

48. *Banquet at the Nuremberg town hall, 25 September 1649, celebrating the peace treaty ending the Thirty Years War: engraving (1649) by G. D. Heumann. The musicians, under the direction of S. T. Staden (right), included 21 singers, 18 instrumentalists and four organists.*

copies. Small groups of instrumentalists played in church, usually with only one player to a part; choirs had hardly more than two singers to a part, as was the case throughout Bavaria. Sheet music might be in use for up to 50 years and was then thrown out and replaced by new works. Printed music generally lasted rather longer than manuscripts, but only a tiny fraction of all this material survived. The repertory was continually changing to accommodate new styles, current tastes and developments.

Nuremberg ranked first among the free imperial cities of Franconia until the beginning of the nineteenth century, although the shifting of trade routes and the effects of the Thirty Years War reduced its European importance. As a Protestant city it had not suffered nearly as severely from the Swedes as large areas of Catholic Bavaria. The Ratsmusik had survived even under the Swedes; this municipal body consisted of five or six *Stadtpfeifer* and their journeymen. Many well-known musicians, began their careers in its ranks. The best-known Nuremberg musician of the first half of the century was Johann Staden (*d* 1634), organist of St Lorenz; he was one of the earliest south German musicians to unite German traditions with the new achievements of the Italians.

Later in the century, organists in the principal Protestant churches included Johann Löhner (1645–1705), whose work clearly shows folk elements, at St Sebald, and Johann Erasmus Kindermann (1616–55) at St Egidius; Kindermann wrote prolifically, and his instrumental music is of some historical significance. A general stylistic feature of the Nuremberg school of the seventeenth century and the early eighteenth is a cantabile style of writing, together with a distinctly conservative approach. Such features characterize the music of Johann Pachelbel (1653–1706), the most important Nuremberg organist-composer of the late seventeenth century, who played the organ at St Sebald for many years.

The citizens of Nuremberg took an interest in music, as shown by the existence around 1700 of several small musical groups and societies. The 'Pegnesische Blumenorden' ('Pegnitz Order of Flowers' – Nuremberg lies on the river Pegnitz), a poets' circle on the model of the Italian academies, stimulated musical creativity: the highly esteemed organist of St Lorenz, Sigmund Theophil Staden (1607–55), wrote the first extant Singspiel, *Seelewig*, for this society in 1644. Löhner emerged in 1679 as the first notable Singspiel composer with *Die triumphirende Treue* (produced in Ansbach in 1679).[14] Since 1667 Nuremberg had had its own opera house, mainly used by touring opera companies. In 1697 Johann Sigismund Kusser, then a well-known figure, mounted operas by Giovanni Battista Bassani of Ferrara and Antonio Giannettini of Bologna in this opera house, using German translations. Nuremberg was among the few German cities where, for a while, German Baroque opera was performed independently of princely patronage.

As in the sixteenth century and the early seventeenth, music printing in Nuremberg regained its importance. The outputs of the younger Christoph Weigel (1703–77) and Balthasar Schmid (1705–49) included works by J. S. Bach, and Johann Ulrich Haffner (1711–67) distributed keyboard music by south German composers. Instrument making flourished as well: violas, horns, trumpets, trombones and organs were made. Johann Christoph Denner (1655–1707) constructed an early keyed chalumeau, a predecessor of the clarinet.

SWABIA

Augsburg and Dillingen

After the hardships of the Thirty Years War the old Protestant imperial city of Augsburg was unable to recover its former prominence, which it had owed largely to its great merchant families, the Fuggers and Welsers. The city's population had decreased by about a third, and considerable financial losses meant that no funds were available for patronage. Gradually, however, the city began to recover. Augsburg goldsmiths in particular did fine work in the new period of prosperity.

After the Peace of Westphalia had established religious equality in 1648, both Catholics and Protestants supported musical activities again. Protestant church music began to thrive. The motets of Adam Gumpelzhaimer (*d* 1625) had been sung at St Anna for a long time, indeed until 1677, when Georg Schmetzer (1642–97), who had gained much experience on his travels, became Kantor and brought a breath of fresh air into the repertory. After the second decade of the eighteenth century, Philipp David Kräuter, a pupil of Bach, and his two successors the Seyferts – Johann Caspar (?1697–1767) and his son Johann Gottfried (1731–72) – were Kantors there and took their lead from the music of north German masters like Bach, J. G. Pisendel in Dresden and Telemann in Hamburg; they were also in touch with J. G. Wagenseil in Vienna. Their work leads from the Baroque, by way of influences from the *Sturm und Drang* movement (and connections with C. P. E. Bach) to early Classicism. Kräuter also encouraged music-making among the citizens; in 1713 he founded a collegium musicum on the model of the one in Leipzig, and 'concerts were given, not publicly but among friends who were themselves well versed in music, and the favourite instruments seem to have been lutes, regals and flutes' (Paul van Stetten, writing in 1779). Some of the music performed had been written in Augsburg. For example, Jakob Scheiffelhut (1647–1709), a *Stadtpfeifer* and organist at the Protestant Barfüsserkirche, wrote attractive suites in the French style for three to five instruments, as well as church music.

Catholic church music at the cathedral was directed by Johann Melchior Gletle (1626–83), a Swiss, and his successor Johann Melchior Caesar (1648–92); several of their printed collections of music appeared in Augsburg between 1667 and 1691. Both also contributed to the genre of the quodlibet, which was specially popular in Augsburg and culminated in the songs and short cantatas of the Augsburg *Tafelkonfekt* ('Table Confection', 1733–46), intended for both secular and monastic use, by Johann Valentin Rathgeber, a Benedictine at the abbey of Banz. Like the *Tafelkonfekt*, which was popular in the best sense of the word, many sacred and instrumental works by musicians throughout southern Germany and beyond were circulated in editions printed in Augsburg. Throughout virtually the whole of the eighteenth century, Augsburg was the leading centre of music publishing south of the Main.

The musicians of the Prince-Bishop of Augsburg's court were based not in the city itself but at his seat in Dillingen. Here, on the site of an ancient university, Johann Baptist Gerer (*d* 1728), canon of St Peter and the prince-bishop's Kapellmeister, wrote the music for several Jesuit dramas. His successor Johann Franz Anton Maichelbeck (1702–50), who was a skilful painter as well as a musician, was noted for his printed works for keyboard and organ. During the reign of Prince-Bishop Joseph, Landgrave of Hesse, from 1740, there was a revival of music; operas were performed at Dillingen in his honour. Around 1750 his Hofmusik consisted of 14 musicians and five trumpeters, and the bishop himself sometimes sang in concerts.

The monasteries

As in Old Bavaria and in some religious houses of Franconia, intensive musical activity was characteristic of Swabian monasteries. Foremost among them was the imperial Benedictine monastery of Ottobeuren, whose imposing church was built in 1748–60. Part of its extensive collection of musical documents, discovered only recently, dates from before 1700. Relations with imperial Vienna and Bohemia are clearly evident in its sacred repertory.

Baroque monastic drama in Swabia, composed by members of the monasteries, had a long tradition. Over 100 texts were printed, but the music for only a few works has survived. An extensive organbook of 1695, containing music by Froberger, Georg Muffat, Kerll and their contemporaries, is instructive as regards the organ repertory, which was particularly important in Ottobeuren. Tangible evidence of its richness is provided by the two famous choir organs built by K. J. Riepp in 1754–66.[15]

The composer Meinrad Spiess (1685–1761), who also had a great reputation as a music theorist, directed the music at the Benedictine abbey of Irsee, near Kaufbeuren, in Swabia. From 1743 he was a member of the first musicological society in Germany, founded in 1738 by the Leipzig university lecturer Lorenz Christoph Mizler in collaboration with the Ansbach court Kapellmeister Georg Heinrich Bümler; this 'corresponding society of musical scholars' numbered among its members Telemann, Handel, C. H. Graun and Bach. Spiess, who was also in contact with Leopold Mozart, published in 1745 his widely circulated *Tractatus musicus*, in essence a treatise on composition; it displays his wide knowledge of music in its many quotations and examples from contemporary works. He refers to, among other people, the then little-known Franz Xaver Richter (1709–89), a major figure of the transition between the Baroque and early Classical periods, who later rose to fame in Mannheim and Strasbourg. From 1740 to 1746 Richter was deputy Kapellmeister to the Prince-Abbot of Kempten, an imperial ecclesiastical sovereign subject only to the emperor. The Prince-Abbot's expensive seat, built in 1732–42 and furnished in exquisite taste, is an expression of his dignity. Richter wrote his first symphonic work in Kempten, and it was printed in Paris in 1741. There had already been an excellent Kapellmeister in this Swabian centre of church music before the turn of the century – Thomas Eisenhut (1644–1702), whose motets for one to seven voices with instrumental accompaniment (1674–94) are typical of contemporary south German sacred music. Musical activity was also of a high standard at the Benedictine abbey at Füssen. The chief composer here was the abbot, Gallus Zeiler (1705–55), who published six collections of sacred music and concertos which reveal him as a typical exponent of the Bavarian rococo style. The craft of the violin and lute makers of Füssen also gained a reputation that extended beyond their own region; among them was Johann Paul Alletsee (1684–1733), who was active at the Munich court and was one of the best Bavarian instrument makers in the Baroque era.

*

Because of its great extent and variety, it has been possible here only to scratch the surface of musical life in Franconia and Swabia. These regions had much in common with Old Bavaria as regards musical activity in the monasteries. Protestant church music played no part in Old Bavaria, except for Regensburg, while in large parts of Franconia and certain places in Swabia, such as Augsburg, Kempten and Memmingen, it had a long tradition behind it. The quality and quantity of musical life in the towns and the many small sovereign states depended on their political and economic conditions, and in particular on the initiative and inclinations of influential citizens or of the ruler. The diversity of circumstances in Bavaria during the Baroque period, which was often very great, tended to lead not so much to spectacular peaks of achievement as to a wealth of creative productivity; and although much of the music is now lost there remains considerable scope for continuing study and assessment.

NOTES

[1] E. Katzbichler, *Über das Leben und die weltlichen Vokalwerke des Ercole Bernabei* (diss., U. of Munich, 1963) [incl. thematic catalogue].

[2] G. Haberkamp and B. Zuber, *Die Musikhandschriften Herzog Wilhelms in Bayern, der Grafen zu Toerring-Jettenbach und der Fürsten Fugger von Babenhausen: thematischer Katalog* (Munich, 1988), pp. xxiii ff [introduction by R. Münster].

[3] R. Münster, *Kurfürst Max Emanuel*, i (Munich, 1976), 315.

[4] R. Münster, 'Neu aufgefundene Opern, Oratorien und szenische Kantaten von Pietro Torri', *Musik in Bayern*, xiii (1976), 49.

[5] R. Münster, *Volksmusik in Bayern: ausgewählte Quellen aus sechs Jahrhunderten* (Munich, 1985), 513 [exhibition catalogue, Bavarian State Library].

[6] A. Sandberger, Introduction to *E. F. dall'Abaco: Ausgewählte Werke*, DTB, i (1900); xvi (1908); see also H. Schmid, Introduction to *E. F. dall'Abaco: Ausgewählte Werke, 3. Teil*, DTB, new ser., i (1967).

[7] P. Tenhaef, 'Zum Leben und Schaffen des Eichstätter Hofkapellmeisters Johann Michael Prentz', *Kirchenmusikalisches Jb*, lxx (1986), 27–44; K. Beckmann, *Joseph Meck (1690–1758): Leben und Werk des Eichstätter Hofkapellmeisters* (diss., U. of Bochum, 1975).

[8] For the Munich Lenten meditations see R. Münster, 'Die Münchener Festenmeditationen von 1724 bis 1774 und ihre Komponisten', *Quaestiones in musica: Festschrift Franz Krautwurst zum 75. Geburtstag* (Tutzing, 1989), 339–69.

[9] Münster, *Volksmusik in Bayern*, 81; A. Hartmann, *Volkslieder, in Bayern, Tirol und Salzburg gesammelt, mit vielen Melodien nach dem Volksmund aufgezeichnet*, i: *Volksthümliche Weihnachtslieder* (Leipzig, 1884; repr. 1987).

[10] D. Hofmann, *Die 'Rhitmorum varietas' des Johannes Werlin aus Kloster Seeon* (diss., U. of Augsburg, 1993).

[11] See F. Zobeley, *Die Musikalien der Grafen von Schönborn Wiesentheid*, i: *Das Repertoire des Grafen Rudolf Franz Erwein von Schönborn (1677–1754)* (Tutzing, 1967).

[12] See E. F. Schmid, *Musik am Hofe der Fürsten von Löwenstein-Wertheim-Rosenberg (1720–1750)* (Würzburg, 1953).

[13] G. Weinzierl, 'Repräsentant des Hochbarock in Bamberg: der fürstbischöfliche Hoforganist Georg Arnold', *Musik in Bayern*, xxiii (1988), 23–30.

[14] See *Johann Löhner: Die triumphirende Treue*, ed. W. Braun, DTB, new ser., vi (1984).

[15] For an introduction to the rich repertory of Ottobeuren see G. Haberkamp, *Die Musikhandschriften der Benediktiner-Abtei Ottobeuren* (Munich, 1986).

BIBLIOGRAPHICAL NOTE

Historical and political background

A historical and political survey of Bavaria in the Baroque era and of the economy, sciences, literature, art and music in the entire area that makes up modern Bavaria, may be found in *Das Alte Bayern* and *Franken, Schwaben, Oberpfalz*, volumes ii and iii of the *Handbuch der bayerischen Geschichte*, ed. M. Spindler with the collaboration of others (Munich, 1974, 2/1988; 1971). B. Hubensteiner provides a good deal of information

The Late Baroque Era

in a short space in *Bayerische Geschichte* (Munich, 1977). The period of Elector Max Emanuel is fully covered in the many articles and catalogue entries in *Kurfürst Max Emanuel: Bayern und Europa um 1700*, i: *Zur Geschichte und Kunstgeschichte der Max-Emanuel-Zeit*; ii: *Katalog* (Munich, 1976).

Literature and art

There is no complete history of literature in Bavaria. The relevant articles in Spindler's history (see above) contain much literary information. The two publications *Bayerische Literaturgeschichte*, ed. E. Dünninger and D. Kiesselbach, ii (Munich, 1967), and *Handbuch der Literatur in Bayern*, ed. A. Weber (Regensburg, 1987) consist substantially of monographs on selected writers.

A thorough survey of the literature on art in Bavaria may be found in H. Wichmann's *Bibliographie der Kunst in Bayern*, i–v (Wiesbaden, 1961–83). H. Schindler's *Grosse bayerische Kunstgeschichte*, ii (Munich, 1976) provides an appreciation of the leading figures in painting, sculpture and architecture and of their works. An extensive account of art in Munich is to be found in N. Lieb's *München: Geschichte seiner Kunst* (Munich, 1977). As an introduction to the world of the Bavarian baroque, B. Hubensteiner's *Vom Geist des Barock* (Munich, 1967) may be recommended.

Music

Musik in Bayern, i: *Bayerische Musikgeschichte*, ed. R. Münster and H. Schmid, with the exhibition catalogue *Musik in Bayern*, ii: *Katalog*, ed. F. Göthel (both Tutzing, 1972), represents a first attempt at a comprehensive account of the subject. On Munich, O. Ursprung's well-written musical history, *Münchens musikalische Vergangenheit von der Frühzeit bis Richard Wagner* (Munich, 1927), has not yet been superseded. R. Münster gives an account of the period of Max Emanuel in *Kurfürst Max Emanuel*, i: *Zur Geschichte und Kunstgeschichte der Max-Emanuel-Zeit*, ed. H. Glaser (Munich, 1976), 295–316. An almost complete list of operas performed at the Munich court is included in *Nationalteater: die Bayerische Staatsoper*, ed. H. Zehetmayr and J. Schläder (Munich, 1993), 259–62. There are very few recent full accounts of the musical history of individual cities and regions. Information on Augsburg is contained in a general survey in the collection entitled *Musik in der Reichsstadt Augsburg* (Augsburg, 1965); additional new findings are published in two articles by F. Krautwurst in *Geschichte der Stadt Augsburg von der Römerzeit bis zur Gegenwart*, ed. G. Gottlieb and others (Stuttgart, 1985), 504–14. For Nuremberg, see F. Krautwurst's two contributions to *Nürnberg: Geschichte einer europäischen Stadt*, ed. G. Pfeiffer (Munich, 1971), 287–91, 344–6. For Kempten, see F. Krautwurst's chapter in *Geschichte der Stadt Kempten*, ed. V. Dottermich (Kempten, 1989), 303–22. Because of its inadequate sources, the posthumous work of O. Kaul on music in Würzburg, *Musica Herbipolis* (Marktbreit, 1980), offers only an incomplete survey. However, E. F. Schmid's *Musik am Hofe der Fürsten von Löwenstein-Werthehim-Rosenberg (1720–1750)* (Würzburg, 1953) and F. Zobeley's catalogue *Die Musikalien der Grafen von Schönborn-Wiesentheid*, i: *Das Repertoire des Grafen Rudolf Franz Erwein von Schönborn (1677–1754)* (Tutzing, 1967–82) provide illuminating insights into the musical life of two small Franconian courts. New material is disclosed in two works of documentation published in connection with exhibitions – *Musik in Ingolstadt: zur Geschichte der Musikkultur in Ingolstadt*, published by the Historischer Verein Ingolstadt (Ingolstadt, 1984), and K. W. Littger, *Musik in Eichstätt: Beiträge zur Geschichte der Hofmusik und Katalog* (Tutzing, 1988). K. G. Fellerer's *Beiträge zur Musikgeschichte Freisings von den ältesten christlichen Zeit bis Zur Auflösung des Hofes 1803* (Munich, 1926) remains useful. A wealth of material is offered by the earliest scholar to work on local musical history in Bavaria, Dominikus Mettenleiter, in *Musikgeschichte der Stadt Regensburg* (Regensburg, 1866) and *Musikgeschichte der Oberpfalz* (Regensburg, 1867); new editions with supplementary indexes are in preparation. On the history of Baroque opera in Bavaria, the incomplete survey by R. Brockpähler, *Handbuch der Barockoper in Deutschland* (Emsdetten, 1963) provides information, but requires some revision. For information on individual composers and cities in Bavaria, see the relevant entries in *Grove 6*, *Grove 0* and *MGG*. Editions of music of the Baroque period have been published in the series *Denkmäler der Tonkunst in Bayern* (DTB), i–xxx (Leipzig, 1900–31) and vol.i of the new series (Wiesbaden, 1967). They include compositions by Dall'Abaco, Kerll, Kindermann, J. P. Krieger, Murschhauser, Pachelbel, Pez, Steffani and Torri; selected works by Arnold are in preparation. The documentation series *Musica Bavarica*, ed. R. Münster and A. Kirchberger (Munich, 1967–), is also useful for this period.

Chapter XI

Vienna under Joseph I and Charles VI

SUSAN WOLLENBERG

A clump of houses and palaces
full of vermin, full of visitors,
A mish-mash of all nations that inhabit East-West-South-North . . .
Plenty of ignorance and plenty of students . . .
Plenty of Spaniards, Italians and French,
Many of the last in German breeches,
Plenty of pressing, pushing, pulling, tugging,
This is the quodlibet of Vienna.[1]

Absolutism . . . [in the course of the seventeenth century] only now
made Vienna an imperial city in the real sense. The imperial court
in Vienna was also musically the centre, with which the few smaller
princely courts in the Austrian realm could hardly compete, and
municipal and monastic culture could no longer compete at all,
with regard to quality.[2]

Music was a prime element in the 'Quodlibet of Vienna', and in
particular in the Habsburg tradition, and so musical life at the
Viennese court – the administrative centre of the Habsburg empire –
inevitably forms the main focus of this chapter.[3] What can be deduced about the music cultivated within the imperial household is
important both for its intrinsic interest and as an aid to understanding the musical culture of the city as a whole. The title of a classic
article on the subject of the Emperors Ferdinand III, Leopold I,
Joseph I and Charles VI as composers and patrons of music[4]
suggests one of the prime factors in the Habsburgs' strong and
continuous musical tradition: the imperial rulers were, for several
successive generations in the seventeenth and early eighteenth centuries, immensely gifted and knowledgeable musicians, for whom the
court musical establishment (the Hofkapelle) thus possessed a more
than superficial significance. The emperors themselves regularly
composed and conducted musical works. It has been suggested[5] that
the frequent references to musical matters effected 'by command of

49. Banquet in the Knights' Chamber, Vienna, following the Ceremony of Oaths of Allegiance sworn to Charles as Archduke of Austria, 8 November 1705: engraving (note the musicians' gallery above left)

the sacred imperial Majesty' in court documents convey a sense not so much of the whim of an absolute monarch, exercised for its own sake, but rather of the emperor's genuine abilities influencing the musical life of the court. (This aspect of the Habsburg tradition illuminates the later and better-known involvement of Emperor Joseph II in musical patronage.) Under Charles VI especially, court ceremonial and the music connected with it were systematically planned and carried out on a grand scale. At times, the accounts of court ceremonies when various dignitaries were received can read like a social calendar: like the court circular in the London *Times* nowadays, this kind of information was published in the official newspaper of the time, the *Wiennerisches Diarium* (forerunner of the *Wiener Zeitung*). The names that crop up are often well known from families connected with later eighteenth-century musicians (Haydn, Mozart, Beethoven) – names such as Erdődy, Kinsky, Zinzendorf and Colloredo – providing a reminder of the essential continuity that underlies the obvious changes from the earlier to the later part of the century.

Table XI.1 HABSBURG RULERS c1640–1780		
Ferdinand III (b 1608)	(1637–57)	m (1) Infanta Maria Anna of Spain (2) Maria Leopoldina of Tirol (3) Eleonora II Gonzaga
Leopold I (b 1640)	(1658–1705)	m (1) Margarita Teresa of Spain (2) Claudia Felicitas of Tirol (3) Eleonora of Pfalz-Neuburg
Joseph I (b 1678)	(1705–11)	m Wilhelmine Amalia of Brunswick-Lüneburg
Charles VI (b 1685)	(1711–40)*	m Elisabeth Christine of Brunswick-Wolfenbüttel
Maria Theresa (b 1717)	(1740–80)	m Francis Stephen of Lorraine (d 1765)
Joseph II (b 1741)	from 1765 co-regent (1780–90)	m (1) Infanta Isabella of Parma (2) Josepha of Bavaria

* Charles VI first entered Vienna in January 1712: his court was moved in several stages from Barcelona to Vienna during 1711–12

Two particular aspects of court music deserve consideration. One is the way in which music represented the power and glory of the ruling family. The other is the detail of the day-to-day court ceremonial with which musical composition and performance were closely linked. With respect to the nature of the imperial authority, again a title gives an important clue. The official ordinance book setting out the liturgical protocol under Charles VI was dubbed 'Ordinance Book showing how His Royal Catholic Majesty, the Holy Roman Emperor, celebrates his sacred worship for the year 1715'. This formal style obviously reflects the identification of the emperor with the Roman Catholic church. Religious and political influences were intermingled in the tradition of Habsburg rule, and in the aftermath of the Counter-Reformation the emperor's position was established as a blend of religious patronage and political leadership: his 'sacred majesty' was a thoroughly meaningful epithet. He was in fact the most powerful lay representative of the Catholic church outside Rome. Various bishoprics, cardinalships and abbeys in the Austrian region came under his control (Vienna itself had graduated from bishopric in the fifteenth and early sixteenth centuries, through prince-bishopric, to Metropolitan see under Charles VI from 1722). These were not matters merely of surface significance or purely external effect: the personal and devout religiosity of the Habsburg emperors is well attested. Naturally, their musical and religious zeal found its expression in a strong tradition of church music in Vienna. Most valuable among the original sources providing documentation on this aspect of Habsburg music are the general instructions for the conduct of ecclesiastical music, the *Rubriche generali*, drawn up in Italian (the language of the court) by the imperial *Konzertmeister* Kilian Reinhardt (*c*1653–1729),[6] and presented, with an elaborately humble and loyally expressed dedication, to the Emperor Charles VI in 1727. The sense of loyalty comes out most strongly in Reinhardt's signing himself as 'Most humbly Kilian Reinharth, with 50 years of most humble service given up to the present day' (the long service characteristic of many court musicians in Vienna ensured continuity through several changes of ruler). Like a faithful family retainer, Reinhardt cared deeply about the traditions of the court: they were his way of life. On a higher artistic plane, Charles VI's Kapellmeister, Johann Joseph Fux (1660–1741), expressed his concern to preserve the musical traditions of the Viennese court, including an emphasis on skilled counterpoint, at a time when he sensed a process of disintegration in the air. It was above all in an ecclesiastical context that a sense of order and tradition was most strongly cultivated in Viennese music of this period.

THE CHURCH MUSIC TRADITION

> . . . and with His Imperial Majesty and the Bishop again kneeling, the Agnus Dei is sung . . . there follows the sermon. (From the year 1715 without a sermon.) After that, the Bishop intones the *Te Deum laudamus*, which is sung . . . with trumpets and drums . . .[7]

Within the period 1705–40 considerable continuity was ensured in the musical life of the Viennese court. This was a period of relative political stability after the traumatic events of the seventeenth century. Following the rebuttal of the threat from the East (which was seen as a threat against western Christianity), the crisis point being the Turkish siege of Vienna in 1683, the city soon recovered and strengthened its position so that the 'fifty-seven years from the defeat of the Turks in 1683 until the death of Charles VI in 1740, were an era of unknown peace and security for the city of Vienna . . . a true

The Late Baroque Era

Blütezeit.[8] It was a period of cultural stability, but not stagnation. In music, and in the elements to which it was linked – art and stage design, literature and liturgy, court ceremonial – there were, on the one hand, features creating continuity with the past and, on the other, features embodying change. In the sphere of liturgical practice it might seem that 'the cultivation of church music . . . was much less affected by changes of taste than for example opera and chamber music,'[9] but nevertheless this should not be taken to imply that the period 1705–40 lacked any distinctive liturgical character. Past practices – and repertory – were not simply preserved in a fossilized state but instead they provided a strong foundation for a still evolving liturgy and its music. Much was certainly retained, in early eighteenth-century Vienna, from the earlier periods of Ferdinand III and Leopold I – including the actual choirbooks – but to the already rich accumulation of layers dating from different periods were added new layers of religious observance and musical style. All this was governed by a clear (though complex) code of practice which can be deduced, as Riedel has shown, from a careful synthesis of the extant documentation. In practical terms, the length, type, structure, style, texture and scoring of the pieces chosen for performance in church depended on the precise liturgical and ceremonial requirements of the occasion (in that sense it was truly occasional music). The correlation was very close, and no piece of church music can really be understood without a consideration of its liturgical context.[10]

What of the occasions themselves? The basic liturgical practice followed the generally established post-Tridentine rite, in the celebration of the Mass and various Offices. But it took on also a specifically local and up-to-date character in respect of the occasions that were celebrated. The annual round of church services was arranged to mark not only the statutory occasions recurring in the established calendar – the special feasts and saints' days, for example – but also both the regular and the special occasions peculiar to Vienna and to the Habsburg dynasty. For instance, there were 'family' saints: in Vienna St Leopold, St Joseph and St Charles Borromeus had a special significance, and a local tradition developed in connection with these saints' days. The customary festive mass would be performed 'solenne', with trumpets and timpani. (Fux's *Messa di San Carlo tutta in canone* of 1719, к7, better known as the 'Missa canonica', was intended, with its austere setting, for performance in Advent and Lent, but was apparently dedicated to Emperor Charles VI on his saint's day, hence its title.) Charles VI paid particular attention, in respect of the Bohemian lands under his rule, to the newly canonized St John Nepomuk of Prague: the *Missa sanctificationis Sancti Joannis Nepomuceni* of 1726 by Antonio Caldara (*c*1670–1736) is among many contemporary masses directly related to this cult, though it may well have been a Viennese mass adapted and entitled for local use, not necessarily by the composer.

The Habsburgs' Spanish connections were important: emphasis was thus placed on religious orders, brotherhoods and feast days of Spanish origin (another important patron saint, for example, was Theresa of Avila, *Namenspatronin* of the Infanta – her official title – Maria Theresa). One special ingredient of Viennese church life that derived from the Spanish Habsburgs' tradition was the Order of the Golden Fleece (founded 1429), which had by the eighteenth century become divided into two branches, one Spanish, the other Austrian (with Emperor Charles VI at its head). Membership of the order was granted, ceremonially, to aristocratic and royal figures in recognition of their distinguished service to the Catholic church and the imperial family (as soon as the long-awaited male heir, the future Joseph II, was born to Maria Theresa in 1741, he was created a Knight of the Golden Fleece). Various religious feasts – at Christmas, Easter, Whitsuntide and so on, and certain saints' days – were celebrated in connection with this order (and were known as *Toisonfeste*). On these occasions the emperor and members of the order dressed in special costume, and the music was particularly grand in style, creating a characteristic combination of aural and visual splendour.

The quotation with which this section began is taken from a description of the liturgical procedure for a special occasion of another kind. This was not a Catholic church feast as such, but a political commemoration, celebrating (on 12 May each year) the Liberation of Barcelona (1706). Battles (for example, during the wars against the Turks) coronations, births and birthdays, as well as a host of other events including miscellaneous religious events such as the consecration of local churches – all these occasioned processions and services held on the appropriate days. Thus, under the heading of 'Processione Tempore Belli contro li Turchi' (12 July 1716), Reinhardt recorded that the Emperor Charles VI went in procession from the Augustinerkirche[11] (St Augustine's) to the Stephansdom[12] (St Stephen's); during the procession the 'Litanie de tutt'i Santi' was sung, and at the Stephansdom the Agnus Dei 'con responsorj particolari'. Such occasions helped to establish a sense of the essential integrity of court life, in which historical, political and personal events were bound up with religious ceremonial.

On 22 October 1713 the emperor and empress went in procession from the Augustinerkirche to the Stephansdom, 'for the vow made by His Most Sacred . . . Majesty Charles VI during the time of the plague in Vienna'. The appropriate processional music was sung and, on arrival at the cathedral, the Agnus Dei; solemn mass was heard 'with trumpets and drums, and Intradas, in honour of St Charles Borromeus':

The Late Baroque Era

50. The Karlskirche, Vienna (1716–38), designed by J. B. Fischer von Erlach and completed by his son: engraving by Salomon Kleiner

> After the communion of the celebrant bishop (who was the Bishop of Vienna) both their Majesties were led to the great altar, then immediately after the communion His Imperial Majesty Charles VI made the vow to build a church in honour of St Charles Borromeus, for [his] intercession in the plague, which had already declined.[13]

Thus it was on this occasion that Charles VI – amid the impressive grandeur of the solemn mass with trumpets and timpani – expressed his votive intention to build a church in honour of his patron saint, Charles Borromeus. The Karlskirche (at Karlsplatz, just south of Bösendorferstrasse; see fig.50) still dominates its surroundings today: the emperor, who took a lively interest in the plans and their realization, had it built so that it would be visible from his city-centre residence (the Hofburg).[14] Its symbolism and design were powerfully expressive of the 'spiritual unity of the imperial realm' under his rule.

> The portico is flanked by two free-standing columns . . . [recalling] triumphal columns of ancient Rome. More recondite, as part of the complex programme of allusions, they were supposed to recall the Pillars of Hercules which are Spain's gate to the New World. All served the triumph of the Emperor, who saw himself as the protector of the Church Triumphant . . . To make the message clearer, the two columns are topped by the imperial crown of which

the Cross is only part and apex; the dome is crowned by a globe and Cross, symbols of the universal empire and the universal church.[15]

The foundation stone of the Karlskirche was laid in 1716: by the time the building was completed (1737–8) the emperor had very few years left in which to enjoy it.

In fact, the buildings in which the emperor and his entourage attended services were numerous and varied; and again their use was governed by a protocol that can be deduced from the surviving documentary evidence. A total of some 30 locations in and around Vienna were used for services, and para-liturgical performances, in which the Hofkapelle – in the sense of the court musicians – took part. The Hofkapelle in the sense of the chapel itself refers to only one of these locations – the 'Grosse Hofkapelle', or 'Capella grande', in the main Hofburg, used regularly during the winter season when the court was in residence there. The spring and summer palaces (Schloss Laxenburg and the Neue Favorita) just outside the city were also furnished with chapels. Vienna was a city full of churches and clerics: 'If one takes the numerous monasteries and convents in Vienna and surrounding areas together [with the papal nuncio and various bishops resident there] one can well assert that in this city the representation of high-ranking clergy was greater than in any other residence of the world at that time – excepting Rome'.[16]

Certain churches and chapels were connected with certain classes of feast days or types of service. Many of the buildings were extended and refitted in the late seventeenth and early eighteenth centuries: in some cases, Gothic originals were given Baroque façades and interiors (only to be 'regothicized' in the nineteenth century), as with the Dorotheerkirche (Baroque additions, 1705);[17] this was a period of growth and change in the churches themselves. New organs were installed, as at the Michaelerkirche (1714; the emperor came to hear the instrument at its inaugural use).[18] The Hofburgkapelle, the Augustinerkirche and the Stephansdom were the places of worship most frequently used by the imperial court, but many other places were closely connected with the imperial 'öffentliche Hofgottesdienste', for example the Minoritenkirche (church of the Minorites), where Charles VI attended services and processions on the day of the Seven Sorrows (Sieben Schmerzen Mariae, the Friday after Passion Sunday). Of particular importance in the environs of Vienna was the monastery at Klosterneuburg, where St Leopold's day (Leopoldstag) was celebrated annually on 14 November in the presence of the emperor; a special feature was the use of Emperor Leopold I's setting of the Vespers. The various services held in the

Stiftskirche (the monastery church) and the Leopoldskapelle (the St Leopold chapel) stretched over two days. It was presumably partly in connection with this annual stay at Klosterneuburg that the emperor formed the plan of establishing a residence next to the monastery, modelled on the Escorial; the unfinished building can still be seen at Klosterneuburg today.[19]

The variety of locations both within and outside Vienna, whether used by the court or only occasionally, meant that the court musicians had to be extremely adaptable. The size, layout and acoustics of the rooms, the arrangements for positioning of the musicians, the organs available – all these were factors subject to considerable variation from one place to another (the arrangements also meant that the court's sacred musical repertory was brought into the public domain, through outdoor processional performances as well as within the churches). Responsibility for the direction of the imperial Hofkapelle was among the most demanding and prestigious of such posts in Europe: those who occupied the positions of Hofkapellmeister and vice-Hofkapellmeister were by dint of their positions automatically distinguished, so that Fux's words in reply to Johann Mattheson's request for biographical details contain (as well as an acknowledged element of pique)[20] a sense of this distinction: 'Suffice it to say that I was considered worthy to be first Kapellmeister to Charles VI'.

The 'accumulation of layers' seen in the liturgy, and in the architectural aspects of the buildings used for worship, was matched musically in a significant and special way. An important point emerging from a study of the church music repertory is that – unlike, for example, the norm in the production of opera – a strong core of older compositions was retained in the church repertory alongside newer works. Composers represented in early eighteenth-century Viennese sources range from Palestrina to Caldara. And, of course, much of the music was expected to be re-used often: some of the extant sources show signs of this frequent use. This situation meant that new music could be directly modelled on older styles, as well as influenced by more modern elements, for example from contemporary Italian opera. The leading court composers, among them Fux and Caldara, contributed prolifically to both opera and church music. Style-consciousness was strongly felt, as Fux's *Gradus ad Parnassum* (1725) shows.[21] It is mistaken to assume (as a superficial knowledge of Fux's *Gradus* might suggest) that the 'Palestrina style' – in a fossilized state, moreover – predominated in Viennese church music. In practice this was merely one of a variety of styles, old and new, including monophonic chant[22] and 'a capella' counterpoint (the latter unaccompanied or austerely accompanied) – these more restrained styles were used especially during Lent and Advent – as well as more modern 'concertante' writing featuring solo voices and obbligato instrumental parts.

Among the forces used, the instruments included strings, cornetts, trombones, bassoons, organ and theorbo; the choir varied from four-part, five-part and six-part to festive (eight-part) double-choir settings. Castratos were heard as soprano and alto soloists, and boy choristers sang in the 'ripieno' choir. Instrumental music had an established place in the services: for example 'Gradual sonatas' for instrumental ensemble were substituted for vocal settings of the Gradual, and 'Intradas' with trumpets and timpani were added on grand occasions such as the *Toisonfeste*. The sound of the trumpets was a recurring motif (its significance will be discussed further): Riedel referred to the genre of the 'trumpet mass' (*Trompeten-Messen*), of which Fux's *Missa brevis* K5, is an accessible example.[23] Thus the total impression of the repertory over the church year is that it offered a vivid aural experience made up of a wide range of different kinds of sound. One interesting detail that surfaces in Riedel's study is that 'authorial unity' was, in Viennese church music as in other areas at that time, not an important consideration; so, for example, masses might be put together for performance from a variety of movements by different composers. In addition, the variety of composers heard within a service afforded an absorbing stylistic experience for connoisseurs among the listeners. Another point that has been established by scholars in relation to the Catholic Baroque repertory in general is that instrumental pieces could be, and were frequently, used for liturgical purposes even when not actually designated as such. Here, too, there is a certain amount of secular-liturgical overlap: there is evidence, for example, that instrumental music originating in operas was adapted 'for use in liturgical and para-liturgical contexts'.[24] All these elements gave the repertory a breadth and eclecticism that its close correlation to its liturgical context, and to a fixed set of genres (such as Mass Ordinary and Proper, psalm settings, *Te Deum*, hymns and litanies), might not immediately suggest. Above all, the complex and varied content of the Viennese church calendar guaranteed composers and performers enormous scope for the cultivation of music in a church context.

OPERA

Drama in music for the most glorious name[day] of Charles VI . . . by command of Her Sacred Imperial and Royal Catholic Majesty Elisabeth Christine, reigning empress . . . 1732. The poetry is by Abbé Pietro Metastasio, imperial poet, the music by Antonio Caldara, vice-Kapellmeister of the imperial chapel . . .[25]

The emperor's 'most glorious' name-day fell on 4 November. This was one of the key dates in the court calendar; apart from the customary religious observances, it would have been quite unthinkable to let it go by without a musico-dramatic performance (which, as the quotation shows, would typically be ordered for the occasion by his spouse). The tradition was established in the seventeenth century, and the imperial family were conditioned to expect such tributes (Joseph I, as heir to the throne, was from the age of three regularly serenaded on his birthday by the Hofkapelle, usually with unstaged vocal chamber compositions).[26] Such days were classed as 'Gala-Tage': on these (birthdays and name-days, betrothals and marriages) the entire court appeared in gala clothing ('Galakleidung'), and during the festive meal *Tafelmusik* would be performed.[27]

Obviously, the concept of 'occasional music', in the sense of music for a specific occasion but not necessarily of ephemeral quality, was central to these proceedings. No secular vocal work of any significance – opera (generally in three-act, sometimes in five- or one-act form) or serenata (unstaged, equivalent to a large-scale cantata) – would be put together unless intended for a particular event or season of the year. Some repeat performances took place, but the repertory more usually consisted of newly composed works. The requirement to produce a regular flow of such works (including Carnival operas for the pre-Lenten season) placed the court musicians under considerable pressure, especially as the imperial recipients were discerning listeners. Four of the principal 'Gala-Tage' in Charles VI's reign fell within a three-month period of the year: the emperor's birthday on 1 October, and his name-day on 4 November (St Charles Borromeus); and Empress Elisabeth Christine's birthday and name-day on 28 August and 19 November (St Elizabeth of Hungary) respectively. The court composers responded prolifically to these demands: Caldara alone, in two decades of service, 'contributed some forty works for these secular festivities' (the majority being operas).[28] Court poets, architects and choreographers contributed to the productions, so that the combined talents of the court artists were magnificently displayed, to the glory of the imperial ruler.

Another central concept is that of a court dynastic style (*Reichsstil*, or *Kaiserstil*) as manifested in the arts. Architectural historians have defined such a style, as seen in the early eighteenth century, with reference to the work of Johann Bernhard Fischer von Erlach (designer of the Karlskirche). It is possible similarly to define a *Reichsstil* in Viennese music. A further reflection of the Habsburgs' political power was afforded by the texts of the court operas, which were customarily constructed in order to portray flatteringly both the qualities supposed to reside in the imperial personage and, in an

51. Auditorium of the Hoftheater, Vienna, designed by Francesco Galli-Bibiena: engraving (1704) by J. A. Pfeffel and C. Engelbrecht

idealized form, the ethos of the court. Indeed, the way in which court life was designed and conducted – the progress through the year (with different seasons spent in varying settings), decorative surroundings and costumes, processions, hunts and a series of ceremonial events – almost seems itself to create the effect of a stage work writ large, with the court personnel enacting the scenes; the theatrical qualities of their own lives perhaps helped them to identify with the characters in the operas they witnessed.

It is pertinent to consider how some of the circumstances mentioned may have been reflected in court opera, and how the music may transcend them. The need to provide large numbers of works was obviously helped by the existence of a standard recipe. Vienna was an important centre of Italian opera, in its typical late Baroque form of *opera seria* as well as in the lighter comic genres. The Habsburg court employed Italians as theatre architects (including the highly influential Galli-Bibiena family, among whom the brothers Ferdinando and Francesco Galli-Bibiena, and Ferdinando's sons Giuseppe, Alessandro and Antonio, were all active in Vienna); as librettists (Apostolo Zeno, Pietro Metastasio, Pietro Pariati); and as composers (Marc'Antonio Ziani, Caldara, Francesco Conti; Fux, born and educated in Lower Austria, was a special exception). In some cases, artistic collaboration had existed earlier in Italy, for example between Caldara and the Galli-Bibiena family; and some of the Italians had established a connection with the Habsburgs during Charles VI's earlier period in Spain (as 'Charles III').[29]

It is to the Vienna court poets Zeno (at court 1718–29) and his successor Metastasio (at court 1730–82) that the late Baroque 're-form' of opera librettos is generally attributed, characterized by the paring down of plot and characters to more dignified effect, and the schematic alternation of recitative with 'exit' arias to form a series of short scenes within the acts, the arias being the centre of the emotional interest. The recipe worked extremely well in its context. While Metastasio's librettos in particular were widely set throughout Europe, and throughout the eighteenth century, it is interesting to realize that composers based in Vienna were among his original collaborators (although direct consultation is not thought to have taken place: the librettos were probably finished and delivered, and the composers then set them to music). It has been noted that Caldara was responsible for the original settings of 'all but two of the twenty-five full-length opera seria librettos written for the Habsburg court by the Imperial poets, Apostolo Zeno and Pietro Metastasio, during the twenty-year period between . . . 1716 and . . . 1736'.[30] Included in the Vienna court opera recipe were end-of-act ballets and, to conclude the whole work, a *licenza*, a specially constructed final scene in praise of the ruler. Typically, parallels would be drawn in the *licenza* between the heroic characters of the opera and the ruler in whose honour the work was performed; or the ruler would be addressed directly, as befitted the occasion (for example, at the end of Fux's Dido opera *Elisa* of 1719, to a libretto by Pariati, Elisa addresses the empress on her birthday).

Although the chorus tended to be given a relatively restricted role, choral sections were doubly important, in carrying the 'message' (greeting and praising the ruler) and in serving as a recurrent musi-cal element (both Fux and Caldara used the chorus structurally in this way). So in Caldara's *Adriano in Siria* the opening chorus, which recurs throughout the first scene, repeats the doubly appropriate greeting 'vivi all'Impero' (without an emperor in the audience it would be impossible to recreate fully the impact of such scenes). The plot of *Adriano in Siria* (based somewhat tenuously on the exploits of the Emperor Hadrian) typically sets up large emotional and political conflicts to test its central character, finally resolving them in such a

way as to show the emperor's capacity for magnanimity – the generosity of the conqueror towards the conquered, and of the victor in love
towards his rival. The action revolves round a classic set of six main
characters, with two emotionally intertwined couples, a vengeful
father and a confidant to the emperor (in the valedictory *licenza* the
parallel is neatly drawn between the Ancient Roman emperors and
the then current ruler of the Holy Roman Empire).

Apart from its textual messages, such an opera can be seen as
conveying political meanings in its musical fabric. The recurring
character types in festive operas were associated with particular
singers: among them were the famed 'veteran Gaetano Orsini, an
alto castrato who had been appointed to the court in 1699', and who
took the title role in *Adriano*[31] (again, many of the singers were
Italians, though in *Adriano* one of the leading female roles was taken
by Theresa Holzhauser, wife of the court composer Georg Reutter
the younger). The arias written for these singers were often extremely
virtuoso, characterized by a wide vocal range and extensive florid
passages (in performance, the da capo form that Caldara overwhelmingly favoured for arias would have given the singers further opportunities for ornamental decoration in the repeat). Thus the arias
served to display, gratifyingly, the much-vaunted excellence of the
court singers, at the same time expressing (often very vividly, within
the conventions of the period) the character's emotional state. The
presence of these celebrated singers, earning high salaries at court,
enhanced the court's image, as well as giving pleasure to the listeners. Among the nobility in the audience there were customarily
distinguished visitors to the court: Caldara's *Adriano in Siria* was
performed in November 1732 'in the large theatre of the court' in the
presence of the Tunisian ambassador, while Fux's *Enea negli Elisi* was
performed in the gardens of the Favorita in August 1731 in the
presence of the Turkish ambassador, 'who not only enjoyed the
music but was also pleased by the courteous attention which he
received'.[32]

Instrumental writing too was designed to display the skills of
particular performers. Its brilliance suggests both the high standard
expected by the Kapellmeister and the levels of expertise available to
him: this was a virtuoso orchestra. The general impression is of a
desire for orchestral discipline founded on a uniform style of performance. This well-drilled professionalism helped display the qualities of
the court orchestra and its directors and reflect the grandeur of the
court, as well as perhaps serving to emulate or outdo the acknowledged excellence of other groups under court patronage, such as the
famous French bands (just as the Schönbrunn palace designed by
Fischer von Erlach was intended 'not only to emulate but to surpass
the grandeur of Versailles'). Thus a characteristic of Viennese

Baroque operas is their attention to instrumental colour and detail. In the overtures and ballets there were, obviously, opportunities for purely instrumental effects (Caldara's overture to *Adriano in Siria* includes showy solo passages for violin, trumpets and cello accompanied by solo double bass). But the arias too afforded opportunities for instrumental solo and ensemble effects; and these were exploited both in the introductory and intervening ritornellos and in the accompaniments to the vocal sections: again, the writing reflects both the technical capabilities of the performers and the expressive possibilities of the texts. Choral and ballet scenes were enhanced by appropriate instrumentation, such as hunting-horns (in Fux's *Elisa*) and martial trumpets. Arias were enlivened by virtuoso parts for unusual solo instruments, such as a pair of bassoons (in Fux's *Julo Ascanio, re d'Alba*). As with the church music, the cumulative aural experience of this repertory was a rich one.

Two features typical of Baroque opera generally are specially notable in the Vienna court operas. One is the ploy of using solo voices and instruments in virtuoso competition; the other, related to it, is the 'planting' of references in the text to evoke a particular instrumentation. The Viennese speciality seems to have been the 'trumpet aria'. It has been remarked that 'Caldara's most demanding trumpet parts are to be found in those arias that pit one trumpeter against a *prima donna* or *primo uomo*'.[33] Similar instances are found in Fux's operas: an aria for Bacchus (in *La corona d'Arianna*, 1726) has solo trumpet and voice trilling in a series of parallel 10ths, while in *Costanza e Fortezza* (1723) Porsenna's Act 1 aria 'Tosca armata tromba' again refers to, and evokes, the sound of battle. The Vienna operas (and indeed the oratorios) contain a compendium of brilliant trumpet writing which was linked to the prestige of the court. It was in the use of 'choirs' of trumpets and timpani that the trumpet motif took on a more specific symbolic meaning in relation to the Habsburg court. 'Constantia et Fortitudine' was the imperial motto (worked into Fux's opera of 1723; its allegorical ballets featured dancers personifying Costanza and Fortezza). The coinage struck in 1712 to honour the new emperor (Charles VI) showed the two pillars of Hercules, bearing the words 'Constantia' and 'Fortitudo'. As Brown has pointed out,[34] the association of the emperor's motto with the Herculean rocks or pillars found its most famous visual representation in the two columns of Fischer von Erlach's Karlskirche. Brown goes on to suggest that the antiphonal choirs of trumpets and timpani in the overture to Fux's *Costanza e Fortezza* are, correspondingly, the most direct musical parallel.

> Less obvious, but no less significant is the reservation, almost without exception, of the double-trumpet-choir scoring for the

52. 'Costanza e Fortezza' by J. J. Fux, performed in an open-air amphitheatre at Prague Castle, 28 August 1723, for the coronation of Emperor Charles VI and his wife as King and Queen of Bohemia. The set, designed by Giuseppe Galli-Bibiena, shows Horatius's defence of the bridge over the River Tiber; Caldara conducted the unusually large forces which included 200 instrumentalists and 100 singers

operas celebrating the Emperor's nameday – arguably the most important of all *Gala-Tage* . . . Caldara's double-choir *introduzioni* reinforced the twin aspects of the Imperial motto. Even the uninitiated must have perceived something of the splendour, majesty and might of the Habsburg empire embodied in the sheer sound of these compositions.

The Viennese cultivation of counterpoint is another 'imperial' feature of court operas. Contrapuntal writing evidently came easily to these composers. Their string writing, for example, generally shows a capacity for creating interesting, independent textural strands within a strongly directed harmonic structure; and at times the counterpoint becomes more overt, as in the aria 'Saggio guerriero antico' (*Adriano*, Act 2) which Caldara appositely constructed as a fugue. This was a homage to the emperor's tastes; learned counterpoint had traditionally been among the intellectual interests of the Viennese emperors, long before Fux's *Gradus* and its counterpart, his 'Missa canonica', were dedicated to Charles VI. Tarquinio's aria 'Con il Regno pria si plachi' (*Costanza e Fortezza*, Act 2) is set up as a double fugue in relaxed, Handelian manner. Indeed, the adjective 'Handelian' presents itself as appropriate for much of the music emanating from early eighteenth-century Vienna, perhaps partly because this music shares with Handel's a mature command of the Italian sonata-concerto style, made up of sequential phrases, 'walking' basses, echo effects, lively melodic figures and motoric rhythms.[35] It is potentially an exciting, energetic style: coupled with the imaginative use of orchestral colour (and especially the thrilling sound of the trumpet in its high registers) it helped to create the effect of a *Reichsstil*.

It was in the famous outdoor performances of opera that this style made its most vivid impact. Johann Joachim Quantz's observations a propos his participation in the sumptuous performance of *Costanza e Fortezza* at Prague in 1723 in a specially built open-air theatre (libretto by Pariati, for the coronation of the Habsburg emperor and empress as King and Queen of Bohemia, and coinciding with the empress's birthday) are pertinent:

> The concertante effects and interweaving of the violins with one another, which occurred in the ritornellos, although it consisted for the most part of passages which on paper may here and there have looked quite stiff and dry, nevertheless had, in the open air and with such lavish resources, a very good effect, indeed perhaps better than a more 'galant' [style of] melody ornamented with many decorative figures and quick notes would have had in such circumstances . . .[36]

The correlation of the musical forces and compositional style with

ISOLE orride, e disabitate ocupate da diversi Mostri per incanto di ALCINA.

53. *Naval battle during the open-air performance of Fux's opera 'Angelica vincitrice d'Alcina', 14 September 1716, in the gardens of the Favorita, in celebration of the birth of Prince Leopold: design by Giuseppe and Ferdinando Galli-Bibiena*

the acoustic, size and layout of the place of performance formed an important consideration in eighteenth-century performance practice in general.

It was an open-air performance of Fux's 'magic' opera *Angelica vincitrice d'Alcina* (1716, for the birth of Prince Leopold), in the naturally scenic gardens of the Favorita palace, that evoked Lady Mary Wortley Montagu's oft-quoted description:

> Nothing of that kind ever was more magnificent; and I can easily believe, what I was told, that the decorations and habits cost the emperor thirty thousand pound sterling. The stage was built over a very large canal, and, at the beginning of the second act, divided into two parts, discovering the water, on which there immediately came from different parts two fleets of little gilded vessels, that gave the representation of a naval fight . . . The story of the opera was the enchantment of Alcina, which gives opportunities for great variety of machines and changes of the scenes, which are performed with a surprising swiftness . . . No house could hold such large decorations; but the ladies all sitting in the open air, exposes them to great inconveniences; for there is but one canopy for the imperial family; and, the first night it was represented, a heavy shower of rain happening, the opera was broke off, and the company crowded away in such confusion, that I was almost squeezed to death.[37]

An antidote to the heroic court opera was provided by the comic intermezzos performed as entr'actes (the most famous example, Pergolesi's *La serva padrona*, was originally composed for the birthday celebrations of Elisabeth Christine in Naples, 1733). Italian intermezzos developing the *buffo* style were introduced into court opera at Carnival 1713 with *L'ammalato immaginario* by Francesco Conti (1681–1732): Conti remained important in the production of intermezzos throughout the early eighteenth century. In addition, popular parodistic comedies that mocked the conventions of heroic court opera were performed in the Kärntnertortheater (built *c*1709); this bourgeois theatre was controlled by a court licence forbidding the performance of opera as such, but allowing 'Comoedien mit einigen untermischt gesungenen intermedien'. The terms of the licence were freely exploited through the practice whereby local composers reworked operas for the general public (including operas by non-Viennese composers, such as Keiser and Handel); thus it was that Handel's *Giulio Cesare* and *Tamerlano* were introduced to the Viennese public in 1731–2.

ORATORIO AND CANTATA

While opera was the dominant, and clearly the most expensive, genre, Vienna's importance as a centre of Italian oratorio should also be mentioned. Again, traditions had been laid down in the seventeenth century. From Good Friday 1660 (with the performance of Emperor Leopold I's *Il sagrifizio d'Abramo*) oratorios were regularly performed in Vienna: it has been described as 'the most important centre of sacred dramatic music in the Italian language outside Italy'.[38] Italian oratorio was cultivated in Vienna mainly, though not exclusively, by Italian librettists and composers. The court poets were involved: thus Pariati (employed at court 1714–33) provided texts for seven of Fux's oratorios, including *La fede sacrilega nella morte del Precursor S Giovanni Battista*. Zeno and Metastasio were active in promoting 'reform' librettos for oratorios as well as for operas; they established a preference for biblical subjects (Old Testament stories were favoured, and Passion texts had a special place in the repertory). The introduction of divine personages was avoided, and the action adhered to the classical dramatic unities. The series of oratorio texts on this model produced by Metastasio from 1730 were first set by Viennese court composers – Caldara, Georg Reutter the younger (1708–72), Giuseppe Porsile (1680–1750), and Luca Antonio Predieri (1688–1767). All Zeno's oratorios received their first performances in Vienna; Caldara set 11 out of the total of 17 (others were set by Conti, Porsile and G. M. Bononcini). The musical ingredients were similar to those of Italian opera (but forming two sections rather than three acts). The skilled counterpoint, expressive harmonies and instrumental colour that lent magnificence to the court operas similarly gave an impressive dignity and vividness to the oratorios. Unusual accompanimental colouring included the chalumeau, trombone and bassoon, used in various arias of Caldara's *Joaz* (1726). It is also possible that political meanings were derived from these oratorios, just as with the operas; in the final chorus of *Joaz* the Levites greet the newly crowned king and declare that he will reign with God, a sentiment obviously apposite to the court of the Holy Roman Emperor.

With the genre of the *sepolcro*, a special (though not original) Viennese idea had been developed in the seventeenth century and was continued in the early eighteenth century. *Sepolcri* – settings of Passion texts – such as Caldara's *Cristo condannato* of 1717, subtitled 'Oratorio per il SSmo Sepolcro', were enacted at the holy sepulchre set up in the Hofburgkapelle.[39] These performances traditionally took place on Gründonnerstag (Maundy Thursday) and Karfreitag (Good Friday). The requirement to provide oratorios for particular occasions created another source of pressure for the musicians of the Hofkapelle: Pritchard has observed,[40] and the sources give evidence, that 'occasionally an oratorio was finished only within days of the performance'. The performers were those who sang in the court operas too: Francesco Borosini, for example, who performed in *Cristo condannato* in 1717 and in *Joaz* in 1726, was also involved in the Prague performance of Fux's *Costanza e Fortezza* in 1723, in which connection Quantz recalled him as 'a lively tenor, as well as a skilled actor'.[41]

The importance of Vienna for the cultivation of vocal chamber music had also been established much earlier in the seventeenth century, and with the accession of Joseph I it seems to have received fresh impetus. The rise of the Italian secular cantata in Vienna in the early years of the eighteenth century has been traced (as background to Caldara) in terms of a 'vigorous upsurge of cantata writing',[42] in which the inevitably italianate stylistic bias was modified by Viennese characteristics, notably, again, a penchant for colourful instrumentation (in response to the players available). A kind of intimacy that was perhaps possible only in the small-scale secular cantata for court performance (rather than in the grand, fully staged opera) is illustrated by Caldara's *Giuoco del quadriglio* of 1734,[43] which features four card-playing female characters. Two of the four soprano parts were designed for the emperor's daughters, the Archduchesses Maria Theresa (as Clarice) and Maria Anna (as Livia), and their real characters were perhaps intended to be reflected in the different styles of music: Clarice's aria is written in a stately manner with elaborate coloratura, for Maria Theresa; and Livia's aria adopts a more 'galant' manner, in a lively, triple dance-metre, for her younger sister.

In producing large numbers of works for specific occasions, to honour court personages and to suit particular performers, composers such as Fux and Caldara brilliantly exploited, and transcended, the needs of the occasion. The very existence of the set conventions governing the various musical genres of the late Baroque period makes it all the more possible to appreciate the extent of individual thinking, as in Caldara's formal inventiveness, or in his penchant for imparting motivic unity to sections within a work. Within the conventional formulae of late Baroque recitative, Caldara's personal hallmark is a gift for creating tense, fast-paced sections of dialogue. The modernity discernible in this, and in other facets of Viennese Baroque music (some of the overtures, for example, come close to the style of the later symphony), is revealing in relation to imperial patronage; while paying plentiful homage to Baroque convention and imperial symbolism, the court composers in Vienna were able to experiment with their own ideas and with the newer 'galant' styles, in a musical environment ideally 'full of accomplishment and potential'. In this environment they felt free during the 1730s to write in a way that pushed the music 'from a high-Baroque into a mid-century idiom'.[44]

PERFORMERS AND COMPOSERS

> Hee being invited went over into Germany and hath ever since bin
> there and now resides at Vienna, in full payment for all the masters
> wee have received out of those countrys.[45]

The eighteenth century was characterized generally by international
movements of musicians, so that, for example, a German-born composer trained in Italy might subsequently make his career in London.
In early eighteenth-century Vienna this trend helped to enrich the
musical establishment at the court. The period 1705–40 was a golden
age for the Vienna Hofkapelle; and (as the quotation above suggests)
musicians were recruited not only from local resources but from a
variety of European centres. Italy was not the only source, though it
was an important one. Connections with England (through Handel)
have already been mentioned. Nicola Matteis the younger (*d* 1760;
his father did much to introduce the Italian violin style to England)
left London for Vienna around 1700 to begin his career at court as a
violinist (later he was involved in composing ballets for the court
operas). In 1701 the court protocols recorded that 'The English
fiddler Nicola Matteis asks to fetch his children out of England and
to bring them here, so that they can come out of that unCatholic
land', for which application he received a grant towards his travel
expenses. Several performers and composers worked in England as
well as in Vienna (such as Borosini and Bononcini); and the
Habsburgs were allied politically with England during the early
eighteenth century.

The connection with Italy was thoroughly well established.
Generations of Habsburg rulers had been served by Italian musicians at court; there was also a tradition of giving study leave and
financial assistance to non-Italians at court to enable them to train in
Italy. Court agents acted on the Habsburgs' behalf in Italy, looking
for suitable musicians to import. In the early eighteenth century the
conditions and rewards of service at the Habsburg court evidently
attracted many excellent Italians to Vienna. Pier Francesco Tosi
(*c*1653–1732), the famed castrato, singing-master and later the
author of the *Opinioni de' cantori antichi e moderni*, a treatise on singing,
came to Vienna via London (where he had been involved in concerts
and teaching) to serve as court composer to Emperor Joseph I from
1705 to 1711. The Italian style was not absorbed second-hand: it
came to Vienna direct from its source. Musicians brought with them
their composing and performing expertise, acquired through experience in various Italian cultural centres. Francesco Conti (1681–1732)
came in 1701 as a brilliant theorbo player from Florence (inspiring

some remarkable solos for theorbo in Viennese court compositions). Both Antonio Caldara and his predecessor in Vienna, Marc'Antonio Ziani (*c*1653–1715), had previously served as *maestro di cappella* to the Duke of Mantua (it has been suggested that this position acted as 'the stepping-stone to the Emperor's court').[46] Earlier, Caldara had been engaged at St Mark's, Venice; and towards the end of his Italian period (1709–16) he became *maestro di cappella* to Prince Ruspoli in Rome.[47] By this time Caldara had already won the future emperor's approval with the wedding composition for Barcelona (1708), and eventually he found the opportunity to take up a formal appointment at the Viennese court, in 1716. His starting salary was 1600 florins (less than that of a leading singer such as Orsini, who was at court from 1711 on a salary of 1800 florins; Fux as Kapellmeister from 1715 earned 3100 florins).[48] It seems that Caldara brought his Italian compositions with him to Vienna; little of his music survives in Italian libraries, but a number of his autograph scores of Italian provenance are extant in Viennese collections.[49] From Vienna his fame (and music) spread widely.

A very different career pattern is illustrated by the case of Gottlieb Muffat (1690–1770). His father, Georg, travelled and worked in different areas of Europe, bringing Italian and French styles, under Corelli's and Lully's influences, to German-speaking regions: in 1690 Georg was at the coronation of Joseph I in Augsburg, and presented to the Emperor Leopold a collection of keyboard compositions, the *Apparatus musico-organisticus*. But Georg was never rewarded with an official appointment at Vienna; if this was his ambition, it was to be realized in the career of his son, Gottlieb. Gottlieb Muffat's musical training, and subsequent activity as composer, organist and keyboard teacher, were intensively centred on the Viennese court. He entered the Hofkapelle as a pupil (*Hofscholar*) in 1711, and moved up to the ranks of the *Hoforganisten* in 1717. Promotion to second organist came in 1729 (and to first organist, following the accession of Maria Theresa, in 1741). Muffat remained in court service until his retirement on a pension in 1763. His works reflect his court duties. He published a set of organ versets (intended as sample pieces, for liturgical use and for practice – much of the organ music used in church services would have been improvised on this kind of model, or assembled for the occasion from various sources) and a collection of keyboard suites, the *Componimenti musicali*, intended as entertainment and for keyboard-teaching purposes. There are signs of a forward-looking approach in his suites (which combine French and Italian influences), and in some respects he helped to bring the Viennese keyboard suite to the point where it was ready to be absorbed into the new sonata forms.[50]

Although early eighteenth-century Vienna produced no keyboard music equal in international renown and posthumous influence to that of Johann Jacob Froberger (*d* 1667), the most illustrious Viennese keyboard composer of the seventeenth century, there were several evidently highly skilled keyboard performers and composers working in a tradition handed down from Froberger and ultimately from Girolamo Frescobaldi. As in the church repertory, diverse chronological and stylistic layers can be seen in the surviving local collections of keyboard music from the time, which show considerable breadth. Copies of music from outside Vienna include ricercares by Luigi Battiferri and Giovanni Battista Fontana, works of Frescobaldi and Michelangelo Rossi, Handel's suites and fugues, and works by Johann Kuhnau and J. C. F. Fischer. In the works of Viennese keyboard composers themselves a full range of genres is represented, including strict contrapuntal pieces, toccatas and preludes, liturgical versets, organ masses, suites and variations, all displaying an electic choice of forms and titles.

Table XI.2 LEADING COURT MUSICIANS 1705–40

Emperor	*Hofkapellmeister*	*Vizehofkapellmeister*	*Others*
Joseph I (1705–11)	Antonio Pancotti (1700–09)	Marc'Antonio Ziani (1700–11)	Kilian Reinhardt (*Konzertmeister* to 1729)
Charles VI (1711–40)	Ziani (1712–15)	Johann Joseph Fux (1711–15) previously *Hofkompositor*	Francesco Conti (*Hofkompositor* 1713–32)
	Fux (1715–40)	Antonio Caldara (1716–36)	Gottlieb Muffat (*Hoforganist* 1717–63)

General features of court employment include the long service already mentioned (exemplified by Muffat) and the linked opportunities for promotion, whereby for example Fux, who had entered court service as court composer in 1698 (from a post at the Schottenkirche, which acted as another possible stepping-stone to an appointment at the Hofkapelle), was promoted in 1711 to vice-Kapellmeister under Ziani, and on Ziani's death in 1715 to Kapellmeister. Several posts tended to be held concurrently: the post of Kapellmeister at the Stephansdom was usually held in conjunction with a court appointment (Fux served as assistant, then as chief Kapellmeister at the Stephansdom from 1705 to 1715), as was a subsidiary duty at the Kapelle of Joseph I's widow, Wilhelmine Amalia, who employed Fux as her Kapellmeister from 1713 to 1718. Gottlieb Muffat later worked as her organist (it was usual for members of the imperial household to keep up their own private chapels).

Teaching might include members of the imperial family; among Muffat's pupils were the two archduchesses, Maria Theresa and Maria Anna. Several members of musical families might find employment at the Hofkapelle over a period of time: various Muffats and Reinhardts appear in the court records for the period 1705–40. French and Slavic, as well as Italian and German, names appear in the lists of court musicians: these might represent local families of foreign extraction, or newly imported talent.

A regular part of the activities of the Hofkapelle was the opportunity to travel with the court on official journeys to parts of the empire, thus helping to transmit the Viennese musical repertory and its influence to outlying regions.[51] The usual religious and secular court feasts (saints' days, birthdays) were celebrated en route with music. So the emperor's entry into Graz on 23 June 1728 (somewhat hampered by heavy rain) was marked by a performance of the *Te Deum* at the Jesuit church of St Aegidius (now the cathedral), with music provided by the Hofkapelle, including the imperial trumpeters and timpanists, and with the customary festive salutes. During the court's extended stay in Graz, the Hofkapelle performed in church music (vocal and instrumental), *Tafelmusik* to accompany ceremonial meals, and – for the empress's birthday, celebrated early, on 10 August – an open-air production of a festive opera, designed by Giuseppe Galli-Bibiena, with a libretto by the court poet Giovanni Claudio Pasquini (1695–1763) and music by Caldara in collaboration with his pupil Georg Reutter the younger. The work was an Iphigenia opera, *La forza dell'amicizia, ovvero Pilade ed Oreste*. The soloists were the leading court singers, among them Theresa Holzhauser (soprano), Orsini (alto), Borosini (tenor) and Praun (bass). A repeat performance was held indoors (because of the strong winds), in the university theatre. On specially grand occasions away from Vienna, such as the Prague coronation performance of *Costanza e Fortezza*, the large numbers of the Hofkapelle who travelled in several convoys were reinforced 'on location' by musicians who were either from the area or had travelled from elsewhere (like Quantz and his companions) to be able to take part.

In spite of the inevitable military drain on resources (in 1716, the year Lady Mary Wortley Montagu attended the production of *Angelica*, it was Prince Eugene's 'constant complaint in the first six months [of that year] that the army could not move for lack of essential funds'),[52] a large and active musical establishment was maintained at the Viennese court in this period (it was left to Maria Theresa to face the necessity of reducing the strength of the Hofkapelle). During the period 1705–40 the size of the court orchestra increased, so that, for example, while the string section had approximately doubled from 15 to 29 members between 1690 (around the mid-point of Giovanni Battista Draghi's tenure as Kapellmeister) and 1705, by 1728 (midway through Fux's tenure as Kapellmeister) the strings numbered 41. Another remarkable rise is seen in the number of trumpets, which with the timpani constituted various special, and partly interrelated, groups, the most prestigious evidently being the *Musikalische Trompeter und Hör-Paucker*:

> It has been a correctly accepted truism that the Imperial trumpeters obtained a prestige and a degree of self-governance that would not have been tolerated for any other group of employees at the European courts . . . In the first forty years of the eighteenth century, a school of clarino [high trumpet] playing that was unrivalled by any equivalent in Italy, North-Central Germany, or England, established itself in Vienna.[53]

Other groups included the six trumpeters and one timpanist who, appropriately costumed, belonged to the emperor's bodyguard, the *Kaiserliche Leib-Garde*.[54] The numbers of trumpets in the *Musikalische Trompeter und Hör-Paucker* had increased from five in 1705 to 15 by 1712, and were thereafter kept up at about this level throughout the period, before the drastic reductions imposed in Maria Theresa's reign.

Once more a note of caution must be sounded in attempting to interpret the available statistics. Court records were not necessarily kept consistently, and were affected by administrative peculiarities. Not all orchestral players, or choral singers, were necessarily used at once: recent research in performing practice has established that a rota system was the norm. Doublings were common (performers playing more than one instrument), so that the absence of a particular instrument in the lists does not necessarily indicate that it was not part of the orchestra. Performers were listed, and paid, after they had ceased to be active; but, on the other hand, aging castratos were still singing late in their careers, so that no assumptions can be made. But the general impression is certainly that of a flourishing musical establishment, making Vienna a centre of excellence to which musicians gravitated.

*

Emperor Charles VI, in wanting 'the ecclesiastical dignity of Vienna to be worthy of the sacred and secular dignity of the Emperor who held his court there . . . strove also, resplendently, to make the architectural setting of this court fit for an emperor'.[55] This statement could be applied equally to the music of the court. The Habsburgs had created an intellectual climate in which music and the fine arts were expected to be encouraged, and to thrive. This cultured outlook, together with the pedagogic legacy of Fux, provided a basis for the later emergence of Vienna as the centre of the Classical style. When Joseph Haydn came to Vienna as a choirboy around 1740 (followed some five years later by his brother Michael), the Kapellmeister of the Stephansdom was Georg Reutter the younger, providing a direct link with the court tradition; the works of Fux and Caldara were still being performed in Vienna; and the textbook from which Haydn (and Mozart, and later Beethoven) studied and taught counterpoint[56] was the *Gradus ad Parnassum* of Charles VI's Kapellmeister, Fux.[57]

NOTES

[1] 'Quodlibet of Vienna' (*c*1730, published 1751).

[2] R. Flotzinger and G. Gruber, eds. *Musikgeschichte Österreichs*, i: *Von den Anfängen zum Barock* (Graz, 1977), 324.

[3] The reign of Charles VI (1711–40) also inevitably dominates in relation to the short, less fully documented reign of his elder brother Joseph (1705–11); see Table XI.1.

[4] G. Adler, 'Die Kaiser Ferdinand III., Leopold I., Joseph I. und Karl VI. als Tonsetzer und Förderer der Musik', *VMw*, viii (1892), 252–74.

[5] F. Riedel, *Kirchenmusik am Hofe Karls VI. (1711–1740): Untersuchungen zum Verhältnis von Zeremoniell und musikalischem Stil im Barockzeitalter* (Munich and Salzburg, 1977), 13.

[6] *Rubriche generali per le funzione ecclesiastiche musicali di tutto l'anno . . . ad uso, e servizio dell'Agust[issi]ma Austriaca, ed imp[eria]le capella* (MS, *A-Wn*). Reinhardt (who was music librarian and copyist at the court from 1683) had successfully petitioned Emperor Leopold I for a title which would discourage the musicians from regarding him merely as a servant; he was thenceforth known as 'Konzertmeister'; For more details (and on several other musical members of the Reinhardt family) see *Grove 6*.

[7] Reinhardt, *Rubriche generali*.

[8] A. P. Brown, 'Caldara's Trumpet Music for the Imperial Celebrations of Charles VI and Elisabeth Christine', *Antonio Caldara: Essays on his Life and Times*, ed. B. Pritchard (Aldershot, 1987), 3. Brown's statement remains true of Vienna even taking into consideration that Charles was involved in renewed war with the Turks (1716–18, culminating in the signing of a trade treaty) and in sustained efforts to obtain guarantees of the Pragmatic Sanction ensuring the Habsburg succession through Maria Theresa. Nevertheless, during this period his energies were also directed to establishing Vienna as a centre of High Baroque Catholic culture.

[9] Riedel, *Kirchenmusik*, 68.

[10] Strict protocol governed the type of music suitable; Riedel provides much detail on this, particularly in the calendars appended to his main text, where specific days and services throughout the year are linked with the music known to have been used.

[11] Also designated the Hofkirche zu St Augustin, adjoining the Hofburg.

[12] The cathedral (where Haydn was later a choirboy); the way can still easily be traced through the streets of Vienna today.

[13] Reinhardt, *Rubriche generali*. To celebrate the ending of the plague, on 13 March 1714 the emperor 'in gratitude for the cessation of the plague' again went 'in Procession from the Augustinerkirche to the cathedral. And by imperial command, the whole of the university, the whole of the clergy, and all the artists, who appeared with their standards, as is customary for the Procession for the Feast of Corpus Christi, the musicians sang the Litany of All Saints, with "Hear our prayer", and without trumpets and drums, in procession. In St Stephen's, after the Agnus Dei had been sung with its responds, there was the sermon. And afterwards, to the bishop's intonation, the *Te Deum laudamus* was sung in most solemn style, with trumpets and drums, and intradas, in honour of St Charles Borromeus . . . with cannon and rifle shots'; the typical military gestures associated with the *Te Deum*, and the mention (elsewhere) of added musical resources for the occasion (*musici stranieri*), are of particular interest.

[14] The Karlskirche was designed by Johann Bernhard Fischer von Erlach (1656–1723) and completed by Joseph Emanuel Fischer von Erlach.

[15] I. Barea, *Vienna: Legend and Reality* (London, 1966), 73–4.

[16] Riedel, *Kirchenmusik*, 12.

[17] Monastery of St Dorothea in the Dorotheergasse; the Emperor Charles VI attended High Mass there annually on the feast of St Dorothea (Riedel, *Kirchenmusik*, 42).

[18] The Michaelerkirche (Hofpfarrkirche) was connected with the Spanish brotherhood 'zu Ehren des Allerheiligsten Sakramentes', which was in turn closely connected to Emperor Charles VI's former Spanish court (Riedel, *Kirchenmusik*, 43).

[19] One Baroque feature was the building of 'Oratorien' for the emperor and other highly placed personages: rather like an opera box, this gave them a prime seat and a private place from which to be observed and to observe the proceedings. In the Stephansdom and at the monastery church of Klosterneuburg the emperor's 'Oratorium' was placed opposite the musicians' gallery: the original layout of Klosterneuburg survived into this century (Riedel, *Kirchenmusik*, 59).

[20] On Fux's quarrel with Mattheson see *Grove 6*.

[21] Facsimile edition in *Fux: Sämtliche Werke*, ed. H. Federhofer and O. Wessely, vii/1 (Kassel, 1967); partial Eng. trans. in A. Mann, *The Study of Counterpoint* (1965). See also S. Wollenberg, 'The Unknown "Gradus"', *ML*, li (1970), 423; and S. Wollenberg, 'Johann Joseph Fux, *Gradus ad Parnassum* (1725): Concluding Chapters', *Music Analysis*, xi (1992), 209–43 [incl. Eng. trans.].

[22] Riedel found evidence also of fauxbourdon (*falso bordone*).

[23] Ed. J.-H. Lederer, *Fux: Sämtliche Werke*, i/3 (Kassel, 1974); Fux shares with Mozart the distinction of having acquired a Köchel catalogue, hence the κ numbering.

[24] Brown, 'Caldara's Trumpet Music', 22–3 and nn. 26–7 on pp. 47–8. Among the extensive detail recorded in Reinhardt's *Rubriche* for Christmas Day is the mention of a Christmas sonata ('Suonata di Natale').

[25] Quoted from the manuscript score of Caldara's opera *Adriano in Siria (A-Wn)*.

[26] Seifert has estimated that in the reign of Emperor Leopold I over 400 dramatic works were sung at the Viennese court (about a quarter were spiritual works, oratorios and related genres such as *sepolcri*, performed during Lent and at Easter; the remainder were secular, operas and serenatas); see Flotzinger and Gruber, *Musikgeschichte Österreichs*, i, 328ff.

[27] Reinhardt (*Rubriche generali*) has for example a reference to 'service at table, with overtures, with and without trumpets and drums. With concertos for one and for more voices in turn, at pleasure, for as long as was wanted. The musicians in a special gallery'.

[28] Brown, 'Caldara's Trumpet Music', 10.

[29] *Grove O* has useful entries on librettists and stage designers, including those mentioned here.

[30] Introduction to the facsimile of Caldara's *L'olimpiade*, ed. H. M. Brown, Italian Opera 1640–1770, xxxii (New York, 1979).

[31] Brian Pritchard's article 'Caldara's "Adriano in Siria"', *MT*, cxxvii (1986), 379–82, is a good introduction to the work.

[32] Quoted (from the *Wiennerisches Diarium*) in E. Wellesz, *Fux* (London, 1965), 52; as Wellesz observes, 'Times had changed; Turkey was no longer a threat to the Empire'. It is interesting to find Turkish colour incorporated in Viennese Baroque music; Fux and Caldara composed janissary music, pre-echoing Mozart.

[33] Brown, 'Caldara's Trumpet Music', 40; Brown cites a series of aria verses which directly invite this kind of setting (e.g. 'Date, o trombe, il suon guerriero').

[34] Ibid, 44. It has been noted (in connection with the wedding opera for Charles and Elisabeth Christine and for the latter's name-day, *Il più bel nome*, composed by Caldara to a libretto by Pariati for the celebrations in Barcelona, 1708) that plots such as this one, 'dealing with Hercules' tenth, Spanish labor are found in several operas for Charles . . . He officially assumed the figure of the mythic hero': see U. Kirkendale, 'The War of the Spanish Succession Reflected in the Works of Antonio Caldara', *AcM*, xxxvi (1964), 221–33. The plot of *Costanza e Fortezza*, on the theme of Porsenna's siege of Rome, presumably evoked parallels with Vienna's history.

[35] There were several threads connecting Handel with the Vienna court (among them the fact that Handel incorporated in his own works borrowings from the music of the Vienna court organist Gottlieb Muffat).

[36] *Herrn Johann Joachim Quantzens Lebenslauf, von ihm Selbst entworfen* (Berlin, 1754), quoted in A. Liess, *Fuxiana* (Vienna, 1958), 41–5 [incl. comments on individual singers].

[37] Reproduced in Wellesz, *Fux*, 42–3. The letters of Lady Mary Wortley Montagu (ed. by her great-grandson, Lord Wharncliffe, 2 vols., London, 1893) give a vivid picture of life in early eighteenth-century Vienna; the extract quoted here occurs in vol.i, p.238.

[38] *Grove 6*, xiii, 664 ('Oratorio').

[39] An extended account of the oratorio and *sepolcro* in eighteenth-century Vienna is provided by H. Smither, *A History of the Oratorio*, i: *The Oratorio in the Baroque Era: Italy, Vienna, Paris* (Chapel Hill, 1977), 365–415.

[40] 'Caldara's "Adriano in Siria"', 379.

[41] See n.36.

[42] L. E. Bennett, 'Italian Cantatas in Vienna, 1700–1711: an Overview of Stylistic Traits', in Pritchard, ed., *Caldara: Essays*, 189.

[43] Ed. in DTÖ, lxxv, Jg.xxxix (1932).

[44] Brown, 'Caldara's Trumpet Music', 7; 22.

[45] Roger North on the English-born Nicola Matteis the younger; quoted in A. McCredie, 'Nicola Matteis, the Younger: Caldara's Collaborator and Ballet Composer in the Service of the Emperor, Charles VI', in Pritchard, ed., *Caldara: Essays*, 157.

[46] U. Kirkendale, 'The War of the Spanish Succession', 223; Caldara was employed in Mantua from 1700 to 1707.

[47] On Caldara's activities in Rome and Venice see Chapters II and III respectively; by the time he came to Vienna, Caldara's work included 17 oratorios for Venice, Mantua and Rome.

[48] C. Ingrao, *In Quest and Crisis: Emperor Joseph I and the Habsburg Monarchy* (West Lafayette, 1979), p.xi, has a useful note on coinage and comparative value.

[49] B. L. Greenwood, 'Antonio Caldara: a Checklist of his Manuscripts in Europe, Great Britain, and the United States of America', *Studies in Music*, vii (1973), 28–39.

[50] See S. Wollenberg, 'The Keyboard Suites of Gottlieb Muffat', *PRMA*, cii (1975–6), 83–91.

[51] Riedel has documented in detail the musical performances on one such tour, the *Erbhuldigungsreise* to Styria in 1728 (*Florilegium musicologicum: Festschrift Hellmut Federhofer zum 75. Geburtstag*, Tutzing, 1988, pp.275–86). The information here on Graz derives from Riedel.

[52] J. W. Stoye, 'Emperor Charles VI: the Early Years of the Reign', *Transactions of the Royal Historical Society*, 5th ser., xii (1963), 71; Stoye stresses that Charles VI made potentially effective attempts to form a workable economic and administrative policy.

[53] Brown, 'Caldara's Trumpet Music', 7.

[54] Ibid, 5; Brown gives useful tables of trumpeters and drummers, pp.6, 8–9.

[55] Stoye, 'Emperor Charles VI', 84.

[56] See, particularly, A. Mann, *Theory and Practice: the Great Composers as Teachers and Students* (New York and London, 1987).

[57] The author wishes to thank the following for their valuable advice in connection with this chapter: Robert Evans (Brasenose College, Oxford), Peter Hainsworth (Lady Margaret Hall, Oxford), Brian Pritchard (University of Canterbury, New Zealand) and J. W. Stoye (Magdalen College, Oxford).

BIBLIOGRAPHICAL NOTE

Music

Very little literature exists in English specifically on music in Vienna in the early eighteenth century. There are partial accounts, tending to focus on individual composers' lives and works; particularly useful among these are E. Wellesz, *Fux* (London, 1965), and B. Pritchard, ed., *Antonio Caldara: Essays on his Life and Times* (Aldershot, 1987); one of the best and most relevant essays in the latter volume is A. P. Brown's 'Caldara's Trumpet Music for the Imperial Celebrations of Charles VI and Elisabeth Christine' (pp.3–48). A companion volume to Pritchard's *Caldara*, and a welcome addition to the literature, is H. White, ed., *Johann Joseph Fux and the Music of the Austro-Italian Baroque* (Aldershot, 1992). General histories of music draw in references to Viennese music of this period, notably the relevant volumes of the *New*

Oxford History of Music, v: *Opera and Church Music 1630–1750*, ed. A. Lewis and N. Fortune (London, 1975), and vi: *Concert Music 1630–1750*, ed. G. Abraham (Oxford, 1986). But the specific literature in English is more usually concerned with social, historical, artistic and architectural aspects of the Viennese Baroque than with its music. One relevant factor may be that the art and architecture of the Austrian Baroque are still readily visible, the music less easily accessible. Another factor is the weight that has inevitably been attached to later developments, from the Viennese Classical period onwards: the recognition of Vienna as a musical centre usually and understandably stems from the achievements of later periods.

For specialized literature on the music we must turn primarily to sources in German, which offer excellent but often very densely constructed accounts, such as L. von Köchel, *Die Kaiserliche Hof-Musikkapelle in Wien von 1543–1867* (Vienna, 1869, repr. 1976); R. Flotzinger and G. Gruber, eds., *Musikgeschichte Österreichs*, i: *Von den Anfängen zum Barock* (Graz, 1977), and ii: *Vom Barock zur Gegenwart* (Graz, 1979); and the invaluable and magisterial account by F. Riedel, *Kirchenmusik am Hofe Karls VI. (1711–1740): Untersuchungen zum Verhältnis von Zeremoniell und musikalischem Stil im Barockzeitalter* (Munich and Salzburg, 1977). Further perspectives can be found in S. Wollenberg, 'The Austro-German Courts', *Companion to Baroque Music*, ed. J. A. Sadie (London, 1990), 229–39. Many of the books mentioned offer helpful illustrative material that includes maps and charts, such as Riedel's plan of churches in Vienna (p.311); they also provide references to further reading.

Other literature

The Habsburg monarchy has been the subject of extensive, often romanticized, literary treatment, again tending to focus on later periods. In fact, the reigns of Charles VI and of his predecessor Joseph I present something of a gap in the literature, only partly (though usefully) filled by C. Ingrao, *In Quest and Crisis: Emperor Joseph I and the Habsburg Monarchy* (West Lafayette, 1979), and J. W. Stoye, 'Emperor Charles VI: the Early Years of the Reign', *Transactions of the Royal Historical Society*, 5th ser., xii (1963), 63–84. For excellent authoritative background to this era, R. J. W. Evans's *The Making of the Habsburg Monarchy 1550–1700* (Oxford, 1979) is indispensable. Again, these have helpful references to further reading. In addition to the literature in English, there are numerous German sources covering the Habsburg monarchy, such as F. Matsche, *Die Kunst im Dienst der Staatsidee Kaiser Karls VI.* (Berlin, 1981).

The subject of Vienna itself has also exerted considerable literary attraction. I. Barea's *Vienna: Legend and Reality* (London, 1966) is still, 25 years after publication, stimulating and wide-ranging. More specialized works on Vienna of musical interest include theatre studies: R. A. Griffin's *High Baroque Culture and Theatre in Vienna* (New York, 1972; particularly valuable for its illustrations); and two items by F. Hadamowsky, 'Barocktheater am Wiener Kaiserhof, mit einem Spielplan (1625–1740)', *Jb der Gesellschaft für Wiener Theaterforschung, 1951–2* (Vienna, 1955), 7–117, and *Die Familie Galli-Bibiena in Wien* (Vienna, 1962). For further specialized bibliography the article 'Vienna' and articles on individual composers (such as Fux and Caldara) in *Grove 6* and *Grove 0* are helpful.

Editions

There are a number of standard collected editions of the music, such as those in the series *Denkmäler der Tonkunst in Österreich* (DTÖ), and *J. J. Fux: Sämtliche Werke*, ed. Johann-Joseph-Fux-Gesellschaft (Kassel & Basle and Graz, 1959–), as well as facsimile editions of works by Viennese court composers in the series *The Italian Cantata in the Seventeenth Century*, xvi (New York, 1985), Caldara's *L'olimpiade* in the series

The Late Baroque Era

Italian Opera 1640–1770, ed. H. M. Brown, xxxii (New York, 1979), and his *Joaz* in *The Italian Oratorio 1650–1800*, xii (New York, 1986), and works by Conti and Caldara in the series *The Symphony*, B II: *Italians in Vienna* (New York, 1983). But this is music that really needs to be appreciated in performance; and performances are relatively rare. Perhaps the increased coverage of the Austrian Baroque in general histories of music, together with the now established role of groups specializing in 'authentic' Baroque performing styles and instruments, will create a more receptive climate for this neglected repertory.

Chapter XII

London: Commercial Wealth and Cultural Expansion

DONALD BURROWS

The death of Henry Purcell on 21 November 1695, while still at the height of his powers and scarcely approaching middle age, is a landmark in the creative history of London's music-making that cannot be ignored. Yet, taking a broader view, that year is not as significant a turning-point as 1688 or 1702, years that marked changes of occupancy in the English throne. The fact that those dates are apparently 'political' rather than 'musical' immediately points up the central significance of court tastes and court patronage to professional musical life in London. Purcell's career in his last years had been profoundly affected by a change of direction at court. King William III's command, relayed through the Dean of the Chapel Royal on 23 February 1689,[1]

> That there shall be no musick [i.e. musical instruments] in the Chappell, but the Organ.

demolished at a stroke the 'Symphony Anthem' repertory to which Purcell had contributed extensively during the preceding decade and which had been the most interesting part of the musical tradition in which he had been educated as a chorister and young organist. Although Purcell continued to hold offices at the Chapel Royal and Westminster Abbey after 1689, and the new king and queen appointed him to their 'Private Music' of chamber players, he sought more stimulating musical outlets elsewhere, principally in the London theatres. In the 1690s he continued writing music, varying in scope from incidental songs to extensive scores, for dramatic productions at the Dorset Gardens and Drury Lane theatres.

Taken together, the court, the larger London ecclesiastical establishments (especially the choirs of the Chapel Royal, Westminster Abbey and the newly rebuilt St Paul's Cathedral) and the theatres provided the major centres of relatively stable employment for professional musicians in London.[2] These sources of employment were in various ways interconnected, for the leading church musicians held appointments at the Chapel Royal in plurality with places in the other major choirs, while instrumentalists might combine places as Royal Musicians (i.e. members of the band under the Master of the King's Musick) with service in the theatres. Although strictly independent of the court, London theatre life was dependent on the goodwill of the Lord Chamberlain as licensing officer and censor, and it could be materially enhanced by the presence of royalty at performances.

We may regret the sudden termination of the 'Symphony Anthem' tradition and, indeed, regret also William III's general lack of interest in music, but London's musicians were in some ways well prepared for the change in public taste that accompanied the political upheaval of the 1680s. English music, though working within its own traditions, was always susceptible to foreign influences. During Charles II's reign, when London life presented some appearance of cultural unity (fuelled, no doubt, by the desire to exorcise the mid-century bloodshed of the Civil War), French influences had been to the fore, led by the tastes that the king had developed in exile. During the 1690s, while there was some suspicion of Dutch influences and 'mercantile' attitudes, British political opinion was nevertheless generally united with William III in his mistrust of the French. The tastes of musicians had shifted in the same direction, but well in advance: a preface acclaiming the 'most fame'd Italian Masters' at the expense of the 'levity and balladry' of the French had appeared in the front of Purcell's first set of trio sonatas in 1683. This preface, and the music that followed, were no doubt written under the influence of music from Italian composers of the generation of G. B. Vitali (*c*1644–1692): in the years following Purcell's death new waves of Italian influences, particularly from Italian opera and Corelli's instrumental music, continued to have decisive effects on the course of musical tastes and performances in London. Such was the strength in the growth of London's musical scene – a factor probably not entirely unconnected with an expansion of wealth across a broad band of the middle and upper classes – that new areas of performance in the fashionable Italian genres added to, rather than replaced, existing performance traditions and opportunities.

1695–1714

The theatre

In 1695 Thomas Betterton broke away from the Drury Lane company and set up a second regular theatre company in London at Lincoln's Inn Fields Theatre, with Congreve as his librettist, John

London: Commercial Wealth and Cultural Expansion

Eccles as his principal composer and Anne Bracegirdle as his principal singer. Apart from the welcome multiplication in the number of dramatic performances (and, incidentally, the liberation of London's theatre programmes from the dominating hand of Drury Lane's manager, Christopher Rich), the general pattern of theatre music within which Purcell had worked did not change very much. Betterton had the better company of performers, but was limited by the physical constraints of his theatre: at Drury Lane, Rich was still able to produce revivals of the spectacular 'semi-operas' that were beyond Betterton's range. All plays from both companies contained some songs, and a few included substantial musical scores: masques, sometimes of considerable duration, were frequently added incidentally to full-length farces, tragedies and comedies, or played as afterpieces. The principal composers apart from Eccles (c1668–1735, who was then a promising young talent just coming into his own) were Daniel Purcell (d 1717) and Gottfried Finger (c1660–1730). The subjects of the masques were mythological, classical or historical (in various combinations): typical examples produced at Lincoln's Inn Fields were *The Loves of Mars and Venus* (1696, Peter Motteux, music by Daniel Purcell and Finger) and *Rinaldo and Armida* (1698, John Dennis, music by Eccles). The latter was a substantial work, and a complete evening's entertainment by itself: its success provoked Drury Lane to rustle up something in reply. This took the form of *The Island Princess . . . made into an Opera*, a new semi-opera by Peter Motteux (1663–1718) with music by Jeremiah Clarke, Daniel Purcell and others.

In March 1700 four prizes were offered in a contest sponsored by 'several persons of quality' for the best setting of Congreve's masque text *The Judgment of Paris*. Judging took place in March 1701, and the setting by John Weldon (1676–1736) was given the first prize. Weldon's music was competent enough (it also included one simple and popular 'hit song'), and the composer probably enjoyed the support of some influential noblemen, including the Duke of Bedford. But Weldon had hitherto been primarily a church composer, and his success was accompanied by suspicions of the power of influence rather than the merits of music-dramatic prowess: Finger (who was awarded fourth prize) reacted by leaving London for good and returning to his native Germany. Eccles and Daniel Purcell were awarded second and third prizes respectively. The original performances of *The Judgment of Paris* were given at Dorset Gardens,[3] but the masques were subsequently used by the companies at the two major theatres as afterpieces. By 1701, however, masques were rather losing favour in the theatres, probably because neither of the companies was flourishing or in a position to finance lavish new productions.[4] Apart from incidental songs within plays, music tended instead to appear in the theatre programmes among various novelties that were disjunct from the drama proper: at Drury Lane the novelties might be Italian violinists or French dancers – or rope-dancers and contortionists.

An important change of direction in theatre programmes, towards a more complete 'music drama' in the form of opera, came as the result of the advent of a new manager and a new building into London's theatrical scene. John Vanbrugh intended to open his theatre in 1705 with a pair of 'Italian' operas:

> The Play-House in the Hay-Market . . . is almost finish'd, in the mean time two Operas translated from the Italian by good Hands, are setting to Musick, one by Mr. Daniel Purcell, which is called Orlando Furioso, and another by Mr. Clayton, both Opera's are to be perform'd . . . at the Opening of the House
> [*The Diverting-Post*, 28 October 1704]

The theatre building was further from completion than this newspaper report suggested, and in the meantime Rich lured Thomas Clayton's opera to his own theatre: *Arsinoe, Queen of Cyprus* opened at Drury Lane on 16 January 1705, and had considerable success. *Arsinoe* is interesting for its Italian origins,[5] but its main significance lay in the fact that it was the first all-sung full-length production in London. Clayton (1673–1725) had closed the gap with 'semi-opera' completely by employing recitative instead of spoken dialogue:

> The Design of this Entertainment being to introduce the *Italian* manner of Musick on the *English* stage, which has not been before attempted: I was oblig'd to have an *Italian* Opera translated . . . The Musick being Recitative, may not, at first, meet with that general Acceptation as is to be hop'd for, from the Audience's being better acquainted with it: But if this Attempt shall be a means of bringing this manner of Musick to be us'd in my Native country, I shall think all my Study and Pains very well employ'd.[6]

It would be easy to draw over-simple conclusions about the extent of Italian musical influence in London in 1705 from Clayton's preface. Certainly the introduction of recitative in place of dialogue was Italian-influenced: Italian opera had, after all, a century of experience in this technique of facilitating continuous musical drama. Yet Clayton obviously anticipated some hostility to his work simply because the medium of Italian opera itself was not yet familiar to many members of a London audience. This situation appeared to be confirmed when Vanbrugh eventually opened his theatre on 9 April 1705 with an Italian opera sung in Italian, *Gli amori di Ergasto* by

Jakob Greber (*d* 1731). A contemporary summed up London's reception to the performance thus:

> a Foreign Opera, Perform'd by a new set of Singers, Arriv'd from *Italy*; (the worst that e're came from thence) for it lasted but 5 Days, and they being lik'd but indifferently by the Gentry; they in a little time marcht back to their own Country.[7]

At Drury Lane, Rich had much better success by putting on with his regular company an English version of another Italian opera, *Camilla*, by Giovanni Bononcini (1670–1747).

Yet Italian opera, sung in Italian, eventually won through with the London public. The decade following 1705 was a period of turmoil and confusion in the London theatres, both in the domestic arrangements of the theatre companies and in the genres performed. The early years saw performances of the last successful new English semi-opera, *The British Enchanters* (February 1706, George Granville, music by Eccles), and the first thoroughly English full-length original all-sung opera, *Rosamond* (March 1707, Joseph Addison, music by Clayton). It was rather an accident that the second landmark was held by *Rosamond*, for Eccles had composed a score for Congreve's *Semele* (musically superior to Clayton's *Rosamond*) in anticipation of the opening of Vanbrugh's theatre in the Haymarket in 1705, but it was never performed. By the time full English opera arrived, the taste for all-sung dramatic performances had begun to move on the path that led to Italian opera in Italian, while in English-language performances it was the 'mixed' varieties of drama-with-music (rather than all-sung drama) that continued to enjoy reliable success in the theatres.

The significant steps towards the establishment of full Italian opera in London relied not so much on the acceptance of the technical shift into all-sung drama as on the introduction of good-quality Italian singers performing in their own language. It was the success of the castratos Valentini and Nicolini in operas at the Queen's Theatre, Haymarket, that turned the London theatre-going public decisively towards Italian opera. In *Pyrrhus and Demetrius* (December 1708, adapted from an opera set by Alessandro Scarlatti for Naples in 1694) the leading men sang in their own language, the rest of the cast singing partly in Italian and partly in English. With *Almahide* (January 1710, also adapted from a previous Italian opera, with music mainly by Bononcini) the change to all-Italian performances was complete: henceforth for most of the audience the bilingual word-book, available on sale at the theatre, was an essential adjunct to the performances.

The intellectual and cultural background to the gradual establishment of Italian opera during the first decade of the eighteenth century was a very subtle one, for the growing awareness of modern Italian genres had developed through several channels. In July 1703 Italian intermezzos or 'interludes and mimical entertainments of singing and dancing' had been performed in concerts at York Buildings. Opportunities for leisured gentlemen to take a 'grand tour' in the first decade of the eighteenth century were rather limited by a continental war, but the high levels of diplomatic activity that accompanied that war brought the younger and more mobile sections of the upper classes into direct contact with 'Italian' opera houses in continental Europe. Another important factor, and one that also may not have been unconnected with the battles raging in continental Europe, was the immigration of talented musicians. In putting together *Arsinoe* Clayton had been assisted by two foreign musicians, the Frenchman Charles Dieupart (*d c*1740) and the Italian Nicola Haym (1678–1729). If Finger returned to Germany, the account was restored in the opposite direction by London's acquisition of Johann Pepusch (1667–1752), Johann Galliard (*c*1687–1749) and Johann Lampe (*c*1703–1751). All five of these men stayed to develop significant careers in London: paradoxically, Pepusch and Galliard were among the principal contributors to English-language theatre music in the second decade of the century. The artistic traffic seems to have been all in one direction: English composers did not attempt Italian opera, for reasons that are now difficult to guess.

The institutional history of the London theatre companies following the entry of Vanbrugh and his theatre into the picture is complicated by its own internal politics: managements grouped and regrouped, negotiating with the Lord Chamberlain for the rights of their performing companies and for possession of the two major patent theatres at Drury Lane and the Haymarket.[8] The distinctions between musicians and 'comedians' – and the accompanying rights to perform dramas with and without musical elements – became important factors in the negotiations. The formation of a separate opera company by Vanbrugh in 1707 might have been seen by contemporaries initially as one move in his game against Rich, but it had momentous consequences. Hitherto, drama with a strong musical component had functioned as one element in the regular and varied programmes of the theatre companies. By taking opera out of this system and establishing it separately, Vanbrugh removed it from the institutional and financial base that had previously supported musical theatre in London. Vanbrugh liberated opera to its own independence, but at the sacrifice of a broadly based financial security. It may however be doubted whether the establishment of Italian opera in London could have been effected without such a division: in the nature of the case, the leading Italian performers could not have been integrated into English-language repertory productions in other genres.

The creation of Vanbrugh's company was also important because, in addition to the solo singers, it institutionalized a regular orchestra of about 25 players. Initially, 14 of these needed the Lord Chamberlain's permission to move over into the 'opera' orchestra because they were under a conflicting contract to Rich at Drury Lane. After many vicissitudes over the coupling of companies and buildings, the Lord Chamberlain's orders in November 1710 settled the 'comedians' at Drury Lane and the Opera Company (now under the management of Aaron Hill) at the Queen's Theatre, Haymarket. The institutional pattern for the future was thus established. It was at this moment that the 25-year-old Handel (1685–1759) arrived in London. His first operas at the Haymarket – *Rinaldo, Il pastor fido* and *Teseo* – happily provided the original artistic successes that justified the existence of the opera company.

Concert life and church music

Advertisements in newspapers of the period reveal that London had a flourishing concert life, but one in which regular patterns are difficult to discern. York Buildings and Stationers' Hall were the two most active concert venues in central London and, although it is rare to find precise details given in the advertisements, it seems that programmes were mainly of about one and a half to two hours' duration. Typical advertisements promised 'A Concert of Vocal and Instrumental Musick by the Best Masters'. Regular formulae of this type were usually accompanied by the identification of the principal works to be performed or the names of the principal performers: these, plus the occasional 'novelty' element, presumably constituted the attractions for individual concerts, though we have no reliable evidence as to whether attendances fluctuated greatly in response to particular attractions or whether fluctuations were numerically marginal to a predictable pool of habitual concert-goers.

Sometimes a complete substantial work is named as the main piece of the programme, often as a repeat performance of a recent work commemorating a court festivity or public event. The continued performance of Henry Purcell's music, along with the most recent works of contemporary composers, is notable. The general flavour of the concerts can be gained from a few samples of advertisements for concerts in York Buildings:

> the Song which was sung before Her Royal Highness, on Her Birth Day last, with other Variety of New Vocal and Instrumental Musick, Compos'd by Dr Turner, and for his Benefit.
> [4 May 1698]

> an entertainment of new Musick, Vocal and Instrumental; Mr
> Pate, Mr Leveridge, Mr Freeman, Mr Bowen, and all the best
> masters performing their parts. Composed by Mr Daniel Purcell for
> his benefit.
>
> [7 June 1698]

> a Consort of Vocal and Instrumental Musick, particularly that
> celebrated Song, set by the late Mr Henry Purcell, (for the
> Yorkshire Feast) the best Masters of each Profession in England
> performing their Parts: For the benefit of the Widow of Mr Thomas
> Williams, who perform'd in the Theatre Royal.
>
> [10 March 1701]

(The Yorkshire Feast Song was repeated on 14 June 'for the Benefit
of the Widdow and seven Children of Mr Charles Powel, late Servant
to his Majesty, and his late Highness the Duke of Gloucester'.)

> a consort for the benefit of Mrs Eliz. Hemmings, including 'New
> Cantatas, with other Songs and Italian Pieces lately brought from
> Italy . . . she will also Accompany to her own Voice on the
> Harpsecord, being the first time of her appearing in Publick.
>
> [21 April 1710]

Most of the concerts seem to have been individual enterprises
rather than part of regular concert series, but there are hints of such
regular series as well. In November 1697 the violinist James
Kremberg 'lately come out of Italy' announced the inauguration of a
weekly concert series at Hickford's Dancing School: 'Hickford's
Room' subsequently became an important concert venue. A concert
at York Buildings in March 1699 was advertised 'for the Benefit of
Mr. William Hall, who formerly had the Consort of Musick at his
House in Norfolk Street'. It is rather tantalizing that little is known
about Hall's previous activities. Similarly, one would like to have
known more about the chamber concerts (supposedly attended by
the Duchess of Queensbury and attracting such performers as
Handel and Pepusch) run by Thomas Britton in the loft above his
coal store in Clerkenwell, beyond the rather gossipy account that
John Hawkins put together 70 years after the event.[9]
During the summer and early autumn the central concert venues
gave place to, or were supplemented by, performances in the spa-
centres that surrounded the metropolis: Richmond, Hampstead,
Lambeth and Islington (Sadler's Wells). The annual pattern of concert activity in central London mirrored that of the theatres, which
concentrated their programmes into the 'dark months' and the
spring, when the landed classes were 'in town' (in the summer these
essential patrons returned to their country estates). Concert pro-

grammes were held on weekday evenings, with frequency but with little regularity as to particular nights. However, as the musical component of London's theatre programmes expanded after 1705 it obviously became prudent for concert-givers to avoid opera nights, when many of the best performers and a good part of the audience would be elsewhere: by 1710 advertisements for concerts at York Buildings were at pains to point out 'There being no Play that Evening at either of the Houses, there will be [as performers at the concert] the best Hands in the Kingdom.'[10] During 1711–12 the concert scene was enlivened by a subscription series run by Clayton, Haym and Dieupart – three musicians momentarily displaced from their opera posts by the internal politics of the opera company.

Vocal performers at concerts might come from theatre or church circles, and indeed there seems to have been a considerable amount of overlap between the two: this was, after all, a period in which the leading church composers such as Weldon, John Blow (1649–1708), Clarke and William Croft (1678–1727) also wrote music for theatrical performances. As Italian opera gradually took hold as the most prestigious music-making in the London theatres, so some first-rate English singers of the rising generation that had hitherto embarked on stage careers turned elsewhere: thus the choirs of the Chapel Royal, Westminster Abbey and St Paul's in the first decade of the eighteenth century gained the outstanding altos Richard Elford and Francis Hughes and the tenor John Freeman.

Mention has been made in passing of works composed to commemorate particular events. These were mainly secular odes or extended pieces of church music, and their performances employed concerted groups of singers and instrumentalists. The patronage of the court was an important factor in this area of music-making. Perhaps rather surprisingly, William III retained (or perhaps just tolerated) the continuation of regular annual court odes to celebrate the New Year and the monarch's birthday, for which composers of the calibre of Blow and Daniel Purcell composed music.[11] Although the 'Symphony Anthem' had been driven from its natural habitat at court, London's professional musicians seem to have provided their own venue elsewhere for the continuance of concerted church music. Since 1683 the celebrations of St Cecilia's Day mounted in London by 'The Musical Society' had included the performance of an ode.[12] During the 1690s a church service was added to the celebrations, and in 1693 this included a sermon in which Ralph Battell, the sub-dean of the Chapel Royal, ventured to counter a commentary in the Geneva Bible attacking the use of musical instruments in church.[13] The next year, the St Cecilia's Day service included the first performance of Purcell's *Te Deum* and *Jubilate* in D major, accompanied by an orchestra of trumpets and strings.[14] In the following two years Blow and William Turner (1651–1740) produced similar works for the Cecilian celebrations. Thereafter the flow of concerted church music continued as various public occasions called forth 'Symphony Anthems', now probably accompanied by a rather larger group of instruments and voices than had been characteristic of Purcell's anthems in the 1680s. Blow produced an orchestrally accompanied anthem for the service at St Paul's Cathedral in 1697 that combined celebration of the Peace of Ryswick with a commemoration of the completion of the choir of Wren's new cathedral, and he followed this with another important anthem in 1698 for the charity service of the Corporation of the Sons of the Clergy in the same cathedral. In 1701 and 1702 Blow's orchestrally accompanied anthems were heard at the edifying performances of music and oratory organized by Cavendish Weedon at Stationers' Hall.[15]

With the death of Queen Mary in 1694 London's musicians had lost an important patron at court. Their hopes now turned mainly to Princess Anne, who was generally regarded as sympathetic to the performing arts but was powerless to exert much effective patronage until her accession as queen in 1702. When her chance came, Anne did not fail the musicians. The musical establishments of the Chapel Royal and the Royal Musicians, which had become rather run down under William, were restored to their former strengths. One innovation in the first part of Anne's reign was the introduction of grand Thanksgiving Services at St Paul's Cathedral marking the victories that John, Duke of Marlborough, produced with annual efficiency in the continental war: these services involved the performance of orchestrally accompanied canticles and anthems in the grandest manner. When, in the later part of her reign, the royal thanksgivings continued in the relative privacy of the Chapel Royal building at St James's Palace, the London musicians appear to have taken the situation into their own hands by re-introducing concerted canticles and anthems into the annual Sons of the Clergy service, thus maintaining a public forum for the continuing tradition of orchestrally accompanied church music.

The court was directly responsible for the regular employment of more than 60 professional musicians,[16] though admittedly all of these needed to supplement their court income elsewhere. The best Chapel Royal singers, as already noted, usually held simultaneous places in other major choirs, while the best string players found their services in demand at concerts or in the opera-house orchestra. Early in Anne's reign financial arrangements were made to enable the full musical establishment of the Chapel Royal to accompany the queen on her annual circuit away from St James's Palace to the royal palaces at Kensington, Hampton Court and Windsor. There seems little doubt that the queen took an active interest in the musical life of her chapel. But she never attended the new Italian operas at the London theatres, and this may be variously accounted for in terms of court diplomacy or the queen's health and personal circumstances. However, she heard private performances given by members of the opera company (including Handel and the leading castrato Nicolini) on her birthdays in 1711 and 1712, apparently in place of the normal court ode. Although ill-health prevented the queen from attending in person, the final thanksgiving service of her reign, at St Paul's Cathedral on 7 July 1713, was the grandest of all: and Handel's 'Utrecht' *Te Deum* and *Jubilate*, performed on that occasion, provides a fitting final tribute to her musical patronage.

1714–30

London's musical life during the two decades following the accession of King George I in 1714 was dominated by the varying fortunes of Italian opera, for reasons that were partly social and partly musical. Opera was patronized by royalty and the aristocracy, but not exclusively: the same performances were also enjoyed by Londoners of modest affluence who could afford the price of a ticket. While the financial security of the successive opera companies undoubtedly relied mainly on a relatively small number of high-level annual subscriptions, walk-in ticket sales seem to have been important as well, and were taken into account when opera budgets were being projected.[17] Normal ticket prices for the operas were initially 8s. for boxes, 5s. for the pit and 3s. 6d. for the gallery,[18] but in the 1720s a new price structure was introduced, with pit and boxes at half a guinea (10s. 6d.) and gallery seats at 5s. Seats in stage boxes, when available, cost one guinea. The opera performances no doubt attracted their share of social climbers, but it would be wrong to conclude that the majority of the audience attended only for social reasons: there seems to have been a genuine enthusiasm and interest for the operas and their performers. This is apparent from the attention paid to the operas in newspapers, which reported the affairs (business-like or scandalous) of the opera companies and from time to time published satirical or critical articles on the subject of the genre and the singers.

In terms of London's musical history in the broader sense, the injection of creative energy that can be directly attributed to the Italian opera performances was very significant. At the Haymarket audiences heard the best singers in Europe, particularly among the castratos and sopranos, and the operas attracted to London an array of important composer-performers. The new influx of talented foreign musicians was not limited to singers and composers, for string players also came to take up leading positions in the opera orchestra, or to seek a career on the back of the general enthusiasm for things Italian. Thus the Castrucci brothers, Pietro (1679–1752) and Prospero (d 1760), and Francesco Geminiani (1687–1762), all violinists, took up careers in London during the period around 1715, and Giacobbe Cervetto (d 1783) came as a cellist and instrument-dealer a decade later. At the same time, Italian-style sonatas and concertos maintained and increased their popularity, both in performance and publication: the catalogue of the publisher John Walsh contained a great number of works of these types. By 1720 the seventeenth-century world of instrumental music had been left behind: the consort and the viola da gamba had become rather antiquarian interests, outbid by the music of Corelli and Vivaldi.

Since support for Italian opera in London relied significantly on patrons who were involved in, or immediately affected by, developments in public life, it is perhaps not surprising that political events had a fairly direct effect on the fortunes of the opera companies. At no time was opera entirely financially secure in London: continuance into the next season always relied upon the willingness of the subscribers to underwrite a potential loss, and anything that diverted or divided the patrons threatened the future of the opera company.

George I's reign began well for the Haymarket company. It was rumoured initially that George I would not be supporting the operas, but the king gave the lie to this by attending an opera within a week of his coronation:[19] during the following months the Prince and Princess of Wales were regular operagoers. The Jacobite rebellion of 1715, unlike its successor 30 years later, did not really shake the confidence of London society, but the division in public life that was symbolized and accelerated by the public estrangement between the king and the Prince of Wales two years later had much more serious effects. Supporters of the Prince of Wales were forbidden the king's court, and it is doubtful whether social mixing of the two parties would have been acceptable at the opera house. Coming at a time when the opera company was in any case facing a loss of artistic impetus accompanied by an accumulating financial crisis, the division in patronage was catastrophic: the doors closed in June 1717, and no Italian opera was heard at the Haymarket for three years. Handel, the principal resident composer for the opera company but now with no immediate alternative means of similar employment,[20] apparently secured private patronage from James Brydges, the Earl of Carnarvon (though more frequently known today by his later title, Duke of Chandos). *Acis and Galatea*, *Esther* and the 'Chandos' Anthems, all written for Brydges, were the happy by-products of Handel's changing fortunes. However, by the spring of 1719 Handel was travelling in continental Europe to collect singers for a new London opera company, the Royal Academy of Music.

London: Commercial Wealth and Cultural Expansion

The Royal Academy was an attempt to put Italian opera in London on a more permanent footing. Instead of leaving responsibility for the opera company to theatre managers (who had hitherto generally lasted only a year or two before retiring in the face of impossible under-capitalization or sheer exhaustion), a public company was created by royal charter, under the terms of which the operas were managed by directors.[21] The governor of the company was the Lord Chamberlain, and the members of the corporation named in the charter included seven dukes, 13 earls and three viscounts – but also 18 plain 'esquires'. Members holding shares to the value of £200 were entitled to one vote in the business affairs of the company, and an annual subsidy of £1000 was promised by the king. The charter gave the Academy the right to present operas for a period of 21 years. Although the structure of the Academy was that of a joint stock company (a fact that did not escape the attention of satirists during the period of the 'South Sea Bubble'), it may be doubted whether anyone with a knowledge of the affairs of the previous London opera companies seriously expected the company to make a profit: the real objects were security, continuity and the preservation of an artistic activity that carried both social and musical prestige. There is no reason to doubt the genuine enthusiasm of the Academy's founders for Italian opera. The level of support from the king was perhaps diplomatic rather than enthusiastic. The royal grant of £1000 per year was respectable, but not sufficient to guarantee financial security in itself: it matched only the level of the annual salary of a singer of Nicolini's calibre. The king supported the Academy's performances regularly by his presence, and perhaps felt that he was reviving in some degree his father's support for Italian opera in Venice and Hanover.[22] The London audience was attentive to the quality of the actor-singers, the dramas themselves were generally coherent within the terms of their own conventions, and dual-language word-books enabled the audiences to follow what was happening on stage.

At an early meeting of the directors of the Royal Academy, a minute recorded their wish 'that Mr Hendell be Ma[ste]r of the Orchestra with a Sallary'. In the wider context of musical history, the permanent living monument to the London opera companies lies in the operas that Handel composed and produced for them between 1710 and 1741: 34 complete operas, including *Rinaldo* and *Amadigi* for the first Haymarket companies, and *Giulio Cesare* and *Tamerlano* for the Academy in the 1720s. Yet it is important to remember that the programmes of the opera companies were not dominated by Handel's works,[23] nor was Handel the only composer working with the companies. In 1716–17 Attilio Ariosti (1666–?1729) was acclaimed for his opera *Tito Manlio*:[24] in the 1720s, Handel,

54. Vignette (with the text 'Si caro, caro si') from Handel's 'Admeto' showing by implication the last scene from the opera where the lovers Admetus and Alcestis (played by Senesino and Faustina Bordoni) are united: from the title-page of a satirical pamphlet published on 8 March 1727 (a few weeks after the première at the King's Theatre)

Bononcini and Filippo Amadei (*fl* 1690–1730) were active together as 'house composers', and even contributed one act each to a joint opera, *Muzio Scevola* (1721). The repertory programmes of the opera companies included works by other composers not resident in London, and the 'new' operas themselves were usually based on pre-existing librettos that had been set by other composers. Composers were named in the opera word-books, but the distinction between original work and newly composed adaptation was a fine one: Handel contributed a considerable creative input to many of the pasticcio operas, for example. The adaptation of librettos for London productions was skilfully done, and particularly happy results came from the collaboration between Handel as composer and Nicola Haym as librettist/adapter. Haym was a performer and composer in addition to being a native Italian with literary interests, and this all-round talent seems to have been the ideal combination for an operatic collaborator.[25] Occasionally Handel and Bononcini seem to have been set up as rivals, and no doubt the qualities of the successive acts of *Muzio Scevola* produced some lively discussion during the intervals between them. But, as far as most of the opera audience was concerned, the comparisons that really mattered were between the singers. Nicolini and Senesino, the successive leading castratos, probably attracted more notice than Handel. The leading ladies were also important, and the employment of two prima donnas together in the later 1720s provoked lively controversy (and eventually unseemly scenes) among the audience.

Events in political life inevitably influenced the programmes of the opera house: *Radamisto*, Handel's first opera for the Royal Academy in 1720, was timed to coincide with the reconciliation between the king and the Prince of Wales (which resolved the patronage conflict of 1717), while the subject of Handel's *Riccardo Primo* in 1727 seems to have been chosen in celebration of the accession of King George II. It is conceivable that the subject matter of some other operas may have had political overtones, though the references are more speculative. Excessive identification of characters in an opera with any individual or party grouping would have caused problems among the patrons, and to some extent the opera house was regarded as a uniting force within the Body Politic.

While Italian opera was the new and vital element in London's musical life, other established elements continued, and with considerable success. The theoretical monopoly of the opera company over London's musical theatrical entertainment soon collapsed in practice. During 1716–17 John Rich gave 36 performances of English-language operas or semi-operas at Lincoln's Inn Fields, including *Camilla* (in English) and Galliard's *Calypso and Telemachus*. Two further masques by Galliard, to texts by Lewis Theobald, followed in 1718: *Pan and Syrinx* and *Decius and Paulina*. At Drury Lane Rich put on masques and pantomimes as afterpieces to the main programmes, the masque *Venus and Adonis* (music by Pepusch) proving a particular attraction in 1715. The importance of *The Beggar's Opera* (1728, John Gay, music by Pepusch) lies less in its occasional satirical references to Italian opera – which upon examination appear to be relatively few and incidental – than in the fact that it established a new wave of successful English drama with an essential musical component. It is doubtful whether *The Beggar's Opera* was regarded as an alternative entertainment by the habitués of the opera house, but they might well have attended it as an additional treat. It seems likely that the rival theatres could successfully syphon off the 'walk-in' audience from the opera house during periods when the opera companies were becoming stale or facing internal difficulties: in this respect, the success of *The Beggar's Opera* in 1728 was a repeat of the success of *Camilla* in 1717.[26] Although *Camilla* was, in contrast to *The Beggar's Opera*, an all-sung performance, the arias were short and sufficiently memorable to appeal to a broader audience than that of the opera house alone.

55. 'The Stage Medley': satirical engraving aimed at the taste of the town and its admiration for John Gay's 'The Beggar's Opera' (music arranged by J. C. Pepusch), first performed at Lincoln's Inn Fields theatre, 29 January 1728 (top left are portraits of Lavinia Fenton and Thomas Walker, the first Polly Peachum and Macheath)

London: Commercial Wealth and Cultural Expansion

The Hanoverian period began quite well for those musicians employed by the court. Although he was a 'foreign' king, George I (in contrast to William III) maintained the full musical establishments and the traditional practices of the Chapel Royal and the Royal Musicians, retaining the level of staffing and activity that had been built up during Queen Anne's reign. The English court odes, which had experienced a slight hiatus during Anne's last years, probably partly owing to her ill-health, resumed their annual timetable. In the first years of his reign George I also maintained and extended the system by which the Chapel Royal accompanied the court on its annual round of visits to Kensington, Hampton Court and Windsor. Following the Peace of Utrecht, there were no more continental battles to be celebrated with thanksgiving services. There was only one large ceremonial thanksgiving service in the reign, attended by the king at St Paul's Cathedral in January 1715; this celebrated the king's peaceable accession to the throne, rather prematurely in view of the Jacobite rebellion later that year. It was the last such grandiose public celebration until George III went to St Paul's in 1789 to give thanks for his recovery from illness. Composers and performers after 1715 thus lost one platform for the further development of orchestrally accompanied church music, but a new opportunity arose instead within the Chapel Royal itself, where the practice of enhancing with such music the first Sunday service after the king's safe return from his visits to Hanover developed in the 1720s. The performance of orchestrally accompanied anthems and canticles was in any case by 1720 an established tradition at the annual festival service of the Corporation of the Sons of the Clergy at St Paul's Cathedral.

Any official awkwardness at the beginning of the reign between the king and Handel over the latter's defection from his duties in Hanover seems to have been overcome fairly quickly, but nevertheless it seems that a deliberate effort was made at court to favour English-born composers in the first years of George I's reign. William Croft's *Te Deum* was performed at the 1715 thanksgiving service, and Croft provided the music for various royal entertainments at Hampton Court during 1717–18. During 1719–21 the king heard orchestrally accompanied church music by Croft, Clayton and the young Maurice Greene (1696–1755) at services in the Chapel Royal. Thereafter, however, Handel seems to have made something of a comeback in this area, taking over the music for the Chapel Royal services celebrating George I's return to St James's Palace in 1722, 1724 and 1726 and then providing the anthems – *Zadok the priest*, *The king shall rejoice*, *Let thy hand be strengthened* and *My heart is inditing* – for the coronation of George II in 1727. Croft, the senior English Chapel Royal composer, died shortly before the coronation, and it was apparently the new king's own choice that Handel should be preferred to Greene (Croft's obvious successor) as the composer for the coronation music. The 1727 coronation was a spectacular event, much more influential than the previous coronation in 1714, because the new king had an established position after 13 years' residence in London. Handel's music was rightly recognized as setting a new standard for English ceremonial music, just as his 'Utrecht' canticles had done in 1714. Handel's 1727 coronation anthems also turned out to have wider ramifications in the history of music in London: they were an important ingredient in the successful brew of English theatre oratorio that Handel was to create five years later.

One significant development during the 1720s was the growth of an antiquarian interest in music, and indeed an interest in the history of music itself. The following advertisement appeared in 1726:

> Proposals for Printing by Subscription, The Whole History of Musick, from its Original to the present Time. By *N. Haym*. This Work has never been hitherto attempted, the many Treatises of the Art already publish'd containing no more than only the Theory (very often unintelligible even to Professors) without any Attempt at the Lives of the Ancient or Modern Masters of Musick, or at the Rise, Progress and Changes of the Science which are the most considerable Parts of this History . . . This History will be published in two volumes in *Quarto* and adorn'd with several Copper-Plates, not only of the Heads of the most eminent Masters and the Statues, Bass-Relievos, Medals and Intaglios relating to this Art, but also of all the Instruments of Musick of the Ancients.[27]

Three years later it was reported that the project was nearing completion:

> Mr. *Haym* has finish'd his History of Music from the earliest Time to this Day. This Work will be in Two Vols. 8vo, embellished with a great Number of Copper Plates engraved by the best Hands. The Author has [s]par'd no Pains to give it in as great Perfection as possible; and as it is a History of Science, its State in the several Ages of the World, and of the most eminent Professors of all Nations, the reading of it must necessarily be very agreable and instructive. As this is the first complete History of Music that was ever written, 'tis presum'd it will meet with an Encouragement suitable to the Excellency of the Performance.[28]

Unfortunately Haym died in July 1729, and it seems that no-one else carried the publication through to completion: had they done so, Haym would have made history by anticipating the historiographical works of Burney and Hawkins by half a century.[29] As it is, we owe our only portraits of Thomas Tallis and William Byrd to copies that were apparently made as illustrations in preparation for this projected book.

By 1729 other innovations in London's concert life reflected an interest in the music of the past that would surely have supported the publication of Haym's *History*, had it materialized. In January 1726 an 'Academy of Vocal Music' was formed, to hold fortnightly meetings for musical performance at the Crown Tavern, near St Clement's church in the Strand.[30] Samson Estwick, one of its founder members, headed his copy of the madrigal *Dolorosi martir* by Luca Marenzio (1553–99) as follows:

> A Musick Meeting being held at ye Crown Tavern near St Clements Mr Galliard at ye head of it, & chiefly for Grave ancient vocell Musick. Wee began it wth ye following Song of Lucas de Marenzio Jan 7 – 1725/6.[31]

Estwick, by then an aging canon of St Paul's Cathedral, had been a chaplain of Christ Church, Oxford, in the 1690s: both the idea of a musical society on a 'club' basis and the taste for 'old-style' music seem to have been influenced by the musical practices of a group that had grown up around Henry Aldrich at Oxford at the end of the seventeenth century.

A decline in the number of concert advertisements from this period suggests that London's musical life in the early 1720s was dominated by operatic events; indeed, the establishment in the later 1720s of musical societies, such as the Academy of Vocal Music, and of concert clubs may well reflect a deliberate attempt to redress the balance. Taverns, which often had large rooms suitable for music-making by ensembles of moderate size, became the venues for semi-private concert clubs.[32] During his early years in London Handel had joined musicians from St Paul's Cathedral choir at the Queen's Arms Tavern (whose facilities included a harpsichord) in their informal music-making: according to received anecdote, Handel on one occasion played through Johann Mattheson's *Pièces de clavecin* very soon after their publication in 1714 to the assembled company at the tavern.[33] In 1724 Maurice Greene, in association with another young professional musician, Talbot Young, founded a concert series (the 'Castle Society') at the Castle Tavern, and this gave Greene a platform for the performance of works of the ode or oratorio type. We may also guess that the latest Italian concertos formed the favoured repertory for societies that had an instrumental ensemble. The very name of the Academy of Vocal Music reveals that that particular society did not have a resident orchestral group, so their bias towards madrigalian-type works such as Marenzio's *Dolorosi martir* is comprehensible. The members at the first meeting of the Academy consisted of ten leading singers from the choirs of St Paul's Cathedral, Westminster Abbey and the Chapel Royal, plus Pepusch, Greene, Galliard and 'The Children of St Paul's Cathedral'. Two months later Bononcini, Haym and Geminiani had been added to their number, and other leading musicians, professional and amateur, gradually joined. Geminiani presumably took part in the meetings as a singer (or listener) and not as a violinist. He was also director of another musical society, the Appollini Philo-Musicae et Architecturae Societas, which was apparently originally founded as a masonic lodge at the Queen's Head Tavern near Temple Bar in 1724.[34]

THE 1730s

During the 1730s various developments shook the relatively stable pattern of musical life that had built up during the previous decade, while at the same time spinning off new musical forms that had importance for the future. There is a strong parallel with the course of British politics at the same period: in just the same way as Walpole's 'Whig consensus', which had brought stability and prosperity to the country throughout the 1720s, broke up gradually from the time of the defeat of his Excise Bill in 1733, so divisions appeared both within the patronage base for London's music-making and within the ranks of the musicians themselves. It might even be argued that the established politicians and musicians fell victim to the same force – the new outlook of a rising generation that was finding its feet in the early 1730s.

Quite apart from internal strains within the Royal Academy of Music – strains between the two leading ladies, or between the leading castrato (Senesino) and the leading composer (Handel) – the opera venture was looking rather tired by 1730. The original patrons were by then perhaps just beginning to realize what it meant to support the company for 21 years, and there was probably some doubt as to whether the next generation was willing to shoulder the responsibility. At court in the early 1730s the events of 1717 repeated themselves in the next generation, as a rift developed between the king and Frederick, Prince of Wales. The younger members of the royal family were quite musical. Mercier's group portrait of the prince and his three sisters shows them involved in collective music-making (fig.56): at least two of the participants seem to have regarded music as more than a polite accomplishment. The eldest sister, Princess Anne, may well have received systematic musical instruction from Handel. It is too simplistic to suggest that the

56. *Frederick, Prince of Wales, and his Sisters: group portrait (1733) by Philip Mercier; the prince plays the cello, his eldest sister Princess Anne the harpsichord and Princess Caroline the mandore (or 'Milanese mandolin'), while Princess Amelia is seated to the right, reading from Milton (in the background is the Dutch House at Kew where Anne, the Princess Royal, was living before her marriage to Prince William of Orange in 1734)*

formation of a second opera company in London (the Opera of the Nobility, 1733–7) was motivated exactly by the interests of the opposition party that gathered around the Prince of Wales, for in most seasons the prince supported both Handel's company and the Nobility opera.[35] Nevertheless, the creation of the second opera company no doubt does reflect the presence in London of a new generation of patrons and connoisseurs, impatient with the establishment that the Royal Academy might be seen to represent.

The division among London's professional musicians was exposed in the unlikely arena of the Academy of Vocal Music. In 1731 a controversy arose over the authorship of a madrigal *In una siepe ombrosa*, said to have been introduced to the Academy by Maurice Greene three years previously as a composition of Bononcini's. It is uncertain whether Bononcini himself ever laid claim to the work, which was certainly composed by Antonio Lotti (*c*1667–1740), a

Venetian, but the controversy was blown up to considerable proportions, and involved the publication of the texts from an exchange of letters on the subject between the Academy and Lotti.[36] The initial round of the controversy may have been signalled by this newspaper report of an Academy programme:

> On Thursday last [14 January 1731] in the Evening, at the Academy of Vocal and Instrumental Musick, (Mr. Gates, Master of the Children of the Chapel Royal being Director for the Night, and a numerous Assembly of Nobility and Gentry being present) were performed, with universal Applause, the following Compositions:
> 1. A Madrigal for 5 Voices, by Abbot Stefani, late President of the Academy.
> 2. A Piece of Vocal and Instrumental Musick, by Sig. Faux [Fux], Chapel Master to the Emperor.
> 3. A Madrigal for 5 Voices, by Sig. Antonio Lotti, Chapel Master to the Doge of Venice.
> 4. Mr. Handell's Great Te Deum and Jubilate.[37]

Two things about this programme are of interest. The programme contained an item requiring orchestral accompaniment – 'Mr. Handell's Great [i.e. 'Utrecht'] Te Deum and Jubilate'.[38] Secondly, the director for the night's programme was Bernard Gates (*c*1685–1773), a member of the choirs of the Chapel Royal and Westminster Abbey and Master of the Children of the Chapel Royal.

As Hawkins later reported the result of the controversy,[39] the weight of opprobrium fell first on to Greene, organist of St Paul's Cathedral, and organist and composer of the Chapel Royal:

> Not able to endure the slights of those who had marked and remembered his pertinacious behaviour in this business, Dr. Greene left the academy, and drew off with him the boys of St. Paul's cathedral, and some other persons, his immediate dependents; and fixing on the great room called the Apollo at the Devil tavern, for the performance of a concert, under his sole management, gave occasion to a saying not so witty as sarcastical, viz., that Dr. Greene was gone to the Devil.

For their part, the remaining members of the Academy decided to avoid future controversy by retrenching into the performance of music that did not involve living composers, agreeing on 26 May 1731 to perform only 'ancient' music, defined thus: 'By ye composition of the Ancients is meant of such as lived before ye end of the 16th century'. (The strictness of this limitation did not survive long in practice.) The Academy of Vocal Music thus became the

Academy of Ancient Music, though in so doing it did not become immune from dispute: there was another argument in 1734 which resulted in the departure of Gates himself, who took the Chapel Royal boys with him.

Behind the original 1731 controversy it is difficult to discount the suspicion of some ill feeling between Greene and Gates, respectively the Organist and the Master of the Children of the Chapel Royal, and the conflict may have been played out in terms of their affiliation to the contemporary repertory, with Greene supporting Bononcini and Gates supporting Handel's music. That the major composers themselves were directly involved or set in opposition is less likely, but it is possible that the Academy controversy was used in some sort of campaign against Bononcini, who might in any case have felt aggrieved that the presidency of the Academy did not fall to him after the death of Steffani in 1728. Since 1724, when he had retired from an active career as opera composer for the Royal Academy of Music, Bononcini had received a handsome pension as a household musician to Henrietta, younger Duchess of Marlborough. The Lotti controversy at the Academy of Vocal Music seems to have signalled the beginning of difficulties in London for Bononcini that eventually precipitated his permanent departure from England: he fell out with his patron, and was constrained in his attempt to produce performances of his music in the London theatres during 1732.[40] All this might perhaps be of rather marginal significance were it not for a reference in a pamphlet written in May 1732:

> As for *Lincolns Inn* Playhouse, I am infor'd her Grace the D——ss of M———h, has advanc'd very largely towards a new Subscription for *Italian* Opera's, to be there under the direction of *Bononcini* and *Arrigoni*;[41]

so perhaps Bononcini was involved in the initial plans that led to the formation of the Opera of the Nobility, but was for some reason cold-shouldered from London before the venture came to fruition.

When the Opera of the Nobility did open, during the season of 1733–4, the company performed at Lincoln's Inn Fields theatre with Nicola Porpora (1686–1768) as the leading resident composer. The new company had attracted most of the soloists from the Haymarket, including Senesino, thus forcing Handel to assemble a new team for his own performances. After one season the Nobility Opera took over the premier opera house in the Haymarket from Handel, who moved his performances to John Rich's new theatre at Covent Garden. Thereafter the two opera companies mounted rival programmes until 1737. It has generally been assumed that, since Handel moved back to the Haymarket in 1737 and nothing further was heard of the Opera of the Nobility under that name, Handel simply won the competitive battle and the rival company went under. It is probable, however, that the true situation was more subtle and that some agreed re-unification took place, producing a position much closer to that enjoyed by the original Royal Academy.[42] Certainly theatrical experience had proved by 1737 that London patronage could not effectively support two companies. It is probably not entirely coincidental that the reduction to one company coincided with a formal reconciliation between the king and the Prince of Wales.

Looking at the course of events during the 1730s, it is difficult to resist the conclusion that royal patronage still had a very important effect on London's professional musicians. The divisions within the royal family gave spice to the rather destructive competition between the two opera companies, and it seems that Handel's company received active personal support from Princess Anne and Queen Caroline.[43] While Princess Anne was in London during 1733–4, the Prince of Wales supported both opera companies. After the princess's marriage in 1734 she moved to her husband's home in Holland, and for the next two seasons her brother supported the Nobility Opera only. The prince's own marriage in 1736 seems to have signalled the beginning of the official reconciliation process within the royal family, and from then onwards the prince supported both companies again, though it remained the case that no love was lost between the prince and his mother, Queen Caroline. There is strong circumstantial evidence that the queen took an active and influential interest in the musical life of the court. During four summers in the 1730s the complete choral establishment of the Chapel Royal accompanied the court on its peregrinations to Hampton Court, Kensington and Windsor. After the queen's death in 1737 this practice was discontinued, and the king was accompanied only by the minimum establishment of priests and servants. Similarly, the attendance of the royal family at musical theatre performances declined dramatically from 1738.

The royal weddings of 1734 and 1736 gave opportunities for musical ceremonial display, but in the relatively private circumstances of the Chapels Royal. The queen's funeral in 1737 at Westminster Abbey was a more public event. At each of these royal occasions the big orchestrally accompanied music was Handel's. The responsibility for the orchestrally accompanied Chapel Royal music on the king's return from Hanover had, however, passed in the new reign to Maurice Greene. On the death of John Eccles in 1735, Greene succeeded him as Master of the King's Musick and assumed responsibility for the annual court odes. Before reaching the age of 40 Greene had therefore secured all the major 'career' posts available to a court musician, as the head of the establishments of the Royal Musicians and the Chapel Royal, as well as retaining his position as organist at St Paul's Cathedral. While admittedly the most glamorous musical occasions at court went to Handel, Greene nevertheless had a quite good base for the performance of his own music. Apart from the obvious opportunities provided by Chapel Royal services and the court odes, the Apollo academy was a 'club' forum for the performance of dramatic pastorals (such as *Florimel, or Love's Revenge* and *Phoebe*) that showed Greene's melodious creative powers to their best advantage. Two younger musicians who were associated with Greene at the Apollo, Michael Festing (*d* 1752) and William Boyce (1711–79), similarly reaped the benefits of this creative outlet for their own music.

The most significant and far-reaching innovation in London's musical life during the decade arose almost accidentally from the confused situation among London's opera companies and the professional musicians. Towards the end of the 1731–2 opera season Bernard Gates arranged some 'club' performances at the Crown and Anchor Tavern of Handel's oratorio *Esther*, originally written some 14 years before for James Brydges's musicians. Gates's singers were drawn mainly from the boys of the Chapel Royal, and the performances probably involved costumes and some form of scenic representation. There was talk of transferring the production to a London theatre (according to one account, an idea encouraged by Princess Anne), but the Bishop of London, in his role as sub-dean of the Chapel Royal, forbade his charges to perform theatrically on the public stage 'even with books [i.e. music] in the children's hands'.[44] In May 1732 Thomas Arne senior advertised forthcoming performances of another work that Handel had written for Brydges, *Acis and Galatea*, in the Little Theatre, Haymarket, directly across the road from the opera house in which Handel himself was performing. Handel's response was to mount his own production of *Acis and Galatea* at the end of his opera season, in a new mixed Italian-English version performed by his opera company. He followed this with a similarly revised version of *Esther*, apparently combining the forces of his opera company with English singers mainly from the Chapel Royal choir. Handel's advertisement promoted the performance as follows:

The Sacred Story of ESTHER:
an
Oratorio in English.
Formerly composed by Mr. Handel, and now revised by him, with several Additions, and to be performed by a great Number of the best Voices and Instruments.
N.B. There will be no Action on the Stage, but the House will be fitted up in a decent Manner, for the Audience. The Musick to be disposed after the Manner of the Coronation Service.[45]

A contemporary described how he

> found this sacred *Drama* a mere Consort, no Scenary, Dress or
> Action, so necessary to a *Drama; but H——l*, was plac'd in a Pulpit,
> I suppose they call that (their Oratory) by him sate *Senesino Strada
> Bertolli*, and *Turner Robinson*, in their own Habits; before him stood
> sundry sweet Singers of this our *Israel*, and *Strada* gave us a
> *Hallelujah* of half an Hour long; *Senesino* and *Bertolli* made rare work
> with the *English* Tongue you would have sworn it had been *Welch*; I
> would have wish'd it *Italian*, that they might have sang with more
> ease to themselves, since, but for the Name of *English*, it might as
> well have been *Hebrew*.[46]

Nevertheless, the innovation of English-language theatre oratorio,
with its combination of first-rate soloists and the grand 'English'
style of the coronation anthem choruses, went down well with the
London opera-house audience, and Handel included concert performances of English-language works of the oratorio, serenata or ode
genres in his subsequent theatre seasons. Their inclusion was, however, rather irregular: Handel's first obligation during the 1730s was
still towards giving the patrons the Italian operas they expected. The
English works were written or re-structured to fulfil the conventional
three-act time-span of current operatic practice.

Indeed, it might be argued that Handel's first English-language
theatre productions survived in his repertory for the very reason that
they were mixed into seasons that drew on an audience with fairly
well-established theatre-going habits. Completely new and independent ventures into English-language music theatre did not seem to
attract even the fickle permanent base that was associated with
Italian opera. The Little Haymarket Theatre during the 1731–2
season saw the first attempt for more than a decade to produce a
new, full-length, all-sung English opera. *Amelia*, with music by
Lampe to a libretto by Henry Carey, was sufficiently successful to
warrant the extension of the original six subscription performances of
March 1732 with four additional performances in the following
month. The name part was sung by Susanna Arne, sister of the
composer Thomas Augustine Arne (1710–78) and later famous as an
actress and singer under her married name as 'Mrs Cibber'. No
doubt her father's production of Handel's *Acis and Galatea* in May
was floated upon a certain optimism created by the success of *Amelia*
and its leading singer. Arne gave only two performances of *Acis* –
hardly a serious rival to Handel's season across the road, though no
doubt rather provoking to Handel at the time – but his son moved on
to greater ambitions in the next season:

We hear that Mr Arne, junior has taken the Theatre-Royal in

London: Commercial Wealth and Cultural Expansion

Lincoln's Inn Field of Mr. Rich, to represent English Operas after the Italian manner, on Mondays and Thursdays during this winter season; in which Mrs Barbier will perform the principal Men's Characters, and Miss Arne the principal Women's and that he will open with a new English Opera on Monday, the 20th of this Instant.[47]

Although Arne managed the company, the first opera of the season, *Teraminta*, was by another composer of the younger generation, John Christopher Smith the younger (1712–95), formerly a pupil of Handel and the son of his principal music copyist. The season included Arne's version of Addison's *Rosamond* and closed in April 1733 with a single performance of Smith's *Ulysses*. Meanwhile, during the same season Lampe also mounted English operas of his own composition at the Little Theatre, Haymarket, beginning with *Britannia* four days before Arne opened his season and featuring the gimmick of 'transparent scenery'. Another new Lampe opera, *Dione*, followed, and then revivals of *Amelia*. Taking the two companies' programmes together, the season saw more than a modest success for an attempt

57. Music-making in an English home: painting (c1750), artist unknown

to launch English opera, but the initiative then promptly died as London's opera public turned its attention elsewhere, to the new rivalry between two Italian opera companies. If London could not sustain two Italian companies for long, its patience with two English opera companies was even less secure.

Handel's oratorio performances at the end of the 1734–5 season introduced a further novelty to the London theatres – organ concertos. These were normally performed at the beginning or end of Parts of the oratorios, or as interval music. Independent of the fame of Handel's own execution of the concertos, the works themselves soon became accessible through publication. On the death of John Walsh senior in 1734, his son (also John) inherited the music publishing business and seems to have improved an already thriving concern. He also made some sort of deal whereby he became Handel's 'official' publisher,[48] and the organ concertos appeared in 1738 as Handel's 'Opus 4' in an edition approved by the composer. Even more remarkably, Walsh produced a full score of Handel's setting of Dryden's ode *Alexander's Feast* the next year, and Handel's op.6 *Concerti grossi* – one of the peaks of Baroque instrumental music, composed in 1739 – appeared in 1740.

Rather more surprising, and of considerable significance from both European and English perspectives, were the first publications of Domenico Scarlatti's keyboard works at the same period. The first edition of Scarlatti's *Essercizi* was published in London in 1738, just ahead of a Venetian edition. More influential in London, however, was the collection that appeared early the next year:

> XLII Suites de Pièces Pour le Clavecin. En Deux Volumes. Composées par Domenico Scarlatti . . . NB. I think the following Pieces for their Delicacy of Stile, and Masterly Composition, worthy the Attention of the Curious, Which I have Carefully revised and corrected from the Errors of the Press. Thos. Roseingrave, London.

Roseingrave (1690–1766), appointed first organist of St George's, Hanover Square, in 1725 but dismissed in 1738–9 after showing signs of mental instability, had followed Scarlatti round Venice, Rome and Naples as a disciple in 1710–13. Carrying his enthusiasm for Scarlatti's music back to London, Roseingrave's successful promotion of his idol's music is reflected in a subscription list of 95 names for the publication, including Arne, Boyce, Greene, Pepusch and John Stanley. Another subscriber was Charles Avison (1709–70) of Newcastle-upon-Tyne, who published a set of 12 concerti grossi in 1744 derived from the music of Scarlatti's keyboard pieces.

The late 1730s also saw another important development, and one

58. George Frideric Handel: marble statue (1738) by Louis François Roubiliac commissioned for Vauxhall Gardens by Jonathan Tyers, the proprietor

that seems to hint at a cooling of the divisions among professional musicians that had characterized the earlier part of the decade. In 1738, following the discovery that the children of Jean Christian Kytch, the first oboe player from Handel's opera orchestra, were living in poverty after their father's death, the musicians rallied round to found a charity, the Fund for the Support of Decay'd Musicians and their Families. Handel, Festing and Greene were among the founder members.

THE 1740s

As Handel moved gradually into English-language works, his music and personality increasingly dominated wider areas of London's musical life. The mutual acceptance between the composer and the city of his adoption is symbolized by the statue commissioned by

The Late Baroque Era

Jonathan Tyers for Vauxhall Gardens in 1738 (fig.58). The composer is not portrayed as a distant foreign figure associated with an aristocratic form of entertainment: while kings and lords were commemorated in formal or military attire, and frequently on horseback, Handel is depicted at his ease, without his wig and with one shoe off, one shoe on, composing tunes (Apollo-style) with a lyre. The venue for the statue is itself significant: the new and elaborately arranged Vauxhall pleasure gardens, along with the spa-centres noted during the first decade of the century, provided for the less formal entertainment of the Londoner (see fig. 59). There could be heard instrumental music and vocal solos, often songs from the shows currently playing in the theatres. Across the river from Vauxhall Gardens in 1749, Handel's music gathered at an open-air performance what was probably the largest London musical audience of the eighteenth century, for the *Music for the Royal Fireworks* at Green Park, celebrating the Peace of Aix-la-Chapelle.

Handel's move from Italian to English works in his theatre career was accompanied by a transition from the old system of 'patronage' opera management to impresario management by the composer himself. In a sense this could be seen as a return to the old system of the theatre managers, though Handel was responsible only for his own performances and not for the general management and programmes of the theatres in which he performed. The decisive break in Handel's career came in 1741–2, when he took himself away from London for one season. Before this Dublin visit Handel was primarily a composer of staged Italian operas: after his return to London in 1743 he gave no more staged performances and no more Italian works, but concentrated on theatre concert oratorio.[49] In the first years he ran the seasons mainly on a subscription basis, but in 1747 he discontinued the subscription system and relied thenceforth on supporting his performances from direct ticket sales. The overall success of Handel's ventures with London audiences over the next 20 years (though coloured by peaks and troughs in individual seasons) was such that he died in comfortable financial circumstances, having attained the status of a public figure worthy of a resting-place in Westminster Abbey. He gave his last opera performance in London in February 1741: the date may be significant as marking the termination of what Handel might have seen as his 21-year obligation to the Royal Academy of Music. Italian opera continued in London, but in other hands. A new management was formed under Lord Middlesex,[50] and Handel apparently resisted various pressures that were directed towards securing his involvement. The new opera company's achievements were not negligible – Galuppi and Gluck came to London to contribute to the programmes – but somehow they lacked the lustre of the great days of the Academy in the 1720s

59. Song sheet from George Bickham's 'The Musical Entertainer', i (1737), with 'The Adieu to the Spring-Gardens' by Boyce; the engraved headpiece (after H. F. Gravelot) shows the Grove and Orchestra at Vauxhall Gardens in the artificial light of evening; the figure seated at the table, with a hat, probably represents Frederick, Prince of Wales

or of Handel's Covent Garden productions in the 1730s. The patrons also soon ran into the same financial difficulties as their ancestors.

London's musical life continued to be affected considerably by public events: the Jacobite rebellion of 1745 produced a short-term panic in London that kept audiences away, severely restricting the quantity of theatre and concert performances. The last years of the decade saw a peaceful plateau of achievement and stability: the Jacobite threat had been countered, the European war had been terminated by the Peace of Aix-la-Chapelle, and Britain's troubles on the continent of America had not yet begun. If Handel's *Judas Maccabaeus* (1746–7) celebrated the victory over the Jacobite rebels, his *Solomon* (1749–50) reflects the period of security and stability that followed. Although the musical routines of court life – such as the performance of regular odes or occasional commemorative anthems – continued, royal influence on music-making seems to have diminished somewhat, because of a reduction in the musical (or music-related) activities undertaken or encouraged by members of the royal family. As already noted, the full Chapel Royal ceased to travel with the king after 1738, and the newspapers reported few visits to the theatres or to Handel's oratorios by the king or the Prince of Wales in the 1740s,[51] in spite of the obvious topical reference of Handel's 'victory' oratorios such as *Judas Maccabaeus*.

Nevertheless, court employment remained an important source of security for many singers and instrumentalists, while theatre musicians looked after their own security by mounting mixed programmes of miscellaneous items as 'benefit concerts'. The benefit system was an accepted practice in the theatres for leading singers or composers: a named person would receive the proceeds of a specified performance of a dramatic work during a regular repertory run. Miscellaneous musical programmes had for long been performed as 'benefits' in the concert rooms and peripheral concert venues (some examples are to be found in the York Buildings concert advertisements quoted above) and, with less frequency, in the theatres. Handel had mounted such a benefit concert of his own works at the Haymarket theatre in 1738, and during the 1740s individual singers and instrumentalists increasingly arranged miscellaneous musical programmes for their own benefit concerts in the theatres, presumably including as many attractions – well-known pieces of music, well-known solo performers, or novelties – as they could manage to collect. Some of the most ambitious programmes were associated with the annual benefit concert for the Fund for the Support of Decay'd Musicians.

Of the younger composers working regularly in London in the 1740s, the most remarkable was certainly Thomas Augustine Arne. Since 1734 Arne had been a house composer for Drury Lane

Theatre, contributing musical scores of various magnitude from incidental songs to complete masques. The 1740s saw some of his best work. *Alfred*, first performed at the Prince of Wales's country residence at Cliveden, Bucks., in 1740 and introduced into the London theatre seasons in 1745, included Arne's most famous song, *Rule, Britannia*; his settings of *Blow, blow thou winter wind* and *Where the bee sucks* were written for revivals of Shakespeare's *As you Like it* and *The Tempest* at Drury Lane in 1740 and 1746 respectively. In 1745 he was also engaged as resident composer for Vauxhall Gardens. Arne enjoyed a successful career with his songs there, and also at Ranelagh and Marylebone Gardens. The structure of his career is in direct contrast to Greene's: Arne made his way in the commercial world of London's theatre music without a professional base in the Chapel Royal (from which his Roman Catholicism debarred him) and without regular employment or pensions from the court.

William Boyce, Arne's junior by one year, managed to some extent to span the two cultures. He held offices as Organist and Composer at the Chapel Royal from 1736, supplementing these with two organist's posts in the City of London – at St Michael's Cornhill (from 1736) and All Hallows the Great (from 1749); yet he also embarked on a successful career as a theatre composer at Drury Lane in 1749, contributing first a couple of songs for a revival of a farce by David Garrick and then writing a more extensive score for *The Chaplet*, a 'musical entertainment' that gained a place as one of the favourite afterpieces in theatrical programmes. Boyce's earlier serenata *Solomon* was more appropriate for 'club concert' than for theatrical performance: its first known performance took place in Dublin in 1741, but another was given soon afterwards in London by the Society of Apollo, and the work was published in full score in 1743.

Another important publication of Boyce's music was his set of 12 trio sonatas (1747). But for the most significant publications of instrumental music by a London-based composer during the decade we have to look to John Stanley (1712–86). His set of six concertos (concerti grossi) op.2, published in 1742, is among the finest produced by an English composer in the eighteenth century. Similarly, three sets of ten organ voluntaries opp.5–7 (1748–54) quickly and deservedly attained 'classic' status in a musical genre previously represented in the eighteenth century by the less ambitious publications of Philip Hart (1704) and Roseingrave (1728). Some of Stanley's voluntaries were composed before or around the time of his appointment as organist to the Temple church in 1734, and show a remarkably early and complete absorption of the Vivaldian style into a typically English medium. Stanley's compositional skill is by no means derivative, however, and we can understand why even Handel may have gone to hear the blind organist at the Temple church. The first set (op.5) seems to contain his most recent music, most of it probably composed not long before its publication in 1748.[52]

*

Looking back from 1750 over the course of half a century, the structure of London's music-making had perhaps not changed all that much: as in 1700, the choice for a professional musician lay between a career in court employment, in ecclesiastical establishments or in the theatre. But London's musical scene, already highly active in 1700, had expanded enormously during the half-century. While some of the expansion involved new ventures into opera and oratorio, much may be seen as a simple multiplication of opportunities that were already there at the beginning of the century. By 1750 the number of concert and music-theatre performances in London was probably larger than in any other European city. While influxes of foreign musicians had enlivened musical life in London throughout the period, the native talents of Croft, Green and Arne also made a good showing. Many foreign influences were intelligently and positively absorbed by the musical community. Some Italian string players settled permanently in Britain, and their English pupils took their places in the next generation of orchestral musicians. In 1742 Galliard published an English translation of a 'classic' Italian treatise on singing – Pier Francesco Tosi's *Opinioni de' cantori antichi e moderni*. Handel promoted and trained new English theatre singers in his oratorios, along with some Italians who could adapt to the English language. Between oratorio, theatre and the pleasure gardens an English soloist might carve a respectable career for himself or herself. The wealth of London as a commercial centre, and the relatively high proportion of this wealth that filtered into the 'middle' classes, provided a sound economic base for cultural activity: London was a busy city and counted music within its 'busy-ness'.

NOTES

[1] Years are given in modern style (beginning 1 January), but dates according to the Old Style calendar currently in use in London throughout the period.

[2] 'London' here includes the Cities of London and Westminster, and the immediately surrounding areas. For individual church appointments within the smaller area of the City of London itself, see D. Dawe, *Organists of the City of London 1666–1850* (Padstow, 1983). Control of professional music-making within the City (waits and dancing-masters) was in theory exercised by the Worshipful Company of Musicians: see Dawe, pp.10–13.

[3] A detailed description of the performances is given in a letter of 26 March 1701 from Congreve to Joseph Keally, printed in B. Dobrée, ed., *The Mourning Bride: Poems and Miscellanies by William Congreve* (London, 1928), 488–9.

[4] The last new masque was probably *Peleus and Thetis*, in Granville's *The Jew of Venice* (Lincoln's Inn Fields, January 1701).

[5] The original Italian libretto was written by Tomaso Stanzano for a production in Bologna, 1676; the English text for 1705 was the work of Motteux.

[6] *Arsinoe* libretto, Preface.

[7] J. Downes, *Roscius Anglicanus* (London, 1708), 48.

[8] R. Hume, 'The Sponsorship of Opera in London, 1704–1720', *Modern Philology*, lxxxv (1988), 420–32.

[9] *HawkinsH*, 788–92. See also E. Ward, *A Complete and Humorous Account of all the Remarkable Clubs and Societies in the Cities of London and Westminster* (London, 1745).

[10] Advertisement for concert on 31 March 1710, *The Tatler* (18 March)

[11] R. McGuinness, *English Court Odes 1660–1820* (Oxford, 1971).

[12] To judge from the lists 'Stewards, the 'Musical Society' was managed by a combination of professional musicians and interested connoisseurs.

[13] R. Battell, *The Lawfulness and Expediency of Church-Musick asserted in a Sermon preached at St Bride's Church, upon the 22nd of November 1693* (London, 1694).

[14] The famous setting of these canticles, though henceforward closely identified with the St Cecilia service, may have been composed with an eye on the possibility of a performance at court. It was the only orchestrally accompanied church music that King William III heard after that performed at his coronation: see D. Burrows, *Handel and the English Chapel Royal in the Reigns of Queen Anne and King George I* (diss., Open U., 1981), i, 28–9.

[15] B. Wood, 'Cavendish Weedon, Impresario Extraordinary', *The Consort*, no.33 (1977), 222–4.

[16] 26 singers in the Chapel Royal, plus organists and composers; 24 string players under the Master of the Queen's/King's Musick; and 16 trumpet players under the Serjant Trumpeter. In addition, trumpets, drums and oboes were employed in units of the guards.

[17] J. Milhous and R. D. Hume 'New Light on Handel and the Royal Academy of Music', *Theatre Journal*, xxxv (1983), 149–67, esp. 156; see also J. Milhous and R. Hume, 'Handel's Opera Finances in 1732', *MT*, cxxv (1984), 86–9.

[18] Under Owen Swiney's management in 1708–9 the First Gallery price was 2s. 6d., the Second Gallery 1s. 6d. Audience capacities are difficult to calculate: Covent Garden and the later Lincoln's Inn Fields theatre may have held 1400, and the Haymarket opera house about 1000.

[19] The pasticcio *Arminio* (26 October 1714).

[20] Handel's national status before his naturalization as a British subject in 1727 presumably debarred him from court appointments, though he was able to receive royal pensions.

[21] J. Milhous and R. D. Hume, 'The Charter for the Royal Academy of Music', *ML*, lxvii (1986), 50–58.

[22] R. Hatton, *George I, Elector and King* (London, 1978), 46–7; C. Timms, 'George I's Venetian Palace and Theatre Boxes in the 1720s', *Music and Theatre: Essays in Honour of Winton Dean* (Cambridge, 1987), 95–9; D. Burrows and R. D. Hume, 'George I, the Haymarket Opera Company and Handel's "Water Music"', *EM*, xix (1991), 323–41.

[23] For some relative statistics of performances of Handel and non-Handel operas in the earlier period, see Hume, 'The Sponsorship of Opera', 428.

[24] L. Lindgren, 'Ariosti's London Years, 1716–1729', *ML*, lxii (1981), 331–51.

[25] L. Lindgren, 'The Accomplishments of the Learned and Ingenious Nicola Francesco Haym (1678–1729)', *Studi musicali*, xvi (1987), 247–380. Haym was the leading continuo cellist for the Haymarket opera during Handel's first years in London, and served as performer-composer to several patrons, including the Duke of Bedford and James Brydges: for the latter he composed a repertory of English anthems.

[26] L. Lindgren, '"Camilla" and "The Beggar's Opera"', *Philological Quarterly*, lix (1980), 44–61.

[27] J. Wiford, *Monthly Catalogue* (June 1926).

[28] *The Flying-Post, or Weekly Medley* (29 March 1729).

[29] See also C. Hogwood, 'Thomas Tudway's History of Music', *Music in the Eighteenth Century: Essays in Memory of Charles Cudworth* (Cambridge, 1983), 19–47. Interesting as Tudway's work is as an example of historical writing about music, Haym's would nevertheless have been a more significant landmark: Tudway's *History* was mainly concerned with church music, and it was written for a private patron, not for publication.

[30] The first minute-book of the Academy is now *GB-Lbl* Add. 11732.

[31] *GB-Dc* MS E15, f.1.

[32] Taverns should be distinguished from inns (which normally had residential accommo-

dation) and ale-houses (which were less salubrious, and normally provided only small-beer as refreshment).

[33] *HawkinsH*, 852.

[34] The society's minute-book is now *GB-Lbl* Add. 23202. The formal institutionalization of freemasonry was one of the historical landmarks of London's history in the period under review: the minutes reveal some doubt about the legitimization of this society within the masonic structure.

[35] C. Taylor, 'Handel and Frederick, Prince of Wales', *MT*, cxxv (1984), 89–92.

[36] L. Lindgren, 'The Three Great Noises fatal to the Interests of Bononcini', *MQ*, lxi (1975), 560–83.

[37] *Daily Journal* (16 Jan 1731).

[38] Handel himself was apparently never a member of the Academy.

[39] *HawkinsH*, 884.

[40] Lindgren, 'The Three Great Noises'.

[41] *See and Seem Blind*, pp.25–6.

[42] R. D. Hume, 'Handel and Opera Management in London in the 1730s', *ML*, lxvii (1986), 347–62.

[43] R. Sedgwick, ed., *Lord Hervey's Memoirs* (London, 1963), 42–3.

[44] C. Burney, *An Account of the Musical Performances . . . in Commemoration of Handel* (London, 1785), 100–01.

[45] *Daily Journal* (19 April 1732).

[46] *See and Seem Blind*, pp.15–16.

[47] *The Craftsman* (4 Nov 1732).

[48] D. Burrows, 'Walsh's Editions of Opera 1–5: the Texts and their Sources', *Music in the Eighteenth Century*, 79–102. Eighteenth-century composers had, in practice, little defence of their copyright, in spite of the existence of royal privileges; in London, which had a flourishing market for printed music, it was no doubt prudent for a major composer to align himself with the most successful publisher.

[49] His repertory included works that were not strictly oratorios (e.g. *Acis and Galatea*, *Semele*) but were performed in the same manner and within the regular repertory seasons.

[50] C. Taylor, 'From Losses to Lawsuit: Patronage of Italian Opera in London by Lord Middlesex, 1739–1745', *ML*, lxviii (1987), 1–25; C. Taylor, 'Handel's Disengagement from the Italian Opera', *Handel Tercentenary Collection*, ed. S. Sadie and A. Hicks (London, 1987), 165–181.

[51] See the table of attendances in P. Daub, *Music at the Court of George II (r.1727–1760)* (diss., Cornell U., 1985), 80.

[52] B. Cooper, 'New Light on John Stanley's Organ Music', *PRMA*, ci (1974–5), 101–6.

BIBLIOGRAPHICAL NOTE

General background

General histories of the period, with their emphasis on political history, tend to divide at the change in the royal house in 1714: thus, for example, C. Hill's *The Century of Revolution, 1603–1714* (London, 1961) is followed by J. B. Owen's *The Eighteenth Century, 1714–1815* (London, 1974). The same division is found in the more detailed volumes of *The Oxford History of England*: G. Clark, *The Later Stuarts 1660–1714* (Oxford, 1956) and B. Williams, *The Whig Supremacy 1714–1760* (Oxford, 1962).

As introductory biographies of the British monarchs of the period, J. P. Kenyon's *The Stuarts: a Study in English Kingship* (London, 1958) and J. H. Plumb's *The First Four Georges* (London, 1956, 1966) are both excellent, and two of the individual monarchs have been well served by detailed modern scholarship in E. Gregg, *Queen Anne* (London, 1980) and R. Hatton, *George I, Elector and King* (London, 1978). Since patronage and public events exerted a considerable influence on London's musical life during the period, these biographies are of more than usual relevance.

London: Commercial Wealth and Cultural Expansion

Biographical studies of the noble patrons do not necessarily pay much attention to their musical interests, though such interests naturally feature in C. H. C. and M. I. Baker's *The Life and Circumstances of James Brydges, First Duke of Chandos* (Oxford, 1949) and J. Johnson's *Princely Chandos* (Gloucester, 1984). In its own field, A. S. Turbeville's *English Men and Manners in the Eighteenth Century* (London, 1929, repr. 1964) still has no successor, and the same is true of M. D. George's *London Life in the Eighteenth Century* (London, 1925). However, a valuable, less specialized survey of the period is available in R. Porter, *English Society in the Eighteenth Century* (Harmondsworth, 1982). The growth of interest in artistic patronage that was enabled by Britain's growing economic stability is well outlined in B. Denvir, *The Eighteenth Century: Art, Design and Society 1689–1789* (London, 1983); of relevance also are J. H. Plumb, *The Commercialisation of Leisure in the 18th Century* (Reading, 1973) and N. McKendrick, J. Brewer and J. H. Plumb, *The Birth of a Consumer Society* (London, 1982).

The musical world

London-based English music receives fair treatment within the relevant volumes of the *New Oxford History of Music*: volume v, *Opera and Church Music 1630–1750*, ed. A. Lewis and N. Fortune (London, 1975) and volume vi, *Concert Music 1630–1750*, ed. G. Abraham (Oxford, 1986); and in the relevant chapters of E. Walker's *A History of Music in England*, rev. J. A. Westrup (Oxford, 1952). Modern scholarly treatment of the period is provided in *The Eighteenth Century*, volume iv of *Blackwell's History of Music in Britain*, ed. H. D. Johnstone and R. Fiske (Oxford, 1990), which also includes a detailed specialist bibliography.

Although much important research on the musical life of the period has been undertaken in recent years, most of the fruits have been published in journal articles or dissertations that are not easily available to the general reader. This is specially true of the important work done by Judith Milhous and Robert D. Hume on the programmes and managements of the 'musical' theatre companies: their joint edition of *Vice Chamberlain Coke's Theatrical Papers 1706–1715* (Carbondale, IL, 1982) takes us straight into the tangled history of the London theatres at the period. C. A. Price's *Music in the Restoration Theatre* (Ann Arbor, 1979) outlines the changing programmes of the respective theatres in the early period, and the specific topic of opera is taken up by R. D. Hume's 'Opera in London, 1695–1706', in *British Theatre and the Other Arts, 1660–1800*, ed. S. S. Kenny (Washington DC, 1984). Other references to articles by Milhous and Hume are given in the above notes. An important general survey of the theatre music of the period is R. Fiske, *English Theatre Music in the Eighteenth Century* (London, 1973, 2/1986). The programmes of the theatres themselves can be followed through the various volumes of *The London Stage*, ed. W. van Lennep, E. L. Avery and A. H. Scouten (Carbondale, IL, 1960–68), and the careers of individual performers can be followed from P. H. Highfill jr and others, *A Biographical Dictionary of Actors, Actresses, Musicians, Dancers, Managers and other Stage Personnel in London 1660–1800* (Carbondale, IL, 1973–). Individual performers, composers, librettists and operas are also well covered in *Grove O*. Fiske's treatment of London's theatre music excludes the repertory of Handel's performances, which is dealt with in W. Dean and J. M. Knapp, *Handel's Operas 1704–1726* (Oxford, 1987); W. Dean, *Handel and the Opera Seria* (London, 1970); and W. Dean, *Handel's Dramatic Oratorios and Masques* (London, 1959).

Other areas of music-making are less well represented in accessible literature. C. Dearnley's *English Church Music 1650–1750* (London, 1970) remains the only book in its field, though the music of the leading London composers is dealt with in J. S. Bumpus, *A History of English Cathedral Music* (London, 1908). There is, as yet, no modern study devoted to London's musical clubs and concert societies, though one specialist strand of this activity is dealt with in W. H. Husk, *An Account of the Musical Celebrations on St Cecilia's Day* (London, 1857, 3/1862), and the cultural ambience that promoted the growth of interest in 'ancient' music is well outlined in W. Weber, *The Rise of Musical Classics in Eighteenth-Century England* (Oxford, 1992). O. E. Deutsch, *Handel: a Documentary Biography* (London, 1955), now revised and expanded in *Händel-Handbuch: gleichzeitig Supplement zu Hallische Händel-Ausgabe*, Dokumente zu Leben und Schaffen, iv (Leipzig and Kassel, 1985), includes a wealth of primary material from the period, much of it having wider relevance beyond the music of Handel.

Biographies of Handel abound: among the most recent is C. Hogwood, *Handel* (London, 1984), and D. Burrows, *Handel* (London, 1993); H. C. Robbins Landon's *Handel and his World* (London, 1984) and J. Keates's *Handel, the Man and his Music* (London, 1985) also have points of interest. The only other books on individual composers and their music are H. Langley, *Doctor Arne* (Cambridge, 1938), and D. R. Martin, *The Operas and Operatic Style of John Frederick Lampe* (Detroit, 1985). For more recent information on Arne, and for biographical studies of significant figures such as Blow, Croft, Greene, Boyce and Stanley, recourse must be made first to the articles on these composers in *Grove 6*, which also has articles on specific musical clubs and societies and a general article on music-making in London. Although journal articles have not in general been included in this review, an exception must be made for L. Lindgren's 'The Accomplishments of the Learned and Ingenious Nicola Francesco Haym (1678–1729)', *Studi musicali*, xvi (1987), 247–380.

An interesting contemporary voice from the early part of the period is easily accessible in J. Wilson, ed., *Roger North on Music* (London, 1959). Any historian of the period must acknowledge his indebtedness to *BurneyH* and *HawkinsH* – and recognize that much of their material is based on anecdote or distant recollection.

Chapter XIII

The Dutch Republic

RUDOLF RASCH

The contribution of the Netherlands to the history of music is less conspicuous than those of its larger neighbours – Germany, France and England. Its chief period of fame was during the later fifteenth century and the sixteenth, when five generations of Netherlands composers were responsible for developing the Renaissance polyphonic style that reached its climax in the works of Roland de Lassus (*d* 1594). Most of them came from the Southern Netherlands and the nearby Walloon and northern French territories, but they were active not only in the cities of northern Europe but also in Spain, Italy and the Austrian empire.

The second half of the sixteenth century was a time of drastic and dramatic change in the political, cultural and religious map of Europe. The Netherlands gained a separate political identity, comprising two separate states: the Northern Netherlands, or Republic of the Seven United Provinces (the subject of this chapter), with Calvinist Protestantism as its main religion; and the Southern Netherlands, still a part of the Spanish Habsburg empire and devoted to Catholicism and the ideals of the Counter-Reformation.[1] These political developments had a profound and long-lasting influence on musical life. While the Southern Netherlands developed along similar lines to the Catholic countries to the south and east, where church and court were the main focuses of musical life, the Northern Netherlands adopted a more isolated position, in which neither church nor court served to stimulate musical developments to any great extent.

The Calvinist Church of the new Dutch Republic allowed only music that had direct biblical inspiration, which effectively restricted the repertory to 150 psalms and a few hymns, preferably sung homophonically by the congregation as a whole, not solely by church musicians. The organ was banned from services, if not from the church altogether. As for the court, the stadholders of the House of Orange – William the Silent (stadholder 1572–84), Maurice (1585–1625), Frederick Henry (1625–47) and William II (1647–50) – maintained courts, but music played only a minor role in official court life.

The Late Baroque Era

With the death of William II a few months before the birth of his only son, later William III, there was a hiatus in court life; William III became stadholder in 1672 (and King of England in 1689), but his interest in music was limited. Another hiatus followed his death in 1702, until the accession of William IV in 1747. Under his son, William V (1751–95), there was for the first time a real interest in music at court and a chapel of musicians was maintained.

Although the seven United Provinces were allied under the banner of Calvinism, it was trade that influenced cultural life more than anything else, except perhaps religion. Trade and religion had opposite effects. Trade activities tended to be concentrated in the western provinces – Holland and Zeeland – in general and in the Republic's capital, Amsterdam, in particular, while religion stimulated the whole of the Republic. These counteracting forces had consequences for musical life: Amsterdam was by far the most important musical centre of the Northern Netherlands, especially as regards secular music and the music trade; but secondary centres remained important, such as the cities of Alkmaar, Haarlem, Leiden, The Hague, Rotterdam and Dordrecht in Holland, Middleburg in Zeeland, and Utrecht, Nijmegen, Zutphen and Groningen in the eastern and northern provinces. Musical life in the Northern Netherlands during the Baroque era, with neither church nor court to support it, was centred mainly on bourgeois society. At the same time, the music trade too was of prime importance. In the survey that follows these two factors reappear repeatedly.

Although some areas of musical activity – notably church music and public concerts – reflect indigenous trends, foreign influences have always been strong, if not dominant, in the cultural life of the Northern Netherlands. The upheavals in European politics in the seventeenth and eighteenth centuries only rarely interfered with cultural exchanges: the wars that the Netherlands fought with England and France in the second half of the seventeenth century did not prevent music from those countries becoming popular in the Netherlands (most notably in the case of Jean-Baptiste Lully, employed by the French court). On the other hand, political ties between countries could, of course, facilitate the exchange of musical influences.

The relationship between the level of musical activity in the Netherlands and the economical and political climate has always been very clear. After the troubled years of the 1670s (French troops invaded in 1672), the 1680s and 90s saw a period of growing prosperity and prominence, reinforced by the special link (through William III) between the Dutch Republic and the United Kingdom. The Nine Years War (or League of Augsburg, 1689–98) did not change that; the battlegrounds were in the Southern Netherlands, or still further away. During this period there was a conspicuous and definite shift in musical activities: foreign musicians arrived, operas were performed, musical settings of Dutch texts received a new impetus and there was a rapid rise in the international music trade. After the death of William III in 1702, and especially after the Peace of Utrecht, which ended the War of the Spanish Succession in 1715, the Dutch Republic's role as a major contender in European politics came to an end. At the same time, musical activities there gradually declined, in both number and significance.

THE DUTCH REFORMED CHURCH

The services of the Dutch Reformed Church featured two musical activities – organ playing and congregational psalm singing. Additionally, the organ was admitted as a non-liturgical concert instrument. The Dordrecht synod of the Dutch Reformed Church which met in 1574, soon after the church's organization, first attacked organ playing during services with the argument that instrumental music did not belong to Christian worship;[2] it was seen, rather, as a Jewish or Catholic 'superstition'. This led to a curious situation in which most organs came into the possession of municipal councils and organists were employed by the city, not by the church (in Haarlem that is still the case today). Organists played before and after the services, normally arrangements of psalm and hymn tunes, and also gave concerts. But during the first half of the seventeenth century accompaniment by the organ of psalm singing during the service became increasingly common, and former objections to it were laid aside. During the eighteenth century, moreover, the accompaniment of congregational psalm-singing was among the chief duties of every organist in the Dutch Reformed Church.

When the Amsterdam church council decided in 1680 to allow the organ accompaniment of congregational psalm-singing, it was one of the last major cities to do so. There were a number of Reformed churches in Amsterdam, but not all had organs at that period. The two main churches, the Oude Kerk and the Nieuwe Kerk, had two organs each; one of the smaller churches, the Nieuwezijdskapel, had one. While the Wester Kerk gained an organ in 1686, the four other churches in Amsterdam (the Zuider, Ooster, Eilands and Amstel) were not to have organs until the nineteenth century.

Some of the organists are also known to have been composers; of the others, little more than their names are known. Among the composer-organists, Sybrand van Noordt (1679–92) and Conrad Friedrich Hurlebusch (1742–65) worked at the Oude Kerk; Jan Janszoon Backer was at the Nieuwezijdskapel (1668–91) and at the

The Late Baroque Era

Wester Kerk (1691–1708); and Leonard Frischmuth was also at the Nieuwezijdskapel (1763–4).[3] Organists often moved from one church to another, gaining in rank as they did so. The ranking order at the time was (from low to high): Nieuwezijdskapel, Wester Kerk, Oude Kerk, Nieuwe Kerk. Some organists stayed long at their posts, up to about 50 years. Amsterdam also housed churches of other religious communities, such as Lutherans and Catholics, which also employed organists.

Important organists from outside Amsterdam, known from their musical compositions or from their writings about music, included Quirinus Blankenburg and Gerhardus Havingha. Quirinus Gerbrandszoon van Blankenburg (1654–1739), one of the more colourful personalities in the musical history of the Netherlands,[4] was born in Gouda and was employed as an organist and carillonist at a number of churches in Rotterdam, Gorinchem and The Hague; his works include the cantata *L'apologie des femmes*, organ settings of the complete psalms (see below) and some smaller keyboard works. In 1739, shortly before his death, he published a treatise on music in Dutch, *Elementa musica*, which he claimed was the result of more than 60 years of study. It includes a *Fuga obligata*, on a theme also used by Handel.[5] Gerhardus Havingha (1696–1753), born in Groningen, was chiefly employed at the Laurenskerk in Alkmaar.[6] Soon after his arrival in 1722 he proposed a thorough reconstruction of the organ on contemporary German principles (including equal temperament) by Franz Caspar Schnitger (German influence was specially strong in Groningen). Although the plan was approved by the city magistrate and carried out it met with a lot of opposition from the citizens of Alkmaar, and Havingha defended his case in an apologia, *Oorspronk en voortgang der orgelen* (1727).[7]

Singing in the Dutch Reformed Church was – and still is – an activity in which the whole congregation took part, supported only by a precentor (*voorzanger*) who as a rule was not a trained musician but a sexton, schoolmaster or simple craftsman.[8] The repertory consisted of the 150 psalms and a few hymns; the melodies were those of the Genevan psalter, the texts translations by Petrus Dathenus of the French psalm texts by Marot and De Bèze. Although Dathenus's translation (first published in 1566) lacked every quality essential to a metrical psalter, it remained in use until the second half the eighteenth century (and is still used today by some religious groups in the Netherlands). The seventeenth century saw dozens of new versifications, but none replaced Dathenus's version, which, though defective, was regarded as authoritative. After 1750 a few new translations appeared that paved the way for the completely revised Dutch Reformed Psalm Book of 1773, such as those by the Konstgenootschap (Society of Arts) entitled *Laus Deo, salus populo*

(Amsterdam, 1760) and by Joannes Eusebius Voet (The Hague, 1763).

Although the texts of psalms around 1700 were the same as in 1566, when Dathenus's psalter appeared, the melodies were certainly not, neither as regards pitch nor rhythm. Seventeenth-century performing practice had introduced a number of sharpened leading-notes into the sixteenth-century modal melodies, and their rhythm was altered too: while the Genevan melodies called for semibreves and minims in regular alternation, it became increasingly common practice in the eighteenth-century Netherlands to give all notes an equal length, perhaps as a consequence of the slower tempo of congregational singing; another rhythmic variant involved singing the first and last notes of each line long and the others short.

Composing complete keyboard harmonizations of the psalms was of little interest to the seventeenth-century Dutch organist, though more so for his eighteenth-century counterpart. Indeed, a number of eighteenth-century organists published their collected accompaniments in 'chorale books' or 'organ psalmbooks'. The most important ones of the first half of the eighteenth century are those by Gerhard Fredrik Witvogel (*c*1669–1746), organist of the Lutheran church in Amsterdam (*De zangwysen van de CL Psalmen Davids*, 1731), Blankenburg (*Clavecimbel en orgel-boek der gereformeerde Psalmen*, 1732) and Hurlebusch (*De 150 Psalmen Davids*, 1746). As well as adding a good number of sharps, they have a lot of ornamental notes to be played by the organist while the congregation sang the unornamented melody. Complete settings for organ of the psalter became very fashionable during the second half of the century, especially after the introduction of the official revised Psalm Book of 1773.

For non-liturgical organ recitals, organists presumably played psalm and hymn arrangements, as well 'free' compositions such as fantasias and toccatas. During the eighteenth century a tradition developed of using the organ to imitate natural and other non-musical sounds, such as birdsong and the noise of battle. In addition, organ transcriptions of popular tunes, suites, sonatas and concertos became popular; there was relatively little original repertory. In the seventeenth century organ concerts often took place daily, but in the eighteenth they were given less frequently, possibly twice a week.

CONCERT LIFE AND OPERA

Collegia musica

The main groups performing ensemble music in the seventeenth century were the civic musicians and the collegia musica. The role of the civic musician may be considered a remnant of an earlier tradition; that moved gradually towards extinction during the last decades of the seventeenth century. The collegium musicum, on the other hand, was a new phenomenon of the early years of the Republic and lasted as an institution until the end of the eighteenth century.

A collegium musicum usually consisted of about a dozen mostly well-to-do citizens who gathered once a week to make music, often under the direction of the local organist or other local professional musician. Collegia musica of this kind existed in Amsterdam, Utrecht, Arnhem, Nijmegen, Zutphen, Leeuwarden and Leiden, among other places. Often they had a semi-official status and could make use of rooms provided by the municipal government. During the eighteenth century two collegia – in Utrecht and Arnhem – developed from amateur groups into semi-professional, concert-giving bodies. But organized concerts for a paying public did not begin until the mid-eighteenth century, when virtuoso performers travelling from abroad began to visit the Netherlands.

In Amsterdam a collegium musicum had existed since the beginning of the seventeenth century under the direction of Jan Pieterszoon Sweelinck (1562–1621), the organist of the Oude Kerk and a leading composer of keyboard and vocal music.[9] No evidence is available concerning later collegia musica there. There are a few records of very early concerts, to which the public were charged admission: they took place in the Stadsschouwburg (City Theatre) during the summer months, when there were no plays, and are documented in 1643, 1648 and 1662;[10] in 1662 the concerts were given by a group of musicians from the French court, under the direction of Bernard Dommaille.

Opera

Opera began to thrive in the Netherlands at the end of the seventeenth century.[11] The Amsterdam Stadsschouwburg was closed for five years during the Franco-Dutch War; when it reopened in 1677 Lully's *Isis* was given, probably by French musicians, within a year of its Paris première. At Christmas 1680 Dirck ('Teodoro') Strijcker, son of the former Dutch consul in Venice, established a theatre for Italian opera in Amsterdam which survived only until early in 1682. Among the operas performed there were *Le fatiche d'Ercole per Deianira* (1681), by the Venetian composer P. A. Ziani, and *Helena rapita da Paride* (1682) by Domenico Freschi (also from Venice), with additions by P. A. Fiocco. Fiocco, another Venetian, may have travelled via Hanover to Amsterdam to assist Strijcker.[12] The librettos of these operas were published in Dutch.

In 1686 the Dutch poet Thomas Arendsz adapted and translated

Quinault's libretto for Lully's *Roland* as a stage play. In the summer of 1687 a number of other French operas by Lully were performed at the Stadsschouwburg: *Amadis* was given 25 times, *Cadmus et Hermione* 16 times and *Atys* 11 times. The following summer (1688) three more were staged: *Le triomphe de Bacchus et de l'Amour*, *Persée* and *Proserpine*; and two of Quinault's librettos – *Amadis* and *Cadmus* – were published in Dutch translation. Many complete Lully operas and collections of *airs* or instrumental items from them were published in Amsterdam, mostly between about 1682 and 1710, notably by such publishers as Joan Philip Heus, Anthony Pointel, Amadée Le Chevalier and Estienne Roger. No new performances of Lully operas seem to have been given in Amsterdam after 1687, but in The Hague they continued to be staged at infrequent intervals between 1700 and about 1730. Lully's music clearly had a substantial impact on Dutch musical life around 1700.

Besides French opera, an indigenous form of music theatre – the *zangspel* or *muziekspel*, a light genre with a mixture of speech and song – flourished briefly. Poets such as Dirck Buysero, Goverd Bidloo, Abraham Alewijn (1664–1721) and Kornelis Zweerts (1669–1742) produced about a dozen librettos of this kind, which were set to music by composers such as Carolus Hacquart (*c*1640–?1700), Johannes Schenck (1660–*c*1712), Hendrik Anders (*c*1657–1714) and Servaas de Konink (1654–1701). Hacquart, born in Bruges, went north around 1670, first to Amsterdam and later (*c*1680) to The Hague, where he moved in court circles.[13] Schenck was born of German descent in Amsterdam, and in 1696 moved to the palatine court in Düsseldorf, where he remained until 1716; he was famous as a viola da gamba player and composed mostly for this instrument.[14] Hacquart's music for *De triomfeerende min* (text by Buysero, written to celebrate the Peace of Nijmegen in 1678, but probably not performed then) and Schenck's for *Bacchus, Ceres en Venus* (text by Bidloo, 1686, given about a dozen times) survive because they were printed; but nothing remains (or, at the most, a few fragments) of the *zangspelen* by Anders and De Konink. Although opera flourished in The Hague for most of the period 1700–33, there was no comparable activity in Amsterdam until the mid-eighteenth century; music and dance, however, did play important roles in the stage plays given there.

Concerts

During the 1730s a number of large-scale public performances of music took place in the Netherlands. In 1736, when the centenary of the University of Utrecht was celebrated, the Collegium Musicum Ultrajectinum was responsible for the musical part of the festivities. The orchestra, under the direction of the conductor of the collegium, the organist J. C. F. Fischer, consisted of a nucleus of amateur collegium members supplemented by professional musicians from Utrecht and elsewhere. They played an 'Introductio et Symphonia' by Fischer for strings and woodwind (horns, oboes and flutes) and a cantata by Carl Georg Geilfuss.[15] The centenary of the Amsterdam Stadsschouwburg, celebrated in 1738, included a performance of a substantial amount of orchestral music. The pieces played included concertos by Vivaldi and Willem de Fesch, and music by lesser-known composers such as J. J. Agrell, Bernhard Hupfeld and Giovanni Chinzer.[16]

In spite of P. A. Locatelli's presence in Amsterdam (see below), no tradition of public concerts seems to have existed before the middle of the eighteenth century. The earliest ones were organized by impresarios, such as Ignazio Raimondi between 1762 and 1780. Their continuance was ensured only with the foundation of the Felix Meritis Society in 1777. In The Hague, too, the first public concerts took place in the middle of the century. Advertisements in local newspapers are a useful source of information about them. One of the first concerts, on 9 May 1749, was given by the violinist Pieter Hellendaal (1721–99), among the most important Dutch composers and performers of the eighteenth century. At a time when many musical positions in the Netherlands were taken by foreigners, Hellendaal, who had studied with Tartini in Padua around 1740, spent most of his career in England.[17] His works include concerti grossi, violin sonatas (often virtuoso), cello sonatas, catches and glees.

It was in The Hague, however, that the best-known instrumental works from the late Baroque era in the Netherlands were produced – the six *Concerti armonici* that were published anonymously in 1740 by Carlo Ricciotti (*c*1681–1756), an Italian active in The Hague from 1702. The concertos have been attributed (in manuscript copies, early reprints, catalogues etc.) variously to Handel, G. B. Pergolesi, Ricciotti, Willem de Fesch and others. But in 1979 the autograph manuscript was discovered in Twickel castle, in Overijssel, and it became clear that one of the castle's eighteenth-century owners, Count Unico Wilhelm van Wassenaer (1692–1766), had composed them.[18] They were probably written for private performance in The Hague by an aristocratic amateur collegium musicum under Ricciotti's direction in which the count participated.

Another leading Dutch violinist and composer who had most of his career in England was Willem de Fesch (1687–1761).[19] Born in Alkmaar, he first worked as a musician in Amsterdam; he married Carl Rosier's daughter Maria Anna (see below). After a spell as music director of Antwerp Cathedral, he departed for England, where he became well known as a performer and as a composer of solo and trio sonatas, cello sonatas, concerti grossi and vocal works.

THE INFLUX OF FOREIGN MUSICIANS

Towards the end of the seventeenth century the population of Amsterdam took on a cosmopolitan air. Its liberal religious and commercial climate attracted many tradespeople and craftsmen from Germany, France and Italy. The Revocation of the Edict of Nantes by the French King Louis XIV in 1685 gave a major impetus to the influx of thousands of Huguenots into the Dutch Republic. The personal union between the Netherlands and the United Kingdom, though forging close links between the two countries, seems not to have brought many Englishmen to settle in the Republic, however.

Musicians were among the immigrants. The musical history of the Netherlands is in some large part the history of musical foreigners. The popular musical genres around 1700 – Dutch songs with continuo accompaniment, Dutch *zangspel* and trio sonatas – were dominated by a group of four musicians, all foreigners: Servaas de Konink (from Flanders), Nicolas Ferdinand le Grand (possibly from France), David Petersen (from Lübeck) and Hendrik Anders (from Thuringia). These composers cooperated with two Dutch poets and librettists, Abraham Alewijn and Kornelis Zweerts.

David Petersen (1651–1737), born in Lübeck, arrived in Amsterdam around 1675 and was famous as a violinist: his *Speelstukken* for violin and figured bass (1683) demand considerable performing ability. Later, he provided the music for Alewijn's *Zede-en Harpgezangen* (1694). Hendrik Anders (1657–1714), born in Overweissbach, Thuringia, was appointed organist of the Lutheran church in 1683 but was dismissed in 1694 for misbehaviour and in 1696 became city carillonist. He composed two sets of suites and overtures for instrumental ensemble,[20] several *zangspelen*, and Dutch songs with continuo accompaniment; he died in extreme poverty. In 1698 he founded a professional collegium musicum – to be distinguished from the amateur ones – together with Carl Rosier (and his daughters Maria Petronella and Maria Anna), Nicolas Ferdinand le Grand, Nicolas Desrosiers, Jacobus Cockuyt (or Cocquu) and Michel Parent. Two observations may be made concerning this collegium. First, its participants were exclusively foreign. Carl Rosier (1640–1725) was born in Liège and was first employed in Bonn, before reaching the Netherlands in about 1675.[21] Desrosiers and Cockuyt were of French origin. Parent (1665–1710), though born in Amsterdam was also of French origin and was not only a musician but also a woodwind instrument maker. Secondly, there was a close relationship between the collegium and the musicians of the city theatre: Anders, Le Grand, Cockuyt and Parent were all employed by the theatre at some time, although the relevant documentation gives a less than clear picture of their activities.

Servaas de Konink (1654–1701), born in Dendermonde, Flanders, settled in Amsterdam around 1685.[22] He composed the music for the *zangspel De vryadje van Cloris en Roosje* (text by Buysero, 1688), which until the later eighteenth century was performed almost every year at the Amsterdam Stadsschouwburg. During the years 1696–9, Estienne Roger published no fewer than seven volumes of his music, which included choruses for Racine's *Athalie* (1697), concertato motets, Dutch songs[23] and chamber music (notably trios and sonatas). His son, also Servaas de Konink (1683–1718), was also employed by the theatre as a musician. Nicolas Ferdinand le Grand (*d* 1710) probably arrived in Amsterdam from either France or the Southern Netherlands in the 1680s. He composed only vocal music – Dutch songs,[24] solo cantatas and other vocal chamber music, including several items (1708) in which the texts deal with the War of the Spanish Succession.[25] There are several cross-relations among these musicians who were of similar ages: De Konink, Anders and Le Grand provided music for the songbook *Verscheide nieuwe zangen* (1697), with texts by Zweerts; De Konink, Petersen and Anders collaborated on *Boertige en ernstige minnezangen* (1705, 1709), with texts by Alewijn, Zweerts and others; and Anders edited the second edition (1709) of De Konink's *Hollandsche minne- en drinkliederen*.

The eighteenth century saw a new and continuous stream of foreign musicians arriving in the Netherlands, either for short visits – like Mozart's and Beethoven's, during the second half of the century – or for prolonged stays. The most famous of the latter type was Pietro Antonio Locatelli (1695–1764), born in Bergamo, who settled in Amsterdam in 1729 after travels as a violin virtuoso and remained there all his life.[26] During that time he sometimes gave performances, but always on private, not public, occasions. A possible reason for his move to Amsterdam was the strength of its music printing and publishing industry: the *XII concerti grossi* op.1 were published in a revised edition by Michel-Charles le Cène in 1729, the first outcome of a prolonged cooperation between the two men (see below). The large-scale works, such as *L'arte del violino* op.3 (1733, a set of 12 violin concertos with the 24 famous solo capriccios), were generally financed by Le Cène; the smaller ones, such as the sonatas for one or two violins or flutes, were printed by Le Cène but published by Locatelli himself. It seems that Locatelli also acted as a copy-editor for Le Cène.

The careers of some German musicians in Amsterdam are typical of the Dutch careers of German musicians in general. Elias Bronnemüller (?c1675–1762) arrived in the Dutch Republic around 1700 and worked first in The Hague before settling in Amsterdam; he published three volumes of keyboard and chamber music in Amsterdam (1709–12). Many German musicians were employed as organists. A competition held in 1719 for the organist's post at the Lutheran Nieuwe Kerk in Amsterdam illustrates the measure of attraction that such positions held for foreigners. There were nine applicants, of whom only three were Dutch (Abraham Giesken and Hendrik Lageman of Amsterdam, and Theodorus Dikte of Leiden). The other six came from abroad, mostly from northern Germany: Varel, near Oldenburg (Gerhard Fredrik Witvogel); Hamburg (Johann Colver, Laurentius Laurenti); and Helmerstadt (Friedrich Ebeling). Some came from further: Dresden (Emanuel Benisch) and Stockholm (Christian Steinberg). Laurenti was appointed.

In addition to Hurlebusch and Frischmuth, other Germans who worked in the Republic include Johann Philipp Albrecht Fischer (1698–1778), born in Ingersleben, Thuringia, who was organist of the Lutheran church in Utrecht before becoming organist and carillonist of Utrecht Cathedral in 1737 (the posts of organist and carillonist at a church were often held by the same person). He wrote a number of books on music theory and on bells, and his *Kort en grondig onderwijs van de transpositie* (Utrecht, 1728) contains instructions for tuning a keyboard in equal temperament. This (like Havingha's work in Alkmaar) shows that equal temperament was by then already gaining ground in the Netherlands.[27]

Jacob Wilhelm Lustig (1706–96), born in Hamburg, is another German organist working in the Netherlands who is perhaps better known for his writings than for his compositions.[28] Appointed organist at the Martinikerk in Groningen in 1728, he dominated the musical life of the city in the eighteenth century and wrote books on keyboard playing (*Idee van 't clavier*, 1740) and music theory (*Muzykaale spraakkunst*, 1754). In addition, he translated several German works into Dutch, notably Quantz's flute treatise, F. W. Marpurg's harpsichord method and some of Charles Burney's reports on contemporary European musical life (probably working from a German translation of Burney's text and adding numerous comments, which provide fascinating anecdotal detail).

THE MUSIC TRADE

During the seventeenth century a number of music printers, such as Paulus Matthysz, Cornelis de Leeuw and Broer Jansz, were active in Amsterdam, but their output was mainly destined for and absorbed by a local or regional market.[29] No international publishing house, such as that of Phalèse in Louvain and Antwerp in the Southern Netherlands (which was active from 1542 to 1672), existed in the North before the final decade of the century. At that time Estienne Roger (c1665–1722), active in Amsterdam from 1696 to 1722, was the most important music printer and publisher in the whole of

60. The Music Lovers: painting (1755) by Julius Quinkhard showing music-making in an Amsterdam home, with the trio sonata combination of flute, violin and bass viol

Europe.[30] Like many others, Roger was not born in the Netherlands. A Protestant from Caen in Normandy, he came with his family after the revocation of the Edict of Nantes in 1685 and entered the book trade in 1695 in association with a compatriot, Jean-Louis de Lorme. The earliest imprints to bear his name date from 1696; early in 1697 he became an independent entrepreneur. From 1699 his shop was established in the Kalverstraat, now a typical Amsterdam shopping-street.

Roger changed the face of music publishing for ever. First, the sheer amount of music that he managed to publish is impressive. Catalogue listings, which appeared nearly every year, trace closely the growth of his business, with 10–30 new publications each year. His repertory was international and was produced in such a way that it could be sold everywhere in Europe. His catalogues contain items in all the popular genres of the times – *airs*, operas (complete or selections), sonatas for all instruments, trios, concerti grossi, keyboard music and much else. He published music by the foremost composers of France, Italy, Germany and England; Netherlands composers played only a minor role in his business. The composers most often mentioned in his survey catalogue of 1716 (which lists his entire stock) are Corelli, Lully and Schickhardt.

The six volumes of trio sonatas, solo violin sonatas and concerti grossi by Arcangelo Corelli (1653–1713), the most famous Italian composer of instrumental music around 1700, served as classic models for instrumental composition for half a century, and Roger's editions procured for them an unprecedentedly wide dissemination.[31] His editions of opp.1–5 were reprints of earlier Italian editions; in 1710 he published op.5 with added written-out ornamentation, 'as Corelli himself played them', and for op.6, the renowned concerti grossi, he provided a posthumous first edition in 1714. By 1710 Roger had become the publisher of other celebrated Italian composers, among them Vivaldi, Albinoni and Dall'Abaco. The popularity of Lully's music outside France, especially in the Netherlands, was unimpeded by political opposition between the two countries, and Roger issued a number of his works reprinted from French editions. Johann Christian Schickhardt (*c*1682–1762), an itinerant German musician, was employed in many posts in Germany, the Netherlands, England and Scandinavia;[32] as a composer he provided Roger with a continuous stream of new works for publication, notably sonatas for one or more flutes, violins, or oboes and other chamber music.

Most music printing in the seventeenth century used typography – a process that was possible using a normal book press – but Roger introduced a system of printing from engraved plates on a regular basis (music printing from plates had previously been rare). He was helped by recent technological developments that enabled him to print from plates made of pewter (an alloy of tin and lead), which could be corrected and re-used far more easily than the older, harder copper plates. Moreover, plates could be stored and used for reprints, something that was not possible in typographic setting; this facilitated smaller print runs, and a larger number of titles could be printed. In addition, the most superior paper in Europe at the time was being manufactured by French refugees in the Netherlands.

A consequence of reprinting from the same plates was that it became less feasible to date prints, and indeed many eighteenth-century music editions are without dates. Instead, a publisher's number was used to identify each print, and in this respect too Roger was a pioneer: all the publications in his catalogue of 1716 carry a serial number,[33] and all subsequent editions are numbered in order of their issue. Roger was also one of the first music publishers to make extensive use of agents in other cities and countries, such as Rotterdam (Pieter van der Veer), London, Brussels, Liège, Cologne, Hamburg and Paris. Through his activities the music trade was soon to become an international one.

Although Roger was by far the most important music publisher in the Netherlands, he was by no means the only one. From 1708 to 1711 Amsterdam was the battleground for a 'music war' between Roger and a compatriot, the printer Pierre Mortier.[34] Mortier, who had already been in the book trade for some time, reprinted, without authority, the most popular items in Roger's lists and offered them for sale at a lower price than Roger's. At the same time, he claimed that his editions contained fewer errors than Roger's (at that time there was barely any protection for works that originated outside the country). Among Mortier's reprints are works by Corelli, Albinoni, Taglietti and Le Grand, and the *Hollandsche minne- en drinkliederen* by De Konink; the last was edited by Anders, which may suggest a cooperation between Mortier and Anders.

In all, Mortier reprinted about 70 of Roger's editions. Naturally, Roger fought back: he declared in advertisements that Mortier's publications were full of errors and that he would sell his own for the same price as Mortier's if his customers could show printed evidence of a lower price. The 'music war' came to a sudden end early in 1711, when Mortier died. Before the auction sale of Mortier's stock could take place, Roger reached an agreement with Mortier's widow and bought the entire stock. Indeed, in many of Roger's later catalogues there are titles printed by Mortier: a comparison of the Mortier and Roger prints shows that in some cases Roger must have used Mortier's plates for re-impressions under his own name, by way of recognition of Mortier's work.

Roger married Marie-Suzanne de Magneville in 1691. Of their two daughters, Jeanne (1701–22) formally owned her father's business from 1716 and inherited it after his death on 7 July 1722, but she died the same year, on 10 December, having barely reached the age of 21. She disinherited her sister Françoise (1694–1723) because she felt neglected by her during her last illness. Françoise had married another Huguenot refugee, the book-trader Michel-Charles le Cène. Eventually, Jeanne's heir, Roger's employee Gerrit Drinkman, sold the business to her brother-in-law, Le Cène. He continued Roger's business along much the same lines, but with much less fervour. During his 20-odd years as a music publisher (he died in 1743) Le Cène issued about 100 titles; in a comparable period Roger had produced about 600. Le Cène's most important catalogue, of 1737, lists 587 numbered titles and about 100 unnumbered ones. It was at about this time that Locatelli cooperated with Le Cène as a kind of assistant editor, correcting proofs. Le Cène's slower pace in publishing, especially in his later years, becomes apparent from the publication history of a set of six keyboard sonatas by the Italian composer and scholar Giovanni Battista ('Padre') Martini (1706–84).[35] In 1736 Martini was considering publishing these works in Amsterdam – still regarded as the mecca of music publishing – and contacted Le Cène via the composer Giuseppe Tartini, who was already on Le Cène's lists. Long and tiring negotiations began. The first manuscripts were sent to Amsterdam in 1740; by the end of 1741 Martini called on Locatelli to help speed up the printing process; the sonatas appeared in the summer of 1742; and Martini received his free author's copies only in January 1743, almost eight years after his first attempts to publish the sonatas.

Martini nevertheless offered Le Cène another work for publication – a set of keyboard works with obbligato violin accompaniment, a genre that was quickly gaining popularity during the 1740s. Le Cène died, however, in May 1743, and his business fell into the hands of G. J. de la Coste. La Coste agreed to publish the volume, and this marked the beginning of a repetition of the long and tedious printing and publishing process of Martini's first Amsterdam edition. The engraving was continued by La Coste's successor, Antoine Chareau, but the publication was never to appear. Despite Locatelli's repeated interventions, in 1748 Martini was forced to give up hope of a second Amsterdam impression. Around mid-century the most important stocks of music prints in Amsterdam came into the hands of Jan Covens, but by this time the business could no longer boast any of the international splendour it had possessed in the days of Estienne Roger.

*

The musical history of the Netherlands in the late Baroque era in its own way presents a microcosm of musical history in the whole of Europe. Its character is individual, but that character is best defined as a mixture, or pasticcio, of foreign influences. There were musicians from all over the continent: Germans, Italians, Frenchmen, Southern Netherlanders. Although few important works were composed within the borders of the Dutch Republic, most of the greatest works from the rest of Europe were known there, printed there for the first time or reprinted there, and then disseminated or re-disseminated from there. Largely through the strength of its music trade, Dutch musical life in the early eighteenth century acted as a kind of linking factor between the distinctive musical cultures of other European countries

NOTES

[1] For musical life at the Brussels court of Maximilian II Emanuel, Governor of the Spanish Netherlands from 1692, see Chapter X, 'Courts and Monasteries in Bavaria'.

[2] H. Bruinsma, 'The Organ Controversy in the Netherlands Reformation to 1640', *JAMS*, vii (1954), 205–12.

[3] Also at the Oude Kerk were Simeon van Ulft (1692), Nicolaas de Koning (1692–1723), Everard Haverkamp (1723–8) and Johannes Uhlhorn (1728–42); at the Nieuwe Kerk, Hendrik Rijpelberg (1692), Simeon van Ulft (1692–1702), Jan Jacob de Graaf (1702–38) and Berend Hendrik Linsen (1739–89); at the Wester Kerk, Jurriaan Beuf (1686–91) and Johannes Clermont (1708–43); and at the Nieuwezijdskapel, Nicolaas de Koning (1691–2), Jan Jacob de Graaf (1692–1702), Jasper Swaan (1703–17), Jacobus van Hoorn (1717–50) and Johannes Chalon (1754–63).

[4] D. J. Balfoort, 'Quirinus Gideon van Blankenburg', *Jaarboek 'Die Haghe' 1938* (1939), 153–224.

[5] Blankenburg accused Handel of stealing the theme from him, but Handel's fugue, written about 1720, predates Blankenburg's claim to it (1725), so Blankenburg himself must have been the 'thief' (he was misled by the fact that Handel's fugue was published only in 1735).

[6] J. W. Enschedé, 'Gerhardus Havingha en het orgel in de Sint Laurenskerk te Alkmaar', *TVNM*, viii/3 (1907), 181–261.

[7] Havingha is also noted for his set of keyboard suites (1724) which includes pieces in uncommon keys such as A$\sharp$ minor and B$\flat$ minor.

[8] See J. R. Luth, *'Daer wert om 't seerste uytgekreten . . .'* (Kampen, 1986).

[9] A. Dekker, 'J. Pzn. Sweelinck en zijn collegium musicum', *Mens en melodie*, xxvi (1971), 290–92.

[10] R. A. Rasch, 'De muziek in de Amsterdamse Schouwburg 1638–1664', *Spiegel Historiae*, xxii (1987), 165–70.

[11] Several accounts of this topic by R. A. Rasch are in preparation; see also H. J. Westerling, 'De oudste Amsterdamsche opera, geopend dinsdag 31 december 1680, en de opera te Buiksloot van 1686', *De gids* (1919), no.83, pp.277–94; J. Fransen, *Les comédiens français en Hollande au XVIIe et au XVIIIe siècles* (Paris, 1925); and S. A. M. Bottenheim, *De opera in Nederland* (Amsterdam, 1946, 2/1983).

[12] Fiocco later settled in Brussels, where he and several of his sons became well known as composers and performers: see Chapter X, 'Courts and Monasteries in Bavaria'.

[13] P. Andriessen, *Carel Hacquart (+ 1640–1701?)* (Brussels, 1974).

[14] K. H. Pauls, 'Der kurpfälzische Kammermusikus Johannes Schenk', *Mf*, xv (1962), 157–171; xix (1966), 288–9. Schenck's publications include *Tyd- en konst-oeffeningen* op.2 (c1688); *Scherzi musicali* op.6 (1698); *Le nymphe di Rheno* op.8 (1701); *L'echo du Danube* op.9 (1703); and *Les bizarreries de la goûte* op.10 (c1710).

[15] The MS scores survive in the archives of the collegium, which still exists in Utrecht.

[16] The MS scores survive in the University Library, Amsterdam; because Vivaldi's concerto is the first in the MS it has been thought that he was personally present for the occasion, but there is no evidence for such a visit.

[17] L. Haasnoot, *Leven en werken van Pieter Hellendaal (1721–1799)* (diss., U. of Amsterdam, 1983); Hellendaal arrived in England in 1751 and was active in London concert life, before becoming an organist at King's Lynn (1760) and in Cambridge (1762).

[18] A. Dunning, *Count Unico Wilhelm van Wassenaer (1692–1766)* (Buren, 1980); R. A. Rasch and K. Vlaardingerbroek, eds., *Unico Wilhelm van Wassenaer (1692–1766): componist en staatsman* (Zutphen, 1993).

[19] F. van den Bremt, *Willem de Fesch (1687–1757?)* (Louvain, 1949); R. Tusler, ed., *Willem de Fesch (1687–c.1760)* (Alkmaar, 1987).

[20] *Trioos* op.1 (1696) and *Symphoniae introductoriae* op.2 (1698).

[21] Rosier left the Netherlands in 1699 to become Kapellmeister of Cologne Cathedral.

[22] R. A. Rasch, 'De Dendermondse componist Servaas de Konink (1654–1701)', *Gedenkschriften van de oudheidkundige kring van het land van Dendermonde*, 4th ser., x (1990), 5–35.

[23] *Hollandsche minne- en drinkliederen* op.3 (1697).

[24] *Tweede deel der mengelzangen* (texts by Zweerts, 1695); *Harderszangen* (texts by Alewijn, 1699).

[25] *Triomf der Batavieren* (1708).

[26] A. Koole, *Leven en werken van Pietro Antonio Locatelli da Bergamo 1695–1764* (Amsterdam, 1949); A. Dunning, *Pietro Antonio Locatelli* (Buren, 1981) [in Ger.]

[27] Until well into the nineteenth century organs were normally tuned to the old-fashioned mean-tone temperament, which limited modulation and the range of available keys.

[28] J. du Saar, *Het leven en de werken van Jacob Wilhelm Lustig* (Amsterdam, 1948).

[29] R. A. Rasch, 'Musica dîs curae est: the Life and Works of the Amsterdam Music Printer Paulus Matthysz (1613/4–1684)', *Quaerendo*, iv (1974), 86–99; R. A. Rasch, 'Cornelis de Leeuw (c. 1613-c. 1661)', *TVNM*, xxvii/1 (1977), 1–27.

[30] F. Lesure, *Bibliographie des éditions musicales publiées par Estienne Roger et Michel-Charles le Cène (Amsterdam, 1696–1743)* (Paris, 1969); K. Hortschansky, 'Die Datierung der frühen Musikdrucke Etienne Rogers', *TVNM*, xxii (1972), 252–86.

[31] Four volumes of trio sonatas, opp.1–4 (1681, 1685, 1689, 1694); one of solo violin sonatas, op.5 (1700); and one of concerti grossi, op.6 (1714).

[32] D. Lasocki, 'Johann Christain Schickhardt (ca. 1682–1762)', *TVNM*, xxvii/1 (1977), 28–55.

[33] After no.348 the numbering includes chronological information: nos.348–416 were issued in 1715–16.

[34] R. A. Rasch, 'De muziekoorlog tussen Estienne Roger en Pieter Mortier (1708–1711)', *De zeventiende eeuw*, vi (1990), 89–97.

[35] See the literature cited in n.26.

BIBLIOGRAPHICAL NOTE

Much of the literature on the musical history of the Netherlands is in Dutch. General collections of source material have been published during the nineteenth century under the title *Bouwsteenen* (3 vols., Amsterdam, 1868–81) and during the twentieth as *Bouwstenen voor een geschiedenis der toonkunst in de Nederlanden* (4 vols., 1965–86; with a certain concentration on organs and organists). Articles on all areas of Dutch musical history can be found in the journal of the Society for Dutch Musical History, *Tijdschrift van de Vereniging voor nederlandse muziekgeschiedenis* (*TVNM*; from 1881); the Dutch music periodical *Mens en melodie* (from 1945) is also valuable. The seventeenth and eighteenth centuries have still not been explored systematically. A classic, though superficial, work is D. J. Balfoort's *Het muziekleven in Nederland in de 17de en 18de eeuw* (Amsterdam, 1938; repr. 1981); it is, however, in need of revision. Two general histories of music in the Netherlands include chapters on the seventeenth and eighteenth centuries: W. H. Thijsse, *Zeven eeuwen nederlandse muziek* (Rijswijk, 1949); and C. van den Borren, *Geschiedenis van de muziek in de Nederlanden* (Amsterdam, 1949–51). Two works by the banker, music collector and amateur musicologist D. F. Scheurleer, though not directly concerned with the period, nevertheless contain much information: *Het muziekleven van Amsterdam in de 17de eeuw* (Amsterdam, 1904); and *Het muziekleven in Nederland in de tweede helft der 18de eeuw in verband met Mozart's verblijf aldaar* (The Hague, 1909). The best text on the history of Calvinist church music in the Dutch Republic is J. R. Luth, *'Daer wert om 't seerste uytgekreten . . .'* (Kampen, 1986).

There are a number of studies of individual musicians: on Blankenburg, D. J. Balfoort's 'Quirinus Gideon van Blankenburg', *Jaarboek 'Die Haghe' 1938* (1939), 153–224; on De Fesch, F. van den Bremt's *Willem de Fesch (1687–1757?)* (Louvain,

1949) and R. Tusler, ed., *Willem de Fesch (1687–c.1760)* (Alkmaar, 1987); on Havingha, J. W. Enschedé's 'Gerhardus Havingha en het orgel in de Sint Laurenskerk te Alkmaar', *TVNM*, viii/3 (1907), 181–261; on Hacquart, P. Andriessen's *Carel Hacquart (+1640–1701?)* (Brussels, 1974); on Hellendaal, L. Haasnoot's *Leven en werken van Pieter Hellendaal (1721–1799)* (diss., U. of Amsterdam, 1983); on Locatelli, A. Koole's *Leven en werken van Pietro Antonio Locatelli da Bergamo 1695–1764* (Amsterdam, 1949) and A. Dunning's *Pietro Antonio Locatelli* (Buren, 1981; in German); on Lustig, J. du Saar's *Het leven en de werken van Jacob Wilhelm Lustig* (Amsterdam, 1948); on Rosier, U. Niemöller's *Carl Rosier (1640?–1725)* (Cologne, 1957); on Schenck, K. H. Pauls's 'Der kurpfälzische Kammermusikus Johannes Schenk', *Mf*, xv (1962), 157–71, and xix (1966), 288–9; on Schickhardt, D. Lasocki's 'Johann Christian Schickhardt (ca.1682–1762)', *TVNM*, xxvii/1 (1977), 28–55; on Van Wassenaer, A. Dunning's *Count Unico Wilhelm van Wassenaer (1692–1766)* (Buren, 1980), and R. Rasch and K. Vlaardingerbroek, eds., *Unico Wilhelm van Wassenaer (1692–1766): componist en staatsman* (Zutphen, 1993); and on Witvogel, A. Dunning's *De muziekuitgever Gerhard Fredrik Witvogel en zijn fonds* (Utrecht, 1966). Articles on individual composers and cities in the Dutch Republic can also be found in *Grove 6* and *Grove O*.

There are two classic studies of the collegia musica that flourished in the eighteenth century: on that of Utrecht, J. C. M. van Riemsdijk's *Het stads-muziekcollegie te Utrecht (Collegium musicum ultrajectinum) 1631–1881* (Utrecht, 1881); and on that of Arnhem, J. W. Staats Evers's *Het St. Caecilia-concert te Arnhem* (Arnhem, 1874). Early opera in the Netherlands is surveyed in S. A. M. Bottenheim's *De opera in Nederland* (Amsterdam, 1946). Roger's activities as a music printer and dealer are discussed in F. Lesure, *Bibliographie des éditions musicales publiées par Estienne Roger et Michel-Charles le Cène (Amsterdam, 1696–1743)* (Paris, 1969) and K. Hortschansky, 'Die Datierung der frühen Musikdrucke Etienne Rogers', *TVNM*, xxii (1972), 252–86. Information on organ and other musical instrument making in the Netherlands in the late Baroque period can be found in two publications by A. J. Gierveld: *Het nederlandse huisorgel in de 17de en 18de eeuw* (Utrecht, 1977); and 'The Harpsichord and Clavichord in the Dutch Republic', *TVNM*, xxxi/2 (1981), 117–66. D. J. Balfoort's *De hollandsche vioolmakers* (Amsterdam, 1931) deals with violin making, and A. Lehr's *Van paardebel tot speelklok: de geschiedenis van de klokgietkunst in de Lage Landen* (Zaltbommel, 1971) has information on bells.

Chapter XIV

The Iberian Peninsula

LOUISE K. STEIN

The Iberian peninsula found itself in new circumstances by the middle of the eighteenth century. The constituent parts of the Spanish kingdom, and the roles of Spain and Portugal in European politics, as well as their relationships to each other, had changed entirely since the seventeenth century. The kingdoms of Castile, Aragon, Portugal, Naples, Sicily, Milan, the Americas and the Netherlands had formerly all belonged, with varying degrees of independence, to Spain; but as a result of manipulation by the other European powers, Spain's empire and central place in European affairs had been gradually eroded. When Charles II, the last of the Spanish Habsburgs, died in 1700, Philippe of Anjou (Louis XIV's grandson) became King Philip V of Spain, but that solution was contested by the Grand Alliance, which led to the War of the Spanish Succession (1701–14). Coinciding with and contributing to Spain's decline, Portugal had arisen as an independent contender in European politics, confident in its newly claimed wealth from Brazil. Portuguese sovereignty was officially granted in 1668, and thereafter her kings astutely forged anti-Spanish political and commercial alliances and steered Portugal's culture away from its ingrained Castilian traditions. For Portugal the late Baroque era was a new beginning, but for most Spaniards it was a time of destabilization of the social order and devaluation of the national cultural currency.

The musical history of eighteenth-century Spain and Portugal has generally been described with buoyant optimism, because Iberian music of this epoch begins to meet our well-conditioned expectations by conforming to a European profile. But changed political circumstances gave rise to different lines of development and different musical results in the two countries, largely because of different social conditions. Whether we choose to lament the demise of the Spanish musical Baroque (as did many Spaniards) or to celebrate the victory of a foreign aesthetic (as did most Portuguese intellectuals), it is clear that social and historical circumstances in the Iberian peninsula were essential to and not incidental to the transformation of music and musical life.

The Late Baroque Era

SPAIN

Tradition and the estilo español

The polemical plurality of styles that characterized early eighteenth-century Spanish music would have been inconceivable to the musicians working some 25 years earlier, during the reign of Philip IV (1621–65), patron of the painter Diego Velázquez (1599–1660), the dramatist Pedro Calderón de la Barca (1600–81) and the composer Juan Hidalgo (1614–85) – artists at the heart of the Spanish Baroque era. Hidalgo's generation created a prolonged period of relative artistic stability and stylistic homogeneity by consistently cultivating a national style, the *estilo español*. In vernacular genres such as secular songs (*tonos humanos, tonadas, romances, jácaras* etc.), Spanish dances and sacred *villancicos*, which were produced in profusion across the peninsula, the *estilo español* predominated, although several influential composers (Carlos Patiño, Juan Hidalgo, Cristóbal Galán) can be said to have shaped musical conventions within particular genres. It had developed in close association with the classic Spanish literary forms of the *romance* and the *comedia nueva*, and it drew its primary characteristics from native, popular traditions.

The survival of Spanish Baroque musical language, genres and conventions to the end of the seventeenth century (even longer in the Spanish New World) was a matter of aesthetic preference. Consolidated in an epoch of proud nationalism, the *estilo español* retained its attraction for contemporary audiences long after the passing of its creators. But its life as a stylistic model was prolonged more by administrative indolence than by vigorous patronage. At the highest levels of government, attempts at much-needed bureaucratic reform did not succeed, and cultural institutions had experienced few changes or administrative innovations toward the end of the Habsburg era. The mechanisms for commissioning and financing musical performance, and the ceremonies and entertainments that presented music to the public, were developed early in the seventeenth century and preserved along with the decaying legacy of the Counter-Reformation and the faded political philosophies and worn emblems of the Spanish Habsburg empire. The stability of the mid-seventeenth century finally lapsed into neglect by the end of the century.

Paradoxically, economic and educational weaknesses contributed to the survival of the late-seventeenth-century Spanish musical repertory, especially in church and at court. The correspondence of leading composers of sacred music is replete with requests for copies of their polyphonic settings for religious feasts, because fewer and fewer churches (beyond the two dozen or so principal cathedrals), provincial convents and monasteries had resident composers or musical establishments capable of providing polyphony on a regular basis. Musical education had declined to such an extent at court that competent male singers and instrumentalists for the royal chapel could not be found in Spain to replace those who, having remained in their posts for decades, finally retired or died. During the reign of Philip IV the chapel had been overwhelmingly staffed by musicians born and trained in Spain, but by the 1680s and 1690s its administrators resorted to hiring more musicians, mostly singers and string players, from outside Spain. Those who came from the Spanish territories in Italy were already citizens of the empire, with easy access to royal employment because of previous service to Spanish courts abroad. They were largely expected to conform to established practice, for the nature of court ritual and entertainment did not change. The *comedias* regularly performed at the palace still contained well-known songs, some that had retained their popularity for several generations. On royal birthdays and other occasions the court of Charles II celebrated, as that of his father had done, with partly sung zarzuelas and semi-operas. Revivals of works by Calderón (*d* 1681) and Hidalgo (*d* 1685) were still a mainstay of the court repertory. The dynastic marriage of Charles II and the French princess Marie-Louise of Orléans was commemorated not with a new work but with Calderón and Hidalgo's *La púrpura de la rosa*, a short pastoral opera originally written in 1659 for another Habsburg-Bourbon union – the wedding of María Teresa of Spain to Louis XIV. More often than not important public ceremonies and occasions at court were celebrated with existing works. In music as in theatre throughout Spain, the repertory of the last decades of the seventeenth century reflects stability and conformity; only a few composers demonstrated any sort of formal, technical or topical innovation.

It is not altogether surprising that the Spanish musical establishment was dedicated to a traditional aesthetic and depended on worn administrative mechanisms which limited the degree to which foreign ideas and techniques could be absorbed. A general distrust of foreigners and consequent suspicion of their ideas permeated Spanish culture: composers did not travel abroad for musical education or for employment; and those foreign musicians who came to Spain came only to serve their royal patrons. In the royal chapels, in the cathedrals and in the theatres, Spanish music prevailed.

The effects of patronage

The death of Hidalgo in 1685 marks the close of the central period of the Spanish Baroque in music, but there was no sudden or widespread rejection of the fundamental approach to composition. New theatrical music at court was provided by one of his pupils, Juan de

Navas (*fl* 1659–1709), and then by an innovative competitor, Sebastián Durón (1660–1716), who already had a considerable reputation as a church composer. Navas was chosen to succeed Hidalgo as harpist and theatrical composer because his music was judged closest to Hidalgo's in style and spirit. While Navas and Durón still cultivated the *estilo español*, some of their compositions show a new flexibility in text setting and, in concerted settings with stronger tonal organization, an expansion of musical phrases to accommodate obbligato instrumental parts. It is precisely the subtle changes in text setting – increased vocal ornamentation, some fragmentation of the text and internal word repetition – that constitute innovation by a few composers in the 1690s (Navas, Durón and Juan de Serqueira), distinguishing their music from that of Hidalgo's generation. Later critics judged these traits to be the result of foreign influence, perhaps conveyed through contact with Italian singers in the royal chapel.

Very little is known about Spanish instrumental ensemble music in the late seventeenth century because only a few collections and instrumental tutors for harp, organ and guitar survive. But there is reason to believe that instrumental ensembles at court absorbed non-Spanish forms and techniques more easily. A few documents from the post-Hidalgo period concerning the royal chamber musicians suggest that imported musicians influenced chamber music at court with informal, somewhat improvisatory settings that allowed for a greater degree of innovation. The documents mention instrumental 'tonatas' (sonatas) and new violin music composed by a recently hired Italian, who claimed to be the only court musician responsible for providing such pieces. Probably these were trio and solo sonatas, although none has survived. Another source of foreign influence and fashion were the frequent but intimate dancing-parties held by the French wives of the Spanish monarchs, first Marie-Louise of Orléans and then Maria Luisa of Savoy (Philip V's consort) at which French dances were enjoyed; it is perhaps significant that Marie-Louise of Orléans was criticized, rebuked and even accused of treachery for introducing French customs.

If the French consorts of the Spanish monarchs found the Spanish court austere, its etiquette severe and their new surroundings somewhat cold, the reception given their musical employees was even colder. The isolation of foreigners at court near the beginning of the period is demonstrated by the experience of the 38 French musicians who accompanied Marie-Louise of Orléans to Madrid when she married Charles II in 1679. This distinguished group, led by the librettist and stage designer Henry Guichard, the composer Michel Farinel (*b* 1649) and the violinist Guillaume Dumanoir (1615–97), included singers, instrumentalists, a dancing-master and other personnel more than sufficient for the requirements of chamber music and independent opera productions. For the short period they spent in Spain (less than a year), the French musicians aroused the envy of their Spanish colleagues because they dressed well and the queen regularly and liberally rewarded them with expensive gifts and money, as was the French custom. Effectively, they worked in a separate sphere, in closer contact with their patroness, enjoying privileges not extended to the regular court musicians but remaining on the fringes of court life.

This sort of special treatment was to become an increasingly important feature of musical patronage in Spain. In 1702, 13 French musicians accompanied Maria Luisa of Savoy to Barcelona when she married Philip V, some of them continuing on to Madrid as musicians of the queen's chamber. After eight months of petitions to various palace officials, it was resolved that they could not be assigned regular salaries but that a few could be retained with money from the queen's private expense account. Again, the French musicians worked largely apart from the salaried court musicians, which points to their limited musical influence.

As part of the misguided plan to transform the Madrid court into an Iberian Versailles, one of Philip V's first concerns on his arrival in Spain was to import French musicians. From Louis XIV he requested several prominent musicians in succession, without result. Finally, the well-known composer Henry Desmarets (1661–1741), forced by scandal to relinquish his post at the Jesuit College in Paris, was sent to Madrid with six musicians on loan from Versailles. We know that they performed several *divertissements* for the royal wedding in Barcelona and for the celebrations in Madrid when Philip and Maria Luisa made their formal entry. But this group lasted only a few years in Spain; in 1705, after the siege of Barcelona by the Habsburg forces, they were disbanded and sent back to France. It is likely that, amid the court's severe financial difficulties and the insecurities of war, the musicians feared for their future: not only might they find themselves trapped in Spain with little income and surrounded by the violence of war, but they were also serving a king who could lose his throne.

While the political history of eighteenth-century Spain was shaped over a period of 70 years by a series of reforms that gradually modernized the monarchy to meet contemporary French standards, the cultural and musical history of the same period did not run directly parallel, largely because imported French culture had to compete with both Spanish tradition and Italian. Although the change in dynasty and the Bourbons' new cultural politics seem to have had no immediate consequences in provincial musical life, the effects in Madrid were felt from the start. The reforms at court were many, but the process of cultural transformation was slowed by Madrid's heavy cultural bureaucracy. Public entertainments in Madrid had traditionally been dependent on royal patronage to some extent, for the Habsburgs had exploited them as a means of distracting, comforting, impressing and educating the populace. Some performances of spectacular royal productions at the palace were open to the public during the later seventeenth century, and provision was made for crowds to observe the court's outdoor entertainments. Staged *autos sacramentales* and other traditional Corpus Christi events – even the religious music performed during Corpus Christi week, for example – had been aimed at a royal audience. The *autos* were offered by the city of Madrid as a gift to the king, court composers normally wrote the music for them, and musicians and singers from the royal chapel performed in the processions and special masses during Corpus week. Because the crown traditionally subsidized these entertainments, the city could rely on having a royal audience and financial advantage to help retain the best actors, singers and musicians during the entire theatre season.

After 1705, however, Philip V decided that the royal funds usually set aside for the *autos sacramentales* should instead be spent on the war effort (Habsburg attacks and invasions escalated after 1705, both within Spain and in Spanish territories in Italy and the Netherlands). But, more significantly, the *autos sacramentales* were no longer to be performed especially for the monarch. Philip V, head of the 'Most Catholic' monarchy and 'Vicar of God' to the Spanish clergy, thus renounced participation in the public symbolism of the Eucharist that Calderón's religious allegories had always represented. The populace were to view the *autos* in the public theatres, not in the plazas of royal and municipal buildings. This separation of royal and public spheres became charactertistic of Philip V's reign, especially after his marriage to Isabella Farnese in 1714, and it was accentuated in the reign of Ferdinand VI, with important consequences for music. Philip V's initial popularity waned as his advisers failed to comprehend the essential role of populist culture in Spain as a symbol of the shared ideals and destiny of the ruler and his subjects.

Administrative reforms and new appointees gradually created changes in the institutional environment, but Philip V's musical taste did not banish traditional Spanish styles and genres from the court during the first years of his reign. Beginning in 1701, a series of reforms of the royal chapel and household provided for the redistribution of musical instruments and personnel to accommodate the foreign musical styles and textures favoured by the new patrons. The first action of consequence to Spanish musicians was the reform of the royal chapel in 1701, which assigned a fixed salary to each position within the chapel, unified the salary scale and instituted a competitive ranking by audition and merit within each group of voices or instruments. The merit system ensured that Philip V's musicians worked in an explicitly competitive situation; this represented a substantive break with the past, in that the court musician was transformed from a servant with no possibility of personal gain or social mobility into an artist who served with some degree of self-determination and considerably more autonomy.

Changes in the economic and social status of composers and performers were facilitated by a new attitude at court towards patronage. As has been noted, the French musicians who came to Spain were treated rather differently from their Spanish counterparts and operated on the fringes of the court bureaucracy. Throughout the eighteenth century this sort of private, elite patronage grew, spreading from the court to wealthy aristocratic households. The Bourbons did not set out to monopolize and centralize musical and theatrical patronage in the way the Habsburgs had done; this meant that court composers could also write music for public theatres, singers and instrumentalists from the royal chapels could perform for hire beyond their regular duties, and royal musicians could compose and perform specially for aristocratic patrons.

A few musicians were consistently and extraordinarily rewarded with money, expensive gifts, political favour and social status. The employment in Spain of Domenico Scarlatti (and later of the singer Farinelli; see below) illustrates this point. Scarlatti went to the Iberian peninsula (*c*1720) as *mestre de capela* to King John V of Portugal and music teacher to Princess María Bárbara de Braganza. When his pupil married Ferdinand of Spain in 1728, Scarlatti travelled with her and thus began his service to the Spanish royal household. Although he had composed both sacred and secular vocal music in Rome and for John V in Lisbon, he seems to have produced only keyboard sonatas during his years in Spain, because María Bárbara was devoted to the harpsichord and it was she who determined his duties. The sonatas were collected and preserved in elegant volumes for her, and only two collections were published in Scarlatti's lifetime (London, 1738–9, the first dedicated to John V of Portugal). Scarlatti earned the great respect of fellow musicians, yet it is unclear whether he was required to perform with them or if he travelled with the court from palace to palace only to serve the princess (who became queen in 1746). He does not seem to have been burdened with any responsibilities beyond composing sonatas and working with his pupil, who made sure that he enjoyed a very private employment with many comforts and privileges.

The Late Baroque Era

Theatre music

While the new style of patronage worked in the favour of many royal musicians and gave others flexibility and broader employment opportunities, it also provoked some unfortunate consequences. The Bourbons failed to respect some of the cherished practices and relationships between crown and city that had been essential to providing a cultural life for commoners. Once royal control of public entertainments had been discarded, the void was filled temporarily by greedy, ambitious foreign entrepreneurs who, in the eyes of many, tarnished the monarch's image through corrupt management. The state of theatrical music at this period illustrates the interrelationship of private taste, popular support, and aristocratic and royal intervention in commercial and musical affairs. Soon after Philip V disdained the *autos*, another royal decree ordained a major change in the musical-theatrical economy. Since 1703 an Italian acting troupe had been performing for the king in the Coliseo theatre in the Buen Retiro palace and also for a small, paying public in a large, private mansion not far from the palace. Breaking the venerable laws and regulations governing commercial theatre in Madrid, in 1707 the king granted exclusive use of the Coliseo to the Italian troupe; moreover, he decreed that they could keep all their profits, exempting them from contributing the usual percentages to the administrators of commercial theatres and thus to the municipal hospitals. With this royal backing, and the novelty of their repertory, the Italians had an immediate (though temporary) advantage over the Spanish companies. As courtiers and aristocrats were bound to follow the king in all matters of taste and fashion, the Italians quickly garnered devotees from the wealthiest levels of Madrid society and accordingly charged inflated ticket prices.

Even as the introduction of Italian culture was invited, facilitated and enforced by the monarchy, court commissions for Spanish works continued. The best dramatists of the period, Antonio Zamora (*c*1660–?1728) and José de Cañizares (1676–1750), wrote for the king as well as for other patrons and the public. Zarzuelas were not suddenly replaced by operas at court: the large, partly sung works of 1707–9 are musical and dramatic hybrids. Da capo arias with texts in the shorter Italian metres and indications for minuets and concerted ritornellos rub shoulders with *coplas* and *estribillos* in Spanish style. Indeed, the extant scores and anthologies, whether by court composers such as the young violón player Antonio Literes (1673–1747) or the leading composers at the public theatres, Juan de Serqueira (*fl* 1656–1723) and Joseph Peyró (*fl* 1701–20), demonstrate the juxtaposition of pieces in traditional Spanish style with those in a selfconsciously applied foreign idiom. The same diversity characterized the music of the zarzuelas and *comedias* performed in the public theatres during this period: the introduction of Italian and French music thus effected not a wholesale replacement of existing genres but a gradual adaptation of them.

The Italians' early commercial triumph was anything but lasting and unproblematic. In 1708 a troupe known as the Trufaldines reconditioned an existing site near the royal palace, the Caños del Peral, to serve as their commercial theatre, but by 1714 they were in disarray and financially ruined. During the worst years of the war the court and the aristocracy had left Madrid (many Spanish grandees fled to country estates to avoid having to pledge support to either side). The loss of revenue was exacerbated in 1714 when the queen died and the theatres were closed during the official period of mourning. In 1716, again by royal decree, a newly formed Italian company was assigned exclusive use of the Caños del Peral theatre without having to pay rent to the city. When Madrid objected, the king declared that ticket prices would be raised to cover a minimum rental, and that the Italians would perform at night rather than in the afternoons, so as not to compete directly with the Spanish theatres. This illegal arrangement was allowed because the great supporter of the Italians, Count Alberoni, was the brother of the king's first minister, the notorious Cardinal Alberoni.

There is little record of what was performed at the Caños del Peral in the early years, but the Trufaldines specialized in Italian comedies. Although it is often stated that they performed operas, most of the original Trufaldines and of the second Italian troupe had earned their reputations as comedians, not as singers. It is possible that they performed comic operas with small casts, but unlikely that they took on contemporary *opera seria*. At court in 1717, six violinists, three cellists and an oboist from the royal chapel are documented as having performed without special compensation in 46 Italian and only two Spanish *comedias*. While this detail sheds some light on the size of the orchestra and proportion of Italian to Spanish works given at court, it does not mention the theatre. Likewise, 11 instrumentalists supplied the orchestra for the 'Italian comedies' performed privately three times a week in the king's chamber between 1715 and 1717, but there are no details of public performances. The frequency of Italian performances at court suggests that the Italian company mounted not full-scale *opera seria* but shorter *buffa* works. The scant documentation about the Caños del Peral theatre indicates, however, that it was equipped with machinery, wings, scenery and props and was much more modern than the older public theatres in Madrid.

An important chapter in the history of public Italian opera in Madrid opened with the arrival in 1719 of the Marquis Annibale Scotti, a special envoy from Parma, who was named protector and manager of the Italian theatre and its performers. Scotti set out to make Italian opera a commercial enterprise by bringing in new companies and extensively renovating the theatre so that it could accommodate *opera seria*. Between 1719 and 1728 it was an opera theatre with Italian performers (a 'Capriccio boscareccio' by Gioacchino Landi dedicated to Queen Isabella Farnese is the only work known to have been performed there). But with their royal protection, Scotti's Italian companies refused to respect the agreement of 1716, antagonizing municipal officials, and, notwithstanding the queen's largesse and royal subsidies, public opera soon failed. That the queen was universally despised by the populace and the Spanish grandees may have worked against the Italian companies she financed. Italian opera succeeded little with most of the theatre-going public, especially when the court was away (in 1728–33 it was in Seville following the marriage of Prince Ferdinand and María Bárbara). It was too expensive, not because the productions were more spectacular than at the Spanish theatres but because Italian singers expected earnings that would allow them to live extravagantly – a financial demand that had never been made by Spanish actors and singers, who for generations had suffered the vicissitudes of both poverty and diminishing royal favour.

In 1735 most of the Italian singers departed for Lisbon, where a fine reception and high salaries could be counted on. From 1735–7 a Spanish company formed of the best female singers performed 'operas' in Spanish translation at the Caños del Peral theatre, so that Madrid might recoup the losses of Scotti's poor management. The actress-singers in this exclusively female company brought the public back to the Caños del Peral theatre, probably because of their immense popularity in the Cruz and Príncipe theatres. Their easy success with settings by Francesco Corradini (*c*1700–after 1749), Francesco Corselli (*c*1702–1778) and Giovanni Battista Mele (1701–after 1752) of Metastasio librettos, given in translation and probably without sung dialogue, reinforces the theory that popular audiences objected not to the music of Italian opera but to its performers and politics. Both at court and in the public theatres, Spanish tradition had established that sung roles in dramatic works (even for such characters as Jupiter and Apollo) were taken by women. Before the advent of Italian opera in Madrid, castratos were heard only in sacred music; on the Spanish stage they became objects of ridicule and favourite targets for xenophobic satire. Because the scores do not survive, we cannot be sure that these works were wholly sung: the librettos include sections clearly labelled as arias, duos and recitatives, just as in partly sung zarzuelas. During the same period, similar 'operas' in Spanish were produced at the Cruz and Príncipe theatres.

61. Group portrait (c1751) by Jacopo Amigoni showing (left to right) the librettist Pietro Metastasio, the soprano Teresa Castellini, the castrato Farinelli, the artist, and Farinelli's dog and page

Scotti's last attempt at the administration of public Italian opera began with the greatest optimism in a new and much larger opera theatre on the site of Los Caños: six operas (five of them *opere serie* with texts by Metastasio), including works by Hasse and Schiassi, were performed by a highly professional group of Italian singers in 1738–9, but the season ended abruptly in failure, and by the autumn of 1739 the theatre had closed its doors, with opera in Italian ceasing to be a commercial activity. The Spanish female companies performed a few 'operas' in Spanish by Corradini and José de Nebra (1702–68) there again in 1743–5, but later in the century the theatre became a ballroom.

Unlike many European countries where opera was a central fixture of society and public life, opera in Spain soon became a private institution. In 1734 the Alcázar palace, the traditional residence of the Spanish monarchs, was destroyed by fire, and the Bourbon court moved to the neglected Buen Retiro, which effectively detached the cultural life of Isabella Farnese's italianized court from the public domain. Performances in the Coliseo at the Buen Retiro supported many of the Italian singers formerly employed by Scotti at the Caños del Peral theatre.

With the complete redecoration of the Buen Retiro's interior in

French Rococo style, the renovation of the Coliseo theatre for Italian opera began. In 1737 the famous castrato Farinelli (Carlo Broschi) finished a season in London and left the opera stages of Europe to become the Spanish court's most valued and privileged employee. At first it seems that he sang only for Philip V as a therapy for the monarch's manic depression, but soon he was entrusted with control of royal entertainments and with unlimited funds for the enrichment of the court opera. With Farinelli's guidance, the Coliseo became one of the most splendid theatres in Europe. The Neapolitan painter Jacopo Amigoni, a representative of the Venetian school, became court painter in 1739 and designed the sets for Farinelli's productions. The best Italian singers were lured to Spain, where they lived well as pampered guests, performing in only a few operas but many more serenatas, *feste teatrali* and private concerts. The resident Italian composers Corselli and Corradini composed or adapted settings of librettos chosen by Farinelli, in some cases arranging pasticcios from scores sent from Italy. The king and queen travelled from palace to palace (Buen Retiro, Aranjuez, La Granja, El Escorial, El Pardo) with their private company of expert Italian singers: *opera seria*, the very spectacle of power for the absolutist monarchy, was for Philip V's last years not an instrument of public policy or regal authority but the private comfort of an ailing, disturbed monarch and his embittered queen.

The spread of the Italian style

When Philip V died in 1746, the state of affairs for musicians in Spain was a healthy one. The number of musicians in royal service, in aristocratic households and in the municipal theatres in Madrid and many other cities had increased. The musical archives of Spanish cathedrals demonstrate that composers had expanded the sacred music repertory. Although it is difficult to generalize about Spanish cathedral music because the immense repertory is largely unstudied, it is safe to say that stylistic diversity prevailed. Some composers preferred conservative counterpoint and the grand polychoral manner for their Latin works while continuing to exploit the *estilo español* and popular topics in their *villancicos*; others mixed traditional sacred idioms with theatrical arias and recitatives; and still others adapted *villancicos*, or substituted sacred cantatas with alternating recitatives and arias. The imported or 'modern' style and its genres, though first introduced in the court and capital, reached other cities and cathedrals before mid-century; its diffusion was aided by music publishing (a significant addition to Spanish musical commerce), notably by Joseph de Torres's Imprenta de Música in Madrid. Familiarity with new musical styles and genres was also furthered gradually by church musicians who travelled to audition for or to start new employment and, to some extent, by the repertories of itinerant theatrical musicians.

Political change, a new social order and the modernization of institutions brought a devaluation of traditional Spanish music and its assumptions, but not without some protest from musicians and intellectuals. The first widespread musical polemic concerned the degree of freedom allowable in composing sacred music to Latin texts. This controversy, incited by a passage in the Gloria of Francisco Valls's *Missa scala aretina* of 1702, involved over 50 church composers and organists. Valls, *maestro de capilla* at Barcelona Cathedral, justified his composition with arguments defending modern practice (as opposed to ancient theoretical rules), artistic licence and the primacy of musical expression, taking a position that might have seemed old-fashioned to many of his European contemporaries. The geographical and chronological extension of this polemic demonstrates the extremely conservative attitude towards Latin sacred music that had prevailed during the Counter-Reformation in Spain, even when vernacular sacred music was flourishing and gaining in flexibility of style. While history has demonstrated that the 'progressives' eventually made out the stronger case, the controversy should not be dismissed as the product of a sterile minority: the conservative approach to sacred music continued to predominate as a feature of confirmed orthodoxy throughout much of the Iberian peninsula and the Spanish New World.

The musical evidence of manuscript scores and anthologies bears witness to a diversity of style and approach that became the stock-in-trade of the practical musician. As we have noted, a few court composers early in the century, influenced by the Italians with whom they worked, produced works that represented the last stages of a national style. Soon after the institutional environment of the court began to change, the new, Italian-influenced style filtered out to the public sphere, in part because court musicians also wrote for public performances and for wealthy patrons, and their works circulated. Composers for the *comedias* and zarzuelas in the Cruz and Príncipe theatres modified these genres, first by including arias and recitatives in the modern style and later by emulating *opera seria*. Finally, the genre with spoken dialogue known as the *zarzuela heróica* absorbed both the dramatic conventions and the musical style of contemporary *opera seria*, as demonstrated by *Viento es la dicha de Amor* (1743), composed by José de Nebra to a text by Antonio de Zamora. One compositional manner did not completely displace another, nor were traditional materials abruptly discarded. Just as texts of older *comedias* and *autos* by Calderón were adapted for 'modern' eighteenth-century performance by substituting da capo aria texts, favourite seventeenth-century songs were 'modernized': by setting well-known

62. *Frontispiece of Pablo Minguet y Yrol's 'Reglas, y advertencias generales que enseñan el modo de tañer todos les instrumentos mejores' (Madrid, n.d.)*

tunes in different contexts, *tonos* were turned into arias, with new instrumental ritornellos, obbligato instrumental parts, added vocal ornamentation, and regularized rhythm and phrase structures. Adaptations such as these meant that eighteenth-century Spanish music lost much of the syncopation, hemiola and rhetorical economy that had characterized the *estilo español*.

By 1736 proficiency in the Italian style was so necessary for both amateurs and professionals that Joseph de Torres y Martínez Bravo, *maestro* of the royal chapel 1718–38, added to the second edition of his *Reglas generales de acompañar* a section on continuo realization for 'modern' Italian music. Ever cognisant of practical realities, Torres declared in favour of the foreign style, yet republished his 1702 text devoted to the 'rigorous Spanish style'. He modestly described himself as a 'foreigner' in the realm of the new musical language, which he had learnt through published Italian and French manuals and Italian colleagues. Although much of his music was lost in the 1734 Alcázar fire, Torres is a central and representative figure of the period. His career began at the close of the Hidalgo epoch, yet he achieved distinguished status as *maestro de capilla* to Philip V amid the stylistic diversity of the period. Several times between 1712 and 1718 the patriarch of the royal chapel had complained to the king about the chaotic state of the chapel since the upheavals of 1706 and the exodus of Sebastián Durón (banished for political reasons). After an extensive search, the patriarch repeatedly suggested Torres as the best candidate for the post (though he was not a cleric). The duties of *maestro* included composing texts and music for the *villancicos* of Christmas, Epiphany, Corpus Christi and the monthly Forty Hours devotion, in addition to Latin pieces for the entire liturgy. Since 1706 Torres had been supplying most of the new works for chapel services and had demonstrated 'understanding of all kinds of music, native and foreign'. Moreover, his works (many of them in print) in several musical idioms were already in use at many cathedrals and were also widely appreciated in 'Italy and other foreign lands'. Finally, Torres was agreed to be the best general musician because he composed all 'genres and species of music of all nations'. He was described as the only composer in Spain to equal Sebastián Durón and surpass Antonio Literes (considered a great composer but not as 'general' as Torres). Torres was not named *maestro* however until 1718, his ascent hindered by the fact that he was a Spaniard. The queen preferred Felipe Falconi, a lesser musician who accompanied her from Parma and received a higher salary, although his duties were few. Even before Torres was ready to retire, Corselli, also from Parma, was promised in advance the post of *maestro* shortly after his arrival in Madrid. As a teacher, performer and composer, Torres provided a strong link with the past, which was useful to the patriarch of the chapel but irrelevant to Isabella Farnese. In the 35 years of chapel membership that preceded his appointment, Torres had participated in all three phases of the shift from the *estilo español* to the *estilo extranjero*; the circumstances of his promotion in 1718–20 however reveal that 'modernity' had by then become essential to professional survival.

After the fire that destroyed the royal music archive in 1734, Torres, Literes, José de Nebra and Corselli were directed to compose new music for the chapel. Their output illustrates perfectly how the social and political reforms of the early eighteenth century had transformed musicians' roles. In addition to sacred works for the chapel, they had all composed theatrical music for court and public performances, and had worked on commission for aristocratic patrons. Between them they could provide the chapel with music in all the styles and textures characteristic of the period. Torres composed in several idioms and brought his contrapuntal skill to bear on the modern style, while Corselli was a thoroughly Italian exponent of the thinly textured, ornate operatic idiom. Literes belonged to the first generation of Spanish composers who had selfconsciously adopted the foreign style early in the century; he is distinguished by the elegance of his settings of Spanish texts and by the restrained, focussed quality of his italianate pieces. José de Nebra, an organist in the chapel and *vicemaestro* from 1751, was the most popular composer for the Spanish public theatres in mid-century and the first to attempt a successful revival of native musical elements within a context dominated by the foreign style. His vernacular settings demonstrate a complete mastery of the modern idiom, yet he was a pivotal figure in the downfall of the Italians and the reform of the royal chapel that was engineered by Cardinal Mendoza and the Marquis of Ensenada during the reign of Ferdinand VI.

Torres's chapter on the accompaniment of music in the 'estilo Italiano' begins with a graceful rhetorical defence of the Italian style in Spain, claiming it as a natural outcome of musical progress and a sign of artistic vigour. What Torres promoted as musical achievement, other writers deplored. The polemic was not incited by a particular piece: the fuel for its fire had been accumulating for many years before the first words were exchanged in print. The prolific Benedictine intellectual Benito Feijoo is the best known among those who lamented the end of an independent Spanish music. In his essay *La música de los templos* (1725), Feijoo criticized the imported music as 'noisy', extravagant and lacking in traditional Spanish gravity. He mocked arguments in favour of musical progress by stating that his compatriots had made themselves 'slaves' to foreign taste and to a false notion of cultural 'progress'. For Feijoo, the loss of the national idiom was such that music had 'degenerated' into an unrecognizable hybrid, a process begun by Durón, the first to 'open the door' to some of the Italian novelties. Feijoo found the new music full of disturbing chromaticism, with too rapid harmonic rhythms, overextended harmonic progressions and excessively frequent modulations such that the 'harmony becomes exasperating'. He praised Literes for a moderate, refined use of italianate devices to enhance textual expression, claiming that his music was, at least, rational and dignified. Other critics, among them the theorist and composer Pablo Nassarre (*d* 1730), complained that excessive internal word repetition in the arias destroyed the integrity of the poetry and the rhetoric of textual expression. Writers in the popular press satirized the coloratura of the Italian vocal style. While these criticisms seem pedantic and unfounded if applied to the repertory of the best composers in Europe at the same period, they make sense when applied to works by Spanish composers who were still learning a foreign musical language. Some Spanish texts do not lend themselves to fragmentation or melismatic treatment, so the vocal lines sound awkward; selfconsciously applied harmonic progressions and long harmonic sequences seem to lack direction; and modulations intended as dramatic often sound clumsy and out of proportion to the banality of the motivic material.

The polemic about the foreign and the national styles aids our understanding that the italianization of Spanish music was not merely a natural, predestined or internally motivated evolution. An area of stylistic plurality, dominated by the Spanish Baroque heritage in the first decades of the century, was transformed through the agency of new patrons, politics and institutional reform into an area of confrontation, competition and demarcation. This was not purely a matter of aesthetic preference. It was immensely significant, because the role of music in many social, religious and physical settings made it an audible national culture; and for many, the association between those who patronized foreign music and the musical style was enough to condemn it. The emancipation of music from tradition, and the political separation of elite music from popular, produced a sense of cultural dislocation in some composers and intellectuals, a longing for a reconstructed national Spanish culture 'a lo castizo'.

PORTUGAL

The history of music in eighteenth-century Portugal bears considerable superficial resemblance to that of Spain, but there are fundamental differences, grounded in the strikingly different political and social climate. Throughout the seventeenth century high culture in Portugal had languished for lack of both national identity and economic support, such that Portugal did not develop an independent Baroque musical style, despite gaining political independence from Spain in 1668. The successful restoration of the economy, increased exploitation of Brazil and the development of trade relationships with Britain and Europe were the essential objectives of the period, although Portuguese involvement in the War of the Spanish Succession before 1713 slowed somewhat the processes of economic and cultural reconstruction. In the eighteenth century, royal financial support, the patronage of the elite and the development of a strong merchant class revitalized musical institutions, providing new employment opportunities for Portuguese musicians and a general improvement in the social place of music in Portugal, especially in the capital city.

The late seventeenth-century contribution of Portugal to the musical Baroque was almost completely absorbed by that of Habsburg Spain, as Portuguese composers cultivated the same styles, forms and genres as the Spaniards, and most of their *vilancicos* and secular songs have Spanish texts. Seventeenth-century Portuguese composers continued to produce Latin church music in the severe *stile antico*, as did many of their Spanish and New World contemporaries. In Portugal this was the legacy of musical training at the Evora Cathedral school of sacred music, which produced a number of distinguished pupils.

In addition, the orthodoxy of music for the divine service responded to the leadership of the first independent Portuguese sovereign, King John IV, who patronized only composers of sacred music and vigorously defended traditional counterpoint and the Palestrina style. An association between the decency, majesty and purity of the *a cappella* style and the decorum of worship became a Portuguese tradition.

While the reforms in Spain virtually ensured stylistic diversity in Philip V's royal chapel, the reforms of the Portuguese monarchs not only precluded the modern theatrical style but, as of 1723, prohibited vernacular genres (including the *vilancico*) in church. King John V (ruled 1706–50) directed his energies and a great deal of his wealth to religious matters, the most elaborate of his projects being the construction of the Monastery of Mafra, which consumed nearly all of his reign. John V's royal chapel was awarded the status of a collegiate church (1710) and then raised (1716) to the Metropolitan and Patriarchal See, after many petitions and a unique diplomatic mission to Rome. Lisbon thus enjoyed special honour as a haven for the faithful, with two dioceses and a vigorous Holy Inquisition. Royal patronage of music was directed to the royal chapel and to the musical establishments of other Lisbon churches. John V strengthened musical education by establishing schools for the study of sacred music, beginning in 1713 with the Seminário da Patriarcal next to his chapel, and by sending several of the most gifted Portuguese composers to study in Rome, financed by the Lisbon Patriarchy. He also obtained copies of the choirbooks used in the papal chapel in order that his religious ceremony should assume Vatican orthodoxy. As part of this process, singers from the papal chapel were brought to Lisbon. The hiring of the composer Domenico Scarlatti away from the Cappella Giulia at the Vatican was certainly a response to the same religious zeal. John V's motivations for the rapid italianization of his musical establishment were quite different from those that had inspired Philip V's wholly secular and political attempts to hire distinguished French musicians. Where Philip V found it necessary to satisfy and emulate Louis XIV, John V sought respect and recognition from Rome and to enhance his devotion to his church with elaborate ceremony.

A new class of performers and a new standard of musical excellence were created as a result of John V's attention to sacred music. By hiring excellent Italian singers for the chapel, he also supplied performers for the frequent oratorios, serenatas and other Italian *feste* that were given. With substantial Italian presence and the lack of a strong national theatrical tradition, it is significant that opera was slow to become established in Lisbon. In the first decades of the eighteenth century there are still references to *comedias* performed in public, and between 1700 and 1730 more than a dozen Spanish works were performed for royal birthdays and other celebrations at court or in the palaces of the nobility. This continued Spanish presence at a period in which Portuguese leaders were working to eradicate ties with Spain might give the impression that the long-established Spanish genres retained some appeal above and beyond political considerations. In fact, about half the private performances of zarzuelas in Lisbon were sponsored either by the Spanish envoys or by the Marquis de Valença, an outspoken traditionalist who published a defence of classical Spanish drama in 1747. Patronage for the zarzuela may reflect only the political and cultural investment of a determined conservative minority. It is surprising, nevertheless, that between 1718 and 1728 Philip V's ambassadors should have chosen zarzuelas by Spanish composers from the current repertory of the Madrid public theatres precisely when the genre was beginning to lose ground as a court entertainment in Spain.

The primacy of Italian music at the Lisbon court was well established through other genres before the first operas were performed there. In its notices concerning the royal court, the *Gazeta de Lisboa* informs us that serenatas were given there for royal celebrations from 1716, yet perhaps as few as five operas were staged at court during John V's reign, and these were not *opere serie* but comic operas. The first was *La pazienza di Socrate*, by Francisco António de Almeida to a libretto adapted by Alexandre de Gusmão, performed during Carnival in 1733 and 1734 – the fruit of a collaboration between two figures of great cultural and political significance. Almeida (*c*1702–1755), one of the first composers sent to Rome by John V, had returned to Lisbon as organist at the Patriarchal See after composing oratorios, concertos and sacred music in Rome. Alexandre de Gusmão (1695–1753), a Brazilian, made an enormous contribution to his era, in many different fields. He had served Portuguese interests in Paris for five years, and deployed his diplomatic skill in Rome for seven years on behalf of John V's royal chapel. He was one of the liberal members of the new Portuguese Academy of History, a purveyor of French neoclassicism whose literary credits include the first Portuguese translation of Molière. By 1730 he had become the king's closest and most valued confidential adviser, and a powerful and respected political figure. *La pazienza di Socrate* is an Italian 'dramma comico' by an esteemed Portuguese composer of italianate music and a powerful *estrangueirado*, whose libretto adapted a somewhat old-fashioned Italian one (by Nicolò Minato) that had been widely successful as far away as the imperial court in Vienna. Circumstances could not have been more auspicious; they certainly differed in the extreme from those at the court of Philip V. Almeida and Gusmão were highly placed in a political and artistic sense, so it is likely that their backing was essential to legitimize the new genre.

The Late Baroque Era

By European standards the performing conditions for this opera were unusual, but they may have removed the stigma of 'immorality' that was evidently attached to theatre. As in Rome, opera at the Lisbon court were performed entirely by males, including castratos in *travesti* roles singing as female characters. The audience was segregated too – only ladies were seated in the theatre, although a select few gentlemen watched from the wings (a privilege granted by the queen's special permission). When another comic opera by Almeida (*La risa di Democrito*) was performed at the palace for Carnival 1735, the ladies and selected court officials and nobles, including the Count of Ericeira, were permitted to sit in the audience, while a few nobles were again granted the privilege of standing in the wings. Social and political favour dictated the location of the male viewers (the ladies were politically unimportant). With perspective scenery, those who watched from the sides of the stage would have had an imperfect view and a distorted comprehension of the whole; the spectacle could be fully contemplated only by the 'chosen'. Segregation of the sexes remained a feature of opera in Lisbon for most of the period, to prevent the theatres from becoming places of assignation and centres of immorality. With the example set at court, the reconstruction of Portugal included a number of such measures designed to 'order' society and reform the moral fibre of its citizens.

In Lisbon, where political friction and open controversy were subdued both by John V's unquestioned authority and by the common goal of national revitalization, an intellectual elite of declared *estrangeirados* sought to bring Portugal into line with their perception of the European profile. Fashions in the capital followed foreign models and supported imported performers. Francisco Xavier de Meneses, 4th Count of Ericeira (1673–1743) and a leader in this movement of cultural 'progress', petitioned to reopen the public theatre in 1730 after a royal order had forced its closure in 1727. Perhaps clinging to the age-old belief that actors and public spectacle were inherently unholy, immoral and dangerous to society, the king had determined that the royal hospital should desist from contact with theatrical personnel. Ericeira's petition was designed to assuage any fear of moral contamination and to ensure that the royal hospital would again benefit from the proceeds of the theatre. One of the theologians who was consulted objected to the association between theatre and hospital, particularly because of the sinful demeanour on stage and after hours of the Spanish actresses who had last performed there. It appears the king was unswayed, even when an Italian company offered to recondition the Pátio das Comedias and perform opera there. For a short time theatrical entertainment was replaced by dances and by vocal and instrumental concerts given in private homes by amateurs and professionals.

The arguments of progressive aristocrats apparently persuaded the king to lift his prohibition, for by 1737 the Pátio das Comedias was functioning again, with a company that specialized in Italian comedy but also performed spoken plays in Spanish, Portuguese and French. In the reconditioned theatre of the Academia da Trinidade, and then at the Teatro Novo da Rua dos Condes (constructed in 1738 on property belonging to the Count of Ericeira), Italian *opera seria* was presented for the public between 1735 and 1742. Operas by the Italian composers Gaetano Maria Schiassi (later hired by the royal chapel), Leonardo Leo and Rinaldo di Capua were well attended and commercially successful, although the proceeds usually did not cover all expenses. European visitors were gratified that the works were well performed, with sets designed by an experienced Italian artist and with excellent Italian singers (male and female), lured to Lisbon by high salaries and leisurely working conditions.

Just as the Spanish theatres in Madrid had responded to the presence of commercial Italian opera by presenting translations, adaptations and hybrids that incorporated Italian conventions, 'operas' in Portuguese were similarly created for Lisbon. The most esteemed Portuguese popular dramatist of the eighteenth century, António José da Silva (1705–39), wrote eight *óperas* – prose plays, with inserted musical numbers clearly marked *aria*, *recitado* and *minuete*; they were not operas in the strict sense, but partly sung, in the Iberian tradition. At least 16 such works were performed at the Bairro Alto and Mouraria theatres for a largely middle-class audience, who were delighted by the frequent and elaborate scenic effects. Da Silva's texts are loaded with social satire, theatrical parody and burlesque; those that have the excuse of a serious main plot employ a ridiculously pompous language for the noble characters and everyday colloquial Portuguese, spiced with puns and slang, for the comic ones. The principal composer in this genre was António Teixeira (1707–after 1759), a chaplain and singer at the Patriarchy who had learnt the Italian style in Rome as a result of the king's patronage.

The competition between the commercial theatres in Lisbon (each presenting several performances per week) ensured that the public enjoyed a variety of theatrical and musical entertainment during this brief and concentrated period in the reign of John V. As the aging king became ill and even more devout, he once again converted his antipathy toward the stage into law, so that public theatrical performances in Lisbon were prohibited between 1742 and 1750. The effects of this decree were not altogether destructive. Composers such as Schiassi, Almeida and Teixeira reverted to church music and oratorio; concerts (but not dances) in private homes once again became the refuge of singers and musicians. When John V died in

The Late Baroque Era

1750 the taste for opera and musical comedy had already been inculcated in his subjects, nobles and commoners alike. Portuguese aristocrats and entrepreneurs had developed the administrative mechanisms for commercial survival and contacts with opera centres in Italy. King José I (ruled 1750–77) began immediately to build a first-rate establishment that was to make Lisbon famous as an operatic paradise in the latter half of the 'enlightened' century.

BIBLIOGRAPHICAL NOTE

Music

An enormous amount of research and analysis has yet to be completed before our knowledge of Iberian music and culture matches that for the rest of Europe. Much of this chapter is based on unpublished primary sources. In recent years several invaluable studies have appeared, chief among them M. C. de Brito, *Opera in Portugal in the Eighteenth Century* (Cambridge, 1989), a richly detailed documentary study with a chronology of public and private performances. The same author's 'Le rôle de l'opéra dans la lutte entre l'obscurantisme et les Lumières au Portugal (1731–1742)', *La musique et le rite, sacré et profane, IMSCR*, xiii Strasbourg 1982, ii, 543–4 is also important. L. K. Stein's *Songs of Mortals, Dialogues of the Gods: Music and Theatre in Seventeenth-Century Spain* (Oxford, 1993) focusses on the genres, conventions and legacy of the Hidalgo era. A. Martín Moreno's survey of Spanish music in the eighteenth century in volume iv of the *Historia de la música española* (Madrid, 1985) is extremely useful, unprecedented for its breadth and detail, and includes an exhaustive bibliography and list of editions. J. A. Rinnander's *One God, One Farinelli: Enlightenment Elites and the Containment of the Theatrical Impulse* (diss., U. of California, San Diego, 1985) is a major contribution to the study of Farinelli and his patrons, supplementing C. Morales Borrero's edition of Carlo Broschi Farinelli, *Fiestas reales en el reinado de Fernando VI* (Madrid, 1972). J. J. Carreras López's *La música en las catedrales en el siglo XVIII: Francisco J. García 'El Españoleto' (1730–1809)* (Saragossa, 1983) is a significant contribution to the study of cathedral music and reform in the eighteenth century. W. M. Bussey's *French and Italian Influence on the Zarzuela 1700–1770* (Ann Arbor, 1982) brings together a wealth of information from primary sources and concise analyses of several important zarzuelas, although the introductory section on the late seventeenth century contains a number of errors. R. Vieira Nery's *Para a história do barroco musical Português* (Lisbon, 1980) is an extremely useful overview.

The treatment of the eighteenth century in E. Cotarelo y Mori's *Historia de la zarzuela ó sea el drama lírico en españa desde su orígen a fines del siglo XIX* (Madrid, 1934) and *Orígen y establecimiento de la ópera en España hasta 1800* (Madrid, 1917) is still useful for factual references, as is the essay on music at court, 1700–1759, in J. Subirá, *El teatro del real palacio* (Madrid, 1950), 17–52. Subirá's *La música en la Casa de Alba* (Madrid, 1927) is essential for its coverage of primary sources that have since been lost.

Among the many shorter studies and editions of eighteenth-century Iberian music and musical theory, the following selections relate to specific points in the foregoing chapter. *Salir el amor del mundo* (1696), a zarzuela by Sebastián Durón, is available in an edition by A. Martín Moreno (Málaga, 1979), and another of Durón's works is the subject of L. Stein's 'Un manuscrito de música teatral reaparecido: *Veneno es de* amor la envidia', *Revista de musicología*, v (1982), 225–33. Selected songs and cantatas from early eighteenth-century sources are available in *Spanish Art Song in the Seventeenth Century*, ed. J. H. Baron (Madison, 1985), and in *Cantatas y canciones*, ed. M. Querol Gavaldá (Barcelona, 1973). M. Querol Gavaldá's edition of *Teatro musical de Calderón* (Barcelona, 1981) makes available selections from an important early eighteenth-century anthology; the many errors in its seriously flawed introduction are corrected in L. K. Stein's 'El "manuscrito novena": sus textos, su contexto histórico-musical y el músico Joseph Peyró', *Revista de musicología*, iii (1980), 197–234. J. López-Calo's edition of Francisco Valls's *Missa Scala Aretina* (London, 1978) includes a useful concise introduction to the work and the controversy and is supplemented by López-Calo's 'Músicos españoles del pasado: la controversia de Valls', *Tesoro sacro musical* (1968, 1969, 1971). A. Martín Moreno's *El Padre Feijoo y las ideologías musicales del siglo XVIII en España* (Orense, 1976) is an important contribution to the study of Feijoo and the eighteenth-century musical polemics. B. Lolo's *La música en la Real Capilla de Madrid: José de Torres y Martínez Bravo* (Madrid, 1990) provides an overview of the royal chapel and Bourbon reforms, and a detailed consideration of Torres's career and achievements. The two editions of Torres's *Reglas generales de acompañar, en órgano, clavicordio, y harpa* (Madrid, 1702 and 1736) have been issued together in facsimile (Madrid, 1983), and Pablo Nassarre's *Escuela música segun la práctica moderna* (Saragossa, 1723–4) is published in facsimile with an excellent introduction by L. Siemens (Saragossa, 1980). Francisco António de Almeida's comic opera *La spinalba, ovvero il vecchio matto* has been published in a transcription by P. Salzmann, Portugaliae Musica, xii (Lisbon, 1969).

Indispensable works on the Spanish theatre in the early eighteenth century include R. Andioc, *Teatro y sociedad en el Madrid del siglo XVIII* (Madrid, 1976, 2/1987), and N. D. Shergold and J. E. Varey, *Teatros y comedias en Madrid: 1699–1719, estudio y documentos* (London, 1986). The standard work on the Portuguese eighteenth-century theatre is still T. Braga, *Historia do theatro portuguez*, iii: *A baixa comedia e a ópera no seculo XVIII* (Oporto, 1871). The works of António José da Silva are available in his *Obras completas*, with preface and notes by J. Pereira Tavares (Lisbon, 1957–8).

History, thought and culture

Essential reading for an understanding of the baroque in Spain and Portugal are J. A. Maravall, *Culture of the Baroque: Analysis of a Historical Structure*, trans. T. Cochran, foreword by W. Godzich and N. Spadaccini (Minneapolis, 1986; 1st Sp. edn Madrid, 1975), and A. Domínguez Ortiz, *La sociedad española en el siglo XVII* (Madrid, 1963–70). J. L. Abellán's *Historia crítica del pensamiento español*, iii: *Del barroco a la ilustración* (Madrid, 1981) is a useful overview with excerpts from Spanish writers. A. Pagden's *Spanish Imperialism and the Political Imagination* (New Haven and London, 1990) considers the Spanish empire as reality and concept with penetrating insight. Standard histories in English are J. Lynch, *Spain under the Habsburgs*, ii: *Spain and America 1598–1700* (Oxford, 2/1981; New York, 1984); J. Lynch, *Bourbon Spain 1700–1808* (Oxford, 1989), 1–195; S. G. Payne, *A History of Spain and Portugal* (Madison, 1973), ii, 351–415; and W. N. Hargreaves-Mawdsley, *Eighteenth-Century Spain 1700–1788: a Political, Diplomatic and Institutional History* (London, 1979), 1–83. H. Kamen's *Spain in the Later Seventeenth Century, 1665–1700* (London, 1980) offers a solid and detailed history with a refreshing point of view, and the same author's *The War of Succession in Spain 1700–1715* (London and Bloomington, 1969) is indispensable. Y. Bottineau's *L'art de cour dans l'Espagne de Philippe V, 1700–1746* (Bordeaux, 1962; Sp. trans., 1986) is the most comprehensive treatment to date of the fine arts at the court of Philip V, although it must be used carefully.

Historical studies in English of this era in Portugal include A. H. de Oliveira Marques, *History of Portugal* (New York, 2/1976), i, 322–33, 379–425; V. Magalhães

Godinho, 'Portugal and her Empire', *The New Cambridge Modern History*, v: *The Ascendancy of France, 1648–88* (Cambridge, 1961), 384–97; and V. Magalhães Godinho, 'Portugal and her Empire 1680–1720', *The New Cambridge Modern History*, vi: *The Rise of Great Britain and Russia, 1688–1725* (Cambridge, 1970), 509–40. Excellent introductions to the Portuguese Enlightenment are provided by the articles 'Estrangeirados' and 'Luzes' by A. Coimbra Martins in the *Dicionário de História de Portugal*, ed. J. Serrão, ii (Lisbon, 1965), 122–9, 836–56; this four-volume dictionary is to be recommended for the high quality of its biographical and historical articles and for their excellent bibliographies.

Chapter XV

Warsaw, Moscow and St Petersburg

MILOŠ VELIMIROVIĆ

Most of the territories of eastern Europe are settled by people of Slavonic ethnic groups who communicate in languages that are closely related to one another but distinct from Germanic and Romance languages. Thus a 'linguistic barrier' has separated most of these populations from the cultural trends of western and central Europe. The one unifying factor – the use of Latin in religious services of the Roman Catholic church – represented an important link with the West for some western Slavs (Poles, Czechs and Slovaks), as well as for some southern Slavs (Croats and Slovenes). Those Slavs – that is Great Russians, Little Russians (now Ukrainians) and White Russians (Byelorussians) – who embraced Eastern Orthodox church teachings, perhaps the most significant of which are the use of the vernacular in services and the existence of a national church hierarchy, developed resistance to Roman missionaries, and for these groups submission to the Roman pope came to be viewed as a loss of national autonomy.

From the mid-seventeenth century to the mid-eighteenth, the time period of this chapter, most of the southern Slavs (Serbs and Bulgarians), some areas of present-day Hungary and Romania and the coastline of the Black Sea were under Turkish domination as parts of the Ottoman Empire, barely subsisting and with no incentives for artistic life; the western parts of the former Yugoslavia, as well as the territories of Bohemia (with their capital, Prague) and Slovakia, came under Austrian domination and within its cultural orbit. Poland and Russia were independent countries, yet beset by internal strife and perennial wars with their neighbours. Thus one of the basic points to keep in mind about these areas is the lack of stability and the constantly shifting state borders. Our discussion of the musical life in these countries examines some basic data for Warsaw, Moscow and St Petersburg.

The Late Baroque Era

WARSAW

Warsaw became the capital city of Poland only during the first decade of the seventeenth century, when it already had about 35 000 inhabitants and had overtaken the population of the former capital, Kraków, for centuries the residence of Polish kings. Even before this, in 1570, the Sejm (the national parliament of the nobility and gentry) had established its residence in Warsaw, after the 1569 Union of Lublin, which sanctioned the union of Poland and Lithuania (with its own capital, Vilnius). As the Sejm of these states began to meet regularly, the importance of Warsaw increased rapidly.

After the death in 1572 of Sigismund II, the last king of the Jagellonian dynasty (which had ruled since 1382), Poland became an elective monarchy with legislative powers vested in the Sejm. After the rule of two elected kings, the new king elected in 1587 was Sigismund III Vasa (reigned until 1632), son of John III of Sweden and of Catherine, daughter of the Polish king Sigismund I (reigned 1506–48), and was thus the grandson of a ruler from the previous dynasty. It was Sigismund III who moved the capital from Kraków to Warsaw, and it was his court that entertained a substantial presence of Italian musicians (Luca Marenzio, G. F. Anerio, Asprilio Pacelli and Marco Scacchi). During Sigismund III's reign Polish troops invaded Russia, assisting the pretender known as 'False Dmitry' as he waged war against Boris Godunov (tsar, 1598–1605), and by 1613 a new dynasty had come to power in Russia – the Romanovs (who were to rule for the next three centuries).

Musical life at the Polish court flourished particularly during the reign of Sigismund's son Władysław IV Vasa (1632–48): many more musicians joined the royal chapel, and in 1637 the king (who had seen an opera in Florence in about 1625) established in Warsaw Castle a theatre, in which no fewer than 11 operas were staged during his reign. It is curious to note that the royal residence was contained in a special wing of the castle; other wings were reserved for meetings of the Sejm, which viewed the ruler as a 'tenant' in the spacious castle. The theatre, referred to in sources as a 'gran sala di teatro', was located in the south wing, and a Frenchman (using the pseudonym 'L'Abbé F. D. S.') described it as 'une salle en galerie des plus grandes de l'Europe pour jouer les comédies'. It was 48 metres long and 12 metres wide, with the stage itself 24 metres deep. On the sides of the stage were balconies for the orchestra, and dressing-rooms were located behind the stage. Along the long walls were two rows of 16 windows; the machinery needed for stage effects was also available. Only the king and ambassadors were seated on chairs; the rest of the audience stood during performances, with only a few benches available.

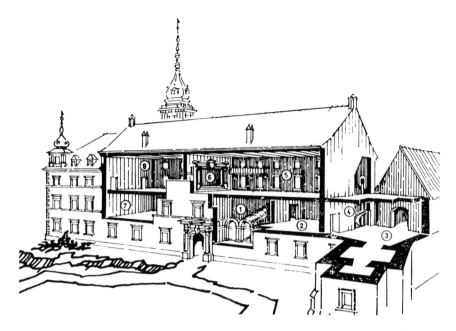

63. *Theatre in the royal castle, Warsaw, in the time of Władysław IV (reconstruction): (1) main entrance, (5) area for spectators, (6) stage, (7) below stage, (8) backstage; from Jerzy Lileyko, 'Zamek warszawski 1569–1763' ('The Warsaw Castle') (1984)*

Besides Italian musicians, who brought new musical practices to Poland, a few Polish musicians and composers were active at this period, which is generally viewed as the 'golden age' of Polish music. Among those who attained great renown were Adam Jarzębski (*c*1590–1649) and Marcin Mielczewski (*c*1600–1651), as well as Franciszek Lilius (*c*1600–1657, of Italian descent) and the talented Bartołomiej Pękiel (*d* 1670), who shared the direction of the chapel with Scacchi and who, after the mid-1650s lived in Kraków for the rest of his life.

Jarzębski travelled abroad and was active as a violinist in Berlin in 1612; he visited Italy in 1615 and returned in 1619 to Warsaw where, about 1640, he wrote a most interesting document, *Gościniec* ('The Road', a survey of Warsaw), in which he described the theatre and the opulent staging of operas. Among his works are a series of dances with names like 'Berlinessa', 'Norimberga', 'Tamburetta' and 'Ben trovata'. None of these Polish composers apparently wrote any operas, in spite of their knowledge of Venetian attainments: Mielczewski, for example, apparently introduced the Venetian rondo concertato to Poland. While only two of his works were printed in his lifetime, many were copied by hand, and it is in these works that the rhythmic patterns of the Polish mazurka are first seen. Some Kraków composers' works were also performed in Warsaw. Pękiel joined the royal chapel in 1637; he soon became Scacchi's deputy and after 1651 was in charge of all the music. During his stay in Warsaw he composed the outstanding *Audite mortales*, for six-part choir, strings and continuo, and the *Missa Lombardesca*. His *Missa pulcherrima*, reckoned the finest Polish composition of the century, dates from his later years in Kraków.

Władysław IV was succeeded by his brother John II Casimir (1648–68), during whose reign Poland was exposed to the many ravages and calamities that resulted from the wars with Sweden and the Cossack uprisings in the Ukraine. In 1654 the Cossacks recognized Moscow's supremacy, and much of the Ukraine, including Smolensk and Kiev, was lost to the Russians. In 1655 the Swedes devastated the city of Warsaw, and, as a result of the plague that followed, the population was reduced from 50 000 in 1650 to around 15 000 by 1669. Many musicians departed to Kraków and other cities, and theatrical life in Warsaw in the 1650s came to a standstill. It was unfortunate that just at this time the nobility and gentry in the Sejm introduced the rule of unanimity for passing any measures, so that after 1652 a single nobleman could – and did – use his *liberum veto*, which led to a total paralysis of political life.

As for the remainder of the seventeenth century, the brief reign of Michael Wisniowecki (1669–73) was followed by that of John III Sobieski (*b* 1629; ruled 1675–96), who is best remembered for his military exploits and as the 'saviour' of Vienna, defeating the besieging Turks there in 1683 and thus repulsing the Ottoman Empire's last attempt to gain a foothold in central Europe. Sobieski's wife Maria Casimira, who was of French descent, appears to have been responsible for the influx of French culture into Warsaw and the reinforcement of contacts with France that had started somewhat earlier (by 1662 Corneille's works, and later Racine's, had already been performed in Poland). Sobieski built a summer palace on the outskirts of Warsaw, the charming Willanow, with a large library that demonstrates his wide-ranging interests.

After the tragic events of the Swedish invasion in the 1650s and Pękiel's departure to Kraków, musical life at the Warsaw court declined. From the 1660s the new leader of the royal musicians was Jacek Różycki (*d* 1707), who was in charge of the royal chapel for more than 40 years under several rulers. Though an able leader, he can no longer be reckoned the composer of some operas performed during the revival of operatic seasons in the later years of Sobieski's reign. On 28 March 1691 the opera *Per goder in amor ci vuol costanza* was staged, with music by Augustino Viviani and libretto by the elder Giovanni Battista Lampugnani, a musician and secretary of the papal nuncio in Warsaw. Lampugnani appears also to have been the author of two subsequent stage works: *Amor vuol in giusto*, performed in 1694 for the wedding of Sobieski's daughter Teresa Kunigunda to the Elector of Saxony, Friedrich August I; and *Transito di B. Casimiro*, performed in 1695, probably on the king's birthday. Polish scholars presume that Viviani may have composed the music for both works, though there is no record to support this.[1] While there are traces of a few Polish composers in Warsaw in this period and in the early eighteenth century, most were active either in Kraków or in various monasteries, and it is not possible to place their activities in Warsaw during their lifetimes. Among them were Damian Stachowicz (*c*1658–1699), Stanisław Sylwester Szarzyński (*fl* 1692–1712) and Grzegorz Gerwazy Gorczycki (*c*1667–1734).

The position of royal musicians underwent a thorough change with the accession to the Polish throne in 1697 of Augustus II ('the Strong') of the house of Wettin, Elector of Saxony, who resided in Dresden (ruled as Polish king until 1733); he was so eager to ascend the Polish throne that he abandoned the Protestant religion of his country and converted to Catholicism. Jacek Różycki appears to have been confirmed as leader of the royal musicians, but he now had to share responsibility with Johann Christoph Schmidt (1664–1728), the Kapellmeister in Dresden, as the two orchestras merged. Moreover, the castle in Warsaw was occupied for only part of the year, as Augustus divided his time between the two capitals, moving in the summer to Warsaw and staying there for a few months, usually until the beginning of Advent (only exceptionally until the beginning of Lent), when he returned to Dresden.

With Augustus II, the so-called Saxon period of Polish history began; it lasted from 1697 to 1763 and encompassed the reigns of Augustus II and his son Augustus III (1733–63). During this period a new royal palace was built in Warsaw, and the famous Saxon park was established, which to this day is a favourite retreat in the centre of the city. As Warsaw was only a 'part-time' capital, its royal musicians were placed in a difficult position. Augustus II actually established two orchestras, the main one in Dresden, which occasionally travelled to Warsaw (as recorded in the memoirs of Franz Benda and Quantz, both of whom mention in their autobiographies that they resided for a while in Warsaw), and the king's 'Polish chapel' or 'small orchestra', which consisted of well-known musicians, foreign and Polish. In addition, there was a special military band known as the Janissary music, in which only the Poles played. The musical life of Warsaw in the first half of the eighteenth century has to be seen in conjunction with that of Dresden (see Chapter 7), as more than one musician had to 'commute' according to the royal schedule of activities.

During the early years of the eighteenth century Poland became involved in the Northern War being fought by the Swedes and Russians under the expansive leadership of Peter the Great. Recuperating slowly after the Swedish 'deluge' of the 1650s, Warsaw recovered by 1700 to reach over 20 000 inhabitants, and by the end of the reign of Augustus III it had no fewer than 30 000, as a prelude to a much more rapid expansion in the second half of the century.

By 1699 Augustus II had already brought to Warsaw a company of comedians from Zelle who staged plays with music. By 1700 he engaged a French troupe, which came to Warsaw for a five-year stay; it consisted of 18 female and 13 male singers, 15 dancers and more than 20 orchestral musicians, and it staged operas in Warsaw Castle and in Sobieski's Willanow Palace. Yet another French group arrived in 1708, but records indicate only four players of string instruments, with eight actors and six actresses. After 1702 there was also apparently an Italian company in Warsaw; since the king was a music lover it comes as no surprise that for 15 years, from 1715, this Italian company under the leadership of Tommaso Ristori was in royal service, commuting between Dresden and Warsaw (it was this company that the king 'lent' to the Russian Empress Anna to perform operas at her coronation in Moscow in 1731; see below). Polish scholars view the presence of such troupes in Warsaw as affording an opportunity for audiences to hear the contemporary works of such composers as Lully and Campra, as well as Rameau's cantatas and ballets by Jean-Féry Rebel.

By 1724 the construction of an opera house, the Operalnia, had been initiated, next to the completed new royal palace. When it opened it had a 'parterre pour la noblesse' and 'bancs élevés pour la bourgeoisie', surrounded by 14 boxes on the lower level and 15 on the upper, where the largest one in the centre was designated for ambassadors. While the building was not viewed as an architectural attainment of artistic merit, it did perform a valuable role in the musical life of Warsaw, since admittance was free of charge; the local populace, however, appears to have attended in small numbers, primarily because performances were in foreign languages – French and Italian. Besides opera, ballets were also staged in this theatre. In 1727 the Dresden royal dancers staged *Proserpina*; it is curious to note that the local population viewed such dancing as 'indecent', so that many refrained from attending subsequent performances, much to the regret of the French choreographer, who tried to attract back the local audience by staging dances more to their taste, even to the extent of including dances with Polish rhythmic patterns.

Whether Johann Adolf Hasse ever came to Warsaw still remains a moot point, though his operas were definitely staged there in the 1750s. Musicians also took an active part in festivities such as birthday celebrations for the king and queen, anniversaries of the coronation and royal arrivals in the city. During Lent, oratorios were performed with music by Hasse, Giovanni Alberto Ristori (Tommaso's son) and Michael Breunich. Performances were not restricted to the church in the castle but were also given in the cathedral of St John and other places, such as the Capuchin monastery. Outside the royal castle, the cathedral was pre-eminent for music performances, and the Augustinian church is said to have had space for three orchestras to perform polychoral music.

According to the custom of the time, many Polish noblemen had residences in Warsaw besides those on their widespread estates. During the Saxon period a few of the nobility had their own janissary bands for military music, which was quite popular in the city. Furthermore, in at least one instance, on 3 March 1699 in the palace garden of the governor of Płock, there was a carousel with trumpeters, drummers and even bagpipe players.

The question of music education has not been so far investigated sufficiently, but the presence of up to 50 musicians at the court of Władysław IV in the first half of the seventeenth century suggests strongly that, in addition to the Italian presence, there must have been opportunities for Poles to learn music. Many members of the royal chapel were entrusted with training young boys as singers for the church services. The Kraków 'Rorantists' choir and its tradition may well have been emulated in Warsaw and other localities, despite the lack of supporting documentation. Several Polish rulers were said to have been proficient in music and to have played one or more musical instruments.

That Jesuits had schools in Poland is well known, but there is no available record of such a school in Warsaw. The children of the nobility, particularly after 1741, were educated in the Collegium Nobilium established by the Piarist scholar Stanisław Konarski. Here they would be taught Latin, French, German and, if required, Italian. Besides a long list of subjects that included mathematics, history and horse-riding, there were classes in dancing and music. In the schedule of daily activities it was specified that from 1 p.m. to 3 p.m. physical education training included dancing and music; even in the schools for the daughters of the nobility, by 1750 a special teacher (a German lady, Strumle) taught dancing, including the 'Polish dance' (i.e. the polonaise).

From the Saxon period there are also records of the establishment of guilds of professional musicians associated with specific churches, and there seems to have been strict delineation of their duties and activities: they were banned from participating in lay entertainments, with punishments involving fines that consisted of a certain amount of wax to be given to the church for trespassing against royal decrees. Some public entertainments involving students are recorded, but no details are given of the instruments that were played or the names of songs and dances. Nevertheless, some Polish melodies probably date from this period and are of interest as they contain strong hints of mazurka rhythms.

MOSCOW

Among the most characteristic developments in the musical life of Moscow during the seventeenth century was the affirmation and flourishing of polyphonic choral music and its acceptance into the religious practices of the Russian Orthodox church, and an increasing interest in performing instrumental music, primarily at the imperial court and in the homes of the nobility. Both these trends were fostered by the steadily growing number of foreign musicians entering service in Russia. The contemporary Western styles they brought with them exerted considerable influence and led even to performances of opera, which by the first half of the eighteenth century were progressing so rapidly that by mid-century Moscow and St Petersburg were on the threshold of becoming visible rivals to well-established musical centres with much longer traditions of professional musicianship. The pace of developments within Russia was, in part at least, conditioned by the turbulent events of its political history and by cultural and trade links with western European countries. While in earlier centuries the basic (if incorrect) impression of Russia was that of an isolated and 'barbarous' country in eastern Europe, the contacts made particularly between Russia and England in the second half of the sixteenth century represented a turning-point in trade, as a growing number of reports about Russia by English merchants began to acquaint the West with some aspects of that remote and unfamiliar kind of society.

Knowledge of musical practices in Moscow before the mid-seventeenth century is restricted to information about vocal music in Russian Orthodox services in churches and monasteries, and to folk music, which was practised by large numbers of minstrels, known as *skomorokhi*. Many were itinerant musicians, playing a variety of indigenous instruments, while some were settled, even respected, tax-paying members of communities. The presence of *skomorokhi* was noted at church fairs and folk festivals, while the best known entertained rulers and nobles as hired servants; they may be viewed as Russian counterparts of Western medieval *jongleurs*, who also performed acrobatics and all sorts of tricks as part of their entertainments. The Russian church did not view *skomorokhi* as acceptable members of the congregations, and in the first half of the seventeenth century in particular there were many attempts to eliminate them from an active role in society. By the late 1640s the reigning tsar,

Alexey Mikhailovich, the second ruler of the Romanov dynasty, had issued more than one edict banning their public performances: under pressure from the church, which often excommunicated these entertainers, thus preventing their burial in the consecrated grounds of church cemeteries, the tsar ordered that all musical instruments in Moscow be taken away from their owners and be collected and burnt on a pyre across the River Moskva. Olearius, a traveller who left descriptions of Russia rich with details of the time, recorded that some five chariots filled with musical instruments were taken to the pyre. But such a number suggests clearly that in a city which by that time had some 100 000 inhabitants there must have remained many instruments for home entertainment. In fact, Olearius mentioned that a close relative of the tsar, Nikita Romanov, had in his possession a number of keyboard instruments (including a 'positiv') which he played well and which no-one dared to take away from him. It is curious indeed that this tsar, at first so puritanically inclined, was to give some of Nikita's instruments to another nobleman, Vorotinsky, a few years after Nikita's death in 1654, and that the very same tsar was to introduce opera into Russia in 1672.

Some other data about the musical life of Moscow in earlier decades are revealing. The period from 1598 to 1613 in Russian history is known as the Time of Troubles, an interregnum after the death of the last member of the original Rurik dynasty and the election as tsar of Mikhail Fyodorovich Romanov, with whom a new dynasty came to the Russian throne and was to reign until 1917. Into the interregnum falls the brief rule of Boris Godunov (1598–1605), as well as the Polish invasion of Moscow, when a number of Polish musicians, among them an organist, Gabriel, are known to have played in the Kremlin, the fortification and settlement that was soon to become the centre of the growing city, surrounded by merchants' and craftsmen's quarters. At the outset, foreigners were not immediately restricted to a specific area, but in the early 1640s at the instigation of the church, which was suspicious of non-Eastern-Orthodox residents, their homes were badly damaged; after a period of uncertainty, in 1652 a special quarter was designated 'Nemetskaya Sloboda' (literally, 'German Quarter', with the implication that it was a tax-free area). Foreigners were henceforth expected to settle there, where they could have their own churches and schools and enjoy limited mingling with the Russian population. However, even in later years some *skomorokhi* were making their living by entertaining the residents of the foreign quarters.

During the reign of Mikhail Fyodorovich, the first Romanov (1613–45), a special 'entertainment palace' (*poteshnaya palata*) was built in the Kremlin complex, close to the imperial residence. The tsar had in his service two Dutch organists, Johann and Melchert

Loon (or Luhn), who had four Russians as their *tsimbalniki* (possibly harpsichordists) – Andrey Andreyev, Tomila Mikhailov Besov, Boris Ovsonov and Melenty Stepanov – the earliest known Russian players of western instruments in the seventeenth century. The tsar also had two Polish organists in his service for an extended period – Jerzy Proskurowski (who served 1625–44) and Fedor (or Bogdan) Zawalski (1638–44). By the the second half of the century the presence of an organ in the entertainment palace was taken for granted in descriptions of events that occurred in that building which record that groups of people were standing 'where the organ is located'.

The reign of Mikhail's successor Alexey Mikhailovich (1645–76) was fraught with difficulties, wars, revolts and riots. In the mid-1650s wars with Poland resulted in the Russian reconquest of the city of Smolensk, and in 1654 the Ukrainian Cossacks accepted the supremacy of the Russian tsar. Within the internal life of the church, the new patriarch, Nikon, elected in 1652, was to become a controversial figure whose views were to have a significant bearing on the future course of Russian church music.

Church music

Before the sixteenth century Russian church music was monophonic and was copied by hand using a neumatic notation that had its roots in Byzantine neumatic notation. During the sixteenth century there was an explosive growth in copying music manuscripts for religious services, and, alongside the traditional monophonic hymn repertory, there appeared the first polyphonic settings, also notated in a rapidly evolving (though still neumatic) notation. Since events connected with notation were to become a focal point of controversies in the mid-seventeenth century, a brief summary of the essence of the problems is necessary.

In the Russian alphabet, besides letters with a specific sound, there are two 'mute' letters, referred to as 'soft' and 'hard' signs, which, while designating no specific 'sound' nevertheless had some 'duration'. During the sixteenth century, and certainly in the first half of the seventeenth, these signs were interpreted as 'semi-vowels', giving the 'soft' sign the value of the sound 'e' (in European pronunciation) and the 'hard' sign the sound 'o' (a practice which may be much older than has been suggested). This enunciation distorted the words which, when sung, differed from the same words in colloquial speech. This type of pronunciation was given the name *khomoniya* (or *khomovoye peniye*: 'chanting according to *khomoniya*') and was viewed by conservative groups as 'traditional'. When reformers wanted to 'correct' the church books and bring the pronunciation into line with contemporary speech, a conflict arose: reformers viewed *khomoniya* as mistakes and corruptions that required correction, and, under Nikon, orders were issued to send all church books to Moscow to be corrected.

In the meantime, an already existing polyphonic practice, however humble in its manifestations, was considerably strengthened in the 1650s when singers from Kiev and south-western areas came to Moscow, bringing with them polyphonic traditions strongly influenced by western, notably Polish, musical practices which emanated from an area of constantly shifting state borders. Their repertory contained the first examples of *partesnye kontserty* (sacred polychoral settings) written in Western staff notation; to grasp the significance of this one must keep in mind the rigidity with which some circles in Russia viewed anything Western as a renunciation of orthodoxy and a step towards submission of the Russian church to the Roman papacy.

Russian neumatic notation had become quite complex in the sixteenth century, and around 1600 a reform by Ivan Shaydur attempted to clarify the meaning of the neumes. By Nikon's time liturgical practices had become complicated; when 'run-on' services were established, there was simultaneous reading of one text and singing by the choir of another (to abridge the services!), and the religious message became incomprehensible as words were mispronounced in *khomoniya* settings. From the mid-1650s several church councils were assembled to deal with these problems. Conservatives were even more shocked by Nikon's benign views of polyphony. Of all the councils, probably the most important was one of 1666–7 at which a new reform of neumatic notation was promulgated, clarifying the meaning of neumes; the author of the treatise codifying the notational reform was Alexander Mezenets, a former employee of the Moscow Printing Press (originally founded in the 1550s), who was assisted by several monks and singers.

The most important factors, however, were the dissent against the correction of texts and the opposition to polyphonic music; in addition to these, the interpretation of some points of dogma led to a schism which split the Russian church into the 'official' church and the so-called Old Believers, or schismatics (*raskolniki*), who resisted all change. It is of no small interest that towards the end of the seventeenth century a need arose for a new type of musical manuscript, the *dvoyeznamennik* (i.e. with two notations), containing melodies written in both reformed neumatic notation and Western staff notation. These manuscripts now serve as a key to the comprehension of the late neumatic forms of a peculiarly Russian notational system.

The penetration of Western musical concepts was immeasurably strengthened by the appearance in Moscow in the 1670s of a musical treatise, *Idea grammatikii musikiskoy* ('The Idea of Musical Grammar'), by the Ukrainian writer Nikolay Diletsky (*fl c*1670–1680s), who may have spent a few years in Poland, as well as in Lithuania (where the treatise first appeared), in the border city of Smolensk and in Moscow, where he is believed to have been employed as a choral director by Count Stroganov. His treatise is the first in Russian to define the concepts of major and minor modes and to cite music examples extracted from a number of Polish composers' works (including Mielczewski); Diletsky was also the first significant composer of polyphonic and polychoral works in Russia. His treatise was followed by a number of other writings, and as a composer he was shortly joined by the somewhat younger Vasily Titov (*d* ?1710), whose activities extended into the years of the rule of Peter the Great, whom Titov glorified after Peter's famous victory over the Swedes at Poltava in 1709. Up to the mid-eighteenth century no fewer than 500 *partesnye kontserty* were composed for large ensembles, requiring skilful singers educated in church schools and in patriarchal and imperial chapels. Only a handful have been transcribed, but those few that are currently accessible demonstrate the considerable talent of composers whose style was ultimately rooted in the choral works of Heinrich Schütz and his contemporaries.

At this period a new type of work, *kantï*, began to appear and flourished particularly in the first half of the eighteenth century. Usually for three voices and performed with occasional doubling of melodic lines by instruments, *kantï* (from the Latin *cantus*: 'song') texts embraced both religious and secular topics; some are panegyrics for rulers, others have texts of lyrical content.

An overview of sacred music in the first half of the eighteenth century indicates that polyphonic works were cultivated at the imperial court and in large cathedrals, whereas parish churches and monasteries remained the repositories of older monophonic chant. It is curious that, after Titov's death, hardly any names of Russian composers of church music are known. The new fashion for the theatre and for secular music had by then won the upper hand.

Music at court

The presence of foreign musicians at the Russian court alongside native entertainers (*skomorokhi*) has already been mentioned for the period up to the mid-seventeenth century. While their repertory is unknown, one may surmise, keeping in mind their origin, that they performed works of contemporary composers that they may have known from their native lands. During the second half of the seventeenth century – the reigns of Alexey (1645–76) and his son Fyodor (1676–82) and the temporary regency of Sofia until the reign of Peter the Great (1689–1725) – there were several significant events in musical life at the court. The 1670s witnessed the sudden appearance of operatic productions and a considerably reduced presence of music after Alexey's death. Throughout the period church music made great strides in integrating traditional monophonic and imported polyphonic trends.

Although Tsar Alexey banned musical instruments and minstrels when he was nearly 20, as he travelled and had the opportunity to observe life in areas outside his immediate domain, new impressions seem to have softened his resistance to professional music-making. After the Russians regained Smolensk in about 1654, a man believed to have been a resident there, Simon Gutovsky (1626–85), possibly a minor member of the local Polish gentry, entered the tsar's service as 'master of organs' and for the remaining 30 years of his life appears to have contributed enormously to the performance of music at court; he was even more influential as an organ builder in Russia, training several young men in the craft. Gutovsky's skills and his workshop must have acquired great renown, as in 1662 he was commissioned to make an instrument to be presented by the Russian Embassy in that year as a gift to the Persian Shah Abbas II. Gutovsky was ordered to join the embassy and go to Ispahan with three of his young assistants and an armed guard (who was to keep an eye on the luggage containing parts of the organ, which was to be assembled in Persia). Since Gutovsky returned only two years later, it is presumed that during his stay he may have trained a young Persian to play the instrument. The description of the organ mentions that it had 27 pipes as a decorative façade, while inside there were some 200-odd pipes with four stops; the pipes were made of 'English lead' (a blend of lead and other metals). Gutovsky's organ must have made a great impression, because in 1668 he was commissioned to make an even larger one for Persia. In that year his workshop was documented as being in the former quarters of the late Nikita Romanov.

From 1672 to 1676 Gutovsky and eight of his pupils were members of the orchestra that played during opera performances at court. For these, a large organ was requisitioned from 'Timofey' Gasenkruch (apparently a local German); when in later years an offer was made to return the instrument to Gasenkruch, he refused to take it back, since he felt it had been damaged by frequent moves from the Kremlin to the nearby summer home of Preobrazhenskoye and back, and he claimed that long ago it had been worth more than 1000 rubles.

In 1673 Gutovsky made a 'clavichord' for a one-year-old baby – the future Peter the Great. In addition to being an organ builder and performer, Gutovsky is said to have invented in 1677 a new tool to aid music printing, a technique that was not used in his lifetime (the Russian church started printing music books only in 1772). After Gutovsky's death two of his sons continued the art of organ building in Moscow and appeared as performers. Although there were Protestant churches in the German Quarter, it appears that there were no organs in them before 1695, when an instrument was installed there.

Mention has already been made of the 'positiv' owned by Nikita Romanov. There were, however, instruments owned by noblemen besides the tsar and his relatives. Several members of the Golitsïn family appear to have owned organs and other instruments: Count Miloslavsky (whose daughter Mariya was Alexey's first wife) had no fewer than 14 trumpeters in his service; Count Stroganov, who employed Diletsky, also had instruments; and Peter's adviser Lefort and friend Menshikov both possessed organs and other instruments (when Peter learnt of Lefort's death in 1699 he was concerned about the disposal of the organs in Lefort's palace). It is also noteworthy that a magnate of this period, Count P. Yaguzhinsky, not only had musicians in his service but was himself the son of a Lithuanian organist who moved to Moscow in 1687, first as a teacher and later as an organist at the Lutheran church in the German Quarter. Besides having organs made in Moscow, Peter ordered several organs from Germany. In 1691 he placed an order in Hamburg with the organ builder Arp Schnitger for an organ, which was delivered in four large crates and had 16 stops. Schnitger also sent another instrument to Moscow in 1697 to a German named Ernhorn, living in the German Quarter.

Just as Gutovsky had been summoned to participate in the court orchestra, Ivan Finalis (possibly of Hungarian origin), the organist of the Roman Catholic church in Moscow at the beginning of the eighteenth century, did double duty as a performer in a theatre on the Red Square during the first decade of the century. It is not clear whether there was more than one Catholic church (Jesuits had their own place of worship with organs by 1699), nor, if so, whether the same organist appeared in both.[2] It is noteworthy that in the first illustrated Russian primer, by Karion Istomin (c1694), one of the objects depicted as starting with the letter 'o' is an organ.

Dramatic music and the beginnings of opera

In the 1650s Russian delegations were sent to Italy (Venice, 1656 and 1661; Florence, 1659) and England (1661), where they encountered theatrical performances. V. Likhachev's description of opera in Florence is very elaborate, full of details about the scenery and its changes, and the entrances and exits of singers, and shows his incomplete understanding of it, through not having experienced anything comparable in his own country. But this situation was soon to change. Tsar Alexey, a devout ruler, became a widower when his first wife Mariya Miloslavska died in childbirth in 1669 (when

Alexey was only 40) after 24 years of marriage. On 1 February 1671 he remarried, taking as second wife Nataliya Kirilovna Naryshkina, daughter of a landowner of Tatar origin who lived far from Moscow and had entrusted his daughter as a ward to the highly educated and extremely able Artamon Matveyev. Matveyev had a wide range of interests and a large library of foreign books, and was married to Mary Hamilton, daughter of a Scots loyalist who had left England after the death of Charles I. Their home had a small domestic theatre with musicians, for entertainment.

To accommodate the tastes and desires of his new bride, the tsar ordered his colonel, Nicolas von Staden, to travel abroad and bring musicians and singers to Moscow. Staden had limited success, as the singers reneged, fearing they might not subsequently be allowed to leave Russia; later, however, he did bring four musicians from Danzig (now Gdańsk) who could play seven musical instruments. In the meantime, without waiting for Staden's return, the German pastor of the Protestant church in the German Quarter, Johann Godfried Gregori (c1630–1675), was commanded to prepare a play based on the story of Esther to be staged in a specially built theatre, which was erected in a very short time in the village of Preobrazhenskoye (where Alexey enjoyed hunting with his falcons), with no expense spared in making it plush and comfortable. Gregori was also commissioned to stage a play at the court. The result of his endeavours was the *Comedy of Artaxerxes* ('comedy' in the sense of 'actus', or 'play'), staged for the first time on 16 October 1672, with an orchestra in which Gutovsky, his pupils and probably other musicians participated. The music for this work does not survive, but Gregori's text does, both in the original German and in a Russian translation; the work was probably performed in German, while a Russian translation was prepared and presented to the tsar to enable him to follow the action. The cast numbered more than 60, with many pupils acting in it; the role of Esther was taken by a man, a certain M. Berner. The play had seven acts and lasted a full ten hours, and the tsar followed it with rapt attention, seated in his special chair with soft cushions; the remainder of the audience sat on benches, while for the tsarina a special box with a wooden screen was built to keep her out of sight of the assembled spectators. Another interesting point about this play was that it had four 'interscenia' – intermezzos performed in the *commedia dell'arte* fashion, that is without written text – the only information being that they contained the quarrel of a man and his wife and included a character named Mishelov (literally, 'Mouse-trap'), the intrigant, who is killed at the end of the play. Throughout the text of the main play by Gregori there are clear changes in rhythm and indications that parts of the text were intended to be sung.

The Late Baroque Era

Theatrical performances continued until Alexey's death in 1676; among the staged works were *Judith* (some of the music in a revision of a century later survives, but the original version is lost); the ballet *Orpheus*, in which the surrounding pyramids join in the dancing; and pieces such as *David and Goliath* and *Bacchus and Venus* (which included ballet numbers), all of which were staged at this period, though no composers' names are known.

These successful theatrical experiments served as impetus for the creation of Russian dramatic works by the educator and poet Simeon Polotsky (1629–80; before taking orders in 1656 he was known as Samuil Gavrilovich Petrovsky-Sitnianovich). Among his plays with music is one about the Fiery Furnace, based in part on the traditional 'Play of the Furnace' – a paraliturgical drama popular in the preceding two centuries in Russian cathedrals, where it was staged not later than the last Sunday before Christmas. Polotsky was also the author of the rhythmicized psalter (*Rifmotvornaya psaltir*, or metrical psalms), for which three-part musical settings were made by Vasily Titov.

One type of theatrical entertainment with popular potential was the school drama; it was probably for a school theatre that Polotsky wrote his dramatic works, since he was educated in both Kiev and Vilnius (where he attended the Jesuit school, 1650–54) and would have been exposed to school dramas. That the Jesuits came to Moscow and had a school there is also well known, and it appears that not later than 1699, for at least a few seasons, dramas were staged in their school in the German Quarter. A special place of honour belongs to the nativity drama by Dmitry, the Metropolitan of Rostov (1651–1709, formerly Daniil Savvich Tuptalo). Born near Kiev and educated at the academy there, he was appointed Metropolitan of Rostov, where he founded a school in which 200 students studied free of charge and had to learn to read, write and sing from musical notation. His nativity drama was staged during the first year of the school's existence, in 1702–3. By 1705, however, the school had closed as a result of financial problems. The nativity drama, recently reconstructed and published,[3] is testimony to the role of dramatic music as a pedagogical device.

Peter the Great, though known to have had a good singing voice and to have sung with church choirs during services, was interested in music only for its military purposes, despite his exposure to opera and the theatre during his travels to western Europe. Nevertheless, in 1702, at Peter's own instigation, a new theatrical troupe arrived in Moscow under the leadership of Johann Kunst, and for some four or five years plays with musical accompaniment were staged in a newly built public theatre on Red Square. Since they were given in languages foreign to Russian audiences, however, the public lost interest, the attendances dwindled from more than 400 to less than 100, and the performances ended in 1706–7. With the demise of Kunst's theatre (he died in 1705 and was succeeded by Fuerst for the remaining seasons), Peter's sister Nataliya Alexeyevna attempted to mount performances using Kunst's stage equipment and decorations, which she had acquired wholesale.

During Peter's reign a new type of entertainment was introduced to Moscow – occasional welcoming ceremonies, and parades to celebrate successful military ventures and victories. For these public events a special architecture evolved as numerous arches were erected in the city, with noblemen competing as to who could sponsor or have constructed a more elaborate or richly decorated arch. For welcoming ceremonies, music was specially composed and sung: on one such occasion in 1723, to celebrate Peter's victorious return from Persia, the students of the School of Surgery staged a 'comedy' appropriate for the occasion. When Peter founded a new city, St Petersburg, in May 1703, it was clear that it was to become the new capital. By 1711–12 the imperial residence was ready to move out of Moscow (but when Peter died in Moscow in 1725, the School of Surgery again staged a special play, to mark his death). Even with a new capital gaining in eminence, Moscow was still growing and experiencing the modernization that was inevitable in the course of events.

The musical repertory at this period was enriched by *kantï*, which may have had their roots in performances of Protestant chorales in the Baltic territories. As was noted above, a number of the *kantï* composed during Peter's reign were songs that openly praised the ruler, filled with the Latin exclamation 'Vivat'; the melodic lines that emulate trumpet calls clearly indicate the taste for military-style settings. Peter also favoured regimental bands: in 1702 the elite Preobrazhensky guard had some 40 drummers and 32 'flute-players': most other bands were smaller, with 10–12 musicians. In the decisive battle at Poltava in 1709, when Peter defeated Charles XII of Sweden, the Russians apparently captured (and subsequently had at their disposal) some 120 musicians, including trumpeters, oboists, flautists, drummers and cymbal players, and needed 54 carts to transport the musical instruments they had seized.

Although the musical importance of Moscow diminished after 1712, later rulers still went to Moscow for coronation ceremonies. Patriarchal residence lost its importance when in 1721 Peter abolished the patriarchate and established a Holy Synod of bishops, presided over by a civilian procurator-general appointed by the tsar. The former patriarchal choir became the synodal choir of the Russian church. The most significant musical events in Moscow after Peter's death and before the mid-eighteenth century were the elaborate musical festivities for the coronation of the Empress Anna in 1731. For this occasion, the opera company of the Polish king and Elector of Saxony, Augustus II, arrived in Moscow, with 13 actors and nine singers under the leadership of the aged Tommaso Ristori and his son, the composer Giovanni Alberto Ristori (1692–1753), whose opera *Calandro* was given – the first full-scale Italian opera performance in Russia. Ristori's company was followed by another, recruited by Johann Huebner. For the Empress Elizabeth's coronation in 1742, Hasse's *La clemenza di Tito* was staged (with some modifications) in a theatre specially built for the occasion and was followed by lavish fireworks. To facilitate the staging, the new empress lent singers from her imperial chapel, and the Italian words were transliterated into the Russian alphabet for easier reading by the choir, which numbered 50.

A significant role in Moscow's future was to be played by the university, which was founded in 1755 by Lomonosov, a gigantic figure among Russian intellectuals in a period so rich with interesting personalities. By that time, many noblemen and their families had established residences in the new capital of St Petersburg, besides maintaining homes in Moscow; it is possible to infer that the private musical bands of some households followed wherever the 'master' of the house went, keeping the musicians well occupied in providing entertainment, whether in Moscow or in St Petersburg.

ST PETERSBURG

After having visited the Netherlands, England and a few large European cities during 1697–8, Peter decided to build a new city on the shores of the Gulf of Finland, at the very place where the River Neva (flowing from Lake Ladoga) joined the waters of the Baltic Sea. This was to be his 'window on Europe', through which the Russian navy and merchant fleet was to have unimpeded access to other countries, instead of having to sail round Scandinavia through icy waters or having to travel over lands enmeshed in territorial disputes. In May 1703 the building began, first with a fortress that would serve as a military outpost in the perennial wars with Sweden; then numerous other buildings started to sprout along both shores of the river, which also had a number of canals that were eventually to prompt the name 'Venice of the North,' much to Peter's pride and joy. The commander of this enterprise was one of Peter's closest friends, Alexander Danilovich Menshikov (1673–1729), whose vanity, cupidity and love of luxury were proverbial, in contrast with the much more modest way of life that Peter seems to have preferred for himself.

The construction process was relatively slow at first, though up to

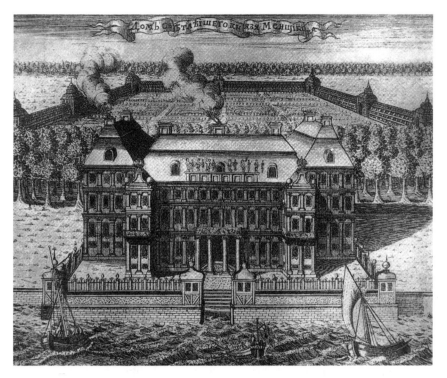

64. Prince Menshikov's palace on the Vasilevsky Island in St Petersburg, the centre of social entertainment during the reign of Peter the Great: engraving (c1714) by A. Zubov; from 'Russkaya arkhitektura pervoy polovini XVIII veka' ('Russian Architecture of the First Half of the 18th Century'), ed. I. Grabar (1954)

100 000 people were summoned to start erecting houses on the marshy soil, and the human losses were staggering. Most of the first buildings were raised on piles, and periodic floods damaged the early structures often beyond repair. Nevertheless, within about five or six years stone buildings were started, and Menshikov was to begin his own palace, which for decades remained one of the most opulent structures and served as a centre for numerous social activities (while Peter resided in a small, modest wooden house). In spite of military action along the Baltic coast, by 1712 Peter had decided to move from Moscow and establish his residence in the city, which he named after his own patron-saint, St Peter; in observance of his admiration for things German, it came to be known as St Petersburg (rather than Petrograd, as it was to be known much later), while the common people called it simply 'Piter'.

Once the decision to move from Moscow into the rapidly growing city was made, regardless of preferences and in the face of objections, the whole imperial family had to follow, as did courtiers and foreign representatives. Merchants and tradesmen, craftsmen, professionals and the state bureaucracy also followed. The growth of the city was nothing short of stupendous, so that by the middle of the eighteenth century its population numbered 74 000; with the surrounding suburbs and nearby settlements the total was close to 140 000 (Moscow had a population of *c*146 000 by 1750).

Peter had no interest in art music, though he seems to have appreciated singing. According to Staehlin, Count Yaguzhinsky recalls how towards the end of his life Peter came to like the sound of the Polish bagpipe ('Bock-Pfeiffe'), and that he even learnt how to play it, producing a 'very loud and harsh sound'. 'He was so attached to this kind of music that he held the Italian in little estimation, nay, banished it from his court, as well as the French, for which he had real aversion.'[4] Yet despite his preference for military music and a somewhat sentimental attachment to church services and chant, (which he appears to have known well), he was fully willing to see theatrical performances staged at the relatively small theatre created in Moscow in 1707 by his sister Nataliya Alexeyevna out of the paraphernalia of the then defunct Kunst-Fuerst theatre. She seems to have had literary ambitions and is now credited with a few plays, which were staged in her theatre, first in Moscow and from about 1708–9 in St Petersburg (she was undoubtedly influenced by the performances of Kunst's company that she saw in Red Square, and her ambitions, it is said, were such that she even directed the performances).

According to the Hanover emissary C. F. Weber, Nataliya established her theatre in St Petersburg in an empty building, which was reconstructed with boxes and a 'parterre'; access was relatively inexpensive – five kopeks per person (some say it was free of charge). Ten actors and actresses, all Russians who had never been abroad, were in her employ. Some plays were serious, others featured a Harlequin. The theatre was served by an orchestra of 16 musicians, all Russians, who (according to reports by foreigners) 'played without any artistry'. After Nataliya's death in June 1716 all the scripts and books used in her theatre were sent for storage to the St Petersburg Printing Press building. At the time of her death Peter was on his second extended trip to western Europe; when he returned in October 1717, Nataliya's official funeral took place with great pomp, with a burial at the richly endowed Lavra of Alexander Nevsky (founded in 1710), located at the far end of the Nevsky Prospekt, some three miles from its starting-point by the Admiralty building on the Neva.

Up to the time of Peter's death in January 1725, there are almost no records of musical activities in the city. Among the entertainments he enjoyed was a show by a 'strong-man', who came with his tightrope walkers. At the same time there are references to dances taking place in Menshikov's palace: Peter's young niece Anna Ioannovna (later Empress Anna) had a French tutor who taught her not only the language but also dances, from which the presence of musicians may be inferred.

Almost all the musicians and musical performers during the first half of the eighteenth century in St Petersburg were foreigners who entered Russian service either directly (having been hired by Russian emissaries) or after accompanying some foreign dignitary on a trip to Russia and then deciding to stay. This does not, however, apply to the choral singers at Russian Orthodox church services, who were trained in the churches and monasteries. That many of the church singers were well trained, unlike the amateurs at some of the theatres, is particularly clear from a letter written about 1732 by the Empress Anna to a church dignitary:

> I am about to stage a comedy in which there ought to be three men who know how to sing, but I don't have any good singers at present and hope that among your boys a few good ones may be selected. So, for this occasion order that a few singers with good voices be sent here so that they could, in the prescribed time, learn what they have to sing. And after the performance of the comedy I shall send them back.[5]

The training of singers, as well as the copying of church music manuscripts, may be observed in some miniature paintings and carvings of the period.

Peter's rather coarse sense of humour led him to favour parody and outright ridicule on the stage, sometimes involving dwarfs and giants. One such example was the mock-wedding in 1715 of a 'Prince-Pope' Nikita Zotov, for which it appears that Peter himself prepared a list of participants, prescribing costumes and the kinds of instrument that each was to 'play'. Some records indicate that up to 400 people took part in this 'entertainment'; a list of at least 170 names, apparently in Peter's handwriting, still exists. The 'bridegroom' was to be dressed like a cardinal, while five distinguished members of Peter's court – Menshikov, Admiral Apraksin, and the generals Bruce, Weyde and Vitztum – were to be dressed as 'Burgmeisters of Hamburg' and play on the 'ryle' (a corruption of the term 'lyre', used to describe a small, three-string instrument); Chinese clothing was to be worn by Count Golikov, by the two counts Dolgoruky (Jakob and Grigory) and by the two counts Golitsïn (Peter and Dmitry), all of whom were to play on 'dudochki' (small pipes like bagpipes); dressed as Turks were Tolstoy and Bestuzhov, playing brass cymbals. Even foreign emissaries were included:

dressed in German shepherd's clothing were the imperial ambassador Bleyer, Weber (the minister from Hanover), Achenbach and the Resident from Holland, all of whom had to play flutes; some eight older persons were excused from playing musical instruments – 'these will not play since because of their age they cannot hold anything in their hands'. It is curious to note that a number of people were to wear 'American' clothing while beating on wooden boards and other devices. Physicians, secretaries, shipbuilders and naval officers were included in the list. Peter himself was dressed as a sailor; he ordered a priest who was more than 90 years old to officiate at the mock-wedding, after which a banquet followed.[6]

Into the social life of St Petersburg Peter introduced 'assemblies', which can probably be described as parties for the populace at large, where people gathered, mingled and were entertained in all conceivable manners. Some of these gatherings during the winter season involved sledding on specially constructed predecessors of a somewhat simple roller-coaster; others, in warm weather, corresponded to the Mediterranean custom of walking along the 'corso', to see who else was there and to be seen at the *gul'yaniya* (public merry-making). That some musical entertainment was included can be taken for granted. At some of the dancing-parties, Russian dances as well as the 'minovet' (minuet) were enjoyed.

If musical events in Russia in the second half of the seventeenth century had been relatively few and somewhat restricted in public access, and if at the same time the number of foreign artisans and professional people in Moscow had already reached tens of thousands before the reign of Peter the Great, with the founding of St Petersburg the floodgates were opened, and the first half of the eighteenth century witnessed a steadily increasing influx of foreign musicians into Russia. Most were attracted by princely honoraria and the growing riches not only of the Russian imperial court but also of the 'nouveau-riche' aristocracy which started emulating Western manners from the seventeenth century onwards and was to reach a high degree of sophistication in the second half of the eighteenth century, during the reign of Catherine the Great. The presence of foreigners with their skills (whether artistic or scientific) was a strong impetus for the Russians themselves to begin mastering the arts and sciences, and the rapid growth of creativity in all branches of learning borders on the astounding. Much as this progress may be interpreted as a manifestation of the desire to 'catch up' with western European levels of achievements, one does observe a steady increase in the development of native talent, as well as in creative output, which, by any standard, was soon able to compete with contemporary creativity in the West.

While opera performances in Russia in the seventeenth century had been few and primitive, with the reign of Empress Anna (1730–40) an uninterrupted sequence of operatic events at the imperial court began, with, at times, the simultaneous appearance of foreign companies, of individual virtuoso performers and of Italian, German and French composers. Even before the landmark date of 1735, when Francesco Araia (1709–70) arrived in St Petersburg, there were substantial numbers of foreign musicians in imperial service, and a number of noblemen followed suit by engaging some of them to instruct their Russian serfs in the art of playing musical instruments. Mooser, in his work of capital significance for the study of music in Russia in the eighteenth century, makes it clear that in the period between about 1731 and 1734 no fewer than 40-odd librettos of comedies (some of them intermezzos used by well-known composers in the West) were published in Russian translation for the benefit of the theatre-going public.[7]

Opera performances had intrigued seventeenth-century Russian travellers, who left fascinating accounts of their impressions of such experiences. By the same token, Western and other travellers to Russia recorded their reactions to the life and customs of Moscow and St Petersburg, affording interesting comparisons with their own musical traditions. It is thus curious to note that a late seventeenth-century Russian traveller who described opera in Venice recorded that female singers appeared on stage while at the same time they were excluded from participating in amusements in Moscow. Probably the earliest known record of female participation on the stage in Russia dates from about 1705, the time of Kunst's theatre in Red Square in Moscow, when the 'wife of a general physician' Hermine Pogenkampf and her sister Johanna von Willing, though not professionals, sang their roles on stage. From the 1730s onwards the presence of female singers is taken as a matter of course. Most were foreigners. A significant date in this respect was 1731, when the Polish King Augustus II's opera company, performing in Moscow, included among its singers Ludovica Seyfried (who had sung in Vienna in 1725 in Fux's *Costanza e Fortezza*), Margherita Ermini and Rosalia Fantasia. This 'loan' of musicians by the Polish king is an important indicator for the spread of the new taste for opera that was to serve as a spur for its flowering in Russia.

During the seventeenth century in Russia, the standard musical instruments in use were those associated with indigenous folk music. When Western musicians were first imported, their tools were listed in detail, giving an interesting picture of the types of musical instrument being brought into new surroundings. The picture of Russian musicians painted by the Englishman Samuel Collins, the personal physician of Tsar Alexey Mikhailovich in the 1660s, offers the following insight:

Russians use *volynki* [bagpipes] and small string instruments somewhat similar to the lute. Their military music consists of drums (their dull sounds correspond very much to the dark Russian character) and of trumpets, which probably only recently came to be used since the Russians play them worse then our swineherds do their horns. For hunting they use brass horns which emit very loud and unpleasant sounds. In a word, if you wish to entertain a Russian with music, take a couple of Billingsgate nightingales, a few owls, a few starlings, a couple of hungry wolves, seven swine, as many cats with their wives, and have them all sing; such a concert will make a Russian more enthusiastic than all Italian music, all light French airs, English marches or Scottish jigs.[8]

Only a few years later when Colonel von Staden fulfilled the tsar's order to hire musicians, he reported in a letter from Mittau (26 August 1672) that he had hired a few of the Duke of Courland's court musicians, listing them by name as Friederich Platenschläger, Iacob Philips, Gottfried Berge and Christopher Ackhermann, each of whom played several instruments – 'Orgeln, Trompeten, Trompeten-Marinen, Cinchen, Dulcian und Posaunen, Violen und Viol de Gambe'. This includes at least some of the instruments that must have been played at the *Comedy of Artaxerxes* performance given in October 1672 in the tsar's theatre at Preobrazhenskoye, alongside a few local musicians under Gutovsky. At Peter's staging in 1715 of the 'mock-wedding' discussed above, more than 30 varieties of instrument, indigenous and imported, are mentioned, including a 'Post-horn' and hunting horns, flutes and oboes, trumpets and organs, violins and balalaikas, recorders and a variety of percussion instruments. But when the Polish opera company arrived in 1731 it had an orchestra with western European instruments, and these were, of course, present in growing numbers at the imperial theatre in St Petersburg.

As far as written music is concerned, Samuel Collins (referring to the 1660s) made an interesting remark:

They have music schools where they educate children thoroughly and strictly. Their notation is very strange and borrowed probably from the Greeks or Slavs. In scales there is little differentiation: instead of fa, sol, la, they sing ga, ga, ge, and to hear the voice one may think their throats are closed or that they are being strangled.[9]

With the introduction of Western staff notation into polychoral music in the mid-seventeenth century and the presence of Western musical instruments, some knowledge of the Western principles of notation must have existed; thus some scores must have been written out to enable the dramatic works staged in the 1670s and later to have had instrumental accompaniment.

65. *'Palata uchitel'-naya' (school): painted woodcarving on the inner surface of a box lid, late 17th or early 18th century; from 'Russkoye iskusstvo pervoy chetverti XVII veka' ('Russian Art from the First Quarter of the 18th Century') (1974)*

When a printing press was established in St Petersburg as a counterpart to Moscow's patriarchal press, its life was short, from 1711 to 1727, and religious books were still printed only in Moscow. Yet it was at Peter's behest that an academy of sciences, with its own press, was established in St Petersburg. Between 1735 and 1738 the Italian musician Giovanni Verocai, a member of the Russian court orchestra, had his 12 sonatas for violin and continuo published in Russia; at that time the academy did not yet have facilities for music printing (which were obtained only later, from Germany), and this edition was not engraved but etched on plates. According to Mooser, it is an incunabulum of Russian music printing, and was followed by works of Luigi Madonis (*c*1690–*c*1770) and Domenico Dall'Oglio (*c*1700–1764). In 1739 the mathematician Leonhard Euler had his *Tentamen novae theoriae musicae* published by the academy in St Petersburg, which was thus the first music theory treatise to be published in Russia – one that, curiously enough, appears to have opposed the idea of equal temperament in tuning.[10]

The number of foreign companies of musicians that continued to arrive in Russia from the 1730s onwards increased at a rapid pace. Besides Ristori's musicians, all of whom were in the service of the Polish King Augustus II, in the same year, 1731, Johann Huebner engaged a group of singers from Hamburg who performed for some time in Moscow, with six singers and nine instrumentalists (see above). They were followed in 1733 by an Italian company, of which Luigi Madonis was a member; they performed intermezzos and comedies in St Petersburg in the 'newly erected' theatre, since the old wooden structure built under Peter the Great in 1723 had fallen into disrepair. One member of that company, Pietro Mira, was sent to Italy in 1735 to recruit more musicians, and it was he who brought Francesco Araia to St Petersburg in a company that also included six musicians, eight singers, 11 'comedians', five dancers and four 'technicians' (decorators and a machinist).

Records are scant concerning the availability in St Petersburg of foreign music publications, although Matveyev, who headed the foreign office in the 1670s, is known to have had books on music in his library (which contained more than 80 books in foreign languages). Peter's son, the unlucky Alexis (1692–1718), had a good library of his own that included Freylingshausen's *Geistreiches Gesangbuch*, published in Halle in 1704; he also owned no fewer than 44 church music manuscripts, which comprised half of all his books, and 25 of his books were in foreign languages (the collection of printed books from his library is now said to be in the University Library in Helsinki).[11]

The year 1735, when Araia arrived in St Petersburg from Italy, has already been noted as a landmark. There were at least two other significant events that took place in the same year. One was the founding of a Russian council to encourage the use of ordinary Russian speech in literature instead of the stilted language used in ecclesiastical literature. The instigator for the founding of this council, as well as its first secretary, was Vasily Kirilovich Tredyakovsky (1703–68), a poet, who in his youth studied for two years (1723–5) at the Slavonic-Greek-Latin Academy in Moscow (founded in 1685), then spent a year in the Netherlands, three more years at the Sorbonne in Paris and several months in Hamburg, before returning to Russia just as Anna became ruler. Tredyakovsky was to be the official translator of plays and operas into German and Russian throughout Anna's reign.

The second notable event of 1735 was the arrival in June of Jakob von Staehlin in St Petersburg. His writings on music in Russia in the eighteenth century, of which he was a first-hand witness, are often referred to, but information about his life and attainments is scant in standard western European reference books. He was born in Memmingen, Swabia, on 10 May 1709 and went to school in Zittau, where he not only learnt foreign languages, dancing and music but excelled in making fireworks (a skill he learnt from an Italian named Montallegro). For three years, 1732–5, Staehlin was a student of literature and the arts in Leipzig, where (according to a letter of his addressed to his son in 1784) he sang under J. S. Bach and became a close friend of C. P. E. Bach. He also developed his skills as an engraver of posters with lengthy texts and descriptions of the picture represented in the engraving. For the accession in 1734 of Augustus III to the Polish throne he apparently made a special engraving and, as is customary with engravers, signed his name on it. The presiding officer of the Academy of Sciences in St Petersburg, Korf, noted Staehlin's name on several engravings of allegories and invited him to Russia to teach rhetoric and poetry in the 'history-classes' of the academy, with a salary of 400 rubles. On 13 April[12] 1735 Staehlin left Leipzig for Berlin and Lübeck, where he boarded a ship to St Petersburg, arriving on 25 June for a stay of 50 years in Russia.[13]

Araia arrived 'in the summer' of the same year for what was going to be (with some interruptions) a quarter-century stay in St Petersburg, and the two men doubtless met and communicated. Staehlin's extensive memoir about music in Russia was written close to 30 years after his arrival, as a retrospective recollection of events he had witnessed;[14] it is only one of a number of his writings that deal with Russian art and ballet, as well as music. One of Staehlin's duties was to supervise all the engravers, and he had many others. The first thing he wrote in Russia was a much delayed review of the first performance of Araia's opera *La forza dell'amore e dell'odio*, which was staged on 29 January 1736. The review appeared in the *Sanktpeterburgskiye vedomosti* ('St Petersburg Gazette') in 1738, in three instalments, entitled 'Historical Description of that Theatrical Performance that is called Opera'.

Araia's opera inaugurated the theatre auditorium in what is de-scribed as 'Third Winter Palace' (the present one is the fifth), erected in 1735 and from 1736 the centre of imperial court opera perform-ances for decades to come. This theatre was seen by Francesco Algarotti in 1739 when out of curiosity he made a brief visit to St Petersburg, sailing on a British ship. He apparently did not comment on music in Russia. It is curious, however, that in his description of the approaches to St Petersburg he noted that 'sailing several hours through these frightful and silent woods' he had the first glimpse of the city: 'all of a sudden the river bends, the scene changes instantly as in an opera, and we behold the Imperial City', which on closer inspection left on him an impression of 'bastard architecture', with its mix of French- and Dutch-style buildings interspersed with wood-en huts and houses of various sizes. As for the theatre, Algarotti noted that it was 'twice as large as the Paris opera'. His impressions from this trip are presented in a series of letters to Lord Hervey.[15]

Staehlin and musicians from the opera orchestra were actively involved in the staging of Hasse's *La clemenza di Tito* for the celebration of the Empress Elizabeth's coronation in Moscow in 1742. Although they seem to have acquired a copy of Hasse's score, much of the music for the Moscow performance was written by Luigi Madonis and Domenico Dall'Oglio (both violinists and composers in the orchestra under Araia), although Hasse's music was retained for the main arias. A year later, in August 1743, Staehlin wrote about his participation in these events and indicated that he was the author of the Prologue to the opera (written and performed in Italian), that he designed the stage decorations, corrected the librettos in Italian and French, taught the young boys how to move on the stage, at rehearsals played the lute as well as the flute, and planned and oversaw the execution of fireworks, which were described as superior to any ever seen in Moscow.

At the time of the Empress Anna's death and the Empress Elizabeth's accession to the Russian throne, the opportunities for musicians in Russia were no longer unknown to professionals in western Europe, as a number of players and singers had already had a chance to visit and perform there. Quite a few returned to their native lands, bringing memories and stories of their experiences among the Russians. Others stayed, and attracted many more to join them. This richly increasing number of musicians in Russia is one of the aspects of Anna's legacy to her successors, who were to expand and greatly add to that heritage.

NOTES

[1] This composer is something of a mystery: attempts to identify him with Giovanni Bonaventura Viviani (1638–after 1692) hinge on reconciling references linking the latter with Pistoia until *c*1690 or later.

[2] J. M. Badalić and V. D. Kuzmina, *Pamyatniki russkoy shkolnoy dramy XVIII veka* [The Monuments of Eighteenth-Century Russian School Drama] (Moscow, 1968), 6–8. See also the interesting reports of Jesuits in Moscow, including a mention of music and concerts, in *Pisma i doneseniya Iezuitov o Rossii kontsa XVII i nachala XVIII veka* [Jesuit Letters and Documents concerning Russia from the End of the Seventeenth and the Beginning of the Eighteenth Centuries] (St Petersburg, 1904), 9, 218; it is clear from the letter (23 Sept 1698) addressed in Latin to superiors in Bohemia (p.218) that the Moscow missionaries were proud of being able to use foreign musicians from diplomatic missions while at the same time educating young children to play, so that in the absence of professionals there would still be some music at services.

[3] Dmitry Mitropolit Rostovskii, *Rozhdestvenskaya drama, ili Rostovskoye deystvo* [A Christmas Drama, or The Rostov Mystery-Play], ed. Ye. Levashov (Moscow, 1989). This allegorical play has 43 individual roles, a large mixed choir and a large children's choir; it opens with the words of Human Nature, and there are seven pairs of 'contrasts' (Love and Envy, Golden Age and Iron Age, Joy and Weeping etc.), each assigned to a solo voice.

[4] J. Staehlin von Storcksburg, *Originalanekdoten von Peter der Grossen* (Leipzig, 1785); Eng. trans. (London, 1788), 318–22.

[5] T. Livanova, *Ocherki i materialï po istorii russkoy muzïkal'noy kul'turï* [Essays and Documents on the History of Russian Musical Culture], i (Moscow, 1938), 336ff, quoting from Pekarski's history of the Academy of Sciences in St Petersburg (1873).

[6] ibid, 329–34, cited from Golikov's 1792 publication of supplements to the activities of Peter the Great.

[7] R.-A. Mooser, *Annales de la musique et des musiciens en Russie au XVIIIe siècle*, i (Geneva, 1948), 385–7, lists 41 Russian librettos, one Italian and one German of comedies and intermezzos performed in St Petersburg, 1733–5. T. P. Samsonova, 'Sobraniye opernïkh libretto XVIII veka v Biblioteke akademii nauk SSSR' [The Collection of Opera Librettos of the Eighteenth Century in the Library of the Academy of Sciences of the USSR], *Kniga i biblioteki v Rossii v XIV – pervoy polovine XIX veka* [The Book and Libraries in Russia from the Fourteenth Century to the First Half of the Nineteenth] (Leningrad, 1982), 68–81, notes that each libretto was printed in 100 copies! Only nine of the Russian librettos were intermezzos with music; the others were comedies without music.

[8] The original English text is inaccessible. The Russian text appears in Livanova, *Ocherki i materialï*, 321, as a citation from the Russian translation published in 1816; the English given here is a re-translation.

[9] ibid.

[10] S. S. Tserlyuk-Askadskaya, 'Leonard Eiler kak teoretik muzïki' [Leonhard Euler as a Theoretician of Music], *XVIII vek* [Eighteenth Century], xvi (1989), 219–33, besides including a bibliography on Euler more comprehensive than those in *MGG* or *Grove 6*, claims that in *RU-Span* there are two additional unpublished music treatises by Euler, *Tractatus de musica* and *Theoriae musicae capita septem*; the author of the article surmises that the latter may be an earlier draft of that published in 1739.

[11] See I. N. Lebedeva, 'Biblioteka Tsarevicha Alekseya Petrovicha' [Prince Alexey Petrovich's Library], *Kniga i knigotorgovliya v Rossii v XVI-XVIII vv.* [Books and Book-trade in Russia from the Sixteenth to the Eighteenth Centuries] (Leningrad, 1984), 56–64.

[12] Dates here (and below) are given in Old Style, i.e. according to the Russian calendar; to convert Old-Style dates in the eighteenth century to New Style, i.e. according to the Western (Gregorian) calendar, 11 days must be added (e.g. 13 April O.S. = 24 April N.S.).

[13] Information about Staehlin's contacts with Bach and the date of his departure from Leipzig to St Petersburg is gleaned from K. V. Malinovsky, 'Yakob fon Shtelin i yego zapiski po istorii russkoy zhivopisy XVIII veka' [Jacob von Staehlin and his Notes on the History of Russian Painting of the Eighteenth Century], *Russkoye iskusstvo barokko* [Russian Art of the Baroque] (Moscow, 1977), 173–9.

[14] See n.4 above.

[15] Algarotti's letters are quoted from J. Cracraft, *The Petrine Revolution in Russian Architecture* (Chicago and London, 1988), 229; and from M. Curtiss, *A Forgotten Empress: Anna Ivanovna and her Era, 1730–1740* (New York, 1974), 212.

BIBLIOGRAPHICAL NOTE

Almost all surveys of the history of music in Poland and in Russia pay lip-service to musical developments before the nineteenth century; in addition, studies in western European languages often lack information on the musical life of these countries before 1800. A glance at the sizable bibliographies accompanying articles on any one of these countries or their capital cities in *MGG* or *Grove 6*, reveals that the bulk of studies on developments before 1800 is written in the languages of these countries. Those bibliographies nevertheless represent good starting-points for deeper study.

Poland

For basic information on the historical, political and cultural background of Poland there is *The Cambridge History of Poland*, ed. W. F. Reddaway and others (Cambridge, 1950–51). Supplementary information about literature, theatres, cities, architecture etc. is easily located in encyclopedias. Warsaw Castle, the focal point of many musical events in the seventeenth century, is described in an excellent booklet by J. Lileyko, trans. D. Evans, *A Companion Guide to the Royal Castle in Warsaw* (Warsaw, 1980).

Polish composers of the Baroque are surveyed in A. Sowiński's *Les musiciens polonais et slaves* (Paris, 1857), which must be supplemented with more recent bio-bibliographical data. A very useful introduction in English to the subject is *An Outline History of Polish Music*, prepared by a group of scholars and edited by G. Michalski (Warsaw, 1979, rev. 2/1984); another useful booklet is L. Erhardt, *Musik in Poland* (Warsaw, 1975). Most Polish musicologists have presented reports and papers at international conferences on various aspects of the history of Polish music, but all the best monographs are in Polish. Much Polish music of the Baroque period is available in modern edition, and a few works have also been recorded, notably works by Jarzębski, Mielczewski and Pękiel.

The so-called Saxon period in Poland is deeply interwoven with the musical life of Dresden, for which one of the basic guides is still M. Fürstenau's *Zur Geschichte der Musik und des Theaters am Hofe zu Dresden* (Dresden, 1861–2; repr. 1971). For musical life in Warsaw, J. Prosnak's *Kultura muzyczna Warszawy XVIII wieku* [Warsaw's Musical Culture in the Eighteenth Century] (Kraków, 1955) is a rich mine of data for the period. Information about musicians' guilds is to be found in Z. Chaniecki's *Organizacje zawodowe muzyków na ziemiach polskich do konca XVIII wieku* [Organizations of Musicians' Guilds in Polish Lands up to the End of the Eighteenth Century] (Kraków, 1980). For details of the personnel of the royal chapel and of the numerous musical establishments in the homes of the nobility, consult the article 'Kapelé' in *Słownik muzyków polskich* [A Dictionary of Polish Musicians] (Warsaw, 1964), i, 216–67, which lists chronologically, by locality and by orchestra, all musicians by name and by the dates of their residences; the list includes no fewer than 85 noblemen's orchestras, as well as some church orchestras, and is immensely helpful in tracing the employment of a large number of musicians from the sixteenth to the eighteenth centuries. Articles on individual Polish composers and cities are to be found in *Grove 6* and *Grove O*.

Russia

On Russia and its two capital cities there is a profusion of books in Russian, on both a popular and a scholarly level. Almost every area of interest, however specialist, is covered, and the wealth of archival documentation is overwhelming. For information in English on the historical, political and cultural background of the period, *The Cambridge Encyclopedia of Russia and the Soviet Union* (London, 1982) and P. Dukes, ed., *Russia and Europe* (London, 1991) contain a number of relevant articles.

The reign of Peter the Great (1689–1725), which represents the beginning of the 'modern era' in Russia, serves as a convenient reference point. Most events of artistic interest before this time are in the literature likely to be unjustly deemed 'unworthy' of musicological interest or investigation; and most books on the history of music in Russia condense a tremendous number of events into a few sentences, claiming that the 'real' history of Russian music begins in the nineteenth century with Glinka. But the first two volumes of R.-A. Mooser's *Annales de la musique et des musiciens en Russie au XVIIIe siècle* (Geneva, 1948–51), published more than 40 years ago, richly document the period covered by this chapter, dealing primarily with foreign musicians in Russia (with some information on Russians); as an introduction to the musical events of eighteenth-century Russia in a Western language it is unsurpassed, though some of its details require revision in the light of more recent research. The seventeenth century is served less well. Isolated aspects are dealt with by O. Dolskaya-Ackerly's thorough doctoral dissertation on *kantï* and E. V. Williams's magnificent study of bells and bell-making, *The Russian Bells* (Princeton, 1985), which covers a broader period of Russian history than the present chapter.

Among wider and more general surveys, N. Findeyzen's *Ocherki po istorii muzïki v Rossii s drevneyshikh vremyon do kontsa XVIII veka* [Essays on the History of Music in Russia from the Earliest Times to the End of the Eighteenth Century] (Moscow and Leningrad, 1928–9) is probably the finest history of Russian music before Glinka (though, like Mooser's work, it is in need of some correction; an English translation, with additions and corrections, is in preparation). The evolution of Russian church music has been well covered by J. von Gardner in his contribution to *MGG* ('Russland'), which has not yet been superseded in any Western language; Russian studies of the subject, while enriching the documentation, have so far failed to produce a satisfying overview of the complex developments. Opera after 1672 has received more attention from theatre historians than musicologists, because of the dearth of musical sources and documentation. Descriptive material abounds, however, and S. K. Bogoyavlensky's coverage of documents for the period 1672–1708, 'Moskovskiy teatr pri Tsaryakh Alexiye i Petriye' [The Moscow Theatre under Tsars Alexey and Peter], *Chteniya v Imperatorskom obshchestve istorii i drevnostey rossiiskkh*, ii (1914), has not been superseded (recent studies of Gregori and his contemporaries focus on literary aspects).

Musicological studies in the Soviet Union have flourished in the last three decades and have produced a veritable explosion of publications in Russian. The music extracts in S. L. Ginzburg's *Istoriya russkoy muzïki notnikh obraztsakh* [A History of Russian Music in Examples] (Moscow, 2/1968–70) provide a useful starting-point for further study of the music, while the series of music editions *Pamyatniki russkogo muzïkal'nogo iskusstva* [Monuments of Russian Musical Art], ed. Yu. Keldïsh (Moscow, 1972–), of which ten volumes have so far appeared, has made available music in editions that essentially emulate the scholarly German *Denkmäler* series: besides a volume of *kantï*, the series includes Diletsky's treatise (ed. with extensive commentary by V. Protopopov, 1979) and several scores from the second half of the eighteenth century.

Among recent surveys of the history of music in Russia, that by Yu. V. Keldïsh, the doyen of Soviet musicologists, *Russkaya muzïka XVIII veka* [Russian Music in the Eighteenth Century] (Moscow, 1965), is an excellent volume, which serves in many ways as a supplement to Mooser's work; T. N. Livanova's *Russkaya muzïkal'naya kul'tura XVIII veka* [Russian Musical Culture in the Eighteenth Century] (Moscow, 1952–3) looks at music in relation to the literature, theatre and social life of the period; A. A. Gozenpud's *Muzïkal'nïy teatr v Rossii ot istokov do Glinki* [Musical Theatre in Russia from its Origins up to Glinka] (Leningrad, 1959) deals with the more specific history of theatre music; and L. I. Royzman's *Organ v istorii russkoy muzïkal'noy kul'tury* [Organs in the History of Russian Musical Culture] (Moscow, 1979) contains a wealth of material on individual musicians, organs and other instruments. Since 1983 a group of scholars associated with the Institute for Art History in Moscow have begun what is to be a ten-volume survey of Russian music, *Istoriya russkoy muzïki v desyati tomakh* [A History of Russian Music in Ten Volumes] (Moscow, 1983–); the first two volumes, edited by Yu. V. Keldïsh, cover the period of the present chapter. Readers without a knowledge of Russian may consult G. Seaman, *History of Russian Music*, i: *From its Origins to Dargomyzhsky* (Oxford, 1967), which includes material on cultural, social and political life, many music examples and an extensive bibliography. There are also articles in *Grove 6* and *Grove O* on individual Russian composers and cities.

Chronology

The Late Baroque Era

MUSIC AND MUSICIANS	POLITICS, WAR, RULERS
1671 *Scipione affricano* (1664) by Francesco Cavalli (1602–76) inaugurates the Teatro Tordinona, Rome. *Tragédie-ballet, Psyché*, by Jean-Baptiste Lully (1632–87) and Molière (1622–73) (with Philippe Quinault and Pierre Corneille), given in Paris. *Pomone*, by Robert Cambert (*c*1627–1677), given in Paris.	**1671** Emperor Leopold I promises neutrality if France attacks Holland as long as Louis XIV does not invade Spain or the Empire.
1672 Heinrich Schütz (87) dies, Dresden. Jacques Champion de Chambonnières (*c*70) dies, Paris. Lully acquires ownership of the Académie Royale de Musique. John Banister (*c*1625–1679) presents first known concerts where admission is charged, in London. *Los celos hacen estrellas* (earliest surviving zarzuela with music), by Juan Hidalgo (*c*1614–1685), given in Madrid.	**1672** William of Orange (later William III of England) elected Stadholder of Holland. Third Anglo-Dutch War, (–1674): English defeated at Texel in 1673 and withdraw with gains in 1674.
1673 Marc-Antoine Charpentier (1643–1704) and Molière collaborate on *Le malade imaginaire*, Lully and Quinault on the first *tragédie en musique, Cadmus et Hermione*, both given in Paris.	**1673** Emperor Leopold I declares war on France after allying with the Dutch.
1674 Giacomo Carissimi (68) dies, Rome. Pelham Humfrey (*c*27) dies, Windsor. Lully's *Alceste* performed in Paris. A new Theatre Royal, Drury Lane, opens in London.	**1674** John Sobieski elected King of Poland after defeating the Turks at Korzim in 1673. Triple Alliance of Austria, Holland and Spain, later joined by the papacy and Brandenburg, against the French.
1675 Matthew Locke (*c*1621–1677) and G. B. Draghi (*c*1640–1708) compose music for Shadwell's English version of Lully's *Psyché* (1671).	**1675** Turenne's death and Condé's retirement bring an end to French military victories and expansion.
1676 Cavalli (73) dies, Venice. Lully's *Atys* given, Saint-Germain-en-Laye. Thomas Mace (*c*1612–*c*1706) publishes *Musick's Monument* in London.	**1676** Denmark declares war on Sweden but defeated by Charles XI at Lunden.
1677 Cambert (*c*50) dies, London. Locke (*c*55) dies, London. Pope Innocent XI bans theatre and opera in Rome. Lully's *Isis* stirs controversy at première at Saint-Germain-en-Laye.	**1677** William of Orange marries Princess Mary, elder daughter of James, Duke of York, brother and heir of Charles II of England, a declared Roman Catholic.
1678 Giovanni Maria Bononcini (*c*36) dies, Modena. Teatro S Giovanni Grisostomo opens in Venice. Opera house in the Gänsemarkt, Hamburg, opens. Thomas Britton institutes weekly musical meetings, open to the public, in London. Carolus Hacquart (*c*1640–?1701) and Dirck Buysero collaborate on *De triomfeerende min* (earliest Dutch opera) in Amsterdam.	**1678** Peace of Nijmegen ends the Franco-Dutch war (begun 1672). France returns all Dutch conquests and repeals Colbert's anti-Dutch tariff of 1667. France makes peace with Spain. Popish Plot (–1679), an alleged conspiracy, leads to the passing of the Test Act in England, the exile of James, Duke of York, and the Exclusion Crisis (an attempt to exclude James's succession).

LITERATURE, PHILOSOPHY, RELIGION	SCIENCE, TECHNOLOGY, DISCOVERY	FINE AND DECORATIVE ARTS, ARCHITECTURE
1671 William Wycherly (1641–75) writes *Love in a Wood* and *The Gentleman Dancing Master*.	**1671** Gottfried Wilhelm von Leibniz (1646–1716) begins work on his calculating machine.	**1671** Pierre Puget (1620–94) begins the *Milo of Crotona* (–1682) for Versailles.
1672 The Synod of Jerusalem, the most important modern Council of the Eastern Church, repudiates movement towards accommodating Calvinism.	**1672** Otto von Guericke (1602–86) describes his invention of the vacuum pump. Isaac Newton (1642–1726) establishes the existence of distinct coloured rays in white light. Jacques Marquette and Louis Joliet explore north of the River Missouri, near modern Chicago (–1673).	**1672** Willem van der Velde (1611–93) and his son (1653–1707) settle in England and paint maritime scenes.
1674 Nicolas Malebranche (1638–1715) publishes *La recherche de la vérité*, which tends towards pantheism.	**1673** Christiaan Huygens (1629–95) solves the problem of the compound pendulum and states the laws of centrifugal force. Leibniz works towards the discovery of differential and integral calculus (–1675).	**1673** Edward Pierce (*c*1635–95) executes a marble bust of Sir Christopher Wren.
1675 Philipp Spener (1635–1705) publishes *Pia desideria*, aimed at fostering a revival in German Protestantism (later known as the Pietist movement).	**1674** John Mayow (1641–79) describes respiration, and recognizes the existence of oxygen.	**1674** Baciccio (Giovanni Battista Gaulli, 1639–1708) paints the illusionist *Adoration of the Name of Jesus* on the ceiling of Il Gesù, Rome (–1679), and the nave vault, a masterpiece of Baroque illusionist decoration.
1676 Sir George Etherege (*c*1634–1691) writes his comedy *The Man of Mode*.	**1675** Royal Observatory, Greenwich, founded, with John Flamsteed (1646–1719) as Astronomer Royal.	**1675** Pedro Roldan (1624–1700) completes the reredos for La Caridad, Seville. François Girardon (1628–1715) begins the monument to Richelieu in the church of the Sorbonne, Paris. Christopher Wren (1632–1723) builds St Paul's Cathedral (–1709).
1677 Jean Racine (1639–99) writes his last tragedy, *Phèdre*, before abandoning the theatre to become historiographer to Louis XIV.	**1676** Ole Rømer (1644–1710) demonstrates the first proof of the finite velocity of light.	
1678 Ralph Cudworth (1617–88), a 'Cambridge Platonist', publishes *The True Intellectual System of the Universe*, arguing that the only real source of knowledge is Christianity. John Bunyan (1628–88) publishes the first part of *The Pilgrim's Progress*.	**1678** René de La Salle (1643–87) explores the Great Lakes of Canada (–1679).	**1677** Liberal Bruant (*c*1635–1697) completes the Hôtel des Invalides, Paris.

The Late Baroque Era

MUSIC AND MUSICIANS	POLITICS, WAR, RULERS
1679 Johann Heinrich Schmelzer (*c*1620–1680) becomes first Austrian-born Habsburg Kapellmeister of this century. Henry Purcell (1659–95) succeeds John Blow (1649–1708) as organist at Westminster Abbey, London. First opera by Alessandro Scarlatti (1660–1725), *Gli equivoci nel sembiante*, given in Rome.	**1679** Sweden signs peace treaties with Brandenburg and Denmark, regaining most of her lost territories. King Charles II of Spain marries Marie-Louise of Orléans.
1680 Schmelzer (*c*60) dies, Prague. York Buildings (housing a public concert room) erected in London.	**1680** Death of Ferdinand I, Elector of Bavaria; succeeded by his son Maximilian II Emanuel.
1681 Lully appointed *secrétaire du roi*. Christoph Bernhard (1628–92) appointed Dresden Hofkapellmeister. Arcangelo Corelli (1653–1713) publishes op.1 in Rome. Opéra du Quai du Foin (later Théâtre de la Monnaie) opens, Brussels.	
1682 Murder of Alessandro Stradella (37), nr Genoa. Draghi appointed Viennese Hofkapellmeister. 53-part *Missa salisburgensis* performed in Salzburg.	
1683 Lully composes his *De profundis* in Paris. Purcell's *[12] Sonnata's of III Parts* published, London.	**1683** By the League of the Hague, the Emperor Leopold I and King Charles II of Spain join the existing Dutch-Swedish alliance against France. Siege of Vienna (by the Turks) relieved; Turkish armies defeated at Kahlenberg by John III Sobieski of Poland and Charles of Lorraine.
1684 Nicolo Amati (87) dies, Cremona. Alessandro Scarlatti appointed viceregal *maestro di cappella* and music director of the Teatro S Bartolomeo, Naples. Johann Kuhnau (1660–1722) appointed organist at the Thomaskirche, Leipzig. Heinrich Biber (1664–1704) appointed Kapellmeister at Salzburg.	**1684** Treaty of Regensburg ends five years of French legalistic and diplomatic aggression.
1685 Juan Hidalgo (*c*70) dies, Madrid. Corelli's op.2 published, Rome. Lully's *Roland* given, Versailles. John Playford (1623–86) publishes *The Division Violin*, London.	**1685** Death of Charles II of England; succeeded by his brother, the Roman Catholic James II. The Duke of Monmouth, Charles's illegitimate son, leads an unsuccessful rebellion. Revocation of the Edict of Nantes causes widespread emigration of French Huguenots. The Protestant Great Elector of Brandenburg withdraws from his alliance with France.
1686 Playford (63) dies, London. Giovanni Legrenzi (1626–90) appointed *maestro di cappella* at St Mark's, Venice. Lully's *Armide* given and Marin Marais (1656–1728) publishes his first volume of *Pièces de violes*, Paris.	**1686** The League of Augsburg formed between the Habsburg emperor, Spain, Sweden, Saxony, the Palatinate and Brandenburg against Louis XIV.
1687 Lully (54) dies, Paris. Constantijn Huygens (90) dies, The Hague. Elisabeth-Claude Jacquet de La Guerre (*c*1666–1729) publishes first collection of *Pièces de clavecin* and Jean Rousseau (1644–?*c*1700) his *Traité de la viole*, in Paris.	**1687** Battle of Mohacs. Turks defeated by Charles of Lorraine. Diet of Pressburg ratifies the Hungarian crown as hereditary in the male Habsburg line.

LITERATURE, PHILOSOPHY, RELIGION	SCIENCE, TECHNOLOGY, DISCOVERY	FINE AND DECORATIVE ARTS, ARCHITECTURE
1679 Olaus Rudbeckius (1630–1702) claims Sweden as the lost Atlantis in *Atland eller Manhem*.	**1679** Edmond Halley (1656–1742) publishes his catalogue of the stars of the southern hemisphere as observed in St Helena. Denis Papin (1647–1712) demonstrates that the boiling-point of water depends on pressure.	**1679** Antoine Coysevoix (1640–1720) works on a relief of Louis XIV for the Salon de Guerre at Versailles. Charles Lebrun (1619–90) paints scenes from the life of Louis XIV for the Galerie des Glaces, Versailles (–1684).
1680 The Comédie Française founded in Paris. César-Pierre Richelet (1641–98) publishes his *Dictionnaire françois*, compiled on philosophical principles.	**1680** Jean Picard (1620–82) states that the pole-star varies its position.	**1680** Jules Hardouin-Mansart (1646–1708) works on Les Invalides, Paris (–1691).
1681 Jean Mabillon (1632–1707) writes *De re diplomatica*, putting palaeography on a scientific footing. John Dryden (1631–1700) publishes *Absalom and Achitophel* (–1682), an allegory about the Exclusion Crisis.	**1681** Publication of work by Giovanni Borelli (1608–79), explaining muscular movements according to laws of statics and dynamics.	**1681** Rombout Verhulst (1624–98) completes the monument to Admiral de Ruyter in the Nieuwe Kerk, Amsterdam.
1682 Thomas Otway (1652–85) writes the tragedy *Venice Preserv'd* in blank verse. The first German learned periodical, *Acta eruditorum* (–1782), founded.	**1682** Nehemiah Grew (1641–1712) publishes *Anatomy of Plants*, noting that stamens are male organs.	**1682** Artus II Quellin (1625–1700) works on the rood screen of Bruges Cathedral; his son Artus III (1653–86) completes monument to Thomas Thynne in Westminster Abbey, London. Carlo Fontana (1634–1714) designs S Marcello al Corso, Rome.
1684 Giovanni Marana (1642–93) publishes *L'espion dans les cours des princes chrétiens*, the model for Montesquieu's *Lettres persanes*. Pierre Bayle (1647–1706) founds the *Nouvelles de la République des lettres*.	**1684** Newton's *Principia* demonstrates the law of gravity.	**1683** Wren builds St James's, Piccadilly, London.
1686 Bernard le Bovier, Sieur de Fontenelle (1657–1757), writes *Entretiens sur la pluralité des mondes*, which popularized scientific enquiry.	**1686** John Ray (1628–1705) produces *Historia plantarum* (–1704), listing all known plants in Europe.	**1685** Claudio Coello (1642–93), of the Madrid school, paints *Charles II Adoring the Host* (–1690), an outstanding example of Baroque illusionism.
1687 Christian Thomasius (1655–1728), appointed at Leipzig, was the first German academic to lecture in the vernacular.	**1687** Sir Hans Sloane (1660–1753) visits Jamaica (–1688) and collects *c*800 new species of plants, which he later catalogues.	**1687** Sir Godfrey Kneller (1646–1723) paints *The Chinese Convert*.

The Late Baroque Era

MUSIC AND MUSICIANS	POLITICS, WAR, RULERS
1688 Carlo Pallavicino (*c*48) dies, Dresden. Charpentier composes *David et Jonathas* for the Jesuit Collège de Clermont, Paris.	**1688** Death of Frederick William, the Great Elector; his son Frederick III succeeds as Elector of Brandenburg. Louis XIV begins the War of the League of Augsburg by invading the Palatinate. Glorious Revolution in England (–1689): after the birth of a son to James II, the Whig lords invite William of Orange to invade England; James II 'abdicates', and William and Mary proclaimed joint monarchs.
1689 Michel-Richard de Lalande (1657– 1726) appointed *surintendant de la musique de la chambre* at Versailles. Corelli's op.3 published, Rome. Giovanni Battista Vitali (1632–92) publishes his contrapuntal *tour de force*, *Artifici musicali*, in Modena. Jean-Henri D'Anglebert (1635–91) publishes *Pièces de clavecin* (incorporating a treatise on accompaniment and table of ornaments). Kuhnau's *Neuer Clavier-Übung*, i, published, Leipzig. Purcell's *Dido and Aeneas* given, London.	
	1689 Peter I, joint Tsar of Russia since 1682, overthrows his sister Sofia and becomes sole ruler.
1690 Domenico Gabrielli (*c*40) dies, Bologna. Legrenzi (63) dies, Venice. François Couperin (1668–1733) offers *Pièces d'orgue* to the Paris public. Wolfgang Caspar Printz (1641–1717) publishes first history of music in German, in Dresden.	**1690** Battle of the Boyne: William III defeats James II, who had invaded Ireland with French support.
1691 Gartentheater in Herrenhausen opens in Hanover. Purcell's semi-opera *King Arthur* given, London.	
1692 Teatro Capranica opens in Rome. Marais' *Pièces en trio* published in Paris (the first engraved French trio suites). Purcell's *The Fairy Queen* given, London.	**1692** Maximilian II Emanuel, Elector of Bavaria, becomes Governor of the Spanish Netherlands.
1693 Johann Kaspar Kerll (65) dies, Munich. Couperin appointed *organiste du roi* at Versailles. Opera house in Leipzig opens. Charpentier's *Médée* given, Paris. John Lenton (*d* ?1718) writes *The Gentleman's Diversion* (earliest violin tutor) in London. Public concerts inaugurated in Edinburgh.	**1693** Liège besieged by French troops in the presence of Louis XIV, who begins tentative overtures for peace.
1694 André Campra (1660–1744) appointed *maître de musique* at Notre Dame, Paris. Corelli's op.4 published in Rome. Alessandro Scarlatti's *Il Pirro e Demetrio* given, Naples. La Guerre's *Céphale et Procris* (only *tragédie en musique* by a woman) and the regent's *Philomèle* given, Paris.	**1694** Death of Queen Mary; William III continues to reign alone.

LITERATURE, PHILOSOPHY, RELIGION	SCIENCE, TECHNOLOGY, DISCOVERY	FINE AND DECORATIVE ARTS, ARCHITECTURE
		1688 Carlo Antonio Carlone (*d* 1708) designs the monastery of St Florian, Austria (–1705).
1689 The English Parliament passes the Act of Toleration granting freedom of worship to all dissenters except Roman Catholics and Unitarians.		**1689** Meindert Hobbema (1638–1709) paints *The Avenue at Middelharnis.*
1690 John Locke (1632–1704) publishes his *Essay Concerning Human Understanding*, attacking the Platonist conception of 'innate ideas' and arguing that all ideas come from experience. The Accademia dell'Arcadia founded in Rome, around Queen Christina of Sweden (*d* 1689), was the last manifestation of the pastoral tradition and the earliest inkling of the Enlightenment in Italy.	**1690** Papin devises an engine operated by a steam piston. Huygens describes the wave theory of light and establishes the fundamental laws of optics. Leibniz writes his *Protogaea* (published 1749) explaining the probable evolution of the Earth.	**1691** Andrea Pozzo (1642–1709) begins his illusionist ceiling decoration *Allegory of the Missionary Work of the Jesuits* in St Ignatius, Rome (–1694).
1691 Claude Fleury (1640–1723) begins the *Histoire ecclésiastique* in 20 volumes (–1720), the first large-scale history of the church.	**1692** Posthumous publication of *General History of the Air* by Robert Boyle (1627–91).	**1692** Luca Giordano (1634–1705) paints the ceiling of the grand staircase in the Escorial (–1694).
	1693 Halley compiles data for calculating distances from the sun.	**1693** José Churriguera (1650–1725) designs the High Altar of S Esteban, Salamanca (–1700), giving his name to an extravagant style of architecture.
1694 *Dictionnaire de l'Académie Française* published, with a supplement by Thomas Corneille, *Dictionnaire des arts et sciences. The Double Dealer* by William Congreve (1670–1729) published, concerning social pressures on love and marriage.	**1694** Rudolph Jacob Camerarius (1665–1721) writes his famous letter *De sexu plantarum*, on sexuality in plants.	**1694** Wren begins Greenwich Hospital.

The Late Baroque Era

MUSIC AND MUSICIANS	POLITICS, WAR, RULERS
1695 Purcell (36) dies, London. Johann Pachelbel (1653–1706) appointed organist at the Sebaldkirche, Nuremberg, and Jeremiah Clarke (c1674–1707) at St Paul's Cathedral, London. Collasse's *Ballet des saisons* (precursor of *opéra-ballet*) given, Paris. Georg Muffat (1653–1704) publishes *Florilegium primum* in Augsburg. Purcell's *The Indian Queen* given, London.	**1695** William III leads an army in Holland and captures Namur from the French. End of press censorship in England.
1696 Couperin granted a coat of arms. The orchestra at S Petronio, Bologna, disbanded for five years and the performances of G. A. V. Aldrovandini's comic opera *Gl'inganni amorosi scoperti in villa* (in Bolognese dialect) censored. *Il trionfo di Camilla* by Giovanni Bononcini (1642–78) given, Naples. Printz's influential treatise *Phrynis Mitilenaeus, oder Satyrischer Componist* published in Dresden and Leipzig. Purcell's *Choice Collection of Lessons* for harpsichord published in London.	**1696** Death of John III Sobieski, King of Poland.
1697 Campra's *L'Europe galante* given, Paris. Reinhard Keiser (1674–1739) arrives in Hamburg. August II sets up royal chapels in Warsaw and Dresden (united in 1720 in Warsaw). Purcell's *Ten Sonata's in Four Parts* published in London. Estienne Roger (c1665–1722) opens music-printing firm in Amsterdam.	**1697** Election of August II of Saxony to the Polish throne. Treaty of Ryswick ends the War of the League of Augsburg Death of Charles XI of Sweden; succeeded by his son Charles XII. Peter the Great visits Prussia, the Netherlands, England and Vienna (–1698); on his return he instigates a vast programme of reform.
1698 Charpentier appointed *maître de musique* at Sainte Chapelle, Paris. Johann Joseph Fux (1660–1741) appointed court composer to Leopold I in Vienna. Giuseppe Torelli (1658–1709) publishes *Concerti musicali* op.6 (containing two early solo violin concertos) in Augsburg. Muffat's *Florilegium secundum* (with treatise on bowing and ornamentation) published in Passau.	**1698** Death of Ernst August, Elector of Hanover; succeeded by Georg Ludwig, the future King George I of England.
1699 Antonio Caldara (c1670–1736) appointed *maestro di cappella* at Mantua.	**1699** Treaty of Karlowitz signed by Austria, Russia, Poland and Venice with Turkey.

LITERATURE, PHILOSOPHY, RELIGION	SCIENCE, TECHNOLOGY, DISCOVERY	FINE AND DECORATIVE ARTS, ARCHITECTURE
1695 Pierre Bayle's *Dictionnaire historique et critique* (–1697) published, used by anti-Christian Deists and *philosophes* in France and England.	**1695** Grew isolates magnesium sulphate ('Epsom salts').	
1696 Death of Mme de Sévigné (*b* 1626), whose letters describe Paris under Louis XVI with charm, wit and great powers of observation. Sir John Vanbrugh (1664–1726), dramatist and architect, produces *The Relapse*, with great success. John Toland (1670–1722) publishes his classic *Christianity not Mysterious*, which argues against revelation and the supernatural.		**1696** Andreas Schlüter (*c*1660–1714) works on the bronze equestrian monument to the Great Elector at Schloss Charlottenburg, Berlin (–1708).
1697 Charles Perrault (1628–1703) publishes *Contes de ma mère l'Oye*, a collection of fairytales.		**1697** Nicodemus Tessin the younger (1654–1728) begins the royal palace in Stockholm.
1698 Jeremy Collier (1650–1726), a non-Juror, publishes *Short View of the Immorality and Profaneness of the English Stage*, attacking Restoration dramatists.	**1698** Thomas Savery (*c*1650–1715) patents his water-raising engine.	**1698** Hardouin-Mansart works on the Place Vendôme, Paris.
1699 Gottfried Arnold (1666–1714) begins the *Unparteiische Kirchen- und Ketzer-Historie*, important for German Protestant mysticism (–1700).	**1699** William Dampier (1652–1715) explores the coastlines of Australia and New Guinea (–1701).	**1699** Leonardo de Figueroa (*c*1650–1730) begins S Luis, Seville (–1731). Sir John Vanbrugh (1664–1726) designs Castle Howard, Yorkshire (–1726).

The Late Baroque Era

MUSIC AND MUSICIANS	POLITICS, WAR, RULERS
1700 Draghi (*c*65) dies, Vienna. Blow appointed first Composer of the Chapel Royal and John Eccles (*c*1668–1735) Master of the King's Musick, London. Corelli's op.5 violin sonatas published in Rome. Kuhnau's satirical novel *Der musicalische Quack-Salber* and his *Musicalische Vorstellung einiger biblischer Historien* (programmatic keyboard sonatas) published in Dresden. A contest for the best setting of Congreve's masque *The Judgment of Paris* held in London, with prize won by John Weldon (1676–1736); Eccles, Daniel Purcell (*d* 1717) and Gottfried Finger (*c*1660–1730) also competed.	**1700** Death of Charles II of Spain; Louis XIV's grandson Philippe of Anjou designated his heir, to the chagrin of Austria. Crown Treaty between Leopold I and Elector Frederick III of Brandenburg, who is recognized as King of Prussia.
1701 Kuhnau elected Kantor of Thomaskirche, Leipzig. The first dictionaries of music, by Sébastien de Brossard and Tomás Baltazar Janovka, published in Paris and Prague. *La púrpura de la rosa* by Tomás de Torrejón y Velasco (1644–1728), the earliest New World opera, given, Lima.	**1701** War of the Spanish Succession (–1713): Britain, the Netherlands and Austria form the Grand Alliance against France, who is supported by Bavaria, Cologne, Savoy and Portugal; the war is fought in Italy, Germany, the Netherlands and Spain.
1702 Giovanni and Antonio Maria Bononcini (1677–1726) visit Berlin. Keiser appointed director of the Theater am Gänsemarkt, Hamburg, and Georg Philipp Telemann (1681–1767) of the Leipzig Opera. The Danish Royal Opera House opens in Copenhagen. Sebastián Durón (1660–1716) appointed *maestro de capilla* at the Spanish court. François Raguenet (*c*1660–1722) publishes *Paralèle des italiens et des françois* in Paris.	**1702** Death of William III; succeeded in England by his sister-in-law, Anne. In the Northern Netherlands the States-General under Heinsius takes control. John Churchill, Duke of Marlborough (1650–1722), takes William's place as the political and military leader against France.
1703 Antonio Vivaldi (1678–1741) appointed *maestro di violino* at the Ospedale della Pietà, Venice. Johann Sebastian Bach (1685–1750) takes up organ post at the Neukirche, Arnstadt. George Frideric Handel (1685–1759) moves to Hamburg.	**1703** Portugal and Savoy join the Grand Alliance against France in the War of the Spanish Succession.
1704 Charpentier (*c*59) dies, Paris. Muffat (50) dies, Passau. Biber (59) dies, Salzburg. Lalande appointed *maître de la chapelle de musique* at Versailles. Jeremiah Clarke and William Croft (1678–1727) jointly appointed organists of the English Chapel Royal.	**1704** Marlborough and Prince Eugene of Savoy defeat the French and Bavarians at Blenheim. Gibraltar captured by the British. Election of Stanislaus Leszczyński as King of Poland at the instigation of Charles XII of Sweden.

LITERATURE, PHILOSOPHY, RELIGION	SCIENCE, TECHNOLOGY, DISCOVERY	FINE AND DECORATIVE ARTS, ARCHITECTURE
1700 *Don Quixote* (1605) by Cervantes translated into English by Peter Anthony Motteux (1660–1718). Congreve's comedy *The Way of the World* produced.	**1700** Pierre Le Moyne (1661–1706) establishes the first European settlement in Louisiana. Berlin Academy of Science founded, with Leibniz as president.	**1700** Giovanni Viscardi (1647–1713) designs the Mariahilfkirche, Freystadt (–1708). Enrico Zuccalli (1642–1724) begins the palace at Schleissheim, Munich (–1725).
1701 Daniel Defoe (1660–1731) writes *The True-born Englishman*, a popular satirical poem attacking English prejudice against William III.	**1701** Jethro Tull (1674–1741) invents the seed-drill.	**1701** Hyacinthe Rigaud (1649–1743) paints his classic state portrait of Louis XIV.
1702 Defoe is imprisoned for writing *The Shortest Way with Dissenters*, which attacked the High Church.	**1702** Wilhelm Homberg (1652–1715) first prepares boric acid.	**1702** Jakob Prandtauer (1660–1726) designs Melk Abbey (–1714).
		1703 Christoph Dientzenhofer (1655–1722) builds St Nicholas, Prague (completed by his son, 1750).
1704 Antoine Gallaud (1646–1715) translates the *Arabian Nights* into French, the first translation into any European language (–1717). Jonathan Swift (1667–1745) publishes *The Battle of the Books* and *A Tale of a Tub*, celebrated satires on learning and religion.	**1704** Newton's *Optics* published, defending the emission theory of light. John Harris (1667–1719) publishes the *Lexicon technicum*, the first scientific encyclopaedia.	**1704** The north front of Chatsworth, Derbyshire, begun by Thomas Archer (1668–1743). Pozzo, now settled in Vienna, paints the ceiling of the garden palace, Liechtenstein (–1707).

The Late Baroque Era

MUSIC AND MUSICIANS	POLITICS, WAR, RULERS
1705 Bach goes to Lübeck to hear Buxtehude play. Vivaldi's op.1 trio sonatas published. Handel's first opera, *Almira*, given, Hamburg.	**1705** Death of Emperor Leopold I; succeeded by his son Joseph I, whose brother is recognized in Catalonia, Valencia and Aragon as Charles III of Spain.
1706 Pachelbel (52) dies, Nuremberg. Jean-Philippe Rameau (1683–1764) arrives in Paris and publishes his first book of *Pièces de clavecin*. Handel travels to Italy. Jean-Baptiste Morin (1677–1754) publishes the first book of French cantatas in Paris. Bononcini's *Camilla* (1696) given (in English), London.	**1706** Marlborough defeats the French at Ramillies and conquers the Spanish Netherlands. French also defeated at Turin and driven from Piedmont by Prince Eugene.
1707 Buxtehude (c70) dies, Lübeck. Bach appointed organist at the Blasiuskirche, Mühlhausen. Handel's oratorio *Il trionfo del Tempo e del Disinganno* performed in Rome, and his opera *Rodrigo* in Florence. Alessandro Scarlatti's *Il Mitridate Eupatore* and *Il trionfo della libertà* given, Venice.	**1707** Act of Union between England and Scotland to form Great Britain, providing for the Hanoverian succession and a single parliament.
1708 Blow (59) dies, London. Bach appointed Weimar court organist. Handel's *La Resurrezione* performed in Rome. A new court opera house is built in Vienna.	**1708** Marlborough and Prince Eugene defeat the French at Oudenaarde: Charles XII defeats the Russians at Holowczyn and invades Ukraine.
1709 Torelli (50) dies, Bologna. Collasse (40) dies, Versailles. Agostino Steffani (1654–1728) appointed Apostolic Vicar of North Germany, at Hanover. A comic opera, *Patrò Calienno de la Costa* (in Neapolitan dialect) by Antonio Orefice (*fl* 1708–34), given, Naples.	**1709** Charles XII defeated by Peter the Great at Poltava and exiled to Turkey. French defeated at Malplaquet by Marlborough and Prince Eugene.
1710 Bernardo Pasquini (72) dies, Rome. Handel travels to Hanover and then to London after performances of his *Agrippina* in Venice. The Teatro Marsigli-Rossi opens in Bologna. Campra's comic *opéra-ballet Les fêtes vénitiennes* given, Paris. *Idaspe*, by Francesco Mancini (1672–1737), given, London.	
1711 Michel Pignolet de Montéclair (1667–1737) publishes *Méthode facile pour apprendre à jouer du violon* (first French violin tutor) in Paris. Handel returns to Hanover after performances of *Rinaldo*, London. Vivaldi's *L'estro armonico* op.3 published in Amsterdam.	**1711** Death of Emperor Joseph I; succeeded by his brother Charles III of Spain, as Emperor Charles VI.

LITERATURE, PHILOSOPHY, RELIGION	SCIENCE, TECHNOLOGY, DISCOVERY	FINE AND DECORATIVE ARTS, ARCHITECTURE
1705 Vanbrugh's comedy *The Confederacy* produced in London.	**1705** Halley (correctly) predicts the return in 1758 of the comet last seen in 1682. Posthumous publication of Ray's *Historia insectorum*, which broke new ground in entomology.	**1705** Vanbrugh begins Blenheim Palace for the Duke of Marlborough.
	1706 *Adversarium anatomica* by Giovanni Morgagni (1682–1771) published.	
	1707 E. W. Tschirnhausen (1651–1708) discovers the hard-paste porcelain process.	
1708 Gian Vincenzo Gravina (1664–1718) writes *Della ragione poetica*, a treatise defining poetry as form of rational knowledge and claiming for it a civilizing power.	**1708** Georg Stahl (1660–1734) publishes his influential *Theoria medica vera*.	**1708** Giovanni Pellegrini (1675–1741) begins painting his finest works at Kimbolton Castle. Camillo Rusconi (1658–1728) produces the statues of apostles in St John Lateran, Rome (–1718).
	1709 Abraham Darby (1678–1717) uses a coke-fired furnace to manufacture iron at Coalbrookdale.	**1709** Johann Friedrich Böttger (*d* 1719) first uses Tschirnhausen's process for making hard-paste porcelain; the famous Meissen factory founded soon afterwards.
1710 George Berkeley (1685–1753) produces *A Treatise Concerning the Principles of Human Knowledge*, arguing that material objects affirmed as real are only perceived ('Esse est percipi').	**1710** Jakob Christoph Le Blon (1667–1741) invents three-colour printing using separate engraved metal plates.	
1711 Anthony Ashley Cooper, 3rd Earl of Shaftesbury (1671–1713), writes *Characteristics of Men, Manners, Opinions and Times*, in opposition to Hobbes. Joseph Addison (1672–1719) and Richard Steele (1672–1729) produce *The Spectator*, which helped create a new image of polite behaviour.		**1711** João Ludovice (1673–1752) commissioned by John V to build a convent at Mafra in Portugal (–1770). Johann Dientzenhofer (1663–1726) builds his masterpiece Schloss Pommersfelden, Franconia (–1718). Matthäus Pöppelmann (1662–1736) builds the Zwinger, Dresden (–1720), for the Elector of Saxony.

The Late Baroque Era

MUSIC AND MUSICIANS	POLITICS, WAR, RULERS
1712 Marc'Antonio Ziani (c1653–1715) appointed Hofkapellmeister in Vienna. Handel settles in London.	
1713 Corelli (59) dies, Rome. André Cardinal Destouches (1672–1749) appointed *inspecteur général* of the Académie Royale de Musique, Paris. Couperin's first book of *Pièces de clavecin* published in Paris. Johann Mattheson (1681–1764) publishes *Das neu-eröffnete Orchestre* in Hamburg. Maria Margherita Grimani becomes first woman composer to have an opera, *Pallade e Marte*, performed at the Hoftheater in Vienna.	**1713** Death of Frederick I of Prussia; succeeded by his son Frederick William I. Treaty of Utrecht ends the War of the Spanish Succession. Philip V recognized as King of Spain. France recognizes the Protestant Succession in Britain. Emperor Charles VI reveals his Pragmatic Sanction, guaranteeing the Habsburg succession, male or female, in the provinces of the Austrian monarchy; after 1717 his heir is his daughter Maria Theresa.
1714 Domenico Scarlatti (1685–1757) appointed *maestro* of the Cappella Giulia in Rome. Francesco Geminiani (1687–1762) arrives in London. Corelli's op.6 concerti grossi published in Rome. Bach begins his first cycle of sacred cantatas in Weimar. Vivaldi's violin concertos *La stravaganza* op.4 published in Amsterdam.	**1714** Peace of Rastatt. France recognizes Habsburg territories in Italy, Austria gains the Spanish Netherlands and the Electors of Bavaria and Cologne restored. Death of Queen Anne of England; succeeded by the Elector of Hanover as George I, great-grandson of James I.
1715 Fux appointed Hofkapellmeister in Vienna. The Three Choirs Festival (Gloucester, Hereford and Worcester) founded.	**1715** Death of Louis XIV; succeeded by his five-year-old great-grandson Louis XV, under the regency of the Duke of Orléans. First Jacobite Rebellion, the 'Fifteen': Scottish supporters of the Pretender 'James III' (son of James II) defeated at Sherrifmuir and Preston.
1716 The Opéra-Comique opens at the Foire St Laurent, the Nouveau Théâtre Italien at the Palais-Royal and the Comédie-Italienne at the Hôtel de Bourgogne, in Paris.	
1717 François Francoeur (1698–1787) appointed leader of the Vingt-quatre Violons and Couperin *ordinaire de la chambre pour le clavecin* in Paris. Bach completes the *Orgelbüchlein* at Weimar before being appointed Kapellmeister at Cöthen. Handel is in residence at Cannons, Edgware; *Water Music* performed at a royal barge party on the Thames.	
	1718 Peace of Passarowitz ends the Austro-Turkish war. Quadruple Alliance between France, Austria, England and Holland against Spain's seizure of Sicily; Spain defeated by an English fleet, under Admiral Byng. Death of Charles XII of Sweden; succeeded by his sister Ulrica Eleanor, who in 1720 abdicates in favour of her husband, Frederick I, Prince of Hessen-Kassel.
1718 Maurice Greene (1696–1755) appointed organist at St Paul's Cathedral, London. Handel's *Acis and Galatea* and oratorio *Esther* performed at Cannons.	

LITERATURE, PHILOSOPHY, RELIGION	SCIENCE, TECHNOLOGY, DISCOVERY	FINE AND DECORATIVE ARTS, ARCHITECTURE
1712 Biblioteca Nacional, Madrid, founded by Philip V. *The Rape of the Lock* by Alexander Pope (1688–1744) published.	**1712** Thomas Newcomen (1663–1729) erects the first well-documented steam engine.	
1713 Scipione Maffei (1675–1755) writes his tragedy *La Merope*, which attracts a wide European audience.	**1713** Posthumous publication of *Ars conjectandi* by Jacques Bernouilli (1654–1705), a treatise on probability.	
1714 Gottfried Wilhelm von Leibniz (1646–1716) writes the *Monadologie* (published 1720), the only systematic account of his metaphysical doctrines.	**1714** Gabriel Daniel Fahrenheit (1686–1736) constructs a mercury thermometer.	**1714** James Gibbs (1682–1754) builds St Mary-le-Strand, London (–1717).
1715 Alain-René Lesage (1668–1747) begins *Gil Blas*, a picaresque novel much admired in France and England (–1735).	**1715** Brook Taylor (1685–1731) establishes the calculus of finite differences.	**1716** Joseph Effner (1687–1745) builds the Pagodenburg, a pavilion with a chinoiserie interior in the Nymphenburg park, Munich. Johann Fischer von Erlach (1656–1723) begins the Karlskirche, Vienna. Sir James Thornhill (c1675–1734) paints scenes from the life of St Paul in the dome of St Paul's Cathedral (–1719).
		1717 Jean-Antoine Watteau (1684–1721), a key figure of Rococo art, submits *The Embarkation for Cythera* to the Académie; the term 'fête galante' is coined to describe it. Robert de Cotte (1656–1735) builds the early Rococo Hôtel de Bouvallais, Paris.
1718 Accademia de Scienze, Lettere ed Arti founded in Palermo, Sicily.	**1718** Abraham Demoivre (1667–1754) publishes his *Doctrine of Chances* on probability, which later leads to the notion of the normal distribution curve. Friedrich Hoffmann (1660–1742) publishes his *Medicinae rationalis systematicae* (–1720).	

The Late Baroque Era

MUSIC AND MUSICIANS	POLITICS, WAR, RULERS
1719 Bononcini recruited by Handel for the Royal Academy of Music in London. Dresden court theatre opens with *Giove in Argo* (1717) by Antonio Lotti (*c*1667–1740). Bernhard Christoph Breitkopf (1695–1777) establishes printing and publishing firm in Leipzig.	
1720 Domenico Scarlatti and Carlos de Seixas (1704–42) take up appointments at the Portuguese court. Benedetto Marcello (1686–1739) publishes satire on Italian opera, *Il teatro alla moda*, in Venice. Bach completes *Clavier-Büchelein* in Cöthen. Royal Academy of Music opens in London with Porta's *Numitore* and Handel's *Radamisto*. Leipzig Opera closes.	**1720** Peace between Quadruple Alliance and Spain. Philip V and Charles VI renounce claims to Italy and Spain, provided that Charles allow Philip's son to succeed in Parma, Piacenza and Tuscany. 'South Sea Bubble' disaster ruins thousands in England. In France, John Law's Mississippi Company fails, producing national bankruptcy.
1721 Telemann appointed Kantor of the Hamburg Johanneum and music director of the main city churches. Marcello publishes his satire on castrato singers. *Il flagello dei musici*, in Venice. The Comédie-Italienne in Paris becomes the Comédiens du Roi. Bach completes the presentation copy of the six Brandenburg Concertos in Cöthen.	**1721** End of Great Northern War: by the Treaty of Rystad, Russia acquires Livonia, Estonia and other lands from Sweden but restores Finland to Sweden.
1722 Kuhnau (62) dies, Leipzig. Rameau settles in Paris and publishes his *Traité de l'harmonie*. Telemann appointed music director of the Hamburg Opera. Bach publishes first volume of *Das wohltemperirte Clavier* in Cöthen. Mattheson founds *Critica musica*, the first periodical devoted to music.	
1723 Bach appointed Kantor and *director musices* of the Thomaskirche, Leipzig; his *Magnificat* performed there. Pier Francesco Tosi (*c*1653–1732) publishes his *Opinioni de' cantori antichi e moderni* in Bologna. Fux's *Costanza e Fortezza* and the *Melodrama de Sancto Wenceslao* by Jan Dismas Zelenka (1679–1745) performed in Prague in coronation celebrations of Charles VI.	**1723** Louis XV attains majority.
1724 Domenico Sarro (1679–1744) becomes the first to set an original Metastasio libretto, *Didone abbandonata*, Naples. Bach begins his second cycle of church cantatas; his *St John Passion* performed at the Leipzig Nicolaikirche. Handel's *Giulio Cesare in Egitto* given, London.	**1724** Treaty of Constantinople between Turkey and Russia, against Persia.

LITERATURE, PHILOSOPHY, RELIGION	SCIENCE, TECHNOLOGY, DISCOVERY	FINE AND DECORATIVE ARTS, ARCHITECTURE
1719 Defoe writes *Robinson Crusoe*, claimed as the first English novel, highly influential and widely imitated. Baron Ludwig Holberg (1684–1754) publishes *Peder Paars*, the first great Danish classic and a brilliant satire on contemporary manners.		**1719** Porcelain factories established at Vienna and Venice. Balthasar Neumann (1687–1753) rebuilds the bishop's Residenz at Würzburg (–1744), with its famous ceremonial staircase (1735).
1720 Christian Wolff (1679–1754) writes his early Enlightenment treatise on ethics, *Vernünftige Gedanken von der Menschen Tun und Lassen*.	**1720** Lady Mary Wortley Montagu (1689–1762) introduces smallpox inoculation to Britain.	**1720** Johann Lukas von Hildebrandt (1668–1745) begins the Upper Belvedere, Vienna (–1723).
1721 Charles Louis de Secondat, Baron de Montesquieu (1689–1755), publishes anonymously his satirical *Lettres persanes*.		**1721** Narciso Tomé (*c*1690–1742) designs the Transparente (–1732) in Toledo Cathedral, a sacramental chapel without walls.
	1722 René Réaumur (1683–1757) publishes *L'art de convertir le fer forgé en acier*, which leads to the establishment of steel-making in France.	**1722** Gibbs begins St Martin-in-the-Fields, London (–1726).
1723 Pietro Giannone (1676–1748) publishes the *Storia civile del regno di Napoli*, identifying the church as a retrogressive force. Voltaire (1694–1778) publishes *La Henriade*, an epic poem on the career of Henry of Navarre. Lodovico Muratori (1672–1750) begins publishing the monumental *Rerum italicarum scriptores*, which assembles Italian historical documents 500–1500 (–1750).		**1723** Fischer von Erlach begins the Hofbibliothek, Vienna (completed by his son Joseph). Effner completes Schloss Nymphenburg, Munich. Nicholas Hawksmoor (1661–1736) builds Christ Church, Spitalfields, London (–1729).
1724 Pietro Metastasio (1698–1782) writes the libretto *Didone abbandonata*.	**1724** Herman Boerhaave (1668–1738) publishes his *Elementia chemiae* (–1732), the authoritative manual of chemistry for a century.	

MUSIC AND MUSICIANS	POLITICS, WAR, RULERS
1725 Alessandro Scarlatti (65) dies, Naples. Anne Danican Philidor (1681–1728) inaugurates the Concert Spirituel, Paris. The Caecilienbrüderschaft founded in Vienna. Bach completes *Clavierbüchlein*, ii (for his wife Anna Magdalena), in Leipzig. Fux's *Gradus ad Parnassum* published in Vienna. Vivaldi's 'Four Seasons' concertos published in his op.8 in Amsterdam.	**1725** Louis XV breaks his engagement to the Spanish Infanta and marries Maria Leszczyńska of Poland; Spain, offended, draws closer to Austria. Death of Peter the Great; succeeded by his wife Catherine I, who is succeeded by Peter II in 1727.
1726 Lalande (68) dies, Versailles. Johann Joachim Quantz (1697–1733) visits Paris. The Concert Italien founded in Paris. The Academy of Vocal Music founded in London. Couperin's *Les nations* published in Paris.	**1726** Cardinal Fleury (1653–1743) becomes Chief Minister of France.
1727 Quantz visits London. Faustina Bordoni (1700–81) and Francesca Cuzzoni (*c*1698–1770) argue violently on stage in London. Philidor inaugurates the Concert Français and Evrard Titon du Tillet (1677–1762) publishes biographies of French composers, in his *Description du Parnasse François*, in Paris. Bach conducts early version of the *St Matthew Passion* in Leipzig.	**1727** Death of George I of England; succeeded by his son George II.
1728 Steffani (73) dies, Frankfurt. Marais (72) dies, Paris. Quantz appointed flute teacher to the future Frederick the Great. Johann David Heinichen (1683–1729) publishes his *Der General-Bass in den Composition*. *The Beggar's Opera* (ballad opera by Johann Christoph Pepusch and John Gay) given, London. Handel's Royal Academy dissolved.	
1729 La Guerre (*c*62) dies, Paris. Pietro Antonio Locatelli (1695–1764) moves to Amsterdam, Domenico Scarlatti to Seville. Handel and J. J. Heidegger launch the Second Royal Academy of Music, London. J. S Bach becomes director of Leipzig Collegium Musicum. Lalande's *grands motets* published posthumously in Paris.	**1729** Treaty of Seville: Spain joins England, France and the Netherlands to promote Spanish interests in Italy and to suppress the Austrian East Indian Company.
1730 Alessandro Grandi (?44) dies, Bergamo. Leonardo Vinci (*c*40) dies, Naples. Johann Adolf Hasse (1699–1783) invited to Dresden as Hofkapellmeister. Marguerite-Antoinette Couperin succeeds her father as *ordinaire de la chambre pour le clavecin*, becoming the first female instrumentalist to hold a court post, at Versailles.	**1730** Death of Peter II of Russia; succeeded by Anne, daughter of Ivan V. Death of Frederick IV of Denmark; succeeded by his son Christian VI.

LITERATURE, PHILOSOPHY, RELIGION	SCIENCE, TECHNOLOGY, DISCOVERY	FINE AND DECORATIVE ARTS, ARCHITECTURE
1725 Giovanni Battista Vico (1668–1744) publishes *Principii di una scienza nuova*, a philosophy of history using language and ritual as key to historical understanding.	**1725** St Petersburg Academy of Science founded by Empress Catherine I. Posthumous publication of *Historia coelestis Britannica* by Flamsteed, which forms the basis of modern star catalogues.	**1725** Lord Burlington (1694–1753) builds Chiswick House, based on Palladio's Rotonda.
1726 Swift publishes the satire *Gulliver's Travels*. James Thomson (1700–48) begins *The Seasons* (–1730), one of the most popular and influential English poems.	**1726** John Harrison (1693–1774) devises the grid-iron pendulum.	**1726** Georg Bähr (1666–1728) builds the Frauen-kirche, Dresden (–1741).

1727 Giovanni Battista Tiepolo (1696–1770) decorates the Udine archbishop's palace with a fresco cycle (–1728). |
1728 Ephraim Chambers (*d* 1740) publishes his *Cyclopaedia*, the first true English encyclopedia.	**1728** Vitus Bering (1681–1741) leads the First Kamchatkan Expedition to determine whether Asia and America are connected by land. Harrison designs the marine chronometer.	**1728** Still-life paintings by Jean-Baptiste-Siméon Chardin (1699–1779) gain him entry to the Académie. The Rococo pilgrimage church of Steinhausen (–1751) built by Dominikus Zimmermann (1685–1766) in Bavaria.
1729 Academia de Buenas Letras, Barcelona, founded.	**1729** James Bradley (1693–1762) discovers that the apparent seasonal shifts of the stars arise from the annual shift in the earth's orbit.	**1729** John Wood the elder (*c*1705–1754) begins building Queen Square, Bath, in Palladian style (–1736).
1730 Matthew Tindal (1655–1733) writes the 'Bible' of Deism, *Christianity as Old as Creation*.	**1730** John Hadley (1682–1744) and Thomas Godfrey (1704–49) independently design the reflecting quadrant, the ancestor of the modern sextant. Charles Towns-hend (1674–1738) intro-duces crop rotation.	

The Late Baroque Era

MUSIC AND MUSICIANS	POLITICS, WAR, RULERS
1731 Hasse marries Bordoni and they arrive in Dresden. Public concerts inaugurated in Stockholm. Bach's first part of the *Clavierübung* published in Leipzig. The opera *Calandro* (1726) by Giovanni Alberto Ristori (1692–1753) given, Moscow.	**1731** Charles VI seizes Parma and Piacenza. European war averted by Treaty of Vienna between England, Holland, Spain and Austria.
1732 Lodovico Giustini (1685–1743) publishes *Sonate da cimbalo di piano e forte* in Florence. The comic opera *Lo frate 'nnamorato* by Giovanni Battista Pergolesi (1710–36) and Hasse's *Issipile* given, Naples. Montéclair's controversial sacred opera *Jephté* given, Paris. John Frederick Lampe (*c*1703–1751), Henry Carey (1687–1743) and Thomas Augustine Arne (1710–78) organize a season of 'English operas after the Italian manner' in London. Handel's *Ezio* and *Sosarme* and his oratorio *Esther* performed in London. Titon du Tillet's *Le Parnasse François* published in Paris. Johann Gottfried Walther (1684–1748) publishes *Musicalisches Lexicon* (first German music dictionary) in Leipzig.	
1733 Couperin (64) dies, Paris. Nicola Porpora (1686–1768) appointed director of the Opera of the Nobility in London. Pergolesi's *La serva padrona* given as intermezzo to his *Il prigionier superbo* in Naples. Rameau's *Hippolyte et Aricie* given, Paris. Handel's *Orlando* (and later *Arianna in Creta*) and oratorio *Deborah* performed, in competition with Porpora's *Arianna in Nasso*, in London. The Kyrie and Gloria of Bach's *Mass in B minor* performed, Dresden. Telemann's *Musique de table* published in Hamburg. Locatelli's *L'arte del violino* published in Amsterdam.	**1733** Pragmatic Sanction guaranteed by the Diet of German Princes, but the Electors of Saxony, Bavaria and the Palatinate refuse to recognize it. Death of August II of Saxony and Poland. War of Polish Succession: Elector August III of Saxony recognized as King of Poland by Russia and Austria, but France supports Stanislaus Leszczyński.
1734 Fire destroys the royal music library in Madrid. Bach's *Christmas Oratorio* performed in Leipzig. Handel plays organ concertos between the acts of his oratorios, and his concerti grossi op.3 published, in London.	
1735 Eccles (*c*67) dies, nr London. Greene succeeds him as Master of the King's Musick. Rameau's *Les Indes galantes* given, Paris. Handel's *Ariodante* and *Alcina* given, London.	**1735** Treaty of Vienna (ratified 1738): Charles VI receives Parma and Piacenza, while Don Carlos succeeds in Naples and Sicily (but not in Spain). Stanislaus renounces claim to Poland and receives Lorraine, after Duke Francis Stephen of Lorraine (future husband of Maria Theresa) has received Tuscany on death of present Grand Duke.

LITERATURE, PHILOSOPHY, RELIGION	SCIENCE, TECHNOLOGY, DISCOVERY	FINE AND DECORATIVE ARTS, ARCHITECTURE
1731 *The Gentleman's Magazine* (–1907) started by Edward Cave (1691–1754) in London.	**1731** Réaumur establishes his thermometric scale of 0°–80°, using an alcohol thermometer.	
1732 Johann Christoff Gottsched (1700–66) publishes the literary periodical (–1744) *Beyträge zur Kritische Historie der deutsche Sprache*, an attempt to establish a single German educated language.		**1732** Nicola Salvi (1697–1751) designs the Trevi Fountain, Rome (–1762). Niccolo di Nazzoni (*d* 1773) builds S Pedro dos Clérigos, Oporto (–1750).
1733 Pope begins his *Essay on Man* (–1734), a series of moral and philosophical poems.	**1733** Stephen Hales (1677–1761) publishes his *Haemastaticks*, on the physiology of circulation, and measures blood pressure. Charles Dufay (1698–1739) differentiates between vitreous and resinous electricity.	**1733** The Asam brothers build the church of St John Nepomuk, Munich (–1746).
1734 Voltaire's *Lettres philosophiques*, inspired by his stay in England, attacks the abuses of the *ancien régime* in the name of tolerance and liberty.	**1734** Réaumur's *Mémoires pour servir a l'histoire des insectes* (–1742) published.	**1734** William Hogarth (1697–1764) paints *A Rake's Progress* (–1735). François Cuvilliés (1695–1768) creates the Amalienburg pavilion in the Nymphenburg park, Munich (–1739).
	1735 Carl Linnaeus (1707–78) introduces a binomial system of scientific nomenclature for plants and animals. Benoit de Maillet (1656–1738) publishes his influential ultra-neptunian theory of the earth.	**1735** Equestrian monument to William III in Queen Square, Bristol, commissioned to Michael Rysbrack (1694–1770). William Kent (1685–1748) designs Holkham Hall, Norfolk (–1759), the ultimate English Palladian achievement.

The Late Baroque Era

MUSIC AND MUSICIANS	POLITICS, WAR, RULERS
1736 Pergolesi (26) dies, Pozzuoli. Caldara (*c*65) dies, Vienna. Bach appointed honorary Dresden Hofkomponist. Pergolesi composes *Stabat mater* at Pozzuoli. Bach's revised *St Matthew Passion* performed at the Thomaskirche, Leipzig. Handel's *Atalanta* and *Alexander's Feast* performed at the newly designated Theatre Royal, Covent Garden, London. Montéclair's *Principes de musique* published in Paris.	**1736** Russo-Turkish War (–1739), in which Charles VI allies with Russia.
1737 Antonio Stradivari (93) dies, Cremona. Montéclair (69) dies, St Denis. Telemann visits Paris. Lorenz Christoph Mizler von Kolof (1711–78) becomes the first German lecturer on music, at the University of Leipzig, and founds a monthly magazine, *Neu-eröffnete musikalische Bibliothek*. Johann Adolph Scheibe (1708–76) publishes critical remarks about Bach in the first issue of *Critischer Musikus* in Hamburg. Teatro S Carlo built in Naples. The Opera of the Nobility and the Second Royal Academy both close in London.	**1737** Death of Gian Gastone de' Medici, the last Grand Duke of Tuscany; succeeded by Francis Stephen of Lorraine, hence duchy passes into the Habsburg family.
1738 Mouret (56) dies, Charenton. Carl Philipp Emanuel Bach (1714–88) enters the service of the future Frederick the Great. Domenico Scarlatti and Seixas ennobled; Francesco Corselli (*c*1702–78) appointed Spanish court *maestro de capilla*. Mizler founds the Korrespondierenden Sozietät der Musicalischen Wissenschaften in Leipzig. The Fund for the Support of Decayed Musicians (The Royal Society of Musicians) founded in London. Michel Corrette (1709–95) publishes *L'école d'Orphée* and Telemann his *Nouveaux quatuors*, in Paris. In response to Scheibe (see **1737**), J. A. Birnbaum publishes a defence of Bach, in Leipzig. Handel's organ concertos op.4 and Domenico Scarlatti's *Essercizi per gravicembalo* published in London. Luigi Madonis (*c*1690–*c*1770) publishes 'symphonies' in St Petersburg.	**1738** Treaty of Vienna ratified. France recognizes Pragmatic Sanctions.
1739 Marcello (53) dies, Brescia. Keiser (65) dies, Hamburg. Rameau's *Dardanus* and *Les fêtes d'Hébé* given, Paris. Handel's *Saul*, *Israel in Egypt* and *Ode for St Cecilia's Day* performed, London. Bach's third part of the *Clavierübung* published in Leipzig and Mattheson's *Der vollkommene Capellmeister* in Hamburg.	**1739** End of Russo-Turkish war, which had weakened Charles VI. Russia becomes a rival in the Balkans, and his enemies in the West gather to break up the Habsburg monarchy on succession of Maria Theresa (1740).

LITERATURE, PHILOSOPHY, RELIGION	SCIENCE, TECHNOLOGY, DISCOVERY	FINE AND DECORATIVE ARTS, ARCHITECTURE
1736 Joseph Butler (1692–1752) writes *Analogy of Religion*, a defence of Christianity which discredited the Deists.	**1736** Anders Celsius (1701–44) joins an Académie Française expedition to Lapland to measure the arc of the meridian. Leonhard Euler (1707–83) introduces analytical methods into mechanics.	
	1737 Manuscripts of Jan Swammerdam (1637–80) on insects published as *Biblia naturae*.	**1737** The Salon established as a biennial event in Paris. Gibbs designs the Radcliffe Camera, Oxford (–1749).
1738 John Wesley (1703–91) begins his evangelical journeys throughout Britain. Papal Bull, *In eminenti*, issued by Clement XII against freemasonry.	**1738** Daniel Bernoulli (1700–82), son of Jacques Bernoulli, publishes his *Hydrodynamica*. *Ichthyologia* by Peter Artedi (1705–35) published, the first systematic study of fish.	**1738** Louis François Roubiliac (1702/5–62) executes statue of Handel for Vauxhall Gardens, London.
1739 Samuel Richardson (1689–1761) writes his influential epistolary novel *Pamela*.		**1739** Interior of the pavilion added to the Hôtel de Soubise, Paris, completed by Germain Boffrand (1667–1754).

The Late Baroque Era

MUSIC AND MUSICIANS	POLITICS, WAR, RULERS
1740 Carl Heinrich Graun (1703–59) appointed Kapellmeister and C.P.E. Bach court harpsichordist to Frederick the Great. Joseph Haydn (1732–1809) appointed a singer at the Stephansdom, Vienna. Handel's concerti grossi op.6 and James Grassineau's *A Musical Dictionary* published in London. The allegorical *Défense de la basse de viole contre les entreprises du violon et les prétentions du violoncelle* by Hubert Le Blanc published in Amsterdam.	**1740** War of Austrian Succession: Prussia, France and Bavaria against Austria and England (–1748). Death of Frederick William of Prussia; succeeded by his son Frederick II ('the Great'). Death of Emperor Charles VI; succeeded by his daughter Maria Theresa. Death of Empress Anne of Russia; succeeded by her great-nephew Ivan VI, an infant of three months. Death of Pope Clement XII; succeeded by Benedict XIV.
1741 Vivaldi (63) dies, Vienna. Fux (*c*80) dies, Vienna. Quantz accepts Berlin court appointment. Bach presents copy of the *Goldberg Variations* to Count von Keyserlingk in Dresden. Handel travels to Dublin for charity concerts. *Artaserse*, the first opera by Christoph Willibald Gluck (1714–87), given, Milan. Handel's last opera, *Deidamia*, given, London. Rameau's *Pièces de clavecin en concerts* and Corrette's cello method published in Paris. Bach's fourth part of the *Clavier-übung* published in Nuremberg.	**1741** Empress Elizabeth usurps the Russian throne.
1742 Seixas (38) dies, Lisbon. Frederick the Great builds an opera house at Sanssouci in Potsdam; a new court opera house built in Mannheim. Handel's *Messiah* performed, Dublin. C. P. E. Bach's Prussian Sonatas published in Nuremberg.	**1742** Charles VII of Bavaria elected Holy Roman Emperor. Prague occupied by Bavarian and French troops.
1743 François Rebel (1701–75) and Francoeur appointed joint directors of the Académie Royale de Musique, Paris. The Musikalische Gesellschaft oder Akademie founded in Cologne and the Grosses Concert in Leipzig. Handel's *Samson* and *Messiah* performed, London. J.-J. Rousseau's *Dissertation sur la musique moderne* published in Paris.	**1743** Maria Theresa crowned Queen of Bohemia. George II is the last European monarch to ride into battle at the head of his troops, at Dettingen. Mme de Pompadour becomes Louis XV's mistress and for over 20 years influences French politics and diplomacy.
1744 Bartolomeo Giuseppe Guarneri 'del Gesù' (46) dies, Cremona. Campra (83) dies, Versailles. Francoeur succeeds François Collin de Blamont (1690–1760) as *surintendant de la musique de chambre* at Versailles. The Opéra-Comique closes in Paris. Handel's *Semele* and *Joseph* performed, London. C. P. E. Bach's Württemberg Sonatas published in Nuremberg.	**1744** Frederick the Great invades Saxony.

LITERATURE, PHILOSOPHY, RELIGION	SCIENCE, TECHNOLOGY, DISCOVERY	FINE AND DECORATIVE ARTS, ARCHITECTURE
1740 Completion of *A Treatise on Human Nature* by David Hume (1711–76). Louis, Duke of Saint-Simon (1675–1755), composes his *Mémoires* of Louis XIV (–1750).	**1740** Dijon Academy of Science founded. The circumnavigation of the globe by Lord Anson (1697–1762) in the *Centurion* (–1744).	**1740** Palace of Dos Aquas, Valencia, remodelled (–1744).
1741 First German translation of a Shakespeare play (*Julius Caesar*), by Caspar Wilhelm von Borck (1704–47).	**1741** Stockholm Academy of Science founded.	**1741** Summer Palace, St Petersburg, begun by Bartolommeo Rastrelli (1700–71).
1742 In *Cartas eruditas* (–1760) Benito Feijoo (1677–1764) contributes to the intellectual emancipation of Spain.	**1742** Celsius proposes a centigrade thermometer.	**1742** Jacques Dubois (1693–1763), a leading representative of the Rococo, becomes a master cabinet maker. Hogarth paints *Marriage à la Mode* (–1746). *Diana Resting after her Bath* by François Boucher (1703–30).
1743 *The Mourning Turtle Dove*, poems on the death of her husband by Hedwig Charlotta Nordenflycht (1718–93), published.	**1743** Copenhagen Academy of Science founded.	**1743** The pilgrimage church of Vierzehn-heiligen begun by Neumann. Capo-di-Monte porcelain factory established in Naples.
1744 George Berkeley (1685–1753) publishes *Siris*, a scientific and philosophical meditation. Third edition of Vico's *Scienza nuova*, the first survey of the social evolution of mankind.		**1744** The Abbey of Ottobeuren, the masterpiece of Michael Fischer (1692–1766), begun. Zimmermann begins the pilgrimage church of Die Wies.

MUSIC AND MUSICIANS	POLITICS, WAR, RULERS
1745 Antoine Forqueray (*c*73) dies, Mantes. Zelenka (66) dies, Dresden. Gluck visits London. The Gentlemen's Concerts founded in Manchester. Rameau's *La princesse de Navarre* and *Platée* given, Versailles. Frederick the Great builds a small theatre for comic operas at Sanssouci in Potsdam. Handel's *Hercules* and *Belshazzar* performed, London.	**1745** Death of Charles VII of Bavaria; succeeded by Maximilian III Joseph. Maria Theresa's husband, Francis Stephen of Lorraine, elected Holy Roman Emperor. Second Jacobite Rebellion (–1746): Prince Charles Edward Stuart attempts to gain the English throne but is defeated at Culloden (1746).
1746 Wilhelm Friedemann Bach (1710–84) appointed organist of the Liebfrauenkirche, Halle. A public opera house opens in Dresden.	**1746** Death of Philip V of Spain; succeeded by Ferdinand VI. Death of Christian VI of Denmark-Norway; succeeded by Frederick V.
1747 Bononcini (76) dies, Vienna. J. S. Bach plays for Frederick the Great, improvising on the king's theme (which inspired the *Musical Offering*), at Potsdam. Mme de Pompadour builds a theatre in the Petits-Cabinets and Rameau's *Les fêtes de l'Hymen et de l'Amour* given, Versailles. Handel's *Judas Maccabaeus* performed, London.	
1748 J. G. Walther (63) dies, Weimar. J.-N.-P. Royer and Gabriel Capperan assume direction of the Concert Spirituel, Paris. Rameau's *Zaïs* and *Pygmalion* given, Paris. The Operalnia opens in Warsaw. Handel's *Joshua* and *Alexander Balus* performed, London. The Holywell Music Room opens in Oxford.	**1748** Treaty of Aix-la-Chapelle ends the War of Austrian Succession, with Austria having lost Silesia to Prussia.
1749 Louis-Nicolas Clérambault (72) dies, Paris. Destouches (76) dies, Paris. The Académie Royale de Musique is taken over by the City of Paris. Rameau's *Naïs* and *Zoroastre* given, Paris. The Musikübende Gesellschaft founded in Berlin. Handel's *Susanna* and *Solomon* and his *Music for the Royal Fireworks* performed, London.	**1749** Maria Theresa unites Austria and Bohemia after the death of the Bohemian Chancellor, Kinsky.
1750 J. S. Bach (65) dies, Leipzig, leaving the *Art of Fugue* unfinished.	**1750** Death of John V of Portugal; succeeded by Joseph I. Britain joins Austro-Russian alliance, hostile to Prussia.

LITERATURE, PHILOSOPHY, RELIGION	SCIENCE, TECHNOLOGY, DISCOVERY	FINE AND DECORATIVE ARTS, ARCHITECTURE
	1745 Invention of the 'Leyden jar' for storing electricity by Pieter van Musschenbroek (1692–1761).	**1745** Chelsea porcelain factory, the first in England, established. Sanssouci palace, Potsdam, begun by Georg von Knobelsdorff (1699–1753).
	1746 Albrecht von Haller (1708–77) publishes his pioneering work on human anatomy.	**1746** Antonio Canaletto (1720–75) arrives in London.
1747 Samuel Johnson (1709–84) begins his *Dictionary of the English Language* (–1755).		**1747** St Andrew's Cathedral, Kiev, begun by Rastrelli. Strawberry Hill, Twickenham, begun by Horace Walpole (1717–97) in the Gothic style.
1748 Montesquieu publishes *De l'esprit des Lois*, the first great synthesis of political economy. *Der Messias* (–1773) by Friedrich Gottlieb Klopstock (1724–1803) appears anonymously, inaugurating a new era in German poetry.	**1748** Osmosis discovered by Abbé Nollet (1700–70). Discovery of the ruined city of Pompeii.	**1748** Lancelot ('Capability') Brown (1716–83) plans his first independent landscape garden design, at Warwick Castle.
1749 *The History of Tom Jones, a Foundling* by Henry Fielding (1705–54) establishes the novel of action in England.	**1749** Publication of the first volume of *Histoire naturelle*, in which Georges Buffon (1707–88) differentiates the sciences of anthropology, geology and archaeology.	
		1750 Tiepolo commissioned to decorate the archbishop's palace at Würzburg. *Robert Andrews and his Wife* painted by Thomas Gainsborough (1727–88). Battersea Enamel factory set up.
	1750 Göttingen Academy of Science founded.	

Index

Index